CONTENTS

KU-043-266

ACKNOWLEDGMENTS

Producing a book of this size and scope involves the combined efforts of many people. We at The Waite Group would like to thank the authors, editors, and production staff who worked together to create the first reference book for QBasic.

First and foremost, we would like to thank Robert Arnson, whose dedication and expertise made this a thorough, complete book that complements an accessible new programming language. Because neither MS-DOS 5 nor QBasic was a released product while this book was in production, Bob Arnson was writing about a moving target. His talent and patience are much appreciated.

We also gratefully acknowledge coauthors Christy Gemmel and Harry Henderson for their extensive contributions.

Thanks to Dean Holmes, Acquisitions Manager at Microsoft Press, for giving us the opportunity to produce the first official reference on the QBasic language. We would also like to thank the people at Microsoft Press who made this book possible: Darcie Furlan, Peggy Herman, Susan McRhoton, Debbie Kem, Judith Bloch, Ruth Pettis, David Rygmyr, Eric Stroo, Suzanne Viescas, and Jean Zimmer. Special thanks must go to Ron Lamb, who managed the project for Microsoft Press, and to Mary DeJong, for her meticulous technical edit.

The Waite Group
December 1990

INTRODUCTION

How to Use This Book

We wrote this book with a special approach in mind—to let you gain access to the most general information first, followed by more specific information. For example, if you are just getting started with QBasic or if you are familiar with another version of Basic and you want to identify those areas of QBasic that are different, you might want a general overview of the entire language—its features and its limitations, its power and its potential. The chapter tutorials give you this information in a style that is both comprehensive and readable.

If you understand the big picture and you need to use a command, you'll want to read about it in greater detail. The reference section of each chapter discusses the purpose, syntax, and usage of every statement and function; the reference sections provide authoritative information about each entry, including programming tips and warnings. The discussions of statements and functions are arranged by subject area rather than alphabetically, as they are in most reference books. This organization lets you understand the relationships of the statements in a specific area to quickly grasp their interactions rather than having to search for scattered entries throughout the book. You can also use the two alphabetic jump tables of keywords and concepts on the inside front and back covers of this book to quickly focus on a specific topic. The jump table at the front of the book is an alphabetic list containing each keyword, statement, and function and the page on which you can find the relevant information; this critical listing is frequently omitted from reference books and manuals. The jump table at the back of the book lists each QBasic keyword, statement, and function by category with the page number on which the item is found.

How We Wrote This Book

We developed the outline of this book by organizing all QBasic keywords into related groups. Next we studied each statement and function and agreed on the best example for it. Then we wrote the reference pages for each command. Short sample programs for the keywords were designed specifically to showcase the commands in an interesting, helpful, and useful manner.

We then used the reference pages to produce the tutorial for each chapter. We condensed the most important elements of each command category into a succinct, instructive summary that shows you how to use the commands together.

Each step of this process further refined the information, pulling out the most salient facts and filtering out the finer details. Finally, we produced the jump tables for the inside front and back covers.

Refinement and a Microscope Analogy

Think of this book as a microscope with different powers of magnification. You can start at the lowest level, with the jump tables on the inside front and back covers, read the tutorials to learn the interrelationships of commands, and finally, view each element of QBasic under the powerful magnification of the reference entries. The index is a lens that gives you a finely detailed list of all the topics that form the QBasic language.

SECTION I

CORE

CHAPTER 1

Variables and Types

Introduction

QBasic programmers are lucky: They can let QBasic manage the details of their programming while they concentrate on problem solving and program design. QBasic lets you use symbolic names for the locations at which QBasic stores values. These locations are known as *variables*. You can name a variable to describe the meaning of the value you want to store. You might, for example, choose the variable name *pastDueAmount* to store the past-due amount a customer owes.

Select self-describing variable names so that you and others who read your programs will immediately recognize the meaning of the values stored in the variables. Some people abbreviate variable names to save typing time. That's acceptable up to a point; however, variable names can be confusing if they're abbreviated too much. If you abbreviate the variable name *pastDueAmount* to *pastAmt*, for example, its purpose is still clear. However, if you further abbreviate the variable name to *pAmt*, you might later think that it means "payment amount."

QBasic variable names must conform to the following conventions:

- The first character of a variable name must be a letter (A–Z), either uppercase or lowercase.
- The remaining characters of a variable name can be letters (A–Z), either uppercase or lowercase, the digits 0–9, or periods (.).
- The last character of a variable name may be a special character (%, &, !, #, or $) that indicates the type of value to be stored in the variable.
- A variable name can be up to 40 characters in length.
- A variable name must not be the same as a QBasic reserved word.

You can think of a variable name as the title on an office door. The title tells you the function of the person inside but not the person's name. In fact, the person who does the job can change without the title changing. The variable *president$*, for example, might contain the value "Smith." However, in the future the value in the variable *president$* might be "Jones." The variable name hasn't changed, yet its contents have.

When you create a program's variables, you must choose between two distinct types of variables—numeric and character. In QBasic, as in most other computer languages, a numeric variable can be one of several types. Each type defines a range of values the variable can contain. A numeric variable can be an integer, a long integer, a single-precision value, or a double-precision value. A character variable can be one of two types: a variable-length string or a fixed-length string. You use the statements and functions described in this chapter to define variables and to convert values to different types of variables. Chapter 5, "Strings," discusses string management.

This tutorial summarizes variables and types and offers some suggestions for their use. Table 1-1 lists in alphabetic order the keywords, statements, and functions used to define and work with variables.

Keyword, statement, or function	Description
CONST	Defines a mnemonic name for values that don't change
DEF*type*	Defines characters that specify default variable types
DOUBLE	Creates a double-precision variable
HEX$	Returns a string containing the hexadecimal value of an integer value
INTEGER	Creates an integer variable
LET	Assigns a value to a variable
LONG	Creates a long-integer variable
OCT$	Returns a string containing the octal value of an integer value
SINGLE	Creates a single-precision variable
STRING	Creates a string variable
SWAP	Exchanges values between two variables
TYPE...END TYPE	Defines a new variable type

Table 1-1.
Variable-typing keywords, statements, and functions.

Defining Mnemonic Names for Constant Values

Because much programming involves numeric codes, QBasic provides the CONST statement to let you assign meaningful names, called constants, to these codes. The COLOR statement, for example, accepts parameters that are values in the range 0 through 31. Each number specifies a different color. Values 16 through 31 specify the same colors as 0 through 15, but with the blinking attribute. You can define constants to represent some of those values, as shown in the following statements:

```
CONST BLACK = 0, BLUE = 1, GREEN = 2, CYAN = 3
CONST RED = 4, MAGENTA = 5, BROWN = 6, WHITE = 7
CONST BLINKING = 16
```

These statements let you easily change colors on the screen without having to memorize the entire code table—for example,

```
COLOR WHITE, BLUE
PRINT "This text is white on a blue background."

COLOR BLINKING + RED, WHITE
PRINT "This text is blinking red on a white background."
```

The CONST statement is also useful for providing names for constant values you might later want to change. Although the standard screen by default displays 25 lines of text, EGA adapters also support 43 lines of text. VGA adapters support 25, 43, and 50 lines of text. To enable users with those adapters to take advantage of more lines on the screen, you can define a constant *HEIGHT* that should be set to 25 for a standard screen, 43 for an EGA screen, or 50 for a VGA screen.

In QBasic, a constant's value can be either a constant value or a constant expression. Any literal number or string of characters is a constant value. For example, the literal number 69 is a constant-integer value, and the string of characters "QBasic Programmer's Reference" is a constant character-string value. An expression that contains only constant elements is called a constant expression—for example,

```
69 + 128 * 2
```

is a constant expression because each element is a constant value. However, the expression

```
69 + 128 * FACTOR
```

is a constant expression only if *FACTOR* has been defined as a constant value. If *FACTOR* is a variable, the above expression is not a constant expression.

Constants that are defined with an expression can contain only literal numbers, literal strings, and other constants; they cannot contain variables or functions. For example, you can define the constant *BLINKINGRED* as shown below because it is a combination of other constants:

```
CONST RED = 4, BLINKING = 16
CONST BLINKINGRED = RED + BLINKING
```

Variable Types

QBasic provides five simple variable types—integer, long integer, single precision, double precision, and string. You can declare a variable as one of these types in an AS clause in the QBasic statements listed in Table 1-2. See the entries of those statements for more details.

COMMON	DIM	STATIC
DECLARE SUB	FUNCTION	SUB
DECLARE FUNCTION	REDIM	TYPE...END TYPE
DEF FN	SHARED	

Table 1-2.
QBasic statements in which variables can be declared.

You can declare a variable's type in one of two ways: either with an AS clause or with a type-declaration character. To declare a type by using an AS clause, follow the variable name with the AS keyword and the keyword of the desired type. For example, the following statement declares the variable *total* as double precision:

```
COMMON total AS DOUBLE
```

Table 1-3 lists the AS clauses for the five simple types.

Type declaration	Purpose
AS INTEGER	Declares an integer variable
AS LONG	Declares a long-integer variable
AS SINGLE	Declares a single-precision variable
AS DOUBLE	Declares a double-precision variable
AS STRING	Declares a string variable

Table 1-3.
Type declarations with the AS keyword.

To declare a variable's type by using a type-declaration character, follow the variable name with one of the type-declaration characters: %, &, !, #, or $. When you do this, QBasic assigns that variable a type according to Table 1-4.

Type-declaration character	Purpose
%	Declares an integer variable
&	Declares a long-integer variable
!	Declares a single-precision variable
#	Declares a double-precision variable
$	Declares a string variable

Table 1-4.
Type-declaration characters.

For example, the statement

```
total# = 128.69
```

assigns the value 128.69 to the double-precision variable named *total#*. Remember, the type-declaration character is part of the variable name, and you must always include it in references to the name. For example, consider the following statements:

```
total# = 128.69
total = 100.55
```

Note that the variable *total* without the # type-declaration character is a different variable from *total#*. In fact, you can use a single name for five different variables:

```
total%        ' an integer variable
total&        ' a long-integer variable
total!        ' a single-precision variable
total#        ' a double-precision variable
total$        ' a string variable
```

The type-declaration character is useful for reminding you what type a variable is. You know, for example, that a variable named *total#* holds a double-precision value.

Creating Default Types for Variables

QBasic does not require you to explicitly declare a variable. Instead of using AS or a type-declaration character, you can use a DEF*type* statement that sets the default data type. The first time you use a new variable, QBasic assigns it whatever type is specified by a DEF*type* statement.

DEF*type* statements specify letters or letter ranges. Any variable names that begin with the specified letters and that do not end in a type-declaration character are assigned the type specified by the DEF*type* keyword. The DEF*type* keyword can be DEFINT, DEFLNG, DEFSNG, DEFDBL, or DEFSTR. For example, in the following program segment the variable *total* is assigned the integer type:

```
DEFINT M-Z
total=12
```

Converting Decimal to Hexadecimal or Octal

When you display the value of a variable using the PRINT statement, QBasic displays it as a decimal (base 10) number. However, QBasic provides two functions that let you display numbers in other bases. The HEX$ function converts a decimal number to a string that represents the value in base 16 (hexadecimal), and OCT$ converts a decimal number to a string that represents the value in base 8 (octal).

Representing numbers in hexadecimal and octal can be useful when you work with assembly-language routines. Most likely, you will not often use these functions. After all, very few invoices or balance sheets must be printed with hexadecimal or octal values.

Assigning Values to Variables

Variables wouldn't be of much use if you couldn't assign values to them. In old versions of Basic you had to use the LET statement to assign values to variables.

Often, for example, you will need to increment a variable that acts as a counter. You can do so in QBasic with the following statement:

```
counter = counter + 1
```

You can assign string constants or other string variables to string variables. You can also assign to a string variable the result of a concatenation operation:

```
language$ = "QBasic "
title$ = language$ + "Programmer's Reference"
```

After a program executes these statements, the variable *title$* contains the value "QBasic Programmer's Reference."

Exchanging Values Between Two Variables

The SWAP statement exchanges the values of two different variables and is especially useful in some sorting algorithms. The SWAP statement is equivalent to three assignment statements organized into a single statement. For example,

```
SWAP currentTotal, subTotal
```

exchanges the values of the variables *currentTotal* and *subTotal* and is equivalent to the following statements:

```
temp = subTotal
subTotal = currentTotal
currentTotal = temp
```

Defining Compound-Variable Types

Some items are usually grouped together: For example, month, day, and year form a date; and title, first name, middle name, and last name form a full name. Perhaps the most natural way to store the three separate elements of today's date would be to use three variables: *month*, *day*, and *year*. QBasic includes the TYPE...END TYPE statement to enable programmers to create types that accommodate record variables consisting of several elements.

To create a record structure for the parts of a person's name, you might use a TYPE...END TYPE statement, as in the following statement:

```
TYPE CompleteName
    title AS STRING * 4
    first AS STRING * 16
    middle AS STRING * 16
    last AS STRING * 20
END TYPE
```

After you create the above structure, you could define a new variable as that structure type, as in the following statement:

```
DIM customerName AS CompleteName
```

Now you can assign values to the variables in the record variable *customerName*, as in the following statements:

```
customerName.title = "Mr."
customerName.first = "John"
customerName.middle = "Q."
customerName.last = "Public"
```

You can also create arrays of record variables. The following program segment declares an array of record variables that are defined by the *CompleteName* type and then assigns values to the variables:

```
TYPE CompleteName
    title AS STRING * 4
    first AS STRING * 16
    middle AS STRING * 16
    last AS STRING * 20
END TYPE

DIM customerName(2) AS CompleteName

customerName(1).title = "Mr."
customerName(1).first = "John"
customerName(1).middle = "Q."
customerName(1).last = "Public"

customerName(2).title = "Ms."
customerName(2).first = "Jane"
customerName(2).middle = ""
customerName(2).last = "Doe"
```

Figure 1-1 shows a graphic representation of the array of record variables declared above.

	title	Mr.
customerName(1).	first	John
	middle	Q.
	last	Public

	title	Ms.
customerName(2).	first	Jane
	middle	
	last	Doe

Figure 1-1.
Values in an array of record variables.

You can also define structures that contain other structures as members. This is a useful technique for reusing basic structures you have already defined, such as the previous structure for names. Other, more complicated, structures might contain these basic structures. The following program segment, for example, declares an array of record variables of the defined type *Patients*. The structure *Patients* contains the variable *patientName*, which is a record variable of type *CompleteName*.

```
TYPE CompleteName
    title AS STRING * 4
    first AS STRING * 16
    middle AS STRING * 16
    last AS STRING * 20
END TYPE

TYPE Patients
    patientName AS CompleteName
    address AS STRING * 128
END TYPE

DIM patient(100) AS Patients

patient(1).patientName.title = "Ms."
patient(1).patientName.first = "Anna"
patient(1).patientName.middle = "Marie"
patient(1).patientName.last = "Smith"
patient(1).address = "1695 Park Street"

patient(2).patientName.title = "Mr."
patient(2).patientName.first = "George"
patient(2).patientName.middle = "John"
patient(2).patientName.last = "Jones"
patient(2).address = "1024 Disk Drive"
```

Figure 1-2 shows a graphic representation of the structure within a structure of the above record variables.

patient(1).	patientName.	title	Ms.
		first	Anna
		middle	Marie
		last	Smith
	address	1695 Park Street	

patient(2).	patientName.	title	Mr.
		first	George
		middle	John
		last	Jones
	address	1024 Disk Drive	

Figure 1-2.
Values in a structure within a structure.

The TYPE...END TYPE statement allows you to specify a wide variety of types for the elements. QBasic provides programmers the flexibility to define types with the TYPE...END TYPE statement.

Related Reading

Lafore, Robert. *The Waite Group's Microsoft C Programming for the PC,* rev. ed. Indianapolis, Ind.: Howard W. Sams and Co., 1989.

Norton, Peter, and Richard Wilton. *The* New *Peter Norton Programmer's Guide to the IBM PC and PS/2*. Redmond, Wash.: Microsoft Press, 1988.

CONST

Purpose

The CONST statement lets you give symbolic, meaningful names to numeric and string constant values. For example, you could use the CONST statement to assign the name PI to the number 3.141592653.

Syntax

CONST *NAME* = *expr* [, *NAME* = *expr*...]

NAME is a constant's name. It must be distinct from any keyword, variable, or subprogram name.

expr is a numeric or string expression containing only a constant value or a constant expression.

Usage

```
CONST PI = 3.141592653
```
Assigns the name PI to the value 3.141592653.

```
CONST FALSE = 0, TRUE = NOT FALSE
```
Defines two symbolic constants, FALSE and TRUE.

Description

Programming in QBasic often requires the use of numeric codes, which can represent everything from screen colors to keyboard keys. The CONST statement lets you assign meaningful names to these codes.

The constant is the word to which you want to assign the specified expression. You can use a type-declaration character (%, &, !, #, or $) at the end of the name to specify the constant's type, but this character is not considered part of the name. For example, if you specify

```
CONST ARRAYSIZE% = 2500
```

to assign the value 2500 to *ARRAYSIZE%*, you can use the constant in statements without the ending type-declaration character, as in the following statements:

```
DIM patients(100 TO ARRAYSIZE)
```

```
FOR i% = 1 TO ARRAYSIZE
```

If you omit a type-declaration character, QBasic assigns a type to the constant that matches the type of the specified expression. If the expression is the value "gobbledygook," for example, QBasic types the constant as a string. If the expression is numeric, QBasic determines the smallest type that can hold it and assigns a type of integer, long integer, single precision, or double precision. For example, in the statement

```
CONST ANNUALSALES = 298500
```

QBasic first determines that 298500 is not in the range of the integer type, and then it checks whether the value is in the range of the long-integer type. Because it is in the range, *ANNUALSALES* is typed as a long-integer constant.

In the following statement, 0.015 is a floating-point number:

```
CONST SERVICECHARGE = 0.015
```

Because the constant cannot be an integer or a long integer, QBasic checks only the ranges of the single-precision and double-precision types. Because it fits in the range of the single-precision type, SERVICECHARGE becomes a single-precision constant.

The specified expression can be a QBasic expression that contains string or numeric constants, other constants defined by a CONST statement, and arithmetic and logical operators except exponentiation. It cannot contain variables, program-defined functions, or QBasic functions and statements such as CHR$, SIN, and SEEK.

Before you use a constant, you must define it with a CONST statement. The following statement, for example, generates a runtime error because you used the constant FALSE before you defined it.

```
CONST TRUE = NOT FALSE, FALSE = 0
```

The proper way to define these symbolic constants TRUE and FALSE is

```
CONST FALSE = 0, TRUE = NOT FALSE
```

If you define a constant by using a CONST statement inside a subprogram or a user-defined function, you can use the constant name only within the subprogram or function. (That is, it's a "local" constant.) Use local constants for constants that are applicable to only one subprogram or function. If, for example, you create a subprogram to track the number of transactions completed, you need to include the following statement in the subprogram to make the constant local:

```
CONST MAXTRANSACTIONS = 1024
```

If you define a constant by using a CONST statement in the main program (outside a subprogram or a user-defined function), you can use the constant name throughout the program. (That is, it's a "global" constant.) Use global constants, such as TRUE and FALSE, for constants that are applicable throughout a program.

You can use a constant anywhere you would normally use a variable or an expression.

Comments

The type of a constant is not affected by DEF*type* statements (DEFDBL, DEFINT, DEFLNG, DEFSNG, and DEFSTR). You can specify the type of a constant only by adding a type-declaration character to the end of the constant—for example,

```
DEFDBL A-Z

CONST MINAMOUNT = 125.50
maxAmount& = 9999
```

MINAMOUNT is a single-precision constant, and *maxAmount* is a long-integer variable.

Errors

If you create an expression that cannot be constant, QBasic displays an "Invalid constant" error message. If you attempt to modify the name of a constant defined in a CONST statement, QBasic displays a "Duplicate definition" error message. If you use the exponentiation operator (^) in an expression in a CONST statement, QBasic displays an "Illegal function call" error message.

Tips

Using the CONST statement offers several advantages over using variables or literals:

- Using constants lets you see the meanings of specific values rather than the values themselves. Using the constant *F1* to represent the value for the F1 function key, for example, is clearer than using the value 59.

- When you define a constant outside a subprogram or user-defined function, it is available to the entire module; a variable declared outside the subprogram or function can be accessed only with a SHARED statement.

- The value of a constant defined in a CONST statement cannot be accidentally changed; a variable's value can be changed easily.

- Using constants declared in a CONST statement lets you make changes to a program more easily than if you use literals. If you originally designed a program to work with a 25-line screen, for example, you might declare the constant *SCREENLINES* as follows:

```
CONST SCREENLINES = 25
```

Later, to expand the program to work with a VGA screen with 50 lines, you need only change the statement to the following:

```
CONST SCREENLINES = 50
```

It is common practice to capitalize the names of constants. This practice helps show you when your program is using a constant instead of a variable.

Example

The following program uses the CONST statement to provide symbolic names for the ASCII codes of certain keystrokes.

```
' define constants that contain the ASCII codes of some keystrokes
CONST ESC = 27, ENTER = 13, CTRLBACKSPACE = 127

CLS
PRINT "Type something... (press Ctrl - Backspace to quit)."
PRINT
LOCATE , , 1                      ' turn on cursor
```

(continued)

continued

```
DO
    DO                              ' loop until a key is pressed
        inky$ = INKEY$
    LOOP WHILE inky$ = ""

    SELECT CASE ASC(inky$)
        CASE ENTER                  ' if key is Enter, print [ENTER]
            PRINT " [ENTER]"

        CASE ESC                    ' if key is Esc, print [ESC]
            PRINT " [ESC] ";

        CASE CTRLBACKSPACE          ' if key is Ctrl-Backspace, exit loop
            PRINT " [CTRL-BACKSPACE] ";
            EXIT DO

        CASE ELSE                   ' otherwise, display the key
            PRINT inky$;
    END SELECT
LOOP
```

DEF*type*

See also
DIM, DOUBLE, INTEGER, LONG, SINGLE

Purpose
QBasic's DEF*type* statements set the default type for variables and user-defined functions that don't include a type-declaration character or that aren't specifically declared by an AS clause.

Syntax
DEFDBL *letters* [, *letters*...]
DEFINT *letters* [, *letters*...]
DEFLNG *letters* [, *letters*...]
DEFSNG *letters* [, *letters*...]
DEFSTR *letters* [, *letters*...]

letters is either a single letter or a range of letters specified by two letters separated by a hyphen.

Usage
```
DEFLNG S, T
```
Declares all variables that begin with the letter S or T to be long integers.

CHAPTER 1: Variables and Types   **15**

```
DEFINT A-Z
```
Declares all variables to be integers.

Description

QBasic does not require you to define the type and size of variables and functions before you use them. If you don't specify a type, QBasic assigns a type to a variable the first time you use it. This gives you the freedom to create a new variable whenever you need it without having to first declare it. The DEF*type* statements set the default types that are used when QBasic automatically assigns a type to a variable. The type depends on which DEF*type* keyword you use. The five DEF*type* keywords in QBasic are shown in Table 1-5.

Any variable that hasn't already been defined and whose name begins with any letter specified in a DEF*type* statement is assigned the type specified by the DEF*type* keyword. (See Table 1-5.) DEF*type* affects variables that begin with the specified letters in lowercase or in uppercase.

With the DEF*type* statement	The default variable type is
<none>, DEFSNG	Single precision
DEFDBL	Double precision
DEFINT	Integer
DEFLNG	Long integer
DEFSTR	String

Table 1-5.
*DEF*type *keywords.*

Comments

Because the types of all elements in a record variable defined by a TYPE...END TYPE statement are explicitly defined by AS clauses, they are not affected by QBasic's DEF*type* statements.

Adding a type-declaration character (%, &, !, #, or $) to a variable name defines the variable as a specific type. Adding an ampersand (&) to the end of a variable, for example, defines it as a long integer. Also, if you declare the type of a variable by using an AS clause, that variable is defined as the type you specify. For example, in the statement

```
DIM freeSpace AS LONG
```

the variable *freeSpace* is a long integer. This explicit typing overrides any defaults created by DEF*type* statements.

Tips

■ Because they are of different types, *i%*, *i&*, *i!*, *i#*, and *i$* are distinct variable names, and each can hold a different value. However, using different variables with such similar names can be confusing, so you should avoid doing so.

■ If you use a DEF*type* statement to set the type of a function defined by a DEF FN statement, remember that the name of the function begins immediately to the right of the letters FN. If you create a function named *FNAverage*, for example, you use the statement *DEFDBL A* to define *FNAverage* as double precision.

Example

The following program uses DEF*type* statements to set the default variable type for loop variables, total amounts, and prompt strings.

```
DEFDBL A, G     ' amt, grandTotal are double precision
DEFINT I        ' i is an integer
DEFLNG X        ' x is a long integer
DEFSNG S        ' subTotal is single precision
DEFSTR Y        ' yesNo is a string

CLS

' initialize variables
grandTotal = 0#
x = 1

DO
    PRINT "How many items on receipt"; x;   ' get number of items on the receipt
    INPUT itemsOnReceipt

    subTotal = 0!                       ' initialize subtotal
    FOR i = 1 TO itemsOnReceipt         ' for each item on receipt
        PRINT "Enter amount of item"; i;
        INPUT ; amt                     ' get item amount
        subTotal = subTotal + amt       ' add item amount to subTotal
        grandTotal = grandTotal + amt   ' add item amount to grandTotal
        PRINT TAB(70); USING "##,###.##"; subTotal
    NEXT

    PRINT TAB(70); "---------"          ' print current grand total
    PRINT TAB(70); USING "##,###.##"; grandTotal
    PRINT

    INPUT "Do you want to add up more receipts"; yesNo   ' prompt if user
    x = x + 1                                            ' wants more receipts
LOOP UNTIL UCASE$(yesNo) = "N"                           ' else quit program
```

DOUBLE

See also

COMMON, DECLARE, DEF FN, DIM, FUNCTION, INTEGER, LONG, REDIM, SHARED, SINGLE, STATIC, STRING, SUB, TYPE...END TYPE

Purpose

The DOUBLE keyword specifies in an AS clause the type of a variable or function as double-precision floating point. Use the DOUBLE keyword when you must use large, accurate numbers, as in scientific and business calculations.

Syntax

var AS DOUBLE

var is the name of a variable; the exact syntax depends on the statement in which you declare the variable.

Usage

```
DIM total AS DOUBLE
```
Defines *total* as a double-precision variable.

```
DECLARE FUNCTION CubeRoot# (number AS DOUBLE)
```
Declares a function that takes a double-precision argument.

Description

The DOUBLE keyword can be used in any QBasic statement that includes an AS clause. Table 1-6 lists the statements that use the AS clause. (For details, see the entries of the statements in the table.)

COMMON	DIM	STATIC
DECLARE SUB	FUNCTION	SUB
DECLARE FUNCTION	REDIM	TYPE...END TYPE
DEF FN	SHARED	

Table 1-6.
QBasic statements that use the AS clause.

Variables declared as double precision can hold floating-point values (values that have numbers after a decimal point) accurately to 15 significant digits. This means that although a double-precision variable can hold much larger values, only 15 digits are accurate. Because double-precision variables can use exponential notation (that is, scientific notation), they can hold extremely large values. Values for positive double-precision numbers range from 4.940656458412465D−324 through 1.797693134862315D+308. Values for negative double-precision numbers range from −1.797693134862315D+308 through −4.940656458412465D−324.

Exponential notation for double-precision numbers is expressed as follows:

±*mantissa*D±*exponent*

An example of this format is the number 4.107D+6, which is equivalent to 4.107×10^6 and to 4,107,000.

Note that, in keeping with the mathematical definition of scientific notation, when the exponent is negative, the value of the expression is fractional—not negative— as in the following expression:

$$4.107D-6 = 4.107 \times 10^{-6} = 0.000004107$$

Errors

If you assign to a double-precision variable a value outside the range of the double-precision type, QBasic displays an "Overflow" error message.

Tips

Rather than declaring a variable using the clause AS DOUBLE, you can add the type-declaration character # to the end of the variable name. Remember, however, that the pound sign (#) becomes part of the name and that you must include it every time you use the variable.

Also, you can use a DEFDBL statement to declare that all variables whose names begin with certain letters be double precision. (See the DEF*type* entry.)

HEX$

See also

OCT$

Purpose

The HEX$ function converts an integer or long-integer expression to a string that contains the hexadecimal (base 16) value of the expression. You might use the HEX$ function if you work with assembly-language routines.

Syntax

HEX$(*num*)

num is the numeric variable or expression that HEX$ converts.

Usage

```
PRINT HEX$(65536)
```
Displays the hexadecimal value of the decimal integer 65536, which is 10000.

Description

People are most comfortable when using decimal numbers (base 10). But other base systems, such as binary (base 2), octal (base 8), and hexadecimal (base 16) work better for digital processing. QBasic provides the HEX$ function to convert decimal numbers to strings containing the representation of the numbers in hexadecimal.

The specified value is a numeric variable or expression of any numeric type; QBasic converts it to an integer or a long integer. Note that QBasic ignores any fractional part of the value.

Errors

If the specified value is not in the range −2147483648 through 2147483647, QBasic displays an "Overflow" error message.

Example

The following example uses the PEEK and HEX$ functions to print the hexadecimal representation of a key status value in memory.

```
CLS
DEF SEG = 0          ' access the "BIOS data area"

PRINT "Press the Shift keys, Ctrl keys, Alt keys, "
PRINT "    Num Lock, Caps Lock, and Scroll Lock."
PRINT "Press Esc to quit."

DO
    LOCATE 4, 1     ' position the cursor

    ' get the data at address 0417 hexadecimal, convert it to hexadecimal
    PRINT RIGHT$("0" + HEX$(PEEK(&H417)), 2)
LOOP UNTIL INKEY$ = CHR$(27)
```

INTEGER

See also

COMMON, DECLARE, DEF FN, DIM, DOUBLE, FUNCTION, LONG, REDIM, SHARED, SINGLE, STATIC, STRING, SUB, TYPE...END TYPE

Purpose

The INTEGER keyword specifies in an AS clause the type of a variable or function as integer. Use the INTEGER keyword when you need to use only small whole numbers (integers) for operations such as accessing screen coordinates.

Syntax

var AS INTEGER

var is the name of a variable; the exact syntax depends on the statement in which you declare the variable.

Usage

```
DIM age AS INTEGER
```
Defines *age* as an integer variable.

```
DECLARE FUNCTION Cube (number AS INTEGER)
```
Declares a function that takes an integer argument.

Description

The INTEGER keyword can be used in any QBasic statement that includes an AS clause. Table 1-6, in the DOUBLE entry, lists the statements that use the AS clause. (See the entries of the statements in the table for details.)

Variables declared as INTEGER can hold whole numbers in the range −32768 through 32767. If you need to use a larger range of whole numbers, you must use the LONG keyword. (See the LONG entry.)

Comments

Mathematical operations on integer and long-integer variables are executed much faster than they are executed on single-precision and double-precision variables. Integer and long-integer variables can be directly represented in the registers of the CPU; however, the three parts of single-precision and double-precision variables (sign, mantissa, and exponent) must be calculated, causing slower mathematical operations. Use integer or long-integer variables whenever possible.

Errors

If you assign to an integer variable a value outside the range of the integer type, QBasic displays an "Overflow" error message.

Tips

Rather than declaring a variable using the clause AS INTEGER, you can add the type-declaration character % to the end of the variable name. Remember, however, that the percent sign (%) becomes part of the name and that you must include it every time you use the variable.

Also, you can use a DEFINT statement to declare that all variables whose names begin with certain letters be integers. (See the DEF*type* entry.)

LET

See also

LSET, TYPE...END TYPE

Purpose

The LET statement assigns the value of an expression to a variable, an array element, or a user-defined TYPE...END TYPE variable or element. Use LET to initialize variables or to change their current value.

Syntax

[LET] *var* = *expr*

var is the name of the variable that is assigned the value of *expr*.

The LET keyword is optional.

Usage

```
LET a = 0
```
Assigns the value 0 to the variable *a*.

```
x = x + 1
```
Increments the variable *x* by 1.

```
item(5) = 4.8
```
Assigns the value 4.8 to element 5 of the array *item*.

```
item.partnum = "26-3004B"
```
Assigns the string "26-3004B" to the element *partnum* in the user-defined record variable *item*.

Description

The LET statement is the QBasic assignment operator; it lets you assign values to variables. You can use it to assign the initial values of the variables in a program or to change the values of variables later in the program. For example, programmers often assign initial values at the beginning of a program, as follows:

```
x = 0: y = 0: z = 0
```

QBasic lets you use the same variable on both sides of the equal sign. This lets you make changes relative to the variable's current value. The statement $x = x + 1$, for example, increments the value of x by 1. In the statement $y = 5 * y$, QBasic calculates the expression $5 * y$ and then assigns the resulting value to y.

Both the variable and the expression in a LET statement can be record variables defined by a TYPE...END TYPE statement; however, both must be declared as the same user-defined type. For example, the DIM statements

```
DIM newItem AS Inventory
DIM item AS Inventory
```

declare two record variables of the same type, allowing you to execute the following assignment statement:

```
item = newItem
```

Note that this works only when the AS clause is the same for both record variables. If the AS clauses are different, you can use the LSET statement to assign the contents of one record variable to the other. (See the LSET entry in Chapter 17, "Files," for details.)

Example

The following example uses the LET assignment statement to build a table of the square and square root of the numbers 1–20.

```
CLS

PRINT "        Number    Square root"
PRINT "Number  Squared  of Number"
PRINT

FOR i% = 1 TO 20
    LET square# = i% ^ 2         ' assign square# the square of i
    LET squareRoot# = SQR(i%)    ' assign squareRoot# the square root of i
    PRINT USING "##     ####  #.#####"; i%; square#; squareRoot#
NEXT
```

LONG

See also

COMMON, DECLARE, DEF FN, DIM, DOUBLE, FUNCTION, INTEGER, REDIM, SHARED, SINGLE, STATIC, STRING, SUB, TYPE...END TYPE

Purpose

The LONG keyword specifies in an AS clause the type of a variable or function as long integer. Use the LONG keyword when you need to use large whole numbers (integers), such as large whole-dollar amounts.

Syntax

var AS LONG

var is the name of a variable; the exact syntax depends on the statement in which you declare the variable.

Usage

```
DIM deficit AS LONG
```
Defines *deficit* as a long-integer variable.

```
DECLARE FUNCTION Cube (number AS LONG)
```
Declares a function that takes a long-integer argument.

Description

The LONG keyword can be used in any QBasic statement that includes an AS clause. Table 1-6, in the DOUBLE entry, lists the statements that use the AS clause. (See the entries of the statements in the table for details.)

Variables declared as LONG can hold whole numbers that are in the range −2147483648 through 2147483647. If you need to use a larger range of whole numbers, you must declare the variable with the DOUBLE keyword. Double-precision variables hold floating-point numbers (values that have numbers after a decimal point), but, of course, you can use the variable to hold whole numbers as well. (See the DOUBLE entry.)

Comments

Mathematical operations on integer and long-integer variables are executed much faster than they are executed on single-precision and double-precision variables. Integer and long-integer variables can be directly represented in the registers of the CPU; however, the three parts of single-precision and double-precision variables (sign, mantissa, and exponent) must be calculated, causing slower mathematical operations. Use integer or long-integer variables whenever possible.

Errors

If you assign to a long-integer variable a value outside the range of the long-integer type, QBasic displays an "Overflow" error message.

Tips

Rather than declaring a variable using the clause AS LONG, you can add the type-declaration character & to the end of the name. Remember, however, that the ampersand (&) becomes part of the name and that you must include it every time you use the variable.

Also, you can use a DEFLNG statement to declare that all variables whose names begin with certain letters be long integers. (See the DEF*type* entry.)

OCT$

See also
HEX$

Purpose

The OCT$ function converts an integer or long-integer expression to a string that contains the octal (base 8) value of the expression. You might use the OCT$ function if you work with assembly-language routines.

Syntax

OCT$(*num*)

num is the numeric variable or expression that OCT$ converts.

Usage

```
PRINT OCT$(511)
```
Displays the octal value of the decimal integer 511, which is 777.

Description

People are most comfortable when using decimal numbers (base 10). But other base systems, such as binary (base 2), octal (base 8), and hexadecimal (base 16) work better for digital processing. QBasic provides the OCT$ function to convert decimal numbers to strings containing the representation of the numbers in octal.

The specified value is a numeric variable or expression of any numeric type; QBasic converts it to an integer or a long integer. Note that QBasic ignores any fractional part of the value.

Errors

If the specified value is not in the range −2147483648 through 2147483647, QBasic displays an "Overflow" error message.

Example

The following example uses the OCT$ function to print the octal representation of decimal numbers input by the user.

```
CLS

PRINT "To quit, press Enter or enter 0."
PRINT

DO
    INPUT "Enter a decimal integer"; dec%
    IF dec% <= 0 THEN EXIT DO

    PRINT dec%; "decimal is "; OCT$(dec%); " octal"
    PRINT
LOOP UNTIL dec% = 0
```

SINGLE

See also

COMMON, DECLARE, DEF FN, DIM, DOUBLE, FUNCTION, INTEGER, LONG, REDIM, SHARED, STATIC, STRING, SUB, TYPE...END TYPE

Purpose

The SINGLE keyword specifies in an AS clause the type of a variable or function as single-precision floating point. Use the SINGLE keyword when you need to use decimal numbers such as small dollar amounts.

Syntax

var AS SINGLE

var is the name of a variable; the exact syntax depends on the statement in which you declare the variable.

Usage

```
DIM total AS SINGLE
```
Defines *total* as a single-precision variable.

```
DECLARE FUNCTION CubeRoot# (number AS SINGLE)
```
Declares a function that takes a single-precision argument.

Description

The SINGLE keyword can be used in any QBasic statement that includes an AS clause. Table 1-6, in the DOUBLE entry, lists the statements that use the AS clause. (See the entries of the statements in the table for details.)

Variables declared as single precision can hold floating-point values (values that have numbers after a decimal point) accurate to seven significant digits. This means that although a single-precision variable can hold much larger values, only seven digits are accurate. Because single-precision variables can use exponential notation (that is, scientific notation), they can hold large values. Values for positive single-precision numbers range from 1.401298E−45 through 3.402823E+38. Values for negative single-precision numbers range from −3.402823E+38 through −1.401298E−45.

An example of exponential notation is the number 4.107E+4. This number is equivalent to 4.107×10^4 and to 41,070. Note that, in keeping with the mathematical definition of scientific notation, when the exponent is negative, the value of the expression is fractional—not negative—as in the following expression:

$$4.107E\text{-}4 = 4.107 \times 10^{-4} = 0.0004107$$

Errors

If you assign to a single-precision variable a value outside the range of the single-precision type, QBasic displays an "Overflow" error message.

Tips

Rather than declaring a variable using the clause AS SINGLE, you can add the type-declaration character ! to the end of the name. Remember, however, that the exclamation mark (!) becomes part of the name and that you must include it every time you use the variable.

You can use a DEFSNG statement to declare all variables whose names begin with certain letters as single precision. (See the DEF*type* entry for details.)

Remember that the default variable type in QBasic is single precision. You can change the default by adding DEF*type* statements to your program.

STRING

See also

COMMON, DECLARE, DEF FN, DEF*type*, DIM, FIELD, FUNCTION, REDIM, SHARED, STATIC, STR$, SUB, TYPE...END TYPE

Purpose

The STRING keyword specifies in an AS clause the type of a variable or function as string. A variable of the type string contains a series of characters. Use the STRING keyword when you need to use character strings for operations such as reading a user's name.

Syntax

var AS STRING

var is the name of a variable; the exact syntax depends on the statement in which you declare the variable.

Usage

```
DIM name AS INTEGER
```
Defines *name* as a string variable.

```
DECLARE FUNCTION InKeys$ (key AS STRING)
```
Declares a function that takes a string argument and returns a string value.

Description

The STRING keyword can be used in any QBasic statement that includes an AS clause. Table 1-6, in the DOUBLE entry, lists the statements that use the AS clause. (See the entries of the statements in the table for details.)

Variables declared as STRING can hold any of the 128 characters in the ASCII character set or the 128 characters in the IBM extended character set. A string can contain up to 32,767 characters. See Chapter 5, "Strings," for more information.

Errors

If you assign to a string variable a string with more than 32,767 characters, QBasic displays an "Overflow" error message.

If you attempt to assign a numeric value to a string variable, QBasic displays a "Type mismatch" error message.

Tips

Rather than declaring a variable using the clause AS STRING, you can add the type-declaration character $ to the end of the variable name. Remember, however, that the dollar sign ($) becomes part of the name and that you must include it every time you use the variable.

You can use a DEFSTR statement to declare that all variables whose names begin with certain letters are strings. (See the DEF*type* entry for details.)

SWAP

See also

TYPE...END TYPE

Purpose

The SWAP statement exchanges the values of two variables, array elements, record variables defined by a TYPE...END TYPE statement, or record-variable elements. Use the SWAP statement to swap values between variables quickly—for example, during a sort.

Syntax

SWAP *var1, var2*

var1 and *var2* are variables that contain the values the SWAP statement exchanges.

Usage

```
SWAP currentTotal, subTotal
```
Exchanges the values of *currentTotal* and *subTotal*.

Description

QBasic's SWAP statement combines a three-step operation into one step. For example,

```
SWAP currentTotal, subTotal
```

is equivalent to the following statements:

```
temp = subTotal
subTotal = currentTotal
currentTotal = temp
```

Note that the latter operation requires the use of a temporary variable.

The two variables can be simple variables, array elements, record variables defined by a TYPE...END TYPE statement or record-variable elements, but they must be of the same type. If they are not, QBasic displays a "Type mismatch" error message.

Example

The following example uses the SWAP statement to perform a "bubble sort" on a 10-element integer array. A bubble sort is so named because values rise to their proper positions just as bubbles float to a surface. Although a bubble sort is one of the easiest sort algorithms to program, it is a bit slow.

```
CLS

DEFINT A-Z

CONST FALSE = 0, TRUE = NOT FALSE              ' define TRUE and FALSE

DIM array(1 TO 10) AS INTEGER                  ' declare a 10-element array

PRINT "Enter 10 integer values, pressing Enter after each value."
PRINT

FOR i = 1 TO 10
    INPUT array(i)          ' assign integers to the elements of array
NEXT
PRINT

' perform a bubble sort
DO
    switch = FALSE
    FOR i = 1 TO 9
        'check whether two adjacent numbers are out of order
        IF array(i) > array(i + 1) THEN
            SWAP array(i), array(i + 1)        ' if out of order, swap
            switch = TRUE
        END IF
    NEXT
LOOP WHILE switch

PRINT : PRINT "Here they are, sorted:": PRINT

FOR i = 1 TO 10
    PRINT array(i);
NEXT
```

TYPE...END TYPE

See also

COMMON, DECLARE, DEF FN, DIM, FUNCTION, REDIM, SHARED, STATIC, SUB, SWAP

Purpose

QBasic's TYPE...END TYPE statement lets you create a data type (sometimes referred to as a user-defined type) that is a structure consisting of one or more variables. You can use TYPE...END TYPE statements to simplify data management. For example, you could create a variable named *inventory* that holds several different variables relating to inventory data.

Syntax

TYPE *Structure*
    element AS *type*
    ⋮
END TYPE

Structure is the name of the type.

element is the name of a variable that is of type *type*.

Usage

```
TYPE Patients
    first AS STRING * 15
    last AS STRING * 20
    birthdate AS STRING * 6
END TYPE
```

Creates a user-defined type named *Patients*.

```
TYPE Family
    address AS STRING * 30
    patient1 AS Patients
    patient2 AS Patients
    patient3 AS Patients
END TYPE
```

Creates a user-defined type named *Family* that contains elements that are of the user-defined type named *Patients*.

Description

Almost all modern computer languages let you create new data types; usually, you create a type that enables a single variable to hold several variables at once. For example, in developing a program for doctors to handle their insurance billing, you probably would want a single variable to contain the patient's name, address, social security number, medicare number, and so on.

When you define a type with the TYPE...END TYPE statement, you first give the type a name. This is the name you must refer to when you later define variables to be of this new type. The type name must be a legal QBasic identifier and must not be used by any other variable.

Then you define each element of the user-defined type. The element name can be the same as that of another variable, user-defined type, element, function, or subprogram name, but it cannot be the name of another element in the same TYPE...END TYPE statement; also, it cannot be the name of an array and it cannot contain periods.

You must then assign each element a type. This can be the keyword DOUBLE, INTEGER, LONG, or SINGLE, a fixed-length string (STRING*x) type, or the name of another user-defined type, but it cannot be a standard, variable-length string.

You can define a particular type only once in a module, and you cannot use TYPE...END TYPE statements in subprograms or functions. Therefore, the best place to put a TYPE...END TYPE statement is at the beginning of the module.

Defining a user-defined type does not create any variables; you must create variables of the type (called record variables) by using the COMMON, DIM, REDIM, SHARED, or STATIC statement. You can also use the AS clause in a DECLARE SUB, DECLARE FUNCTION, DEF FN, FUNCTION, or SUB statement to indicate that a variable you are passing is of a certain record type.

Figure 1-3 shows an example of a TYPE...END TYPE statement and a record-variable declaration.

```
TYPE Dates ───────────── Dates is the type name
    month AS INTEGER ⎤
    day AS INTEGER   ⎬─── month, day, and year are element names
    year AS INTEGER  ⎦    INTEGER is the type of the elements
END TYPE
```

```
DIM birth AS Dates ─────── birth is a record variable of type Dates
```

Figure 1-3.
An example TYPE...END TYPE statement and record-variable declaration.

You must use a special syntax to access an element in a record variable: Specify the record-variable name followed by a period (.) and then the element name. For example, in the record variable *birth*, which is declared in Figure 1-3, you would use the following statement to set the value of the element *month* to 9:

```
birth.month = 9
```

Use the same syntax to use an element of a record variable in the condition of an IF statement; for example,

```
IF 1990 - birth.year >= 18 THEN
    PRINT "OK to vote"
END IF
```

Comments
Although you cannot use arrays in a TYPE...END TYPE statement, you can create arrays that contain records defined by a TYPE...END TYPE statement.

Errors
If you create an element name that contains periods, QBasic returns an "Identifier cannot include period" error message.

Example
The following example uses a TYPE...END TYPE statement to create a record type that takes information about the planets and holds it in a single variable. You can use the program to write information to and then to read information from the data file SOL.DAT.

```
TYPE Planets                    ' type to hold planet information
    nam AS STRING * 20          ' planet name
    diameter AS LONG            ' planet diameter
    perihelion AS DOUBLE        ' orbital point closest to sun
    aphelion AS DOUBLE          ' orbital point farthest from sun
    highTemp AS SINGLE          ' highest surface temperature
    lowTemp AS SINGLE           ' lowest surface temperature
    yearDiscovered AS INTEGER   ' year planet was discovered
END TYPE

DIM planet AS Planets           ' define the variable planet

CLS
OPEN "SOL.DAT" FOR RANDOM AS #1 LEN = 50     ' open the data file

DO
    PRINT : PRINT : PRINT
    INPUT "Information on which planet [1-9]"; planetNum%  ' get number

    ' if out of range or user presses Enter, then exit the loop
    IF planetNum% < 1 OR planetNum% > 9 THEN EXIT DO

    GET #1, planetNum%, planet                ' get data from file

    PRINT : PRINT "Information on planet "; planet.nam      ' print header
    PRINT STRING$(79, 45): PRINT

    ' if the record is empty, then get all the information from the user
    IF planet.nam = STRING$(20, 0) THEN
        INPUT "Name"; planet.nam
        INPUT "Diameter (km)"; planet.diameter
        INPUT "Perihelion (km)"; planet.perihelion
        INPUT "Aphelion (km)"; planet.aphelion
        INPUT "High temperature (Celsius)"; planet.highTemp
        INPUT "Low temperature (Celsius)"; planet.lowTemp
        INPUT "Discovered in"; planet.yearDiscovered

        ' write the information to the file
        PUT #1, planetNum%, planet

        PRINT : PRINT "Information saved": PRINT : PRINT

    ' if record is not empty, then display it on the screen
    ELSE
        PRINT "Diameter is"; planet.diameter; "kilometers"
        PRINT "Perihelion is"; planet.perihelion; "kilometers"
        PRINT "Aphelion is"; planet.aphelion; "kilometers"
        PRINT "High temperature is"; planet.highTemp; "degrees"
        PRINT "Low temperature is"; planet.lowTemp; "degrees"
        PRINT "Discovered in"; planet.yearDiscovered
    END IF
LOOP            ' go back to beginning of loop

CLOSE
```

CHAPTER 2

Flow Control

Introduction

Few programs execute in one continuous sequence from the first statement to the last. Typically, a program performs different tasks; the tasks it performs depend upon the data it generates or the instructions it receives from the user. A well-structured program contains a separate section of code for each task, and execution branches to the appropriate section whenever the associated task must be performed.

Often a program must also perform a single task repeatedly. One program might execute a global search-and-replace on a 1000-page novel, changing every occurrence of the heroine's name from "Cindy" to "Sue." Another might print all the payroll checks for a company's employees. These types of operations, in fact, make computers particularly useful in business: Computers execute the same sequence of statements again and again without complaint, performing those boring and repetitive jobs that humans dislike.

This chapter discusses the ways that QBasic lets you control the sequence in which statements are executed. Table 2-1 lists these flow-control statements in alphabetic order.

Statement	Description
DO...LOOP	Repeats a block of statements while or until a given logical condition is true.
EXIT	Transfers control from a subprogram, user-defined function, or loop structure before the normal exit conditions are met.
FOR...NEXT	Repeats a block of statements a specified number of times.
GOTO	Executes an unconditional branch to a specified program line.
ON...GOSUB	Branches to a subroutine at one of several specified lines. On completion of the subroutine, control returns to the statement following the ON...GOSUB statement.
ON...GOTO	Branches to one of several specified lines.
WHILE...WEND	Repeats a block of statements while a given logical condition is true.

Table 2-1.
Flow-control statements in alphabetic order.

Branching

If a program consists of several sections, each of which performs a particular task, the program must be able to transfer control from one section to another. One way to transfer control in QBasic is to use a statement that performs branching. Unconditional branching always transfers control; conditional branching transfers control only if a certain condition is met.

Unconditional Branching

The simplest way to direct the flow of execution to another part of the program is to use an unconditional branch. You can use the GOTO statement for this; for example,

```
GOTO Finish
```

transfers control to the line that contains the label *Finish*. You can also use GOTO with a line number (if your program uses line numbers). The target line must be in the same portion of the program as the GOTO statement; you cannot use GOTO to branch into a subprogram or user-defined function. You can, however, use GOTO inside functions and subprograms, provided the target line is in the same function or subprogram.

GOTO differs from a function call: After the branch is made, the program executes statements following the target line either until it encounters another branching statement or until the program ends. Program execution doesn't return to the line following the GOTO statement, as it does with GOSUB. (See Chapter 4, "Procedures.") Note the one exception—when you use GOTO with the ON ERROR GOTO statement (defined in Chapter 9, "Error Trapping") to define an error-handling routine. In this case, when a subsequent RESUME statement is encountered, control returns to the section of the program from which the branch was made.

Conditional Branching

Although by itself GOTO is unconditional, it can be used as part of a conditional statement. For example, the following statements cause the program to branch to line 1000 only when the first letter contained in the string variable *response$* is a Y:

```
240 INPUT "Report to printer"; response$
250 IF UCASE$(LEFT$(response$, 1)) = "Y" THEN 1000
```

Note that the keyword GOTO is implicit when you use an IF...THEN statement. However, if the target statement has a label rather than a line number, you must include the GOTO keyword, as shown in the following statement:

```
250 IF UCASE$(LEFT$(response$, 1)) = "Y" THEN GOTO Print
```

Another version of the GOTO statement is also conditional. The ON...GOTO statement can direct the program to branch to one of several lines; the value of a variable or an expression determines which line. In the statement

```
900 ON selection% GOTO 1000, 2000, 3000, Start, Finish
```

control branches to one of five line numbers or labels in response to the value of the integer variable *selection%*. If *selection%* contains the value 1, the program branches to line 1000; if *selection%* contains the value 2, the program branches to line 2000; and so on. If *selection%* contains the value 0 or, in this case, a value greater than 5, no branching occurs, and control continues with the statement following line 900. Always be sure the variable *selection%* is the value 0 or greater. If the variable is negative, QBasic displays an "Illegal function call" error message.

Subroutines

The ON...GOSUB statement is similar to the ON...GOTO statement except that control returns to the statement following the ON...GOSUB statement after the subroutine finishes.

The ON...GOTO and ON...GOSUB statements are provided only to preserve compatibility with earlier versions of Basic. In QBasic, the preferred method of conditionally executing blocks of statements is to use the SELECT CASE statement. (See Chapter 3, "Decisions and Operators.") The SELECT CASE statement is more flexible than and has none of the limitations of ON...GOTO and ON...GOSUB.

Loops

A loop is a sequence of statements that a program executes more than once in succession. QBasic provides two kinds of loops. The first, which is controlled by the FOR...NEXT statement, is a loop that repeats a fixed number of times. (The program specifies the number of repetitions when the loop begins.)

In the second type of loop, the actual number of iterations is not specified in advance—it is determined by the result of a logical test that is made during every pass through the loop. Execution continues until a certain condition is met.

The FOR...NEXT Statement

In a FOR...NEXT statement, QBasic repeats the statements between the keywords FOR and NEXT a specified number of times. You determine the number of repetitions by assigning a range of values to the variable that is the loop counter; for example,

```
FOR count% = 1 TO 10
    PRINT count%;
NEXT count%
```

sets the initial value of the counter to 1 and then executes the loop. The loop increments the counter on each iteration until the counter is greater than its maximum value, which in this case is 10. Because the single statement in the body of the loop prints only the value of the counter, the output of the program is a series of numbers, 1 through 10.

QBasic lets you use the STEP clause to specify the value of the increment of the FOR...NEXT loop. The default increment is 1. For example, the following loop counts to 10 by twos:

```
FOR count% = 1 TO 10 STEP 2
    PRINT count%;
NEXT count%
```

This loop generates the output

```
1 3 5 7 9
```

You can also use the STEP clause to decrement the loop counter. The following program counts backward by threes:

```
FOR count% = 10 TO 1 STEP -3
    PRINT count%;
NEXT count%
```

This loop generates the output

```
10 7 4 1
```

You can use as many statement lines as you want in the body of the loop; the entire sequence repeats until the value of the counter is outside the specified range. When this happens, the program continues with the statement that follows the NEXT keyword.

The WHILE...WEND Statement

You can use the WHILE...WEND statement for those situations in which your program must execute a series of statements an indeterminate number of times. When QBasic first encounters the WHILE keyword, it tests the value of the associated logical expression or variable, and if the value of the expression or variable is true (nonzero), it executes the subsequent statements. When the program finds the matching WEND keyword, it returns control to the top of the loop and tests the value of the associated expression or variable again. If the value is still true, the process is repeated; if it is false (zero), program execution continues with the statement that follows the WEND keyword. (See Chapter 3, "Decisions and Operators," for an explanation of what makes an expression logically true or false.) The following program, for example,

```
count% = 1
WHILE count% <= 10
    PRINT count%;
    count% = count% + 1
WEND
```

generates the output

```
1 2 3 4 5 6 7 8 9 10
```

This kind of loop is called an "entry-condition" loop because the test is made at the top of the loop. If the test expression is already false when the WHILE keyword is first encountered (for example, if count% is initially 11), the program bypasses the loop completely and no statements within it are executed.

Because all QBasic numeric variables and functions return values that can be interpreted logically as well as numerically, the WHILE...WEND statement has many applications. The following example opens a sequential access file of unknown length and uses a WHILE...WEND statement to read from the file until the end of the file is encountered:

```
OPEN file$ FOR INPUT AS #1
WHILE NOT EOF(1)
    LINE INPUT #1, record$
    PRINT record$
WEND
```

The DO...LOOP Statement

The DO...LOOP statement is more powerful and flexible than WHILE...WEND. You can easily rewrite the previous example by using a DO...LOOP statement:

```
OPEN file$ FOR INPUT AS #1
DO WHILE NOT EOF(1)
    LINE INPUT #1, record$
    PRINT record$
LOOP
```

This is almost identical to the WHILE...WEND version, including the rudimentary test for the end of the file. In addition to repeating a series of statements while a condition is true, a DO...LOOP statement can also repeat statements only while a condition is false; that is, it loops until the condition is true. The syntax of the DO...LOOP statement, in fact, lets you state this explicitly by using the keyword UNTIL in the DO...LOOP statement, as shown in the following example:

```
OPEN file$ FOR INPUT AS #1
DO UNTIL EOF(1)
    LINE INPUT #1, record$
    PRINT record$
LOOP
```

Both DO...LOOP statements in the two previous examples are, like WHILE...WEND statements, entry-condition loops; this means that if the test fails when the loop is first entered (if the file is empty, for example), the statements inside the loop are never executed. However, a loop created by a DO...LOOP statement can also be an exit-condition loop, in which the body of the loop is always executed at least once; for example,

```
DO
    PRINT SPACE$(81 - POS(0))
LOOP WHILE CSRLIN < 23
```

always clears to the end of the current line, even if the cursor is already on or below line 23 of the display. You can also use UNTIL in place of WHILE in an exit-condition loop, as shown in the following example:

```
PRINT "Ready printer, press P to continue"
DO
    ready$ = UCASE$(INPUT$(1))
LOOP UNTIL ready$ = "P"
```

The preceding examples show that the DO...LOOP statement is far more versatile than the WHILE...WEND statement. Because of its versatility, the DO...LOOP statement has become the preferred method of constructing loops that involve logical tests.

Breaking Out of Loops

QBasic lets you exit a loop at a statement within the body of a loop in addition to exiting at its usual exit point, even if the normal exit condition has not been met. An EXIT DO statement interrupts the execution of a DO...LOOP statement from any point between the keywords DO and LOOP and resumes execution at the statement following the keyword LOOP. The EXIT FOR statement performs the same operation in a FOR...NEXT statement.

The following set of statements uses a FOR...NEXT statement to scan for a character that has been set at a random location in a string of blank spaces. If the character is found, the program uses an EXIT FOR statement to exit the loop; this leaves the $i\%$ counter indicating the location of the target character.

```
RANDOMIZE TIMER

a$ = SPACE$(10000)
x% = INT(RND * 10000) + 1
MID$(a$, x%, 1) = CHR$(INT(RND * 223) + 32)

FOR i% = 1 TO 10000
    IF MID$(a$, i%, 1) <> " " THEN EXIT FOR
NEXT i%
IF i% > 10000 THEN
    PRINT "Not found!"
ELSE
    PRINT i%; MID$(a$, i%, 1)
END IF
```

QBasic provides similar EXIT statements for escaping from user-defined functions and subprograms. EXIT DEF, for example, lets a program exit a DEF FN function call before the END DEF statement is executed; EXIT SUB and EXIT FUNCTION perform the same service for subprograms and user-defined functions. (See Chapter 4, "Procedures," for details of subprograms and functions.) No equivalent exit statement exists for the WHILE...WEND statement.

DO...LOOP

See also
EXIT, FOR...NEXT, WHILE...WEND

Purpose
The DO...LOOP statement repeats the execution of a block of statements while (or until) an exit or entry condition is met. Use DO...LOOP to count up or down, iterate a value, or repeat a procedure while a given condition is true or until it becomes false.

Syntax
The DO...LOOP statement has two possible syntaxes; the syntax depends on whether you test for the exit condition at the beginning or at the end of the loop.

To test at the beginning of a loop, use the following syntax:

```
DO [{WHILE ¦ UNTIL} expr]
     [statements]
LOOP
```

If the exit condition is already met on entry into the structure, the loop is not executed.

To test at the end of a loop, use the following syntax:

```
DO
     [statements]
LOOP [{WHILE ¦ UNTIL} expr]
```

The body of the loop is always executed at least once, whether or not the exit condition is met on entry into the structure.

statements are the one or more QBasic program statements that are repeated. Notice that they are optional—empty loops, which do nothing until an external event (such as a keypress) occurs, are permissible.

expr is any logical expression; that is, it must evaluate to either true (a nonzero value) or false (a value of zero).

If you use the WHILE keyword, the loop repeats while the expression remains true. If you use UNTIL, the loop repeats while the expression remains false (that is, until the expression is true).

Usage

```
DO
LOOP WHILE INKEY$ = ""
```
Suspends program execution until a key is pressed.

```
DO UNTIL PLAY(1) = 0
LOOP
```
Suspends program execution until the background music buffer is empty.

```
DO
    x% = INT(RND * 80) + 1
    y% = INT(RND * 24) + 1
    LOCATE y%, x%
    PRINT "*";
LOOP UNTIL INKEY$ = CHR$(27)
```

Prints asterisks at random locations on the screen until the user presses Esc.

Description

The DO...LOOP statement lets you execute a loop either while a given condition is true or until the condition is true. The DO...LOOP statement also lets you test for the exit condition at either the beginning or the end of the loop. If you place the test condition at the beginning of the loop and if the exit condition is already met, the loop is not executed. If, however, you place the test condition at the end of the loop, the body of the loop is always executed at least once, even if the exit condition is already met.

Be sure that any loop you create will eventually end. If you create a loop whose exit condition is never met, the program will run indefinitely.

You can use the EXIT DO statement in the middle of a loop to exit the loop before the exit condition is met. EXIT DO transfers control to the first statement after the keyword LOOP.

Although QBasic returns −1 to represent a true expression, in practice any nonzero value evaluates as true; therefore, you can use any numeric variable or function as the expression in a DO...LOOP statement.

Errors

Every DO statement in a program must have a corresponding LOOP statement, just as every LOOP must have a preceding DO. If the program executes a LOOP statement without having encountered a previous DO, QBasic displays a "LOOP without DO" error message. Conversely, an unmatched DO statement causes QBasic to display a "DO without LOOP" error message.

Warnings

Although the GOTO statement does not produce an immediate error, do not use it to exit the body of a DO...LOOP statement.

If you repeatedly exit a loop with GOTO, the program stack will grow uncontrollably, eventually producing an "Out of stack space" error message. If you must exit a loop prematurely, use the EXIT DO statement.

Example

The following program uses a DO...LOOP statement to create a game. The program displays a character representing a skier. The skier moves down the screen between two lines of a "track"; if the skier hits either edge of the track, the program ends. The user can avoid hitting the track by moving the skier left and right with the left and right direction keys.

```
CLS : RANDOMIZE TIMER
ySkier% = 21: xSkier% = 55                    ' coordinates for the skier
yTrack% = 24: xTrack% = 51                    ' coordinates for the track
rightDirection$ = CHR$(0) + CHR$(77): leftDirection$ = CHR$(0) + CHR$(75)
track$ = CHR$(176) + "      " + CHR$(176)

DO
    LOCATE 1, 1: PRINT "Score ="; score&      ' print score
    score& = score& + 1

    LOCATE yTrack%, xTrack%: PRINT track$     ' print track
    change% = INT((RND * 3) - 1)
    xTrack% = xTrack% + change%               ' change position of track

    r$ = INKEY$
    IF r$ = leftDirection$ THEN xSkier% = xSkier% - 1     ' move skier left
    IF r$ = rightDirection$ THEN xSkier% = xSkier% + 1    ' move skier right

    LOCATE ySkier%, xSkier%: PRINT CHR$(2);    ' print skier
LOOP WHILE SCREEN(ySkier% + 1, xSkier%) <> 176 ' exit loop if skier hits track

END
```

EXIT

See also
DEF FN, DO...LOOP, FOR...NEXT, FUNCTION, SUB

Purpose
EXIT transfers control out of a loop or procedure either before the exit condition is met or before the end of the procedure is reached. Use this statement if you want your program to respond to a separate event that might occur before the loop finishes executing.

Syntax
EXIT {DEF ┆ DO ┆ FOR ┆ FUNCTION ┆ SUB}

Use EXIT with one of the five QBasic keywords in the preceding syntax line. You must include one of the keywords in braces; the keyword you must include depends on the type of loop or procedure in which you use the EXIT statement.

Usage
```
DO WHILE x% < 100
    PRINT x%, x% ^ 2
    IF INKEY$ = "Q" THEN EXIT DO
    x% = x% + 1
LOOP
```
Uses EXIT DO to exit a loop if the user types the letter Q.

Description

The EXIT DO and EXIT FOR statements can be used to exit a loop defined by either a DO...LOOP statement or a FOR...NEXT statement. When a program executes either of these statements, control transfers to the first statement after the loop.

If a program contains nested FOR...NEXT or DO...LOOP statements, EXIT exits only the current loop. Statements in any loop outside of the one in which the EXIT instruction occurs continue to execute until that loop terminates or another EXIT statement is encountered.

The EXIT DEF, EXIT FUNCTION, and EXIT SUB statements can be used to exit a procedure defined by a DEF FN, a FUNCTION, or a SUB statement. When a program uses any of these statements, control returns to the statement following the call to the procedure. If a program uses EXIT DEF or EXIT FUNCTION before an assignment has been made to the function, the function returns an indeterminate value.

Example

The following QBasic program calls a function that checks a string the user entered to see whether the string is a valid filename. The function tests the characters in the string and the length of the string. The string can be a filename with or without an extension. If any test fails, the function uses the EXIT FUNCTION statement to return prematurely; this sets a validation flag to false.

```
DECLARE FUNCTION ValidName% (fileSpec$)

CONST FALSE = 0, TRUE = NOT FALSE

CLS
PRINT "Enter a filename for testing: ";
LINE INPUT f$
PRINT : PRINT "That is a";

IF ValidName%(f$) THEN
    PRINT " legal filename."
ELSE
    PRINT "n illegal filename."
END IF
END

' test filename for invalid characters and length
FUNCTION ValidName% (fileSpec$) STATIC
    length% = LEN(fileSpec$)
    invalid$ = ""
    ValidName% = FALSE

    FOR i% = 0 TO 32          ' create string of all invalid characters
        invalid$ = invalid$ + CHR$(i%)
    NEXT
    invalid$ = invalid$ + "/\[]:|<>+=;," + CHR$(34)
```

(continued)

continued

```
    FOR i% = 1 TO length%     ' check for any invalid characters
        IF INSTR(invalid$, MID$(fileSpec$, i%, 1)) > 0 THEN
            EXIT FOR
        END IF
    NEXT i%

    IF i% < length% + 1 THEN EXIT FUNCTION  ' string has an invalid character
    ValidName% = TRUE                       ' string has no invalid characters

    dot% = INSTR(fileSpec$, ".")            ' check for an extension
    IF dot% = 0 THEN
        IF length% > 8 THEN                 ' check length of string
            ValidName% = FALSE
        END IF
    ELSEIF dot% > 9 OR dot% < (length% - 3) THEN  ' check length of extension
        ValidName% = FALSE
    END IF
END FUNCTION
```

FOR...NEXT

See also
DO...LOOP, EXIT, WHILE...WEND

Purpose
A FOR...NEXT loop executes a sequence of program statements a specified number of times. Use the FOR...NEXT statement to specify the number of times you want the statements to be repeated—for example, to print the numbers 1 through 100.

Syntax
FOR *cntr* = *initval* TO *finalval* [STEP *incr*]
    [*statements*]
NEXT [*cntr* [, *cntr*...]]

cntr is a numeric variable that counts the number of times the loop executes. It can be of type integer, long integer, single-precision, or double-precision and can be an element of an array.

initval is the value assigned to the counter when the loop begins; *initval* can be a constant, a variable, or an expression.

finalval is the value for which the loop tests *cntr* at the beginning of each pass. If the counter value is greater than *finalval* (or less than *finalval* if *incr* is a negative value), execution of the loop ceases and control transfers to the statement following the keyword NEXT. *finalval* can be a constant, a variable, or an expression.

incr is the amount by which the counter variable is increased (or decreased, if *incr* is a negative value) after every iteration of the loop. It can be a constant, a variable, or an expression; if you omit it, QBasic uses a value of 1.

When FOR...NEXT loops are nested within each other, you can combine the NEXT statement of each loop into a single NEXT statement by including after the keyword NEXT the name of every counter.

Usage

```
FOR third! = 1 TO 10 STEP 1 / 3
    PRINT third!;
NEXT third!
```

This loop counts from 1 to 10 in steps of ⅓. The loop terminates after 28 iterations.

```
FOR counter% = 20 TO 1 STEP -1
    PRINT TAB(5); counter%
NEXT counter%
PRINT TAB(5); counter%
PRINT "BLAST OFF!"
```

This loop executes 20 times; the STEP instruction decrements the value of the counter variable by 1 at each iteration. (Note that when the loop terminates, the counter contains the value 0, not 1.)

Description

The FOR...NEXT statement repeats execution of a block of statements a specified number of times. On entry into a FOR...NEXT loop, QBasic first stores the value of the specified final value and then sets the counter variable to the value of the specified initial value. QBasic also checks for a STEP instruction to see whether the loop counter is to be incremented or decremented on successive iterations of the loop. If no STEP instruction is given, QBasic increments the counter variable by 1.

If, at this preliminary stage, the counter value is greater than the final value and the increment is positive, QBasic does not execute the loop. Instead, control transfers to the statement following the NEXT statement. Similarly, if the increment is negative and the initial counter value is less than the final value, the loop is not executed.

If the counter value is within the range specified by the initial and final values, QBasic executes the program lines following the FOR statement until it encounters the NEXT statement. Then it adjusts the counter variable by the value given in the STEP instruction. If the increment is positive, the value is added to the counter variable; if it is negative, the value is subtracted from the counter variable.

Note that the actual test is always made after the FOR keyword, at the beginning of the loop. The NEXT statement merely adjusts the counter value before it returns control to the FOR statement. This order means that on completion of the loop, the counter value is always greater (if the increment is positive) or less (if the increment is negative) than the specified final value.

If, when control returns to the FOR statement, the value of the counter is greater than the final value (or less if the increment is negative), control transfers to the statement that follows the loop. Otherwise, the loop executes again.

You can nest FOR...NEXT loops. For example, if you nest a loop that counts from 1 through 10 in a loop that counts from 1 through 5, the program counts from 1 through 10 five times. By including in one NEXT statement the name of the counter of each loop in a nested FOR...NEXT loop, you can combine the NEXT statements of the loops. The following two segments of code, for example, are syntactically equivalent:

```
FOR row% = 1 TO 24
    LOCATE row%, 1
    FOR stripe% = 1 TO 20
        FOR colors% = 9 TO 12
            COLOR colors%
            PRINT "*";
        NEXT colors%
    NEXT stripe%
NEXT row%

FOR row% = 1 TO 24
    LOCATE row%, 1
    FOR stripe% = 1 TO 20
        FOR colors% = 9 TO 12
            COLOR colors%
            PRINT "*";
NEXT colors%, stripe%, row%
```

Errors

Each FOR statement must have a corresponding NEXT statement just as every NEXT statement must have a preceding FOR. If you omit the NEXT statement, QBasic displays a "FOR without NEXT" error message. If QBasic encounters a NEXT statement without a preceding FOR, it displays a "NEXT without FOR" error message. The "NEXT without FOR" error also occurs if you inadvertently cross loops. The following code fragment shows a typical mistake that produces such an error:

```
FOR i% = 1 TO 20
    PRINT i%
    FOR j% = 1 TO 10
        PRINT j%;
    NEXT i%  ┐
    PRINT    ┘────── These two lines have been transposed
NEXT j%  ─────
```

Tips

Note that QBasic sets the final value for the loop before it initializes the counter to the starting value. The following program fragment, for example, prints the numbers 1 through 10 (not 1 through 6, as you might suppose):

```
i% = 5
FOR i% = 1 TO i% + 5
    PRINT i%;
NEXT
```

You must close nested loops in the reverse order from that in which you opened them. You cannot close a FOR...NEXT loop until you've closed all other loops nested inside it.

If you do not specifically name a variable in the NEXT statement, QBasic uses the counter specified by the most recent FOR statement.

Example

FOR...NEXT loops are ideal for tasks that repeat a series of actions an exact number of times. The following program prints large text for title screens and banners. The displayed text is encoded into DATA statements that are read into the program by a series of FOR...NEXT loops.

```
CONST FALSE = 0, TRUE = NOT FALSE
DEF SEG = &H40: IF PEEK(&H49) = 7 THEN mono% = TRUE   ' check for monochrome

CLS : DEF SEG : RESTORE Text

READ row%, column%, hue%, numColumns%
IF NOT mono% THEN COLOR hue%

' print each letter of the banner one column at a time
FOR newColumn% = 1 TO numColumns%
    READ item$
    IF item$ = "F" THEN item$ = "12345678"          ' if "F," fill the column
    FOR i% = 1 TO LEN(item$)
        IF MID$(item$, i%, 1) = "*" THEN EXIT FOR   ' if "*," start next letter
        space% = VAL(MID$(item$, i%, 1))            ' index of the space to fill
        LOCATE row% + space%, column%
        PRINT CHR$(219);                            ' fill the space
    NEXT i%
    IF i% = 1 THEN                          ' change color for the next letter
        hue% = hue% + 1
        IF hue% = 7 THEN hue% = 9
        IF hue% > 14 THEN hue% = 1
        IF NOT mono% THEN COLOR hue%
    END IF
    column% = column% + 1
NEXT newColumn%
COLOR 14, 0: LOCATE 15, 28: PRINT "P R O G R A M M E R ' S"
COLOR 11, 0: LOCATE 16, 31: PRINT "R E F E R E N C E"
END

' Data Division
Text:
DATA    3, 18, 9, 42
DATA    F, F, 1238, 168, 1678, 18, F, F, *              ' "O"
DATA    F, F, 1248, 148, 148, 148, F, 1235678, *        ' "B"
DATA    F, F, 124, 14, 14, F, F, *                      ' "A"
DATA    123478, 123478, 148, 148, 1245678, 1245678, *   ' "S"
DATA    F, F, *                                         ' "I"
DATA    F, F, 18, 18, 1278, 1278                        ' "C"
```

GOTO

Purpose

The GOTO statement can be used to branch to a particular section of code. In QBasic, you rarely need to use GOTO; it is retained to provide compatibility with programs written in earlier versions of Basic.

Syntax

GOTO {*line* ¦ *label*}

line or *label* specifies the destination of the GOTO statement. The destination must be a line in the current module. Execution branches to the statement at *line* or *label* and continues from that point until either another GOTO statement is encountered or until the program ends.

Usage

```
GOTO 1000
```
Branches to the statement at line 1000 in the current module.

```
GOTO PrintOut
```
Branches to the line labeled *PrintOut* and continues execution from there.

Description

GOTO forces QBasic to branch to the line number or label specified; control always transfers to the destination line. If the destination line contains a remark or a DATA statement, control passes to the next executable statement.

You cannot use GOTO to branch into or out of a subprogram or user-defined function; you can, however, use GOTO to direct control flow within these procedures.

IF...THEN statements (described in Chapter 3, "Decisions and Operators") can include an implied GOTO statement after the THEN clause, as in the following example:

```
IF y% = 50 THEN 1000
```

In this case, execution branches to line 1000 when $y\%$ equals 50. This implicit GOTO works only with line numbers, however; if the destination line has a label, you must insert the GOTO keyword:

```
IF x% >= 100 THEN GOTO OverFlow
```

Example

QBasic control structures such as multi-line IF statements and DO loops have lessened the need for GOTO statements. The following example uses a GOTO statement to check that the user entered a valid name. The subprogram following the example uses structured programming to perform the same task. Structured programming produces compact and efficient code and is much easier to maintain.

```
 10  lc$ = "abcdefghijklmnopqrstuvwxyz "
 20  uc$ = UCASE$(lc$)
 30  nu$ = "0123456789-+/."
 40  valid$ = uc$ + lc$           ' a string containing all valid characters
 50  buffer$ = ""                 ' buffer for name
 60  max% = 30                    ' maximum number of characters

 70  CLS : LOCATE 10, 1, 1: PRINT "Type your name > ";
 80  length% = 0
 90  keyStroke$ = INKEY$
100  IF keyStroke$ = "" THEN 90            ' loop until user types a character
110  IF keyStroke$ = CHR$(13) THEN 230     ' exit when user presses Enter

120  IF keyStroke$ <> CHR$(8) THEN 180     ' branch if user does not press Backspace
130  IF length% = 0 THEN 90
140  PRINT CHR$(29); " "; CHR$(29);
150  length% = length% - 1
160  buffer$ = LEFT$(buffer$, length%)
170  GOTO 90

180  IF length% = max% OR INSTR(valid$, keyStroke$) = 0 THEN 90
190  buffer$ = buffer$ + keyStroke$
200  PRINT keyStroke$;
210  length% = length% + 1
220  GOTO 90

230  LOCATE 20, 1: PRINT buffer$
240  END
```

```
' this program does the same as previous program using structured programming
SUB GetInput (max%, buffer$) STATIC
    SHARED valid$
    length% = 0
    DO
        DO
            keyStroke$ = INKEY$
        LOOP WHILE keyStroke$ = ""     ' loop until user types a character
        IF keyStroke$ = CHR$(8) THEN   ' check whether user pressed Backspace
            IF length% > 0 THEN
                length% = length% - 1
                PRINT CHR$(29); " "; CHR$(29);
                buffer$ = LEFT$(buffer$, length%)
            END IF
        ELSE
            IF length% < max% AND INSTR(valid$, keyStroke$) THEN
                buffer$ = buffer$ + keyStroke$
                PRINT keyStroke$; : length% = length% + 1
            END IF
        END IF
    LOOP UNTIL keyStroke$ = CHR$(13)   ' exit when user presses Enter
END SUB
```

ON...GOSUB

See also

GOSUB...RETURN, ON...GOTO, SELECT CASE

Purpose

The ON...GOSUB statement branches control to one of several QBasic subroutines; the value of an expression determines the subroutine to which the statement branches. It is similar to the ON...GOTO statement except that control eventually returns to the section of the program from which it branched.

Syntax

ON *expr* GOSUB {*line1* ¦ *label1*} [, {*line2* ¦ *label2*}...]

expr is a numeric variable or expression. QBasic converts *expr* to an integer and then applies the value to the list of line numbers or labels. The list is used as a jump table that specifies the line to which the program branches. If *expr* evaluates to 1, control branches to the line specified by *line1* or *label1*; if *expr* evaluates to 2, control branches to the line specified by *line2* or *label2*; and so on. Note that the list can be a mixture of labels and line numbers.

Usage

```
ON INT(RND * 2) + 1 GOSUB Heads, Tails
```

Branches to one of two subroutines; the subroutine is determined by the value of a random number.

Description

ON...GOSUB is an alternative to the ON...GOTO statement. Like ON...GOTO, it lets your program branch to one of several line numbers or labels; the line number or label to which it branches depends on the value of an expression. Execution continues from there. Unlike ON...GOTO, the target address is the start of a QBasic subroutine. When the program encounters the RETURN statement that marks the end of the subroutine, control returns to the statement following the ON...GOSUB statement.

If the expression evaluates to 0 or is a number greater than the number of entries in the jump table, control passes to the statement that follows ON...GOSUB and none of the subroutines are executed.

You do not need to use a different line number or label for every entry in the jump table; the same line number or label can serve in several entries. In the following example, the program branches to line number 200 when the variable *where%* contains the value 2, 4, or 7:

```
ON where% GOSUB Start, 200, 300, 200, File, Printer, 200, Finish
```

Comments

Although QBasic accepts integers in the range 0 through 255 as the value of the expression in an ON...GOSUB statement, you cannot branch to more than 60 line numbers and labels in the list of addresses. In practice, you are even more limited because you must fit the entire statement—line or label list included—into a single program line.

Errors

If the expression used in the ON argument evaluates to a number less than 0 or greater than 255, QBasic displays an "Illegal function call" error message.

Example

Because ON...GOSUB can branch to different subroutines in response to different values of an expression, it's ideal for programming multiple-choice tests and menus. The following program displays a multiple-choice question and then uses an ON...GOSUB statement to execute the routine that corresponds to the response that it receives.

```
COLOR 0, 2: CLS : COLOR 14, 4: PRINT SPACE$(240)
LOCATE 2, 30: PRINT "****MULTIPLE CHOICE****";
LOCATE 4, 1: PRINT STRING$(80, "_"); : COLOR 0, 2
LOCATE 10, 25: PRINT "Are you enjoying this program?";

DO
    PLAY "L62 O4 T250 D G G D G# A A O3 D G G D A A# A# O2 D G G D A# B B"
    LOCATE 13, 29, 1: PRINT "<Y>es, <N>o, <M>aybe";
    LOCATE 15, 40
    r$ = UCASE$(INPUT$(1))                      ' get input from user
    ON INSTR("YNM", r$) GOSUB Yes, No, Maybe    ' branch to Yes, No, or Maybe
LOOP WHILE response$ = ""
LOCATE 18, 40 - (LEN(response$) \ 2)
PRINT response$;
PLAY tune$
END

Maybe:
    tune$ = "T255 L15 O1 A D C E F A O2 D E F A E C"
    response$ = "You sound undecided!"
    RETURN
Yes:
    tune$ = "L8 O2 T240 D.. E. P16 ML A G B."
    response$ = "You sound very positive!"
    RETURN
No:
    tune$ = "T200 O314 G C D E L2 F L4 E C L2 D P64 D L4 E L1C"
    response$ = "You sound very negative!"
    RETURN
```

ON...GOTO

See also

GOTO, ON...GOSUB, SELECT CASE

Purpose

The ON...GOTO statement branches control to one of several lines. A program often needs to perform one of a set of different tasks; the event that occurs while the program is executing determines the task. This event might be the result of either a test or input from the user. The ON...GOTO statement is the traditional means of testing an event and transferring control to the appropriate address.

Syntax

ON *expr* GOTO {*line1* ¦ *label1*} [, {*line2* ¦ *label2*}...]

expr is a numeric variable or expression. QBasic converts it to an integer value and then applies the value to the list of line numbers or labels. The list is used as a jump table that specifies the lines to which the program branches. If *expr* evaluates to 1, control branches to the line specified by *line1* or *label1*; if *expr* evaluates to 2, control passes to the line specified by *line2* or *label2*, and so on. Note that the list can be a combination of labels and line numbers.

Usage

```
ON INT(RND * 3) + 1 GOTO One, Two, Three
```
Randomly branches to a destination routine starting at the label *One*, *Two*, or *Three*.

Description

Using the ON...GOTO statement is the traditional way of creating jump tables in Basic. The value of the expression supplied to it is an index to the list of line numbers or labels that follow the GOTO keyword. When the statement executes, QBasic evaluates the expression and then transfers control to the line specified by the corresponding table entry. If the expression evaluates to 0 or is greater than the number of entries in the table, no branch is made and control passes to the next statement after the ON...GOTO statement.

You do not need to use a different line number or label for every entry in the jump table; the same line number or label can serve as several entries. In the following example, the program branches to line 200 when *where%* contains the value 2, 4, or 7:

```
ON where% GOTO Start, 200, 300, 200, File, Printer, 200, Finish
```

You cannot use an ON...GOTO statement to transfer execution into or out of either a subprogram or a user-defined function. You can, however, use this statement to direct control flow within these procedures.

QBasic provides a more flexible way of constructing jump tables with the SELECT CASE statement. One benefit of SELECT CASE is that it lets you specify a range of values that causes the program to branch to a single address. (See Chapter 3, "Decisions and Operators," for more details.)

Comments

Although QBasic accepts integers in the range 0 through 255 as the value of the expression in an ON...GOTO statement, you cannot branch to more than 60 line numbers or labels in the list of addresses. In practice, you are even more limited because you must fit the entire statement—line or label list included—into a single program line.

Errors

If the expression used in the ON argument evaluates to a number less than 0 or greater than 255, QBasic displays an "Illegal function call" error message.

Example

In games or computer-aided instruction software, you need to be able to reward a successful player. The following program uses an ON...GOTO statement to instruct your computer to play a piece of music with a duration that corresponds to the size of the score obtained by a call to the RND function.

```
RANDOMIZE TIMER:  ' force a new random number each time

CLS : LOCATE 10, 30: PRINT "YOUR SCORE ...";
score% = RND * 5000
PRINT score%

ON (score% \ 1000) + 1 GOTO Shortest, Shorter, Longer, Longest

Shortest:
    PLAY "L4 T200 ML O2 G E G F D O1 B O2 C.. MN"
    SYSTEM
Shorter:
    PLAY "P32 L4 T200 ML O1 G O2 C D E2 C E O2 D C D E F"
    SYSTEM
Longer:
    PLAY "L4 T200 ML O1 G O2 C D E.. P16 MS E ML E D C D. D"
    SYSTEM
Longest:
    PLAY "L4 T200 ML O1 G O2 C D E.. P16 MS E ML E D C D C O1 A P48"
    SYSTEM
END
```

WHILE...WEND

See also

DO...LOOP, FOR...NEXT

Purpose

The WHILE...WEND statement repeats a series of statements only while a given condition is true (for example, until the end of a file is reached).

Syntax

```
WHILE logicalexpr
    [statements]
WEND
```

logicalexpr is any numeric variable or expression that evaluates to true (a nonzero value) or false (zero). While *logicalexpr* is true, QBasic executes the statements in the loop between the WHILE and WEND keywords. When *logicalexpr* becomes false, control transfers to the statement that follows WEND. Execution continues from there.

Usage

```
WHILE INKEY$ = ""
WEND
```

Loops continuously until the user presses a key.

```
WHILE NOT EOF(1)
    LINE INPUT #1, buffer$
    PRINT buffer$
WEND
```

Reads successive lines from a sequential file into the string variable *buffer$* and displays the lines on the screen. This continues until the loop reaches the end of the file.

Description

WHILE...WEND is called an entry-condition loop because the logical test is performed at the beginning of the loop. If the expression is already false when the WHILE statement is first encountered, QBasic bypasses the loop and does not execute the statements within it.

The body of a WHILE...WEND loop can contain any number of statements. WHILE...WEND loops can also include other WHILE...WEND loops; these can be nested to any level. QBasic includes the DO...LOOP statement, which provides greater flexibility than the WHILE...WEND statement.

Errors

Every WHILE in a program must have a corresponding WEND, just as every WEND must have a preceding WHILE. If a program executes a WEND statement without having encountered a previous WHILE, it returns a "WEND without WHILE" error message. Conversely, an unmatched WHILE statement causes QBasic to display a "WHILE without WEND" error message.

Example

Because it executes until a specified condition becomes true, a WHILE...WEND loop is particularly suitable for procedures that need to monitor external events, such as user input. The following program uses WHILE...WEND statements to switch between two graphics displays; one display changes to the other in response to a keypress.

```
' this program requires at least a Color Graphics Adapter
SCREEN 1: LINE (0, 0)-(320, 200), 1, BF
VIEW (32, 4)-(288, 196), 0, 15
CLS 1
esc$ = CHR$(27)
WHILE keyPress$ <> esc$
    LINE (78, 75)-(178, 75), 3                  ' draw top line
    LINE (78, 125)-(178, 125), 3                ' draw bottom line
    PSET (78, 75), 3: DRAW "C3 H8 BD16 E8"      ' draw arrows
    PSET (178, 75), 3: DRAW "C3 E8 BD16 H8"
    PSET (86, 125), 3: DRAW "C3 BU8 G8 F8"
    PSET (170, 125), 3: DRAW "C3 BU8 F8 G8"
    keyPress$ = ""
    WHILE keyPress$ = ""
        keyPress$ = INKEY$
    WEND
    IF keyPress$ <> esc$ THEN
        PSET (78, 75), 0: DRAW "C0 H8 BD16 E8"  ' erase arrows
        PSET (178, 75), 0: DRAW "C0 E8 BD16 H8"
        PSET (86, 125), 3: DRAW "C0 BU8 G8 F8"
        PSET (170, 125), 3: DRAW "C0 BU8 F8 G8"
        keyPress$ = ""
        WHILE keyPress$ = ""
            keyPress$ = INKEY$
        WEND
    END IF
WEND
END
```

CHAPTER 3

Decisions and Operators

Introduction

Decisions. The average person makes thousands of decisions every day. Changing situations and new stimuli force everyone into constantly shifting actions and reactions. Programs, too, must confront new information and alter their performance accordingly. Computers would be of little use if their responses were always fixed and unalterable.

Decision-making structures are vital to programming. Something as simple (yet important) as accepting a user's choice from a menu requires decision making. For example, if the user enters an "A" (for Add), the program adds new information; however, if the user enters a "Q" (for Quit), the program ends. The statements, functions, and operators of the decisions category of QBasic let you create programs that can make these important decisions.

This tutorial summarizes QBasic's decision-making abilities and offers some suggestions for their use. Table 3-1, below, is a list of QBasic's decision-making statements, functions, and operators.

Statement, function, or operator	Description
AND	Logical conjunction operator
+	String concatenation operator
EQV	Logical equivalency operator
IF	Conditional statement
IMP	Logical implication operator
MOD	Arithmetic modulo operator
NOT	Logical negation operator
OR	Logical disjunction operator
SELECT CASE	Conditional comparison statement
XOR	Logical "exclusive or" operator

Table 3-1.
QBasic's decision-making statements, functions, and operators.

IF—The General-Purpose Decision Maker

In QBasic, as in English, you use the IF statement to make general-purpose decisions. Consider the following sentence:

> If the sun is shining, I will go on a picnic; otherwise, I will stay inside.

You can rephrase the sentence to include the words "then" and "else":

> If the sun is shining, then I will go on a picnic; else, I will stay inside.

Now you can translate this phrase into QBasic statements:

```
IF sunShining THEN
    GOTO Picnic
ELSE
    GOTO Indoors
END IF
```

The expression that follows the IF keyword (in this case, *sunShining*) is called the *antecedent*.

The actions of the IF statement are straightforward. If the antecedent is true, the statements following the THEN keyword are executed; if the antecedent is false, however, the statements following the ELSE keyword are executed. In the example, if the expression *sunShining* is true, the program branches to *Picnic*. If the expression is false, the program branches to *Indoors*.

How does QBasic know what is "true" and what is "false"? For QBasic, true and false are merely numbers—false is 0, and true is any number except 0. In the previous example, *sunShining* could be a variable that is 0 when the sun isn't shining and any other number when it is. Internally, QBasic generates the value −1 for true; however, any number other than 0 will be recognized as true.

Relational Operators

Let's look at QBasic's relational operators, which are =, <>, >, <, >=, and <=. Table 3-2 defines these operators.

Relational operator	Math symbol	Example	Meaning
=	=	x = y	Equal to
<>	≠	x <> y	Not equal to
>	>	x > y	Greater than
<	<	x < y	Less than
>=	≥	x >= y	Greater than or equal to
<=	≤	x <= y	Less than or equal to

Table 3-2.
Relational operators.

With QBasic's idea of true and false in mind, let's examine how the relational operators work. Remember that QBasic returns the value −1 if an expression is true and 0 if an expression is false. All of these operators compare one value to another.

Equality

The operator = checks for equality. When QBasic encounters the expression

$x = y$

it compares x with y. If x equals y, the expression is true; otherwise, the expression is false. For example, the expression *150 = 200* is false.

Inequality

The operator <> checks for inequality. When QBasic encounters the expression

$x <> y$

it compares x with y. If x does not equal y, the expression is true; otherwise, the expression is false. For example, the expression *150 <> 200* is true.

Greater Than

The operator > checks for relative values. The expression

$x > y$

is true if x is greater than y. If y is greater, the expression is false.

Less Than

Like the operator >, the operator < checks for relative values. The expression

$x < y$

is true if x is less than y; if y is less than x, the expression is false. For example, the expression *150 < 200* is true.

Greater Than or Equal To

The operator >= checks for relative values and equality. The expression

$x >= y$

compares the values of x and y. If x is greater than or equal to y, the expression is true; otherwise, the expression is false. For example, the expression *150 >= 200* is false and the expression *100 >= 100* is true.

Less Than or Equal To

Like the operator >=, the operator <= checks for relative values and equality. The expression

$x <= y$

is true if x is less than or equal to y. Otherwise, the expression is false.

Examples Using Relational Operators

Let's assume that *temp* is a variable that contains the temperature. To be sure that you don't go on a picnic unless the temperature is higher than 75 degrees Fahrenheit, you might use the following IF statement:

```
IF temp > 75 THEN
    GOTO Picnic
ELSE
    GOTO Indoors
ENDIF
```

If you want to go to the health club's spa whenever the water temperature at the beach is 60 degrees or less, you could make your decision with the following IF statement:

```
IF waterTemp <= 60 THEN
    GOTO Spa
ELSE
    GOTO Beach
END IF
```

You might want to vary your activities depending on the weather. Let's assume the following: If it's raining, you'll go to the movies; if the sun is shining, you'll go to the beach; if it's snowing, you'll build a snowman; and if you can't do any of these things, you'll merely take a nap. You can represent this in QBasic by using the ELSEIF keyword in an IF...THEN statement:

```
IF weather = sunny THEN
    GOTO Beach
ELSEIF weather = raining THEN
    GOTO Movie
ELSEIF weather = snowing THEN
    GOTO BuildSnowman
ELSE
    GOTO TakeNap
END IF
```

In this statement, the variable *weather* represents one of many possible values for the weather. QBasic evaluates each IF and ELSEIF statement and tries to find a match. This example contains only three statements; however, if you use many ELSEIF statements, your program might be hard to read and understand. Fortunately, QBasic offers an alternative—the SELECT CASE statement. (See the SELECT CASE entry later in this chapter.)

The Logical Operators— AND, EQV, IMP, NOT, OR, and XOR

One of the virtues of QBasic is that it lets you combine simple expressions to create complex expressions. You combine simple expressions with the logical operators AND, EQV, IMP, NOT, OR, and XOR. The operators you will use most often are AND and OR.

Let's expand the previous picnic example to include more details. For example, let's specify that the sun must be shining and the temperature must be more than 75 degrees before you go on a picnic:

```
IF sunShining AND temp > 75 THEN
    GOTO Picnic
ELSE
    GOTO Indoors
ENDIF
```

Notice that the AND operator works in almost the same way as it does in an English sentence. You must include one operand on each side of the AND, as in the following expression:

```
this AND that
```

The AND operator returns a value of true only when both operands are true. In the previous example, the sun must be shining *and* the temperature must be greater than 75 degrees before you can go on a picnic.

The OR operator returns a value of true if either operand is true. For example, if the temperature of the water at the local beach is below 60 degrees *or* the sun isn't shining, you will go to the health club's spa. The following QBasic IF statement expresses those conditions:

```
IF waterTemp < 60 OR sunNotShining THEN
    GOTO Spa
ELSE
    GOTO Beach
END IF
```

The NOT operator is different from the other logical operators—it is a unary operator, which means that it requires only one operand. The NOT operator, as its name implies, reverses the value of the operand. If the operand is true, the result of a NOT operation is false; if the operand is false, the result of a NOT operation is true. Thus you can rephrase the previous expression as follows:

```
IF waterTemp < 60 OR NOT sunShining THEN
    GOTO Spa
ELSE
    GOTO Beach
END IF
```

The EQV, IMP, and XOR logical operators let you construct complex expressions because they test two expressions at once. The EQV operator returns true if both its operands have a value of true or both have a value of false. The IMP operator returns a result of false only if the first operand is true and the second is false. Finally, the XOR operator returns true when only one of the operands is true; if both of the operands are true (or both are false), XOR returns false.

SELECT CASE

QBasic's SELECT CASE statement doesn't do anything that the IF statement can't—it merely uses a clearer format. For example, the following statements use a SELECT CASE statement to perform the same task as a previous example that used the IF statement:

```
SELECT CASE weather
    CASE sunny
        GOTO Beach
    CASE raining
        GOTO Movie
    CASE snowing
        GOTO BuildSnowman
    CASE ELSE
        GOTO TakeNap
END SELECT
```

Suppose that you also want to go inside if it is windy. To specify this, you need to change an ELSEIF clause in the IF statement as follows:

```
ELSEIF weather = raining OR weather = windy THEN
    GOTO Inside
```

However, with SELECT CASE you can simply add *windy* to the appropriate case clause:

```
CASE raining, windy
    GOTO Inside
```

The MOD Operator

The MOD operator is related to the integer division operator (\). MOD returns the remainder from an integer division operation. For example, *5 MOD 2* is 1, because 5 divided by 2 is 2 with a remainder of 1.

Programmers often use the MOD operator as an "evenly divisible" operator. For example, to determine whether a year is a leap year, you must know whether it is divisible by 4 but not by 100 (unless it's also divisible by 400). You can use the MOD operator to check for divisibility, as the following statements illustrate:

```
CLS
DIM year AS INTEGER, by4 AS INTEGER, by100 AS INTEGER, by400 AS INTEGER

INPUT "Enter a year in four digits (for example: 1989)"; year

by4 = year MOD 4          ' evenly divisible by 4?
by100 = year MOD 100      ' evenly divisible by 100?
by400 = year MOD 400      ' evenly divisible by 400?

IF (by4 = 0 AND by100 <> 0) OR by400 = 0 THEN
    PRINT "Yes,"; year; "is a leap year."
ELSE
    PRINT "No,"; year; "is not a leap year."
END IF
```

The + (Concatenation) Operator

BASIC is well known for its advanced string-handling capabilities. For example, QBasic has built-in support for combining (or concatenating) two strings. Not only can QBasic's + operator add two numbers, it can also "add" two strings. Concatenation is often used to combine the separate elements of a name into a single string. For example, after the following statements,

```
title$ = "Dr."
first$ = "Heywood"
last$ = "Floyd"

whole$ = title$ + " " + first$ + " " + last$
```

the value of *whole$* is "Dr. Heywood Floyd". Note that the last statement also concatenates spaces in the string in order to separate the parts of the name.

Related Reading

Bergmann, Merrie, et al. *The Logic Book*. New York, N.Y.: Random House, 1980.

Prata, Stephen, with Harry Henderson. *The Waite Group's Microsoft QuickBASIC Primer Plus*. Redmond, Wash.: Microsoft Press, 1990.

AND

See also
EQV, IF, IMP, MOD, NOT, OR, XOR

Purpose
The AND operator is both a logical and an arithmetic operator. As a logical operator, it returns a value of true only if both its operands have a value of true. As an arithmetic operator, it performs AND operations with the corresponding bits of two values.

Syntax
IF *op1* AND *op2* THEN …

or

result% = *op1* AND *op2*

The *op1* and *op2* operands in the first syntax can be logical expressions or values of any numeric type (integer, long integer, single precision, or double precision). The operands in the second syntax can be of any numeric type, but the result is always an integer or a long integer.

result% is the variable that contains the result of an arithmetic AND operation.

Usage
```
IF rich% AND famous% THEN
    PRINT "Are you single?"
END IF
```
If the variables *rich%* and *famous%* are both true (nonzero), the message is displayed.

Description
You can use QBasic's AND operator in a logical expression to tell you whether both operands are true. For example,
```
var1 > 2 AND var2 < 4
```
is true only when the expressions *var1 > 2* and *var2 < 4* are both true.

The AND operator can also be used arithmetically to perform a bit-by-bit comparison of the operands. If the corresponding bits in the operands are 1, the resulting bit is 1; otherwise (if one or both of the bits is 0), the result is 0. See the truth table in Table 3-3.

p	q	p AND q
1	1	1
1	0	0
0	1	0
0	0	0

Table 3-3.
AND truth table.

Figure 3-1 demonstrates the use of the arithmetic AND operator.

Figure 3-1.
Arithmetic AND.

The AND operator accepts single-precision and double-precision operands; however, it converts them to either an integer or a long integer before processing them. The result of the AND operation is always an integer or a long integer.

Errors
The operands in an AND operation can be of any numeric type (integer, long integer, single precision, or double precision) in the range −2147483648 through 2147483647. If either operand is out of range, QBasic displays an "Overflow" error message.

Example
The following example shows how you can use the AND operator to determine eligibility for a loan.

```
CLS
PRINT "Loan Application": PRINT

INPUT "Amount of desired loan"; amt#
INPUT "Does the applicant have a good credit history (Y/N)"; goodCreditHistory$
INPUT "Is the applicant working full-time (Y/N)"; fullTime$

PRINT
IF UCASE$(goodCreditHistory$) = "Y" AND UCASE$(fullTime$) = "Y" THEN
    PRINT "Because the applicant has a good credit history and ";
    PRINT "is working full-time,"
    PRINT "the application for"; amt#; "is approved."
ELSE
    PRINT "The applicant does not meet our qualifications;  ";
    PRINT "the application is denied."
END IF
```

+ (Concatenation)

See also
CONST, FRE

Purpose
The + operator, when used with strings, combines (concatenates) two or more strings into one string. Use the + operator, for example, to combine a first name and a last name into a single string.

Syntax
result$ = string1$ + string2$* [+ *string3$] ...

result$* is a string variable that contains the concatenation of *string1$, *string2$*, *string3$*, and so on.

Usage
```
overall$ = prefix$ + baseName$
```
Combines the contents of *prefix$* and *baseName$* into *overall$*.

```
fullName$ = firstName$ + " " + lastName$
```
Combines the contents of *firstName$* and *lastName$* (separated with a space) into *fullName$*.

Description
QBasic's + operator lets you perform string concatenation, the process of combining several strings or string expressions into a single, longer string. For example,

```
"ABCDE" + "FGHIJ"
```

results in the single string "ABCDEFGHIJ". The + operator enables you to combine many strings in a single operation; for example,

```
"ABCDE" + "FGHIJ" + "KLMNO" + "PQRST" + "UVWXYZ"
```

results in the single string "ABCDEFGHIJKLMNOPQRSTUVWXYZ".

Comments

QBasic doesn't permit string concatenation in a CONST statement. (See the CONST entry in Chapter 1, "Types and Variables," for details.)

When you concatenate a variable-length string with another string, QBasic creates a new string containing the original two strings. This is true even if you merely add characters to the same string. For example, the following string concatenation adds characters to *longString$*:

```
longString$ = longString$ + "*-*-*-*-*"
```

QBasic creates a new string, copies the previous contents of *longString$* to it, adds "*-*-*-*-*" to it, gives the new string the name *longString$*, and then deletes the old *longString$* to make room for other strings. However, during the process QBasic needs enough string space for two copies of *longString$*. For example, assume that you have 20,000 bytes of free string space and that *longString$* is 10,000 bytes long. If you try to concatenate "*-*-*-*-*" to *longString$*, the compiler returns an "Out of string space" error message because QBasic makes another copy of *longString$*, leaving no room for "*-*-*-*-*".

Example

The following example program uses the + operator to combine the three parts of an employee's name.

```
CLS
LINE INPUT "Enter the employee's first name:     "; firstName$
wholeName$ = firstName$ + " "

LINE INPUT "Enter the employee's middle initial: "; middleInitial$
wholeName$ = wholeName$ + middleInitial$ + ". "

LINE INPUT "Enter the employee's last name:      "; lastName$
wholeName$ = wholeName$ + lastName$

INPUT "Enter the amount of the employee's salary:   "; amt#

PRINT
PRINT "Pay to the order of "; wholeName$; TAB(60);
PRINT USING "##,###.##"; amt#
END
```

EQV

See also

AND, IF, IMP, MOD, NOT, OR, XOR

Purpose

The EQV operator is both a logical and an arithmetic operator. As a logical operator, it returns a value of true only if both its operands have a value of true or both have a value of false. As an arithmetic operator, it performs EQV operations with the corresponding bits of two values.

Syntax

IF *op1* EQV *op2* THEN ...

or

result% = *op1* EQV *op2*

The *op1* and *op2* operands in the first syntax can be logical expressions or values of any numeric type (integer, long integer, single precision, or double precision). The operands in the second syntax can be of any numeric type, but the result is always an integer or a long integer.

result% is the variable that contains the result of an arithmetic EQV operation.

Usage

```
IF amt1# > 100# EQV amt2# > 2000# THEN
    PRINT "The amounts are in range"
END IF
```

Tests two double-precision values. If *amt1#* is greater than 100 and *amt2#* is greater than 2000, the expression is true; if *amt1#* is less than 100 and *amt2#* is less than 2000, the expression is also true. The expression is false if one value is true and the other value is false.

Description

You can use QBasic's EQV operator in a logical expression to tell you whether both operands are true or both are false. For example,

```
var1 > 2 EQV var2 < 4
```

is true only when both the expressions *var1 > 2* and *var2 < 4* are true or both are false.

The EQV operator can also be used arithmetically to perform a bit-by-bit comparison of the operands. If the corresponding bits in the operands are both 1 or both 0, the result is 1; otherwise, the result is 0. See the truth table in Table 3-4.

p	q	p EQV q
1	1	1
1	0	0
0	1	0
0	0	1

Table 3-4.
EQV truth table.

QBasic's EQV operator is rarely used in arithmetic expressions. More often it is used in logical expressions.

The EQV operator accepts single-precision and double-precision operands; however, it converts them to either an integer or a long integer before processing them. The result of the EQV operation is always an integer or a long integer.

Errors

The operands in an EQV operation can be of any numeric type (integer, long integer, single precision, or double precision) in the range −2147483648 through 2147483647. If either operand is out of range, QBasic displays an "Overflow" error message.

Example

The following example shows how you can use the EQV operator to determine eligibility for a loan.

```
CLS
PRINT "Loan Application"
PRINT

INPUT "Amount of desired loan"; amt#
INPUT "What is the applicant's annual salary"; salary#

PRINT
IF amt# > 1000 EQV salary > 15000 THEN
    PRINT "Because the applicant is requesting an amount ";
    PRINT "appropriate for his or her salary,"
    PRINT "the application for"; amt#; "is approved."
ELSE
    PRINT "The applicant does not meet our qualifications; ";
    PRINT "the application is denied."
END IF
```

IF

See also

DO...LOOP, ON...GOSUB, ON...GOTO, SELECT CASE

Purpose

The IF statement uses the value of an expression to control the order in which statements are executed. The expression in an IF statement can be a logical comparison; several comparisons can be combined by using the logical operators AND, OR, NOT, XOR, EQV, and IMP.

Syntax

Single line:

IF *expr* THEN *true* ELSE *false*

Block form:

IF *expr1* THEN
    [*true*]
[ELSEIF *expr2* THEN
    [*true*]]
⋮
[ELSEIF *exprx* THEN
    [*true*]]
[ELSE
    [*false*]]
END IF

expr is an expression that yields a result of true or false. The expression can use QBasic's relational operators (=, <>, >, <, >=, <=) and logical operators (AND, OR, NOT, XOR, EQV, IMP) to yield a value of true or false. Your program can represent false by 0 and true by any nonzero value. Therefore, *expr* can also be an integer expression.

true is a block of statements to be executed if *expr* is true. In the single-line IF statement, multiple statements must be on the same line, separated by colons. In the block-form IF statement, multiple statements can be on the same line (separated by colons) or on separate lines.

The statements following the ELSEIF clause, which can appear only in a block-form IF statement, are executed only if *expr1* is false and *expr2* is true. ELSEIF lets you test for many different conditions within a single IF statement.

QBasic executes *false*, which is a block of statements that follow the keyword ELSE, if all preceding IF and ELSEIF expressions are false. The ELSE clause is the catchall clause—if all else fails, QBasic executes the statements following the ELSE keyword.

Usage

```
IF age% < 18 THEN status$ = "Minor"
```

If the value of the variable *age%* is less than 18, the statement sets *status$* to "Minor".

```
IF memSize& < 250 THEN
    PRINT "Sorry, not enough memory."
    BEEP
    SYSTEM
END IF
```

Prints a message, beeps, and then exits the program if the value of the variable *memSize&* is less than 250.

```
IF answer$ = "Y" THEN 10 ELSE 20
```

```
IF answer$ = "Y" THEN GOTO 10 ELSE GOTO 20
```

```
IF answer$ = "Y" THEN
    GOTO 10
ELSE
    GOTO 20
END IF
```

These three statements are equivalent—all jump to line 10 if the value of the variable *answer$* is equal to "Y" and to line 20 if it is not.

```
IF age% >= 16 AND license$ = "NO" THEN
    PRINT "Take your driver's test...and drive carefully."
    GOTO GetDriversLicense
ELSEIF age% > 16 AND license$ = "YES" THEN
    PRINT "Renew your license."
    GOTO RenewLicense
ELSE
    PRINT "Sorry, but you'll have to wait..."
    GOTO TooYoung
END IF
```

Checks the value of the variables *age%* and *license$* and prints the message that corresponds to the combination of those values.

Description

QBasic's IF statement checks to see whether a certain condition has been met. If the condition has been met, QBasic executes the given statements; if the condition has not been met, QBasic executes different statements. The IF statement provides the lowest level of decision making in QBasic; unlike control flow loops, IF statements are executed only once.

When an IF statement branches to another *numbered* line in the program, you can omit the keyword GOTO. If the line has a label, however, you must use GOTO. The following statements illustrate valid usages of the IF statement:

```
IF amountDue# > 1000.0 THEN GOTO 10000
```

```
IF amountDue# > 1000.0 THEN 10000
```

You should use a single-line IF statement when the set of statements that are executed when the expression is true includes only a couple of statements. In fact, when there is only one statement, a single-line IF is more concise and easy to read than a block-form IF, as shown in the following example:

```
IF amountDue# > 1000.0 THEN 10000

IF amountDue# > 1000.0 THEN
    GOTO 10000
END IF
```

The block-form IF statement lets you include whatever statements are needed rather than forcing you to fit statements (separated by colons) on a single line.

QBasic evaluates the IF statement from the top, starting at the first expression and working down. Each block-form IF statement must end with a matching END IF clause. Whenever an expression evaluates to true, QBasic executes the statements on the line following the keyword THEN. If the expressions corresponding to the IF clause and all the ELSEIF clauses are false, QBasic executes the statements following the keyword ELSE. Remember that including statements in the IF, ELSEIF, and ELSE clauses is optional—if you omit statements, QBasic executes nothing if the expression is true. The following block-form IF statement, for example, is legal:

```
IF age% >= 21 THEN
ELSE
    PRINT "You're under arrest!"
END IF
```

Also note that the ELSEIF and ELSE clauses are optional—if the IF expression is false and there are no ELSEIF or ELSE clauses, QBasic continues execution at the first statement following the END IF clause.

A block-form IF can include other block-form statements, such as other IF statements and DO...LOOP statements; a single-line IF cannot. The IF, ELSEIF, ELSE, and END IF clauses of the block-form IF must be the first statements on each line; however, you can precede them with a line number or line label if you must branch to them from another part of the program.

Because QBasic looks at what follows the THEN clause to determine whether the IF statement is a block-form or single-line statement, you cannot add anything except a comment after the THEN keyword in a block-form IF statement.

Errors

If you use a numeric expression as the expression in an IF statement, it must evaluate to a number in the range of a long integer, -2147483648 through 2147483647; if you use a floating-point expression that exceeds this range, QBasic displays an "Overflow" error message.

Tips

To see whether a variable is 0, simply use

```
IF NOT variable%
```

If *variable%* is 0, then *NOT variable%* is true. The simple expression *variable%* in the following statement is true if *variable%* equals any integer value except 0:

```
IF variable%
```

Floating-point operations sometimes generate inaccurate results; therefore, floating-point values that appear equal when printed might actually be minutely different. If you round the floating-point numbers before you compare them, the differences do not affect the comparison.

Example

The following example sounds the speaker (from low to high frequencies) and displays the frequency and range of the tones.

```
CLS
FOR freq% = 100 TO 1000 STEP 10
    IF RND <= .5 THEN dur% = 1 ELSE dur% = 2    ' pick a random duration

    SOUND freq%, dur%
    LOCATE 1, 1
    PRINT USING "##### "; freq%;

    IF freq% < 200 THEN
        PRINT "Very low frequency "
    ELSEIF freq% < 400 THEN
        PRINT "Low frequency       "
    ELSEIF freq% < 600 THEN
        PRINT "Average frequency  "
    ELSEIF freq% < 800 THEN
        PRINT "High frequency     "
    ELSE
        PRINT "Very high frequency"
    END IF
NEXT
END
```

IMP

See also

AND, EQV, IF, MOD, NOT, OR, XOR

Purpose

The IMP operator is both a logical and an arithmetic operator. As a logical operator, it returns a value of false only if its first operand is true and its second operand is false. As an arithmetic operator, it performs IMP operations with the corresponding bits of two values.

Syntax

IF *op1* IMP *op2* THEN ...

or

result% = *op1* IMP *op2*

The *op1* and *op2* operands in the first syntax can be logical expressions or values of any numeric type (integer, long integer, single precision, or double precision). The operands in the second syntax can be of any numeric type, but the result is always an integer or a long integer.

result% is the variable that contains the result of an arithmetic IMP operation.

Usage

```
IF amount > 1000 IMP safetyGoggles$ = "YES" THEN
    PRINT "Ready to proceed"
END IF
```

The expression in the IF statement is false only if *amount* is greater than 1000 and *safetyGoggles$* is not equal to "YES".

Description

You can use QBasic's IMP operator in a logical expression to check for implication. The expression is true if the value of the first operand implies the value of the second one. An expression that uses the IMP operator is true except when the first operand is true and the second is false. For example,

```
var1 > 2 IMP var2 < 4
```

is false only when the expression *var1 > 2* is true and the expression *var2 < 4* is false.

The IMP operator can also be used arithmetically to perform a bit-by-bit comparison of the operands. If a bit in *op1* is 1 and the corresponding bit in *op2* is 0, the result is 0; otherwise, the result is 1. See the truth table in Table 3-5.

p	q	p IMP q
1	1	1
1	0	0
0	1	1
0	0	1

Table 3-5.
IMP truth table.

QBasic's IMP operator is rarely used in arithmetic expressions. More often it is used in logical expressions.

The IMP operator accepts single-precision and double-precision operands; however, it converts them to either an integer or a long integer before processing them. The result of the IMP operation is always an integer or a long integer.

Errors

The operands in an IMP operation can be of any numeric type (integer, long integer, single precision, or double precision) in the range −2147483648 through 2147483647. If either is outside the range, QBasic displays an "Overflow" error message.

Example

This example shows how you can use the IMP operator to determine a person's eligibility for a loan.

```
CLS
PRINT "Loan Application": PRINT

INPUT "Amount of desired loan"; amt#
INPUT "Is the applicant working full-time (Y/N)"; fullTime$

PRINT
IF amt# > 1000 IMP UCASE$(fullTime$) = "Y" THEN
    PRINT "Because the applicant is requesting an amount ";
    PRINT "appropriate for his or her work status,"
    PRINT "the application for"; amt#; "is approved."
ELSE
    PRINT "The applicant doesn't meet our qualifications; "
    PRINT "the application is denied."
END IF
```

MOD

Purpose

The MOD operator is an arithmetic operator that returns the remainder of division between two integers. You can use MOD, for example, to start a new page of a report every 55 lines.

Syntax

remainder% = op1 MOD *op2*

The *op1* and *op2* operands can be of any numeric type (integer, long integer, single precision, or double precision), but the result is always an integer or a long integer.

remainder% is the variable that contains the result of the MOD operation.

Usage

```
IF line% MOD 55 = 0 THEN
    LPRINT CHR$(12);
END IF
```

If the MOD operation generates no remainder, the program sends a formfeed character to the printer.

Description

QBasic's MOD operator divides two operands and returns the remainder of that division. Before the division, the operands are rounded to integers; the result of the division is also rounded to an integer before the remainder is calculated. The result of the MOD operation is always an integer or a long integer.

Errors

The operands in a MOD operation can be of any numeric type (integer, long integer, single precision, or double precision) in the range −2147483648 through 2147483647. If either is outside the range, QBasic displays an "Overflow" error message.

Example

This example uses the MOD operator to stop displaying output at the end of each screenful.

```
x = 1
DO
    PRINT TAB(x MOD 55); "QBasic Programmer's Reference"

    IF x MOD 23 = 0 THEN
        PRINT "Press [Esc] to end the program or any other key to continue...";
        DO
            wait$ = INKEY$
        LOOP WHILE wait$ = ""
        IF wait$ = CHR$(27) THEN EXIT DO
    END IF
    x = x + 1
LOOP
```

NOT

See also

AND, EQV, IF, IMP, MOD, OR, XOR

Purpose

The NOT operator is both a logical and an arithmetic operator. As a logical operator, NOT returns a value of true if its operand has a value of false. As an arithmetic operator, it reverses the bit values of its operand. Use the NOT operator to reverse the truth value of a variable.

Syntax

IF NOT *op* THEN ...

or

result% = NOT *op*

The *op* operand in the first syntax can be a logical expression or a value of any numeric type (integer, long integer, single precision, or double precision). The operand in the second syntax can be of any numeric type, but the result is always an integer or a long integer.

Usage

```
IF NOT printerReady% THEN
    PRINT "Please load paper in the printer and press Enter."
END IF
```

Displays a message when the printer is not ready. The variable *printerReady%* represents the status of the printer and returns true when the printer is ready. Because you need to know when the printer is *not* ready, you simply apply the NOT operator to *printerReady%*.

Description

You can use QBasic's NOT operator in a logical expression to tell you whether an operand is false. For example,

```
NOT var1 > 2
```

is true only when the expression *var1 > 2* is false.

The NOT operator can also be used arithmetically to reverse the bits of the operator. If a bit in the operator is 1, the resulting bit is 0. If it is 0, the result is 1. See the truth table in Table 3-6.

p	NOT p
1	0
0	1

Table 3-6.
NOT truth table.

The NOT operator examines each bit in the operand before it returns a value. If the bit is 1, the resulting bit is 0. If the bit is 0, the resulting bit is 1. Because of the way QBasic stores integers and long integers, using the NOT operator on them is the same as adding 1 to the value and making it negative.

The NOT operator accepts single-precision and double-precision operands; however, it converts them to an integer or a long integer before processing them. The result of the NOT operation is always an integer or a long integer.

Errors

The operand in a NOT operation can be of any numeric type (integer, long integer, single precision, or double precision) in the range −2147483648 through 2147483647. If the operand is outside the range, QBasic displays an "Overflow" error message.

Example

This example uses the NOT operator to reverse the value of the user-defined function *Ok%* so that the program doesn't end until the function returns a true value.

```
DECLARE FUNCTION Ok% (prompt$)
CONST FALSE = 0, TRUE = NOT FALSE

CLS
DO WHILE NOT Ok("Ready to end program.  ")    ' call the Ok function
LOOP                                          ' loop while Ok returns true

SYSTEM

' The Ok function returns TRUE if the user enters "Y"

FUNCTION Ok% (prompt$) STATIC
    LOCATE , , 1                              ' turn on cursor
    PRINT prompt$; "Is this OK?  ";

    DO
        keyboard$ = UCASE$(INKEY$)            ' get a character
    LOOP WHILE NOT (keyboard$ = "N" OR keyboard$ = "Y")

    SELECT CASE keyboard$
        CASE "N"
            PRINT "No"
            Ok% = FALSE

        CASE "Y"
            PRINT "Yes"
            Ok% = TRUE
    END SELECT
END FUNCTION
```

OR

See also
AND, EQV, IF, IMP, MOD, NOT, XOR

Purpose
The OR operator is both a logical and an arithmetic operator. As a logical operator, it returns a value of true if either or both its operands have a value of true. Use the logical OR operator to guarantee that at least one variable is true. As an arithmetic operator, it performs OR operations with the corresponding bits of two values.

Syntax
IF *op1* OR *op2* THEN ...

or

result% = *op1* OR *op2*

The *op1* and *op2* operands in the first syntax can be logical expressions or values of any numeric type (integer, long integer, single precision, or double precision). The operands in the second syntax can be of any numeric type, but the result is always an integer or a long integer.

result% is the variable that contains the result of an arithmetic OR operation.

Usage

```
IF rich% OR famous% THEN
    PRINT "That's good enough--are you single?"
END IF
```

If either or both of the variables *rich%* and *famous%* are true, a message is displayed on the screen.

Description

You can use QBasic's OR operator in a logical expression to tell you whether either or both of the operands are true. For example,

```
var1 > 2 OR var2 < 4
```

is true when the expression *var1 > 2* is true, when the expression *var2 < 4* is true, or when both are true.

This or operation is an "inclusive or"—it is true if either or both of the operands are true. If you need to check whether only one and not both the operands is true, use XOR. (See the XOR entry for details.)

The OR operator can also be used to perform a bit-by-bit comparison of the operands. If either or both of the corresponding bits in the two operands are 1, the resulting bit is 1; otherwise, the resulting bit is 0. See the truth table for OR in Table 3-7.

p	q	p OR q
1	1	1
1	0	1
0	1	1
0	0	0

Table 3-7.
Logical OR truth table.

Figure 3-2 on the following page demonstrates the use of the arithmetic OR operator.

The arithmetic OR statement

```
262 OR 39
```

is calculated using binary as follows:

```
    262 decimal = 100000110 binary
OR   39 decimal = 000100111 binary

    295 decimal = 100100111 binary
                    | | |||
```

One or both of the bits in these
columns are 1

Figure 3-2.
Arithmetic OR.

The OR operator accepts single-precision and double-precision operands; however, it converts them to an integer or a long integer before processing them. The result of the OR operation is always an integer or a long integer.

Errors

The operands in an OR operation can be of any numeric type (integer, long integer, single precision, or double precision) in the range −2147483648 through 2147483647. If either is outside the range, QBasic displays an "Overflow" error message.

Example

The example following shows how you can use the OR operator to determine eligibility for a loan.

```
CLS
PRINT "Loan Application": PRINT

INPUT "Amount of desired loan"; amt#
INPUT "Is the applicant working full-time (Y/N)"; fullTime$
INPUT "Does the applicant have sufficient collateral (Y/N)"; collateral$
PRINT

IF UCASE$(fullTime$) = "Y" OR UCASE$(collateral$) = "Y" THEN
    PRINT "Because the applicant requested a loan that is reasonably secured,"
    PRINT "the application for"; amt#; "is approved."
ELSE
    PRINT "The applicant doesn't meet our qualifications; ";
    PRINT "the application is denied."
END IF
```

SELECT CASE

See also

IF

Purpose

The SELECT CASE statement provides a readable method of comparing an expression to several constants and then executing statements based on the comparison. Use SELECT CASE when you must execute different statements depending on the value of an expression. The SELECT CASE statement offers a readable and more structured alternative to complex IF...ELSE statements.

Syntax

```
SELECT CASE expr
    CASE comp [, comp...]
        [statements]
    [CASE comp [, comp...]
        [statements]]
    [CASE ELSE
        [statements]]
END SELECT
```

expr is any numeric or string expression.

comp is an expression that represents a range of values to which *expr* is compared. *comp* must use one of the following forms:

expr	A single expression
lowexpr TO *highexpr*	A value range
IS *relationexpr*	A range comparison

statements is one or more QBasic statements.

Usage

```
SELECT CASE menu&
    CASE 1
        AddCustomers
    CASE 2
        AddTransactions
END SELECT
```

If *menu&* equals 1, the program executes the subprogram *AddCustomers*; if *menu&* equals 2, the program executes the subprogram *AddTransactions*.

```
SELECT CASE ok$
    CASE "Y", "y"
        DoIt
    CASE "N", "n"
        Cancel
END SELECT
```

If the variable *ok$* equals "Y" or "y", the program executes the subprogram *DoIt*; if *ok$* equals "N" or "n", the program executes the subprogram *Cancel*.

```
SELECT CASE year%
    CASE 1901 TO 1930
        PRINT "Early twentieth century..."
    CASE 1931 TO 1960
        PRINT "Mid-twentieth century..."
    CASE IS > 1961
        PRINT "Late twentieth century or beyond..."
END SELECT
```

If the variable *year%* is between 1901 and 1930, between 1931 and 1960, or greater than 1960, an appropriate message is displayed.

Description

The IF statement (discussed in the IF entry) is the lowest level of decision making in QBasic. IF operates on logical comparisons; SELECT CASE is more efficient in working with range and relational comparisons. Because QBasic's SELECT CASE accepts relational operators, you can make any comparisons with either SELECT CASE or a combination of IF, ELSEIF, and ELSE statements.

The expression in the SELECT CASE clause can be any integer, floating-point, or string expression. For example, in the following clause the value of the expression *LOG(e)* is compared to the constants in the CASE clauses:

```
SELECT CASE LOG(e)
```

SELECT CASE compares the value of the expression to the values or range of values in the CASE clauses. If the expression matches the value or range of values, the statements of that CASE clause are executed. After the block of statements executes, control continues at the first statement following the END SELECT clause.

Following are some examples of valid values for the comparison expression.

A single expression:

CASE 3.141592653# * arc#	Matches the value of pi times *arc#*
CASE 1000&	Matches the long integer 1000
CASE patientName$	Matches the string variable *patientName$*

A value range (*lowexpr* TO *highexpr*, where *lowexpr* must be less than *highexpr*, either numerically smaller or earlier in ascending ASCII order):

CASE 1 TO 10	Matches 1.0 through 10.0
CASE "A" TO "Z"	Matches all capital letters

A range comparison:

CASE IS = 1	Matches numbers equal to 1
CASE 1	Matches numbers equal to 1
CASE IS <= 10	Matches numbers less than or equal to 10
CASE IS <= "Z"	Matches strings less than or equal to Z

The IS keyword gives SELECT CASE all the functionality of the IF statement by letting you use QBasic's relational operators (=, <>, >, <, >=, and <=). Note that a CASE clause using an equal sign is equivalent to a CASE clause that uses a single expression.

If none of the CASE statements' values or ranges of values match the expression, QBasic executes the statements of the CASE ELSE clause (if one exists).

You can make several comparisons (separated by commas) in each CASE clause. If you use multiple comparisons, QBasic executes the associated statements if any of the comparisons match. The commas act like the logical operator OR in the IF statement. However, you cannot simulate the logical operator AND.

Tips

Because you cannot use logical operators with SELECT CASE, the IF statement is a better choice when your program must make logical comparisons (using the logical operators AND, OR, NOT, XOR, EQV, and IMP).

Because floating-point operations can be inaccurate, floating-point numbers that appear equal when printed might actually have minute differences. If you round floating-point numbers before you compare them, the differences will not affect the comparison.

Example

The following example uses the SELECT CASE statement to determine how many characters in a sentence are vowels, how many are consonants, and how many are punctuation marks.

```
CLS
LINE INPUT "Enter a sentence: "; sentence$

vowels = 0: consonants = 0: punctuation = 0    ' initialize counter variables

FOR X = 1 TO LEN(sentence$)                     ' loop through the string
    char$ = UCASE$(MID$(sentence$, X, 1))       ' get a single character

    SELECT CASE char$
        CASE "A", "E", "I", "O", "U"            ' check for vowels
            vowels = vowels + 1
        CASE "A" TO "Z"                         ' consonants
            consonants = consonants + 1         ' includes the vowels, but they
                                                ' are counted first
        CASE ELSE
            punctuation = punctuation + 1       ' all others are punctuation marks
    END SELECT
NEXT

' print totals
PRINT "In the sentence containing"; LEN(sentence$); "characters,"
PRINT "there are"; vowels; "vowels,"; consonants; "consonants and";
PRINT punctuation; "punctuation marks"
```

XOR

See also

AND, EQV, IF, IMP, MOD, NOT, OR

Purpose

The XOR operator is both a logical and an arithmetic operator. As a logical operator, it returns a value of true if either, but not both, of its operands has a value of true. Use the XOR operator to guarantee that only one variable is true; this prevents conflicting options from being true. As an arithmetic operator, it performs XOR operations with the corresponding bits of two values.

Syntax

IF *op1* XOR *op2* THEN …

or

result% = *op1* XOR *op2*

The *op1* and *op2* operands in the first syntax can be logical expressions or values of any numeric type (integer, long integer, single precision, or double precision). The operands in the second syntax can be of any numeric type, but the result is always an integer or a long integer.

result% is the variable that contains the result of an arithmetic XOR operation.

Usage

```
IF hardDisk% XOR floppyDisk% THEN
    PRINT "You can now install the program."
END IF
```

If either (but not both) of the variables *hardDisk%* and *floppyDisk%* is true, the message is displayed.

Description

You can use QBasic's XOR operator in a logical expression to tell you whether one (but not both) of the operands is true. For example,

```
var1 > 2 XOR var2 < 4
```

is true only when the expression *var1 > 2* is true and *var2 < 4* is false or when the expression *var1 > 2* is false and *var2 < 4* is true.

The XOR operator can also be used to perform a bit-by-bit comparison of the operands. If the corresponding bits in the operands have different values, the resulting bit is 1; if they have the same values, the resulting bit is 0. See Table 3-8.

p	q	p XOR q
1	1	0
1	0	1
0	1	1
0	0	0

Table 3-8.
XOR truth table.

Figure 3-3 shows an example of an arithmetic use of the XOR operator.

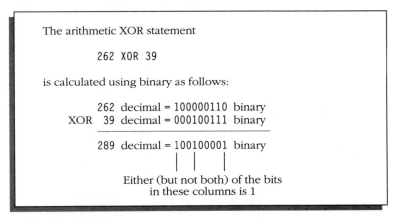

Figure 3-3.
Arithmetic XOR.

The XOR operator accepts single-precision and double-precision operands; however, it converts them to an integer or a long integer before processing them. The result of the XOR operation is always an integer or a long integer.

Errors

The operands in an XOR operation can be of any numeric type (integer, long integer, single precision, or double precision) in the range −2147483648 through 2147483647. If either is outside the range, QBasic displays an "Overflow" error message.

Example

The following example shows how to use the XOR operator in the UNTIL clause of a DO...LOOP statement to loop until the user chooses only one of the two types of loans.

```
CLS
PRINT "Type of Loan": PRINT

DO
    DO
        INPUT "Would you like a fixed-interest-rate loan (Y/N)"; fixed$
        INPUT "Would you like an adjustable-interest-rate loan (Y/N)"; adj$
        PRINT
    LOOP UNTIL UCASE$(fixed$) = "Y" XOR UCASE$(adj$) = "Y"

    IF UCASE$(fixed$) = "Y" THEN
        PRINT "You have chosen a fixed-interest-rate loan."
    ELSE
        PRINT "You have chosen an adjustable-interest-rate loan."
    END IF
    INPUT "Have you changed your mind (Y/N)"; change$
LOOP UNTIL UCASE$(change$) = "N"
```

CHAPTER 4

Procedures

Introduction

Early versions of Basic don't offer structured features; if programmers aren't careful, their programs can become difficult to read and maintain. Also, programs that use early versions of Basic are limited to the size of the largest source file that the interpreter can process.

QBasic has neither of these problems. It contains all the structured features of the structured programming languages such as C and Pascal. You can define your own functions and subprograms, and pass them the variables and arguments that they require. You can also control the scope of variables, sharing them with other procedures only if it's necessary.

This chapter discusses the structured features of QBasic in detail. Table 4-1 lists the QBasic procedure statements and functions in alphabetic order.

Statement or function	Description
CALL	Transfers control to a QBasic subprogram
CHAIN	Transfers control to another program
COMMON	Declares variables that can be passed to a separate, chained program
DECLARE	Defines the name and parameter list of a procedure specified by a SUB or FUNCTION statement
DEF FN	Defines a user-defined function compatible with those written in early versions of Basic
FUNCTION	Defines a QBasic function
GOSUB...RETURN	Branches to a subroutine
SHARED	Specifies variables that can be shared by functions, subprograms, and statements in the module-level code
STATIC	Specifies the local variables in a function or subprogram that retain their values between calls to the function or a subprogram
SUB	Defines a subprogram

Table 4-1.
Procedure statements and functions.

DIM, SHARED, and COMMON Statements

You can dimension variables and arrays in the main program. If you want the variables and arrays to be available to all the procedures in the program, use the DIM statement with the SHARED keyword. Without the SHARED keyword, the dimensioned variables are visible to the subprograms and functions only if you specify the variables in a SHARED statement in each procedure that uses them. The DIM statement that includes the SHARED keyword does not make these variables available to procedures in other programs; only a COMMON statement can do that.

Variables specified by a COMMON statement are not visible to the subprograms and functions in the program. To make them visible, either you must include the keyword SHARED in the COMMON statement or you can include a separate SHARED statement in every procedure that needs to access variables specified in the COMMON statement.

Variable Type Definitions

You can define complex variable types by using the TYPE...END TYPE statement. (See Chapter 1, "Types and Variables," for information about user-defined types.) In the DIM statement that declares a variable of a user-defined type, you must include the SHARED keyword if you want the variable to be visible to procedures in the program—for example,

```
DIM SHARED stockRecord AS RecordType
```

If the program doesn't include this statement, the subprograms and functions themselves must include the statement

```
SHARED stockRecord AS RecordType
```

to gain access to the contents of the variable *stockRecord*.

Subprograms

A subprogram is a type of procedure. Because it is a self-contained block of code that performs a single programming task, you can easily use the same subprogram in many different programs.

Unlike the traditional Basic subroutine, which it is intended to replace, a subprogram defined by a SUB statement has only one entry point—at the first executable statement of the procedure. However, a subprogram can have more than one exit point because, in addition to the END SUB statement that marks the normal exit point, QBasic also provides an EXIT SUB statement that forces an early termination of the subprogram. The variables of a subprogram (except those passed to it or specified in a SHARED statement) are local to the subprogram.

By default, variables that are local to a subprogram (or to a function, as explained below) are created each time the procedure is called and are destroyed each time control returns to the line that called the procedure. Local variables are unique to the procedure that uses them and cannot be accessed by any other subprogram, even if it contains variables of the same name. This enables subprograms to call themselves recursively, with each iteration using its own set of variables.

In some cases, however, you might want a subprogram to retain the values of its local variables between calls. To do so, use QBasic's STATIC statement. If you define the entire procedure as static, none of its variables is destroyed when the procedure completes; if you make only one or two variables static, the rest remain transient. Note, however, that two types of variables are always static—those that are passed to the subprogram as arguments and those that are specified in a SHARED statement.

Calling Subprograms

You can execute a subprogram by issuing a CALL statement. The following statement, for example, is a call to a subprogram named *VGASave*:

```
CALL VGASave(picName$)
```

picName$, the variable in parentheses, is a string argument that is passed to the called subprogram. When *VGASave* completes execution, any changes made to *picName$* in the subprogram are returned to the statement that called it.

The DECLARE statement can be used to specify the number and type of variables used in a call to a subprogram. Here is a DECLARE statement for *VGASave*:

```
DECLARE SUB VGASave (pictureName AS STRING)
```

This statement tells the compiler that when you call *VGASave* you are calling a subprogram (and not a function) and that the subprogram requires a single argument, which must be a string.

It is good practice to include DECLARE statements for every subprogram or function you call. Indeed, if you write a program in the QBasic environment, the "smart" editor generates these statements. Using DECLARE, in fact, makes the CALL statement unnecessary and lets you call *VGASave* merely by naming it:

```
VGASave picName$
```

Notice that if you omit the CALL statement, you must not use parentheses around the argument list.

Subroutines

Subroutines are the traditional way of storing code that must be executed repeatedly during the course of a program. To branch to a subroutine, you use the following statement syntax:

GOSUB *location*

In this statement, *location* is the line number or label of a statement in the subroutine code. It does not need to be the first statement in the subroutine, although entering at some other point is poor programming style. The program continues from the entry point until it encounters a RETURN statement, which causes execution to resume with the statement following the GOSUB statement.

Avoid using the GOSUB statement. In QBasic, subroutines have been largely replaced by the more powerful subprograms; however, they still have their uses, particularly in event trapping. (See the various ON *event* GOSUB statements.)

User-Defined Functions

Functions are merely procedures that return a value. QBasic not only provides many built-in functions; it also lets you design your own. The two types of QBasic functions are the functions defined by DEF FN (a carryover from BASICA) and the more powerful function procedure, which is defined by the FUNCTION statement.

FUNCTION Procedures

A procedure defined by a FUNCTION statement is similar to a subprogram except that it returns a value. In addition, it also must be named as though it were a variable of the same type as the returned value. For example, you might declare a function that returns a long integer as follows:

```
DECLARE FUNCTION BinDec& (binry AS STRING)
```

The DECLARE statement specifies the number and type of variables you should include in a *BinDec&* call. You don't use a CALL statement; instead, you must assign the value returned by the function to another variable, as in the following example:

```
decimal& = BinDec&(binaryNumber$)
```

You can also use a procedure defined by FUNCTION in a QBasic statement or as an argument to another function or statement—for example,

```
PRINT BinDec&("01010011")
OUT speaker%, CINT(BinDec&(mask$))
```

Like subprograms, procedures defined by FUNCTION take arguments and use local variables (except for those passed to it or specified in a SHARED statement). You must make variables static with the STATIC statement if you want to preserve their values between calls. Because variables are local to each function and because a function can be used as an argument to another function, you can call functions recursively.

DEF FN Functions

Functions defined by a DEF FN statement are to procedures defined by FUNCTION what subroutines are to subprograms. QBasic includes them for compatibility with older versions of Basic, in which DEF FN is the only user-defined function.

Variables named in a DEF FN statement are not local by default, as they are in a FUNCTION statement. To isolate DEF FN variables, you must make them static; otherwise, their scope extends to the entire main program. In short, DEF FN statements do nothing more than FUNCTION statements, and they are more difficult to use.

Use subprograms and functions rather than subroutines and DEF FN functions; their modular nature makes them easy to develop and test in isolation.

Chaining

Instead of returning control to DOS, a QBasic program can transfer control to another program when it finishes. You can accomplish this in one of two ways. Simply use the RUN statement to execute a second program or, if you don't specify a filename, to start the same program again. Or, use the CHAIN statement to start a second program. The difference between these two commands is that CHAIN lets you pass selected variables to the new program.

To pass information to another program, you must use CHAIN in conjunction with the COMMON statement. Variables specified by a COMMON statement can be transferred to any program that contains a matching COMMON statement.

CALL

See also
CALL ABSOLUTE, DECLARE, FUNCTION

Purpose
The CALL statement lets you execute subprograms from anywhere in your program.

Syntax
[CALL] *name* [[(] *arg* [, *arg* ...] [)]]

name can contain up to 40 characters and must match the name of the subprogram being called.

arg is an optional argument (variable, constant, or expression) that is passed to the subprogram. Multiple arguments are separated by commas.

CALL is a keyword that is optional if you use a DECLARE statement to define the types of variables for the call to the subprogram. If you omit CALL, you must also omit the parentheses around the argument list.

Usage
```
CALL ShutDoor
```
Executes the procedure *ShutDoor*, which does not take any parameters.

```
CALL Scan(UCASE$(COMMAND$))
```
Executes the subprogram *Scan*, which receives an argument that is the result of a call to the QBasic function UCASE$.

```
VerMenu 8, 28, menu%
```
Executes the subprogram *VerMenu*, which has a related DECLARE statement.

Description
Subprograms are self-contained blocks of statements and, as such, are not part of the main program. Because they are separate entities, you cannot branch to them with GOTO and GOSUB statements. Instead, you must use a CALL statement, which transfers control to a subprogram.

Using the DECLARE statement to define how a subprogram is called removes the need for the CALL keyword and lets you execute the subprogram using only its name. If you omit CALL, you must also omit the parentheses around the argument list. In effect, the subprogram becomes an extension of the QBasic language.

If an argument is a variable, it must be of the type that the subprogram expects. By default, any variables in the CALL statement's argument list are *passed by reference*. This means that QBasic passes to the subprogram the address of the variables—not the values—so that any changes made to the variables in the subprogram are maintained when control returns from the subprogram. You can prevent this by enclosing in parentheses each variable that you don't want modified, as in the following statement:

```
QuickSort observations%(), (day1%), (day6%)
```

This causes QBasic to evaluate the variable in parentheses and to copy the result to a temporary variable, the address of which is then passed to the procedure, leaving the original variable unaffected. This is often called *passing by value*.

Warnings

If you call a subprogram by its name alone, QBasic might mistake the reference for a line label. This can happen if the subprogram name is the first statement on the line and the call does not include any parameters, as in the following example:

```
PrintScreen: LOCATE 24, 65: PRINT "Press a key >";
```

In this line, QBasic will probably mistake the call to the procedure *PrintScreen* as a line label, even if *PrintScreen* has previously been declared as a subprogram.

This mistake does not produce an error message. However, the subprogram never executes, and this might result in long hours of debugging time before you understand why. In such circumstances, always include the CALL keyword, even if you previously used a DECLARE statement.

Example

The following program uses a procedure to draw outlined boxes on the text screen, exactly as the LINE statement does on the graphics screen.

```
DECLARE SUB Panel (switch%, row%, col%, numrows%, numcols%)

CLS
FOR i% = 1 TO 7
    COLOR 15, i%
    Panel 1, i% * 2, i% * 2, 8, 20        ' draw a single-border panel
    Panel 2, i% * 2, 40 + i% * 2, 8, 20   ' draw a double-border panel
NEXT i%
COLOR 7, 0
END

SUB Panel (switch%, row%, col%, numrows%, numcols%) STATIC
    IF numcols% > 81 - col% THEN numcols% = 81 - col%
    IF numrows% > 24 - row% THEN numrows% = 24 - row%

    IF switch% = 1 THEN    ' characters for single-border panel
        top$ = CHR$(218) + STRING$(numcols% - 2, CHR$(196)) + CHR$(191)
        mdl$ = CHR$(179) + STRING$(numcols% - 2, " ") + CHR$(179)
        bot$ = CHR$(192) + STRING$(numcols% - 2, CHR$(196)) + CHR$(217)

    ELSE                   ' characters for double-border panel
        top$ = CHR$(201) + STRING$(numcols% - 2, CHR$(205)) + CHR$(187)
        mdl$ = CHR$(186) + STRING$(numcols% - 2, " ") + CHR$(186)
        bot$ = CHR$(200) + STRING$(numcols% - 2, CHR$(205)) + CHR$(188)
```

(continued)

continued

```
    END IF
    LOCATE row%, col%, 0: PRINT top$;              ' print top of square
    FOR i% = 1 TO numrows% - 2
        LOCATE row% + i%, col%: PRINT mdl$;        ' print middle of square
    NEXT i%
    LOCATE row% + i%, col%: PRINT bot$;            ' print bottom of square
END SUB
```

CHAIN

See also

CALL, COMMON, SHELL

Purpose

When one program's task is finished, the CHAIN statement lets you pass control to another program. Use CHAIN when a programming task is divided among several programs.

Syntax

CHAIN *filename*

filename is the name of the program to which you are chaining. Like all DOS filenames, it can be no more than eight characters long; you can also include a drive letter, directory path, and filename extension. If you enter the name literally, you must enclose it in quotation marks; otherwise, you can use any valid string variable or expression to hold the filename.

Usage

```
CHAIN "A:\BIN\PROGRAM2"
```
Transfers control to the PROGRAM2 program in drive A and directory BIN.

```
CHAIN drive$ + path$ + program$(choice%)
```
Transfers control to the program specified by the concatenation of the variables *drive$*, *path$*, and *program$(choice%)*.

Description

QBasic is a modular language. You can include subprograms and functions in your programs. For large applications, you might find it convenient to divide the task among several different programs, each devoted to one particular aspect of the job. The CHAIN statement lets you transfer control from one such program to another.

You can pass variables that are specified in a COMMON statement in the "chaining" program to the "chained-to program," provided that both programs have matching COMMON statements.

CHAIN handles programs run in the QBasic environement in a manner different from the way it handles programs run from the DOS command line. When you chain programs, the target program must be a QBasic file. QBasic assumes a BAS file extension unless another is specifed.

Warnings

Note that when you chain between programs in QBasic, any files left open by the chaining program remain open when the chained program starts. Because QBasic lets you open the same file more than once, you could accidently reopen files until you generate a "Too many open files" error message.

Example

To simplify programming, large applications are often split into several smaller programs or overlays. The following program presents the top-level menu for such an application. It is flexible enough that you can use it for a variety of applications. After the user chooses a menu option, the program uses a CHAIN statement to execute the program corresponding to the option.

```
' $DYNAMIC

CLS : RESTORE
READ options%                    ' get the number of options in the menu
DIM menu(options%) AS STRING     ' declare an array of strings
READ menu(0)                     ' get the string containing possible choices

FOR i% = 1 TO options%
    READ menu(i%)
    IF i% = 1 THEN column% = 40 - (LEN(menu(i%)) \ 2)
    LOCATE 8 + i%, column%: PRINT menu(i%);              ' print menu option
NEXT i%

LOCATE 9 + i%, column%: PRINT "Press <Esc> to quit";
LOCATE 12 + i%, column% + 3: PRINT "< Your choice";

DO
    LOCATE 12 + i%, column%, 1
    choice$ = INPUT$(1): IF choice$ = CHR$(27) THEN EXIT DO
    choice$ = UCASE$(choice$)
    selection% = INSTR(menu(0), choice$)   ' find the index of the choice
    IF selection% THEN
        PRINT choice$;
        CHAIN "PROG" + LTRIM$(RTRIM$(STR$(selection%)))   ' chain to a program
    END IF
    BEEP
LOOP WHILE 1
END

DATA    6, "CAEDSP"
DATA    "C.  Create a data file", "A.  Add a new record"
DATA    "E.  Edit a record  ", "D.  Delete a record "
DATA    "S.  Sort the file  ", "P.  Print reports   "
```

COMMON

See also
CHAIN, $DYNAMIC, FRE

Purpose
The COMMON statement determines the scope of variables in the list that follows it. COMMON extends the scope of the listed variables to chained programs that have a matching COMMON statement.

Syntax
COMMON SHARED *var* [()] [AS *type*] [, var [()] [AS *type*]...]

SHARED is an option that extends the scope of the variables in the list by making them available to the subprograms and functions in the program and to chained programs. Variables that are declared in a COMMON statement that includes the SHARED keyword can be examined or changed by all subprograms and functions in the main program; therefore, you don't have to declare each as shared inside the subprograms and functions that use them.

var is any legal QBasic variable name and can include a type-declaration character (such as % for integers) to define the type of variable. Using the AS clause instead, however, is more flexible because it lets you include the names of user-defined types in addition to the standard types INTEGER, LONG, SINGLE, DOUBLE, and STRING. Array variables are identified in the COMMON statement by parentheses.

Usage
```
COMMON balance, surName AS STRING
```
Declares a single-precision variable and a variable-length string and makes them available to chained programs.

```
COMMON SHARED ages() AS INTEGER
```
Declares a dynamic integer array and makes it available to all subprograms, functions, and chained programs.

```
DIM lightYears(1 TO 50) AS INTEGER
COMMON lightYears()
```
Declares a static, long-integer array of 50 elements and makes it available to chained programs.

Description
COMMON statements assign storage for global data during program initialization. Therefore, you must place them at the top of the main program, before any executable code. The only statements that can precede COMMON are the metacommands

($DYNAMIC and $STATIC), the declarations of constants and procedures (CONST, DATA, and DECLARE), data type declarations using DEF*type*, or the statements TYPE...END TYPE, SHARED, STATIC, OPTION BASE, and DIM. You must declare static arrays named in the variable list of the COMMON statement with DIM statements before the COMMON statement. Arrays in the COMMON statement that are not declared before COMMON are considered dynamic; this enables you to use the DIM or REDIM statement to dimension or redimension them.

You must include matching COMMON statements in all programs that need to access global data. Note, however, that QBasic does not preserve variable names across programs. Consequently, you can use different names to refer to the same variables in different programs. However, you must maintain the type and position of the variables in the COMMON statement, as shown in Figure 4-1.

Figure 4-1.
Matching common variables.

If you declare a common array in the main program as static, you must also declare it static in all other programs that use it. Similarly, a dynamic array must be dynamic in all participating programs because QBasic stores static and dynamic arrays in different segments of memory.

The number of common variables in a chained to program does not have to be the same as in the chaining program. If, for example, program A declares four common variables and program B uses only the first two, you need to declare only two variables in program B.

```
' Program A
COMMON one AS INTEGER, two AS DOUBLE, three AS STRING, four AS LONG
' Program B
COMMON one AS INTEGER, two AS DOUBLE
```

If, however, program B needs to access variables *one* and *four,* you must declare all four as common in program B, as shown in the following, even though *two* and *three* are not used:

```
' Program A
COMMON one AS INTEGER, two AS DOUBLE, three AS STRING, four AS LONG
' Program B
COMMON one AS INTEGER, x#, y$, four AS LONG
```

Comments

QBasic has no arbitrary limit to the number of variables that you can declare as common; however, because common variables are allocated to DGROUP (the default data segment of your program), you must leave enough of this 32-KB space for the other variables your program uses. Use the statement *FRE("")* to determine the number of free bytes remaining in DGROUP.

Dynamic numeric arrays are an exception to this limit because they use only enough space in DGROUP for the array names. The contents of dynamic arrays are stored in the far heap. The statement *FRE(–1)* returns the number of bytes available on the far heap for dynamic numeric arrays.

Errors

If a common variable has a type different from that of the variable occupying the same position in the COMMON statement of a chained-to program, QBasic displays a "Type mismatch" error message at runtime.

Tips

Do not give the same name to variables declared in different COMMON statements in the same program. Doing this does not always produce the expected "Duplicate definition" error message at runtime and can result in incorrect data being passed between programs. This is a bug that can be very difficult to track down.

You should also keep in mind that common variables are not available to subprograms and functions in the program in which you declare them unless you specify the SHARED option.

Example

The following two programs demonstrate the use of the COMMON statement. The first program prompts for the user's name and then chains to the second program, which calls the subprogram *InTake*. *InTake* is a subprogram that accepts and validates keyboard input.

```
COMMON SHARED abort AS INTEGER, maxlen AS INTEGER, validKeys AS STRING

CONST FALSE = 0, TRUE = NOT FALSE            ' constants used by this program

lc$ = "abcdefghijklmnopqrstuvwxyz"
uc$ = UCASE$(lc$)
nu$ = "0123456789"
punc$ = " .,;:'"

COLOR 14, 0: CLS
LOCATE 12, 1: PRINT "Enter your name > ";   ' prompt for name
COLOR 0, 7
maxlen = 40
validKeys = uc$ + lc$ + punc$               ' string containing valid keys

CHAIN "COMMON2"
```

(continued)

continued

```
DECLARE SUB InTake (buffer$)

COMMON SHARED abort AS INTEGER, maxLen AS INTEGER, validKeys AS STRING

CONST FALSE = 0, TRUE = NOT FALSE     ' constants used by this program

InTake yourname$

LOCATE 15, 1
IF abort THEN
    PLAY "T255 L24 O1 A A A O2 B B B O3 C C C O4 D D D"
    COLOR 12, 0: PRINT "You pressed Esc"
ELSE
    PLAY "T240 O3 L8 G F L4 E L8 E E D E L3 F L4 E"
    PLAY "L8 E L4 D L8 D D C D L3 E L4 C L8 D L4 E"
    PLAY "L8 E E D E L4 F L8 G L4 A L8 A L4 G L8 F L4 E L8 D L4 C"
    COLOR 11, 0: PRINT "Hello, "; yourname$
END IF
LOCATE , , 1
END

SUB InTake (buffer$) STATIC

    bSpace$ = CHR$(8): cr$ = CHR$(13): esc$ = CHR$(27)     ' special keys
    cLeft$ = CHR$(29): cursor$ = CHR$(95): cFlag% = FALSE ' variables for cursor
    ptr% = 0: buffer$ = "": done% = FALSE: abort% = FALSE
    tick& = 0: start% = POS(0)

    PRINT SPACE$(maxLen);
    LOCATE , start%, 0
    DO
        DO                                  ' print a blinking cursor
            IF ABS(TIMER - tick&) > .3 THEN
                tick& = TIMER
                IF cFlag% THEN
                    PRINT " "; cLeft$;          ' erase cursor
                    cFlag% = FALSE
                ELSE
                    PRINT cursor$; cLeft$;      ' draw cursor
                    cFlag% = TRUE
                END IF
            END IF
            key$ = INKEY$                   ' get a character from the user
        LOOP WHILE key$ = ""
        SELECT CASE key$
            CASE esc$          ' if character is Esc
                abort = TRUE
                done% = TRUE
            CASE cr$           ' if character is Enter
                done% = TRUE
```

(continued)

continued

```
                CASE bSpace$          ' if character is Backspace
                    IF ptr% > 0 THEN
                        PRINT " "; cLeft$; cLeft$;
                        ptr% = ptr% - 1
                        buffer$ = LEFT$(buffer$, ptr%)
                    END IF
                CASE ELSE              ' check validity of character
                    IF INSTR(validKeys, key$) AND ptr% < maxLen THEN
                        PRINT key$;
                        ptr% = ptr% + 1
                        buffer$ = buffer$ + key$
                    END IF
            END SELECT
        LOOP UNTIL done%
        PRINT " "; cLeft$;
    END SUB
```

DECLARE

See also

CALL, FUNCTION, SUB

Purpose

The DECLARE statement defines how QBasic function and subprogram procedures are
called. The DECLARE statement specifies the name of a procedure and defines the
✳ number and type of variables that are passed to it as arguments. Using the DECLARE
statement makes the CALL keyword unnecessary.

Syntax

✳ If there are no arguments, it seems that DECLARE must not be used.

DECLARE FUNCTION *Name* [([*params*])]
DECLARE SUB *Name* [([*params*])]

Name is the name of the procedure to be called. It can contain as many as 40 characters
and must correspond to the name of the procedure to which it refers.

params is the list of variables that are the parameters of the procedure. The types of the
variables must be specified in the list.

Usage

```
DECLARE SUB Verify (prompt$, ok%)
```
Defines a subprogram named *Verify* and specifies the types of arguments passed to it.

```
DECLARE FUNCTION Center$ (text AS STRING, maxWidth AS INTEGER)
```
Declares that *Center$* is a user-defined function that takes as arguments a string and an
integer.

Description

DECLARE statements can appear only in the code of the main program and are usually listed at the top of the program, before any executable statements. They define the names of procedures that are called by statements in the program, and they specify the number and type of the variables to be passed as arguments. DECLARE statements are often called *prototypes* of the procedures they refer to.

If the called procedure returns a value, you should define it with the FUNCTION statement, in which case the name of the procedure is interpreted as a variable. Use a type-declaration character (%, &, !, #, or $) to specify the type of the value returned by a FUNCTION statement. If the procedure doesn't return a value, declare the procedure with the SUB keyword.

The names of the variables in the parameter list of the DECLARE statement are not passed to the external procedure and do not need to match the names of the variables used in the called procedure. However, it is important that the types of the variables used in the call to the procedure be the same as those in the corresponding positions of the DECLARE statement's parameter list. You can specify variable types by including a type-declaration character or by using an AS clause with INTEGER, LONG, SINGLE, DOUBLE, STRING, or the name of a user-defined type to declare that the variable is of a particular type. Do not, however, use fixed-length strings as arguments; only variable-length strings may be passed to functions and subprograms.

You can also pass complete arrays to a procedure (to be sorted, for example). In such cases you do not need to specify the number of dimensions in the parameter list of the DECLARE statement; however, if you include the number, the QBasic smart editor will accept it but will then erase it.

Errors

If you call a procedure that has a variable of a type different from the one in the corresponding position in the parameter list of the DECLARE statement, QBasic returns a "Parameter type mismatch" error message. If the number of parameters is greater than or less than the number of parameters listed in the DECLARE statement, QBasic displays an "Argument-count mismatch" error message.

Example

The following example contains two procedures—*BinDec&*, a function, and *DecBin*, a subprogram—that convert numbers between binary and decimal format. The DECLARE statements tell the compiler what kinds of procedures *BinDec&* and *DecBin* are and specify the number and type of arguments that they expect.

```
' declare procedures
DECLARE FUNCTION BinDec& (binry AS STRING)
DECLARE SUB DecBin (decimal AS LONG, bin AS STRING)

decimal& = 123456                   ' a decimal value
DecBin decimal&, bin$               ' convert from decimal to binary
PRINT "Binary  = "; bin$            ' display the result
PRINT "Decimal ="; BinDec&(bin$)    ' convert from binary to decimal
END

' converts a string of binary digits to its decimal equivalent
FUNCTION BinDec& (binary$) STATIC
    decimal& = 0: power% = 0
    binary$ = UCASE$(binary$)
    FOR i% = LEN(binary$) TO 1 STEP -1        ' convert from binary to decimal
        digit% = ASC(MID$(binary$, i%, 1)) - 48
        IF digit% < 0 OR digit% > 1 THEN decimal& = 0: EXIT FOR
        decimal& = decimal& + digit% * 2 ^ (power%)
        power% = power% + 1
    NEXT i%
    BinDec& = decimal&
END FUNCTION

' converts a decimal value to an equivalent string of binary digits
SUB DecBin (decimal&, bin$) STATIC
    bin$ = ""
    h$ = HEX$(decimal&)        ' convert from decimal to hexadecimal
    FOR i% = 1 TO LEN(h$)
        digit% = INSTR("0123456789ABCDEF", MID$(h$, i%, 1)) - 1
        IF digit% < 0 THEN bin$ = "": EXIT FOR
        j% = 8: k% = 4
        DO                     ' convert from hexadecimal to binary
            bin$ = bin$ + RIGHT$(STR$((digit% \ j%) MOD 2), 1)
            j% = j% - (j% \ 2): k% = k% - 1
            IF k% = 0 THEN EXIT DO
        LOOP WHILE j%
    NEXT i%
END SUB
```

DEF FN

See also

FUNCTION, STATIC, SUB

Purpose

DEF FN defines a function. QBasic provides this command so that programs that are written in versions of Basic that support only the DEF FN statement for user-defined functions can be easily ported to QBasic. QBasic extends the DEF FN statement by removing the restriction that confined such functions to a single program line.

Syntax

Single-line functions:

DEF FN*Name* [(*arg* [AS *type*] [, *arg* [AS *type*...])] = *expr*

Multiple-line functions:

DEF FN*Name* [(*arg* [AS *type*] [, *arg* [AS *type*]...])]
    [STATIC *var* [, *var*...]]
    ⋮
    [EXIT DEF]
    ⋮
    FN*Name* = *expr*
    ⋮
END DEF

Name is any legal QBasic variable name; you must always prefix it with the keyword FN, which indicates that it is a function. Because QBasic regards *Name* as a variable, you should include a type-declaration character. If you don't, the value returned will be either the default single precision or the type defined in a DEF*type* statement.

arg is the name of an optional argument that is passed to the function. You should either include a type-declaration character or use the AS keyword with the keyword INTEGER, LONG, SINGLE, DOUBLE, or STRING to define an argument as being of a particular type. You cannot pass arrays, fixed-length strings, or user-defined variable types as arguments to a DEF FN function.

Multiple-line DEF FN functions have two additional features. They can use variables other than those passed to them as arguments; however, these variables are visible to (and may be modified by) statements in the rest of the program. To override this, use the STATIC keyword to explicitly declare the variables local to the function.

By using the EXIT DEF statement, you can allow a multiple-line function to terminate before the END DEF is encountered. If no value has been assigned to FN*Name* when the EXIT DEF executes, the function returns a 0 for numeric types and a null string ("") for string types.

Usage

```
DEF FNBitTest (number%, bit%) = -SGN(number% AND 2 ^ bit%)
```
A single-line DEF FN statement that tests a specified bit of the integer *number%*. It returns −1 (true) if *bit%* is set and 0 (false) if *bit%* is not set.

```
DEF FNMaximum! (a!, b!, c!)
    STATIC max!
    IF a! > b! THEN
        max! = a!
    ELSEIF c! > b! THEN
        max! = c!
    ELSE max! = b!
    END IF
    FNMaximum! = max!
END DEF
```

A multiple-line DEF FN statement that finds the maximum of three values. Note that the variable *max!* is declared in a STATIC statement to make it local to the function.

Description

DEF FN is traditionally used to add specialized functions to the built-in library of functions and statements used in Basic. It lets you assign any expression to a variable whose name begins with the FN keyword; QBasic then evaluates the expression every time the program references that DEF FN function. The following example demonstrates the procedure:

```
DEF FNBitSet(number%, bit%) = number% OR 2 ^ bit%
IF FNBitSet(attribute%, 7) THEN MakeBlink(character%)
```

DEF FN functions are similar to subroutines, but they are much more compact and efficient. However, unlike subroutines, they return a value. You can use DEF FN functions as part of another expression or even call them from inside other functions or statements, as in the following example:

```
DEF FNBitReSet(number%, bit%) = number% AND (32767 - 2 ^ bit%)
PRINT CHR$(FNBitReSet(ASC("a"), 5))
```

In the above example, the ASC function (within the DEF FN) supplies *FNBitReSet* with a value of 97 (the ASCII value of "a"). Setting bit 5 of this number to 0 reduces it by 32 (to 65), and the CHR$ function converts the value 65 to A.

Multiple-line DEF FN statements

QBasic lets you use as many statement lines as you need before assigning a value to the function. If you use multiple lines, however, you must also use the END DEF statement to mark the end of the function and return control to the line that called the function. If you use the EXIT DEF statement, you force the function to terminate prematurely and return without making an assignment to the function.

The FUNCTION statement lets you write user-defined functions that are separate from the main program. Because these functions can also call themselves recursively, they are now the preferred method of creating new functions. You cannot use DEF FN functions recursively.

Errors

QBasic attempts to convert the value returned by a DEF FN statement to the precision specified by the type of the function's name. If it cannot do so because, for example, the expression returns a numeric value and the function is defined as a string, QBasic displays a "Type mismatch" error message.

DEF FN declarations must appear before any statements that reference them. If you call a function before it has been declared, QBasic displays a "Function not defined" error message.

Example

The following program uses a DEF FN statement to define a function that returns a string containing the day of the week for any date from 1901 through 2099. Notice that the variables *numDay!*, *numYear*, and *days$* are declared in a STATIC statement to make them local to the function. To use the function in your own programs, specify parameters in the following ranges:

m% = month (1 - 12), d% = day (1 - 31), y% = year (1901 - 2099)

```
DEF FNWeekDay$ (m%, d%, y%)
    STATIC numDay!, numYear!, days$

    numYear! = y%
    IF numYear! < 1901 OR numYear! > 2099 THEN EXIT DEF

    days$ = "Friday   Saturday Sunday   Monday   Tuesday  WednesdayThursday "
    num! = VAL(MID$("00030306081113161921242426", (m% - 1) * 2 + 1, 2))
    numDay! = numYear! * 365 + INT((y% - 1) \ 4) + (m% - 1) * 28
    numDay! = numDay! + num! - ((m% > 2) AND (y% MOD 4 = 0)) + d%

    FNWeekDay$ = MID$(days$, (numDay! - INT(numDay! \ 7) * 7) * 9 + 1, 9)
END DEF

CLS
PRINT "January 1, 2000, falls on a "; FNWeekDay$(1, 1, 2000)
```

FUNCTION

See also
DECLARE, DEF FN, EXIT, SHARED, STATIC, SUB

Purpose
QBasic includes many predefined functions that either perform mathematical calculations or return information about a variable. If, however, no standard function performs the programming task you require, QBasic provides the FUNCTION statement so that you can define your own.

Syntax
FUNCTION *Name* [(*arg* [AS *type*][, *arg* [AS *type*]]...)] [STATIC]
    [SHARED *var* [, *var...*]]
    [STATIC *var* [, *var...*]]
    ⋮
    [EXIT FUNCTION]
    ⋮
    Name = *expr*
    ⋮
END FUNCTION

Name is the name that you assign to the function. It must be a valid QBasic variable name and include a type-declaration character, if necessary.

arg is the name of a variable that is passed to the function as an argument. It must include a type-declaration character or be declared with the AS clause with INTEGER, LONG, SINGLE, DOUBLE, STRING, or a user-defined type. Arrays passed as arguments must include parentheses after the array name, although you do not need to specify the number of dimensions.

The SHARED statement specifies variables that are in the main program and that the function needs to use, but that are not specifically passed as arguments.

The STATIC statement specifies the local variables whose values are preserved between calls to the function. If you omit this statement, new local variables are created each time the function is called.

The EXIT FUNCTION statement returns control from the function before it reaches the normal exit point (the END FUNCTION statement).

Usage

```
FUNCTION Signed% (unSigned&) STATIC
    IF unSigned& > 32767 THEN
        Signed% = unsigned& - 65536
    ELSE
        Signed% = unsigned&
    END IF
END FUNCTION
```

This function converts an unsigned 4-byte long integer to its 2-byte signed integer equivalent. (This is useful for accessing memory addresses above location 32767.)

Description

A function is a separate set of statements that returns a value. The value returned by a function defined by a FUNCTION statement is usually assigned to another variable on return. However, you can also apply the value directly to another QBasic statement or function. You can even use one function as the argument for another user-defined function or subprogram. The following statement is a valid application of the function *signed%*:

```
PRINT PEEK(Signed%(65000))
```

Because a function always returns a value, QBasic handles the function's name as a variable. The name, therefore, should include the appropriate type-declaration character for the value it returns. If you do not include a type-declaration character, QBasic assumes that the value returned is single precision or of the type defined by a DEF*type* statement.

Functions usually take one or more variables as arguments. Define the types of these variables using either the appropriate type-declaration character or the AS clause with INTEGER, LONG, SINGLE, DOUBLE, STRING, or the name of a user-defined type. When you pass an array variable to a function, include parentheses after the array name; however, you don't need to list the number of dimensions.

You may define any number of local variables within a user-defined function. By default these variables exist only while the function executes, and their contents are lost when control returns to the line that called the function. The STATIC keyword, however, instructs QBasic to preserve the contents of all local variables between calls. This speeds program execution considerably because, after the first invocation, QBasic doesn't need to spend time creating local variables each time the function is called. You can use a STATIC statement instead of the STATIC keyword to preserve only some of the local variable's values.

Local variables, as their name implies, are available only to the specific function in which they are used; they cannot be accessed by other functions or by statements in the code from which the function is called. Similarly, variables defined in the main program are normally invisible to a user-defined function unless they are specifically passed to it as arguments. The SHARED statement lets you override this default condition; use it to specify variables in the main program to which your function needs access. However, remember that any changes you make to the variables inside a function are returned to the main program when it regains control. You must declare shared variables at the start of the function code before any executable statements. If you've already defined a variable as shared in the main program, however, you do not need to define it again in the function in order to use it there.

Errors

Although QBasic regards the function name as a variable, you cannot define the type of the value that it returns with the AS type clause. The following statement, for example, causes QBasic to display an "Expected: (or end-of-statement" error message:

```
FUNCTION HiByte AS INTEGER (number AS INTEGER) STATIC
```

You can, however, use the DEF*type* statement as an alternative method for defining a function type; for example,

```
DEFINT H
FUNCTION HiByte (number AS INTEGER) STATIC
```

correctly defines *HiByte* as an integer function.

Most users, though, prefer the economy of the standard method of assigning a variable type to a function:

```
FUNCTION HiByte% (number%) STATIC
```

Warnings

Whenever you use the STATIC keyword in a FUNCTION, remember that local variables retain the values assigned to them during prior calls to the function. Unless you initialize these variables each time you call the the function, the function might return an incorrect value. This is a common and hard-to-find source of programming errors.

Example

Converting fractions to decimal numbers is easy: Merely divide the numerator by the denominator. It is not as easy, however, to convert decimals to fractions. The following QBasic function performs this operation. The function makes the size of the denominator a variable so that fractions can be calculated to varying degrees of accuracy.

```
' converts a decimal number to a whole number and a fraction
FUNCTION ConDecFrac$ (number!) STATIC
    SHARED den%                          ' value of the denominator
    frac$ = ""
    whole& = INT(number!)                ' get integer portion
    decimal! = number! - whole&          ' get decimal portion
    IF decimal! > 0 THEN
        num% = INT(den% * decimal!)      ' get numerator of fraction
        IF num% = 0 THEN num% = 1
        DO WHILE num% MOD 2 = 0 AND den% MOD 2 = 0
            num% = num% \ 2
            den% = den% \ 2
        LOOP                ' loop while numerator and denominator are both even
        frac$ = STR$(num%) + "/" + LTRIM$(STR$(den%))
    END IF
    ConDecFrac$ = LTRIM$(RTRIM$(STR$(whole&))) + frac$
END FUNCTION
```

GOSUB...RETURN

See also

CLEAR, GOTO, ON...GOSUB, SUB

Purpose

The GOSUB statement directs a program to branch, unconditionally, to a subroutine elsewhere in the same module. RETURN marks an exit from the subroutine; this statement causes execution to resume either at the statement following the one that invoked the subroutine or at another section of the program. Because QBasic now provides self-contained subprograms and functions as more structured alternatives to subroutines, programmers rarely use GOSUB statements. However, QBasic retains the keyword to maintain compatibility with programs written in earlier versions of Basic.

Syntax

GOSUB {line ¦ label}
⋮
RETURN [{line ¦ label}]

line or *label* specifies the destination of a GOSUB statement. Execution then proceeds until a RETURN statement is encountered. At this point, control returns either to the statement following the GOSUB statement or to the line number or label specified in the RETURN statement.

Usage

```
GOSUB Update
```
Branches to the line labeled *Update*.

```
RETURN
```
Exits a subroutine and returns control to the statement following the original GOSUB statement.

```
RETURN Menu
```
Exits a subroutine and branches to the statement labeled *Menu*.

Description

GOSUB instructs QBasic to make an unconditional branch to the line number or label specified; control transfers to the destination line, regardless of the result of previously executed statements.

You cannot use GOSUB to branch into or out of a subprogram or a user-defined function. You can, however, use a GOSUB statement to branch within a subprogram or function, provided that execution returns to a statement in the procedure.

All variables that subroutines use are shared by other statements in the portion of the program that includes the subroutine; any changes made to these variables are maintained when the subroutine exits. Subroutines can contain GOSUB statements that call other subroutines (nesting) or even call themselves (recursion); however, because the address of the statement to be returned to is stored on the stack, your program must allocate sufficient stack space to allow for the level of nesting used. The CLEAR statement lets you specify stack size. (See the CLEAR entry in Chapter 18, "DOS and Program Management," for more details.)

If you use RETURN with a line number or label to exit from a nested subroutine, the return address must be in the same subroutine that called it. If your subroutines are nested more than one level, you can return only to the level that called the subroutine.

Warnings

If you use RETURN with a line number or label, do so with caution; the statements following the target line must then allow for returns from subroutines that were called from any other line in the program.

Example

A subroutine might have more than one exit point, and the RETURN statement can branch control to any point in the program. The following example program includes a subroutine that selectively branches to various destinations, depending on the user's response. The program draws designs on the screen until the user presses a key.

```
        CLEAR : SCREEN 1: COLOR 0, 1: RANDOMIZE TIMER
100
    VIEW
    LINE (0, 0)-(319, 199), 1, BF    ' draw a filled box the size of the screen
    VIEW (32, 4)-(287, 186), 0, 2    ' reduce the size of the graphics screen
    CLS
    xLimit% = 253: yLimit% = 180
    signA% = 0: version% = 1: x1% = 0: y1% = 0
    rate% = INT(RND * 3) + 2                         ' set the rate of change
    colors% = INT(RND * 3) + 1
110
    IF x1% <= 0 THEN x1% = 0: changeX% = signA%      ' set the direction of change
    IF y1% <= 0 THEN y1% = 0: changeY% = signA%
    IF x1% >= xLimit% THEN x1% = xLimit%: changeX% = -signA%
    IF y1% >= yLimit% THEN y1% = yLimit%: changeY% = -signA%
    IF signA% <= 1 THEN signA% = 1: signB% = 1
    IF signA% >= rate% THEN signA% = rate%: signB% = -1

    x2% = 255 - x1%: y2% = 181 - y1%
    IF version% = 1 THEN
        LINE (x1%, y1%)-(x2%, y2%), colors%, B        ' draw the outline of a box
        LINE (x1%, y1%)-(x2%, y2%), 0                  ' draw a black diagonal line
        LINE (x1%, y2%)-(x2%, y1%), 0
        version% = 2
    ELSE
        LINE (x1%, y1%)-(x2%, y2%), 3, B               ' draw the outline of a box
        LINE (x1%, y1%)-(x2%, y2%), colors%            ' draw a diagonal line
        LINE (x2%, y1%)-(x1%, y2%), colors%
        version% = 1
        colors% = INT(RND * 3) + 1                     ' change color
    END IF
    x1% = x1% + changeX%
    y1% = y1% + changeY%
    signA% = signA% + signB%
    GOSUB 900: GOTO 110
120
    SCREEN 0, 0, 0: WIDTH 80: CLS
END


900
    IF INKEY$ <> "" THEN LOCATE 25, 1 ELSE RETURN
    PRINT "Q = Quit  R = Restart  C = Continue";
    key$ = UCASE$(INPUT$(1))
    SELECT CASE key$
        CASE "Q"
            RETURN 120
        CASE "R"
            RETURN 100
        CASE ELSE
            VIEW: LINE (0, 188)-(319, 199), 1, BF
            VIEW (32, 4)-(287, 186), , 2
    END SELECT
RETURN
```

SHARED

See also

COMMON, DIM, FUNCTION, SUB

Purpose

Unless passed as arguments, variables used by subprograms and functions the user defines by SUB and FUNCTION statements are local to those procedures and cannot be accessed by statements in the module-level code. The SHARED statement lets you override the default and make specified variables available to both the procedure and the main program. This lets you return the results of operations within the procedure and lets functions, for example, return more than one value.

Syntax

SHARED *var* [AS *type*][, *var* [AS *type*]...]

var is any valid QBasic variable. A variable (other than the default single-precision type) must either include a type declaration character or be followed by an AS clause with INTEGER, LONG, SINGLE, DOUBLE, STRING (including a fixed-length string), or the name of a user-defined type. If the variable is an array, it must be followed by parentheses, although you don't need to specify the number of dimensions.

SHARED statements must appear at the beginning of the procedure, before any executable statements.

Usage

```
SHARED student%, grades!()
```

Makes the contents of an integer variable and a single-precision array available to the procedure in which the SHARED statement appears.

Description

SHARED statements can appear only in subprograms and user-defined functions; they specify the names of the variables in the main program that the subprogram or function needs to access. These variables are available to only those subprograms and functions in the program that include a SHARED statement. A procedure variable that is not shared can have the same name as a variable in the main program; because the variable is not in the scope of the main program, QBasic considers the procedure variable different from the main program variable.

Specifying variables in a SHARED statement saves you from having to pass them as parameters. As with parameters, any changes made to a variable in the procedure that shares it are maintained when control returns to the main program.

The scope of SHARED statements extends only to the procedure and the main program that contains it.

Tips

You can make specified variables available to all the functions and subprograms in a module by dimensioning them in a DIM statement with the SHARED keyword in the module-level code, as in the following example:

```
DIM SHARED volume!, radius!, diameter!
```

This eliminates the need for using separate SHARED statements in all the procedures that need to access those variables.

Example

In addition to the parameters passed to them and the values returned, you might want selected procedures to share certain standard variables that are defined in the module-level code. The following program uses a function to let the user select a filename. The function uses a SHARED statement to access variables that are defined in the main program.

```
DECLARE FUNCTION GetFile$ (pathName$)

CONST FALSE = 0, TRUE = NOT FALSE          ' constants are global

DIM SHARED abort AS INTEGER
cr$ = CHR$(13): esc$ = CHR$(27): bSpace$ = CHR$(8): cLeft$ = CHR$(29)

filename$ = GetFile$("*.*")
LOCATE 15, 1

IF abort THEN PRINT "Aborted!" ELSE PRINT " You chose "; filename$
END

FUNCTION GetFile$ (path$) STATIC
    SHARED cr$, esc$, bSpace$, cLeft$      ' shared with main program
    abort = FALSE                          ' shared with main program
    buffer$ = "": ptr% = 0
    CLS : FILES path$                      ' print the names of files

    PRINT "Enter the name of a file: ";
    DO
        key$ = UCASE$(INKEY$)
        SELECT CASE key$
            CASE esc$                      ' if Esc, exit loop
                abort = TRUE
                EXIT DO
            CASE bSpace$
                PRINT " "; cLeft$; cLeft$;
                ptr% = ptr% - 1
                buffer$ = LEFT$(buffer$, ptr%)
            CASE ""
```

(continued)

continued

```
            CASE ELSE
                PRINT key$;
                buffer$ = buffer$ + key$
                ptr% = ptr% + 1
            END SELECT
    LOOP UNTIL key$ = CHR$(13)            ' loop until user presses Enter
    GetFile$ = buffer$
END FUNCTION
```

STATIC

See also

COMMON, DIM, SHARED

Purpose

By default, variables in a subprogram or function are dynamic. They are re-created each time the procedure is called. The STATIC statement preserves the contents of selected variables in the procedure, thereby allowing them to retain their values between calls. This lets you use the results of calculations in subsequent calls to the procedure.

Syntax

STATIC *var* [AS *type*][, *var* [AS *type*]...]

var is any valid QBasic variable. A variable (other than the default single-precision type) must either include a type-declaration character or be followed by an AS clause with INTEGER, LONG, SINGLE, DOUBLE, STRING, or the name of a user-defined type. If the variable is an array, it must be followed by parentheses, although you don't need to specify the number of dimensions.

Usage

```
STATIC counter%, total
```

Makes an integer variable and a single-precision variable local to the procedure, and preserves their values after the procedure terminates.

Description

Unless you specify otherwise, all variables named in a function or a subprogram are dynamic. QBasic creates them when the procedure is called (typically, to hold temporary values necessary to the procedure's task) and discards them and their contents when the procedure finishes executing. This type of variable is often called an *automatic* variable; it exists only while the function or subprogram is active and is destroyed on exit, thus freeing the memory assigned to it.

Sometimes, however, you might need to preserve the value of one or more variables between calls so that they can be used the next time the procedure is executed. To do so, use the STATIC statement, followed by a list of the variables whose values you want saved, at the beginning of the procedure, before any executable statements.

Alternatively, you can preserve all variables by using the keyword STATIC in the first line of the procedure definition, after the procedure name and argument list. This makes every local variable in the procedure static.

Static variables retain their contents even while the procedure is inactive. Because QBasic does not need to create them each time you call the procedure, using static variables makes your program run slightly faster than it would otherwise, although less memory is available for other processing.

Dynamic variables are local to the subprogram or function that contains them because they do not exist when the procedure is not being executed. Static variables are also local. Even if a variable of the same name has been dimensioned in a DIM statement with SHARED or declared in a COMMON statement in the main program, QBasic considers it to be a different variable. You cannot define a variable in both a SHARED and a STATIC statement in the same procedure.

Although the STATIC statement is most often used in subprograms and functions, you can also use it inside multiple-line DEF FN functions in the module-level code. This declares the variables local to the DEF FN function so that the variables can have the same name as variables in the rest of the program and yet not interfere with them.

Warnings

Do not confuse the STATIC statement with the $STATIC metacommand. The latter is an instruction to the compiler that allocates memory for arrays; it doesn't affect the existence or scope of variables after the program starts.

Example

The following program demonstrates that the static variable *i%* retains its value between calls to the procedure *Counter* that contains it. Note that it is not affected by the variable of the same name in the main program. The variable *j%*, on the other hand, is a dynamic variable, so it is created with an initial value of 0 each time the procedure executes.

```
DECLARE SUB Counter (count AS INTEGER)

CLS
FOR i% = 0 TO 9
    j% = i%: PRINT
    Counter i%
NEXT i%
END
```

(continued)

continued

```
SUB Counter (count AS INTEGER)
    STATIC i%
    PRINT USING "   # "; count;
    FOR a% = 0 TO 9
        i% = i% + 1
        PRINT USING " ### "; i%;
    NEXT a%
    PRINT TAB(6);
    FOR a% = 0 TO 9
        j% = j% + 1
        PRINT USING " ### "; j%;
    NEXT a%
END SUB
```

SUB

See also

CALL, DECLARE, DEF FN, EXIT, FUNCTION, SHARED, STATIC

Purpose

The SUB statement lets you define subprograms that can be called from anywhere in your program.

Syntax

SUB *Name* [(*arg* [AS *type*] [, *arg* [AS *type*]...])] [STATIC]
    [SHARED *var* [, *var*...]]
    [STATIC *var* [, *var*...]]
    ⋮
    [EXIT SUB]
    ⋮
END SUB

Name is any valid QBasic name, which you use to call the subprogram.

arg is the name of a variable that is passed to the subprogram as an argument. You must indicate the type of this argument (either by using a type-declaration character or by using an AS clause with INTEGER, LONG, SINGLE, DOUBLE, or STRING) or the name of a user-defined type. Arrays passed as arguments must include parentheses after the array name, although you do not need to specify the number of dimensions.

The SHARED statement specifies variables that are in the main program and that the subprogram needs to use but that are not specifically passed as arguments.

The STATIC statement specifies the local variables whose values are preserved between calls to the subprogram.

The EXIT SUB statement returns control from the subprogram before it reaches the normal exit point (the END SUB statement).

Usage

```
SUB CvtSign (unsign&, sign%)
    IF unsign& > 32767 THEN
        sign% = unsign& - 65536
    ELSE
        sign% = unsign&
    END IF
END SUB
```

Finds the signed, 2-byte, equivalent value of *unsign&* (an unsigned long integer) and assigns the value to the parameter *sign%*.

Description

Subprograms are self-contained procedures that you can add to QBasic programs to perform a specific task. Like traditional subroutines, they can be called from anywhere in the current program.

If you create a subprogram with the QBasic editor, QBasic immediately generates the appropriate DECLARE statement.

To execute a subprogram you must call it: Use the subprogram name as the object of the call, and substitute your own arguments for those named in the parameter list, as in the following example:

```
CALL QuickSort(scores%(), LBOUND(scores%), UBOUND(scores%))
```

Notice that arguments do not have to be actual variables. You can also use constants and expressions in the parameter list, provided that they evaluate to the type of argument that the subprogram expects.

If a DECLARE statement for the subprogram exists in the current module, you can omit the CALL keyword in a call to the subprogram. If you do so, however, you must also omit the parentheses around the parameter list:

```
QuickSort scores%(), LBOUND(scores%), UBOUND(scores%)
```

Other than arguments that are passed and variables that are specified in a SHARED statement, all variables are local to the subprogram. You can use any variable names without interfering with variables of the same name in the main program.

Unlike functions, subprograms do not return a value. However, because the arguments that they use are passed by reference, any changes the subprogram makes to the arguments are maintained when the subprogram completes.

Recursion

An important feature of subprograms (and functions) is that they can be recursive; that is, they can call themselves. Recursive procedures use a lot of stack space because each time a subprogram is called QBasic assigns a new set of local variables and stores them on the program stack. Because recursion requires the use of new local variables, do not use the STATIC keyword in recursive procedures.

Recursion is often the most efficient method for programming applications in which large blocks of data must be processed. The following subprogram, for example, uses recursion to sort an array.

```
SUB QuickSort (array%(), start%, finish%)
    top% = start%: bottom% = finish%
    compare% = array%((start% + finish%) \ 2)
    DO
        DO WHILE array%(top%) < compare% AND top% < finish%
            top% = top% + 1
        LOOP
        DO WHILE compare% < array%(bottom%) AND bottom% > start%
            bottom% = bottom% - 1
        LOOP
        IF bottom% > top% THEN
            SWAP array%(top%), array%(bottom%)
            top% = top% + 1: bottom% = bottom% - 1
        END IF
        IF bottom% = top% THEN top% = top% + 1
    LOOP UNTIL top% > bottom%
    IF start% < bottom% THEN QuickSort array%(), start%, bottom%   ' recursion
    IF top% < finish% THEN QuickSort array%(), top%, finish%       ' recursion
END SUB
```

This subprogram uses a quicksort algorithm to sort an integer array into ascending order. You supply it with the name of the array and the upper and lower bounds of the elements to be sorted. The subprogram works by dividing the elements into successively smaller partitions and calling itself recursively to sort each partition until the entire array has been ordered.

Warnings

QBasic sometimes mistakes program labels for calls to subprograms that do not take parameters. This occurs only if the call is the first statement on the line and does not include the CALL keyword, as in the following example:

```
PrintScreen:
```

QBasic is as likely to treat the statement as a line label as it is to treat it as a call to a subprogram. This mistake does not produce an error message. However, the subprogram never executes, and this situation might result in long hours of debugging time before you understand why.

To prevent this error, use an explicit CALL statement in such circumstances, even if the module includes a DECLARE statement for the subprogram.

Example

Programmers often create subprograms that can be used in a wide range of programs. The following QBasic program uses a subprogram to provide a standard menu handler. The calling program supplies the option list (as a string array) and the screen location where the menu is to be drawn. The subprogram draws the menu, handles user input, and returns with the option selected.

```
DECLARE SUB VerMenu (row%, col%, menu%)

CONST FALSE = 0, TRUE = NOT FALSE

DIM SHARED menu$(0 TO 9): menu% = 8
CLS : RESTORE

FOR i% = 1 TO menu%                        ' get menu options
    menu$(0) = menu$(0) + CHR$(i% + 64)
    READ menu$(i%)
    menu$(i%) = CHR$(i% + 64) + ". " + menu$(i%)
    menu$(i%) = LEFT$(menu$(i%) + SPACE$(24), 24)
NEXT i%

VerMenu 8, 28, menu%

LOCATE 20, 10, 1
IF abort% THEN
    PRINT "ABORTED!"
ELSE
    PRINT "Option"; choice%; "selected"
END IF
END

DATA "View current settings", "Read personal mail"
DATA "Read messages", "Send a message", "Download a file"
DATA "Upload a file", "Yell for Sysop", "Goodbye - log off"

SUB VerMenu (row%, col%, menu%) STATIC
    SHARED abort%, choice%

    abort% = FALSE: choice% = 1
    FOR i% = 1 TO menu%
        LOCATE row% + i%, col%, 0
        COLOR 15, 0: PRINT LEFT$(menu$(i%), 1);
        COLOR 7, 0: PRINT MID$(menu$(i%), 2);
    NEXT i%
```

(continued)

continued

```
    DO
        COLOR 14, 4
        hiLine% = row% + choice%
        LOCATE hiLine%, col%: PRINT menu$(choice%);
        DO
            key$ = INKEY$
        LOOP WHILE key$ = ""
        lastChoice% = choice%
        IF LEN(key$) < 2 THEN
            IF key$ = CHR$(13) THEN EXIT DO
            IF key$ = CHR$(27) THEN abort% = TRUE: EXIT DO
            key$ = UCASE$(key$)
            m% = INSTR(menu$(0), key$)
            IF m% > 0 THEN choice% = m%
        ELSE
            scanCode% = ASC(MID$(key$, 2, 1))
            IF scanCode% = 80 THEN choice% = choice% + 1
            IF scanCode% = 72 THEN choice% = choice% - 1
        END IF
        IF choice% > menu% THEN choice% = 1
        IF choice% < 1 THEN choice% = menu%
        IF choice% <> lastChoice% THEN
            LOCATE row% + lastChoice%, col%
            COLOR 15, 0: PRINT LEFT$(menu$(lastChoice%), 1);
            COLOR 7, 0: PRINT MID$(menu$(lastChoice%), 2);
        END IF
    LOOP WHILE 1
    COLOR 7, 0
END SUB
```

CHAPTER 5

Strings

Introduction

Although computers are often associated with "number crunching," much of the data they process involves characters in letters and reports, labels in spreadsheets, names and addresses in mailing lists, and so on.

How QBasic interprets the data in a byte or a group of bytes in memory depends on the type of data that is represented. If your program manipulates numbers, you use numeric variables, such as *total%* and *tax!*, in which the data in each byte of the variable is part of a binary number. The type of variable you define specifies how QBasic groups the bytes in memory and how it interprets their values. For example, *total%* is a 2-byte integer, and *tax!* is a 4-byte, single-precision, floating-point integer. Thus if the value in a particular byte in memory is 65, the value of the variable that contains that byte depends on the type of the variable involved. If the variable is a 2-byte integer, the value of the variable depends on the value of 2 bytes.

On the other hand, if you define a string variable (for example, *firstName$*), each byte in the variable is treated either as an ASCII character with a value in the range 0 through 127 or as an IBM extended character in the range 128 through 255. Thus if a string variable contains the value 65 in a byte, the value is interpreted as an uppercase A rather than as part of a number. This is shown in Figure 5-1. The ASCII character set

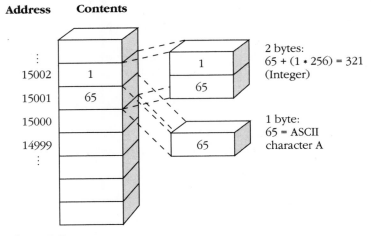

Figure 5-1.
Numeric versus character representation of a value.

and the IBM extended character set contain 256 different characters, each of which corresponds to a specific numeric value. The ASCII set includes uppercase and lowercase letters, numerals, punctuation marks, mathematical symbols, and printer control characters (such as carriage return, linefeed, and formfeed). The IBM extended character set includes graphics characters, mathematical symbols, and characters for foreign languages.

A *string* is simply a series of character values, such as "QBasic" or CHR$(7) + CHR$(12). In the first example, the quotes enclose a string *literal,* the specific characters that make up the word "QBasic." In the second example, the CHR$ function returns the character specified by the ASCII value. This string consists of ASCII character 7 (which sounds a beep) and ASCII character 12 (which either advances the print head to the next page or clears the screen). QBasic offers many statements and functions that handle strings. Table 5-1 lists these functions and statements alphabetically.

Statement or function	Purpose
ASC	Returns the ASCII code (or IBM extended code) of a character or of the first character of a string
CHR$	Returns the character corresponding to the specified ASCII code (or IBM extended code)
INSTR	Returns the position in a string at which a given string begins
LCASE$	Returns a string in lowercase characters
LEFT$	Returns the specified number of characters, beginning at the left end of a string
LEN	Returns the length of a string
MID$ (Function)	Returns the specified number of characters, beginning at the specified position in the string
MID$ (Statement)	Replaces the characters in a string, beginning at the specified position, with the specified characters
RIGHT$	Returns the specified number of characters, beginning at the right end of a string
SPACE$	Returns a string consisting of the specified number of spaces (blanks)
STR$	Returns a string containing the string representation of the specified value
STRING$	Returns a string containing a character repeated the specified number of times
UCASE$	Returns a string in uppercase characters
VAL	Returns the numeric value that the numerals and other special characters in the specified string represent

Table 5-1.
QBasic's string statements and functions.

Defining and Using Strings

Strings are versatile—you can define variables or constants that contain string values, store strings in an array, pass them to (or receive them from) functions or subprograms, and define your own string data types.

String Variables

To define a string variable, first select a name that describes its contents. For example, a variable that will hold the name of a city to be printed on a mailing label might be called *city$*. The dollar-sign ($) suffix indicates that the variable will hold string data. To assign a value to the string, use an equal sign (=) followed by a *string expression*. A string expression can contain a string (in quotes), a call to a string function, the name of another string variable, or a combination of these elements.

You can also use the DEFSTR statement to specify that all variables whose names begin with a particular range of letters will be string variables by default. For example, you might include the following statements in a program:

```
DEFSTR A-Z
city = "San Francisco"
PRINT city$
```

In this example, QBasic treats *city* and *city$* as the same identifier; however, *city!* is still a single-precision numeric variable.

You can also define the type of a variable as string by using the DIM statement with the phrase AS STRING; for example,

```
DIM firstName AS STRING
```

defines *firstName* as a string variable.

Using DIM is a more complicated way to name a variable, but it enables you to declare the type of a variable before using it.

String Constants

You can define a string constant with the CONST keyword. The difference between a string constant and a regular string is that after you define a string constant you can't change its contents; for example, the statement

```
CONST DASHES$ = "---"
```

defines a string that prints three dashes. If you later create a statement that attempts to change the value of *DASHES$*, QBasic displays the "Duplicate definition" error message.

You can also create numeric constants that contain the values of certain characters:

```
CONST FF = 12          ' ASCII value for formfeed
CONST DOBEEP = 7       ' ASCII value for beep
```

Now you can write the string *CHR$(7) + CHR$(12)* as *CHR$(DOBEEP) + CHR$(FF)*. (You cannot use the name BEEP because BEEP is a reserved QBasic keyword.) Because a constant cannot contain a function call as part of its value, you cannot define a string constant DOBEEP as follows:

```
CONST DOBEEP$ = CHR$(7)
```

String Arrays

Chapter 6, "Arrays and Data," describes arrays in detail and explains how to define them. To create a string array, simply use a string variable name in a DIM statement; for example,

```
DIM days$(7)
```

specifies an array named *days$* that contains seven strings. The following example uses this array:

```
DIM days$(7)
days$(1) = "Sunday": days$(2) = "Monday"
days$(3) = "Tuesday": days$(4) = "Wednesday"
days$(5) = "Thursday": days$(6) = "Friday"
days$(7) = "Saturday"

FOR day% = 1 TO 7
    PRINT days$(day%); " ";
NEXT day%
```

The program displays the days of the week.

Variable-Length Strings and String Storage

Most versions of Basic support only strings that can vary in length. Indeed, all the QBasic string variables used thus far can contain as many as 32,767 characters. QBasic stores variable-length strings (along with static arrays, ordinary numeric variables, and the stack) in a 32-KB memory segment called DGROUP—the default data area. QBasic creates a 4-byte string descriptor for each variable-length string: The first two bytes of the descriptor contain the address of the string within DGROUP, and the next 2 bytes contain the string's length. Figure 5-2 shows how QBasic stores variable-length strings.

Separating the descriptor from the contents lets QBasic move strings in memory more efficiently: QBasic updates the address in the descriptor only as necessary.

Understanding how QBasic stores strings lets you manage available string memory in programs that use (and reuse) many strings or string arrays.

If you change the value of a string either by using an assignment statement or by calling one or more of the string functions described in this chapter, QBasic allocates memory as necessary by changing the address in the descriptor and updating the length. Eventually, the memory taken by string values that are no longer being used is reclaimed through a process of "garbage collection."

QBasic performs continuous garbage collection; this frees the memory that holds obsolete strings as soon as a program changes the strings' contents.

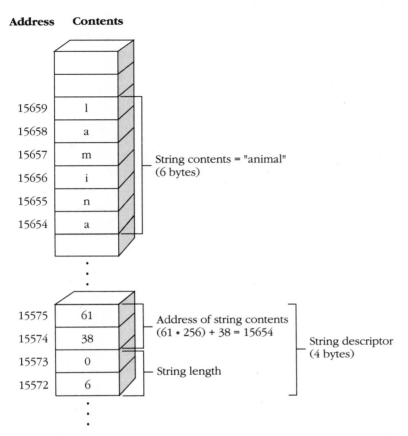

Address   Contents

15659	l
15658	a
15657	m
15656	i
15655	n
15654	a

String contents = "animal"
(6 bytes)

15575	61
15574	38
15573	0
15572	6

Address of string contents
(61 * 256) + 38 = 15654

String length

String descriptor
(4 bytes)

Figure 5-2.
Storage of variable-length strings.

Fixed-Length Strings

QBasic has another kind of string that has a fixed length regardless of how many characters you actually assign to the string. To declare a fixed-length string, use a statement such as the following:

```
DIM fixedStr AS STRING * 10
```

You can't use the $ suffix; the AS STRING qualifier establishes the variable type. Follow the asterisk (*) with the length of the string, in bytes (to a maximum of 32,767). The number of bytes in a string is equal to the number of characters.

The disadvantage of using fixed-length strings is that some space is usually wasted in each fixed-length string because the actual string value stored in the variable usually doesn't fill all the allotted space. Also, you cannot store a string longer than the length you specify.

The value you assign to a fixed-length string is left-justified, with spaces filling any unused character positions to the right. You can use the RSET statement to assign to a variable a value that is right justified in the string and that has leading spaces. (See Chapter 17, "Files," for more details about RSET.) For a fixed-length string, the LEN function returns the defined length, not the actual length.

String-Manipulation Functions

String Comparison

You can test and compare strings much as you do numeric values. A string is "greater than" another string if the first differing character has a larger ASCII value. (The letter A, for example, has a smaller ASCII value than the letter Z, so Z is "greater than" A.) The following table contains some examples of string comparison:

Comparison	Result	Comparison	Result
a$ = "QBasic"		a$ = "microsoft"	
b$ = "Programming"		b$ = "MICROSOFT"	
a$ > b$	True (−1)	a$ > b$	True (−1)
a$ < b$	False (0)		
		a$ = "Q"	
DO WHILE LEN(a$)	True (−1)	b$ = "QBasic"	
LOOP		b$ > a$	True (−1)
		b$ <> a$	True (−1)
a$ = ""			
LEN(a$)	False (0)		

These examples illustrate the following points:

- True comparisons of strings return a value of −1.
- False comparisons of strings return a value of 0.
- To test whether a string has a value (is not null), test the result of the LEN function. A null string has a length of 0, so the result of a test of a null string is false.
- Comparisons are case sensitive: Lowercase letters follow (are "greater than") uppercase letters.
- If all the characters in a shorter string match the corresponding characters in a longer string, the longer string is "greater than" the shorter one.

Extracting Parts of a String

For string comparison and formatting you often need to examine only part of a string. Use the LEFT$ function to retrieve a specified number of characters from the left side (or beginning) of a string. For example, if the variable *language$* equals "QBasic", the statement

```
PRINT LEFT$(language$, 1)
```

displays "Q". Note that all the functions that operate on strings return a modified copy of the string; the string itself is not affected.

Use the RIGHT$ function to examine characters, beginning at the right side of the string. For example,

```
RIGHT$(language$,5)
```

returns the string "Basic".

The RTRIM$ and LTRIM$ functions (discussed in detail in Chapter 17, "Files") remove trailing and leading blanks from a fixed-length string. Removing blanks prevents unintentional gaps in a printout and also prevents problems when you must compare a fixed-length string with a variable-length string. Consider the following example:

```
a$ = "QBasic"          ' variable-length string
DIM b AS STRING * 10   ' fixed-length string
b = "QBasic"           ' left-justified string
PRINT (b > a$)         ' compare the strings
```

Because *b* includes trailing blanks that fill out the fixed-length string to ten characters, *b* is "greater than" *a$* even though their meaningful contents are identical. However, if you use the statement

```
PRINT (RTRIM$(b) > a$)
```

in place of the fourth line in the above example, then *b* is not "greater than" a$.

You can use the MID$ function to extract one or more characters from any position in a string. When you call the MID$ function, specify the string, the position in the string at which extracting is to start, and the number of characters to be extracted. For example, if *a$* equals "Three blind mice", the call

```
MID$(a$, 7, 5)
```

returns "blind".

The MID$ function is perhaps most useful for "looping through" a string and examining each character in turn, as shown in the following statements:

```
a$ = "Three blind mice"
FOR char% = 1 TO LEN(a$)
    thisChar$ = MID$(a$, char%, 1)
    IF thisChar$ = " " THEN
        PRINT              ' go to next line
    ELSE
        PRINT thisChar$;   ' print the character
    END IF
NEXT char%
```

The above example extracts each character with the MID$ function, using the position specified by the loop counter *char%*. If the character is a space, the output is moved to the next line; otherwise, the current character is printed in the next position on the line.

Finding Characters in a String

You will often need to check whether a character or a string is contained in another string. The INSTR function searches for one string within another. The function accepts two strings as parameters and returns the location of the second string within the first string. If the second string isn't contained within the first, INSTR returns 0, providing a value of false for any test—for example,

```
a$ = "QBasic"
b$ = "Basic"
c$ = "Q"
d$ = "Pascal"
PRINT INSTR(a$, b$)                                 ' displays 2
PRINT INSTR(a$, c$)                                 ' displays 1
IF INSTR(a$, d$) THEN PRINT "Pascal is in Basic" ' doesn't display anything
```

In the first PRINT statement, the INSTR function returns the value 2 because "Basic" begins at the second character in the string "QBasic." In the second PRINT statement, INSTR returns the value 1 because position 1 in "QBasic" is "Q." The THEN clause in the IF statement in the above example isn't executed because INSTR returns 0 (that is, the string "Pascal" isn't contained in the string "QBasic"). Note that if there is a match anywhere in the string, the returned value is greater than 0. Because QBasic considers any value other than 0 to be true, you can use INSTR with any statement that requires a condition (IF, WHILE, and so on); the condition is true only if the string is found.

INSTR can also take an optional first parameter that specifies the position in the first string at which INSTR will start looking for the second string. For example, the statement

```
INSTR(4,"one and one make two","one")
```

returns the value 9 because the search starts after the first "one" and returns the position of the second "one."

String Concatenation

QBasic lets you add two strings together (by joining them with the + operator) and assign them to a string variable. This is called *concatenation* and is explained in Chapter 3, "Decisions and Operators."

Making "Filler" Strings

Two QBasic functions, SPACE$ and STRING$, let you create "filler" strings that you can use to format and arrange your output. The SPACE$ function generates the requested number of blank spaces; for example,

```
filler$ = SPACE$(10)
```

assigns a value of 10 spaces to the string *filler$*.

STRING$ is a more general function that returns a string containing a character that is repeated the specified number of times—for example,

```
PRINT STRING$(10,"*")       ' displays **********
PRINT STRING$(10, " ")      ' same as SPACE$(10)
```

Changing the Case of Letters

The UCASE$ function returns a copy of a string with all lowercase characters converted to uppercase; the LCASE$ function returns a copy of a string with all its uppercase characters converted to lowercase:

```
PRINT LCASE$("QBasic")      ' prints qbasic
PRINT UCASE$("QBasic")      ' prints QBASIC
```

Nonalphabetic characters, such as numerals and punctuation marks, are not affected by the UCASE$ and LCASE$ functions.

Changing Part of a String

You've already seen how the MID$ function locates the position of a particular character or characters in a string. QBasic also includes the MID$ statement, which lets you substitute one character or group of characters for another in a string. For example, the following statement pairs display the strings "geodesic", "geocentric", and "geoduck".

```
a$ = "geodesic   "
PRINT a$

MID$(a$, 4) = "centric"
PRINT a$

a$ = "geodesic"  ' restore original value
MID$(a$, 4) = "duck "
PRINT a$
```

The characters in the assigned string replace their counterparts in the string that is specified in the first parameter to MID$, starting in the position given in the second parameter. Thus

```
MID$(a$, 4) = "centric"
```

replaces characters in *a$* with the characters in the string "centric", starting with the fourth character (the "d" in "desic"). If you want to "blank out" parts of the string being replaced, simply include blanks in the replacement string. Because MID$ can't replace beyond the last character in the original string, you must include enough blanks in the original string to accommodate the longest anticipated replacement string. (You can also specify that only part of the replacement string be used; see the MID$ (Statement) entry for details.)

Note that unlike the string-manipulation functions that return modified copies of a string, the MID$ statement changes the original string.

Converting Numbers to Strings

Finally, this section reexamines string and numeric representations. To QBasic, a number and a string are completely different objects. Nevertheless, you often need to convert a string to a number and vice versa. In many applications you might want to get a number from the user in string form so that you can check its validity. You then probably want to convert the input to a number for further processing (calculations). Also, when you display numbers on the screen or in a printed report, you might want to convert the numbers back to strings so that you can easily format them.

Use the VAL function to return the numeric value of a string. Use the STR$ function to return the string that represents a numeric value—for example,

```
PRINT VAL("12.5")
PRINT VAL("9999999999999999")
PRINT STR$(12.5)
PRINT STR$(1.5D8)
```

results in the following output:

```
 12.5
 1D+16
 12.5
 150000000
```

The VAL function essentially interprets the string as though it was typed at the keyboard as a number. The result is usually a number with the same numerals as the string; however in some cases, as in the second example, QBasic applies its rules for representing large numbers. The specified number was too large to be represented in decimal form, so QBasic converted it to exponential (scientific) notation and rounded up to 10 to the 16th power. STR$ usually converts the numerals (and any sign or decimal point) to characters in a string. In the last example, however, because the number fits within the range that can be represented in decimal form, 1.5D8 is converted to 150000000.

Conclusion

You will find that the QBasic string functions are among the tools that you find most useful and reach for most often. QBasic contains other string functions, which are discussed in Chapter 3, "Decisions and Operators;" Chapter 8, "Simple I/O;" Chapter 15, "Printer;" and Chapter 17, "Files." Some string functions in those chapters perform the same task as the string functions presented here. In many cases, you can do a job in more than one way; only experience can help you determine which works best.

Related Reading

Kernighan, Brian, and P. J. Plauger. *Software Tools*. Reading, Mass.: Addison-Wesley, 1976.

Prata, Stephen, with Harry Henderson. *The Waite Group's Microsoft QuickBASIC Primer Plus*. Redmond, Wash.: Microsoft Press, 1990.

ASC

See also
CHR$, STRING$, VAL

Purpose
The ASC function returns the ASCII or IBM extended code value (in the range 0 through 255) for the first character in a string.

Syntax
ASC(*string*)

string can be any string variable, string constant, string literal, or string expression.

Usage
```
PRINT ASC("a")
```
Prints the value of the letter "a", which is 97.

```
PRINT ASC("Apple")
```
Prints the value of the letter "A", which is 65.

Description
The ASC function returns the ASCII character or IBM extended character value of the character specified in a string literal, string constant, or string variable. If a string of more than 1 character is used, ASC returns the value of only the first character.

The CHR$ function is the opposite of the ASC function: CHR$ returns the character whose ASCII value is specified.

Errors
If a null (length 0) string is given as the argument to the ASC function, QBasic displays an "Illegal function call" error message. If the value supplied isn't a string, QBasic displays a "Type mismatch" error message.

Example
The following program creates an encoded string by adding the ASCII value of each character in the message to the value of the corresponding character in the code-key string. Most resulting characters are members of the IBM extended character set and look cryptic indeed! (As an exercise, write a program that decodes the strings encoded by this program.) Figure 5-3, on the following page, shows an example of this program's output.

```
CLS
INPUT "Message text "; text$

DO
    INPUT "Code key "; key$
    IF LEN(key$) < LEN(text$) THEN
        PRINT "Key must be as least as long as message text."
    ELSE EXIT DO
    END IF
LOOP

FOR char% = 1 TO LEN(text$)
    textVal = ASC(MID$(text$, char%, 1))    ' character value for message
    codeVal = ASC(MID$(key$, char%, 1))     ' character value for key
    MID$(text$, char%, 1) = CHR$(codeVal + textVal) ' add values
NEXT char%

PRINT "Encoded text is: "; text$
```

Message text ? This is a secret message.
Code key ? This is the secret code for the secret message.
Encoded text is: ¿ª╥µⱥ╥µⱥ ⱼê╪à ╥║ⱥµàßà ╥⌐╪║äö

Figure 5-3.
Output of ASC sample program.

CHR$

See also
ASC, SPACE$, STRING$

Purpose
The CHR$ function returns the ASCII or IBM extended character that corresponds to the specified ASCII code value. You can use this function to send special control characters to the printer or to draw objects using the IBM extended character set.

Syntax
CHR$(*val*)

val is the value of the ASCII character or IBM extended character that you want. It must be in the range 0 through 255.

Usage
```
LPRINT CHR$(12)
```
Sends a formfeed character to the printer.

```
PRINT CHR$(205)
```
Displays the = symbol.

```
a$ = "quoted"
PRINT CHR$(34)+a$+CHR$(34)
```
Displays "quoted" (including the quotation marks).

Description

There are many characters that you can't easily enter at your keyboard and put in a string, such as most control characters and the IBM extended characters (those characters with ASCII values of 128 and above). The CHR$ function lets you generate all 256 characters of the ASCII and IBM extended character sets. (See the tutorial to learn how to enter graphics and control characters directly from your keyboard instead of specifying them with CHR$.)

The ASC function is the opposite of CHR$: ASC returns the ASCII or IBM extended code value of the first character in the specified string.

Comments

If you want to generate spaces, the SPACE$ function is faster and easier than using a loop that repeatedly prints CHR$(32) or the string " ". If you want to generate a specific number of a particular character, use the STRING$ function.

Errors

If the value specified with CHR$ isn't within the range 0 through 255, QBasic displays an "Illegal function call" error message. If the value is a string variable or literal, QBasic displays a "Type mismatch" error message. (If you specify a non-numeric character or string without quotation marks, the compiler generates no error message, and CHR$ merely returns the null character, or ASCII value 0.)

Example

The following example uses CHR$ to store three different filled-box characters in a string array. The user is asked to input the name and number sold of three items; the program then generates a bar chart that reflects those numbers.

```
DIM bar$(3)
bar$(1) = CHR$(176): bar$(2) = CHR$(177): bar$(3) = CHR$(178) ' three bars

maxItems = 3

TYPE ItemType                  ' data type for each item
    itemName AS STRING * 10
    sold AS INTEGER
END TYPE

DIM sales(3) AS ItemType       ' array to hold names and number sold
```

(continued)

continued

```
CLS
FOR item = 1 TO maxItems
    PRINT "Name of item #"; item;
    INPUT sales(item).itemName
    INPUT "How many were sold "; sold
    sales(item).sold = sold / 1000
NEXT item

'header for chart
PRINT : PRINT "            Number of Items Sold (in thousands)"
PRINT SPACE$(10); "        1         2         3"
PRINT SPACE$(10); "12345678901234567890123456789012345678901234567890": PRINT

FOR item = 1 TO maxItems
    PRINT sales(item).itemName;
    FOR bar = 1 TO sales(item).sold
        PRINT bar$(item);
    NEXT bar
    PRINT : PRINT
NEXT item
```

INSTR

See also

LEFT$, MID$, RIGHT$

Purpose

The INSTR function returns the position of the first occurrence of a particular string in another string. This is useful for searching for text in database fields or for validating user input.

Syntax

INSTR ([*start,*] *string1, string2*)

start is an optional integer that specifies the position at which the search begins. If you don't specify *start*, the search begins at the first character.

string1 is the string that is searched; *string2* is the string that INSTR attempts to find. Both strings can be any string variable, string constant, string literal, or string expression.

Usage

```
PRINT INSTR("San Francisco", "San")
```

Displays the value 1 because "San" occurs at the first character in the string "San Francisco".

```
a$ = "San Francisco"
position% = INSTR(a$, "an")
```
Assigns the variable *position%* the value 2 because "an" first occurs at position 2.

```
PRINT INSTR(5, "San Francisco", "an")
```
Displays the value 7 because "an" first occurs at position 7 when the search begins at position 5.

Description

The INSTR function returns the position of the first occurrence of one string in another string. If you merely want to test for the presence of the string, use a statement such as

```
IF INSTR(a$, b$) THEN
```

This condition is always true if *b$* is contained in *a$* because the value returned by INSTR will be a nonzero value. If you need to know the exact position at which the string was found, you can assign the position to a variable, as follows:

```
found% = INSTR(a$, b$)
```

If INSTR does not find the string, the position returned is 0.

Optionally, you can precede the first string specified in the INSTR function call by a number that indicates the position at which the search starts. You can loop through a string and find all occurrences of the search string, as follows:

```
start% = 1
DO
    position% = INSTR(start%, a$, b$)
    IF position% <> 0 THEN PRINT position%
    start% = position% + 1
LOOP WHILE position% <> 0
```

Errors

If the optional starting position is 0 or less, QBasic displays an "Illegal function call" error message. Specifying a starting position number greater than the length of the string to be searched doesn't result in an error: INSTR simply returns 0 (no match). If either the search string or the string for which you are searching isn't a string variable, string constant, or string literal, QBasic displays a "Type mismatch" error message.

Example

The following program prompts you to enter a string to be searched, a string for which to search in the first string, and a replacement string. The LEFT$ and RIGHT$ functions delete from the string any matching string found. The original string is reassembled with the replacement string substituted for the search string. The DO...LOOP statement repeats the search-and-replace until the INSTR function no longer finds an occurrence of the search string.

```
CLS
INPUT "Enter a string"; aStr$
INPUT "Search for:"; search$
INPUT "Replace with:"; replace$
newPos% = 1

DO WHILE newPos% > 0
    newPos% = INSTR(aStr$, search$)
    IF newPos% > 0 THEN
        temp1$ = LEFT$(aStr$, newPos% - 1)
        temp2$ = RIGHT$(aStr$, (LEN(aStr$) - newPos% - LEN(search$) + 1))
        aStr$ = temp1$ + replace$ + temp2$
    END IF
LOOP
PRINT aStr$
```

LCASE$

See also
CHR$, UCASE$

Purpose
The LCASE$ function returns a copy of a string in which all uppercase letters are converted to lowercase. You can use this function to make string comparisons case insensitive. You can also use it as the first step in normalizing text that was created entirely in uppercase letters.

Syntax
LCASE$(*string*)

string can be any string variable, string constant, string literal, or string expression.

Usage
```
PRINT LCASE$("USING ALL CAPS IS LIKE SHOUTING")
```
Prints the string "using all caps is like shouting".

Description
The LCASE$ function returns a copy of the specified string variable, string constant, string literal, or string expression. In the copy, any letters that were uppercase in the original string are converted to lowercase. The LCASE$ function does not modify nonalphabetic characters.

The UCASE$ function operates similarly except that it converts all lowercase letters to uppercase.

Errors

If the value supplied to the LCASE$ function is not a string, QBasic displays a "Type mismatch" error message. Specifying a null string in a call to LCASE$ does not result in an error; the function merely returns a null string.

Example

The following program accepts a string and converts any uppercase characters to lowercase. Press Enter to exit the loop.

```
DO
    INPUT "Enter a string: "; aString$
    PRINT LCASE$(aString$)
LOOP UNTIL aString$ = ""
```

LEFT$

See also

INSTR, MID$ (Statement), RIGHT$

Purpose

The LEFT$ function returns a copy of a string consisting of the specified number of characters from the left (beginning) of the string. You can combine LEFT$ with INSTR to extract the portion of a string either up to or including a specified substring.

Syntax

LEFT$(*string, num*)

string is a string variable, string constant, string literal, or string expression.

num can be any number in the range 0 through 32767.

Usage

```
a$ = "QBasic Programmers' Association"
PRINT LEFT$(a$,6)
PRINT LEFT$(a$,99)
```
Displays "QBasic" and "QBasic Programmers' Association".

Description

The LEFT$ function returns a string that contains a copy of the number of characters you specify, starting at the beginning of the original string. If you specify a number of characters equal to or greater than the string's length, LEFT$ returns a copy of the entire string; for example,

```
LEFT$(a$, LEN(a$))
```

returns an exact copy of *a$*.

The following example shows how to use LEFT$ with INSTR to return selected portions of a string:

```
a$ = "QBasic Programmers' Association"
b$ = "Basic"
PRINT LEFT$(a$, INSTR(a$, b$) - 1)           ' display the characters to the substring
PRINT LEFT$(a$, INSTR(a$, b$) + LEN(b$) - 1) ' display the characters
                                             ' including the substring
```

The program displays the strings "Q" and "QBasic".

(See the "Example" section in the INSTR entry for a program that uses INSTR with LEFT$ and RIGHT$ to find and replace a portion of a string.)

Errors

If the first value in the call to LEFT$ isn't a string, QBasic displays a "Type mismatch" error message. Specifying a null string or zero characters does not result in an error; LEFT$ merely returns a null string. If you specify fewer than zero characters, QBasic displays an "Illegal function call" error message. If you specify more than 32767 characters, QBasic displays an "Overflow" error message.

Example

The following program extracts the first name from a complete name and constructs the salutation of a letter.

```
INPUT "Enter first and last name together: "; name$
firstSpace% = INSTR(name$, " ")
firstName$ = LEFT$(name$, firstSpace% - 1)
PRINT "Dear "; firstName$; ","
```

LEN

See also

VARPTR, VARSEG

Purpose

The LEN function returns either the number of characters in a string or the number of bytes allocated to a numeric variable.

Syntax

LEN(*var*)

var can be any numeric variable (not a numeric literal) or any string variable, string constant, string literal, or string expression.

Usage

```
a$ = "QBasic"
PRINT LEN(a$)
```

Prints the length of the string *a$*, which is 6.

```
total% = 6
PRINT LEN(total%)
```
Prints the number of bytes allocated to *total%*, which is 2.

Description

The LEN function returns the number of bytes used to store the value of a string variable, string constant, string literal, or string expression. For a string, the value returned by LEN is equal to the number of characters in the string. For a numeric variable or a variable of a user-defined type, the value returned is the number of bytes used to store the value of the variable.

You use LEN most often to obtain the length of a string. A returned value of 0 indicates an empty (null) string. Thus you can force input of a non-null string value by using the following loop:

```
DO
    INPUT choice$
LOOP UNTIL LEN(choice$)
```

The loop repeats until the length of *choice$* is a nonzero value. Conversely, you can create a loop that exits when the user enters a null string (which the user can do by pressing Enter):

```
DO
    INPUT "Choice (or <Enter> to quit)"; choice$
    IF LEN(choice$) = 0 THEN EXIT DO
    ' process the choice
LOOP
```

You can also use the LEN function to obtain the length of a string for use in a loop that processes characters in the string one at a time. This approach is shown in the following FOR loop:

```
FOR char% = 1 TO LEN(a$)
    ch$ = MID$(a$,1,1)   ' get next character
    ' process the character in some way
NEXT char%
```

The primary value of using LEN for numeric variables is that LEN determines the length of a user-defined type; this lets you estimate how many bytes each variable of that type will require. (Note that for an array, LEN returns the number of bytes per element.)

Errors

If you supply a value to LEN that isn't a numeric variable or a string, QBasic displays a "Variable required" error message.

It is important to note that LEN returns only the number of bytes required to store the actual value of a variable, not the total amount of memory used by the variable. Each string, for example, also has a descriptor that uses an additional 4 bytes.

Example

The following program underlines the string that was input by the user. The program uses the LEN function to provide the ending value for the FOR loop that generates the IBM extended character 196, which is used here as an underline character.

```
ul$ = CHR$(196)
INPUT "Type a string to be underlined: "; aString$
PRINT : PRINT aString$
FOR char% = 1 TO LEN(aString$)
    PRINT ul$;
NEXT char%
PRINT
```

MID$ (Function)

See also

LEFT$, LEN, RIGHT$

Purpose

The MID$ function returns a copy of a string. The copy starts at a specified position and includes the given number of characters. You could, for example, use this function to extract the first name of a person from a string containing the full name.

Syntax

MID$(*string, start*[, *num*])

string is any string variable, string constant, string literal, or string expression.

start is the position of the first character to be extracted.

num is the number of characters to be extracted.

Usage

```
PRINT MID$("QBasic Programmer's Reference", 2, 5)
```
Displays the string "Basic".

```
PRINT MID$("QBasic Programmer's Reference", 2)
```
Displays the string "Basic Programmer's Reference".

Description

The MID$ function extracts a substring (a string within another string) from a string. When you call MID$, specify the string from which you want to extract a substring, the position of the first character you want to copy to the substring, and, optionally, the number of characters you want to include in the substring. (If you omit the number of characters, the MID$ function copies characters from the specified starting position to the end of the string.)

If you need to extract characters from either the beginning or the end of the string, use the more convenient LEFT$ and RIGHT$ functions. (See those entries for details.)

The starting position and number of characters specified as arguments to MID$ must be in the range 1 through 32767. If the starting position is greater than the length of the string, MID$ returns a null string. If the number of characters specified is greater than the number of characters from the starting position to the end of the string, the function returns all characters, beginning at the starting position. (Note that you can use the LEN function to obtain the length of a string.)

Errors

If the first item specified in the call to MID$ isn't a string variable, string literal, or string constant, QBasic displays a "Type mismatch" error message. If the starting position or number of characters is less than 1, QBasic displays an "Illegal function call" error message, and if the number is greater than 32767, QBasic displays an "Overflow" error message.

Example

The following program examines each character in the string *aString$* to see whether it is a space. If the character is a space, a PRINT statement moves output to the next line; if it isn't, the program prints the character. The result is that each word in the string is printed on a separate line.

```
INPUT "Type a string: "; aString$

FOR char% = 1 TO LEN(aString$)
    thisChar$ = MID$(aString$, char%, 1)
    IF thisChar$ = " " THEN
        PRINT                    ' go to next line if character is a space
    ELSE PRINT thisChar$;        ' print the character
    END IF
NEXT char%
```

MID$ (Statement)

See also

LEFT$, MID$ (Function), RIGHT$

Purpose

The MID$ statement replaces part of a string with another string. You could, for example, use this statement to replace a misspelled portion of a name with the correct characters.

Syntax

MID$(*string, start*[, *num*]) = *replacement*

string is any string variable.

start is the position of the first character that is to be replaced.

num is the number of characters to use from the replacement string.

replacement is the replacement string variable, string constant, string literal, or string expression.

Usage

```
a$ = "Who put the cat out?"
MID$(a$, 13, 1) = "b"
PRINT a$
```

Prints the string "Who put the bat out?".

```
b$ = "geocentric"
MID$(b$, 4) = "duck    "
PRINT b$
```

Prints the string "geoduck".

Description

The MID$ statement, unlike the MID$ function and the LEFT$ and RIGHT$ functions, actually changes the specified string rather than returning a modified copy of it. When you call MID$, specify the string variable to be modified, the position of the first character to be replaced, and, optionally, the number of characters to be replaced. Follow the call with an equal sign and the replacement string, which can be any string expression (string constant, string variable, string literal, or combination).

The starting position and number of characters to be replaced must be in the range 1 through 32767. The starting position cannot be greater than the length of the target string. If you specify more characters to be replaced than are available in the replacement string, only the available characters will be used. For example, in the statements

```
a$ = "brown rice"
MID$(a$, 7, 5) = "m"
```

the MID$ statement changes "brown rice" to "brown mice".

If the number of characters to be replaced would make the modified string longer than its original length, MID$ replaces characters only to the length of the original string. Thus in the example

```
a$ = "brown rice"
MID$(a$, 6, 14) = "ie points"
```

the variable *a$* has a value of "brownie po".

Errors

If you use a string literal instead of a string variable for the string you want to change, QBasic displays an "Expected: variable" error message. If the variable you specify is not a string variable, QBasic displays a "Type mismatch" error message. If the starting position or number of characters is less than 1, QBasic displays an "Illegal function call" error message; if the number is greater than 32767, QBasic displays an "Overflow" error message.

Example

The following program uses the MID$ function to check each character in a string to see whether it is a vowel. If it is a vowel, the program uses the MID$ statement to replace the character with an asterisk. You might use this program, for example, to develop a word-guessing game.

```
INPUT "Enter a string: "; aString$

FOR char% = 1 TO LEN(aString$)          ' check each character
    ch$ = MID$(aString$, char%, 1)      ' get next character
    IF INSTR("AEIOU", UCASE$(ch$)) THEN ' is it a vowel?
        MID$(aString$, char%, 1) = "*"  ' replace vowel with *
    END IF
NEXT char%

PRINT aString$
```

RIGHT$

See also

INSTR, LEFT$, MID$ (Statement)

Purpose

The RIGHT$ function returns a copy of a string. The copy consists of the specified number of characters from the right (end) of the string. You can use RIGHT$ to extract the last word in a string.

Syntax

RIGHT$(*string, num*)

string can be any string variable, string constant, string literal, or string expression.

num can be any number in the range 0 through 32767.

Usage

```
a$ = "the whole thing"
PRINT RIGHT$(a$, 5)
PRINT RIGHT$(a$, 99)
```

Prints the strings "thing" and "the whole thing".

Description

The RIGHT$ function returns a string that contains a copy of the specified number of characters, beginning with the end of the original string. If the number of characters you specify is equal to or greater than the string's length, RIGHT$ returns a copy of the entire string; for example,

```
RIGHT$(a$, LEN(a$))
```

returns an exact copy of *a$*.

Errors

If the first value you use in the call to RIGHT$ isn't a string, QBasic displays a "Type mismatch" error message. Specifying a null string or zero characters does not result in an error; RIGHT$ merely returns a null string. If you specify fewer than zero characters, QBasic displays an "Illegal function call" error message. If you specify more than 32767 characters, QBasic displays an "Overflow" error message.

Example

The following program changes a string containing a name so that the last name is listed as the first word in the string. This program might be used to format a list of names as a prelude to sorting the names. The program uses the RIGHT$ function to extract the last name from the string.

```
INPUT "Enter a full name: "; name$

length% = LEN(name$)
FOR char% = length% TO 1 STEP -1            ' examine each character
    IF MID$(name$, char%, 1) = " " THEN     ' starting at end of name
        EXIT FOR                            ' found beginning of last name
    END IF
NEXT char%

IF char% <> 0 THEN
    lastName$ = RIGHT$(name$, LEN(name$) - char%)  'extract the last name
    restOfName$ = LEFT$(name$, char% - 1)
    PRINT lastName$; ", "; restOfName$
ELSE
    PRINT "You must enter an entire name"
END IF
```

SPACE$

See also

LSET, PRINT USING, RSET, SPC, TAB

Purpose

The SPACE$ function returns a string that contains a specified number of spaces. This can be useful for indenting text.

Syntax

SPACE$(*num*)

num can be any number in the range 0 through 32767.

Usage

```
PRINT SPACE$(10); "Indented text"
```
Prints the string "Indented text" preceded by 10 spaces.

Description

The SPACE$ function returns a string consisting of the specified number of spaces (ASCII character 32). The number must be in the range 0 through 32767. If the number is not an integer, QBasic rounds it to the nearest integer.

You can use the SPC and TAB statements to achieve similar effects in formatting output. See those entries in Chapter 8, "Simple I/O," for details.

Errors

If the value you specify with SPACE$ isn't numeric, QBasic displays a "Type mismatch" error message. If you use a numeric value that is less than 0, QBasic displays an "Illegal function call" error message. For a numeric value greater than 32767, QBasic displays an "Overflow" error message. Using a value of 0 does not produce an error; SPACE$ merely returns a null string.

Example

The following program defines the function *Indent$*, which accepts an indention value and a string; the program also uses SPACE$ to indent the string when it is displayed. The program uses *Indent$* to format information on a page.

```
DECLARE FUNCTION Indent$ (spaces!, aString$)

CLS
PRINT Indent$(25, "Personal Information");
PRINT Indent$(15, "Page 1"): PRINT
PRINT Indent$(25, "Identification"): PRINT
PRINT Indent$(5, "Name  :"): PRINT
PRINT Indent$(5, "Street:"): PRINT
PRINT Indent$(5, "City  :");
PRINT Indent$(30, "State:");
PRINT Indent$(10, "Zip:")

FUNCTION Indent$ (spaces, aString$)
    Indent$ = SPACE$(spaces) + aString$  'returns an indented string
END FUNCTION
```

STR$

See also
VAL

Purpose
The STR$ function returns a string representation of a number. This lets you manipulate a number as a string and apply the other string functions to it for validation and formatting.

Syntax
STR$(*num*)

num can be any numeric variable, numeric constant, numeric literal, or numeric expression.

Usage
```
num! = 3.1415
PRINT STR$(num!)
```
Prints the string "3.1415".

Description
The STR$ function accepts any valid numeric expression and returns the result as a string.

The VAL function converts in the opposite direction: It accepts a string and returns the number that its characters represent.

Errors
If the value you specify with STR$ is not numeric, QBasic displays a "Type mismatch" error message. If you use a value that starts with numerals but contains characters that aren't valid in a number or expression (for example, a comma), QBasic displays an "Expected:)" error message and highlights the invalid character.

Example
The following example demonstrates how to print a number without leading or trailing spaces. When printing the amount on a check, for example, you should eliminate any leading or trailing spaces that might be used to alter the amount. The first PRINT statement, which displays a numeric variable, includes an unwanted leading space and a trailing space. The second PRINT statement doesn't display the unwanted spaces because the numeric amount has been converted to a string with the STR$ function and then stripped of the spaces with the LTRIM$ and RTRIM$ functions. (See Chapter 17, "Files," for details about LTRIM$ and RTRIM$.)

```
CLS
INPUT "How much money do you want"; num
PRINT "***"; num; "***"; " dollars"

num$ = STR$(num)                ' convert number to a string
num$ = LTRIM$(RTRIM$(num$))     ' strip trailing and leading blank space

PRINT "***"; num$; "***"; " dollars"
```

STRING$

See also
CHR$, SPACE$

Purpose
The STRING$ function returns a string containing a character that is repeated a specified number of times. You can use this function to create underlines, rows of asterisks, bordered windows, and so on.

Syntax
STRING$(*num, code*)

or

STRING$(*num, string*)

num is the number of characters (in the range 0 through 32767) in the resulting string.

code is the ASCII or IBM extended character code for the character you want in the returned string.

string is any string variable, string constant, string literal, or string expression.

Usage
```
PRINT STRING$(10, 42)
```
Prints the string "**********".

```
PRINT STRING$(10,"*")
```
Prints the string "**********".

```
a$ = STRING$(20,"Basic")
```
Assigns the string "BBBBBBBBBBBBBBBBBBBB" to the variable *a$*.

Description
The STRING$ function is useful for creating a string consisting of repeated characters. The first argument in the STRING$ function specifies the number of characters in the string. The second argument is either a character code or a string variable, string constant, string literal, or string expression. The second argument specifies the character

that STRING$ repeats. If the second argument is a string that has more than one character, only the first character is used in the generated string.

Use a string literal in the call to STRING$ if you can easily enter the character from the keyboard. For characters that aren't easy to enter, such as control characters or the IBM extended characters, use the character code instead.

If you use a character code with a value greater than 255, the value "wraps around" so that the value 256 produces the same character 0 produces, and so on. Negative codes also wrap around, so that the value −1 produces the same character 255 produces, and so on.

If you want to generate a string consisting only of spaces, the SPACE$ function is more convenient because you need only specify the number of spaces.

Errors

If the number you specify for the number of characters is negative, QBasic displays an "Illegal function call" error message. If the number is greater than 32767, QBasic displays an "Overflow" error message. Specifying zero characters results in a null string. If you specify a string as the first argument, QBasic displays a "Type mismatch" error message. If you use a character code less than −32768 or greater than 32767, QBasic displays an "Overflow" error message.

Example

The *BoxString* subprogram in the following program defines graphics character constants and then uses CHR$ (for single characters) and STRING$ (for multiple characters) to draw a box around a string. The subprogram checks the requested position of the box and prints a message if the entire box doesn't fit on the standard screen.

```
DECLARE SUB BoxString (row!, col!, aString$)

CLS
msg$ = "QBasic Programmer's Reference"
BoxString 10, 30, msg$

SUB BoxString (row, col, aString$)    ' print a string in a box
    ' graphics characters
    CONST UPPERLEFT = 201
    CONST LOWERLEFT = 200
    CONST UPPERRIGHT = 187
    CONST LOWERRIGHT = 188
    CONST HORIZONTAL = 205
    CONST VERTICAL = 186

    CONST MAXLINE = 22            ' last line at which box can begin
    CONST MAXCOLS = 80            ' maximum number of screen columns
    IF row > MAXLINE THEN
        PRINT "Row must be 22 or fewer characters."
        EXIT SUB
    END IF
```

(continued)

continued

```
        farthestLeft = MAXCOLS - LEN(aString$) - 2

        IF col > farthestLeft THEN    ' too far to the left
            PRINT "Row for string "; aString$; " must be no greater than ";
            PRINT farthestLeft
            EXIT SUB
        END IF
        LOCATE row, col
        line$ = STRING$(LEN(aString$), HORIZONTAL)

        LOCATE row + 1, col
        PRINT CHR$(UPPERLEFT); line$; CHR$(UPPERRIGHT)    ' print top of box

        LOCATE row + 2, col
        PRINT CHR$(VERTICAL); aString$; CHR$(VERTICAL)    ' print sides of box

        LOCATE row + 3, col
        PRINT CHR$(LOWERLEFT); line$; CHR$(LOWERRIGHT);  ' print bottom of box
    END SUB
```

UCASE$

See also
LCASE$

Purpose
The UCASE$ function returns a copy of a string in which all lowercase letters are converted to uppercase. Use this function for checking input that the user might enter in either uppercase or lowercase characters.

Syntax
UCASE$(*string*)

string can be any string variable, string constant, string literal, or string expression.

Usage
```
a$ = "QBasic"
PRINT UCASE$(a$)
```
Prints the string "QBASIC".

Description
The UCASE$ function returns a copy of the specified string variable, constant, literal, or expression in which every lowercase letter in the original string is converted to uppercase. Letters that are already uppercase and nonalphabetic characters are not modified by UCASE$.

The counterpart LCASE$ function returns a copy of a string in which all upper-case letters are converted to lowercase.

By using functions such as LEFT$ and RIGHT$ with the MID$ statement, you can use UCASE$ to selectively change characters in a string to uppercase. For example, the following program segment prints the string "Mary":

```
a$ = "mary"
MID$(a$, 1, 1) = UCASE$(LEFT$(a$, 1))
PRINT a$
```

Errors

If the value supplied to the UCASE$ function is not a string, QBasic displays a "Type mismatch" error message. Sending UCASE$ a null string does not result in an error; the function merely returns a null string.

Example

The following program prompts the user to enter the letter A, B, C, D, or E. The UCASE$ function converts any lowercase input to uppercase so that the program needs to test only uppercase letters in the IF statements that work with the input. The program uses LEFT$ to strip all input characters after the first one; this allows users to enter full words (such as "copy").

```
CLS
PRINT "<Type E to exit program>"
DO
    INPUT "Type A, B, C, D, or E"; choice$
    choice$ = UCASE$(LEFT$(choice$, 1))
    IF INSTR("ABCDE", choice$) THEN
        PRINT "You chose: "; choice$
    END IF
LOOP UNTIL choice$ = "E"
```

VAL

See also

STR$

Purpose

The VAL function returns the number represented by the digits (and other numeric symbols) in a string variable or expression. This function lets a program accept numeric input as a string, use the various string functions to validate the input, and then convert the input back to a number for use in calculations.

Syntax

VAL(*string*)

string can be any string variable, string constant, string literal, or string expression.

Usage

```
INPUT num$
value = VAL(num$)
```

Assigns the numeric value of the string entered to the variable *value*.

Description

The VAL function accepts the value of a string variable and scans it, beginning with the first character, until it encounters a character that cannot be part of a numeric literal (for example, a comma, letter, or dollar sign) or until it reaches the end of the string. The resulting string (which can include digits, a plus or minus sign, a decimal point, or the exponential D or E) is then converted into a valid QBasic numeric value. The following strings are some examples:

Value of string	Result of call to VAL
500	500
4.4E7	44000000
123D-7	.0000123
99999999999999999	1D+17
4,000	4
xvi	0
2b or not 2b	2

Note that you can enter numbers using exponential notation (with D or E). VAL converts the numbers to regular decimal notation unless they have more than 16 digits, in which case they remain in exponential notation. VAL converts numbers with more than 16 digits that are entered in decimal notation to exponential notation.

The STR$ function performs the operation opposite to that of VAL: It returns a string containing the representation of a number.

Comments

VAL provides no error checking. Your program should check for strings input improperly such as "4,000", "50%", "1/2", and so on, and respond appropriately.

Errors

If the expression you specify with VAL is not a string, QBasic displays a "Type mismatch" error message.

Example

The following program accepts input into a string variable and uses VAL to convert the input to a number, which is stored in an array. Both your input and the converted value are displayed after each input. The program checks the length of the input string with the LEN function. If the length is 0 (that is, if only Enter was pressed), the program stops prompting for input.

```
DIM numbers(10)        ' array to hold input numbers
CLS
FOR i% = 1 TO 10
    INPUT "Enter number, press Enter to exit:", num$ ' input value as a string
    IF LEN(num$) = 0 THEN              ' user pressed Enter
        i% = i% - 1                   ' don't count this iteration
        EXIT FOR                      ' exit loop
    END IF

    value = VAL(num$)                 ' convert input to number
    PRINT "===> "; num$, value        ' display string, value
    numbers(i%) = value               ' store number in the array
NEXT i%

total = 0
FOR j% = 1 TO i%
    total = total + numbers(j%)       ' add the values of the array
NEXT j%

IF i% = 0 THEN PRINT "No numbers entered": SYSTEM  'if no numbers entered, exit

average = total / i%                  ' find average
PRINT "*** Total: "; total; " *** Average: "; average
```

CHAPTER 6

Arrays and Data

Introduction

Arrays are efficient tools for storing and retrieving large quantities of data in memory, just as files are efficient tools for storing and retrieving data on disk. Some of the data your program uses is unique, such as a numeric variable to hold a month's sales total or a string variable to hold a user's name. In many cases, however, a program must manipulate many data items that have the same type and purpose. Suppose, for example, you need to process sales totals for 12 months and print 12 strings, each of which contains the name of a month. All the data items in these cases have the same type (single-precision and string) and purpose (sales total and month name).

Clearly, it would be tedious to create variables such as *janTotal*, *febTotal*, *mar Total*, and so on for the sales totals and *jan$*, *feb$*, *mar$*, and so on for the month names. Not only would you have to type all the different variable names into your program, but you would lack an easy way to refer to each total or name in turn. Suppose you want to add all the monthly totals to create a grand total. You have to write a statement such as *grandTotal = janTotal + febTotal + marTotal ... + decTotal*. Or suppose that you are printing reports for the entire year and that you want to print the name of the current month. You have to refer to the proper string variable for each month—for example, if the month is July, you must use the variable *july$*, and so on.

This section discusses how you use arrays as tools for organizing and processing data. An array lets you create an entire set of variables with a common name, such as *totals*. In effect, an array gives you a filing cabinet with many drawers, numbered from 0 (or sometimes 1) through any number you specify. You can retrieve the contents of a specific drawer (or store something there) merely by referring to the array name and the number of the drawer. If you wanted to systematically process the contents of all the drawers, you would use a simple loop (such as a FOR loop) to access each drawer, one at a time.

Table 6-1, on the following page, shows the array-related and data-related statements and functions in alphabetic order.

Statement or function	Purpose
DATA	Specifies a series of data values (usually to be read into arrays)
DIM	Dimensions (declares and allocates memory for) an array or specifies a variable's data type
$DYNAMIC	Directs QBasic to make all numeric arrays and fixed-length string arrays dynamic
ERASE	Reinitializes a static array or deallocates (frees) the memory used by a dynamic array
LBOUND	Returns the lowest valid subscript of a dimension of an array
OPTION BASE	Sets either 0 or 1 as the default lowest subscript
READ	Assigns the next item in a DATA statement to the specified variable
REDIM	Redefines subscript ranges for an array
RESTORE	Specifies the next DATA statement to be used for reading data
$STATIC	Directs QBasic to make all arrays static
UBOUND	Returns the highest valid subscript of a dimension of an array

Table 6-1.
Array-related and data-related statements and functions.

Declaring and Using Arrays

The DIM (dimension) statement declares the name, size, and type of an array. In most cases you simply use the keyword DIM followed by the array name and its dimensions—for example,

```
DIM totals!(12)
DIM months$(12)
```

These statements declare two arrays. One, called *totals!*, can contain the sales total for each month; the other, called *months$*, can contain the name of each month. Note that array names can use the same type-declaration characters that specify the data types of ordinary variables. In this example, *totals!* is an array of single-precision numeric variables and *months$* is an array of strings. Or you can use an AS clause to specify the data type:

```
DIM totals(12) AS SINGLE
DIM months(12) AS STRING
```

Note that you can't use both the type suffixes and the AS clause—you must use one or the other. You can also use a DEF*type* statement (such as DEFINT or DEFSTR) to apply a type to array names. Thus in the two statements

```
DEFSTR A-C
DIM a(5)
```

the array *a* is an array of strings because the DEFSTR statement makes string the default type for variables with names beginning with A, B, or C.

QBasic also lets you implicitly dimension arrays having 10 elements without using a DIM statement. Thus if your program uses

```
grade(5) = 99
```

QBasic acts as though the program contains the statement

```
DIM grade(10)
```

However, using implicitly dimensioned arrays is not recommended: It makes the code less readable.

Dimensions and Subscripts

The number or numbers in parentheses following the array name in the DIM statement specify the number of individual variables (called "elements") in the array as well as the numbers (called "subscripts") that can be used to gain access to the elements. QBasic needs to know the number of elements in an array for two reasons. First, the number of elements multiplied by the size of each element specifies the amount of memory that the compiler allocates, or reserves, for the array. Second, QBasic uses the specified values to check references to the array to prevent attempts to access nonexistent elements.

In the previous example, both the *totals!* and *months$* arrays use the value 12 to specify that there are 12 elements in each array. By default, the subscript of the first element (the base) of every array is the number 0, so these arrays actually have 13 elements with subscripts ranging from 0 through 12. Because January is commonly considered the first—not the zeroth—month, it is more convenient to make 1 the base of the array. By using the statement

```
OPTION BASE 1
```

before you dimension any arrays, you can change the default so that the subscript of the first element of each array is the number 1.

Arrays with Multiple Dimensions

Sometimes you might find it useful to have more than one dimension in an array. For example, suppose you need an array that stores information about the status of a chessboard—such as which piece (if any) is on each square, the relative value of that square to the player, and so on. Because a chessboard is eight squares long by eight squares wide, it is logical to dimension the following array:

```
DIM board%(8, 8)
```

The *board%* array has two dimensions, each containing eight elements; this assumes you have set the base of the array to 1 with an OPTION BASE statement. This array has 8 times 8, or 64, elements. In general, you can think of a two-dimensional array as being like a table or spreadsheet—having a certain number of rows and a certain number of columns.

QBasic lets you specify many dimensions in an array; however, the most you will probably need for ordinary applications is three. Suppose you need a topographic map on which each point specifies an east-west coordinate, a north-south coordinate, and an elevation. If the map measures 10 miles east to west, 10 miles north to south, and 30 thousand feet in elevation, you could declare the following array to represent the map:

```
DIM topo(10, 10, 30)
```

You might think of this as a stack of thirty 10-by-10 grids (or a big, three-dimensional chess set).

Specifying Subscript Ranges

A subscript is a number that specifies the location of an element along a given array dimension. For example, to access the name "February," specify *months$(2)* because "February" is stored in the second element of the array. To access the square in the second row of the fourth column on a chessboard, use the array element *board%(2, 4)*, as shown in Figure 6-1. To access the region at 8 miles east, 7 miles north, and an altitude of 5000 feet from the reference point on the map, use the element *topo(8, 7, 5)*. These examples demonstrate that to access an array element you must provide its location along each dimension.

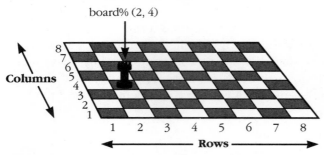

Figure 6-1.
Accessing an array element.

Thus far, our examples assume that every dimension begins at either 0 or 1 (depending on the base set with the OPTION BASE statement). Although this is appropriate in many cases, sometimes you might need to specify a base subscript other than 0 or 1. For example, the Cartesian coordinate system uses the point specified by the coordinates (0, 0) as its center (origin), places negative *x*-coordinates to the left of the *y*-axis, and places negative *y*-coordinates below the *x*-axis. The array that represents this coordinate system must allow negative subscripts; you can specify this by using the TO keyword when specifying the array's dimensions in a DIM statement, as in the following example:

```
DIM cartesian(-100 TO 100, -100 to 100)
```

The above DIM statement declares a two-dimensional array, called *cartesian*, whose subscripts are in the range −100 through 100. You can specify the point specified by (−50, −25) with *cartesian(−50, −25)*, as shown in Figure 6-2.

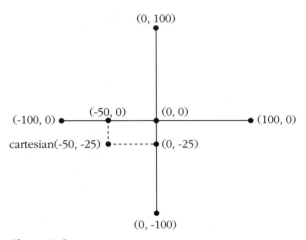

Figure 6-2.
Gaining access to a point in the Cartesian coordinate system.

You can use TO to specify any range of subscripts. Suppose you want to tally the number of students who receive each score on a test that had a minimum score of 40 and a maximum score of 100. The following statement creates the array *totals%*, which can contain this tally:

```
DIM totals%(40 TO 100)
```

Storing Data in an Array

After you create an array, you can assign values to the individual elements by specifying the array name and the subscript of the element, as shown in the following two statements:

```
totals!(1) = 244.45
totals!(2) = 389.90
```

The data for an array might also come from outside the program. If the data is in a file named SALES.DAT, you can transfer the data to the array one value at a time, as shown in the following program segment:

```
OPEN "SALES.DAT" FOR INPUT AS #1
FOR total% = 1 TO 12
    INPUT #1, totals!(total%)
NEXT total%
CLOSE #1
```

Accessing data from files is discussed in Chapter 17, "Files." Notice, however, that because arrays organize data sequentially, in order of the subscripts, a loop such as a FOR loop is all you need to fill the array with data.

You can also use a READ statement to assign data to the elements of an array. You usually use a READ statement if the data items have fixed values that are the same whenever the program is run. Here is one way you can read the month names into the array *months$*:

```
FOR month% = 1 TO 12
    READ months$(month%)
NEXT month%

DATA January, February, March, April
DATA May, June, July, August
DATA September, October, November, December
```

In this example, each time the READ statement executes, it assigns the next string from the DATA statements to an element of *months$*.

Accessing Data in an Array

Recall that you gain access to an element of an array by specifying the subscript along each dimension. Thus the statement

```
PRINT months$(4)
```

displays "April", and the statement

```
currentMonth! = totals!(8)
```

assigns the value stored in the eighth element of *totals!* to the *currentMonth!* variable. If an array has more than one dimension, you must specify a subscript for each dimension. Thus the statement

```
squareVal% = board%(3, 7)
```

references the seventh element in the third set (that is, in row 3 and column 7 on the chessboard) and assigns that element's value to the *squareVal%* variable.

To summarize: After you declare an array with a DIM statement, you can assign either a variable or constant to any element of the array, or you can assign an element's value to any variable that can accept that type of data. QBasic treats each element of an array as a separate variable of whatever data type you have declared for the array.

Arrays of User-Defined Types

One drawback of using arrays is that each array can hold only one kind of data. You can't, for example, store both strings and integers in one array. One solution is to create one array for each kind of data. If, for example, you want to use arrays to store employee names, identification numbers, job titles, and salaries, you have to use one array for each of the four pieces of information. To reference the data for a particular employee, you might use a FOR loop:

```
FOR employee% = 1 TO totalEmployees%
    PRINT names$(employee%)
    PRINT id%(employee%)
    PRINT title$(employee%)
    PRINT salary(employee%)
NEXT employee%
```

Although this method works, it obscures the fact that you're actually dealing with a series of data records, each of which describes information about a particular employee. A better solution is to declare a user-defined type with a TYPE...END TYPE statement and then use an array of records of that type, as in the following example:

```
TYPE EmpRecord
    empName AS STRING
    id AS DOUBLE
    title AS STRING * 32
    salary AS SINGLE
END TYPE

DIM empInfo(1000) AS EmpRecord

FOR employee% = 1 TO totalEmployees
    PRINT empInfo(employee%).name
    PRINT empInfo(employee%).id
    PRINT empInfo(employee%).title
    PRINT empInfo(employee%).salary
NEXT employee%
```

In this example, creating an array of records enables you to assign the information about each employee to one element of the array. (See Chapter 1, "Variables and Types," for more information about user-defined types. Note that although you can have an array of record variables, a record variable cannot contain an array.)

Using Arrays in Subprograms and Functions

Usually you dimension an array in the module-level code unless the array is to be used only in a particular subprogram or function. There are several ways to make an array available to a subprogram or function. In the main program, the DIM statement can include the keyword SHARED, as shown in the following statement:

```
DIM SHARED globalData(100)
```

Using SHARED allows all subprograms and functions to access the array directly (rather than having it passed as a parameter). In other words, the array becomes global.

Or you can use a SHARED statement in a particular subprogram or function to enable the procedure to use an array declared in the main program. Finally, you can pass an array as a parameter to a subprogram or function merely by including its name followed by an empty set of parentheses in the argument list, as in the following:

```
CrossTotal totals()
```

In this case, the subprogram *CrossTotal* would also have an array specified (with an empty set of parentheses) in its parameter list.

Static vs. Dynamic Arrays

If you declare an array using a literal or a constant as a dimension, as shown in the statements on the following page, the array is static.

```
CONST ELEMENTS = 100
DIM n(ELEMENTS)
DIM p(10)
```

Both *n* and *p* are static arrays. QBasic knows exactly what size they must be, and the compiler allocates the appropriate space in memory for each array when it encounters the array's DIM statement. Static arrays have a drawback: You can't change their dimensions later in the program.

On the other hand, if you either use a variable for the dimension or declare the array in a COMMON statement before you dimension it, the array is dynamic. Dynamic arrays have the advantage that the memory for the array is not allocated until runtime. In the following example, the arrays *n* and *grid* are dynamic:

```
COMMON n()
DIM n(500)

rows% = 100
cols% = 50
DIM grid(rows%, cols%)
```

Furthermore, all arrays declared within a subprogram or function are dynamic unless you declare them in a STATIC statement. Because most subprograms or functions don't need to retain variable values between calls, using dynamic arrays ensures that the maximum amount of free memory is available at all times; this consideration is increasingly critical as programs become larger.

Most arrays in QBasic are stored in the far heap in memory. Implicitly dimensioned arrays (arrays that contain 10 elements that are used without first being declared in a DIM statement) and dynamic arrays of variable-length strings are always stored in the default data segment.

You can use the metacommands $STATIC and $DYNAMIC to set the default static or dynamic allocation for the various types of arrays. Following a $STATIC or $DYNAMIC metacommand, QBasic allocates all arrays either statically or dynamically, as specified. (Variable-length strings are still stored in the default data segment, however, and implicitly dimensioned arrays, which are always static, are not affected.)

After you create a dynamic array, you can either use the ERASE statement to deallocate, or free, its memory for other uses or use the REDIM statement to change the array's subscript ranges (but not the number of dimensions). With a static array, ERASE reinitializes the array elements to 0 (or to the null string for string elements), but it does not free any memory. You cannot use the REDIM statement with static arrays.

Related Reading

Prata, Stephen, with Harry Henderson. *The Waite Group's Microsoft QuickBASIC Primer Plus*. Redmond, Wash.: Microsoft Press, 1990.

DATA

See also

CONST, READ, RESTORE

Purpose

DATA statements store constant values that can be read into variables by the READ statement.

Syntax

DATA *val1* [, *val2*...]

val1 and *val2* are literal numeric or string values. Separate multiple values with commas. Enclose string literals in quotation marks only if the string contains commas, colons, or leading or trailing spaces.

Usage

```
DATA North, South, East, West
```
Stores four string constants that can be read only into string variables.

```
DATA 640, 320, 200, 16
```
Stores four numeric constants that can be read into either numeric or string variables.

Description

Each DATA statement contains a list of values separated by commas. If a program has a series of DATA statements, the values contained in all the data statements are treated as one list of data. The first READ statement executed by your program reads the first value from the data list into the specified variable, the second READ transfers the second value, and so on. QBasic always marks its place with a pointer to keep track of the next value to be read. (You can reset this pointer or set it to point to the beginning of a labeled DATA statement by using the RESTORE statement.)

Each data value is interpreted according to the variable type specified in the READ statement. If the variable is numeric, the corresponding data value must consist only of legal numeric characters. If the variable is a string variable, the data value can be a value of any type. (To use a comma in a string data value or preserve leading or trailing spaces, you must enclose the string in quotation marks.) A value consisting of only a comma is treated as a null value; when a READ statement reads a null character, it sets numeric variables to 0 and string variables to the null (empty) string.

QBasic allows DATA statements only in the main program; that is, you can't put them inside subprograms or functions. However, you can place READ statements anywhere in a program's code.

DATA statements are commonly used to hold a series of values that a loop reads into an array. (See the tutorial in this chapter for an example.) However, DATA statements are not always appropriate. If your program uses only a few diverse values,

CONST statements make the program more readable. Also, for large amounts of data, using many DATA statements makes the code unwieldy; therefore, the program probably should read the data from a file, although you must then ensure that the file always accompanies your program.

Errors

If a DATA value being read into a numeric variable has non-numeric characters, QBasic displays a "Syntax error" message. If a READ statement attempts to read past the last DATA value (and a RESTORE statement hasn't reset the read pointer), QBasic displays an "Out of DATA" error message. Having more data than you actually read is not an error; QBasic simply ignores the extra values.

Example

The following program reads a variety of values from DATA statements. Note that all values are read into the string variable *item$*. The numeric value 3.14 is stored in the variable *item$* as a string containing those characters. The quotation marks surrounding the "contains, a" value preserve the comma in the string. If the quotes were removed, the strings "contains" and "a" would be treated as separate data values. Notice that the null value, which is specified by a single comma, is printed as a blank line (because it is an empty string).

Although MAXVAL is the name of a constant, the READ statement treats it as the string "MAXVAL", not as the number 100. If this were read into a numeric value, it would generate a syntax error because MAXVAL cannot be treated as a number.

```
CLS
CONST MAXVAL = 100
FOR i% = 1 TO 5
    READ item$
    PRINT item$
NEXT i%

DATA Saturday, 3.14, "contains, a",, MAXVAL
```

DIM

See also

$DYNAMIC, ERASE, LBOUND, OPTION BASE, REDIM, SHARED, $STATIC, UBOUND

Purpose

The DIM statement declares arrays and allocates storage for them. You can also use DIM to specify the type of a variable.

Syntax

DIM [SHARED] *var* [(*subscripts*)] [AS *type*] [, *var* [(*subscripts*)] [AS *type*]...]

The optional keyword SHARED indicates that the item being declared will be accessible to subprograms or functions in the program.

var is the name of the variable or array.

subscripts indicates the maximum number of subscripts in the array. If the array has more than one dimension, the subscripts for the dimensions must be separated by commas.

AS followed by the name of a type specifies that *var* consists of elements of that data type or is a variable of that data type.

Usage

```
maxX% = 640: maxY% = 480
DIM screen(maxX%, maxY%)
```
Declares a two-dimensional array with variables for subscripts. Because the subscripts are variables, the array is dynamic.

```
DIM names(100) AS STRING * 30
```
Declares an array of fixed-length strings.

```
DIM counter AS LONG
```
Declares a long-integer variable.

Description

The DIM statement is most commonly used to declare an array, which is a variable containing a series of values that are all of the same type. If you use DIM to declare more than one array, separate the declarations with commas.

There are several ways you can define the type of value that an array holds. One way is to include a type-declaration character (%, &, !, #, or $) at the end of the array's name in the DIM statement. Or, you can specify the type by using an AS clause in the DIM statement; this lets you specify either a user-defined type or a fixed-length string type. Finally, you can use a DEF*type* statement, which specifies that variables (including array variables) beginning with certain letters are of a default type.

The number or numbers in parentheses following the array name specify the number of individual variables (called elements) in the array as well as the numbers (called subscripts) that can be used to access the elements in the array. If you include only one number, QBasic assumes that the number is the upper bound of the subscripts. The following DIM statement, for example, declares the array *players$* with subscripts ranging from 0 through 10:

```
DIM players$(10)
```

If you include an OPTION BASE statement to change the default lower bound (the base) from 0 to 1, the subscripts in the above statements range from 1 through 10.

You can specify both the lower and upper bounds of the subscripts by using a TO clause in the parentheses following the array name. The following statement, for example, declares the array *ranking%* with subscripts ranging from −10 through 10:

```
DIM ranking%(-10 TO 10)
```

Sometimes you might find it useful to have more than one dimension in an array. To declare an array with more than one dimension, include the subscripts of each of the dimensions of the array in the parentheses following the array's name and separate the subscripts with commas. For example, the statement

```
DIM sheet(10, 20)
```

declares an array that contains 10 rows and 20 columns. Although QBasic allows as many as 60 dimensions in an array, limit the number of dimensions in an array to three because an array that has more than three dimensions is difficult to conceptualize.

If you include the SHARED keyword in a DIM statement in the main program, you can use the array in any subprogram or function. Otherwise, you must either pass an array declared in the main program as a parameter or specify the array in a SHARED statement within the subprogram or function.

Arrays you declare with literals or constant subscripts are static. The memory for a static array, which is allocated at compile time, cannot be changed during runtime.

On the other hand, arrays you declare with variable subscripts are dynamic. QBasic allocates memory for a dynamic array at runtime; this enables your program to vary the amount of memory the array uses by calling the REDIM statement.

You can also use the DIM statement to declare the type of a variable. This lets you declare variables without assigning them a value, making programs more readable and letting you check the types of the variables more readily. When you use DIM to declare a variable as a particular data type, you cannot include the type-declaration characters (%, !, #, &, and $).

The DIM statement initializes all elements of numeric arrays to 0 and all elements of string arrays to null strings. The fields of user-defined types (including fixed strings) are initialized to 0.

Comments

An array of fixed-length strings cannot be passed as a parameter to a subprogram or function. You can circumvent this limitation by using a SHARED statement to let the subprogram access the array. You can also include the fixed-length strings as fields within a user-defined data type and then use an array of that type.

Errors

If a program contains more than one DIM statement naming a particular array (without an intervening ERASE statement, in the case of a dynamic array) or if the program executes the same DIM statement more than once, QBasic displays a "Duplicate definition" error message.

If the value of a subscript is not in the range −32768 through 32767, QBasic displays an "Overflow" error message.

If an implicitly dimensioned array or any array of variable-length strings attempts to use more memory than is available in the default data segment (DGROUP), QBasic displays an "Out of data space" or "Out of string space" error message. The "Out of data space" error also occurs if the far heap doesn't contain enough memory for any other type of array. If the size of an array stored in DGROUP is greater than 32 KB, QBasic displays a "Subscript out of range" or "Array too large" error message.

If you use a subscript outside the range specified in the array's DIM or REDIM statement, QBasic displays a "Subscript out of range" error message. This usually indicates an error in a loop statement.

Example

The following program uses DIM to declare two integer arrays—one to hold input values and one to hold the number of times each value occurs in the input. After the input is completed, the "mode" (the most commonly occurring value in the input) is calculated and displayed.

```
CONST TRUE = -1, FALSE = 0

CLS
INPUT "Minimum value: "; minVal%          ' get ranges of values to input
INPUT "Maximum value: "; maxVal%
INPUT "How many total values: "; maxInputs    ' get number of values to input

DIM vals%(maxInputs)                       ' array to hold input values
DIM freq%(minVal% TO maxVal%)              ' array to hold frequency of each value

FOR v% = 1 TO maxInputs
    DO                                     ' get and validate an input value
        valid = TRUE
        PRINT "Enter integer value #"; v%; " ("; minVal%; "-"; maxVal%; "):";
        INPUT inputVal%
        IF INT(inputVal%) <> inputVal% THEN
            PRINT "Must be an integer"
            valid = FALSE
        END IF
        IF inputVal% < minVal% OR inputVal% > maxVal% THEN
            PRINT "Must be between "; minVal%; " and "; maxVal%; ", inclusive"
            valid = FALSE
        END IF
    LOOP UNTIL valid = TRUE
    vals%(v%) = inputVal%
    freq%(inputVal%) = freq%(inputVal%) + 1      ' tally the input
NEXT v%
```

(continued)

continued

```
' find the mode
times% = 1
FOR v% = minVal% TO maxVal%
    IF freq%(v%) > times% THEN
        times% = freq%(v%)
        value% = v%
    END IF
NEXT v%

PRINT : PRINT "Mode values: ";
FOR v% = minVal% TO maxVal%             ' allow for more than one mode
    IF freq%(v%) = times% THEN PRINT v%; " ";
NEXT v%

PRINT : PRINT "occur "; times%; " times"
```

$DYNAMIC

See also
$STATIC, REDIM, ERASE

Purpose
The $DYNAMIC metacommand directs QBasic to allocate memory for storing numeric arrays and fixed-length string arrays while the program is running. This metacommand lets the program redimension or erase arrays during execution, allowing for more efficient use of available memory.

Syntax
' $DYNAMIC

or

REM $DYNAMIC

Usage
REM $DYNAMIC

Directs the compiler to make all subsequent arrays dynamic.

Description
If your program includes the $DYNAMIC metacommand, QBasic doesn't allocate memory to arrays until the program starts executing. If you use $DYNAMIC, you can reassign array storage when program requirements change. You can change the size of an array by using the REDIM statement or you can delete the array from memory using the ERASE statement. (See the REDIM and ERASE entries, in this chapter, for details.)

The opposite of $DYNAMIC is the $STATIC metacommand, which forces QBasic to allocate array space when the program is compiled. However, memory allocated to static arrays cannot be released or resized. Use the $DYNAMIC metacommand if you don't know in advance how big your arrays will be. If, however, you know how much array storage a program needs, then use $STATIC—your program will run faster. (See the $STATIC entry for details.)

Errors
If you include the $DYNAMIC metacommand without the REM keyword or a single quotation mark, QBasic displays an "Expected: expression" error message.

ERASE

See also
DIM, $DYNAMIC, REDIM, $STATIC

Purpose
The ERASE statement either reinitializes the elements of a static array or releases the memory used by a dynamic array. Thus you can reuse an array (or the memory it uses) if you no longer need the contents of the array.

Syntax
ERASE *array* [, *array*...]

array is the name of the array to be erased or reinitialized.

Usage
```
sets% = 4
valsPerSet% = 100
DIM inputData(sets%, valsPerSet%)
⋮
ERASE inputData
```
Dimensions the dynamic array *inputData* and releases the memory used by the array.

Description
With a static array, the ERASE statement merely resets all elements to their default value—0 if numeric, or null strings ("") if string. ERASE does not change the dimensions of the static array defined in the DIM statement nor release any memory.

With a dynamic array, however, ERASE deallocates the memory used by the array, thereby freeing the memory for other dynamic arrays. Before you can reuse an erased array, you must dimension it again with DIM. (QBasic offers the REDIM statement as an alternative to erasing and redimensioning a dynamic array. REDIM deallocates, re-dimensions, and reinitializes a dynamic array in one step.)

You can also erase an array of elements of a user-defined data type. All fields in each element, including fixed-length strings, are reinitialized.

Errors

After you erase a dynamic array, any reference to an element results in a "Subscript out of range" error message. You must first use a DIM or REDIM statement to redimension the array. If you specify the name of an array that does not exist, QBasic displays an "Array not defined" error message.

Example

The following program declares a dynamic array, erases it, and shows the amount of memory available for arrays before and after erasing the array. Notice that erasing the array frees all the memory used by the array.

```
DECLARE SUB ShowMem ()
CLS

PRINT "Before declaring array: ",
ShowMem

totalNums% = 2500
DIM dynArr$(totalNums%)    ' a dynamic array of 2500 strings

PRINT "After declaring array: ",
ShowMem

ERASE dynArr$                 ' deallocate dynamic array
PRINT "After erasing array: ",
ShowMem
END

SUB ShowMem
    ' display amount of available memory
    PRINT "Total array space is "; FRE(-1)
END SUB
```

LBOUND

See also

UBOUND

Purpose

The LBOUND function returns the lower bound (lowest valid subscript value) of a dimension of an array. You can use LBOUND with the UBOUND statement to determine the size of an array.

Syntax

LBOUND (*array*[, *dim*])

array is the name of the array.

dim is the number of the array dimension whose lower bound is to be obtained. If you do not specify a dimension, LBOUND returns the lower bound of the first dimension.

Usage

```
DIM items(50, 100)
low1% = LBOUND(items, 1)
low2% = LBOUND(items, 2)
```

Assigns the value 0 to *low1%* and *low2%*.

```
DIM freq(500 TO 1000)
low% = LBOUND(freq)
```

Assigns the value 500 to *low%*.

Description

The LBOUND function returns the lowest legal subscript value of a dimension of the array you specify. If you do not specify a dimension, LBOUND returns the value of the lower bound of the first dimension. The lowest subscript of an array is 0 by default; however, the statement *OPTION BASE 1* makes 1 the lowest value, and a TO clause can specify any lower bound when you dimension or redimension an array.

You can calculate the size of an array by subtracting the value returned by LBOUND from the value returned by UBOUND.

Errors

If the variable you specify in the LBOUND statement isn't an array or if it is an array that has not been dimensioned, QBasic displays an "Array not defined" error message. If you specify a dimension less than 0 or greater than the total number of dimensions in the array or if you specify a dynamic array that has been erased but not redimensioned, QBasic displays a "Subscript out of range" error message. Specifying a dimension of 0 does not result in an error, but LBOUND returns a random value. Be sure you do not use 0 in a call to LBOUND.

Example

The following program passes an array to the subprogram *Total*. The latter uses the LBOUND and UBOUND functions in a FOR loop that accesses the elements of the array and totals their values. This is more concise than supplying the lowest and highest subscript values with the array name in the call to the subprogram.

```
DECLARE SUB Total (anArray%())
DIM values%(5 TO 10)

FOR num% = 5 TO 10
    values%(num%) = num%    ' assign values to the array
NEXT num%

Total values%()             ' get the sum of the elements of the array

SUB Total (anArray%())
    t = 0
    FOR n% = LBOUND(anArray%) TO UBOUND(anArray%)
        t = t + anArray%(n%)
    NEXT n%
    PRINT "Total of array values: "; t
END SUB
```

OPTION BASE

See also
DIM, LBOUND, UBOUND

Purpose
The OPTION BASE statement specifies the default lowest subscript value for arrays; this can be 0 or 1.

Syntax
OPTION BASE [0 ¦ 1]

Usage
OPTION BASE 1
Sets the default lowest array subscript to 1.

Description
Use the OPTION BASE statement with a value of 0 or 1 to set the default lowest array subscript. By default, when you use an array that is not declared in a DIM statement or was not dimensioned with a TO clause, the default lowest subscript for each dimension is 0. By using the statement

OPTION BASE 1

you make 1 the first subscript in each dimension. Although many computer languages start array subscripts at 0, you might often find it more natural to label the first element of a list as number 1 and then to use the subscript 1 as the lower bound of the array that contains the list. Therefore, if you design code that never uses a 0 subscript, using the statement *OPTION BASE 1* offers two advantages: It guards you against inadvertently using the 0 subscript (by generating a "Subscript out of range" error message), and it saves memory by not allocating space for the element you don't use—the zeroth element.

When you include a TO clause for each dimension in a DIM statement, you can specify the lower and upper bounds of an array. Any bounds specified in a TO clause override the default lowest subscript.

Because the default lowest subscript is 0, the statement *OPTION BASE 0* is useful only to indicate to anyone reading the program that the lowest subscript is 0.

Errors

If you use a value other than 0 or 1 with the OPTION BASE statement, QBasic displays an "Expected: 0 or 1" error message. If you attempt to use a second OPTION BASE statement in the same program, QBasic displays an "Array already dimensioned" error message.

Warnings

QBasic ignores an OPTION BASE statement in a chained-to program if a dynamic array is passed to the program through a COMMON statement. In that case, the chained-to program inherits the default lowest subscript from the chained-from program.

Example

The program below shows that the statement *OPTION BASE 1* changes the lowest array subscript to 1.

```
OPTION BASE 1          ' make default lowest subscript 1

DIM matrix(10, 10)
PRINT "First element in the two-dimensional array is matrix";
PRINT "("; LBOUND(matrix, 1); ","; LBOUND(matrix, 2); ")"
```

READ

See also

DATA, RESTORE

Purpose

The READ statement accesses values from one or more DATA statements and assigns the values to specified variables. A READ statement is commonly used inside loops to read values into an array.

Syntax

READ *var* [, *var*...]

var is any simple numeric or string variable type. Be sure to separate multiple variables with commas. (Arrays and user-defined types must be read one element or one field at a time.)

Usage

```
READ n$, a$, num
DATA Gary, Pittsburgh, 1
```

Reads the values "Gary", "Pittsburgh", and 1 into the variables *n$*, *a$*, and *num*.

Description

A READ statement retrieves the values in a DATA statement found in the main program and stores the values in the specified variables. The READ statement always reads values in the order in which they appear in the DATA statements. (Note that you can use the RESTORE statement to reread values from the beginning of a DATA statement.)

When assigning values to variables, the READ statement converts values to the variable's data type as follows:

- Noninteger numeric values read into integer variables are rounded to the nearest integer.

- Numeric variables read into string variables are stored as a string of numerals.

- String values read into fixed-length string variables are truncated if they are too long. If a value is too short, it is left justified and padded on the right with blanks.

Errors

If you attempt to read more values than are available in DATA statements, QBasic displays an "Out of DATA" error message. If you read fewer values than are available, the next READ statement (if one exists) begins reading at the first unread value. QBasic does not check to ensure that all values specified in DATA statements are used. If you attempt to read a string value into a numeric variable, QBasic displays a "Type mismatch" error message.

Warnings

You cannot read an entire user-defined data type (record) into a single variable. That is, if *custRec* is a variable of a user-defined type, you can't use the statement *READ custRec*. You must read the fields one at a time—for example,

```
READ custRec.name, custRec.street, custRec.city
```

Example

The following program uses a READ statement to read integers into an array. The values are then used to draw a star.

```
DIM points%(28)
FOR pt% = 1 TO 28
    READ points%(pt%)    ' read the data values into an array
NEXT pt%

' draw the star
SCREEN 1
PSET (points%(1), points%(2))
FOR pt% = 3 TO 28 STEP 2
    LINE -(points%(pt%), points%(pt% + 1))
NEXT pt%

DATA 100, 100, 150, 100, 175, 75, 200, 100
DATA 250, 100, 200, 125, 250, 150, 200, 150
DATA 175, 175, 150, 150, 125, 150, 100, 150
DATA 150, 125, 100, 100
```

REDIM

See also

DIM, ERASE

Purpose

The REDIM statement deallocates, redimensions, and reinitializes a dynamic array. This lets a program use the same array for different sets of data during processing.

Syntax

REDIM [SHARED] *var* (*subscripts*) [AS *type*] [, *var*(subscripts) [AS *type*]...]

The optional keyword SHARED indicates that the array being declared will be accessible to subprograms or functions in the program.

var is the name of the dynamic array variable to be redimensioned.

subscripts specifies the subscripts for each dimension of the array. If the array has more than one dimension, the subscripts for the dimensions must be separated by commas. The AS clause can specify the type of data the array will hold.

Usage

```
rows% = 10: cols% = 10
DIM matrix(rows%, cols%)
⋮
rows = 20: cols = 15
REDIM matrix(rows, cols)
```

Redimensions the array *matrix*.

Description

The REDIM statement can redimension only dynamic arrays (arrays that either use variables as subscripts in the DIM statement or have been made dynamic with the $DYNAMIC metacommand). QBasic specifies the dimensions for these arrays and allocates their memory at runtime rather than at compile time, as with static arrays. After you have used DIM or $DYNAMIC to establish a dynamic array, you can use REDIM anywhere in your program to reallocate memory and subscript ranges for that array.

The syntax for REDIM is the same as that for DIM. Follow REDIM with the keyword SHARED if you want the array to be accessible to all subprograms and procedures. (Or, you can simply pass the array as a parameter to a subprogram or use a SHARED statement within a subprogram or function to make the array accessible to the subprogram or function.)

As with DIM, you can specify more than one array in the same REDIM statement; merely separate the declarations with commas.

Errors

If you attempt to change the number of dimensions in the redimensioned array, QBasic displays a "Wrong number of dimensions" error message. If you changed the type of data stored in the array, QBasic displays a "Duplicate definition" error message.

Warnings

You cannot use REDIM with a static array. You also cannot change the number of dimensions of the array or the type of data (integer, double, user-defined type, and so on) stored in the array.

Example

The following program declares and fills an array and then uses the REDIM statement to redimension it; the program displays the contents of the array both before and after the redimensioning. The program also demonstrates how to pass an array to a subprogram and how to use LBOUND and UBOUND to. gain access to each element correctly.

```
DECLARE SUB FillMatrix (anArray%())
DECLARE SUB PrintMatrix (anArray%())

CLS
OPTION BASE 1                  ' set lowest array subscript to 1
rows% = 5: cols% = 5
DIM matrix%(rows%, cols%)      ' declare a dynamic array
FillMatrix matrix%()           ' fill the array
PrintMatrix matrix%()          ' display the array

rows% = 6: cols% = 8
REDIM matrix%(rows%, cols%)    ' redimension the array
FillMatrix matrix%()           ' fill the array
PRINT : PRINT
PrintMatrix matrix%()          ' display the array
```

(continued)

continued

```
SUB FillMatrix (anArray%())
    ' fill a two-dimensional array
    FOR row% = LBOUND(anArray%, 1) TO UBOUND(anArray%, 1)
        FOR col% = LBOUND(anArray%, 2) TO UBOUND(anArray%, 2)
            anArray%(row%, col%) = col%
        NEXT col%
    NEXT row%
END SUB

SUB PrintMatrix (anArray%())
    ' print contents of any two-dimensional array
    FOR row% = LBOUND(anArray%, 1) TO UBOUND(anArray%, 1)
        FOR col% = LBOUND(anArray%, 2) TO UBOUND(anArray%, 2)
            PRINT anArray%(row%, col%); " ";
        NEXT col%
    PRINT
    NEXT row%
END SUB
```

RESTORE

See also

DATA, READ

Purpose

The RESTORE statement lets a READ statement either reuse all previously read DATA statements or reread DATA statements, beginning at a specified location. This allows your program to reread data from the beginning of the DATA statements or to read data selectively, based on a particular condition.

Syntax

RESTORE [*line* ¦ *label*]

line or *label* specifies the line that holds the DATA statement to be read next.

Usage

```
RESTORE
```
Rereads data from the beginning of the first DATA statement.

```
RESTORE Monday
```
Rereads data from the DATA statement on the line labeled "Monday".

Description

Normally, a READ statement reads data from the first item in the first DATA statement. Subsequent READ statements read data from DATA statements sequentially. The RESTORE statement lets you define a new starting point for reading data. If you use RESTORE without a line number or line label, the next READ statement gains access to the data at the beginning of the first DATA statement. This is useful for reinitializing data before restarting a process.

If you use RESTORE with a line number or line label, the next READ statement reads the data at the beginning of the DATA statement on the line with the specified number or label. Note that RESTORE doesn't read anything; it merely specifies the DATA statement to be read by the next READ statement.

Errors

If you specify a nonexistent line label or number in a RESTORE statement, QBasic displays a "Label not defined" error message.

Example

The following program labels three different DATA statements and reads the value of *wage!* from one of them, depending on the choice entered by the user. (In practice, you probably would define named constants—with the CONST statement—for the items in the DATA statements of this example. However, if you have several large sets of data items, use labeled DATA statements because they require much less memory.)

```
CLS
PRINT "Regular, Overtime, or Doubletime wage: "
INPUT "R, O, or D"; type$
SELECT CASE UCASE$(type$)
    CASE "R": RESTORE Regular
    CASE "O": RESTORE Overtime
    CASE "D": RESTORE Doubletime
END SELECT

READ wage!
PRINT "Your hourly wage is ";
PRINT USING "$##.##"; wage!

Regular:
DATA 5.00

Overtime:
DATA 7.50

Doubletime:
DATA 10.00
```

$STATIC

See also
$DYNAMIC, REDIM, ERASE

Purpose
The $STATIC metacommand directs QBasic to allocate memory for storing arrays when the program is compiled, not when it is running. Static arrays let your programs run faster, but, because these arrays cannot be redimensioned or deleted, they can result in inefficient memory use.

Syntax
' $STATIC

or

REM $STATIC

Usage
REM $STATIC
Directs the compiler to make all subsequent arrays static.

Description
If your program includes the $STATIC metacommand, QBasic allocates storage space to all explicitly dimensioned arrays when it compiles the program. (Explicit dimensioning means that you specify a specific number of elements in the DIM statement.) Arrays dimensioned by variables or expressions whose values are not known in advance are dynamic arrays, and QBasic allocates memory for their storage after the program starts executing. Because QBasic allocates memory for static arrays before a program starts, the running program doesn't have to waste time building arrays during execution; therefore, a program that uses static arrays executes faster than a program that uses dynamic arrays.

Memory assigned to static arrays cannot be released or resized while the program is running. The REDIM statement cannot be used to change the number of elements in a static array, because the amount of memory allocated to an entire array cannot be changed. The ERASE statement does not free the memory used by a static array; however, it resets all the array's elements to 0 or to null strings.

If your program references an array that has not been explicitly dimensioned by a previous DIM or REDIM statement, QBasic creates the array with 11 elements (numbered 0 through 10). Such arrays, called implicitly dimensioned arrays, are always static, so you cannot redimension or erase them.

Do not confuse the $STATIC metacommand with the STATIC statement. (See the STATIC entry in Chapter 4, "Procedures," for details.)

Errors

If you include the $STATIC metacommand without the REM keyword or a single quotation mark, QBasic displays an "Expected: expression" error message.

UBOUND

See also
LBOUND

Purpose
The UBOUND statement returns the upper bound (highest valid subscript value) of a dimension of an array. You can use UBOUND with the LBOUND statement to determine the size of an array.

Syntax
UBOUND (*array*[, *dim*])

array is the name of the array.

dim is the number of the array dimension whose upper bound is to be obtained. If you do not specify a dimension, UBOUND returns the upper bound of the first dimension.

Usage
```
DIM items(50, 100)
high1% = UBOUND(items, 1)
high2% = UBOUND(items, 2)
```
Assigns the value 50 to *high1%* and the value 100 to *high2%*.

```
DIM freq(500 TO 1000)
high% = UBOUND(freq)
```
Assigns the value 1000 to *high%*.

Description
The UBOUND function returns the highest legal subscript value of a dimension of the array you specify. If you do not specify a dimension, UBOUND returns the value of the upper bound of the first dimension.

You can calculate the size of an array by subtracting the value returned by the LBOUND function from the value returned by UBOUND. The UBOUND function is also useful for finding the upper limit of a loop that works with each element of an array.

Errors

If the variable you specify in the UBOUND statement isn't an array or if it is an array that has not been dimensioned, QBasic displays an "Array not defined" error message. If you specify a dimension less than 0 or greater than the total number of dimensions in the array or if you specify a dynamic array that has been erased but not redimensioned,

QBasic displays a "Subscript out of range" error message. Specifying a dimension of 0 does not result in an error, but UBOUND returns a random value. Be sure you don't use 0 in a call to UBOUND.

Example

The following program uses the user-defined function *Sizeof* to determine the total number of bytes needed to store a specified integer array. When the program calls the function, it passes the array name and the number of dimensions in the array to the function.

For the array in this program, the program displays "The array uses 1890 bytes." Notice that because no lower bound is specified and no *OPTION BASE 1* statement is used, the lower bound for each dimension is 0. Therefore the total number of array elements of type integer is 9 times 7 times 5 times 3; the function multiplies this value by 2 to find the total number of bytes occupied by the array.

```
DECLARE FUNCTION Sizeof (anArray%(), dimensions%)

DIM IntArray%(8, 6, 4, 2)
PRINT "The array uses"; Sizeof(IntArray%(), 4); "bytes."

FUNCTION Sizeof (anArray%(), dimensions%)
    ' return the size of an integer array
    size = 1                    ' holds product of dimensions
    FOR dimen% = 1 TO dimensions%
        subSize% = UBOUND(anArray%, dimen%) - LBOUND(anArray%, dimen%) + 1
        size = size * subSize%
    NEXT dimen%
    Sizeof = size * 2          ' 2 bytes per integer
END FUNCTION
```

CHAPTER 7

Math

Introduction

Most ordinary programming applications use only the standard arithmetic operations—addition, subtraction, multiplication, and division. In fact, you can write many useful programs without having any knowledge of mathematics beyond simple arithmetic.

Nevertheless, QBasic's more advanced math functions are helpful (and sometimes necessary) in many applications. You need to use trigonometric functions in surveying and in CAD (Computer Aided Design) programs. Many games and simulations need a source of random numbers. Business applications require the ability to round numbers to a certain number of digits, and scientific applications often must determine the results of calculations to many places of precision. This tutorial explains the capabilities of QBasic's math functions and offers suggestions for their use. Table 7-1 lists the math statements and functions in alphabetic order.

Statement or function	Purpose
ABS	Returns the absolute (positive) value of a number
ATN	Returns an angle, in radians, whose tangent is the given number
CDBL	Returns a number as a double-precision value
CINT	Returns a number rounded to the nearest integer
CLNG	Returns a number as a long-integer value
COS	Returns the cosine of an angle that is measured in radians
CSNG	Returns a number as a single-precision value
EXP	Returns e (the natural base, which equals 2.718282) to a specified power
FIX	Returns the integer part of a number
INT	Returns the next integer value less than or equal to a number
LOG	Returns the natural logarithm (base e) of a number
RANDOMIZE	Seeds the random-number generator (establishes a random-number sequence)
RND	Returns a value from a random-number sequence
SGN	Returns the sign value of number (−1, 0, or 1)
SIN	Returns the sine of an angle that is measured in radians
SQR	Returns the square root of a number
TAN	Returns the tangent of an angle that is measured in radians

Table 7-1.
QBasic math functions and statements.

Trigonometric Functions and Square Roots

QBasic includes four trigonometric functions: ATN (arctangent), COS (cosine), SIN (sine), and TAN (tangent). The results of these functions depend on relationships between an angle and the parts of a right triangle, as shown in Figure 7-1.

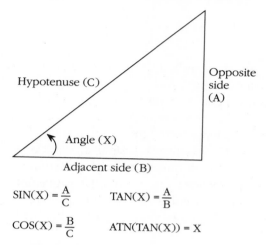

$$SIN(X) = \frac{A}{C} \qquad TAN(X) = \frac{A}{B}$$

$$COS(X) = \frac{B}{C} \qquad ATN(TAN(X)) = X$$

Figure 7-1.
Trigonometric functions.

The QBasic functions SIN, COS, and TAN work with angles expressed in radians. (A radian is an angular measurement equal to the angle formed at the center of a circle by an arc equal to the circle's radius.) To convert from degrees to radians, multiply the number of degrees by the result of π divided by 180. To convert from radians to degrees, multiply the number of radians by the result of 180 divided by π, which is approximately 57.2958. You might want to declare the following constants in programs that perform conversion from degrees to radians:

```
CONST PI = 3.141593
CONST DEGREETORAD = PI / 180
```

(If you need more precision, define *PI* as a double-precision constant and add digits to the value.) Now, if you know how many degrees are in an angle, you can use the expression *angle * DEGREETORAD* to convert from degrees to radians, as shown in the following calculation:

```
result = SIN(angle * DEGREETORAD)
```

This example expresses the values in single precision. The trigonometric functions return single-precision values by default; however, if you specify a double-precision value, the functions return a double-precision result.

Trigonometric functions are useful for calculating an unknown length or height when you know an angle and the length of one side of a right triangle. For example, by using Figure 7-1 as a guide, you can find the height of a tree without climbing it. Drive a stake at angle X into the ground a few feet away from the tree, and use a surveyor's transit to measure the angle to the top of the tree. Then stretch a line to measure side B (the distance to the base of the tree). Now QBasic can calculate the height of the tree, as the following statements show:

```
INPUT "Angle in degrees: "; angleX      ' get angle
INPUT "Length of side B: "; lenB        ' get known side
radiansX = angleX * DEGREETORAD         ' convert angle to radians
tanX = TAN(radiansX)                    ' calculate tangent of angle X
height = tanX * lenB                    ' use algebra to calculate the height
```

This example uses algebra as well as trigonometry to find the height of the tree. Because TAN(X) equals A divided by B, A (the height of the tree) equals TAN(X) times B.

You can derive many other trigonometric functions from the four that QBasic provides. Table 7-2 shows examples in which A is an angle in radians. The SQR function, used in some of the formulas in Table 7-2, returns the square root of any value that is greater than or equal to 0.

Function	Formula
Secant	SEC(A) = 1 / COS(A)
Cosecant	CSC(A) = 1 / SIN(A)
Cotangent	COT(A) = 1 / TAN(A)
Inverse sine	ARCSIN(A) = ATN(A / SQR(−A * A + 1))
Inverse cosine	ARCCOS(A) = PI/2 − ATN(A / SQR(−A * A + 1))
Inverse secant	ARCSEC(A) = ATN(SQR(A * A − 1)) + SGN(SGN(A) − 1) * PI
Inverse cosecant	ARCCSC(A) = ATN(1 / SQR(A * A − 1)) + SGN(SGN(A) − 1) * PI
Inverse cotangent	ARCCOT(A) = ATN(1 / A) − SGN(SGN(A) − 1) * PI
Hyperbolic sine	SINH(A) = (EXP(A) − EXP(−A)) / 2
Hyperbolic cosine	COSH(A) = (EXP(A) + EXP(−A)) / 2
Hyperbolic tangent	TANH(A) = (EXP(A) − EXP(−A)) / (EXP(A) + EXP(−A))
Hyperbolic secant	SECH(A) = 2 / (EXP(A) + EXP(−A))
Hyperbolic cosecant	CSCH(A) = 2 / (EXP(A) − EXP(−A))
Hyperbolic cotangent	COTH(A) = (EXP(A) + EXP(−A)) / (EXP(A) − EXP(−A))

Table 7-2.
Additional trigonometric functions.

Logarithms and Exponents

Two QBasic functions perform operations with logarithms and exponents. The LOG function finds the natural logarithm of a specified number or expression. This is the power to which the base *e* (2.718282) must be raised to equal the specified value. The EXP function is the complement of LOG: It raises *e* to a specified value. To convert from natural logarithms to "common," or base 10, logarithms, divide the natural logarithm of the number by the natural logarithm of 10, as in the following function:

```
FUNCTION LOG10(number)
    LOG10 = LOG(number) / LOG(10)
END FUNCTION
```

Logarithms are often used in scientific models and simulations, such as simulations of population growth.

Numeric Conversion Functions

The next group of math functions converts numbers from one type to another, such as from single precision to double precision or from integer to long integer. This group of functions lets you convert a numeric value to the form expected by a function or subprogram. For example, if the function *Calc* expects two double-precision values as parameters, but you have been working with the single-precision variables *num1!* and *num2!*, you can call the function only by converting the variables, as the following statement shows:

```
result# = Calc(CDBL(num1!), CDBL(num2!))
```

To convert a number to double precision, use the CDBL function; to convert to single precision, use CSNG. To convert a number to an integer, use the CINT function; to convert to a long integer, use CLNG. Because precision increases with the number of significant (meaningful) digits, converting a number to a lower precision might reduce the number's accuracy. On the other hand, although converting a number to a higher precision adds more decimal places, it doesn't necessarily make the number more accurate.

Truncating and Rounding

Three functions let you round or truncate numbers. The INT and FIX functions truncate numbers by eliminating the digits following the decimal point and returning the integer; for example, *INT(3.445)* equals 3. INT and FIX differ only in the way they deal with negative numbers: INT returns the next-lower integer—for example, *INT(-3.52)* equals -4; FIX returns the next-higher integer—*FIX(-3.25)* equals -3. Truncation is useful when you want only the integer portion of a number.

The CINT ("convert integer") function rounds a value to the nearest integer. A positive decimal value greater than 0.5 is rounded to the next-higher integer. For example, *CINT(5.52)* equals 6 but *CINT(5.49)* equals 5; a negative decimal value greater than 0.5 is rounded to the next-lower integer: *CINT(-5.52)* equals −6, but *CINT(-5.49)* equals −5. (A fraction of exactly 0.5 is rounded to the nearest even integer.) Use the CINT function when you don't want to work with fractions but you do want to maintain a high degree of accuracy.

Random Numbers

The last two functions discussed in this section provide programmers with a means of generating random numbers. A random number is merely a number that has no inherent relationship to its predecessor (much as the result of one coin toss is not affected by the previous toss). Random numbers are useful for many games, in which they serve the same purpose as dice in the noncomputer world. Simulations also use them to model unpredictable behavior. The following program segment uses the RANDOMIZE statement and the RND function to print five random numbers:

```
RANDOMIZE 10

FOR randNum% = 1 TO 5
    PRINT RND
NEXT randNum%
```

The above program segment displays the following values:

```
.5749933
.2375866
.5295308
.2520258
.9770579
```

The RANDOMIZE statement seeds (initializes) the random-number generator with a value used in a formula that generates unpredictable results. However, each specific seed always generates the same sequence of random numbers. Although this type of randomness is useful for testing a simulation or game, a playable game requires that numbers be unpredictable as well as mathematically random. To generate a different sequence of random numbers every time you run a program, use the statement *RANDOMIZE TIMER*. The TIMER function returns the number of seconds counted by the system clock since the previous midnight, thus giving the RANDOMIZE statement a reasonably unpredictable seed value.

Related Reading

Graham, Ronald L., Donald E. Knuth, and Oren Patashnik. *Concrete Mathematics*. Reading, Mass: Addison-Wesley, 1989.

Hewitt, Paul G. *Conceptual Physics*. Boston, Mass: Little and Brown, 1985.

ABS

See also

SGN

Purpose

The ABS function returns the absolute value of a numeric constant, variable, or expression. The absolute value is the actual quantity of the number, regardless of its sign. For example, the absolute value of −1 is 1. All absolute values are positive numbers.

Syntax

ABS(*expr*)

expr is a numeric constant, numeric variable, or numeric expression that can be of any numeric type (integer, long integer, single precision, or double precision).

Usage

```
PRINT ABS(-45)
```
Displays 45, the absolute value of −45.

```
difference = ABS(guess1 - guess2)
```
Assigns to the variable *difference* the value of the absolute difference between the values of *guess1* and *guess2*.

Description

The ABS function returns the unsigned value of a numeric constant, variable, or expression. An expression can contain variables or constants of any numeric type. The precision of the value returned by ABS is the same as that used in the expression. For example, *ABS(−1)* returns 1 and *ABS(99.44555)* returns 99.44555.

The ABS function is often used in routines that use approximation to calculate values. For example, a program that calculates cube roots might compare the cube of the current calculated value to the original value. The program accepts the calculation when the absolute value of the difference between the two values is less than a specified tolerance, as demonstrated in the following DO...LOOP statement:

```
DO UNTIL ABS(target - result) < tolerance
    ' perform the calculation
LOOP
```

Such approximation has many other applications; for example, a program might read the current *x*- and *y*-coordinates of a ball on the screen and "bounce" the ball when the absolute value of the distance from a screen edge is small enough.

Errors

If you specify a non-numeric value with ABS, QBasic displays a "Type mismatch" error message.

Example

The following program generates a random "target" on a 100-by-100-square grid and lets you guess the target's *x*- and *y*-coordinates. The program displays the difference between your guess and the target to indicate how close your guess was to the target. When the difference between your guess and the target is less than 5 (the "bull's-eye distance") for both the *x*- and *y*-coordinates, the target is "hit."

```
RANDOMIZE TIMER          ' get random-number sequence
DEFINT A-Z               ' define all variables as integers
targetX = RND * 100      ' random x-coordinate between 0 and 99
targetY = RND * 100      ' random y-coordinate between 0 and 99
bullseye = 5             ' distance within which "hit" occurs
xApproach = 100          ' x distance from target
yApproach = 100          ' y distance from target

CLS
PRINT "Try to hit a target in a 100-by-100-square grid": PRINT
DO UNTIL xApproach <= bullseye AND yApproach <= bullseye
    INPUT "X-coordinate of shot "; xShot
    INPUT "Y-coordinate of shot "; yShot
    xApproach = ABS(targetX - xShot)         ' get absolute distance
    yApproach = ABS(targetY - yShot)
    PRINT "x + y distance from the target is "; xApproach + yApproach: PRINT
LOOP

PRINT "You hit the target!"   ' x and y coordinates were in the bulls-eye
PRINT "Target was at x = "; targetX; "y = "; targetY
```

ATN

See also

COS, SIN, TAN

Purpose

The ATN function returns the arctangent of a numeric constant, numeric variable, or numeric expression. The arctangent is the angle (measured in radians) whose tangent is equal to the specified value.

Syntax

ATN(*expr*)

expr can be any combination of numbers or numeric variables (integer, long integer, single precision, or double precision). The result is expressed in radians, which can be converted to degrees by multiplying by 180 divided by pi, or approximately 57.2958.

Usage

```
PRINT ATN(.8000001)
```
Displays the arctangent of .8000001 in double precision, which is .6747410031991594 radians.

Description

The ATN function returns the size of the angle (in radians) whose tangent is the value of the specified expression. The function returns a single-precision floating-point value by default; however, if the given value is a double-precision value, the arctangent is also a double-precision value. The value returned by ATN will always be between $-\pi/2$ and $\pi/2$. (The value of π is approximately 3.141593.)

The ATN function (as with the other trigonometric functions) is useful for solving problems in geometry, trigonometry, or practical surveying. For example, if you know the lengths of the two sides of a right triangle, you can obtain the tangent of an angle by dividing the length of the opposite side by that of the adjacent side. As shown in the following statement, you can then find the size of the angle in radians by calculating the arctangent of the tangent, and you can convert the result to degrees:

```
angleInRadians = ATN(oppositeSide / adjacentSide)
angleInDegrees = angleInRadians * 57.2958
```

Errors

If you specify a non-numeric value with ATN, QBasic displays a "Type mismatch" error message.

Example

The following program prompts the user to enter the known distance to an object and the known height of the object. The program then displays the angle in degrees between the user's position and the top of the object.

```
CONST RADTODEGREE = 57.2958    ' constant for conversion from radians to degrees

INPUT "Distance to object: "; distance
INPUT "Height of object: "; height
PRINT "Angle from observer to top of object in degrees is: ";

tangA = height / distance      ' tangent of observer angle
angleA = ATN(tangA)            ' find angle by using arctangent
PRINT angleA * RADTODEGREE     ' convert angle to degrees
```

CDBL

See also
CINT, CLNG, CSNG, FIX, INT

Purpose
The CDBL function converts a numeric constant, numeric variable, or numeric expression to a double-precision floating-point value.

Syntax
CDBL(*expr*)

expr is any combination of numbers or numeric variables (integer, long integer, single precision, or double precision).

Usage
```
PRINT CDBL(3 / 7)
```
Displays the value .4285714285714285.

Description
The CDBL function converts a numeric constant, variable, or expression to double precision. Ordinarily, you use this function to force QBasic to perform a calculation in double precision. For example, if a program uses two single-precision variables, *num1!* and *num2!*, the expression *CDBL(num1! / num2!)* returns the result of the division in double precision rather than in the default, single precision.

You can achieve the same effect by assigning the result of a calculation to a double-precision variable; for example, the statement

```
result# = num1! / num2!
```

yields a double-precision result and stores the value in *result#*.

Comments
The CDBL function cannot make an individual number more precise. Although the statement *PRINT CDBL(1.1)* displays the value 1.100000023841858, the extra digits are incorrect. However, the situation is different when determining the results of a calculation because a calculation (such as *3 / 7*) can be carried out to additional decimal places, thus making the result more precise.

In practical and scientific applications, the precision of a calculation depends on the precision of the components used in the calculation. Although you can divide two single-precision numbers to produce a double-precision result, the result is really no more accurate than the single-precision data used. The extra decimal places thus convey a false impression of accuracy. Do not use greater precision than is required by your data.

Errors

If you specify a non-numeric value with CDBL, QBasic displays a "Type mismatch" error message.

Example

The following program demonstrates the methods of converting the result of a calculation to double precision. Notice that assigning the result of a calculation to a double-precision variable produces the same result as using the CDBL function does. Also notice that using CDBL separately with the numerator and denominator offers no advantage over using CDBL with the expression as a whole.

```
INPUT "Numerator: "; numerator
INPUT "Denominator: "; denominator

PRINT numerator / denominator, "(single-precision result)"

result# = numerator / denominator
PRINT result#;
PRINT "(result assigned to double-precision variable)"

PRINT CDBL(numerator / denominator); "(result converted with CDBL)"
PRINT CDBL(numerator) / CDBL(denominator);
PRINT "(result with values converted before dividing)"
```

CINT

See also

FIX, INT

Purpose

The CINT function converts a numeric constant, numeric variable, or numeric expression to an integer value. For example, *CINT(99.7)* is 100.

Syntax

CINT(*expr*)

expr is any combination of numbers or numeric variables (integer, long integer, single precision, or double precision).

Usage

```
a = 100.43
PRINT CINT(a)
```
Displays the value 100.43 converted to an integer, which is 100.

```
PRINT CINT(-1.9)
```
Displays the value −1.9 converted to an integer, which is −2.

Description

Think of the name CINT as meaning "closest integer" because the function converts a numeric constant, variable, or expression to the nearest integer. For positive numbers, fractions greater than 0.5 are rounded to the next-higher integer, and fractions less than 0.5 are rounded to the next-lower integer. The opposite is true for negative numbers: Fractions greater than 0.5 are rounded to the next-lower integer, and fractions less than 0.5 are rounded to the next-higher integer.

You can use CINT with an expression of any numeric type; however, its value must be in the range −32768 through 32767, which is the range for signed integers.

Errors

If the value used with CINT is less than −32768 or greater than 32767, QBasic displays the runtime error message "Overflow." If the value is non-numeric, QBasic displays a "Type mismatch" error message. Using CINT with an integer or long integer value doesn't result in an error: The result is merely the same value as the value given.

Example

The following program prompts you to enter a number and then displays the number after converting it to an integer with the CINT function. Enter 0 (zero) to quit the program.

```
DO
    INPUT "Enter a number (enter 0 to quit): "; number
    PRINT "Closest integer is: "; CINT(number)
LOOP UNTIL number = 0    ' exit when 0 is entered
```

CLNG

See also

CINT, FIX, INT

Purpose

The CLNG function converts a numeric constant, numeric variable, or numeric expression to a long-integer value. Generally, you use this function to convert a value so that you can pass the value to a subprogram or function that is expecting a long integer. Fractions are rounded to the nearest integer.

Syntax

CLNG(*expr*)

expr is any combination of numbers or numeric variables (integer, long integer, single precision, or double precision).

Usage

```
PRINT CLNG(-32768.92)
```
Displays −32769.

```
PRINT CLNG(1483555.513)
```
Displays 1483556.

Description

The CLNG function can be used to convert a numeric variable or expression to a 4-byte long integer. Any fractional part is rounded to the nearest integer before conversion. For positive numbers, fractions greater than 0.5 are rounded to the next-higher integer, and fractions less than 0.5 are rounded to the next-lower integer. The opposite is true for negative numbers: Fractions greater than 0.5 are rounded to the next-lower integer, and fractions less than 0.5 are rounded to the next-higher integer.

To pass an integer variable to a subprogram that expects a long integer, call it with a statement such as

```
LongSub& CLNG(value%)
```

The value used with CLNG cannot have a value of less than −2147483648 or greater than 2147483647 (the range for a long integer).

Errors

If the value used with CLNG is outside the range for a long integer, QBasic displays the runtime error message "Overflow." QBasic displays a "Type mismatch" error message if the value is non-numeric.

Example

The following program uses CLNG in preparing to call a subprogram that calculates population growth for each of three generations. Note that the value you enter, which is stored in *number%*, is of type integer. The subprogram *Populate* expects a long integer, *people&*. The CLNG function in the subprogram call converts the argument *number%* to a long integer before passing it to *Populate*.

```
DECLARE SUB Populate (people&)
DO
    INPUT "Enter number of people: ", number%
    IF number% = 0 THEN EXIT DO
    Populate CLNG(number%)
LOOP

SUB Populate (people&)
    ' show population after three generations (very simplistic)
    CONST KIDSPERCOUPLE = 1.8
```

(continued)

continued

```
    FOR generation% = 1 TO 3
        couples& = people& * .25    ' assume half the people have kids
        kids& = couples& * KIDSPERCOUPLE
        people& = people& + kids&
        PRINT "Population after generation "; generation%; ": "; people&
    NEXT generation%
END SUB
```

COS

See also
ATN, SIN, TAN

Purpose
The COS function returns the cosine of an angle.

Syntax
COS(*angle*)

angle is the angle measurement expressed in radians. You can convert degrees to radians by multiplying the number of degrees by the result of π divided by 180.

Usage
```
PRINT COS(57.2958)
```
Displays the cosine of 57.2958, which is .7336411.

```
PRINT COS(0)
```
Displays the cosine of 0, which is 1.

```
PRINT COS(3.1415)
```
Displays the cosine of 3.1415, which is −1.

Description
The COS function returns the cosine of an angle, which must be expressed in radians. To convert an angle from degrees to radians, use the formula *radians = degrees * pi / 180*, in which pi is 3.141593 in single precision or 3.141592653589793 in double precision.

By default, COS returns a single-precision value; however, if you supply a double-precision value, the return value will also be double precision.

Errors
If you specify a non-numeric value with the COS function, QBasic displays a "Type mismatch" error message. If you don't convert a value in degrees to radians before passing it to the COS function, QBasic does not display an error message; however, the result is wrong.

Example

The following program prints a table of the sines and cosines of 19 different angles. The table shows the relationship between the values and the repetition of the values of the sines and cosines. The program uses a PRINT USING statement to show all values carried to four decimal places.

```
CONST PI = 3.141593
CLS
PRINT : PRINT "Degrees    Radians    Sine      Cosine": PRINT
FOR angle% = 0 TO 360 STEP 20
    radians = angle% * PI / 180    ' convert angle to radians
    PRINT USING "###      "; angle%;
    PRINT USING "#.####   "; radians;
    PRINT USING "##.####  "; SIN(radians); COS(radians)
NEXT angle%
```

CSNG

See also

CDBL, CINT, CLNG, FIX, INT

Purpose

The CSNG function converts a numeric constant, numeric variable, or numeric expression to a single-precision floating-point value. This function can be useful if you occasionally need to pass a variable that isn't single precision to a function or subprogram that expects a single-precision value.

Syntax

CSNG(*expr*)

expr is any combination of numbers or numeric variables (integer, long integer, single precision, or double precision).

Usage

```
doublePrec& = 1.23456789
PRINT CSNG(doublePrec&)
```

Displays the value of *doublePrec&* converted to single precision, which is 1.234568.

Description

The CSNG function converts a numeric constant, variable, or expression to a single-precision floating-point number. It rounds the value to the number of decimal places supported by single precision. Using this function has the same effect as assigning a value to a single-precision variable.

Errors

If you specify a non-numeric value with CSNG, QBasic displays a "Type mismatch" error message.

Warnings

Remember that converting a number from a double-precision or long-integer number to a single-precision number might result in loss of accuracy.

Example

The following program stores in a double-precision variable the number the user inputs. The program first displays the value in double precision and then converts it to single precision and displays the new value.

```
DO
     INPUT "Enter value (enter 0 to exit): "; dbl#
     IF dbl# = 0 THEN EXIT DO
     PRINT "Value as double precision: "; dbl#
     PRINT "Value as single precision: "; CSNG(dbl#)
     PRINT
LOOP
```

EXP

See also

LOG

Purpose

The EXP function raises the natural logarithmic base e to a specified power.

Syntax

EXP(*expr*)

expr is any combination of numbers or numeric variables (integer, long integer, single precision, or double precision).

Usage

```
PRINT EXP(10)
```

Displays the value of e raised to the power 10, which is 22026.46.

Description

The natural logarithm of a number is the power to which the base e (a constant with an approximate value of 2.718282) must be raised to obtain the number. The EXP function is the inverse function of the natural log function. EXP returns the value of e to the specified power. (For more information about natural logarithms, see the entry for the LOG function.)

By default, the EXP function returns a single-precision value. However, if you supply a double-precision value, the returned value is also double precision. For example, EXP(1#) displays 2.718281828459045, which is the value of *e* in double precision.

Errors

If you specify a non-numeric value with EXP, QBasic displays a "Type mismatch" error message.

Example

This program demonstrates the meaning of "exponential growth" by displaying the first 20 powers of *e*:

```
PRINT "Power                          e to the power"
FOR power% = 1 TO 20
    PRINT USING "##"; power%;
    PRINT TAB(25);
    PRINT USING "##########.###"; EXP(power%)
NEXT power%
```

FIX

See also

CINT, INT

Purpose

The FIX function truncates a number and returns the remaining integer. This allows a program to discard fractional parts of numbers so that it can perform faster integer arithmetic.

Syntax

FIX(*expr*)

expr is any combination of numbers or numeric variables (integer, long integer, single precision, or double precision).

Usage

```
PRINT FIX(1.5)
```
Displays the integer portion of 1.5, which is 1.

```
PRINT FIX(-1.25)
```
Displays the integer portion of −1.25, which is −1.

Description

The FIX function returns the integer, or whole, part of a specified numeric constant, literal, or expression. The fractional (decimal) part, if any, is simply truncated—no rounding occurs.

The FIX and INT functions perform the same operation with positive values. With negative values, however, FIX returns the next-higher integer, and INT returns the next-lower integer. Thus *FIX(–0.75)* returns 0, but *INT(–0.75)* returns –1.

Because no rounding is performed, using FIX can result in a considerable loss of accuracy.

Errors
If you specify a non-numeric value with FIX, QBasic displays a "Type mismatch" error message.

Example
The following program lets you observe the behavior of the FIX function with values that you input.

```
DO
    INPUT "Enter a number (enter 0 to exit): "; number
    IF number = 0 THEN EXIT DO
    PRINT "Integer part of "; number; " is "; FIX(number)
LOOP
```

INT

See also
CINT, FIX

Purpose
The INT function truncates the fractional part of a number and returns the remaining integer. This function allows a program to trade accuracy for speed by discarding fractions so that QBasic can use integer arithmetic, which is faster than floating-point arithmetic.

Syntax
INT(*expr*)

expr is any combination of numbers or numeric variables (integer, long integer, single precision, or double precision).

Usage
```
PRINT INT(3.33)
```
Displays the integer portion of 3.33, which is 3.

```
PRINT INT(-1.89)
```
Displays the next-lower integer, which is –2.

Description

The INT function returns the integer, or whole, part of a specified numeric constant, literal, or expression. The fractional (decimal) part, if any, is simply truncated—no rounding occurs.

The FIX and INT functions perform the same operation with positive values. With negative values, however, FIX returns the next-higher integer and INT returns the next-lower integer. Thus *FIX(−0.75)* returns 0, but *INT(−0.75)* returns −1.

Because no rounding is performed, using INT can result in a considerable loss of accuracy.

Errors

If you specify a non-numeric expression with INT, QBasic displays a "Type mismatch" error message.

Example

The following program demonstrates how much more quickly QBasic performs math operations when you convert numbers to integers by using INT. Of course, you must determine whether the loss of accuracy is acceptable in your application.

```
' perform floating-point math
floatA = 1.8975: floatB = 2.113
time1 = TIMER

CLS : PRINT "Seconds elapsed for floating-point math: ";
FOR time% = 1 TO 5000
    temp = floatA * floatB
NEXT time%
time2 = TIMER
PRINT time2 - time1

' perform integer math
intA% = INT(floatA): intB% = INT(floatB)
time1 = TIMER

PRINT "Seconds elapsed for integer math: ";
FOR time% = 1 TO 5000
    temp% = intA% * intB%
NEXT time%
time2 = TIMER
PRINT time2 - time1
```

LOG

See also
EXP

Purpose
The LOG function returns the natural logarithm of a number. (Natural logarithms should not be confused with common logarithms, which are based on 10 rather than on *e*, which is approximately 2.718282.)

Syntax
LOG(*expr*)

expr is any combination of numbers or numeric variables (integer, long integer, single precision, or double precision). However, *expr* must be greater than 0.

Usage
```
PRINT LOG(2.718282)
```
Displays the natural logarithm of *e*, which is 1.

```
PRINT LOG(100)
```
Displays the natural logarithm of 100, which is 4.60517.

Description
The natural logarithm function finds the power to which the constant *e* (2.718282 in single precision) must be raised to obtain a given number. Because *e* to the third power is 20.08554, for example, the natural logarithm of 20.08554 is 3. You can find the natural logarithm of a number by using the LOG function.

The LOG function by default returns the natural logarithm of a number in single precision. However, if the given value is double precision, the function returns a double-precision value.

Errors
If you specify a non-numeric value with EXP, QBasic displays a "Type mismatch" error message. If you use a numeric value that is less than or equal to 0, QBasic displays an "Illegal function call" error message.

Example
The following program displays the base 10 logarithmic curve. The program uses the function *Log10!* to convert the natural logarithm to a base 10 logarithm, which is multiplied by a scaling factor of 100 so that the progression is large enough to show clearly on the screen.

```
DECLARE FUNCTION Log10! (number%)
SCREEN 9            ' EGA or VGA adapter
CONST XMAX = 640

FOR x% = 1 TO XMAX
    PSET (x%, Log10!(x%) * 100)
NEXT x%

FUNCTION Log10! (number%)
    Log10! = LOG(number%) / LOG(10!)
END FUNCTION
```

RANDOMIZE

See also

RND, TIMER

Purpose

Use the RANDOMIZE statement to specify a particular initial value or "seed value" for the random-number generator, thus specifying the random-number series to be used when the program calls the RND function.

If you use the value returned by the TIMER function as the seed, RANDOMIZE generates the unpredictable random numbers that are necessary for applications such as games and simulations. (The TIMER function returns the number of seconds that have elapsed since midnight. For more information, see the TIMER function in Chapter 10, "Timing, Date, and Time.")

Syntax

RANDOMIZE [*expr*]

expr is any combination of numbers or numeric variables (integer, long integer, single precision, or double precision).

If no value is specified, RANDOMIZE prompts the user for a seed value.

Usage

```
RANDOMIZE 10
```
Specifies the value 10 as the seed for the random-number generator.

```
RANDOMIZE TIMER
```
Generates a set of random numbers using the value returned by the TIMER function as the seed.

Description

The RANDOMIZE statement specifies a seed for the random-number generator. (You can then use the RND function to return random values from the set of values generated.)

You can use any type of numeric expression with RANDOMIZE. If you don't specify a value in the statement, QBasic prompts the user for a value in the range −32768 through 32767. If a program doesn't include a RANDOMIZE statement, all calls to the RND function return the values generated by using the seed 0.

Note that additional RANDOMIZE statements in the same program reseed the random-number generator; however, they do not generate the entire random-number sequence from the beginning. If the program generates three random numbers before calling RANDOMIZE with a new seed, the fourth random number is the fourth value in the sequence of the new seed.

For games, the most convenient way to ensure that each run uses a different series of random numbers is to use the statement *RANDOMIZE TIMER*. (The TIMER function returns the number of seconds that have elapsed on the system clock since midnight.)

Errors

If you specify a non-numeric value with RANDOMIZE, QBasic displays a "Type mismatch" error message.

Example

The following program uses RANDOMIZE to initialize the random-number generator and then "flips" the requested number of "coins." The program takes into account the small chance of a coin landing on its edge.

```
RANDOMIZE                ' prompts user for seed
CLS : INPUT "Enter number of coins to flip: ", numFlips%
heads% = 0: tails% = 0
edgies% = 0              ' coins that landed on their edge

FOR flip% = 1 TO numFlips%
    randVal = RND(1)
    IF randVal > .5005 THEN
        heads% = heads% + 1
    ELSEIF randVal < .4995 THEN
        tails% = tails% + 1
    ELSE edgies% = edgies% + 1
    END IF
NEXT flip%

PRINT "Total flips: "; numFlips%
PRINT "Heads = "; heads%
PRINT "Tails: "; tails%
PRINT edgies%; " coins landed on their edge."
```

RND

See also

RANDOMIZE, TIMER

Purpose

The RND function returns a random single-precision floating-point number between 0 and 1. The same sequence of random numbers is generated each time the program runs unless you use the RANDOMIZE statement to specify a different sequence.

Syntax

RND[(*expr*)]

expr, an optional parameter, is any combination of numbers or numeric variables (integer, long integer, single precision, or double precision). The value of *expr* dictates the value returned by RND, as described in the "Description" section below.

Usage

```
PRINT RND
```
Displays a random value.

```
PRINT RND(0)
```
Displays the value of the last random number.

Description

The RND function returns what is called a "pseudo-random" number. This kind of number is generated from a stored value (called a seed) using a formula designed to produce numbers that have no pattern or order and thus appear to be random. Each seed, however, creates a fixed sequence of numbers: For example, if the program contains no previous RANDOMIZE statement, the first three values returned by RND are always .7055475, .533424, and .5795186.

The RANDOMIZE statement changes the seed and thus the sequence generated. You can use RANDOMIZE with a random seed returned by the TIMER function to generate thoroughly random numbers.

The value specified in a call to RND dictates the value RND returns. If the value is greater than 0 or is not specified, RND returns the next random value in the sequence. If the value specified is equal to 0, RND returns the random value that was last returned. Finally, if the value is less than 0, RND returns the random number associated with that value.

Many applications (such as simulations and games) require random integers that fall within a specified range. To create a random integer within the range *lower* through *upper*, use the expression

```
INT((upper - lower + 1) * RND + lower)
```

Errors

If you specify a non-numeric value with RND, QBasic displays a "Type mismatch" error message.

Example

The following program defines a function called *RandInt%* that returns a value returned by RND as an integer in a specified range. The program uses this function to set random *x*- and *y*-coordinates, radius, and color, and uses that information to draw circles of varying position, size, and color on the screen.

The DO...LOOP in the main module continues to draw circles until the user presses any key.

```
DECLARE FUNCTION RandInt% (lowest!, highest!)

SCREEN 9          ' use 9 for EGA, 1 for CGA, and 12 for VGA
maxX = 640        ' use 640 for EGA or VGA, and 320 for CGA
maxY = 350        ' use 350 for EGA, 200 for CGA, and 480 for VGA
colors = 15       ' use 15 for EGA or VGA, 3 for CGA

DO
    x% = RandInt(-maxX, maxX)              ' random x-coordinate
    y% = RandInt(-maxY, maxY)              ' random y-coordinate
    radius = RandInt(5, 50)                ' random radius
    circleColor% = RandInt(0, colors)      ' random color
    CIRCLE (x%, y%), radius, (circleColor%) ' draw circle
    PAINT (x%, y%), circleColor%           ' fill in circle
LOOP WHILE INKEY$ = ""                     ' continue until user presses a key

FUNCTION RandInt% (lowest, highest)
    ' return a random number between lowest and highest
    RandInt = INT((highest - lowest + 1) * RND + lowest)
END FUNCTION
```

SGN

See also

ABS

Purpose

The SGN function returns the value of the sign (negative, positive, or 0) of a number or a numeric expression. You might use this function to quickly determine the direction in which an object on the screen is moving or whether a temperature is above or below 0 degrees.

Syntax

SGN(*expr*)

expr is any combination of numbers or numeric variables (integer, long integer, single precision, or double precision).

Usage

```
PRINT SGN(-145)
```
Displays the sign of −145, which is −1.

```
PRINT SGN(0)
```
Displays the sign of 0, which is 0.

```
PRINT SGN(12645.33)
```
Displays the sign of 12645.33, which is 1.

Description

The SGN function tests whether a value is negative, positive, or 0. For example, the following two tests are equivalent:

```
number < 0
SGN(number) = -1
```

Remember that SGN(0) returns 0, which might not be appropriate if you are treating 0 as a positive value.

Errors

If you specify a non-numeric value with SGN, QBasic displays a "Type mismatch" error message.

Example

The following program generates random numbers centered at 0; approximately half the random numbers are positive and half are negative. The program then uses SGN to detect a number's sign, and a SOUND statement plays a low "A" note for a negative number and a higher "A" note for a positive one. (Durations of the tones are random.)

```
CONST LOW = 220      ' the note "A"
CONST HIGH = 440     ' the note "A" one octave higher

DO
    rndVal = RND(1) - .5          ' distribute random value around 0
    duration = ABS(rndVal * 50)   ' specify the tones duration
    IF SGN(rndVal) = -1 THEN
        SOUND LOW, duration
    ELSE
        SOUND HIGH, duration
    END IF
    SOUND 32767, 9.1              ' about half a second of silence
LOOP WHILE INKEY$ = ""
```

SIN

See also

ATN, COS, TAN

Purpose

The SIN function returns the sine of an angle.

Syntax

SIN(*angle*)

angle is the angle measurement expressed in radians. You can convert degrees to radians by multiplying the number of degrees by the result of π divided by 180.

Usage

```
PRINT SIN(.1)
```

Displays the sine of .1, which is 9.983342E-02.

Description

The SIN function returns the sine of an angle, which must be expressed in radians. To convert an angle from degrees to radians, use the formula *radians = degrees * pi / 180*, in which pi is 3.141593 in single precision or 3.141592653589793 in double precision.

By default, SIN returns a single-precision value. However, if you specify a double-precision value, the return value will also be double precision.

Errors

If you specify a non-numeric value, QBasic displays a "Type mismatch" error message. If you use degrees, no error message is generated; however, the result is wrong.

Example

Imagine that you are a mountaineer who has thrown a grappling hook with a line attached so that the hook is stuck high on a rock. You know the length of the line, and you measure the angle defined by the line and the ground. The following program determines the height of the hook from the ground.

```
CONST PI = 3.141593
CONST DEGREETORAD = PI / 180
CLS

DO
    INPUT "Number of feet of line paid out (enter 0 to quit): ", length
    IF length = 0 THEN EXIT DO
    INPUT "Angle of line to ground (in degrees): ", angle
    radians = angle * DEGREETORAD
    height = length * SIN(radians)
    PRINT "Height of hook is "; height; " feet."
LOOP
```

SQR

Purpose

The SQR function returns the square root of a numeric constant, numeric variable, or numeric expression.

Syntax

SQR(*expr*)

expr is any combination of numbers or numeric variables (integer, long integer, single precision, or double precision), but it must be a positive value (0 or greater).

Usage

```
PRINT SQR(16)
```
Displays the square root of 16, which is 4.

```
PRINT SQR(1000)
```
Displays the square root of 1000, which is 31.62278.

Description

The SQR function returns the square root of a positive numeric value (0 or greater). The value returned is single precision by default. However, if you specify a double-precision value, the return value is also double precision.

QBasic has no function that squares a number; instead, you must use the exponentiation operator for this purpose. Thus the square of the variable *number* can be calculated by *number* ∧ *2* or *number * number*.

Errors

If you specify a non-numeric value for SQR, QBasic displays a "Type mismatch" error message. If the value is numeric but is less than 0, QBasic displays an "Illegal function call" error message.

Example

The following program uses the Pythagorean theorem ($c^2 = a^2 + b^2$, where *a* is the length of the adjacent side, *b* is the length of the opposite side, and *c* is the length of the hypotenuse) to calculate the length of the hypotenuse of a right triangle.

```
CLS
DO
    INPUT "Length of adjacent side (enter 0 to quit): "; adjacent
    IF adjacent = 0 THEN EXIT DO
    INPUT "Length of opposite side: "; opposite
    hypot = SQR(adjacent ^ 2 + opposite ^ 2)
    PRINT "Length of hypotenuse is: "; hypot: PRINT
LOOP
```

TAN

See also
ATN, COS, SIN

Purpose
The TAN function returns the tangent of an angle.

Syntax
TAN(*angle*)

angle is the angle measurement expressed in radians. You can convert degrees to radians by multiplying the number of degrees by the result of π divided by 180.

Usage
```
PRINT TAN(.75)
```
Displays the tangent of .75, which is .9315965.

```
PRINT TAN(3.1415)
```
Displays the tangent of 3.1415, which is −9.265741E-05.

Description
The TAN function returns the tangent of an angle, which must be expressed in radians. To convert an angle from degrees to radians, use the formula *radians = degrees * pi / 180*, in which pi is either 3.141593 in single precision or 3.141592653589793 in double precision.

By default, TAN returns a single-precision value. However, if you specify a double-precision value, the return value is also double precision.

Errors
If you specify a non-numeric value, QBasic displays a "Type mismatch" error message.

Warnings
Avoid using the tangent of 90 degrees, which is equal to infinity. QBasic does not display an "Overflow" error message in this case; it merely returns a very large number.

Example
The following program prints a table of angles and their tangents.

```
CONST PI = 3.141592653589793#        ' pi in double precision
CONST DEGREETORAD = PI / 180

PRINT "Angle in Degrees        Tan(Angle)"

FOR angle% = 0 TO 85 STEP 5
    PRINT USING "##"; angle%; TAB(26);
    PRINT USING "###.######"; TAN(angle% * DEGREETORAD)
NEXT angle%
```

CHAPTER 8

Simple I/O

Introduction

This chapter discusses the interface between QBasic programs and users. It includes the statements and functions that let your programs

- Generate prompts and accept data from the keyboard
- Check for keypresses without interrupting program execution
- Respond to input from the function keys, the direction keys, and nonprinting key combinations
- Display text at any location on the screen
- Display text and numeric values in a variety of formats
- Change the number of rows and columns of text that can be displayed on the screen
- Define the size of the viewport in which text is displayed
- Clear the display or the specified viewport
- Control the size of the cursor

Table 8-1 lists the QBasic input/output statements and functions alphabetically.

Statement or function	Description
CLS	Clears the display or specified viewport
CSRLIN	Returns the current cursor row
INKEY$	Reads a character from the keyboard
INPUT	Prompts for and reads input from the keyboard
INPUT$	Reads a specified number of characters from a file or device; if no file is specified, INPUT$ reads input from the keyboard
LINE INPUT	Prompts for and reads a string of characters from the keyboard
LOCATE	Positions the text cursor at the specified row and column and specifies the size of the cursor
POS	Returns the current cursor column
PRINT	Displays text and data on the screen at the current cursor position
PRINT USING	Displays numeric and string data in a specified format

Table 8-1. *(continued)*
Input/output statements and functions.

Table 8-1. *(continued)*

Statement or function	Description
SPC	Advances the cursor or print head by a specified number of columns relative to the last character printed
TAB	Advances the cursor or print head to the specified column position
VIEW PRINT	Defines the area of the screen to which the program must direct all text output
WIDTH	Defines the number of rows and columns on the screen or other device or sets the width of a file
WRITE	Outputs data (including delimiters) to the screen or a file

Keyboard Input

QBasic provides three methods for retrieving keyboard input. The standard method, using the INPUT statement, pauses the program while the user types characters; execution does not resume until the user presses the Enter key to indicate that input is complete.

QBasic offers two versions of the INPUT statement. One version—simply INPUT—lets the user enter both numeric and character data and then assigns the data to one or more variables of the appropriate type. Another version—the LINE INPUT statement—accepts data entered at the keyboard as one string of characters and then assigns all the characters to a single string variable. The advantage of LINE INPUT is that it enables the program to accept any type of data.

Both the INPUT and LINE INPUT statements can display a prompt that describes the kind of input you want the user to enter. They also let the user edit or make corrections to the data before entering it. Table 8-3 in the INPUT entry lists the key combinations that can be used to edit input.

Another method for retrieving keyboard input—using the INKEY$ function—does not interrupt the program. INKEY$ merely checks to see whether a key has been pressed: If so, it immediately returns the character; if not, it returns a null (or empty) string. This method also lets your program respond to keys that do not produce printable characters, such as the direction keys, Pg Up, Pg Dn, and the function keys. Table 8-2, in the INKEY$ entry, lists the nonprinting keys that INKEY$ can trap.

The third method for retrieving keyboard input—using the INPUT$ function—reads a specified number of characters from an input device, which is usually a file that has been opened for input. However, if you do not specify a file, INPUT$ reads from the keyboard the requisite number of characters. Using INPUT$ with the keyboard is not recommended because it doesn't let the user edit input, it doesn't echo the input on the screen, and it doesn't accept nonprinting characters. Furthermore, the user must enter the exact number of characters specified because INPUT$ does not recognize the Enter key as a signal of input termination.

Text Output

The QBasic PRINT statement displays text and numeric values on the screen. You can use this statement to display literal text and the contents of numeric or string variables. PRINT displays output beginning at the current cursor position and continues until it has displayed all specified characters or variables.

The WRITE statement, which is similar to PRINT, outputs data to the screen in teletype fashion. It updates the cursor position after displaying each character and scrolls the display when output reaches the bottom line of the screen. Unlike PRINT, however, WRITE encloses the strings it displays in quotation marks and separates all items in the list with commas.

Use WRITE primarily to output data to a file; even when you use WRITE to output to the screen, the statement formats the data as if it were writing it to a sequential file.

Formatted Printing

The PRINT statement does not format output. However, another version of the statement does: PRINT USING lets you specify a template string containing the fields in which the statement displays the output. You can then use this template to print a column of figures, for example, in which all decimal points are aligned. PRINT USING is particularly useful for designing reports or lists that must be presented in a readable way.

Two other QBasic functions can also help you format lines of text. The SPC function inserts a specified number of blank spaces into a line that was output by PRINT; this lets you separate printed items and produce a neat display. TAB performs a similar function except that it moves the cursor to a specified position on the line; this function lets you easily indent and align the columns of a report.

The Text Cursor

As previously mentioned, the PRINT, PRINT USING, and WRITE statements output text to the screen at the current cursor position. You can use the LOCATE statement to move the cursor to any position on the screen so that subsequent printing proceeds from that position. The TAB and SPC functions also move the cursor, but only within the current screen row.

LOCATE lets you move the cursor to a specified row and column. It also lets you change the size of the cursor—from invisible to the usual underline to a full block.

QBasic also provides two functions that report the current position of the cursor. POS returns the cursor column, and CSRLIN returns the cursor row.

Figure 8-1.
Rows and columns on the standard text screen.

Screen Dimensions

The standard text screen, which is displayed when QBasic runs a program, can contain up to 2000 characters in a grid of 25 rows by 80 columns. (Figure 8-1 illustrates the organization of the standard text screen.) QBasic lets you change this format, however, by using the WIDTH (Screen) statement, which, despite its name, can also change the height of the screen.

QBasic offers only two widths—80 columns (the default) and 40 columns. The latter displays broader characters. You cannot change the screen height (the number of rows displayed) unless your computer has an EGA, VGA, or MCGA adapter: the default of 25 rows can be increased to 43 with an EGA and to either 43 or 50 with a VGA. The VGA and MCGA adapters can also display text formats of 80 by 30 and 80 by 60 characters, but only in the graphics screen modes 11 and 12. (See the SCREEN (Statement) entry in Chapter 11, "Graphics.")

The WIDTH statement affects the appearance of the output of a program, not the appearance of the QBasic environment. Although 80 columns by 25 rows is the standard mode, you can change the default of the environment by starting QBasic with the /H switch. For example,

```
QBASIC /H
```

instructs QBasic to display the QBasic environment in the highest resolution your video adapter permits, producing a text format of 80 by 43 characters with an EGA and 80 by 50 characters with a VGA.

The Text Viewport

QBasic also lets you restrict text output to only part of the entire screen. This approach can be advantageous when you combine text and graphics on the same screen because it prevents text from overwriting the graphics display.

The VIEW PRINT statement lets you define a specified number of screen rows as the text viewport. After calling the statement, the actions of all PRINT, PRINT USING, and WRITE statements are confined to the text viewport and do not spill into the surrounding areas of the screen. The following statement limits text output to screen rows 20 through 23:

```
VIEW PRINT 20 TO 23
```

You cannot move the text cursor outside the text viewport after you initialize it; therefore, the LOCATE statement works only with row numbers inside the viewport area.

Clearing the Display

In addition to the statements that position text on the screen, QBasic provides one statement that lets you erase that text when you no longer need it. By default, CLS clears the entire screen. You can, however, restrict the action of CLS so that it clears only the text viewport, leaving any graphics on the screen intact. Or, if you have also defined a graphics viewport (discussed in the VIEW entry in Chapter 11, "Graphics"), you can direct CLS to clear only the contents of the graphics viewport.

Related Reading

Davies, Russ. *Mapping the IBM PC and PCjr.* Greensboro, N.C.: Compute! Books, 1985.

Wilton, Richard. *Programmer's Guide to PC and PS/2 Video Systems.* Redmond, Wash.: Microsoft Press, 1987.

CLS

See also
VIEW, VIEW PRINT, WIDTH (Screen)

Purpose
The CLS statement clears the viewport and returns the cursor to the upper left corner of the viewport. All versions of Basic provide this statement; however, QBasic extends the statement's range by letting you clear from the screen only graphics, only text, or both.

Syntax
CLS [0 ¦ 1 ¦ 2]

Usage
CLS

Clears the currently active viewport. If neither a graphics viewport nor a text viewport is defined, the statement clears the entire screen.

CLS 0

Clears the entire screen, regardless of the currently active viewport.

Description
CLS called without an argument does not clear the QBasic screen; it clears the currently active viewport. Often the active viewport is the full screen. However, you can also divide the screen into separate viewports for text (discussed in the VIEW PRINT entry) and graphics (discussed in the VIEW entry); if you do this, the CLS statement clears only the one in use.

QBasic also lets you specify the viewport to be cleared by including an argument with the CLS statement. The statement *CLS 1* clears the graphics viewport, *CLS 2* clears the text viewport, and *CLS 0* clears the entire display.

When you clear the text viewport, QBasic fills it with blank spaces in the current background color and returns the cursor to the upper left corner of the viewport. If no text viewport has been defined, QBasic clears the entire screen and returns the cursor to row 1, column 1 (the home position). Note that when CLS clears a text viewport it does not clear the bottom line of the screen, which is called the function-key display.

To clear the text viewport and set a new background color, use CLS with the COLOR statement. For example, the statements

COLOR , 1
CLS 2

clear the text viewport and create a blue background. All subsequent text is printed on a blue background until you use COLOR again to change it.

When CLS clears the graphics viewport, it resets all pixels to the background color and resets the graphics cursor to its default position, the center of the viewport. If the next graphics statement uses relative addressing (by using the STEP keyword), QBasic calculates the location of the specified point from the center point of the viewport.

Example

The following program uses CLS to change the entire screen to a blue background color. It then fills the screen with asterisks, defines a text viewport, and uses CLS to clear only the text viewport.

```
COLOR , 1                    ' set background color to blue
CLS 0                        ' fill screen with blue background
PRINT STRING$(1920, "*");    ' fill screen with asterisks
LOCATE 25, 1                 ' move to bottom line
PRINT "Press a key";         ' display message
SLEEP                        ' wait until user presses a key
VIEW PRINT 10 TO 20          ' set the text viewport
CLS                          ' clear the text viewport
END
```

CSRLIN

See also

LOCATE, POINT, POS, WIDTH (Screen)

Purpose

The CSRLIN function returns the row number (vertical coordinate) of the text cursor. (Use the POS function to return the cursor's column number.)

Syntax

CSRLIN

Usage

yPosition% = CSRLIN

Assigns the screen row in which the cursor is located to the variable *yPosition%*.

Description

QBasic includes two functions that report the current position of the cursor. The CSRLIN (cursor line) function returns the number of the current cursor row. Usually this number is an integer in the range 1 through 25; however, it might extend to 43 for systems using EGA adapters or to 60 for VGA and MCGA adapters. The POS function returns the column number of the cursor. (See the POS entry.)

Example

Programs that branch to subroutines whenever an event-trapping statement is triggered need to preserve the current cursor position so that the position can be restored when the subroutine returns. The following program uses the TIMER statement and the CSRLIN function to display the time continuously while the program outputs other information to the screen. Updating the clock does not interfere with the output to the screen.

```
CLS : TIMER ON
ON TIMER(1) GOSUB Tick
DO
    LOCATE 2, 1: clr% = clr% + 1
    IF clr% > 7 THEN clr% = 1
    COLOR , clr%
    DO                              ' color the screen one line at a time
        PRINT " ";
        IF INKEY$ <> "" THEN        ' see whether user pressed a key
            xCursor% = POS(0): yCursor% = CSRLIN      ' find position of cursor
            COLOR 14, 4: LOCATE 24, 1: PRINT SPACE$(80);
            COLOR 14, 4: LOCATE 24, 1: PRINT SPACE$(80);
            LOCATE 24, 34, 1: PRINT "Quit (Y/N)? ";
            response$ = UCASE$(INPUT$(1))
            COLOR 7, 0: LOCATE 24, 1: PRINT SPACE$(80);
            COLOR , clr%
            IF response$ = "Y" THEN
                done% = -1
            ELSE
                LOCATE yCursor%, xCursor%, 0
            END IF
        END IF
    LOOP UNTIL CSRLIN > 22
LOOP UNTIL done%
COLOR 7, 0
END

' this subroutine is executed once per second
Tick:
    xStop% = POS(0): yStop% = CSRLIN           ' save the position of the cursor
    COLOR 11, 0: LOCATE 1, 36: PRINT TIME$;
    COLOR , clr%: LOCATE yStop%, xStop%        ' reset the cursor
RETURN
```

INKEY$

See also

INPUT, INPUT$, LINE INPUT, ON KEY(n) GOSUB

Purpose

INKEY$ reads a character from the keyboard. QBasic offers several functions and statements that let a program accept data from the keyboard. In most cases, however, those statements force the program to stop and wait until the user enters information. The INKEY$ function is an exception; it reads a character from the keyboard and returns immediately, whether a character is available or not. INKEY$ also enables your programs to respond to special keys, such as the function keys or the direction keys.

Syntax

INKEY$

Usage

```
response$ = UCASE$(INKEY$)
```

Converts a character from the keyboard to uppercase and then assigns it to *response$*.

Description

When you press a key on the keyboard, your computer stores the character in a buffer until the program is ready to process it. The standard buffer can contain as many as 15 characters. INKEY$ checks the buffer to see whether any keys have already been pressed. If the buffer contains characters, INKEY$ reads the first character and returns it to the program; otherwise, INKEY$ returns a null string. INKEY$ never waits for a keypress, so it never interrupts program execution. (For a sample program that displays the contents of the keyboard buffer, see the "Example" section in the INPUT$ entry.)

INKEY$ returns the 1-byte or 2-byte string representing the key that was pressed. For ASCII characters and IBM extended characters, INKEY$ returns a 1-byte string; for function keys, INKEY$ returns a 2-byte string. For a list of ASCII characters and IBM extended characters, see Appendix C, "ASCII Characters."

The set of function keys includes the direction keys, Pg Up, Pg Dn, Home, End and keys F1 through F10 (F1 through F12 if you have an extended keyboard). The set of function keys also includes the alphanumeric keys combined with the Alt key. When a function key is pressed, INKEY$ returns a 2-byte string consisting of a 0 byte (a character whose ASCII value is 0) followed by the key's scan code.

Every key on the keyboard has a different scan code, even the ASCII keys. However, INKEY$ reads only the scan codes of function keys. The following statements assign to the variable *scan%* the scan code of any function key that has been pressed:

```
ky$ = INKEY$
IF LEN(ky$) > 1 THEN scan% = ASC(MID$(ky$, 2, 1)
```

Table 8-2, on the following page, lists the scan codes of all the function keys that INKEY$ can trap. The list includes only those keys that return a scan code to the QBasic INKEY$ function.

Function keys F11 and F12 are available only with extended keyboards. Alt-minus and Alt-plus can be trapped only on the main keyboard; the − and + keys on the numeric keypad do not return a scan code when used with Alt.

Example

The program following Table 8-2 monitors the keyboard and reports the ASCII values and scan codes of each key pressed. It also displays the character returned if doing so does not disturb the display.

KEYBOARD SCAN CODES

Key	Scan code	Key	Scan code	Key	Scan code
Alt-A	30	Alt-0	129	Ctrl-F9	102
Alt-B	48	Alt--	130	Ctrl-F10	103
Alt-C	46	Alt-=	131	Ctrl-F11	137
Alt-D	32	F1	59	Ctrl-F12	138
Alt-E	18	F2	60	Alt-F1	104
Alt-F	33	F3	61	Alt-F2	105
Alt-G	34	F4	62	Alt-F3	106
Alt-H	35	F5	63	Alt-F4	107
Alt-I	23	F6	64	Alt-F5	108
Alt-J	36	F7	65	Alt-F6	109
Alt-K	37	F8	66	Alt-F7	110
Alt-L	38	F9	67	Alt-F8	111
Alt-M	50	F10	68	Alt-F9	112
Alt-N	49	F11	133	Alt-F10	113
Alt-O	24	F12	134	Alt-F11	139
Alt-P	25	Shift-F1	84	Alt-F12	140
Alt-Q	16	Shift-F2	85	Home	71
Alt-R	19	Shift-F3	86	Up direction	72
Alt-S	31	Shift-F4	87	Pg Up	73
Alt-T	20	Shift-F5	88	Left direction	75
Alt-U	22	Shift-F6	89	Right direction	77
Alt-V	47	Shift-F7	90	End	79
Alt-W	17	Shift-F8	91	Down direction	80
Alt-X	45	Shift-F9	92	Pg Dn	81
Alt-Y	21	Shift-F10	93	Ins	82
Alt-Z	44	Shift-F11	135	Del	83
Alt-1	120	Shift-F12	136	Ctrl-Print Scrn	114
Alt-2	121	Ctrl-F1	94	Ctrl-Left direction	115
Alt-3	122	Ctrl-F2	95		
Alt-4	123	Ctrl-F3	96	Ctrl-Right direction	116
Alt-5	124	Ctrl-F4	97		
Alt-6	125	Ctrl-F5	98	Ctrl-End	117
Alt-7	126	Ctrl-F6	99	Ctrl-Pg Dn	118
Alt-8	127	Ctrl-F7	100	Ctrl-Home	119
Alt-9	128	Ctrl-F8	101	Ctrl-Pg Up	132

Table 8-2.
Scan codes trapped by INKEY$.

```
CLS : LOCATE 10, 1, 0
PRINT "ASCII Code :      Character :      Scan Code :";
DO
    DO
        response$ = INKEY$
    LOOP WHILE response$ = ""         ' wait for keypress
    asciiCode% = ASC(response$)       ' find ASCII code
    LOCATE 10, 14: PRINT USING "###"; asciiCode%;     ' display ASCII code
    LOCATE 10, 30
    IF asciiCode% > 31 THEN           ' display printable characters
        PRINT CHR$(asciiCode%);
    ELSE
        PRINT " ";                    ' erase previous character
    END IF
    LOCATE 10, 45
    IF LEN(response$) > 1 THEN        ' display scan code of function keys
        scanCode% = ASC(MID$(response$, 2, 1))
        PRINT USING "###"; scanCode%;
    ELSE
        PRINT "   ";                  ' erase previous character
    END IF
LOOP UNTIL asciiCode% = 27            ' exit loop if user presses Esc
END
```

INPUT

See also
INKEY$, INPUT$, LINE INPUT

Purpose
The INPUT statement retrieves data from the keyboard and places the data into variables.

Syntax
INPUT [;] ["*prompt*" {;|,}] *var* [, *var*...]

A semicolon immediately after the keyword INPUT keeps the cursor on the same line after the user presses Enter.

prompt is an optional string of text that is displayed immediately before the entry field.

A semicolon immediately after the prompt directs INPUT to display a question mark before the entry field. A comma immediately after the prompt suppresses the question mark. If no prompt is used, INPUT displays only a question mark.

var is the QBasic variable to which input is assigned. A variable can be of any type or precision. It can also be an element of either an array or a user-defined type. To use more than one variable, separate the variable names with commas.

Usage

```
INPUT "What is your reponse", response$
```
Pauses program execution and displays the prompt and a question mark until the user enters a string of characters. The string is then assigned to the variable *response$*.

```
INPUT a%, b!, c&(d%), e$
```
Waits for the user to enter three numbers and a string and then assigns them to variables of the appropriate type.

Description

The INPUT statement lets a program accept characters from the keyboard until input is terminated when the user presses Enter. However, the data items that are entered must match—in type and number—the variables to which they are assigned.

You can add a prompt to the INPUT statement to tell the user what kind of data the program expects. If a semicolon follows the prompt string, INPUT prints a question mark after the prompt. If a comma follows the prompt string, INPUT suppresses the question mark.

INPUT echoes to the screen all printable characters that are entered. It accepts characters until the user presses the Enter key. This carriage return is not considered part of the entered data even though it usually causes the cursor to move to the beginning of the next line. Using a semicolon immediately after the INPUT statement suppresses the carriage return and leaves the cursor on the same line, immediately to the right of the last character entered.

If INPUT requires more than one item, the user must insert a comma between input items. The INPUT statement assumes that a new item starts with the first character after a comma that is not a white-space character (space, tab, linefeed, or carriage return). The user can enclose strings of characters in quote marks if the string must contain leading spaces, colons, or commas.

The INPUT statement lets the user edit the characters in the entry field before entering them, and it provides a set of editing keys for this purpose. Table 8-3 lists the key combinations that move the cursor and that insert and delete characters within the entry field.

Errors

Entering too few items or data of the wrong type does not generate an error. Instead, QBasic displays the "Redo from start" error message. If this occurs, the user must retype all of the items in the input field. INPUT does not assign any data items to variables until all are entered correctly.

Key combination	Description
Left direction key or Ctrl-]	Moves cursor one character to the left
Ctrl-Left direction key or Ctrl-B	Moves cursor one word to the left
Right direction key or Ctrl-\	Moves cursor one character to the right
Ctrl-Right direction key or Ctrl-F	Moves cursor one word to the right
Home or Ctrl-K	Moves cursor to the beginning of the entry field
End or Ctrl-N	Moves cursor to the end of the entry field
Ins or Ctrl-R	Toggles insert mode. When insert mode is on (indicated by a block cursor) and characters are inserted, any characters that follow the cursor are shifted to the right
Tab or Ctrl-I	Tabs cursor to the right
Delete	Deletes the character at the cursor
Ctrl-End or Ctrl-E	Deletes characters from the cursor position through the end of the entry field
Esc or Ctrl-U	Erases the entire entry field
Backspace or Ctrl-H	Deletes the character to the left of the cursor and moves the cursor to the left. If the cursor is in the first position of the entry field, the character at the cursor is deleted
Ctrl-T	Toggles the function-key label display on the status line
Enter or Ctrl-M	Terminates input and stores the data from the input field
Ctrl-Break or Ctrl-C	Aborts input and terminates the program

Table 8-3.
INPUT editing key combinations.

Example

INPUT is most useful when a program needs to accept several data items of different types at the same time. The following program, for example, asks the user to type a name and a complete birthdate. It then uses the information to calculate the number of days remaining until the user's birthday.

```
DECLARE FUNCTION Date2days& (month%, day%, year&)

month1% = VAL(LEFT$(DATE$, 2)):      ' extract current month
day1% = VAL(MID$(DATE$, 4, 2)):      ' extract day of the month
year1& = VAL(RIGHT$(DATE$, 4)):      ' extract current year

CLS : PRINT
PRINT "Enter your name and date of birth"
INPUT "(Name, Month, Day, Year) > ", name$, month2%, day2%, year2&

diff& = Date2days&(month1%, day1%, year1&) - Date2days&(month2%, day2%, year1&)
PRINT : PRINT
```

(continued)

continued

```
IF diff& > 0 THEN
    PRINT diff&; "days since your birthday,"; name$
    PRINT " What presents did you get?"
ELSEIF diff& < 0 THEN
    PRINT ABS(diff&); "days to your birthday,"; name$
    PRINT " What are you expecting?"
ELSE
    PRINT "It's your birthday TODAY, "; name$
    PRINT " - How nice!"
END IF
END

FUNCTION Date2days& (month%, day%, year&) STATIC
    ' convert date to a numeric value
    temp& = year& * 356 + INT((year& - 1) \ 4) + (month% - 1) * 28
    temp2& = VAL(MID$("000303060811131619212426", (month% - 1) * 2 + 1, 2))
    Date2days& = temp& + temp2& - ((month% > 2) AND (year& MOD 4 = 0)) + day%
END FUNCTION
```

INPUT$ (Keyboard)

See also

INKEY$, INPUT, LINE INPUT

Purpose

The INPUT$ (Keyboard) function reads a specified number of characters from the keyboard. Usually INPUT$ is used to read from a file (discussed in the INPUT$ (File I/O) entry in Chapter 17, "Files"); however, if no file number is specified, INPUT$ reads input from the standard input device, which, by default, is the keyboard.

Syntax

INPUT$(*chars*)

chars is the number of characters to be read and must be in the range 0 through 32767.

Usage

buffer$ = INPUT$(5)

Reads five characters from the keyboard and assigns them to the string variable *buffer$*.

Description

INPUT$, like INKEY$, does not echo received characters to the display. Unlike INKEY$, however, INPUT$ can read more than one keypress and halts program execution until the requisite number of bytes have been read. INPUT$ cannot read function keys or the direction keys, or allow the user to edit the input field, as INPUT and LINE INPUT do.

INPUT$ handles control characters (such as tab and carriage return) as printable characters that are passed to the program without affecting the screen display. The function halts program execution either until it reads the specified number of characters or until the user interrupts it by pressing Ctrl-Break.

In its simplest form, INPUT$ is useful for pausing program execution until the user is ready to continue, as the following example shows:

```
PRINT "Press any key to continue";
temp$ = INPUT$(1)
```

INPUT$ is also useful whenever the user must enter an exact number of characters.

Example

Your computer stores information about keystrokes in a buffer until the program is ready to process it. This enables users to enter responses before prompts. The following program displays the contents of the buffer, continuously updating it as keystrokes are entered. The program uses INPUT$ to empty the buffer when it becomes full and when the program finishes.

```
' output display template
COLOR 15, 0: CLS
READ items%
FOR i% = 1 TO items%
    READ row%, col%, display$
    LOCATE row%, col%, 0: PRINT display$;
NEXT i%
LOCATE 11, 68: COLOR 11

' set BIOS segment and display addresses of buffer
DEF SEG = &H40
start% = &H400 + PEEK(&H80): finish% = &H400 + PEEK(&H82)
PRINT RIGHT$("0000" + HEX$(start%), 4); " ";
PRINT RIGHT$("0000" + HEX$(finish%), 4);

DO

    ' display positions of beginning of buffer (head) and next key (tail)
    LOCATE 11, 4: COLOR 11
    head% = &H400 + PEEK(&H1A): tail% = &H400 + PEEK(&H1C)
    PRINT RIGHT$("0000" + HEX$(head%), 4); " ";    ' display location of head
    PRINT RIGHT$("0000" + HEX$(tail%), 4);         ' display location of tail
    COLOR 13: LOCATE 9, 17: PRINT SPACE$(48);
    LOCATE 9, 17 + ((head% - &H41E) \ 2) * 3: PRINT CHR$(25);  ' point to head
    COLOR 12: LOCATE 13, 17: PRINT SPACE$(48);
    LOCATE 13, 17 + ((tail% - &H41E) \ 2) * 3: PRINT CHR$(24); ' point to tail
```

(continued)

continued

```
     ' read and display characters in the buffer
     FOR i% = 0 TO 15
         character% = PEEK(&H1E + (i% * 2))
         scanCode% = PEEK(&H1E + (i% * 2) + 1)
         IF character% < 32 THEN key$ = "  " ELSE key$ = CHR$(character%) + " "
         LOCATE 11, 17 + (i% * 3): COLOR 14: PRINT key$;  ' display character
         LOCATE 14, 17 + (i% * 3): COLOR 9
         PRINT RIGHT$("0" + HEX$(character%), 2);            ' display ASCII code
         LOCATE 15, 17 + (i% * 3): COLOR 10
         PRINT RIGHT$("0" + HEX$(scanCode%), 2);             ' display scan code
     NEXT i%

     ' display the number of characters in the buffer
     IF head% >= tail% THEN
         numkeys% = 16 - ((head% - tail%) \ 2)
     ELSE
         numkeys% = (tail% - head%) \ 2
     END IF
     LOCATE 14, 76: IF numkeys% = 16 THEN numkeys% = 0
     PRINT RIGHT$(" " + LTRIM$(RTRIM$(STR$(numkeys%))), 2);

     ' if buffer is full, use INPUT$ to clear it
     IF numkeys% = 15 THEN
         LOCATE 15, 67: COLOR 28: PRINT "BUFFER FULL";
         dummy$ = INPUT$(16)
         LOCATE , 67: PRINT SPACE$(11);
     END IF
LOOP UNTIL PEEK((tail% - &H400) - 2) = 27                 ' quit when user presses Esc

' restore segment and empty the buffer
DEF SEG : COLOR 7, 0: LOCATE 20, 1, 1
dummy$ = INPUT$(numkeys%)
END

' data for display template
DATA 20, 6, 4, "Head Tail", 6, 33, "Keyboard Buffer"
DATA 6, 67, "Buffer Area", 8, 4, "041A 041C"
DATA 8, 17, "1E 20 22 24 26 28 2A 2C 2E 30 32 34 36 38 3A 3C"
DATA 8, 68, "0480 0482", 10, 3,"-----¦-----"
DATA 10, 16, "¦--¦--¦--¦--¦--¦--¦--¦--¦--¦--¦--¦--¦--¦--¦--¦"
DATA 10, 67, "-----¦-----",11, 3,"          ", 11, 16, " "
DATA 11, 64, " ", 11, 67, "          ", 12, 3, "-----¦-----"
DATA 12, 16, "¦--¦--¦--¦--¦--¦--¦--¦--¦--¦--¦--¦--¦--¦--¦--¦"
DATA 12, 67, "-----¦-----", 14, 3, "ASCII Codes"
DATA 14, 67, "Waiting", 15, 3, "Scan Codes"
DATA 24, 30, "Press Esc to quit"
```

LINE INPUT

See also
INKEY$, INPUT, INPUT$, LINE INPUT #

Purpose
The LINE INPUT statement accepts all data entered as ASCII text and assigns it to a single string variable. This statement lets the user enter any characters—even commas and quotation marks—that are regarded as delimiters by the INPUT statement.

Syntax
LINE INPUT [;] ["*prompt*";] *var*

A semicolon after the keyword INPUT keeps the cursor on the same line after the user presses Enter.

prompt is an optional string of text, displayed immediately before the entry field, that can prompt the user for the required data.

var is a QBasic string variable to which input is assigned.

Usage
```
LINE INPUT "What is your name? "; name$
```
Prompts the user to type a name and assigns the characters entered to the string variable *name$*.

Description
LINE INPUT accepts all printable characters and lets you edit the line before you press Enter. The carriage return is not considered part of the data entered; it ends input and moves the cursor to the beginning of the next line. If you use a semicolon after the LINE INPUT keywords, however, QBasic suppresses the carriage return and leaves the cursor on the same line, positioned immediately to the right of the last character entered.

Unlike INPUT, LINE INPUT does not print a question mark unless you include one as part of the prompt string. The data entry field begins immediately after the last character in the prompt. It is a good idea, therefore, to end the string with at least one blank space so that the prompt and input are clearly separated on the screen.

The variable to which LINE INPUT assigns input can be an ordinary string variable, an element of a string array, or a fixed-length string. If you assign input to a fixed-length string, LINE INPUT discards any characters that exceed the string length. If you enter only a carriage return in response to a LINE INPUT statement, the statement assigns a null string to the variable.

LINE INPUT provides the same editing key combinations as INPUT does. Table 8-3, in the INPUT entry, lists the available key combinations.

Comments

LINE INPUT accepts up to 255 characters. You cannot limit the number of accepted characters. This makes LINE INPUT unsuitable for accepting formatted input in which the user must enter a fixed number of characters (a Social Security number, for example).

Example

The following program uses LINE INPUT to prompt the user to input values separated by commas and store the values in the string variable *text$*. The program then uses the subprogram *CommaParse* to separate the individual values and place them in an array.

```
DECLARE SUB CommaParse (text$, individual$(), total%)

DIM individual$(10)

CLS
LINE INPUT "Enter a string, with commas... "; text$

' separate individual parts of text$ into individual$() array
CommaParse text$, individual$(), total%

FOR i% = 1 TO total%
    PRINT LTRIM$(RTRIM$(individual$(i%)))
NEXT
END

SUB CommaParse (text$, individual$(), total%) STATIC
    i% = 1
    total% = 1

    DO
        j% = INSTR(i%, text$, ",")

        IF j% > 0 THEN
            individual$(total%) = MID$(text$, i%, j% - i%)
            total% = total% + 1
            i% = j% + 1
        ELSE
            individual$(total%) = MID$(text$, i%)
            EXIT SUB
        END IF
    LOOP UNTIL i% > LEN(text$)
END SUB
```

LOCATE

See also

CSRLIN, POS, WIDTH

Purpose

The LOCATE statement positions the cursor on the screen, thus marking the point at which text will subsequently be printed. LOCATE can also control the appearance of the cursor, making it visible or invisible and setting its size within the character cell.

Syntax

LOCATE [*row*][, [*column*][, [*visible*][, [*start*][, *stop*]]]]

row is the number of the row at which the cursor is positioned. Usually this number is an integer in the range 1 through 25, but it can extend through 43 for computers with an EGA adapter or through 50 with a VGA adapter. *row* can be in the range 1 through 60, with VGA and MCGA adapters in screen modes 11 and 12.

column is the number of the column at which the cursor is positioned. It ranges from 1 to 40 or from 1 to 80 depending on the current screen width.

visible determines whether the cursor is displayed or hidden. A value of 1 displays the cursor; 0 hides it.

start and *stop* are the CRT scan lines at which the cursor begins and ends. Values must be in the range 0 through 31.

All arguments are optional and can be numeric constants, variables, or expressions. If you omit any arguments, QBasic uses the previous values of those arguments. If you omit an argument from the middle of the statement, you must insert a comma to hold its place. You do not need to insert commas for arguments missing from the end of the statement.

Usage

```
LOCATE , 30
```
Positions the cursor at column 30 of the current screen row.

```
LOCATE , , 1, 0, 7
```
Makes the cursor visible and sets it to the size of a full character cell without changing its position.

Description

You can use the LOCATE statement simply to position the text cursor on the screen. You can also use the statement to change the appearance of the cursor.

Every video adapter creates characters on the screen by filling certain locations in a character cell. A Color Graphics Adapter (CGA), for example, uses an 8-by-8 grid for each character cell in which the adapter can draw a character. Other adapters (including MDA, MCGA, EGA, and VGA) use character cells with an 8-by-14, 9-by-14, 8-by-16, or 9-by-16 grid. If an adapter uses a character cell with many locations, it can create high-resolution characters.

The LOCATE statement always uses an 8-by-8 grid to form the cursor. If the adapter you are using has a character cell with higher resolution, LOCATE maps the values for the start and stop scan lines of the cursor to the values appropriate to the installed graphics adapter.

Although LOCATE accepts values in the range 0 through 31 for the scan line values, use only values in the range 0 through 7 because the statement maps these values directly to the 8-by-8 grid. Any value greater than 7 is converted to a value in the range 0 through 7.

If the value of the stop scan line is less than the value of the start scan line and you are using an adapter other than VGA (Video Graphics Array), LOCATE splits the cursor into two parts. If you are using a VGA adapter, setting the start scan line greater than the stop scan line produces a cursor that fills the character cell.

Warnings

LOCATE does not move the cursor to the bottom line of the display if the "soft key" display has been activated with KEY ON. (See the KEY entry in Chapter 14, "Keyboard.")

Options for setting the size and visibility of the cursor are effective only in SCREEN 0, the text mode. In graphics modes, LOCATE doesn't display the cursor.

Example

You will find the LOCATE statement most useful when you want to place a prompt at a certain location on the screen. The following program uses LOCATE to move the prompt to the middle of the screen and to set the cursor to full height. The program uses INPUT four times to prompt for strings of text. Before each prompt, it changes the shape of the cursor. The program then displays the strings at the corners of the screen.

```
CLS
LOCATE 10, 1, 1, 0, 7                              ' full-height cursor
INPUT "Enter first string of text : ", entry1$
LOCATE , , 1, 3, 7                                 ' half-height cursor
INPUT "Enter second string of text : ", entry2$
LOCATE , , 1, 5, 7                                 ' quarter-height cursor
INPUT "Enter third string of text : ", entry3$
LOCATE , , 1, 7, 7                                 ' single-line cursor
INPUT "Enter fourth string of text : ", entry4$

' display the strings in the corners of the screen
LOCATE 1, 1, 0                                     ' invisible cursor
PRINT entry1$
LOCATE 1, 80 - LEN(entry2$)
PRINT entry2$
LOCATE 22, 1
PRINT entry3$
LOCATE 22, 80 - LEN(entry4$)
PRINT entry4$
END
```

POS

See also

CSRLIN, LOCATE, LPOS, POINT, WIDTH (Screen)

Purpose

The POS function returns the column number (horizontal coordinate) of the text cursor. (Use the CSRLIN function to return the cursor's row number.)

Syntax

POS(*n*)

n is a dummy argument; although it is not used by the function, its presence is always required. It's easiest to use 0 as the dummy argument.

Usage

```
xPosition% = POS(0)
```

Returns the column number at which the cursor is located and assigns the value to the variable *xPosition%*.

Description

QBasic includes two functions that report the current position of the cursor. The POS function returns the column position of the character that will be output to the display by the next PRINT statement. The value can be in the range 1 through 40 or 1 through 80, depending on the current screen width. The leftmost column is always position number 1. CSRLIN returns the row number of the cursor. (See the CSRLIN entry.)

Tips

POS is useful if you want to clear a line from the cursor position. You can do this with the following statement:

```
PRINT SPACE$((80 - POS(0)) + 1);
```

Also, if you do not want the initial cursor position to change, you can save the position in a variable, clear the line, and then restore the cursor, as follows:

```
p% = POS(0)
PRINT SPACE$((80 - p%) + 1);
LOCATE , p%
```

Similarly, you can also use POS to clear from the beginning of the line to the cursor:

```
p% = POS(0)
LOCATE , 1
PRINT SPACE$(p% - 1);
```

Example

A word processor can wrap incomplete words at the end of a line to the next line. The following text-entry program emulates this feature by testing for the end of the line after the user enters each character. If the program encounters the end of the line while a word is still being entered, that word is removed from the current line and transferred to the beginning of the next one.

```
CLS
LOCATE , , 1: PRINT TAB(33); "WORDWRAPPING"
PRINT STRING$(80, "_")
VIEW PRINT 4 TO 22
DO
    DO
        keyStroke$ = INKEY$
    LOOP WHILE keyStroke$ = ""        ' wait for a keypress
    keyCode% = ASC(keyStroke$)        ' get ASCII value
    IF keyCode% > 31 THEN             ' printable characters
        buffer$ = buffer$ + keyStroke$
        PRINT keyStroke$;
        IF POS(0) > 79 THEN           ' check for end of line
            ptr% = POS(0)             ' find beginning of word
            DO
                ptr% = ptr% - 1
                IF MID$(buffer$, ptr%, 1) = " " THEN EXIT DO
            LOOP UNTIL ptr% = 1
            IF ptr% = 1 THEN          ' don't wrap unbroken lines
                buffer$ = "": PRINT
            ELSE                      ' wrap word to the next line
                temp$ = MID$(buffer$, ptr% + 1)
                LOCATE , 1: PRINT LEFT$(buffer$, ptr%);
                PRINT SPACE$((80 - POS(0)) + 1)
                buffer$ = temp$: PRINT buffer$;
            END IF
        END IF
    ELSEIF keyCode% = 13 THEN         ' if user pressed Enter, start a new line
        buffer$ = "": PRINT
    END IF
LOOP UNTIL keyCode% = 27              ' quit when user presses Esc
END
```

PRINT

See also

LOCATE, PRINT #, PRINT USING, TAB, WRITE

Purpose

PRINT outputs data to the display. Use PRINT to display any message or data.

Syntax

PRINT [*data* [{;|,}*data*...]] [;|,]

data is any numeric or string constant, variable, or expression. If you specify more than one item, separate the items with commas or semicolons.

If you use a semicolon between data items, PRINT displays the next item immediately after the previous one. If you use a comma between data items, PRINT displays the next item in the next print zone. (Each print zone is 14 characters in length.) A semicolon or comma at the end of a PRINT statement keeps the cursor on the same line for the next PRINT statement.

Usage

```
PRINT
```
Moves the text cursor to the beginning of the next line.

```
PRINT "Press a key.";
```
Displays the message in quotes and positions the cursor immediately after the last character printed.

```
PRINT x, x^2, x^3
```
Displays the value of the variable, x, x squared, and x cubed. The text cursor moves to the next print zone after each value is printed.

Description

When you create program lines, you can abbreviate the keyword PRINT as a question mark (?). If you are using the QBasic environment editor, the question mark is translated into PRINT as soon as you enter the line.

PRINT outputs the supplied data to the screen, starting at the current cursor position. If a data item is too long for the part of the line remaining after the cursor, PRINT issues a linefeed before sending the data to the screen. The following PRINT statement, for example, moves the cursor to the beginning of line 11 before printing 60 equal signs:

```
LOCATE 10, 40
PRINT STRING$(60, "=")
```

If the output contains more characters than can fit on one line, PRINT fills the line and continues displaying the output on the following line.

If you use PRINT without supplying any data, QBasic outputs a linefeed character, which moves the cursor to the next line. The contents of the line on which the cursor was positioned are unaffected.

Numeric values displayed by PRINT are always followed by a blank space. If the number is positive, PRINT precedes it with a space; otherwise, it precedes the number with the minus sign (–).

QBasic displays numeric values in fixed-point format if it can. If a single-precision number can be represented with seven digits or less, it is displayed in fixed-point format. Numbers of more than seven digits are displayed in scientific notation. For example,

```
a! = 1234567: PRINT a!
```

displays 1234567, but

```
b! = 12345678: PRINT b!
```

displays 1.234568E+07. This also applies to double-precision numbers except that they are displayed in scientific notation only when the number has more than 16 digits.

Example

PRINT can also display graphics characters from the IBM extended character set. In fact, before the advent of high-resolution graphics support, PRINT was the only statement available for drawing pictures on the screen. The program below uses PRINT to produce kaleidoscopic patterns on the text screen.

The program builds patterns from only five characters:

Character	Code
█	219
▄	220
▌	221
▐	222
▄	223

The program uses a combination of the LOCATE statement and PRINT to display the characters in diagonal lines across the text screen, in six different high-intensity colors. Because the patterns are generated randomly, you see a different sequence each time you press any key except Esc, which stops the program.

```
LOCATE , , 0: RANDOMIZE TIMER
leftEdge% = 1: rightEdge% = 80: top% = 1: bottom% = 25
DO
    COLOR RND * 7 + 8
    character% = RND * 5 + 218
    CLS
    changeX% = RND * 3 + 1: changeY% = SGN((RND * 2) - 2)
    x% = RND * (rightEdge% - leftEdge%) + leftEdge%
    y% = RND * (bottom% - top%) + top%
```

(continued)

continued

```
     DO
         IF x% + changeX% >= rightEdge% OR x% + changeX% <= leftEdge% THEN
             changeX% = -changeX%
         END IF
         IF y% + changeY% >= bottom% OR y% + changeY% <= top% THEN
             changeY% = -changeY%
         END IF
         x% = x% + changeX%: y% = y% + changeY%
         LOCATE y%, x%
         IF SCREEN(y%, x%) = character% THEN
             character% = character% + 1                    ' change character
             IF character% > 223 THEN character% = 219
             clr% = clr% + 1: IF clr% > 15 THEN clr% = 9    ' change color
             COLOR clr%
         END IF
         PRINT CHR$(character%);                            ' print character
         LOCATE y%, rightEdge% - x%: PRINT CHR$(character%);
         LOCATE bottom% - y%, rightEdge% - x%: PRINT CHR$(character%);
         LOCATE bottom% - y%, x%: PRINT CHR$(character%);
         keyStroke$ = INKEY$
     LOOP WHILE keyStroke$ = ""
 LOOP UNTIL keyStroke$ = CHR$(27)
 END
```

PRINT USING

See also

PRINT, PRINT # USING

Purpose

PRINT USING defines a template that specifies the length and format of each item to be displayed and then displays the result on the screen. Use PRINT USING to format data for a screen display in which each variable must fit into a particular field.

Syntax

PRINT USING *templateString*; *var*[; *var*...][,¦;]

templateString is either a string constant (enclosed in quotation marks) or a variable. It can contain literal text, which is printed unchanged, and one or more special formatting characters that determine how the variables or expressions following the template string are to be printed.

A comma at the end of the statement causes the cursor to move to the next print zone on the current line. A semicolon causes the cursor to remain positioned directly after the last character displayed.

Usage

```
payment$ = "**$#####,.##"
checkAmount! = 2449.73
PRINT USING payment$; checkAmount!
```

Displays a payment amount with a comma inserted between every third character to the left of the decimal point. The display is also padded on the left with asterisks to produce a field of 12 characters. The displayed line reads: ***$2,449.73.

```
surName$:"Sutcliffe"
fullName$ = "John Sutcliffe"
PRINT USING "!.&"; fullName$; surName$
```

Prints John Sutcliffe's first-name initial and full surname—J. Sutcliffe. The exclamation mark (!) extracts the first character from *fullName$*; the ampersand (&) displays *surName$* without any formatting. Note that because the period (.) is not part of a numeric field, it is interpreted as a literal character, not a decimal point.

Description

The PRINT USING statement accepts any variables and fits them into the fields of a template string. This template controls the length of each variable, its position in the output line, and the way it is formatted. You can use the template to format both numeric and string data.

Each field in the template is indicated by one or more special formatting characters; usually, the number of formatting characters in a field controls how many characters or digits of the variable are to be printed. See Table 8-4 for a list of formatting characters for strings; see Table 8-5 for a list of formatting characters for numbers.

Character	Description
!	Displays only the first character of the specified string.
&	Displays the entire string regardless of its length.
\ \	Displays as many characters from the beginning of the source string as are in the field deliminated by the backslashes. The backslashes are considered part of the field; therefore the number of characters output will be equal to the number of blank spaces between the backslashes plus 2. If the source string doesn't contain enough characters to fill the field, the string is padded on the right with blank spaces.
_	Indicates that the next character is to be interpreted as a literal character. Use the underscore to include formatting characters in the actual text. For example, "_!" prints an exclamation mark, not the first character of a string.

Table 8-4.
PRINT USING formatting characters for strings.

Character	Description
#	Displays a single numeric digit. Use multiple number symbols to indicate the maximum number of digits to be displayed. Numbers having fewer digits are right-justified within the field and padded with leading spaces.
$$	Appends a single dollar sign immediately to the left of the number in a numeric field. If the number to be displayed is negative, a minus sign is displayed immediately to the left of the dollar sign.
**	Fills any leading spaces in the numeric field with asterisks. Two asterisks must be included, each of which represents a digit position in the field.
**$	Combines the effects of $$ and ** by displaying a dollar sign to the left of the number and filling with asterisks any leading spaces before the dollar sign.
+	Displays the sign of both positive and negative numbers. If the plus character appears at the beginning of the field, the sign is displayed immediately to the left of the number; if it appears at the end, the sign is displayed immediately to the right of the number.
,	Displays a comma in front of every third digit before the decimal. To use this character, place a comma immediately to the left of the decimal point in the print field.
-	Displays negative numbers with a trailing minus sign. Append the hyphen to the field.
.	Marks the position of the decimal point in a numeric field. If any digits to the left of the decimal are specified and the number to be displayed is less than 1, a single leading 0 is displayed. The decimal part of the number is rounded to fit into the number of digits to the right of the decimal point.
^^^^[^]	Prints the number in exponential format. Four carets (^) display a two-digit exponent (E+nn); five carets display a three-digit exponent (E+nnn). Use number symbols (#) in front of the caret symbols to indicate the length of the significant digit field. You can use any numeric formatting character except the comma in an exponential field.

Table 8-5.
PRINT USING formatting characters for numbers.

use space between / fields

If you send more arguments to PRINT USING than there are fields in the template, QBasic does not ignore the excess. Instead, after the contents of the last assigned field have been printed, it will start again at the beginning of the template, inserting the extra variables into the same set of fields. In the following example, the variables a%, c%, and e% are formatted with the first field, and the variables b$, d$, and f$ are formatted with the second field:

```
PRINT USING "### \   \"; a%; b$; c%; d$; e%; f$
```

Notice in this example how important it is that you don't position string variables so that they are fitted into numeric fields, and vice versa.

If a numeric variable contains more digits than will fit into the field of the template assigned to it, the displayed value overflows the template, and a percent sign (%) is inserted in front of the value. PRINT USING does not truncate numeric variables if their fields will not contain them.

Errors

If you specify a numeric value for a string field or a string value for a numeric field, QBasic displays a "Type mismatch" error message. If the number of digits of a field specified in the template of a PRINT USING statement exceeds 24 characters, QBasic displays an "Illegal function call" error message.

Example

PRINT USING is often used to format data so that it fits neatly on the screen display. The following program reads elements of a customer's transactions from DATA statements and then writes them to the screen in the form of an account statement. Note that although the data in this example is read from DATA statements, an accounting application would receive the data from a file or the keyboard.

```
CLS
dateTemp$ = " \\_/\\_/\\"        ' date template
moneyTemp$ = " $$###,.##"         ' money template
tranTemp$ = " ######  \       \ \" + SPACE$(18) + "\"    ' transaction template

READ accountNo&, fullName$, surName$
PRINT TAB(32); "SINGULAR  SOFTWARE": PRINT
PRINT TAB(31); "STATEMENT OF ACCOUNT"
PRINT USING dateTemp$; LEFT$(DATE$, 2); MID$(DATE$, 4, 2); RIGHT$(DATE$, 2);
PRINT TAB(39 - (LEN(surName$) \ 2));
PRINT USING "!.&"; fullName$; surName$;
PRINT TAB(72); USING "#######"; accountNo&
PRINT STRING$(80, "-")
PRINT "   Item    Date     Description";
PRINT TAB(59); "Credit"; TAB(75); "Debit"
PRINT STRING$(80, "-")
total! = 0: length% = 9
DO
    READ item&
    IF item& < 0 THEN EXIT DO
    READ dte$, desc$, debit!, credit!
    PRINT USING tranTemp$; item&; dte$; desc$;
    IF debit! > 0 THEN
        PRINT TAB(70); USING moneyTemp$; debit!
        total! = total! + debit!
    ELSEIF credit! > 0 THEN
        PRINT TAB(55); USING moneyTemp$; credit!
        total! = total! - credit!
    END IF
    length% = length% + 1       ' add one to length of list
LOOP
FOR i% = 1 TO 22 - length%
    PRINT
NEXT i%
PRINT STRING$(80, "-")
PRINT TAB(63); USING "Total: $$###,.##"; total!
END
```

(continued)

continued

```
' account data
DATA 460755, "Jim Bates", "BATES"
DATA 3850, "08/01/89", "b/f", 2862.30, 0
DATA 3863, "08/03/89", "System", 1795, 0
DATA 3864, "08/03/89", "Monitor", 379, 0
DATA 3879, "08/10/89", "Basic", 60, 0
DATA 3888, "08/18/89", "Diskettes", 19.95, 0
DATA 3925, "08/22/89", "Hard drive", 529, 0
DATA 3926, "08/22/89", "Check", 0, 5000
DATA 3933, "08/23/89", "Graphical interface", 116.95, 0
DATA 3976, "08/28/89", "Backup program", 139.95, 0
DATA -1
```

SPC

See also
SPACE$, TAB, WIDTH (Screen)

Purpose
The SPC function moves the cursor or print head forward the specified number of spaces. You can use SPC in PRINT, LPRINT, and PRINT # statements. Use SPC to format output so that you can read it easily.

Syntax
SPC(*col*)

col is the number of character positions the cursor or print head will be advanced. It can be a constant, variable, or expression, but it must evaluate to a positive integer in the range 0 through 32767.

Usage
```
LPRINT "CODE"; SPC(16); "DESCRIPTION"; SPC(19); "LOCATION"
```
Prints the heading of a report. The string "CODE" is separated from "DESCRIPTION" by 16 blank spaces. "DESCRIPTION" is, in turn, separated from "LOCATION" by another 19 spaces.

Description
The SPC function advances the text cursor or print head a specified number of columns (from the column in which the last character is printed) and fills the intervening columns with blank spaces. Use SPC to insert a specific number of spaces between items regardless of the position of the items.

SPC works as though it has a trailing semicolon. If you use SPC at the end of a line of data, it suppresses the normal carriage return and linefeed, leaving the cursor or print head positioned immediately to the right of the last space character printed.

If the width of a data item following a call to SPC is greater than the number of columns remaining on the line, QBasic displays the entire data item on the next line. If the specified number of columns is greater than the width of the current output device, the SPC function uses the number of columns modulo (MOD) the width as the number of spaces to output.

Errors

If you use a value greater than 32767 with the SPC function, QBasic displays an "Overflow" error message. A negative value does not produce an error; QBasic merely ignores the function.

Example

You can use SPC with the PRINT # statement to format data sent to a file. Doing this saves you from having to format the data again when you print the file. The following program writes a simple geometric pattern to a disk file and then displays the contents of the file.

```
CLS
OPEN "DIAGONAL" FOR OUTPUT AS #1
FOR i% = 1 TO 24
    PRINT #1, STRING$(15, CHR$(219)); SPC(i%);
    PRINT #1, STRING$(25, CHR$(219)); SPC(25 - i%);
    PRINT #1, STRING$(15, CHR$(219));
NEXT i%
CLOSE
SHELL "TYPE DIAGONAL"
END
```

TAB

See also

SPC, WIDTH (Screen)

Purpose

The TAB function sets the column position of the next character to be displayed on the current line. You can use TAB with the PRINT, LPRINT, and PRINT # statements. Use TAB when an item must appear in a particular column on the line.

Syntax

TAB(*col*)

col is any numeric constant, variable, or expression. It indicates the column number to which the print head or cursor will move. The number must evaluate to a positive integer in the range 0 through 32767.

Usage

```
PRINT #1, TAB(16) "PRICE:   " TAB(36 - (LEN(price$))) price$
```

Outputs to a sequential file a line of data that contains 36 characters. The line begins with 16 blank spaces, continues with the quoted string, and ends with the contents of the variable *price$* right-justified in the 36-character field.

Description

Use TAB to advance the text cursor or print head to a specific column along a line.

You cannot use TAB to move to a column number greater than the width of the device being printed to. The maximum number of columns per line is usually 80 for both printer and screen. If the specified column number is greater than the current output width, TAB does not return an error; instead, it advances to the position that equals the value of the column modulo (MOD) the width. If TAB receives a negative value, it sets the column number to 1.

TAB works as though it has a trailing semicolon; it suppresses the normal carriage return and linefeed usually added to the end of a PRINT statement. This ensures that the print position is held at the specified column.

Errors

If you use a value greater than 32767 with the TAB function, QBasic displays an "Overflow" error message. A negative value does not produce an error; TAB merely moves the text cursor or print head to the first column of the row.

Example

When you use TAB to format text, TAB ensures that the line contains the proper number of characters by filling intervening columns with blank spaces. The following program displays a formatted page of text that has a border.

```
PRINT CHR$(201); STRING$(77, CHR$(205)); CHR$(187)
FOR i% = 1 TO 5
    PRINT CHR$(186); TAB(79); CHR$(186)
NEXT
message$ = "QBasic Programmer's Reference"
PRINT CHR$(186); TAB(40 - (LEN(message$) \ 2)); message$; TAB(79); CHR$(186)
FOR i% = 1 TO 4
    PRINT CHR$(186); TAB(79); CHR$(186)
NEXT
message$ = "The Ultimate Reference"
PRINT CHR$(186); TAB(40 - (LEN(message$) \ 2)); message$; TAB(79); CHR$(186)
message$ = "for"
PRINT CHR$(186); TAB(40 - (LEN(message$) \ 2)); message$; TAB(79); CHR$(186)
message$ = "QBasic Programmers"
PRINT CHR$(186); TAB(40 - (LEN(message$) \ 2)); message$; TAB(79); CHR$(186)
FOR i% = 1 TO 8
    PRINT CHR$(186); TAB(79); CHR$(186)
NEXT
PRINT CHR$(200); STRING$(77, CHR$(205)); CHR$(188)
END
```

VIEW PRINT

See also

CLS, LOCATE, PRINT, SCREEN (Function), VIEW (Graphics), WIDTH (Screen)

Purpose

The VIEW PRINT statement defines a rectangular area of the screen and confines all text output to within its borders. This area is known as the text viewport. If your program uses both text and graphics, you can create a text viewport to keep the two types of output separate, preventing text from overwriting any pictures that are drawn.

Syntax

VIEW PRINT [*top* TO *bottom*]

top is the number of the row that marks the upper boundary of the viewport; *bottom* is the number of the row that marks the lower boundary. Both parameters have a range of 1 through the maximum number of rows available with the installed video adapter (by default, 25). The value of *bottom* must be greater than that of *top*.

Usage

```
VIEW PRINT 10 TO 24
```

Defines the 15 rows from line 10 through 24 as the area for text output.

Description

Use the VIEW PRINT statement to specify the part of the screen in which text output will appear. VIEW PRINT does not affect the output of graphics statements.

After you define a text viewport with VIEW PRINT, any text output to the screen is confined to the viewport. Note that an output statement executed on the bottom row of the viewport scrolls the viewport up one line exactly as if it were the actual bottom row of the screen.

If the function key display is active, you cannot specify the bottom row of the display as a parameter for VIEW PRINT. See the KEY statement in Chapter 14, "Keyboard," for details about enabling and disabling the function key display.

The number of rows available for the viewport depends on the number of rows your video adapter can display. The number is usually 25; however, if your system has an EGA adapter, you can extend this to 43 (50 rows with a VGA adapter, and 60 rows with a VGA or MCGA adapter in screen modes 11 and 12). See the WIDTH (Screen) entry for details about setting the number of rows on the display.

Errors

After you define a text viewport, you cannot move the text cursor outside the area. For example, if you use the statements

```
VIEW PRINT 1 TO 12
LOCATE 16, 1
```

QBasic displays an "Illegal function call" error message. QBasic displays an "Illegal function call" error message if you use a negative number in the call to VIEW PRINT, if the value of the top row is greater than the value of the bottom row, or if the value of the bottom row exceeds the number of rows available.

Example

VIEW PRINT is commonly used in applications that mix text and graphics on the same display. Defining separate viewports for text and graphics lets you isolate the two forms of output, preventing them from interfering with each other. The following program constructs a pie chart in the graphics viewport from data entered in the text viewport.

```
CONST PI = 3.14159

' dimension arrays for data and pie-chart labels
DIM items(1 TO 7) AS SINGLE, label(1 TO 6) AS STRING

' set up the screen and text viewport
SCREEN 9: LINE (0, 0)-(639, 349), 1, BF
VIEW PRINT 20 TO 25
CLS 2: PRINT "Enter up to six values for the pie chart ";
PRINT "(0 = last item, -1 = quit)": PRINT STRING$(80, "_")
DO

    ' collect pie-chart data in the text viewport (maximum six items)
    VIEW PRINT 22 TO 25
    CLS 2                       ' clear text viewport
    total! = 0
    title$ = LEFT$(title$, 60)
    FOR itemNum% = 1 TO 6
        PRINT "Value for item #"; itemNum%; : INPUT ; items(itemNum%)
        total! = total! + items(itemNum%)
        IF items(itemNum%) = 0 THEN
            PRINT
            INPUT "Title for chart :", title$
            EXIT FOR
        ELSEIF items(itemNum%) < 0 THEN EXIT FOR
        END IF
        PRINT TAB(41); "Label"; : INPUT label(itemNum%)
    NEXT itemNum%
    itemNum% = itemNum% - 1
    IF items(itemNum% + 1) < 0 THEN EXIT DO

    VIEW PRINT                  ' disable text viewport
    ' initialize graphics viewport
    VIEW (10, 5)-(629, 245), 0, 15
    CLS 1                       ' clear graphics viewport
    start! = .0001: units! = 2 * PI / total!
    row% = 2: column% = 12
```

(continued)

continued

```
     ' draw pie chart
     FOR i% = 1 TO itemNum%
         finish! = items(i%) * units! + start!
         IF finish! > 2 * PI THEN finish! = 2 * PI
         CIRCLE (310, 120), 80, i%, -start!, -finish!
         midPoint! = finish! - ((finish! - start!) / 2)
         x = 310 + 40 * COS(midPoint!)
         y = 120 - 40 * SIN(midPoint!)
         PAINT (x, y), i%, i%
         CIRCLE (310, 120), 80, 0, -start!, -finish!

         ' draw key and print labels
         start! = finish!
         LINE (10, column%)-(20, column% + 5), i%, BF
         LOCATE row%, 10: PRINT LEFT$(label(i%), 20)
         row% = row% + 1: column% = column% + 14
     NEXT i%
     LOCATE 17, 40 - (LEN(title$) \ 2): PRINT title$;
 LOOP WHILE 1
 END
```

WIDTH (Screen)

See also

SCREEN (Statement), WIDTH (File), WIDTH LPRINT

Purpose

The WIDTH statement resets the number of columns on the screen. If your computer has a high-resolution video adapter, you can also use WIDTH to increase the number of rows available on the screen.

Syntax

WIDTH [*cols*][, *rows*]

cols is the number of characters in a screen line, either 40 or 80 (the default). *rows* is the number of screen lines; possible settings include 25 (the default), 43, 30, 50, and 60.

Usage

```
WIDTH 40
```
Sets the number of columns to 40.

```
WIDTH ,43
```
Sets the number of rows to 43 without changing the number of columns.

Description

Use WIDTH to select the number of columns and rows of text that can be displayed. Changing the display size also clears the screen.

Possible values for the number of rows depend on the current screen mode and the capabilities of the installed video adapter. The number of columns is always either 40 or 80. Table 8-6 lists the text display sizes available in each screen mode.

Screen mode	Width values	Video adaptor
0	80 by 25	MDA, Hercules, Olivetti, AT&T, CGA, EGA, MCGA, VGA
	80 by 43	EGA, VGA
	80 by 50	VGA
	40 by 25	CGA, EGA, MCGA, VGA
	40 by 43	EGA, VGA
	40 by 50	VGA
1	40 by 25	CGA, EGA, MCGA, VGA
2	80 by 25	CGA, EGA, MCGA, VGA
3	80 by 25	Hercules
4	40 by 25	Olivetti and AT&T
7	40 by 25	EGA, VGA
8	80 by 25	EGA, VGA
9	80 by 25	EGA, VGA
	80 by 43	EGA, VGA
10	80 by 25	EGA, VGA
	80 by 43	EGA, VGA
11	80 by 30	MCGA, VGA
	80 by 60	MCGA, VGA
12	80 by 30	VGA
	80 by 60	VGA
13	40 by 25	MCGA, VGA

Table 8-6.
Valid WIDTH row and column values for QBasic screen modes.

WIDTH is particularly useful in screen modes 9 through 13 (discussed in the SCREEN (Statement) entry in Chapter 11, "Graphics"), in which you can use it to control the height of labels for graphs and charts. Be sure that you use WIDTH to set the character size before you begin drawing; otherwise, it will clear any existing graphics from the screen. Remember also that screen modes 9 through 13 do not allow fewer than 80 columns.

Errors

Trying to set the number of columns to a value other than 40 or 80 or the number of rows to a value that is not supported by your video adapter causes QBasic to display an "Illegal function call" error message.

Example

The following program demonstrates the difference in character size when you change the width of the screen. The program uses WIDTH to change the number of columns in a line from 80 to 40.

```
CONST MESSAGE$ = "QBasic Programmer's Reference"
CLS
WIDTH 80, 25
PRINT MESSAGE$
LOCATE 23, 1
PRINT "Press any key to change the screen width to 40 columns"

DO
LOOP WHILE INKEY$ = ""

WIDTH 40, 25
PRINT MESSAGE$
```

WRITE

See also

PRINT, WRITE #

Purpose

The WRITE statement displays data on the screen. WRITE separates each item with a comma and encloses each string item in quotation marks.

Syntax

WRITE [*expr*]

expr is a list of one or more items of data, separated by commas. These items can be numeric or string variables, constants, or expressions. If you don't specify an expression list, only a carriage return and linefeed are written.

Usage

```
WRITE
```
Advances the cursor to the next line of the display.

```
a% = 6: price = 9.95: tax = 1.15
WRITE a%, "Blender", price * tax
```
Displays three items of data on the screen, beginning at the current cursor position. WRITE displays commas to separate the output items and deletes all blank spaces.

Description

Use WRITE to output data to the screen in teletype fashion, starting at the current cursor position and advancing the cursor to a new line after the data is written. QBasic evaluates numeric expressions in the data list, and WRITE displays the resulting value without leading or trailing spaces. WRITE encloses character strings in quotation marks and separates the items in the list with commas. The commas in the expression list do not move the cursor to the next print zone, as the commas in PRINT do. In fact, WRITE requires that commas be used as the separator between data items.

You cannot suppress the linefeed by adding a semicolon, as you can in a PRINT statement.

Example

The following program compares WRITE and PRINT by using the two statements to output the same data in a variety of ways.

```
CLS
DIM wrd(1 TO 9) AS STRING

FOR i% = 1 TO 9
    READ wrd(i%)              ' read a data item
    PRINT i%, wrd(i%),        ' display item with PRINT
    WRITE i%, wrd(i%)         ' display item with WRITE
NEXT i%
PRINT


' display the data on the screen with PRINT
PRINT wrd(1); wrd(2); wrd(3); wrd(4); wrd(5); wrd(6); wrd(7); wrd(8); wrd(9)


' display the data on the screen with WRITE
WRITE wrd(1), wrd(2), wrd(3), wrd(4), wrd(5), wrd(6), wrd(7), wrd(8), wrd(9)
END

DATA "The ", "moving ", "finger ", "writes ", "and, ", "having "
DATA "writ, ", "moves ", "on."
```

CHAPTER 9

Error Trapping

Introduction

Errors in programs can be divided into two main categories—compiler errors and run-time errors. Compiler errors include syntax errors (for example, a misspelled QBasic keyword) and references to array variables that use an index outside the array's range. QBasic immediately warns you about such errors when you try to run a program in the QBasic environment. Indeed, if you write your programs in the environment, QBasic warns you of syntax errors in a line immediately after you type it in.

Runtime errors are more difficult to find. By definition, they occur only when you run the program, after a successful compilation. Furthermore, a particular error might not occur every time you run the program; it might appear only when a certain combination of circumstances occurs.

A runtime error might not even be your fault: If a user forgets to turn the printer on before the program attempts to print a report, a runtime error can occur. This is the type of error your program must be able to handle; the program must either trap the error or end safely so that the user doesn't lose any data.

This chapter discusses how QBasic lets you trap and handle runtime errors. Table 9-1 is an alphabetic list of QBasic's error-handling statements and functions.

Statement or function	Description
ERDEV	Returns the DOS error code set by the critical error handler and information concerning the device in which an error occurred
ERDEV$	Returns the name of the device that generated an error
ERL	Returns the line number of the statement that caused an error
ERR	Returns the QBasic code of the most recent error
ERROR	Simulates an error
ON ERROR GOTO	Establishes error trapping and specifies an error-handling routine
RESUME	Specifies the return from an error-handling routine

Table 9-1.
QBasic error-handling statements and functions.

Error Trapping

Many runtime errors are first detected by the computer hardware. If your program instructs the CPU to divide a number by 0, for example, the CPU sends DOS an interrupt. Similarly, if your program tries to read a disk when the drive door is open, DOS generates the critical error interrupt, which produces the familiar message

```
Abort, Retry, Fail?
```

QBasic, however, intercepts the interrupts generated by errors and passes the interrupts to its internal error-handling routines. It also collects information about the circumstances that caused the error. QBasic passes this information to the program as a message in a dialog box.

This information can help you understand how to modify your program to prevent the error from occurring in the future. However, the error message cannot prevent the error from stopping the program. To enable your program to handle all errors, use an ON ERROR GOTO statement. This statement activates error trapping and specifies the line number or label that marks the beginning of the error-handling routine in your program. Note that if you use an ON ERROR GOTO statement in a subprogram or function, the line number or label that the statement specifies must be in the main program, not in the subprogram or function.

If you use an ON ERROR GOTO statement, an error will no longer halt your program. Instead, execution will branch to the specified routine, which contains statements to handle errors.

Error Handlers

If your program traps errors, you must write an error-handling routine, called an error handler, that specifies what your program will do if a particular error occurs. QBasic provides functions that return information about the nature of each error. Use these functions in your error handler so that it responds properly to each error. The ERR function returns QBasic's code for the error. The ERDEV function returns the DOS code for the error and information concerning the device in which a hardware error occurred, and the ERDEV$ function returns the name of that device. If your program uses line numbers, the ERL function returns the number of the line in which the error occurred.

After an error occurs, QBasic disables further error trapping until the handling routine finishes. This prevents the program from recursively executing the error handler if another error occurs. However, if an error occurs while the handling routine is executing, the error will not be trapped; this causes the program to terminate and display an error message.

Your program can encounter two types of errors—"recoverable" errors and "fatal" errors. If a recoverable error occurs, your error-handling routine can take the necessary steps to correct it (for example, by instructing the user to turn the printer on).

After offering a solution to the problem, the program can use the RESUME statement to try again to execute the statement that triggered the error. Or the program can ignore the error by using RESUME NEXT to execute the statement following the one that caused the error. However, if the error is fatal and cannot be rectified or ignored, the program should call the RESUME statement with a specified line number or label to direct control to the line number or label of an exit routine that safely terminates execution.

If an error that your routine cannot handle occurs, you can pass control to QBasic by using the following statement within the error-handling routine:

```
ON ERROR GOTO 0
```

This statement causes QBasic to terminate the program and print its own error message. Using this statement outside an error-handling routine disables error trapping without terminating the program.

QBasic also provides a statement that lets you test error-handling routines in programs you are developing. The ERROR statement simulates a specified error, so you do not have to wait for it to occur naturally. When you call the ERROR statement, your program executes the error-handling routine specified by the last ON ERROR GOTO statement exactly as if a real error had occurred.

User Events

In addition to its error-trapping capabilities, QBasic lets you trap for other events that might occur when your program is running. These events are predefined and have statements dedicated to them. For example, ON COM GOSUB transfers execution to a special routine whenever the program receives data from the serial port; ON TIMER GOSUB lets you create a subroutine that is executed whenever a specified number of seconds has elapsed on the system clock.

Related Reading

Duncan, Ray, et al. *The MS-DOS Encyclopedia*. Redmond, Wash.: Microsoft Press, 1988.

The Waite Group. *MS-DOS Papers*. Indianapolis, Ind.: Howard W. Sams & Co., 1988.

ERDEV

See also

ERDEV$, ERR, IOCTL, IOCTL$, ON ERROR GOTO

Purpose

The ERDEV function returns an integer describing the device that produced an error and the error itself. Call this function to determine what kind of error has occurred. Your program can then take the appropriate measures to either rectify the problem or terminate safely.

Syntax

ERDEV

Usage

```
errorCode% = ERDEV
```

Assigns the error code to the integer variable *errorCode%* after a hardware fault has occurred.

Description

The integer value returned by ERDEV contains two separate pieces of information. The lower, or least-significant, byte (LSB) contains the DOS error code that reveals the nature of the error. The upper, or most-significant, byte (MSB) contains selected information from the "device attribute word," a 2-byte collection of flags that is part of the device-driver program in memory. To separate the two components of the information returned by ERDEV, use the following statements:

```
deviceID% = VAL("&H" + LEFT$(HEX$(ERDEV), 2))
errorCode% = VAL("&H" + RIGHT$(HEX$(ERDEV), 2))
```

(Note that the translation to and from hexadecimal format masks the sign bit; this prevents *deviceID%* and *errorCode%* from becoming negative numbers.)

For an interpretation of the information in *deviceID%* (the MSB of the value returned by ERDEV), see Table 9-2. The possible values for *errorCode%* (the LSB of the value returned by ERDEV) are listed in Table 9-3.

Warnings

QBasic retains the information set by the last device error even after you call the ERDEV function. This approach lets you call ERDEV more than once for the same error. Be sure, however, that your program does not read an old value and respond to a nonexistent error. If an error was caused by something other than a device, ERDEV continues to return information about the device that last caused an error. You might find it safer to rely on the ERR function, which always returns the code of the current error.

Bit	Meaning if bit equals 1
0	Device is the standard input device
1	Device is the standard output device
2	Device is the NUL device
3	Device is a clock device
4	Not used (always 0)
5	Device is a non-IBM-type disk drive
6	Device supports I/O control
7	Device is a character device

Table 9-2.
Meaning of the bits in the MSB returned by ERDEV.

Error code	Description
0	Write-protect error
1	Unknown unit
2	Drive not ready
3	Unknown command request
4	Data error (CRC)
5	Bad request structure length
6	Seek error
7	Unknown media type
8	Sector not found
9	Printer out of paper
10	Write fault
11	Read fault
12	General failure
13	Not used
14	Not used
15	Invalid disk change (DOS 3.x only)

Table 9-3.
Error codes in the LSB returned by ERDEV.

Example

ERDEV is most useful in programs that must communicate with user-installed devices. However, you can use it to gather information about standard devices, such as disk drives and printers. The following program uses ERDEV in an error handler to report the meaning of the error code. When you run this program, leave the door of the A drive open so that the OPEN statement produces an error that can be trapped.

```
ON ERROR GOTO Handler

OPEN "A:\ERDEV.DAT" FOR OUTPUT AS #1
END

Handler:
    code% = VAL("&H" + RIGHT$(HEX$(ERDEV), 2))
    SELECT CASE code%
        CASE 0
            PRINT "Write-protect error"
        CASE 1
            PRINT "Unknown unit"
        CASE 2
            PRINT "Drive not ready"
        CASE 3
            PRINT "Unknown command request"
        CASE 4
            PRINT "Data error"
        CASE 5
            PRINT "Bad request structure length"
        CASE 6
            PRINT "Seek error"
        CASE 7
            PRINT "Unknown media type"
        CASE 8
            PRINT "Sector not found"
        CASE 9
            PRINT "Printer out of paper"
        CASE 10
            PRINT "Write fault"
        CASE 11
            PRINT "Read fault"
        CASE 12
            PRINT "General failure"
    END SELECT
    RESUME NEXT
```

ERDEV$

See also

ERDEV, ERR, IOCTL, IOCTL$, ON ERROR GOTO

Purpose

The ERDEV$ function returns the name of the device that generated an error. Call the function to let the program gain information that enables it to either rectify the problem or end without destroying data.

Syntax

ERDEV$

Usage

```
device$ = ERDEV$
```
Assigns to the variable *device$* the name of the device in which an error has occurred.

```
IF ERDEV$ = "LPT1    " THEN PRINT "Error produced by the printer"
```
Prints a message if the printer connected to the parallel port produces an error.

Description

The ERDEV$ function returns the name of the device that caused the error. It returns a two-character string if a block device, such as a disk drive (A: or B:), produced the error. Otherwise, it returns an eight-character string that contains the name of a character device, such as a printer port or a serial port (for example, LPT1 or COM1). Occasionally, one of the devices listed in your CONFIG.SYS file causes an error; in that case, ERDEV$ returns the name of the device.

Warnings

QBasic retains the information set by the last device error even after you call the ERDEV$ function. This approach lets you call ERDEV$ more than once for the same error. Be sure, however, that your program does not read an old value and respond to a nonexistent error. If the error was caused by something other than a device, ERDEV$ continues to return the name of the device that last caused an error.

Example

ERDEV$ is most useful in programs that must interface with user-installed devices. See the example in the ON ERROR GOTO entry for an error-handling routine that uses ERDEV$ to help the user decide how to correct a recoverable error.

ERL

See also

ERDEV, ERDEV$, ERR, ERROR, ON ERROR GOTO, RESUME

Purpose

The ERL function returns the line number of the statement that caused an error. You use ERL primarily as a debugging aid to fix runtime errors that occur in your program.

Syntax

ERL

Usage

```
PRINT ERL
```
Displays the line number of the statement that caused an error.

```
errorLine& = ERL
```
Assigns to *errorLine&* the line number at which the most recent error occurred.

Description

ERL is useful only if your program uses line numbers. It does not work with line labels, nor does it return the number of the source-code line containing an error. If the line that incurred the error does not contain a line number, ERL returns the number of a line before it that does contain a line number. The value ERL returns is a number in the range 0 through 65529, depending on the range of line numbers in your program. QBasic treats any line numbers that are greater than 65529 as line labels, so ERL will not return a value greater than 65529.

Example

Because the user of a program usually has no access to the source code, the ERL function is typically a debugging tool—used during program development and deleted from the finished application. The following debugging routine, intended for inclusion in the test version of a program, reports the type of error that occurred and the line number at which it occurred. (Note that this program returns an error line number of 100—the preceding line number nearest to the statement that causes the error.)

```
1 ON ERROR GOTO Debug

10        ' program code starts here

100

ERROR 73  ' test error handler by generating an error

9999 END

Debug:
    PRINT : PRINT : PRINT
    PRINT "A type"; STR$(ERR); " error has just occurred ";
    PRINT "in line"; STR$(ERL): BEEP: PRINT
    ON ERROR GOTO 0
```

ERR

See also

ERDEV, ERDEV$, ERL, ERROR, ON ERROR GOTO, RESUME

Purpose

The ERR function returns the QBasic error code for the most recent error. You can use this code in an error-handling routine to help identify the problem and determine whether the program can recover from the error.

Syntax

ERR

Usage

```
PRINT ERR
```

Displays the QBasic error code of the most recent error.

```
errCode% = ERR
```

Assigns the value of the most recent error to the integer variable *errCode%*.

```
ERROR ERR
```

Repeats the most recent error that occurred. (Used inside an error handler, this statement halts the program and prints the default message for the error.)

Description

The ERR function returns a value in the range 1 through 255; this number is the QBasic error code of the most recent error. (See Appendix A, "Error Messages and Error Codes," for a complete list of QBasic error codes and their meanings.) If no error has occurred, ERR returns 0.

QBasic uses only the numbers 1 through 76 to specify various errors. If the error is not in a predefined category, QBasic returns error code 21 and displays the message "Unprintable error."

If you simulate an error with the ERROR statement, ERR returns the code that corresponds to the simulated error. ERR can be called from anywhere in the program.

Example

You can use the ERR function to test an error to see whether it can be corrected by the user. The following error-handling routine identifies four recoverable errors and gives the user appropriate instructions.

```
DIM eMessage(0 TO 4) AS STRING

eMessage(0) = "027061068071"              ' error code values
eMessage(1) = " Printer out of paper, please reload"
eMessage(2) = " Disk full, please insert a new disk"
eMessage(3) = " Device is off line, please switch it on"
eMessage(4) = " Drive not ready, please close drive door"

CLS
ON ERROR GOTO Trap
ERROR 61   ' simulate disk-full error to test whether routine works

Finish:
    COLOR 7, 0
END
```

(continued)

continued

```
Trap:
    xPos% = POS(0): yPos% = CSRLIN: COLOR 14, 4
    LOCATE 23, 1: PRINT SPACE$(160);
    errCode$ = RIGHT$("00" + LTRIM$(RTRIM$(STR$(ERR))), 3)
    recoverable% = INSTR(eMessage(0), errCode$)
    LOCATE 23, 6

    IF recoverable% THEN
        recoverable% = recoverable% \ 3 + 1
        PRINT LTRIM$(RTRIM$(ERDEV$));
        PRINT eMessage(recoverable%); " and try again.": BEEP
        PRINT "     Press a key when ready, Esc to abort. > ";
        LOCATE , , 1
        r$ = INPUT$(1)
        IF r$ = CHR$(27) THEN RESUME Finish    ' abort if user presses Esc
        COLOR 7, 0: LOCATE 23, 1: PRINT SPACE$(160);
        LOCATE yPos%, xPos%, 0: RESUME
    ELSE
        PRINT "A type"; STR$(ERR); " error has just occurred!"
        BEEP: PRINT "     "; : ERROR ERR
    END IF
```

ERROR

See also
ERDEV, ERDEV$, ERL, ERR, ON ERROR GOTO, RESUME

Purpose
The ERROR statement simulates the occurrence of a specified error. ERROR is especially useful for debugging error-handling routines. Instead of waiting for a specific error to occur, you can simulate the error to see whether the handler responds to it properly. You can also use ERROR to define your own codes for errors not specified in QBasic's predefined codes.

Syntax
ERROR *errorcode*

errorcode is the number of the error you want to simulate; it must be in the range 1 through 255.

Usage
```
ERROR 10
```
Generates a "Duplicate definition" error.

```
ERROR 251
```
Generates a user-specified error. (QBasic does not define the error code 251.)

ERROR ERR

Repeats the last error. (If used inside an error handler, this statement halts the program and prints the default message for this error.)

Description

The ERROR statement causes the program to behave exactly as if a real error had occurred. If error trapping is enabled, the program branches to the line indicated by the last ON ERROR GOTO statement; otherwise, QBasic halts execution and displays the error message that corresponds to the specified error code.

If the specified value corresponds to a number used by QBasic and error trapping is not enabled, the program stops and generates the appropriate error message; if the value does not correspond to a number, the program stops and displays an "Unprintable error" error message. You can, however, replace this catchall message with one of your own by writing an error-handling routine that traps the error.

You can use the ERROR statement to define your own errors so that you can check your trapping of circumstances or exceptions that you want to prevent but that are not easily caused. To use this technique, be sure the error code you choose is one not reserved by QBasic. Then check for that error code in the error-handling routine.

Errors

If you specify in an ERROR statement a value that is greater than 255 or less than 1, QBasic displays an "Illegal function call" error message.

Example

Most programs impose constraints on the kinds of entries the user can make; for example, a program might refuse to accept inappropriate data even if the data is within the limits of the variable and would not normally cause an input error. The following game program responds to a player's mistakes by using ERROR to define and set a program-defined error.

```
RANDOMIZE TIMER
CLS
PRINT "The object of this game is to keep the man from falling off the"
PRINT "table. Use the left and right arrow keys to help him stay put."
PRINT "< Press any key to continue >"
DO WHILE INKEY$ = ""
LOOP

CLS : LOCATE 12, 25, 0: PRINT STRING$(30, CHR$(223))
x% = 40: counter% = 0: score% = 0: lives% = 5
leftArrow$ = CHR$(0) + CHR$(75)
rightArrow$ = CHR$(0) + CHR$(77)
escape$ = CHR$(27)
ON ERROR GOTO Trap
```

(continued)

continued

```
DO
    LOCATE 1, 38: PRINT USING "#####"; score%
    LOCATE 11, x%: PRINT " ";
    IF counter% > 20 THEN
        x% = x% + SGN(RND - .5) * (difficulty% / 200 + 1)
        score% = score% + 1
        difficulty% = difficulty% + 1     ' make task more difficult
        counter% = 0
    END IF
    keyStroke$ = INKEY$
    IF keyStroke$ = leftArrow$ THEN x% = x% - 1
    IF keyStroke$ = rightArrow$ THEN x% = x% + 1
    IF keyStroke$ = escape$ THEN EXIT DO
    LOCATE 11, x%: PRINT CHR$(2);
    IF x% < 25 THEN ERROR 251     ' error for falling off left side
    IF x% > 55 THEN ERROR 252     ' error for falling off right side
    counter% = counter% + 1
LOOP WHILE lives%
LOCATE 24, 35: PRINT "You lose";
END

Trap:
    LOCATE 11, x%: PRINT " "; : difficulty% = 0: x% = 40
    SELECT CASE ERR
    CASE 251      ' program-defined error for falling off of left side
        LOCATE 24, 25: PRINT "You fell off of the left side!";
        BEEP: LOCATE 24, 25: PRINT SPACE$(30);
        lives% = lives% - 1
        RESUME NEXT
    CASE 252      ' program-defined error for falling off of right side
        LOCATE 24, 25: PRINT "You fell off of the right side!";
        BEEP: LOCATE 24, 25: PRINT SPACE$(31);
        lives% = lives% - 1
        RESUME NEXT
    CASE ELSE
        LOCATE 24, 26: ERROR ERR
    END SELECT
```

ON ERROR GOTO

See also

ERDEV, ERDEV$, ERL, ERR, ERROR, RESUME

Purpose

The ON ERROR GOTO statement enables error handling and specifies the location of the error handler. It lets your program trap runtime errors that usually halt execution so that your program executes an error handler that reports the error and helps the user recover from it.

Syntax

ON ERROR GOTO {*line* ¦ *label*}

line or *label* is the line number or label that indicates the first program line of the error handler.

Usage

```
ON ERROR GOTO Trap
```
Enables error trapping and specifies *Trap* as the label of the error-handling routine.

```
ON ERROR GOTO 0
```
Turns off error handling.

Description

Your program must execute an ON ERROR GOTO statement before the program can trap errors. You can use as many ON ERROR GOTO statements as you have routines to handle them. Whenever the program executes a new ON ERROR GOTO statement, it replaces the information from the previous ON ERROR GOTO statement with new information. The section of code that an ON ERROR GOTO statement specifies is called an error handler or an error-handling routine.

After the program executes an ON ERROR GOTO statement, the occurrence of any subsequent error causes the program to branch to the specified line number or label. The program then executes an error-handling routine until it encounters a RESUME statement, which either returns control to the interrupted task or branches to another part of the program.

If you specify line number 0 in an ON ERROR GOTO statement, ON ERROR GOTO turns off error handling. If the program is already in an error handler when 0 is specified, the program halts and prints the appropriate error message.

Errors

If you specify, in an ON ERROR GOTO statement, a line number or label that does not exist in your program, QBasic displays a "Label not defined" error message.

Example

Many runtime errors can be corrected without terminating the program if the program instructs the user how to fix the problem. The following program uses an ON ERROR GOTO statement so that control branches to an error-handling routine that recognizes two recoverable errors and lets the user correct the problems.

```
CONST FALSE = 0, TRUE = NOT FALSE

ON ERROR GOTO Trap     ' begin error trapping and specify error handler

CLS
ERROR 27    ' simulate printer-out-of-paper error to test whether routine works

Egress:
    COLOR 7, 0: LOCATE 20, 1, 1: RESET
END

Trap:
    device$ = ERDEV$   ' get name of device that caused the error
    recoverable% = FALSE
    COLOR 14, 4

    SELECT CASE ERR
    CASE 27
        message1$ = "PRINTER " + device$ + " IS OUT OF PAPER"
        message2$ = "Load paper and press any key."
        recoverable% = TRUE
    CASE 71
        message1$ = "DISK IN DRIVE " + device$ + "IS NOT READY"
        message2$ = "Check that drive door is closed and press any key."
        recoverable% = TRUE
    CASE ELSE
        message1$ = "A type" + STR$(ERR) + " error has just occurred."
    END SELECT

    IF NOT recoverable% THEN
        LOCATE 24, 1: PRINT SPACE$(80);
        message1$ = message1$ + ", aborting program. Press any key."
        LOCATE 24, 6: PRINT message1$; : BEEP
        r$ = INPUT$(1)
        RESUME Egress
    ELSE
        col% = POS(0): row% = CSRLIN
        LOCATE 23, 1: PRINT SPACE$(160);
        LOCATE 23, 40 - (LEN(message1$) \ 2): PRINT message1$;
        message2$ = message2$ + " Press Esc to quit program."
        LOCATE 24, 40 - (LEN(message2$) \ 2): PRINT message2$;
        r$ = INPUT$(1)
        IF r$ = CHR$(27) THEN RESUME Egress
        COLOR 7, 0: LOCATE 23, 1: PRINT SPACE$(160);
        LOCATE row%, col%
        RESUME
    END IF
```

RESUME

See also

ON ERROR GOTO

Purpose

The RESUME statement redirects program execution from an error-trapping handler. If a runtime error is recoverable, the error-handling routine that traps it must let program execution continue after the error has been corrected.

Syntax

RESUME [*line* ¦ *label*]
RESUME NEXT

line or *label* is the line number or label that indicates the line at which execution continues.

Usage

RESUME
Retries the statement that caused an error.

RESUME NEXT
Skips the statement that caused an error and resumes execution with the next statement.

RESUME Egress
Resumes execution, after an error, with the statement following the label *Egress*.

Description

The RESUME statement returns control to the statement that caused the error, allowing the program to try to proceed. RESUME NEXT skips the statement that caused the error and transfers control to the next statement. The RESUME statement with a line number or label specified branches execution to the specified line.

You can use a RESUME statement only in an error-handling routine that has already been enabled by an ON ERROR GOTO statement. When a runtime error triggers a branch to the handling routine, QBasic disables the trapping of subsequent errors. This prevents the program from recursively executing the error handler if another error occurs. RESUME enables error trapping again so that the error handler specified in the previous ON ERROR GOTO statement will be used in the event of an error.

All error-handling routines must contain at least one RESUME statement to direct control back to the main program. You cannot end the program inside the handler.

RESUME is useful when the error that occurred is recoverable—for example, when the program tries to read from a floppy-disk drive when the drive door is open.

If your error handler is sophisticated enough to recognize this error, it can first instruct the user to close the drive door and then execute a RESUME statement to try the operation again.

If the operation cannot be tried again but the error was not sufficiently serious to warrant terminating the program, your handler can execute a RESUME NEXT statement to ignore the line containing the error and continue processing with the statement that follows.

Avoid using RESUME statements that specify a line number or label. The code at the target line must be capable of handling returns from errors throughout the program. Specifying a line has two main uses: It handles returns from special-purpose error traps built around a particularly vulnerable section of code, and it directs control to a routine that safely terminates the program when all else fails. The target line must be in the main program. You cannot use RESUME with a line number or label to branch into a subprogram or function. However, if the error occurred in a subprogram or function, a RESUME statement without an argument or a RESUME NEXT statement will return control to the subprogram or function.

Errors

If an error-handling routine does not include a RESUME statement, QBasic displays a "No RESUME" error message. If you use RESUME with a line number or label that does not exist, QBasic displays a "Label not defined" error message.

Example

A program can run under several types of computer configurations by first determining the host system's capabilities at runtime and then modifying its behavior accordingly. The simplest way to do this is to use a hardware-specific feature and see whether an error occurs. The following routine uses this technique to see whether the system supports a 43-line display. If the system supports only 25 lines, the program uses a RESUME NEXT statement to continue the program.

```
screenLines% = 43          ' assume 43-line display
ON ERROR GOTO VideoTrap    ' enable error trapping
WIDTH , 43                 ' try to set 43 lines
ON ERROR GOTO 0            ' turn off error trapping

Egress:
    IF screenLines% = 43 THEN WIDTH , 25    ' reset standard screen
END

VideoTrap:
    screenLines% = 25      ' change to 25 lines
    IF ERR = 5 THEN        ' check whether error was illegal function call
        RESUME NEXT        ' continue execution
    ELSE                   ' terminate program if it was any other error
        RESUME Egress
    END IF
```

CHAPTER 10

Timing, Date, and Time

Introduction

QBasic offers several statements and functions that work with the date and time. These statements and functions enable your programs to provide users with information about when a certain event took place or how long it lasted. The most basic of these tasks include displaying the date and time. Other QBasic features let your program time an activity or perform a task at regular intervals.

In most computers, time is clocked by a microchip. On the IBM PC, the timer chip (the Intel 8253-5) interrupts the computer 18.2 times per second. Each interruption is called a clock tick. During each interruption, the ROM BIOS of the computer notes that one more tick has occurred. When you ask for the time, DOS calculates the time by counting the number of ticks that have passed since midnight.

This tutorial summarizes QBasic's timing capabilities and offers some suggestions for their use. Table 10-1 lists QBasic's timing statements and functions alphabetically.

Statement or function	Description
DATE$ (Statement and function)	Sets or returns the current date
ON TIMER GOSUB	Specifies the location of a timer event-handling routine and the number of seconds between executions of the routine
SLEEP	Pauses the program
TIME$ (Statement and function)	Sets or returns the current time
TIMER	Returns the number of seconds since midnight
TIMER ON/OFF/STOP	Enables, disables, or temporarily suspends the timer event trap specified by the ON TIMER statement

Table 10-1.
QBasic timing statements and functions.

Setting and Getting the Current Date

When you start your computer, DOS might ask you to specify the date and time; however, most computers now include clocks that don't stop when you turn off your computer. These clocks maintain the current date and time. DOS uses the date and time to time stamp your files on disk. You see this time stamp when you use the DIR command to produce a directory listing of your files. You can use the DATE$ statement in QBasic to change the date that DOS uses. Be careful when you use DATE$ because any files you create or update will have an incorrect time stamp if you change the date.

To gain access to the current date in QBasic, use DATE$ as a function. DATE$ returns the current date; however, if you've used the DATE$ statement to change the date, the DATE$ function returns the new date.

Setting and Getting the Current Time

In addition to the date, DOS includes the current time on the time stamp of a file when the file is created or updated. The TIME$ statement lets you change the time that DOS uses. When you use TIME$, DOS keeps track of time beginning at the moment you specify. If you change the time with the TIME$ statement, any files you create or update will be stamped with a time based on the time you specified.

To gain access to the current time, use TIME$ as a function. TIME$ returns the current time; however, if you've used the TIME$ statement to change the time, the TIME$ function returns the new time. Computers aren't perfect timekeepers, and their internal clocks are likely to be slightly inaccurate. Because the IBM PC timer ticks 18.2 times a second, the time of day is accurate to approximately $^{54}/_{1000}$ of a second.

If you need to time the length of a specific operation, you can use the QBasic TIMER function. The TIMER function returns the number of seconds past midnight. To use it, call TIMER, perform the operation, and then call TIMER again. The difference between the two results is the number of seconds the operation took to complete.

A program that uses TIMER has a potential problem if a user runs it late at night. Because the TIMER function returns the number of seconds that have elapsed since midnight, TIMER returns the value 0 at midnight. Therefore, if a program is running at 11:59 P.M. and stops at 12:01 A.M., for example, you must adjust the results, as shown in the following program segment:

```
startTime& = TIMER
:
endTime& = TIMER

IF endTime& < startTime& THEN          ' check was executing at midnight
    endTime& = endTime& + 86400        ' adjust time
END IF

PRINT endTime& - startTime&; "seconds elapsed"
```

Pausing the Program

If you want to give the user a chance to read a screen or perform a task, use QBasic's SLEEP statement. SLEEP pauses the program for the length of time you specify. However, users who finish reading the screen or complete their task before the specified time can simply press a key to interrupt the SLEEP statement.

Setting Up and Managing the Timer Event Trap

QBasic also provides a set of statements that set a timer event trap. This event trap lets the program execute a subroutine every time a specified number of seconds has passed. You might use a timer event trap to update the time on the screen every minute or to save the user's file on disk periodically.

QBasic's event-trapping statements for the timer are ON TIMER GOSUB, TIMER ON, TIMER OFF, and TIMER STOP. You must initialize timer event trapping with the ON TIMER GOSUB statement and then enable trapping by using TIMER ON. Forgetting to enable trapping is a common mistake.

The following lines initialize an event trap and enable the program to execute the subroutine at the label *ShowClock* every 60 seconds:

```
ON TIMER(60) GOSUB ShowClock    ' initialize event trap
TIMER ON                        ' enable it
```

Because event trapping slows your program considerably, you might want to turn off event trapping during critical operations in your program, such as serial I/O communications. You turn off timer event trapping with the TIMER OFF statement. While timer event trapping is disabled, your program executes as though the timer event trap didn't exist. You can also turn off the timer event trap with the TIMER STOP statement. When you use the TIMER STOP statement, the program notes whether the specified number of seconds passes, but it doesn't immediately execute the event trap's subroutine. However, when you execute another TIMER ON statement, the program executes the subroutine.

Related Reading

Norton, Peter, and Richard Wilton. *The* New *Peter Norton Programmer's Guide to the IBM PC & PS/2*. Redmond, Wash.: Microsoft Press, 1988.

Prata, Stephen, with Harry Henderson. *The Waite Group's Microsoft QuickBASIC Primer Plus*. Redmond, Wash.: Microsoft Press, 1990.

DATE$ (Statement and function)

See also

TIME$ (Statement and function)

Purpose

The DATE$ statement sets the date kept by the computer to a new date. The DATE$ function returns the current date kept by the computer. You can use DATE$ to print a specified date on report headings.

Syntax

Statement:

DATE$ = *expr*

Function:

DATE$

expr is a string expression that must be in one of the following forms: *mm-dd-yy*, *mm-dd-yyyy*, *mm/dd/yy*, or *mm/dd/yyyy*. *mm* represents the month number, *dd* the day number, *yy* the year within the twentieth century, and *yyyy* the year including the century. QBasic doesn't require a zero in front of a single-digit month or day value.

Usage

```
PRINT "Today is "; DATE$
```
Displays the current date.

```
todaysDate$ = DATE$
```
Assigns the current date to the string variable *todaysDate$*.

```
DATE$ = "01-21-1992"
```
Sets the date to January 21, 1992.

```
DATE$ = todaysDate$
```
Sets the date to the date contained in the variable *todaysDate$*.

Description

You can use DATE$ as both a statement and a function. When you use DATE$ as a statement, QBasic sets the date; when you use DATE$ as a function, QBasic returns the current date.

DATE$ as a statement

Use the DATE$ statement to set the system's date, the date used by both QBasic and DOS. The DATE$ statement requires a syntax that is different from that of most QBasic statements. You must use DATE$ in an assignment statement of which the left side is the DATE$ keyword and the right side is a string that specifies the new date.

DATE$ as a function

Use the DATE$ function to retrieve the current date. The DATE$ function returns the date in the form *mm-dd-yyyy*: two digits for the month (1 through 12), a dash, two digits for the day (1 through 31), a dash, and four digits for the year. Notice that any single-digit number includes a leading zero.

Errors

If you use an invalid date (such as "June 31" or "1979") with the DATE$ statement, QBasic displays an "Illegal function call" error message. If you use an expression other than a string expression in the DATE$ statement, QBasic displays a "Type mismatch" error message.

Warnings

You cannot set a date that is earlier than January 1, 1980, or later than December 31, 2099.

Example

The following program uses the DATE$ statement to change the date to the user's birthday and then the DATE$ function to display the date.

```
DEFINT A-Z

DIM months(12) AS STRING, numMonth AS INTEGER
DIM day AS INTEGER, year AS INTEGER, suffix AS STRING

FOR i% = 1 TO 12              ' get month names from DATA statements
    READ months(i%)
NEXT

INPUT "What is your birthday <day-month>"; birthday$
oldDate$ = DATE$             ' save the current date
DATE$ = birthday$ + "-1990"  ' change the date

numMonth = VAL(LEFT$(DATE$, 2))   ' get month from mm-dd-yyyy
day = VAL(MID$(DATE$, 4, 2))      ' get day from mm-dd-yyyy
year = VAL(RIGHT$(DATE$, 4))      ' get year from mm-dd-yyyy

SELECT CASE day
    CASE 1, 21, 31           ' ordinals that end in "st"
        suffix = "st"

    CASE 2, 22               ' ordinals that end in "nd"
        suffix = "nd"

    CASE 3, 23               ' ordinals that end in "rd"
        suffix = "rd"
```

(continued)

continued

```
    CASE ELSE                        ' ordinals that end in "th"
        suffix = "th"
END SELECT

PRINT USING "Your birthday is & ##&, ####"; months(numMonth); day; suffix; year
DATE$ = oldDate$                     ' reset the date to the current date

DATA "January", "February", "March", "April", "May", "June", "July"
DATA "August", "September", "October", "November", "December"
```

ON TIMER GOSUB

See also
TIMER ON/OFF/STOP

Purpose
QBasic's ON TIMER GOSUB statement specifies the subprogram that a program executes every time a specified number of seconds has passed. You can use the ON TIMER GOSUB statement to specify the subroutine that displays and updates the time at regular intervals.

Syntax
ON TIMER(*time*) GOSUB {*line* ¦ *label*}

time is an integer in the range 1 through 86400 that specifies the number of seconds that must pass before control branches to a subroutine.

line or *label* is the line number or label that specifies the first line of a subroutine.

Usage
```
ON TIMER(60) GOSUB UpdateClock TIMER ON
```
Specifies that the subroutine starting at label *UpdateClock* will be executed every 60 seconds.

Description
The ON TIMER GOSUB statement specifies the location of a timer event-handling routine and the number of seconds between executions of the routine. An event-handling routine is a subroutine that is executed when a specified event occurs. The ON TIMER GOSUB statement specifies the details of a timer event trap, which executes a subroutine every time the number of seconds specified in the ON TIMER GOSUB statement passes. Note that the subroutine must be in the main program.

When the timer event-handling subroutine begins executing, QBasic implicitly executes a TIMER STOP statement so that the event-handling subroutine is not executed recursively. However, because QBasic uses TIMER STOP, if another timer event occurs while the subroutine executes, QBasic keeps track of the event and executes the subroutine at the next TIMER ON statement. When the subroutine encounters a RETURN statement, QBasic executes a TIMER ON statement unless the subroutine executed a TIMER OFF statement.

The event-trapping subroutine can end with a RETURN statement that specifies a line number or label. The statement causes execution to branch to a specified line in your program. This version of the RETURN statement can cause serious problems because the event trap can occur at any point in your program. Also, the RETURN statement that specifies a line or label cannot return control to a subprogram or function. (See the GOSUB...RETURN entry in Chapter 4, "Procedures," for details.)

Errors

In an ON TIMER GOSUB statement, if you specify a line number or label that does not exist or that is in a procedure, QBasic displays a "Label not defined" error message. If you specify more than 86,400 seconds (the number of seconds in 24 hours) or less than 1 second, QBasic displays an "Illegal function call" error message. If you specify a non-numeric expression as the number of seconds, QBasic displays a "Type mismatch" error message.

Tips

Using event trapping slows your programs considerably. Try to avoid using event trapping in routines in which speed is a critical factor.

Example

The following program uses the ON TIMER GOSUB statement to specify the subroutine that updates a time display every 60 seconds.

```
CLS
GOSUB UpdateClock                  ' display the initial time

ON TIMER(60) GOSUB UpdateClock     ' specify location and timing of event trap
TIMER ON                           ' enable timer event trapping

LOCATE 5, 1: PRINT "Press any key to quit"
DO UNTIL INKEY$ <> ""              ' loop until user presses a key
LOOP
END

UpdateClock:
    LOCATE 1, 1
    PRINT DATE$, LEFT$(TIME$, 5)   ' display the hours and minutes
    RETURN
```

SLEEP

See also

ON COM GOSUB, ON KEY(n) GOSUB, ON PEN GOSUB, ON PLAY GOSUB, ON STRIG GOSUB, ON TIMER GOSUB, TIMER

Purpose

The SLEEP statement pauses the program until a specified number of seconds has passed, a key is pressed, or an event occurs. You can use the SLEEP statement to pause a program so that the user has time to read an output screen.

Syntax

SLEEP [*time*]

time is an optional integer expression that specifies the number of seconds the program will pause.

Usage

SLEEP

Pauses the program until the user presses a key or an event occurs.

SLEEP 5

Pauses the program for 5 seconds or until the user presses a key or an event occurs.

Description

The SLEEP statement lets you insert pauses in a program. SLEEP suspends execution until one of the following occurs:

■ The specified number of seconds passes

■ The user presses a key

■ QBasic encounters a trapped event. (See ON COM GOSUB, ON KEY(n) GOSUB, ON PEN GOSUB, ON PLAY GOSUB, ON STRIG GOSUB, or ON TIMER GOSUB.)

The number of seconds specified must be an integer expression; if it is less than 1 (or not specified), the program pauses until either the second or third condition occurs. If the number is a floating-point value, SLEEP converts the number to an integer.

The SLEEP statement responds only to keystrokes and events that occur after the SLEEP statement executes. Therefore, all keystrokes in the keyboard buffer are ignored.

Trapped events can interrupt the SLEEP statement only if they have been enabled by the appropriate ON statement and have not been turned off or suspended by the corresponding OFF or STOP statement.

Comments

The specified number of seconds is an integer expression, and therefore its accuracy is limited to whole seconds. If you need to pause for increments of less than a second, use the TIMER function in a loop statement.

Errors

If you specify a non-numeric expression in a SLEEP statement, QBasic displays a "Type mismatch" error message.

Warnings

You can press any key to interrupt a SLEEP statement, including the Shift, Ctrl, Alt, Caps Lock, Num Lock, and Scroll Lock keys. Therefore, the user cannot press the Shift-PrtSc key combination to produce a screen dump during a pause created by the SLEEP statement.

Example

The following program uses the SLEEP statement to pause the display so that the user has time to read the screen.

```
CLS
PRINT "You have"; FRE(-1); "bytes of free space for arrays."
PRINT "You have"; FRE(-2); "bytes of free stack space."

PRINT
PRINT "Copy this information and then press any key to continue."
PRINT
PRINT "This screen will self-destruct in 10 seconds..."
SLEEP 10
CLS
```

TIME$ (Statement and function)

See also

DATE$ (Statement and function), TIMER ON/OFF/STOP

Purpose

The TIME$ statement sets the time kept by the computer to a new time. The TIME$ function returns the current time kept by the computer. For example, you can use TIME$ to print a specific time on report headings.

Syntax

Statement:

TIME$ = *expr*

Function:

TIME$

expr is a string expression that must appear in one of the following forms:

hh	Sets the hour; minutes and seconds default to 0
hh:mm	Sets the hour and minutes; seconds default to 0
hh:mm:ss	Sets the hour, minutes, and seconds

bh represents the hour (0 through 23), *mm* the minutes (0 through 59), and *ss* the seconds (0 through 59). Note that QBasic doesn't require zeros in front of single-digit hour, minute, or second values.

Usage

```
PRINT "It is now "; TIME$
```
Displays the current time.

```
now$ = TIME$
```
Assigns the current time to the string variable *now$*.

```
TIME$ = "10:35:30"
```
Sets the time to 35½ minutes after 10 A.M.

```
TIME$ = "10"
```
Sets the time to 10 A.M.

```
TIME$ = now$
```
Sets the time to that contained in the variable *now$*.

Description

You can use TIME$ as both a statement and a function. When you use TIME$ as a statement, QBasic sets the time; when you use TIME$ as a function, QBasic returns the current time.

TIME$ as a statement

Use the TIME$ statement to set the current time of the system's internal clock; the clock will begin counting at the time you specify. The TIME$ statement requires a syntax that is different from that of most QBasic statements. You must use TIME$ in an assignment statement of which the left side is the TIME$ keyword and the right side is a string that specifies the new time.

TIME$ as a function

Use the TIME$ function to retrieve the current time. The TIME$ function returns the current time in the form *bh:mm:ss*: two digits for the hour (0 through 23), a colon, two digits for the minutes (0 through 59), a colon, and two digits for the seconds (0 through 59). Notice that any single-digit number includes a leading zero.

Errors

If you use an invalid time (such as "26:65:00") with the TIME$ statement, QBasic displays an "Illegal function call" error message. If you use an expression other than a string expression in the TIME$ statement, QBasic displays a "Type mismatch" error message.

Example

The following program uses the TIME$ statement to change the system time to 3:30 A.M. and then the TIME$ function to display the time.

```
DEFINT A-Z

DIM hour AS INTEGER, minute AS INTEGER, suffix AS STRING

oldTime$ = TIME$                    ' save the current system time
TIME$ = "3:30"                      ' set the time to 3:30 A.M.

hour = VAL(LEFT$(TIME$, 2))         ' get the hour from hh:mm:ss
minute = VAL(MID$(TIME$, 4, 2))     ' get the minute from hh:mm:ss

IF hour = 0 THEN                    ' show midnight as 12 A.M.
    hour = 12
    suffix = "A.M."
ELSEIF hour < 12 THEN
    suffix = "A.M."
ELSE
    hour = hour - 12
    suffix = "P.M."
END IF

PRINT USING "The time is now ##:## &"; hour; minute; suffix

TIME$ = oldTime$                    ' reset time
END
```

TIMER

See also

ON TIMER GOSUB, TIMER ON/OFF/STOP

Purpose

The TIMER function returns the number of seconds that have elapsed since midnight. Use the TIMER function to time the length of specific operations.

Syntax

TIMER

Usage

startTime& = TIMER

Assigns the current number of seconds past midnight to the long integer *startTime&*.

Description

The TIMER function returns values in the range 0 to 86400. Sometimes you need to know how much time certain operations require. The TIMER function provides an easy way to time operations: Merely subtract the TIMER value at the beginning of the operation from the TIMER value at the end; the result is the duration of the operation in seconds.

Comments

Because the value TIMER returns is always changing, programmers often use this function as the argument in the RANDOMIZE statement. (See the RANDOMIZE entry in Chapter 7, "Math," for details.)

Warnings

Because the TIMER function returns the number of seconds that have elapsed since midnight, the timer returns the value 0 at midnight. Therefore, if a program that uses TIMER will be run at midnight, be sure to adjust the results properly.

Example

The following program uses the TIMER function to calculate the time it takes to generate and display 2000 random numbers. The TIMER function is also used in the RANDOMIZE statement to reseed the random-number generator.

```
CLS
startTime& = TIMER

RANDOMIZE TIMER
FOR i% = 1 TO 2000
    PRINT RND * 1000,
NEXT

endTime& = TIMER
PRINT
PRINT endTime& - startTime&; "seconds elapsed"
```

TIMER ON/OFF/STOP

See also

ON TIMER GOSUB

Purpose

The TIMER statements enable, disable, or suspend timer event trapping. Use a TIMER ON statement, for example, to enable event trapping that updates a clock displayed on the screen.

Syntax

```
TIMER ON
TIMER OFF
TIMER STOP
```

Usage

```
ON TIMER(60) GOSUB EveryMinute
TIMER ON
```

Turns on event trapping so that the program executes the subroutine beginning at the label *EveryMinute* every 60 seconds.

```
TIMER OFF
```

Disables event trapping.

Description

After you call the ON TIMER GOSUB statement to specify the details of a timer event trap, you must enable the event trapping by using the TIMER ON statement. Then, after every statement, QBasic checks to see whether the time specified in the ON TIMER statement has elapsed. If it has, QBasic executes the subroutine specified in the ON TIMER GOSUB statement. (See the ON TIMER GOSUB entry in this chapter for details.)

The TIMER OFF statement disables timer event trapping. No event trapping occurs until the program executes another TIMER ON statement.

The TIMER STOP statement suspends timer event trapping. No event trapping occurs until the program executes another TIMER ON statement. However, if an event occurs after the TIMER STOP statement, the program sets a flag so that it "remembers" the event. When the program encounters another TIMER ON statement, the event is trapped.

QBasic executes an implicit TIMER STOP statement whenever it enters a timer event-handling routine. This ensures that another occurrence of the event does not cause the handler to be executed recursively. When the program encounters a RETURN statement and returns to the main program, it reinstates the timer event trap by executing a TIMER ON statement.

Tips

Event-trapping statements increase the size of your executable programs and slow them considerably. Try to avoid using event-trapping statements in routines in which speed is a critical factor.

Example

See the example in the ON TIMER GOSUB entry, in this chapter.

SECTION II

MULTIMEDIA

CHAPTER 11

Graphics

Introduction

One of the strengths of QBasic is its built-in set of graphics commands. QBasic includes support for the additional colors and high-resolution video modes of the new generation of EGA and VGA graphics adapters.

Table 11-1 is an alphabetic list of QBasic's graphics statements and functions.

Statement or function	Description
CIRCLE	Draws a circle, ellipse, arc, or segment at a given location on the screen. You can specify the radius, color, and aspect ratio of the object.
COLOR	Sets the default foreground and background colors for the current screen. In some video modes, it can also set the color of the screen border.
DRAW	Executes a string of instructions that define the size, shape, angle, and color of a graphics figure.
GET (Graphics)	Copies a graphics image from the screen into an array in memory.
LINE	Draws a line connecting two sets of coordinates, or draws a rectangle with the two sets of coordinates specifying its opposite corners.
PAINT	Fills an outlined area of the display with a specified color or pattern.
PALETTE, PALETTE USING	Assigns color values to the display attributes in EGA, VGA, and MCGA systems.
PCOPY	Copies the contents of one screen page to another.
PMAP	Translates between logical and physical pixel coordinates.
POINT	Returns the color of the specified pixel or the coordinates of the graphics cursor.
PRESET	Resets a pixel on the screen to the background color or to a specified color.
PSET	Sets a pixel on the screen to the foreground color or to a specified color.
PUT (Graphics)	Copies a graphics image from an array in memory to a specified location on the screen.
SCREEN (Function)	Returns the character or color attribute for the character at the specified row and column.
SCREEN (Statement)	Sets the current display mode and screen page.
VIEW	Defines the physical coordinates of the current graphics viewport.
WINDOW	Defines a logical coordinate system on which graphics images are plotted.

Table 11-1.
QBasic graphics statements and functions.

Display Adapters

Table 11-2 lists the types of display adapters supported by QBasic.

Name	Abbreviation
Monochrome Display and Printer Adapter	MDPA
Color Graphics Adapter	CGA
Hercules Graphics Card	HGC
Olivetti	—
AT&T	—
Enhanced Graphics Adapter	EGA
Multi-Color Graphics Array	MCGA
Video Graphics Array	VGA

Table 11-2.
Display adapters supported by QBasic.

The MDPA and CGA were the original display adapters used in the IBM PC. The MDPA adapter can display 25 rows of 80-column text on a monochrome display, but it has no graphics capabilities. This 80-by-25-character format is the default text mode for all display adapters.

The CGA supports graphics in addition to text. When used with a color monitor, it can display 25 rows of 80-column text in 16 foreground and 8 background colors. Two graphics modes are available: medium resolution (320-by-200-pixel with 4 colors) and high resolution (640-by-200-pixel with 2 colors).

In addition to 80-by-25-character text, the Hercules Graphics Card (HGC) can display graphics in high resolution (720-by-348-pixel) on a monochrome monitor. To use an HGC adapter to produce graphics in the QBasic environment, you must first install a resident driver program (MS-HERC.COM) in memory. Microsoft does include MS-HERC.COM in the DOS package.

QBasic also supports Olivetti and AT&T adapters. These adapters can display 80-by-25-character text and 640-by-400-pixel graphics. You can choose one of 16 foreground colors, but the background color is always black.

New display adapters introduced higher resolution and more colors yet preserved compatibility with previous standards. The EGA supports the MDPA text mode and the CGA graphics modes and adds further graphics modes. The highest resolution possible with an EGA adapter is 640 by 350 pixels with 16 colors.

The IBM PS/2-series computers introduced two new video adapters. The MCGA is similar to the CGA, but it adds two extra graphics modes: a medium-resolution mode (320-by-200-pixel with 256 colors) and a very-high-resolution mode (640-by-480-pixel with 2 colors). The MCGA does not support the EGA graphics modes. The successor to the EGA is the VGA, which can display all the modes of the MDPA, CGA, EGA, and MCGA, as well as its own 640-by-480-pixel 16-color mode. Additional colors for the

MCGA and VGA adapters are created through the use of analog monitors, which blend colors on the screen to produce a vast range of shades and textures.

Pixels and Resolution

The previous section referred to the capabilities of the adapters in graphics modes by using pixels to indicate their degree of resolution. A pixel is one picture element—the smallest point that can be individually set or reset on the screen. The more pixels available, the higher (or finer) the resolution of the pictures that can be drawn. For example, a medium-resolution display can display 320 by 200 (64,000) pixels; higher resolutions can display 640 by 480 (307,200) pixels.

Another factor that distinguishes adapters is color. Not all adapters can display color; the HGC adapter, for example, can display pixels on the screen in only two ways—either on or off. The CGA and EGA adapters have resolutions that can display pixels in 2, 4, or 16 colors, and the VGA and MCGA adapters can blend colors, thus displaying as many as 256 different shades in a medium-resolution graphics mode.

Table 11-3 lists display resolutions, the number of colors available at each resolution, and the mode and adapters required to produce them.

Resolution	Colors	Mode	Adapters required
320-by-200-pixel	4	1	CGA, MCGA, EGA, VGA
	16	7	EGA, VGA
	256	13	MCGA, VGA
640-by-200-pixel	2	2	CGA, MCGA, EGA, VGA
	16	8	EGA, VGA
640 by 350	4	10	EGA, VGA
	16	9	EGA, VGA
640 by 400	16	4	Olivetti, AT&T
720 by 348	2	3	HGC
640 by 480	2	11	MCGA, VGA
	16	12	VGA

Table 11-3.
Graphics resolution and colors and the mode and adapters required to produce them.

Screen Modes

The QBasic SCREEN statement lets you select from your adapter's available display modes. To switch to a 640-by-350-pixel 16-color EGA mode, for example, you execute the statement *SCREEN 9.*

The screen mode you use defines the graphics resolution and the number of available colors. QBasic offers 11 modes for graphics and 1 mode for text. The Mode column in Table 11-3 lists the numbers that you use with the SCREEN statement to access different graphics screen modes. Specify the text mode by using the statement *SCREEN 0*.

Screen Coordinates

The pixels on a graphics screen are numbered in rows and columns. Columns are numbered from the left of the screen to the right, and rows are numbered from the top to the bottom. The number of rows and columns available depends on the screen resolution: screen mode 2, for example, has 640 columns by 200 rows.

You locate an individual pixel by using a pair of coordinates that specifies the pixel's row and column. The first coordinate, usually referred to as the horizontal (or x) coordinate, is the column number, and the second, the vertical (or y) coordinate, is the row. Figure 11-1 shows the range of pixel coordinates available in screen mode 9. Because coordinate values begin at 0, the pixel at the upper left corner of the screen is specified by the coordinate pair (0, 0) in any graphics mode. In a 640-by-350-pixel-resolution screen (screen mode 9), the pixel in the center of the screen is at the point specified by the coordinates (319, 174).

Figure 11-1.
Pixel coordinates in screen mode 9.

Drawing on the Screen

QBasic provides two statements that can draw individual pixels. The PSET statement draws a pixel of the given color. If you don't specify a color, PSET draws the pixel in the current foreground color. The PRESET statement also draws a pixel of the given color. But if you don't specify a color, PRESET draws the pixel in the background color. Use PRESET to erase pixels. The POINT function returns information about a pixel. If you specify a particular location, POINT returns the current color of the pixel. You can also use POINT to find the current x- or y-coordinate.

Other QBasic graphics statements use coordinates to plot more elaborate figures. The CIRCLE statement draws a circle or ellipse whose center is at the specified coordinate and whose radius is the specified length. You can also specify the color of the circle and draw arcs and segments instead of a complete circle. To draw a circle with the center at the location (50, 50), a radius of 30, and a green outline, use the following statement:

```
CIRCLE (50, 50), 30, 2
```

The LINE statement draws either a straight line between two coordinate pairs or a rectangle whose opposite corners are located at the specified coordinates.

After you have drawn the outline of an object, you can use the PAINT statement to fill the object with a specified color or pattern. PAINT requires you to provide the coordinates of only one point that is within the outline of the shape you want filled. To color the circle drawn earlier in green, for example, use the statement

```
PAINT (50, 50), 2
```

Instead of using specific, or absolute coordinates, you can use relative coordinates. With relative addressing, the *x*- and *y*-coordinates specified in a statement do not refer to actual row and column coordinates on the screen but to the horizontal and vertical distance of the current pixel from the graphics-cursor position. The graphics-cursor position is usually the location of the most recent point drawn by the previous graphics statement; however, if no statement has been executed, the cursor position defaults to the center of the screen.

Relative addressing is useful for constructing elaborate displays because by changing the original location you can move an entire figure to a different part of the screen. To use relative addressing, you need only add the STEP keyword before the coordinates in a graphics statement.

Colors

All the drawing statements accept arguments that let you specify the color of the figure being drawn. However, QBasic also provides two statements that let you control the default colors of the current screen mode.

The COLOR statement specifies the default foreground and background colors for the display. In some screen modes, you can also select the color of the screen border or choose the palette of colors that will be used. The PALETTE and PALETTE USING statements let you change any or all of the colors that can be displayed. This feature is available only for computers using EGA, VGA, or MCGA adapters.

Viewports and Windows

Although the entire screen is available for graphics, you can restrict output to a smaller section, thus leaving the rest of the screen for text output. The area to which graphics output is restricted is called the graphics viewport. Use the VIEW statement to specify the coordinates that define this rectangular viewport. All subsequent graphics statements must refer to locations within the viewport; any coordinates that fall outside this area are not drawn.

After you define a viewport, the *x*- and *y*-coordinates are measured from the upper left corner of the viewport, not the screen. QBasic programs can define more than one viewport during the course of execution, but only one viewport at a time can be active.

Coordinates on the vertical (*y*) axis are measured downward (from the top of the screen). If you prefer to use the Cartesian coordinate system, in which *y*-coordinates are measured from the bottom of the screen and you want to use coordinates in a range that is different from the default range, you can use the WINDOW statement.

The WINDOW statement lets you define a set of logical, or view, coordinates that match the scale of the figure to be drawn. WINDOW maps these coordinates to the physical viewport, for which coordinates correspond to actual pixel locations. After WINDOW has been called, graphics statements such as LINE, CIRCLE, and PAINT accept arguments from your set of logical coordinates, and QBasic translates the arguments into the physical coordinates that correspond to pixels on the screen.

The logical window shown in Figure 11-2, for example, can be defined by using the statement

```
WINDOW (0, 0)-(1000, 1000)
```

to map a logical coordinate system that uses *x* and *y* values in the range 0 through 1000 onto a 640-by-350-pixel viewport. Vertical coordinates in this logical window are plotted from the bottom of the display.

To plot the point (70, 820) in the logical window, use the PSET statement as you would with absolute coordinates, but use logical coordinates instead:

```
PSET (70, 820)
```

QBasic translates the logical coordinates into physical coordinates, thus setting the pixel at the physical location (45, 63).

Because the conversion of logical into physical coordinates is automatic when you use WINDOW, you rarely need to know the actual address of a pixel. However, if you do need to know, the PMAP function returns the physical location of any logical coordinate.

The WINDOW statement lets you easily produce graphs and charts from your data. It also has many advanced uses. You can, for example, define a logical window that uses a smaller range of coordinates than those defining the physical dimensions of the screen. Any graphics images you then plot are "magnified" when compared to the same images plotted using physical coordinates. Furthermore, by expanding, contracting, or displacing the window's coordinates, you can create the effect of panning or zooming the display.

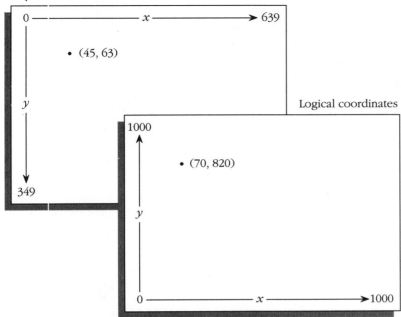
Physical coordinates

Logical coordinates

Figure 11-2.
Mapping logical coordinates to physical coordinates.

Animation

Any image that is drawn on the screen can be captured and stored in memory by the GET statement, which copies the contents of a specified screen area into an array in memory. To restore the captured image at a different screen location, use the PUT statement. PUT copies the contents of an array onto the screen, starting at a specified location. By copying the image to the screen many times and in many different locations, you can produce a variety of animation effects.

Screen Pages

If your adapter provides enough memory, some video modes let you maintain several screens of information; each is stored in a separate "screen page." The SCREEN statement lets you select the "active" page, on which graphics statements draw, and the "visible" page, which the program displays. The two pages need not be the same. You can produce animation by changing visible pages containing an image that occupies a slightly different position on each page.

QBasic also provides the PCOPY statement, which copies the contents of a source page to a destination page. You use this statement to transfer the contents of one screen page to another. For example, if you routinely use a particular page for animation and you want to save a given instance of that page, you can call the PCOPY procedure to copy the image to a page that the program won't alter.

Displaying Graphics by Using the DRAW Statement

The graphics statements already described use a system of "vector" graphics, in which the end points of lines and curves are defined in terms of screen coordinates. The DRAW statement provides another method of drawing on the screen: It lets you define a line in terms of direction and length.

The DRAW statement lets you control the movement of the graphics cursor by using various commands to produce a figure of a specified size, shape, color, and orientation. QBasic provides a wide range of DRAW commands—enough so that the DRAW statement is a versatile graphics language in its own right.

Related Reading

McGregor, Jim, and Alan Watt. *The Art of Graphics for the IBM PC.* Menlo Park, Calif.: Addison-Wesley, 1986.

Wilton, Richard. *Programmer's Guide to PC & PS/2 Video Systems.* Redmond, Wash.: Microsoft Press, 1987.

CIRCLE

See also

COLOR, PAINT, SCREEN (Statement), WINDOW

Purpose

The CIRCLE statement draws a circle of the specified size. Although the default of the statement is the circle, you can use it to draw ellipses, arcs, and segments.

Syntax

CIRCLE [STEP](x, y), radius [, [color] [, [start] [, [stop] [, aspect]]]]

x and y are the screen coordinates of the center of the circle. If you use the STEP keyword, these coordinates are relative to the coordinates of the graphics-cursor position; otherwise, they are absolute references.

radius is the distance from the center of the circle to its circumference; it is measured in the current coordinate system.

color is the color assigned to the circle; if no color is specified, the current foreground color is used.

start and stop are angles (in radians) that specify the beginning and end points of an arc or a segment.

aspect is the aspect ratio, which is the ratio of the vertical radius of the ellipse to the horizontal radius. The default value of aspect is the value that produces a perfect circle in the current screen mode.

Arguments to CIRCLE can be numeric constants, numeric variables, or numeric expressions. Only x, y, and radius are required. The color, start, stop, and aspect parameters are optional and, if omitted, are replaced by the default values. If you omit arguments from the middle of a CIRCLE statement, you must include commas to hold their position; however, you do not need to include commas in place of arguments omitted from the end of the statement.

Usage

```
CIRCLE (160, 100), 40
```
Draws a circle with a radius of 40 pixels at the center of the screen mode 1 display. Because no color is specified, QBasic draws the circle in the current foreground color.

```
CONST PI = 3.14159
CIRCLE STEP(50, -40), 60, 2, -PI, -PI * 2
```
Draws in green an arc with its center 50 pixels to the right and 40 pixels above the graphics-cursor position. The values of the start and stop parameters are negative; therefore, the resulting arc is joined to the center by radii, producing a half circle.

Description

CIRCLE not only draws circles; it can also be used to produce ellipses, arcs, and segments.

To draw a circle, you must specify its location and size. You define its location by using a pair of coordinates to measure the horizontal (x) and vertical (y) distance of the center of the circle from the upper left corner of the display. These distances are measured in the current coordinate system, and the range of possible values is determined by the graphics mode set by the previous SCREEN statement. For example, to position a circle at the center of the screen in screen mode 1 (medium-resolution graphics), you specify x- and y-coordinates of 160 and 100, but in VGA screen modes 11 and 12 you would use coordinates of 320 and 240.

Another way to position a circle is to use the keyword STEP to specify that the x- and y-coordinates are offset from the graphics-cursor position, which is the most recent position of the figure drawn by the previous graphics statement. STEP causes CIRCLE to perform "relative addressing," which has many useful applications. By merely changing the coordinates of the original starting point, a program can completely relocate a large, complex figure.

You define the size of a circle by specifying its radius, which is the distance from the center to the perimeter, drawn along the major (longest) axis of the figure. Measurement is, once again, in the current coordinate system. Circles can be of any size, although any portion of the circle located beyond the screen boundaries is not drawn.

Aspect ratio

To create the appearance of a circle, QBasic actually draws an ellipse, or oval. This approach would not be necessary if the pixels on your screen were equal in height and width; however, because pixels are taller than they are wide, a radius of 50 pixels is shorter horizontally than vertically. Thus a "true" circle would appear taller than it is wide.

Because the size of a pixel on the screen depends on the current screen mode, QBasic calculates a different default aspect ratio for each screen mode in order to produce "round" circles. It does this by using the following formula, in which *xPixels* and *yPixels* are the maximum number of pixels in the x and y axes:

$$aspect = (yPixels \, / \, xPixels) * 4 \, / \, 3$$

In a medium-resolution screen mode (320-by-200-pixel), the default aspect is 0.83333 ($\frac{5}{6}$). In high-resolution mode (640-by-200-pixel), it is half of this, or 0.41667 ($\frac{5}{12}$). Thus to draw an ellipse that appears longer horizontally than vertically, you must specify an aspect ratio that is less than the default for the current screen mode. To draw a tall ellipse, you must specify an aspect value greater than the default, as shown in Figure 11-3. If the specified aspect is less than the default, the radius is measured along the horizontal axis; if the aspect is greater than the default, the radius is measured vertically. So the specified radius is always the value of the longer axis of the ellipse.

An ellipse with an aspect ratio
greater than the default.

An ellipse with an aspect ratio
less than the default.

Figure 11-3.
Effects of specifying an aspect ratio.

Arcs and segments

To draw an arc, you must define a beginning point and an end point. These points are defined by angles measured in radians, starting at the three o'clock position on the perimeter of the circle of which the arc is a part. The number of radians increases in a counterclockwise direction, from 0 at the origin to 6.2832 (or 2 * pi), which is the number of radians that form an entire circle. This is shown in Figure 11-4.

If the start and stop values are negative, the angles they represent are still treated as positive, but the CIRCLE statement draws a radius connecting the start or stop point on the arc to the center of the circle, thus producing a segment. Figure 11-5 shows three examples of the CIRCLE statement.

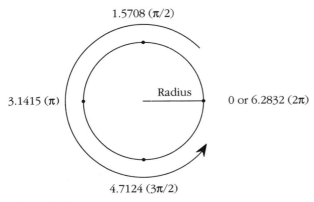

Figure 11-4.
CIRCLE start and stop coordinates.

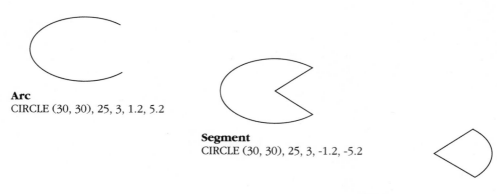

Arc
CIRCLE (30, 30), 25, 3, 1.2, 5.2

Segment
CIRCLE (30, 30), 25, 3, -1.2, -5.2

Segment
CIRCLE (30, 30), 25, 3, -5.2, -1.2

Figure 11-5.
Creating arcs and segments with the CIRCLE statement.

Tips

You can always use CIRCLE with the STEP keyword, even if no previous graphics statement was executed. When QBasic changes screen modes, it sets the graphics cursor to the center of the display and plots subsequent relative coordinates from there.

Example

One of the most useful features of CIRCLE and of most other graphics statements is the STEP keyword, which plots the coordinates of the current figure relative to the position of the graphics cursor. The following program uses STEP in the CIRCLE statement to draw a picture of an extraterrestrial being. You can change the location of this complex graphics image simply by changing the value of the initial coordinates.

```
DEFINT A-Z

x = 160: y = 120                        ' initial coordinates
clr0 = 0: clr1 = 1: clr2 = 2: clr3 = 3  ' values for setting color

SCREEN 1
LINE (0, 0)-(319, 199), clr3, BF        ' paint entire screen

' draw the creature
CIRCLE (x, y), 35, clr0: PAINT STEP(0, 0), clr0, clr0
CIRCLE STEP(-30, -40), 20, clr0: PAINT STEP(0, 0), clr0, clr0
CIRCLE STEP(0, 0), 15, clr2, , , .5: PAINT STEP(0, 0), clr1, clr2
CIRCLE STEP(0, 0), 5, clr3, , , 6: PAINT STEP(0, 0), clr2, clr3
CIRCLE STEP(60, 0), 20, clr0: PAINT STEP(0, 0), clr0, clr0
CIRCLE STEP(0, 0), 20, clr0: CIRCLE STEP(0, 0), 15, clr2
PAINT STEP(0, 0), clr1, clr2: CIRCLE STEP(0, 0), 5, clr3, , , 6
PAINT STEP(0, 0), clr2, clr3
```

(continued)

continued

```
CIRCLE STEP(-15, 10), 11, clr0, 2.1, 3.3
CIRCLE STEP(0, 0), 6, clr0, 2, 3.3: PAINT STEP(-8, -4), clr0, clr0
CIRCLE STEP(-22, 4), 11, clr0, .01, 1.3
CIRCLE STEP(0, 0), 6, clr0, 6.1, 1.3: PAINT STEP(8, -4), clr0, clr0
CIRCLE (x, y + 10), 30, clr2, , , .5: PAINT STEP(0, 0), clr1, clr2

FOR i! = .001 TO .5 STEP .07      ' draw details of creature's mouth
    CIRCLE STEP(0, 0), 25, clr0, , , i!
NEXT i!
END
```

COLOR

See also

PALETTE, SCREEN (Statement)

Purpose

The COLOR statement selects the display attributes of objects on the screen. If your computer has a color monitor, these attributes are translated into actual display colors. On monochrome monitors display attributes control the intensity of the displayed objects. COLOR can also be used to set the display attributes in text mode.

Syntax

COLOR [*foreground*][, [*background*][, *border*]]   (Screen mode 0)
COLOR [*foreground*][, *palette*]   (Screen mode 1)
COLOR [*foreground*][, *background*]   (Screen modes 7-10)
COLOR [*foreground*]   (Screen modes 4, 12, and 13)

foreground is an integer value that specifies the color of the text and graphics displayed on the screen.

background is an integer value that specifies the color of the background of the screen.

border is an integer that specifies the color of the screen's border.

palette is an integer value used in screen mode 1 that specifies which of two sets of colors to use in graphics display.

Usage

```
SCREEN 8
COLOR 1, 14
```
Sets the foreground color to blue and the background color to light yellow.

Description

The number and purpose of the arguments supplied to COLOR vary with the selected screen mode. (See the SCREEN (Statement) entry.) However, all arguments that specify an attribute represent one of the colors listed in Table 11-4.

Attribute number	Color	Attribute number	Color
0	Black	8	Dark gray
1	Blue	9	Light blue
2	Green	10	Light green
3	Cyan	11	Light cyan
4	Red	12	Light red
5	Magenta	13	Light magenta
6	Brown	14	Yellow
7	White	15	Bright white

Table 11-4.
COLOR attribute numbers.

Note that the colors corresponding to attributes 8 through 15 are the same as those corresponding to 0 through 7 except that an added intensity makes them appear brighter.

The COLOR statement performs different tasks; the screen mode in use determines the task.

COLOR with screen mode 0

Screen mode 0 is the text screen mode. In this mode, COLOR controls the appearance of characters printed on the display and the color of the background. Numbers for the foreground color can be in the range 0 through 31. Numbers 0 through 15 are the attribute numbers for the colors; these are listed in Table 11-4. Numbers 16 through 31 are the same colors in the same order, but blinking. Numbers for the background color range from 0 through 7 and represent the first eight colors; these are listed in Table 11-4. For background colors, you cannot specify colors with higher intensity, and you cannot specify colors that blink.

Issuing a COLOR statement in text mode has no effect on characters that are already displayed; however, all subsequent output has the specified foreground and background colors. Use the CLS statement to clear the screen to the new background color.

Colors, of course, are not produced on monochrome monitors. Text displayed with foreground numbers in the range 8 through 15 appear brighter than characters in the range 0 through 7. If you have an MDPA or an HGC adapter, a foreground number of 1 displays underlined text, and a foreground color of 9 displays bright underlined text.

Background numbers 0 through 6 have no effect on monochrome monitors, but number 7 used with a foreground number of 0 changes the display to inverse video.

On computers that use a Color Graphics Adapter (CGA), you can also use COLOR to set the color of the screen border to any color in the range 0 through 15.

COLOR with screen mode 1

Screen mode 1 is the medium-resolution (320-by-200-pixel) graphics mode. Note that the COLOR statement in this mode cannot set the foreground color. It can, however, set the screen background to a color from the full range listed in Table 11-4. Calling the COLOR statement immediately changes the color of the display.

Graphics statements, such as LINE, CIRCLE, and PAINT, that are used in screen mode 1 can draw using one of four (0 through 3) color attributes. The colors assigned to these attributes depend on the color set, or palette, specified in the COLOR statement. Two palettes are available. They are described in Table 11-5.

Attribute number	Palette 0	Palette 1
0	Current background color	Current background color
1	Green	Cyan
2	Red	Magenta
3	Brown	White

Table 11-5.
COLOR attribute numbers for each palette.

If you do not assign an explicit color argument to graphics statements, QBasic draws the graphics statements in the color corresponding to attribute 3. For example,

```
LINE (50, 35)-(216, 60)
```

is plotted in brown if palette 0 is active and in white if palette 1 is active.

When you first select screen mode 1, the default COLOR setting is a black background and palette 1 (cyan, magenta, and white).

COLOR with screen modes 7 through 10

In screen modes 7 through 10, foreground and background colors are by default bright white on black. Screen modes 7, 8, and 9 let you select from 16 attributes (numbers 0 through 15) that specify the colors of the foreground and background.

Modes 7, 8, and 9 can be used only if your EGA or VGA adapter has a color monitor, which lets you display up to 16 different colors at once. In modes 7 and 8, these colors are selected from the 16 color attributes listed in Table 11-4. In mode 9 you can select from an extended palette of 64 color attributes (numbered 0-63), provided that your adapter has more than 64 KB of memory and that your monitor can display 64 colors. Screen mode 10, the monochrome EGA and VGA mode, supports four attributes for the foreground pseudocolor. Table 11-6, on the following page, lists the four available attributes.

Attribute number	Description of pseudocolor
0	Sets no pixels
1	Sets normal intensity
2	Sets blink on
3	Sets high intensity

Table 11-6.
Available attributes for foreground of screen mode 10.

Screen mode 10 supports nine color numbers for the background pseudocolors. Table 11-7 lists these pseudocolors.

Color number	Description of pseudocolor
0	Sets no pixels
1	Blinks between off and normal intensity
2	Blinks between off and high intensity
3	Blinks between normal intensity and off
4	Sets normal intensity, no blink
5	Blinks between normal intensity and high intensity
6	Blinks between high intensity and off
7	Blinks between high intensity and normal intensity
8	Sets high intensity, no blink

Table 11-7.
Available color numbers for background of screen mode 10.

COLOR with screen modes 4, 12, and 13

You can select only foreground attributes in screen modes 4, 12, and 13. To change the default background color from black in modes 12 and 13, use the PALETTE statement to assign the color of your choice to attribute 0. Screen modes 4 and 12 support 16 foreground attributes, and screen mode 13 supports 256 foreground attributes. Each attribute can be assigned to one of 262,144 colors by using the PALETTE or PALETTE USING statement.

Errors

The COLOR statement is not valid in screen modes 2, 3, and 11. If you use it in these modes, QBasic displays an "Illegal function call" error message. QBasic also displays an "Illegal function call" error message if any of the parameters you set are not in the range specified by the screen mode.

Example

The COLOR statement varies depending on the adapter your system uses and the mode the program sets with the SCREEN statement. If you write a program that must be portable between systems, be sure you take the different types of adapters into consideration. The following program contains the COLOR statement in three different formats; the format used depends on the value the user enters.

```
ON ERROR GOTO WrongMode

PRINT "What type of video adapter are you using?"
INPUT "<Enter 1 for CGA, 2 for EGA, and 3 for VGA or MCGA>: ", adapt%

ShowColors:
SELECT CASE adapt%
CASE 1                  ' show background colors of mode 1 for CGA
    SCREEN 1
    PRINT "You can use one of 15 background colors."
    PRINT "Press any key to see them."
    DO WHILE INKEY$ = "": LOOP
    CLS
    FOR i% = 0 TO 14
        COLOR i%
        LOCATE 10, 10: PRINT "Color:"; i%
        SLEEP 1
    NEXT i%
CASE 2                  ' show background and foreground colors for EGA
    SCREEN 7
    PRINT "You can use one of 15 background and"
    PRINT "one of 15 foreground colors."
    PRINT "Press any key to see them."
    DO WHILE INKEY$ = "": LOOP
    FOR i% = 0 TO 14
        COLOR , i%
        CLS
        FOR j% = 0 TO 14
            COLOR j%
            PRINT "Foreground:"; j%; "Background:"; i%
        NEXT j%
        SLEEP 1
    NEXT i%
CASE 3                  ' show foreground colors of VGA or MCGA
    SCREEN 13
    PRINT "You can use one of 256 foreground colors."
    PRINT "Press any key to see them."
    DO WHILE INKEY$ = "": LOOP
    CLS
    FOR i% = 0 TO 255:
        COLOR i%
        PRINT "Color:"; i%
```

(continued)

continued

```
    NEXT i%
END SELECT
END

WrongMode:
IF ERR = 5 THEN
    PRINT "Your system does not support screen modes for that adapter."
    INPUT "Enter a different number: ", adapt%
    RESUME ShowColors
ELSE
    ON ERROR GOTO 0
END IF
```

DRAW

See also
VARPTR$, WINDOW

Purpose
The DRAW statement draws the figure specified in a string expression. DRAW uses a macro language that lets you describe lines in relative terms, by specifying the distance and direction of graphics-cursor movement.

Syntax
DRAW *commandString*

commandString is a string literal, string variable, or string expression that contains a sequence of drawing commands. Enclose literal strings in quotes. You can enter commands in either uppercase or lowercase, and you can separate them with blank spaces or semicolons.

Usage
```
DRAW "C4 U45 R75 D45 L75"
```
Draws a rectangle 45 units high by 75 units wide in color number 4 (red, by default).

```
DRAW box$
```
Draws the figure specified by the commands in the string variable *box$*.

```
DRAW "C=" + VARPTR$(clr%)
```
Sets the color for subsequent DRAW statements to the color specified by the value of the integer variable *clr%*.

Description

The DRAW command accepts a string that contains a list of macro commands. The commands specify graphics-cursor movement, scaling, rotation, and color. The following sections group the macro commands by function.

Cursor movement

The **Mx,y** command is the only DRAW command that specifies coordinates. The M command moves the graphics cursor to the screen location specified by coordinates x and y. If x is preceded by a sign operator, plus (+) or minus (−), cursor movement is relative to the current position of the graphics cursor; otherwise, QBasic assumes x and y are the absolute coordinates of a location on screen. In both cases, QBasic draws a line between the graphics-cursor position and the new location, and this location becomes the new graphics-cursor position. For example, the statement

```
DRAW "M10,25"
```

draws a line from the graphics-cursor position to location (10, 25) on the screen. However, the statement

```
DRAW "M-10,-25"
```

draws a line from the position of the graphics cursor to a point 10 pixels to the left and 25 pixels above the current location.

The **B** command indicates the movement command that follows moves the graphics cursor but does not draw a line. By default, all cursor movements result in a line being drawn from the previous point to the new location. Prefixing a movement command with the B command, however, produces a "blank" move, in which the cursor position is updated but no points are drawn between it and the previous location.

The **N** command indicates the movement command that follows does not update the graphics-cursor position. When the N command prefixes a movement command, the DRAW statement draws the line but then returns the graphics cursor to its original position.

Table 11-8 lists commands that move the graphics cursor in various directions. You control how far the cursor moves in the chosen direction by specifying the length of the resulting line in "units". By default, a unit is equal to one pixel, but you can adjust this by modifying the current scale factor with the S command. (See the next section, "Scaling.") If you do not specify a length, DRAW moves the cursor one unit in the direction specified.

Scaling

Sn, the scale command, specifies a number (in the range 1 through 255) that is divided by four to determine the number of pixels moved for each unit of distance given in a movement command. The default scale value is 4, which makes one unit of movement equal to a single pixel.

The S command is very useful when you want to draw multiple copies of the same figure, but in different sizes.

Command	Description
Un	Move *n* units upward
Dn	Move *n* units downward
Rn	Move *n* units to the right
Ln	Move *n* units to the left
En	Move *n* units diagonally upward and to the right
Fn	Move *n* units diagonally downward and to the right
Gn	Move *n* units diagonally downward and to the left
Hn	Move *n* units diagonally upward and to the left

Table 11-8.
Commands that move the graphics cursor.

Rotation

DRAW lets you rotate the vertical and horizontal axes of a figure by up to a full 360 degrees. By default, the U (up) command moves the graphics cursor upward at an angle of 0 degrees. However, if the axes are rotated 45 degrees, a U command draws a diagonal line upward and to the left. The other direction commands are affected similarly. The DRAW statement includes two rotation commands. These commands affect only the commands following them; they do not rotate any lines that have already been drawn.

The **A**n command rotates the axes in 90-degree steps. The value of *n* can be a number between 0 and 3. DRAW multiplies the value by 90 to calculate the number of degrees to rotate. Angles are measured in a counterclockwise direction, 12:00 being 0 degrees.

The **TA**n command rotates the axes *n* degrees, where *n* is a number in the range −360 through 360. Positive values of *n* rotate the axes in a counterclockwise direction; negative values rotate the axes clockwise. Shifts in the axes remain in effect for subsequent commands.

Color

DRAW includes a command that allows you to specify the color of the line drawn. The possible range of colors is determined by the current screen mode. (See the COLOR entry for details about the colors available in various screen modes.) If you do not specify a color, the DRAW statement defaults to the current foreground color.

The **C**n command sets the color of the lines drawn by direction and movement commands to the color associated with the value *n*.

The **P**c,b command performs the same task as the PAINT statement does; it fills the interior of the figure enclosing the current graphics-cursor position with the color specified by *c*. Specify the border color of the figure with *b*.

If you have just drawn the figure to be painted, you must move the graphics cursor off the border and into the interior of the figure; otherwise, painting will not take place. The best way to do this is to execute a blank move, as in the following example:

```
DRAW "C2 R50 D30 L50 U30"     ' draw a green rectangle
DRAW "BF10"                   ' move cursor inside the figure
DRAW "P3,2"                   ' fill it with cyan
```

Substrings

The **X** ("execute") command lets you specify substrings for DRAW to execute from the current command string. This is an extremely powerful feature of the DRAW macro-language. To use the X command, you must use the VARPTR$ function to supply DRAW with the address of the substring to be executed. (VARPTR$ returns in string format a pointer to the variable; see Chapter 20, "QBasic and Machine Language," for details.) For example, when DRAW encounters the statement

```
"X" + VARPTR$(boat$)
```

in a larger string, DRAW executes the commands specified in the string variable *boat$* before completing the original string. The variable *boat$* can contain its own X commands, thus executing further substrings, which can also contain their own X commands, and so on.

Variables

You can use numeric variables in the DRAW statement in two ways. First you can use the STR$ function to convert their values to string form before using them in a DRAW statement, as shown in the following statements:

```
move$ = "BM" + STR$(x%) + "," + STR$(y%)
DRAW move$
```

You can also use the VARPTR$ function to supply a numeric variable argument within the DRAW statement. If you do this, the command must have an equal sign (=) between it and the VARPTR$ expression. For example,

```
DRAW "G=" + VARPTR$(pixels%)
```

draws a diagonal line down and left. The length of the line (in units) is specified by the value of the integer variable *pixels%*.

Example

The DRAW command is well suited for drawing patterns using fractals, or figures constructed from smaller versions of the same figure. The following program lets you experiment with fractals: By changing the parameters that govern the line length and the number of sides in the subprogram *Flake*, you can draw many intricate and beautiful patterns.

```
DECLARE SUB Fractal (n AS INTEGER)
DECLARE SUB Flake (n AS INTEGER, sides AS INTEGER)
DECLARE SUB IncAngle (increment AS INTEGER)

DIM SHARED angle AS INTEGER
SCREEN 9
Flake 120, 9
END

SUB Flake (n AS INTEGER, sides AS INTEGER) STATIC
    move$ = "BM+" + STR$(n \ 2) + ",+" + STR$(n \ 2)
    DRAW move$                          ' move graphics cursor
    turn% = 360 \ sides
    FOR i% = 1 TO sides
        Fractal n                       ' draw a portion of the fractal
        IncAngle turn%
        DRAW "TA=" + VARPTR$(angle)      ' rotate axes
    NEXT i%
END SUB

SUB Fractal (n AS INTEGER)
    IF n < 4 THEN
        DRAW "U=" + VARPTR$(n)           ' draw a portion of the fractal
    ELSE
        Fractal n / 3                    ' recursively call Fractal subprogram
        IncAngle -60
        DRAW "TA=" + VARPTR$(angle)
        Fractal n / 3
        IncAngle 120
        DRAW "TA=" + VARPTR$(angle)
        Fractal n / 3
        IncAngle -60
        DRAW "TA=" + VARPTR$(angle)
        Fractal n / 3
    END IF
END SUB

SUB IncAngle (increment AS INTEGER) STATIC
    angle = angle + increment
    IF angle > 360 THEN
        angle = angle - 360
    ELSEIF angle < 0 THEN
        angle = angle + 360
    END IF
END SUB
```

GET (Graphics)

See also

PUT (Graphics), SCREEN (Statement), VIEW, WINDOW

Purpose

The GET statement copies a rectangular area of the screen into an array. Its counterpart, the PUT statement, copies the contents of the array back onto the screen at any position that you specify. Together, the statements let you move an image from one part of the display to another without having to draw it again.

Syntax

GET [STEP](*x1*, *y1*)-[STEP](*x2*, *y2*), *array*[(*subscript*)]

x1, *y1*, *x2*, and *y2* are screen coordinates that specify the opposite corners of the rectangular area to be copied. The STEP keyword indicates that the location to which the coordinates refer is relative to the position of the graphics cursor.

array is the name of the numeric array that will hold the image data. You can specify the array element in which storage of the image starts by including *subscript* in parentheses. If you omit the subscript, GET begins storing the image in the first element of the array.

Usage

```
GET STEP(20, -5)-STEP(xInc, yInc), image&(0, 5)
```

Defines a rectangle whose upper left corner is 20 pixels to the right of the graphics cursor and 5 pixels above it. The bottom right corner of the rectangle is offset from the new location of the graphics cursor by *xInc* horizontal pixels and *yInc* vertical pixels. The contents of this rectangle are then copied into column 5 of the two-dimensional array *image&*.

Description

Do not confuse this statement with the file I/O version of GET, which is used to read data from a random-access file. The GET statement for graphics reads data from the screen and then copies it into an array in memory; usually the data is in the form of a figure that has been plotted by one or more of the other graphics statements.

The coordinates of the source rectangle, from which the picture is copied, are specified in the same way they are for the LINE statement. You can use actual pixel numbers measured from the upper left corner of the current viewport. (See the VIEW entry for an explanation of viewport coordinates.) If a WINDOW statement has been executed, you can use the logical coordinate system defined by that statement.

Because GET copies every pixel from the source rectangle into the target array, you must be sure the array is large enough to hold them all. Use the following formula to calculate the size of the array required:

$$bytes = 4 + \text{INT}(((width) * bits\_per\_pixel/bit\_planes) + 7)/8 * bit\_planes * height$$

width is the horizontal extent of the source rectangle. To extract this information from the x-coordinates, use the following formula:

$$width = (x2 - x1) + 1$$

Similarly, you can obtain the value of height, the vertical extent of the source rectangle, by using the following formula:

$$height = (y2 - y1) + 1$$

bits_per_pixel is based on the number of colors available on the display. Table 11-9 lists the bits_per_pixel value for each screen mode.

bit_planes is the number of different areas in memory used to store the color of a pixel. Table 11-9 lists the bit_planes value for each screen mode.

Screen mode	Bits per pixel	Bit planes
1	2	1
2	1	1
3	1	1
4	1	1
7	4	4
8	4	4
9	2	2 (if EGA adapter has 64 KB)
	4	4 (if EGA adapter has more than 64 KB)
10	2	2
11	1	1
12	4	4
13	8	1

Table 11-9.
Bits per pixel and bit planes for each screen mode.

In screen modes 7, 8, 9, and 12, the adapter divides the four bits for the color of each pixel among four separate rows of bits called bit planes; screen mode 10 divides the two bits for the color of each pixel between two bit planes. The values listed in Table 11-9 take this division into account.

The above formula returns the size of the array, in bytes. The actual number of elements required in the array depends on the type of array you use. Table 11-10 lists the element size (in bytes) for different array types.

Array type	Bytes per element
Integer	2
Long integer	4
Single precision	4
Double precision	8

Table 11-10.
Element size for different types of numeric arrays.

To copy the source rectangle defined by the coordinates (50, 20) and (69, 34) in screen 9, for example, you would need to dimension an integer array of 92 elements, as determined by the following calculation:

$$(4 + INT(((20) * (4 / 4) + 7) / 8) * 4 * 15) / 2 = 92$$

After you make the above calculation, you can execute the following statements to copy the source rectangle to *array*:

```
DIM array(0 TO 91) AS INTEGER
GET (50, 20)-(69, 34), array
```

Example

See the PUT entry for an extended example that uses both GET and PUT.

LINE

See also

PALETTE, SCREEN (Statement)

Purpose

The LINE statement uses a straight line of a specified color and style to join two points on the graphics screen. The specified coordinates can also mark the corners of a rectangle, which can be filled with a color.

Syntax

LINE [[STEP](*x1, y1*)]-[STEP](*x2, y2*)[, [*color*][, [B[F]][, *style*]]]

x1, y1, x2, and *y2* are screen coordinates that specify the two ends of the line to be drawn. The optional STEP keyword indicates that the locations to which the coordinates refer are relative to the position of the graphics cursor.

color is the attribute number corresponding to the color in which the line is drawn.

The letter B directs LINE to draw a rectangle using the specified coordinates as the upper left and lower right corners. Adding an F creates a rectangle and fills it with the selected color.

style is a 16-bit value that specifies the style of the line drawn.

You must define the start and end points in the LINE statement by using either absolute or relative coordinates; all other arguments are optional. If you omit any argument that is not the last argument in the parameter list, you must insert a comma to mark its position.

Usage

```
LINE (120, 100)-(30, 15)
```
Draws a line (using the current foreground color) from location (30, 15) to (120, 100).

```
LINE -(100, 50), , B
```
Draws in the current foreground color a rectangle that has one corner at the graphics-cursor position and the opposite corner at the absolute coordinate (100, 50).

```
LINE(x%, y%)-(x% + 20, y% + 12), c%, BF
```
Draws a box 12 pixels high and 20 pixels wide with the upper left corner specified by the integer variables $x\%$ and $y\%$. The box is filled with the color specified by the value contained in $c\%$.

Description

The range of coordinates allowed for the locations specified in a LINE statement depends upon the dimensions of the current screen mode. (See the SCREEN (Statement) entry.) If you use the B or BF parameter, QBasic draws a rectangle whose diagonally opposite corners are the specified points. Otherwise, LINE draws a straight line between the two points. If either of the coordinates refers to a point outside the current viewport, QBasic does not report an error but merely draws the part of the line that is within the viewport.

The order of the two specified locations makes no difference. In fact, the following two statements produce the same line:

```
LINE (35, 18)-(178, 86)
LINE (178, 86)-(35, 18)
```

The number of available colors also depends on the current screen mode. The numbers for the colors correspond to the attribute numbers used by the COLOR statement. (See Table 11-4 in the COLOR entry.) However, if your computer has an EGA, VGA, or MCGA adapter, you can remap the attribute numbers to other colors by using the PALETTE statement.

By default, the lines and the outlines of the rectangles are solid and unbroken. You can, however, draw broken or dotted lines in a variety of styles. You can specify an integer argument whose bits are read (from left to right) as a mask that determines whether a particular pixel on the line is set. You usually specify the argument as a hexadecimal number. For example, &H5555 (21845 decimal) produces a dotted line with alternate pixels set, and &H0707 produces a dashed line, as shown in Figure 11-6.

Hexadecimal	Binary	Line drawn
&H5555	0101010101010101	▪▪▪▪▪▪▪▪
&H0707	0000011100000111	▬▬▬▬

Figure 11-6.
Examples of line styles.

You can define the pattern for both single lines and the sides of rectangles. The pattern does not affect the way that LINE fills the boxes; even if the lines that compose the sides of the rectangle are broken, the paint does not "leak" past the box boundaries.

Example

A powerful feature of the LINE statement is the STEP clause—it lets you draw complex figures without having to calculate the absolute coordinates of each point referenced. The following example uses LINE to draw a three-dimensional bar chart; plotting the coordinates of each bar with STEP makes the program much simpler because each bar is identical in shape and differs only in height.

```
SCREEN 9
LINE (0, 0)-(639, 349), 9, BF      ' paint entire screen blue
VIEW (32, 4)-(607, 345), 0, 15     ' define a viewport
WINDOW SCREEN (0, 0)-(255, 191)    ' define logical coordinate system

READ numItems%
DIM item!(numItems%)

xInt% = 240 \ numItems%            ' initialize interval for x
xWidth% = xInt% - 10
zWidth% = xWidth% * 2

FOR i% = 1 TO numItems%
    READ item!(i%)
    IF item!(i%) > max! THEN max! = item!(i%)
NEXT i%

yInt! = 160 / max!: i% = 1: clr% = 1

FOR x% = 15 TO 239 STEP xInt%      ' draw bars of the chart
    yLen% = item!(i%) * yInt!
    LINE (x%, 180)-(x% + xWidth%, 180 - yLen%), clr%, BF
    LINE -STEP(5, -3), clr%: LINE -STEP(-xWidth%, -0), clr%
    LINE -STEP(-5, 3), clr%: LINE -STEP(xWidth%, 0), clr%
    LINE -STEP(5, -3), clr%: LINE -STEP(0, yLen%), clr%
    LINE -STEP(-5, 3), clr%: i% = i% + 1: clr% = clr% + 1
    IF clr% = 7 THEN clr% = 9
NEXT x%
r$ = INPUT$(1)
END
```

(continued)

continued

```
DATA 12
DATA 356.21, 216.53, 99.9, 25.8, 176, 282. 75
DATA 303.4, 111. 11, 168.3, 271.9, 333.3, 88
```

PAINT

See also

COLOR, PALETTE, SCREEN (Statement)

Purpose

The PAINT statement fills an enclosed figure with a specified color. You can specify either a solid color or a mixture of colors that produces pixel patterns.

Syntax

PAINT [STEP](*x, y*)[, [*color*][, [*border*][, *background*]]]

x and *y* are the coordinates of the point at which painting will start. The optional STEP keyword indicates that the coordinates are relative to the position of the graphics cursor.

color can be either a numeric expression or a string expression. A numeric expression specifies the attribute number corresponding to the color that will fill the area. A string expression defines a new paint pattern. If you omit *color*, PAINT fills the area with the current foreground color.

border is the number corresponding to the color of the area's border. If you omit this parameter, PAINT defaults to the same color as the parameter *color*.

background is a single-character string expression defining a background pattern that can be painted over.

Usage

```
PAINT (319, 174), 14, 4
```

Moves the graphics cursor to the center of a screen mode 9 display and fills the area with yellow (attribute 14) paint. Painting continues until either a red border is encountered or the entire viewport is filled.

Description

To call PAINT to fill a figure, you must first specify the coordinates of a location within the figure at which painting is to start. The range of possible values of the coordinates is determined by the current graphics mode. For example, you can use the coordinates

(159, 99) to position the cursor at the center of the screen in screen mode 1 (medium-resolution graphics); for screen modes 11 and 12, however, you specify the screen center at coordinates (319, 239).

If you use the WINDOW statement to define your own logical coordinate system, QBasic translates the logical coordinates sent to PAINT into physical pixel locations and plots them correctly. (See the WINDOW entry.)

PAINT assumes the border of the figure has already been drawn. It uses a "flood-fill" algorithm to set all the pixels within the border to the specified color attribute. If you do not specify a fill color, PAINT uses the current foreground color. If you do not specify the border color, PAINT fills the space defined by a border with the same color that it uses for painting. Be sure the area to be painted is totally enclosed by the border; if it is not, the paint "leaks."

PAINT uses the program stack to record the location of pixels that are already set, so if the edges of the figure are particularly jagged, your program might report an "Out of stack space" error message. If this happens, use the CLEAR statement to increase the stack size. (See the CLEAR entry in Chapter 18, "DOS and Program Management.")

Paint tiling

You can use a number to specify the solid color with which PAINT fills the enclosed figure. The values you can use are limited to the range of colors available in the current screen mode. By using a string value, however, you can specify a mixture of colors to produce a great variety of shades, textures, and patterns. This process of mixing paint colors is known as "tiling."

To understand how tiling works, you must first know how QBasic produces solid colors in the screen mode you are using. In the 4-color graphics mode (screen mode 1), each pixel is represented by 2 bits of screen memory that specify one of the four colors. In the 2-color graphics mode (screen mode 2), each pixel is represented by 1 bit. In 16-color graphics modes (screen modes 7, 8, 9, and 12), each pixel is represented by 4 bits of screen memory, each of which defines an attribute of color. The 4 bits define a mixture of blue, red, green, and color intensity. The setting of each bit combines with the other bit settings to determine the color of the pixel. For example, a pixel set with bit values of 1010 is displayed in color 10, which is light green. Note that the value of the binary number 1010 is 10 in decimal. As Table 11-11, on the following page, shows, the numbers of the 16 available colors specify the bit setting that creates the color.

If you want to create your own pattern for PAINT, you must design a tile, which is a rectangular grid of pixels that defines the pattern. The grid must always be 8 bits across and can be up to 64 bits high. When you use PAINT with the tile, PAINT draws the tile repeatedly in order to fill an area.

For screen mode 1, each row of the grid must contain the representation of four pixels to fill eight bits. For screen mode 2, each row must contain the representation of 8 pixels. In screen modes 7, 8, 9, and 12, the 4 bits that represent each pixel

Bit setting	Decimal value	Color
0000	0	Black
0001	1	Blue
0010	2	Green
0011	3	Cyan
0100	4	Red
0101	5	Magenta
0110	6	Brown
0111	7	White
1000	8	Gray
1001	9	Light blue
1010	10	Light green
1011	11	Light cyan
1100	12	Light red
1101	13	Light magenta
1110	14	Yellow
1111	15	Bright white

Table 11-11.
Bit settings for colors.

are stored in four different areas of video memory, which are called *bit planes*. Each byte of video memory (or row in the grid), therefore, contains one bit from 8 different pixels.

For example, to produce an intermediate shade of green, you can design a tile in which adjacent pixels are two different intensities of green, as shown in Figure 11-10.

To specify the tile in the PAINT statement, you supply a string in which each byte contains the bits of each bit plane. For example, to produce the tile of 8 pixels defined by the grid in Figure 11-7, you must specify a 4-character string in which the value of each character is the summation of the bits in one of the bit planes:

```
tile$ = CHR$(0) + CHR$(255) + CHR$(0) + CHR$(85)
```

The program on the following page paints three circles, using this tile pattern to paint one of them in a shade of green that is between the two intensities provided by QBasic.

You can, of course, blend different colors in the tile pattern, not merely different shades of the same color. This lets you produce many more interesting shades and textures.

PAINT also lets you create pattern strings as long as 64 characters, with each set of 4 characters defining the pattern for successive rows of 8 pixels. Designing tile patterns can be tedious; however, it is worth the effort because you can use the same patterns in many different programs.

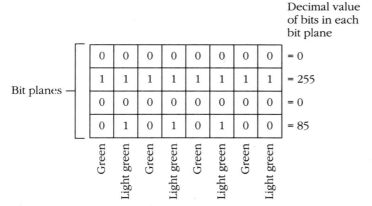

Decimal value
of bits in each
bit plane

Figure 11-7.
A tile pattern of an intermediate shade of green for PAINT.

```
tile$ = CHR$(0) + CHR$(255) + CHR$(0) + CHR$(85)

SCREEN 9
FOR x% = 100 TO 500 STEP 200
    CIRCLE (x%, 174), 80, 4
NEXT x%

PAINT (100, 174), 2, 4
PAINT (300, 174), tile$, 4
PAINT (500, 174), 10, 4
END
```

Example

Paint tiling lets you obtain many more colors and shades than are normally available from the screen mode in use. It lets you create much more interesting and realistic effects than solid colors. The following program draws a mountain landscape and adds just enough color and texture to create "atmosphere."

One problem with paint tiling is blending the outline color with the interior texture of the figure being painted. This program solves the problem by retracing the border (using the LINE statement) with a style option that matches the bit pattern of the tile. This can produce some striking effects, especially if the figure has a complex outline.

```
SCREEN 8
DIM tile$(1 TO 8)
lnStyl% = &H55AA                        ' line style for the fourth pattern
PAINT (319, 99), 15
VIEW (14, 6)-(624, 123), 15, 0
```

(continued)

continued

```
FOR i% = 1 TO 21
    READ x1%, y1%, x2%, y2%, clr%    ' read line coordinates
    LINE (x1%, y1%)-(x2%, y2%), 0    ' draw landscape outline
NEXT i%

FOR i% = 1 TO 8
    READ j%                          ' read number of bytes in tile
    FOR k% = 1 TO j%
        READ byte%                   ' read pixel data
        tile$(i%) = tile$(i%) + CHR$(byte%)  ' build paint tile
    NEXT k%
NEXT i%

FOR i% = 1 TO 8
    READ x%, y%                      ' read coordinate for PAINT
    PAINT (x%, y%), tile$(i%), 0     ' paint enclosed area
NEXT i%

RESTORE                                  ' reset data pointer
FOR i% = 1 TO 21
    READ x1%, y1%, x2%, y2%, clr%        ' read line coordinates and color
    LINE (x1%, y1%)-(x2%, y2%), clr%     ' erase outline
NEXT i%

LINE (400, 90)-(430, 87), 4, , lnStyl%   ' touch up edge of fourth pattern 4
LINE -(520, 84), 4, , lnStyl%
LINE -(610, 82), 4, , lnStyl%
END

' screen coordinates and colors for lines
DATA  0, 75, 130, 66, 5, 130, 66, 150, 65, 9, 150, 65, 215, 60
DATA  9, 215, 60, 305, 65, 9, 305, 65, 380, 55, 9, 380, 55, 395
DATA  50, 9, 395, 50, 415, 55, 9, 415, 55, 460, 62, 9, 460, 62
DATA  520, 68, 9, 520, 68, 610, 75, 9, 0, 58, 130, 66, 9, 305
DATA  65, 610, 80, 5, 615, 98, 305, 98, 1, 305, 98, 380, 93, 1
DATA  380, 93, 400, 90, 1, 400, 90, 430, 87, 2, 430, 87, 520, 84
DATA  2, 520, 84, 610, 82, 2, 0, 90, 400, 90, 1, 0, 98, 610, 112
DATA  2, 615, 104, 285, 104, 14

' values for pattern tiles
DATA  4, 255, 0, 0, 255, 4, 255, 0, 0, 0
DATA  8, 0, 255, 170, 0, 0, 255, 85, 0
DATA  8, 0, 170, 85, 0, 0, 85, 170, 0
DATA  8, 85, 170, 255, 170, 170, 85, 255, 85
DATA  4, 255, 0, 255, 0, 4, 255, 0, 255, 170
DATA  4, 0, 255, 255, 255

' coordinates of areas for painting
DATA  10, 10, 10, 95, 305, 113, 600, 95, 305, 85
DATA  380, 60, 10, 63, 605, 110
```

PALETTE, PALETTE USING

See also

COLOR, SCREEN (Statement)

Purpose

The PALETTE statement changes one color in the available palette to another; PALETTE USING changes every color in the palette. You can use the PALETTE USING statement to produce stunning graphics effects.

Syntax

PALETTE [*color, display*]
PALETTE USING *array*(*subscript*)

color is the attribute number of the color to be changed; *display* is the number of the new color to which the attribute is mapped.

array is the name of an array containing values of the colors to be mapped to the current palette; *subscript* identifies the element of the array at which remapping begins.

Usage

```
PALETTE 6, 14
```

Changes the color associated with attribute 6 from brown to yellow.

```
PALETTE USING clrs&(9)
```

Changes every attribute in the palette to the color value of an element in the array *clrs&*. The remapping begins at the element whose subscript is 9, so attribute 0 is assigned the color value contained in *clrs&*(9).

Description

The collection of display colors available in a specific screen mode is known as its *palette*. Depending on the current screen mode, a palette might contain 2, 4, 16, or even 256 colors. Each of these colors is assigned its own attribute number, which indicates that color's position in the palette. In computers with an EGA, VGA, or MCGA adapter, however, you can remap these attribute numbers to other colors so that, for example, a figure that was originally drawn in red can be changed to blue.

When you select a screen mode for the first time, QBasic assigns a default color number to each attribute in the palette for that mode. In screen modes with 16 colors (screen modes 7, 8, 9, and 12) the default palette is configured as shown in Table 11-12.

PALETTE lets you change the color number assigned to any single attribute in the palette. Doing this causes every pixel on the screen with that attribute to be displayed in the new color. This change also affects subsequent graphics output to the screen: any graphics statements in which you can specify an attribute (LINE, CIRCLE, or PAINT, for example) will draw using the color assigned to the attribute.

Attribute number	Color number	Color
0	0	Black
1	1	Blue
2	2	Green
3	3	Cyan
4	4	Red
5	5	Magenta
6	6	Brown
7	7	White
8	8	Gray
9	9	Light blue
10	10	Light green
11	11	Light cyan
12	12	Light red
13	13	Light magenta
14	14	Yellow
15	15	Bright white

Table 11-12.
Attribute and color numbers for 16-color screen modes.

All changes remain in effect until you either change the screen mode or cancel the changes by using another PALETTE statement. Using PALETTE without arguments restores the attribute of every pixel on the screen to its default color for that screen mode.

PALETTE USING lets you use a single statement to change the colors assigned to all the attributes in the palette. To use this statement, you must first dimension an array that contains at least the same number of elements as there are colors in the current palette. The elements of the array must be the correct type to hold the color values. In EGA modes, an integer array is sufficient; because of the way VGA and MCGA modes create colors, however, these modes require long integers. To specify the color values of the new palette, assign values to the elements of the array. If you do not want to change an attribute, assign a value of −1 instead of a color number to the element.

Although the previous examples use color numbers only in the range 0 through 15, you can assign as many as 64 different colors in EGA modes and 262,144 colors in VGA and MCGA modes.

The color numbers for the EGA modes range from 0 through 63. Although 262,144 different colors are available in the VGA and MCGA modes, their numbers do not range from 0 through 262,143. Instead, you must calculate the value for each color. Each color in these modes is a specific mixture of intensities of the colors blue, green, and red. The color intensity can range from 0 through 63. To calculate a color's value, use the formula on the following page, in which *blue*, *green*, and *red* are values specifying the intensity:

$$value = (65536 * blue) + (256 * green) + red$$

If you want to create a pure, bright blue, for example, use in the calculation an intensity of 63 for *blue* and an intensity of 0 for *green* and for *red*. The result of the calculation is the value 4128768.

Example

Because the PALETTE USING statement changes screen colors without redrawing the figures displayed, it is often used to produce animation effects. The following program cycles through a regular succession of color changes to create the illusion of movement through a tunnel.

```
SCREEN 9
DIM array(0 TO 32) AS INTEGER
PALETTE USING array(0)               ' set every color to the background color
FOR i% = 1 TO 32: array(i%) = (i% MOD 15) + 1: NEXT  ' fill array for palette
LINE (0, 0)-(639, 399), 1, BF
clr% = 0                             ' change foreground color to the background
FOR i% = 440 TO 10 STEP -10          ' paint screen with concentric circles
    clr% = clr% + 1
    IF clr% > 15 THEN clr% = 1       ' give each circle a different color
    IF clr% = 8 THEN clr% = 9
    CIRCLE (320, 200), i%, 0
    PAINT (320, 200), clr%, 0
NEXT i%
PALETTE                              ' restore the default colors
DO
    FOR i% = 15 TO 1 STEP -1
        a1% = array(i%): array(i%) = 0  ' set first color of new palette to 0
        PALETTE USING array(i%)         ' change palettes
        array(i%) = a1%
        IF INKEY$ = CHR$(27) THEN EXIT FOR
    NEXT i%
LOOP UNTIL i%
END
```

PCOPY

See also

SCREEN (Statement)

Purpose

The PCOPY statement copies one screen page to another. Computers with certain graphics adapters can switch among as many as eight different screen pages.

Syntax

PCOPY *source, destination*

source is an integer that specifies the number of the screen page to be copied; *destination* is an integer that specifies the number of the screen page to which the source page is copied.

Usage

```
PCOPY 3, 0
```
Copies the contents of display page 3 to page 0, the first screen page.

Description

To use PCOPY, your computer must have a display adapter that supports multiple screen pages. Systems with EGA and VGA adapters permit as many as eight screen pages in screen modes 0, 7, 8, 9, and 10; CGA and MCGA systems can display as many as eight pages in screen mode 0. Computers with monochrome display adapters are limited to a single screen page and do not support PCOPY. (See the SCREEN (Statement) entry for a complete list of the number of pages available in different graphics modes.)

Errors

If you issue a PCOPY statement in a screen mode that does not support multiple screen pages, QBasic displays an "Illegal function call" error message. Attempting to use PCOPY to copy either to or from a page number that is outside of the range available to the current screen mode also results in an "Illegal function call" error message.

Tips

PCOPY works only in text screen mode 0 and in graphics screen modes 7 and higher, so owners of computers equipped with CGA, Hercules, Olivetti, or AT&T adapters cannot use PCOPY in graphics mode.

Example

When used with the SCREEN statement, PCOPY can store graphics and text on a screen page; you can then copy the screen page to the active display whenever you need it. The following program includes an offline help screen. The user can display Help with a single keypress and then restore the original display with another keypress.

```
' this program will not run on monochrome systems
SCREEN 0, , 1, 0        ' sets active page to page 1, displayed page to page 0

' draw Help screen on the active page
COLOR , 1: CLS : COLOR , 0
FOR row% = 11 TO 16
    LOCATE row%, 29: PRINT SPACE$(24);
NEXT row%
COLOR 0, 3
```

(continued)

continued

```
' draw box
LOCATE 10, 28: PRINT CHR$(201); STRING$(22, 205); CHR$(187);
FOR row% = 11 TO 14
    LOCATE row%, 28: PRINT CHR$(186); SPACE$(22); CHR$(186);
NEXT row%
LOCATE row%, 28: PRINT CHR$(200); STRING$(22, 205);
PRINT CHR$(188): : LOCATE 12, 34

' display the message
FOR i% = 1 TO 11: READ a%: PRINT CHR$(a%); : NEXT
LOCATE 13, 30
FOR i% = 1 TO 20: READ a%: PRINT CHR$(a%); : NEXT


SCREEN , , 0, 0          ' change active page to page 0, the displayed page
COLOR 14, 2: CLS
LOCATE 3, 28: PRINT " PCOPY  DEMONSTRATION ";
LOCATE 5, 1: PRINT STRING$(80, "-"); : COLOR 14, 4
LOCATE 24, 1: PRINT SPACE$(80);
PCOPY 0, 2              ' copy displayed page to page 2
LOCATE 24, 26: PRINT "Press any key for help."

r$ = INPUT$(1)
PCOPY 1, 0             ' copy Help screen to displayed page
LOCATE 24, 1: PRINT SPACE$(80):
LOCATE 24, 29: PRINT "Press any key to resume."

r$ = INPUT$(1)
PCOPY 2, 0            ' restore original page
COLOR 7, 0
END

DATA  73, 84, 39, 83, 32, 65, 76, 76, 32, 73, 78
DATA  84, 72, 69, 32, 81, 66, 97, 115, 105, 99
DATA  32, 82, 69, 70, 69, 82, 69, 78, 67, 69
```

PMAP

See also

VIEW, WINDOW

Purpose

The PMAP function maps a physical coordinate to a logical coordinate or vice versa. If your display contains a mixture of logical and physical coordinates, you can use the PMAP function to convert coordinates from one system to the other.

Syntax

PMAP(*coordinate, action*)

coordinate is a single-precision value that represents one of the coordinates of the pixel to be mapped.

action is an integer value that indicates whether *coordinate* is an *x*- or a *y*-coordinate and whether the coordinate value should be translated from the logical to the physical system or vice versa. *action* can have the following values:

Value	Description
0	Converts the coordinate from a logical coordinate to a physical *x*-coordinate
1	Converts the coordinate from a logical coordinate to a physical *y*-coordinate
2	Converts the coordinate from a physical coordinate to a logical *x*-coordinate
3	Converts the coordinate from a physical coordinate to a logical *y*-coordinate

Usage

```
CIRCLE (PMAP(160, 2), PMAP(100, 3)), 50, 3
```

Draws a circle using physical coordinates for the location of the center. This ensures that the circle is always centered on a 320-by-200-pixel viewport, regardless of the current logical coordinate system.

Description

PMAP does not directly affect pixels on the screen. It merely translates pixel coordinates from one coordinate system for use in graphics statements.

The physical coordinate system is determined by the number of pixels available in the current screen mode and by the limits of the current graphics viewport defined by the most recent VIEW statement. (See the VIEW entry.) If no VIEW statement has been executed, the viewport is the size of the screen.

You can use the WINDOW statement to define your own logical coordinate system and to map it onto the viewport. (See the WINDOW entry.) This lets you use logical coordinates in graphics statements, such as LINE, CIRCLE, PAINT, GET, PUT, PSET, and PRESET.

The value returned by PMAP when translating from logical to physical coordinates will most often be a single-precision variable because the act of translating physical coordinates into logical coordinates rarely produces an integer value.

The following program segment maps a logical coordinate system that has values for *x* and *y* that range from -1000 through 1000 onto a 640-by-200-pixel physical coordinate system:

```
SCREEN 2
WINDOW (-1000, -1000)-(1000, 1000)
```

Figure 11-8 illustrates the mapping of the logical coordinate system onto the physical coordinate system. Notice that the origin of the logical coordinate system, the location specified by (0, 0), is the center of the screen and that the greatest value of y is at the top of the screen. In the physical coordinate system, the origin is at the upper left corner of the screen, and the greatest y value is at the bottom of the screen.

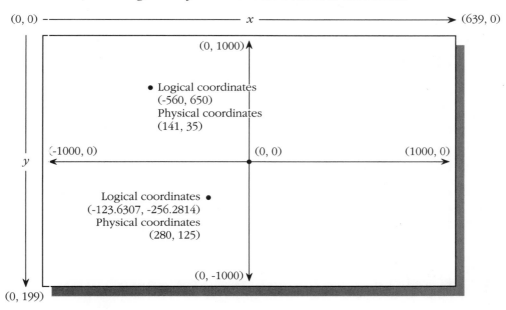

Figure 11-8.
PMAP translates between logical and physical coordinate systems.

Example

The WINDOW statement is particularly useful because it lets you specify a logical coordinate system that is smaller than the physical dimensions of the current viewport. Only those points whose coordinates are within the logical frame of the window can be plotted, thus displaying a small section of what might be a much larger picture. Furthermore, by changing the window's range of logical coordinates you can bring other parts of the display into view, as though you were panning a video camera.

Usually, however, when the camera pans, it focuses on an object that is moving against a stationary background. You can achieve the same effect in QBasic by keeping the object stationary and moving the background instead. To do this, use PMAP to plot the foreground image using physical coordinates, so that the image appears at the same position in the viewport regardless of which part of the logical display is visible in the background. The following program uses the PMAP function to translate physical coordinates to logical coordinates so that each of five windows has the foreground image as its focus.

```
DECLARE SUB DrawWorld ()

SCREEN 9: LINE (0, 0)-(639, 349), 9, BF
x1 = 100: x2 = 256: y1 = 10: y2 = 70        ' define coordinates for window
x% = 10: y% = 10                            ' define coordinates for viewport
xChange = -100: numIter% = 1
DO
    VIEW (x%, y%)-(x% + 300, y% + 155), 0, 15        ' define a viewport
    WINDOW SCREEN (x1, y1)-(x2, y2)                  ' define a window
    DrawWorld                                        ' draw background image
    numIter% = numIter% + 1
    xPhys = PMAP(150, 2): yPhys = PMAP(75, 3)
    IF y1 > 10 THEN                                  ' draw foreground image
        CIRCLE (xPhys, yPhys), 10, 13, -.8, -5.78
    ELSE
        CIRCLE (xPhys, yPhys), 10, 13, -3.9, -2.2
    END IF
    PAINT (PMAP(150, 2), PMAP(68, 3)), 13, 13
    CIRCLE (PMAP(150, 2), PMAP(68, 3)), 1, 1, , , 3
    x% = x% + 320
    IF numIter% = 3 THEN
        x% = 10: y% = 175
        x1 = x1 - 100: x2 = x2 - 100: xChange = -xChange
        y1 = y1 + 22: y2 = y2 + 22
    END IF
    x1 = x1 + xChange: x2 = x2 + xChange
    r$ = INPUT$(1)
LOOP UNTIL numIter% = 5
VIEW (160, 97)-(460, 252), 0, 15
WINDOW SCREEN (0, 0)-(256, 120): DrawWorld           ' draw entire background
CIRCLE (138, 84), 10, 13, -3.9, -2.2                 ' draw foreground image
PAINT (138, 86), 13, 13
CIRCLE (138, 81), 1, 1, , , 3
END

SUB DrawWorld STATIC
    LINE (0, 0)-(256, 27), 14, BF: LINE (0, 28)-(256, 118), 4, B
    LINE (4, 30)-(252, 116), 4, B: LINE (30, 50)-(251, 52), 4, B
    PAINT (128, 51), 4, 4: LINE (3, 72)-(226, 74), 4, B
    PAINT (128, 73), 4, 4: LINE (30, 94)-(251, 96), 4, B
    PAINT (128, 95), 4, 4: PAINT (128, 29), 4, 4
    PAINT (2, 80), 4, 4: PAINT (254, 70), 4, 4
    LINE (208, 27)-(251, 30), 14, BF
    CIRCLE (118, 84), 10, 6: PAINT (118, 84), 6, 6
    CIRCLE (114, 82), 4, 0: CIRCLE (122, 82), 4, 0
    PAINT (114, 82), 15, 0: PAINT (122, 82), 15, 0
    CIRCLE (117, 82), 2, 1: CIRCLE (119, 82), 2, 1
    CIRCLE (118, 86), 2, 0: PAINT (118, 86), 0, 0
END SUB
```

POINT

See also
PALETTE, PMAP, PSET, WINDOW

Purpose
The POINT function returns either the color of a pixel or the value of one of its coordinates. If the function is called with a pair of coordinates, it returns the color attribute number of the pixel at the specified location. If called with a single argument, it returns the x- or y-coordinate of the graphics cursor as either a logical or a physical coordinate.

Syntax
POINT(x, y)

or

POINT(*switch*)

x and y are the horizontal and vertical coordinates of the pixel to be examined.

switch is an integer value in the range 0 through 3 that specifies the graphics cursor coordinate to be returned. *switch* can have the following values:

Value	Description
0	Returns the physical x-coordinate
1	Returns the physical y-coordinate
2	Returns the logical x-coordinate
3	Returns the logical y-coordinate

Usage
```
PRINT POINT(319, 174)
```
Prints the attribute number of the pixel at the center of a 640-by-350-pixel display.

```
lastY! = POINT(3)
```
Assigns to *lastY!* the y-coordinate of the graphics cursor in the logical coordinate system defined by the most recent WINDOW statement.

Description
The POINT function can be used to return the attribute number of a specified pixel. Note that the number of the displayed color might be different if the colors have been remapped by the PALETTE statement. If the given coordinates specify a point outside the current viewport, POINT returns a value of −1.

If you call POINT with a single argument, the function returns one of the coordinates of the graphics cursor. The coordinate can be the x- or the y-coordinate in either the physical or the logical coordinate system.

If no WINDOW statement is in effect, the POINT function returns the physical *x*- and *y*-coordinates of the graphics cursor even if the argument specifies logical coordinates.

The graphics cursor is not a physical object, as the text cursor is. It is merely a term that refers to the most recent point referenced on the graphics screen. Therefore, if you draw a line between two points by calling the statement

```
LINE (10, 10)-(110, 60), 3
```

the graphics cursor is at the endpoint of the line, which is the location (110, 60). The next LINE statement, however, would change the cursor position again. If you select a new screen mode or use CLS to clear the display, the graphics cursor moves to its default location at the center of the current viewport.

The graphics cursor can be outside the boundaries of the current coordinate system. Although QBasic doesn't draw the parts of lines or circles that are outside the viewport, it still plots their endpoints so that the objects can be clipped correctly. In such cases, the graphics cursor position that POINT returns can be greater than the maximum or less than the minimum value defined by the current coordinate system.

Example

Programs that draw patterns often use POINT to test the color of a pixel before changing it to a different color. The following example uses this procedure when drawing diagonal lines to set the color of only those pixels that are currently turned off; the pixels that are turned on are set to the background color. The result is an intricate and everchanging pattern.

```
SCREEN 1: COLOR 0, 1: DEFINT A-Z: RANDOMIZE TIMER

DO
    CLS
    xMin = 0: xMax = 319: yMin = 0: yMax = 199      ' define boundaries
    clr = INT(RND * 3) + 1
    xChange = SGN((RND * 2) - 1.5): yChange = SGN((RND * 2) - 1.5)
    xStart = INT(RND * (xMax - xMin)) + xMin
    yStart = INT(RND * (yMax - yMin)) + yMin
    DO
        IF xStart + xChange > xMax OR xStart + xChange < xMin THEN
            xChange = -xChange
        END IF
        IF yStart + yChange > yMax OR yStart + yChange < yMin THEN
            yChange = -yChange
        END IF
        xStart = xStart + xChange: yStart = yStart + yChange
        x = xStart: y = yStart

        IF POINT(x, y) = 0 THEN                      ' check color of pixel
            LINE (x, y)-(x + 2, y + 3), clr, BF
            x = xMax - xStart: LINE (x, y)-(x + 2, y + 3), clr, BF
```

(continued)

continued

```
        y = yMax - yStart: LINE (x, y)-(x + 2, y + 3), clr, BF
        x = xStart: LINE (x, y)-(x + 2, y + 3), clr, BF
    ELSE
        LINE (x, y)-(x + 2, y + 3), 0, BF
        x = xMax - xStart: LINE (x, y)-(x + 2, y + 3), 0, BF
        y = yMax - yStart: LINE (x, y)-(x + 2, y + 3), 0, BF
        x = xStart: LINE (x, y)-(x + 2, y + 3), 0, BF
    END IF
    r$ = INKEY$
    clr = clr + 1: IF clr > 3 THEN clr = 1
  LOOP WHILE r$ = ""
LOOP UNTIL r$ = CHR$(27)
SCREEN 0: WIDTH 80: COLOR 15, 0: CLS
END
```

PRESET, PSET

See also

COLOR, SCREEN (Statement)

Purpose

PRESET and PSET statements set or reset a single point, or pixel, on the graphics screen. Typically these statements are used within a program's loop structure for plotting graphs and geometric figures.

Syntax

PRESET [STEP](*x*, *y*) [, *attribute*]

PSET [STEP](*x*, *y*) [, *attribute*]

x and *y* are the horizontal and vertical coordinates of the pixel to be set.

attribute is the pixel's display attribute, which defines the color to which the pixel will be set.

The STEP keyword indicates that the location to which the coordinates refer is relative to the position of the graphics cursor.

Usage

```
PRESET (xPos%, yPos%)
```

Moves the graphics cursor to the coordinate specified by the variables *xPos%* and *yPos%* and sets the pixel to the current background color.

```
PSET (160, 100), 3
```

Sets the pixel at the location specified by the coordinates 160 and 100 to the color assigned to attribute 3 in the current palette.

Description

The only difference between PRESET and PSET is that if the attribute parameter is omitted, PRESET sets a pixel with the current background color, whereas PSET sets the pixel with the foreground color. The numbers of the color attribute you can use depend on the current screen mode.

QBasic does not report an error if the specified coordinates are outside the current viewport; however, in this case, no pixel on the screen is either set or reset.

Example

Programs rarely need to set only a single pixel. Sometimes, however, the shape of the figure to be drawn is determined by calculations made while the program is executing and is too complex for the usual LINE or CIRCLE statements. The following program accepts data that is entered and uses it to plot a geometric figure.

The program uses the number of degrees the user specifies to plot a series of points that form a spiral. The user also must choose between points and lines. If lines are specified, the program uses PSET to connect the points of the spiral. After drawing the spiral, the progam uses PRESET to erase it.

```
CLS
INPUT "Enter angle between points, in degrees: ", degrees
PRINT : INPUT "<P>oints or <L>ines"; s$
s$ = UCASE$(LEFT$(s$, 1))

xMax = 319: yMax = 199: SCREEN 1          ' screen limits
CLS
x1 = xMax / 2: y1 = yMax / 2              ' set x1 and y1 to half screen limits
PRINT degrees; "Degrees"
radians = degrees / 57.29578             ' convert degrees to radians
IF s$ = "P" THEN PRINT "Points" ELSE PRINT "Lines"

FOR black% = 0 TO 1                      ' first draw points, then erase them
    FOR angle = 0 TO yMax / 2 STEP radians
        x = angle * COS(angle) + (xMax / 2)
        y = angle * SIN(angle) + (yMax / 2)
        IF x < 0 OR x > xMax OR y < 0 OR y > yMax THEN
            EXIT FOR
        END IF
        r$ = INKEY$: IF r$ = CHR$(27) THEN EXIT FOR
        IF s$ = "P" THEN
            IF black% THEN
                PRESET (x, y)                ' erase points
            ELSE
                PSET (x, y)                  ' draw points
            END IF
        ELSE                                 ' draw (or erase) lines
            IF x = x1 THEN
                IF y1 < y THEN change = 1 ELSE change = -1
```

(continued)

continued

```
                   FOR z = y1 TO y STEP change
                       IF black% THEN
                            PRESET (x1, z)              ' erase lines
                       ELSE
                            PSET (x1, z)               ' draw lines
                       END IF
                   NEXT z
              ELSE
                   slope = (y - y1) / (x - x1)
                   IF ABS(slope) > 1 THEN change = ABS(1 / slope) ELSE change = 1
                   IF x1 > x THEN change = -change
                   FOR z = x1 TO x STEP change
                       IF black% THEN
                            PRESET (z, slope * (z - x1) + y1)        ' erase lines
                       ELSE
                            PSET (z, slope * (z - x1) + y1)         ' draw lines
                       END IF
                   NEXT z
                   x1 = x: y1 = y
              END IF
         END IF
     NEXT angle
NEXT black%
END
```

PUT (Graphics)

See also

GET (Graphics), PSET, WINDOW

Purpose

The PUT statement copies a graphics image from the array in which it has been stored into a specified screen location. Its counterpart, the GET statement, copies an area of the screen into an array. Using these two statements, you can move an image from one part of the display to another.

Syntax

PUT [STEP](*x*, *y*), *array*[(*subscript*)] [, *action*]

x and *y* are the screen coordinates of the upper left corner of the rectangle into which the image is copied. The STEP keyword specifies that the location to which these coordinates refer is relative to the position of the graphics cursor.

array is the name of the numeric array that holds the image data. You can specify the array element from which copying starts by including *subscript* in parentheses. If you omit *subscript*, the image is copied starting with the first element in the array.

action is a constant that specifies how the image is displayed on the screen if another image already exists. If no constant is provided, PUT uses XOR by default. The following list describes the constants.

- AND Performs a logical AND operation with each pixel in the target rectangle and the corresponding pixel in the source array. PUT writes the resulting value to the screen. If corresponding bits of the source and destination pixels are the same, the resulting bit is unchanged. If both of the bits are not 1, the resulting bit is 0, as shown in the following example:

- OR Performs a logical OR operation with each pixel in the target rectangle and the equivalent pixel in the source array. PUT writes the resulting value to the screen. If either of the corresponding bits in the pixel is 1, the resulting bit is 1, as shown in the following example:

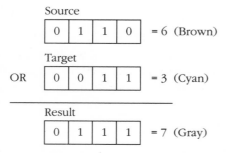

- PRESET Overwrites the target rectangle with the image stored in the source array and logically inverts the image as it is transferred, as shown in the example on the following page.

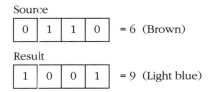

Source

| 0 | 1 | 1 | 0 | = 6 (Brown)

Result

| 1 | 0 | 0 | 1 | = 9 (Light blue)

■ PSET Overwrites the target rectangle with the image stored in the source array.

■ XOR Performs a logical XOR (exclusive or) operation with each pixel in the source array and the corresponding target pixel. PUT writes the resulting value to the screen. XOR inverts the screen image. If either but not both of the corresponding bits in the pixel is 1, the resulting bit is 1, as shown in the following example:

Source

| 0 | 1 | 1 | 0 | = 6 (Brown)

Target

XOR | 0 | 0 | 1 | 1 | = 3 (Cyan)

Result

| 0 | 1 | 0 | 1 | = 5 (Magenta)

Note that using PUT twice in succession with XOR restores the original contents of the target rectangle. This is a useful technique for generating animation effects in which the movement of an image must not destroy its background.

Usage

PUT (160, 100), image%

Copies the image stored in the integer array *image%* into a screen rectangle whose upper left corner is at position (160, 100). PUT performs logical XOR operations with the image and the existing display.

PUT STEP(xInc, yInc), image(0, 5), PSET

Defines a rectangular area of the screen whose upper left corner is offset *xInc* pixels on the *x*-axis and *yInc* pixels on the *y*-axis from the graphics-cursor position. PUT copies the image stored in the fifth column of the two-dimensional array *image* into this area, thus overwriting any previous contents.

Description

The GET statement lets you copy the pixels from a rectangular area of the screen into a numeric array. PUT lets you copy these pixels back onto the screen at any location.

QBasic lets you specify a logical operator with the PUT statement so that you can either combine the stored image with graphics already on the screen or overwrite the current contents of the display. You can, for example, reverse the original image (PRESET), superimpose it onto the existing pixels (OR), or invert each screen pixel that matches a pixel in the source array (XOR).

XOR is particularly useful for animation effects because using PUT twice with the same image at the same location draws and then erases the image, thus restoring that area of the screen to its original state. You can, therefore, make an image appear to move against a constant background by using PUT with XOR twice and then repeating the process at the next location in the sequence.

Warnings

Usually the *x*- and *y*-coordinates you specify in the PUT statement define the upper left corner of the rectangle into which the contents of the array will be copied. However, if you use the WINDOW statement without the SCREEN keyword to define your own logical coordinate system, the vertical axis of the display is reversed and the specified *x*- and *y*-coordinates indicate the lower left corner of the rectangle.

Example

You can use PUT to copy graphics images that have been stored by the GET statement to successive areas of the screen; this produces the effect of animation. The following program implements this technique and lets you use the direction keys to "walk" a pair of footprints around the screen. It also illustrates how images can be stored in and copied from multidimensional arrays.

The first part of the program builds a collection of images from one basic image. Notice how the DRAW statement rotates the original figure to produce images pointing in four directions (corresponding to the four direction keys).

The program uses the loop in the second part of the program to control the animation sequence. Two PUT statements that use XOR are made to each location, one to draw the image and one to erase it. This ensures that the background is restored before the program moves the image to a new location.

```
DIM ftUp%(25), ftDown%(25), ftLeft%(25), ftRight%(25)
DIM feet%(50, 3, 1)
DIM xInc%(3), yInc%(3)      ' arrays for incrementing position
DIM forward%(8)             ' array to figure which foot will be forward

FOR i% = 0 TO 3: READ xInc%(i%), yInc%(i%): NEXT

upArrow$ = CHR$(0) + CHR$(72): downArrow$ = CHR$(0) + CHR$(80)
leftArrow$ = CHR$(0) + CHR$(75): rightArrow$ = CHR$(0) + CHR$(77)
foot$ = "C2 S4 R2 D2 L2 U2 BM+1,+1P2,2BM-1,+3R2 D1 L2 U1 BM+1,+1P2,2"

SCREEN 1: x% = 50: y% = 50
```

(continued)

continued

```
' draw a foot for each direction and get the image
DRAW "BM52,51" + foot$
GET (x% + 2, y% + 1)-(x% + 4, y% + 6), ftUp%
DRAW "BM104,56 TA180" + foot$
GET (x% + 52, y% + 1)-(x% + 54, y% + 6), ftDown%
DRAW "BM152,54 TA90" + foot$
GET (x% + 102, y% + 2)-(x% + 109, y% + 4), ftLeft%
DRAW "BM208,52 TA270" + foot$
GET (x% + 152, y% + 2)-(x% + 159, y% + 4), ftRight%

' display the second foot for each direction
' and the pairs with the opposite foot forward
FOR i% = 1 TO 3
    READ xChange%, yChange%
    PUT (x% + xChange%, y% + yChange%), ftUp%, PSET
    READ xChange%, yChange%
    PUT (x% + xChange%, y% + yChange%), ftDown%, PSET
    READ xChange%, yChange%
    PUT (x% + xChange%, y% + yChange%), ftLeft%, PSET
    READ xChange%, yChange%
    PUT (x% + xChange%, y% + yChange%), ftRight%, PSET
NEXT i%

' get the image for each of the eight pairs of feet
GET (52, 50)-(59, 59), feet%(0, 0, 0)        ' up, left foot front
GET (102, 50)-(109, 59), feet%(0, 1, 0)      ' down, left foot front
GET (151, 51)-(162, 57), feet%(0, 2, 0)      ' left, right foot front
GET (201, 51)-(212, 57), feet%(0, 3, 0)      ' right, right foot front
GET (52, 100)-(59, 109), feet%(0, 0, 1)      ' up, right foot front
GET (102, 100)-(109, 109), feet%(0, 1, 1)    ' down, right foot front
GET (151, 101)-(162, 107), feet%(0, 2, 1)    ' left, left foot front
GET (201, 101)-(212, 107), feet%(0, 3, 1)    ' right, left foot front

' perform animation
CLS : x% = 160: y% = 100
arrow$ = upArrow$ + downArrow$ + leftArrow$ + rightArrow$
PUT (x%, y%), feet%(0, 0, 0), XOR
DO
    DO
        keyStroke$ = INKEY$
    LOOP WHILE keyStroke$ = ""
    move% = INSTR(arrow$, keyStroke$)
    IF move% THEN
        move% = ((move% + 1) \ 2) - 1          ' figure direction to move
        newX% = x% + xInc%(move%): newY% = y% + yInc%(move%)
        IF newX% < 10 OR newX% > 300 OR newY% < 10 OR newY% > 180 THEN
            PLAY "T255 L16 O1 G#"               ' a foot hit the border
        ELSE
```

(continued)

continued

```
          ' erase previous image
          PUT (x%, y%), feet%(0, lastMove%, forward%(lastMove%)), XOR
          thisMove% = move%
          IF thisMove% = lastMove% THEN    ' change which foot will be forward
              IF forward%(thisMove%) = 0 THEN
                  forward%(thisMove%) = 1
              ELSE
                  forward%(thisMove%) = 0
              END IF
          END IF

          ' draw new image
          PUT (newX%, newY%), feet%(0, thisMove%, forward%(thisMove%)), XOR
          lastMove% = thisMove%
          x% = newX%: y% = newY%
        END IF
    END IF
LOOP UNTIL keyStroke$ = CHR$(27)
END

DATA  0, -5, 0, 5, -5, 0, 5, 0
DATA  6, 3, 56, 3, 105, 5, 155, 5, 2, 53, 52, 53, 105, 52, 155
DATA  52, 6, 51, 56, 51, 102, 55, 152, 55
```

SCREEN (Function)

See also

COLOR, LOCATE, SCREEN (Statement)

Purpose

The SCREEN function returns information about a specified location. By default, the function returns the ASCII code of the character at the position (row and column) specified; in text mode, it can also return the color attribute number of that character.

Syntax

SCREEN(*row, column* [, *color*])

row and *column* are integers that specify the position of the character.

color is an optional integer: If you omit it, the SCREEN function returns the ASCII code of the character at that position; if you include a nonzero value for *color*, SCREEN returns the attribute number of the character's color.

Usage

```
PRINT SCREEN(5, 10)
```

Prints the ASCII code of the character currently displayed on the screen at row 5, column 10.

```
clr% = SCREEN(row%, col%, 1)
```
Assigns the attribute number of the character's color at the position specified by *row%* and *col%* to the integer variable *clr%*.

Description

The SCREEN function is the text mode version of the graphics POINT function. The SCREEN function returns information about the character at a specified location on the screen. It returns either the ASCII code of the character displayed there or the attribute number of the character's color.

In monochrome systems, the attribute number controls the intensity of the character and whether it is displayed as reverse video, blinking, or underlined.

The SCREEN function also returns ASCII values in graphics modes. It returns attribute numbers only in screen mode 0, the text mode. (See the SCREEN (Statement) entry for a description of the different screen modes.)

Errors

If you use the VIEW PRINT statement to define a text viewport, the SCREEN function operates only within this viewport. If you attempt to read a character on a line outside the viewport, QBasic displays an "Illegal function call" error message.

Example

The SCREEN function is useful for reading data that was output to the screen by DOS or by another program. The following example uses the function with the SHELL command to determine the volume label of the disk in a specified drive.

```
CLS : LOCATE 10, 1
INPUT "Volume label for which drive"; drive$
IF drive$ <> "" THEN
    drive$ = " " + LEFT$(drive$, 1) + ":"
END IF
VIEW PRINT 20 TO 21
label$ = ""
SHELL "VOL" + drive$        ' call the DOS function VOL
FOR i% = 23 TO 33
    label$ = label$ + CHR$(SCREEN(21, i%))            ' read the label
NEXT i%
VIEW PRINT: LOCATE 22, 1
PRINT "The VOL function returned the label "; label$  ' display the label
END
```

SCREEN (Statement)

See also

COLOR, PALETTE, PCOPY, VIEW, WIDTH (Screen), WINDOW

Purpose

The SCREEN statement defines various screen characteristics. The SCREEN statement lets you select different video modes, each of which controls the number of pixels, colors, and screen pages available for display.

Syntax

SCREEN [*mode*][, [*color*][, [*active*][, *visible*]]]

mode is a number in the range 0 through 13 that specifies the display mode. QBasic does not support modes 5 and 6.

color is a numeric expression that when true (nonzero) disables color display on computers connected to a composite monitor or a color television. *color* is ignored in all modes except 0 and 1.

active is an integer that specifies the screen page to which screen output is written, and *visible* is an integer that specifies the screen page that is currently displayed. The two integers need not be the same.

Usage

```
SCREEN 9, , 1, 0
```

Selects the high-resolution (640-by-350-pixel), 16-color mode available on EGA and VGA adapters. All subsequent graphics statements draw on screen page 0; page 1 becomes the displayed screen page. Notice that although the color argument is not valid in this mode, its place in the parameter list of the statement must be held by a comma.

```
SCREEN 0
```

Disables graphics output and returns to screen mode 0, the text mode.

Description

The screen modes available to your computer are determined by the type of display adapter you have installed. QBasic supports all adapters commonly used with the IBM PC, XT, AT, PS/2, and compatibles. It also supports adapters that are included in Olivetti and AT&T systems. Table 11-13 lists these adapters and the screen modes that they display. Note that many of these video adapters are downwardly compatible with their predecessors and support all previous screen modes.

Some video adapters can store more than one page of screen information at a time in memory. These pages are called screen pages. Screen pages are numbered from 0 through the maximum number available. Not only can you use SCREEN to select the active and visible pages, you can also copy the screen contents from one page to another with the PCOPY statement. Table 11-14 lists the maximum number of screen pages available in each screen mode for different types of video adapters.

Adapter		Available screen modes
MDPA	(Monochrome Display and Printer Adapter)	0
Olivetti		0, 4
AT&T		0, 4
CGA	(Color Graphics Adapter)	0, 1, 2
MCGA	(Multi-Color Graphics Array)	0, 1, 2, 11, 13
HGC	(Hercules Graphics Card)	0, 3
EGA	(Enhanced Graphics Adapter)	0, 1, 2, 7, 8, 9, 10*
VGA	(Video Graphics Array)	0, 1, 2, 7, 8, 9, 10*, 11, 12, 13

* Screen 10 is available only for EGA and VGA adapters that are connected to high-resolution monochrome monitors.

Table 11-13.

Video adapters and the available screen modes.

Screen	MDPA	CGA	MCGA	HGC	Olivetti	AT&T	EGA	VGA	Remarks
0	1	4	8	2	1	1	8	8	80 by 25 text
	-	8	8	-	-	-	8	8	40 by 25 text
	-	-	-	-	-	-	8	8	40 by 43 text
	-	-	-	-	-	-	-	4	40 by 50 text
	-	-	-	-	-	-	4	4	80 by 43 text
	-	-	-	-	-	-	-	4	80 by 50 text
1	-	1	1	-	-	-	1	1	
2	-	1	1	-	-	-	1	1	
3	-	-	-	2	-	-	-	-	Hercules only
4	-	-	-	-	1	1	-	-	
7*	-	-	-	-	-	-	8	8	
8*	-	-	-	-	-	-	4	4	
9*	-	-	-	-	-	-	2	2	
10*	-	-	-	-	-	-	4	4	
11	-	-	1	-	-	-	-	1	
12	-	-	-	-	-	-	-	1	
13	-	-	1	-	-	-	-	1	

* Values for screen modes 7, 8, 9, and 10 assume an EGA or VGA adapter with 256 KB of dedicated memory.

Table 11-14.

Number of screen pages available in each screen mode.

Screen mode 0

Screen mode 0 is the text screen mode and is the default mode of all video adapters. If you have an MDPA, HGC, or an EGA or VGA with a monochrome adapter, the only display size available is 25 rows by 80 columns. Other text formats are available with different adapters and color monitors, as shown in Table 11-14.

Use the WIDTH (Screen) statement to modify the number of rows and columns. (See the WIDTH (Screen) entry in Chapter 8, "Simple I/O.")

Text can be displayed in any combination of 16 foreground and 8 background attributes. On monochrome monitors, the attribute numbers control underlining and two degrees of character intensity; on color monitors, they determine text and background color. Both types of monitors support blinking characters. (See the COLOR entry for more details.) Computers with an EGA, VGA, or MCGA adapter and a color monitor can remap color attributes to different display colors using the PALETTE statement.

Screen mode 1

Screen mode 1 is a medium-resolution (320-by-200-pixel) graphics mode with a text format of 25 rows by 40 columns. Because televisions and composite monitors can display both graphics and text in this mode, color is enabled by default. To disable color, call the SCREEN statement with the third argument set to a nonzero value.

Four colors are available in screen mode 1. The background color can be any of the 16 standard attributes listed in Table 11-4. You can choose between the two color palettes listed in Table 11-5 to specify the three available foreground colors.

As in other screen modes, you can use the PALETTE statement to remap these attributes to display different colors on computers with an EGA, VGA, or MCGA adapter.

Screen mode 2

Screen mode 2 is a high-resolution (640-by-200-pixel) graphics mode with a text format of 25 rows by 80 columns. This mode supports only two colors. Normally these are white (foreground) and black (background), but you can use the PALETTE statement with EGA, VGA, and MCGA systems to map the two colors to any of the 16 standard colors.

Screen mode 3

Screen mode 3 is a high-resolution (720-by-348-pixel) graphics mode with a text format of 25 rows by 80 columns. Screen mode 3 is available only on computers using the Hercules Graphics Card (HGC) adapter. To enable the adapter, you must run the program MS-HERC.COM before using QBasic.

Screen mode 3 supports monochrome graphics only; you cannot remap the foreground and background colors with the PALETTE statement.

Screen mode 4

Screen mode 4 is a high-resolution (640-by-400-pixel) graphics mode with a text format of 25 rows by 80 columns. Screen mode 4 is available only on Olivetti Personal Computers Models M24, M240, M28, M280, M380, M380/C, and M380/T and on AT&T Personal Computers 6300 series. This mode supports 16 foreground colors that can be chosen using the COLOR statement. The background color, which is black, cannot be changed.

Screen mode 7

Screen mode 7 is available only on computers that use an EGA or VGA adapter and is similar to screen mode 1 except that 16 colors are available instead of 4. The colors can be remapped with the PALETTE statement. Screen mode 7 has a resolution of 320 by 200 pixels and a text format of 25 rows by 40 columns. As many as eight screen pages are available in this mode, depending on the amount of video memory in your adapter.

Screen mode 8

Screen mode 8 is an enhanced version of screen mode 2 for computers that use an EGA or VGA adapter. Screen mode 8 has a resolution of 640 by 200 pixels and a text format of 25 rows by 80 columns. This mode supports 16 colors, which can be remapped with the PALETTE statement. Four screen pages are available in this mode to adapters that have 256 KB of display memory.

Screen mode 9

Screen mode 9 is the standard graphics mode for computers with an EGA adapter, although systems with a VGA adapter can also use it. Screen mode 9 has a resolution of 640 by 350 pixels and a text format of either 80 rows by 25 columns or 80 rows by 43 columns.

The number of colors and screen pages available is determined by the amount of video memory that is available in the adapter. Early versions of the EGA include only 64 KB of memory, which supports only one screen page and 4 colors out of a palette of 16. VGA and EGA adapters with 256 KB or more of memory can switch between two pages and display 16 colors from a palette of 64 colors.

Screen mode 10

Screen mode 10 is available only to computers with an EGA and VGA adapter that is connected to a high-resolution monochrome monitor. Screen mode 10 has a resolution of 640 by 350 pixels and a text format of either 80 rows by 25 columns or 80 rows by 43 columns. Four display pages are available to adapters with 256 KB of video memory.

This mode supports four attributes. Each attribute can support one of 9 pseudo-colors, which control such characteristics as intensity and blink. (See the COLOR entry.)

Screen mode 11

Screen mode 11 is available only to computers using a VGA or MCGA adapter. Screen mode 11 has a resolution of 640 by 480 pixels and a text format of either 80 rows by 30 columns or 80 rows by 60 columns. 80-row-by-25-column text is not available.

Only two display attributes are available (one for foreground and one for background), but each can be assigned one of 262,144 colors with the PALETTE statement.

Screen mode 12

Screen mode 12 is available only to computers using a VGA adapter. Like screen mode 11, it has a graphics resolution of 640 by 480 pixels and either an 80-row-by-30-column or 80-row-by-60-column text format. Unlike screen mode 11, however, it supports 16 attributes from a palette of 262,144 colors.

Screen mode 13

Screen mode 13 is a medium-resolution (320-by-200-pixel) mode with a 40-row-by-25-column text format and is available to both VGA and MCGA adapters. In this mode, graphics can·be drawn with any of 256 attributes from a palette of 262,144 colors.

Notes

In graphics modes, changing the number of character columns on the screen by using the WIDTH (Screen) statement has the same effect as changing the screen mode number. Executing the statement WIDTH 40 in mode 2, for example, immediately switches the display to screen mode 1.

    If you select a screen mode other than the current one, QBasic clears the display, exactly as if you had also executed a CLS statement. However, if you use the SCREEN statement to select another page, but you don't change screen modes, QBasic does not clear graphics or text from the screen page. Note, however, that the graphics or text might no longer be visible because the page might no longer be the visible screen page.

Example

See the example in the COLOR entry for a program that demonstrates the SCREEN statement.

VIEW

See also

PMAP, SCREEN (Statement), VIEW PRINT, WINDOW

Purpose

The VIEW statement defines a rectangular area of the screen and confines all subsequent graphics output within its borders. This area is known as the graphics viewport. If your program uses both text and graphics, you can create a graphics viewport to keep the two types of output separate, thus preventing your graphics figures from overwriting any text on the screen.

Syntax

VIEW [[SCREEN] (*x1*, *y1*)-(*x2*, *y2*) [,[*attribute*] [,*border*]]]

The SCREEN keyword controls coordinates that can be used in subsequent graphics statements. If you use the SCREEN keyword, all subsequent graphics statements continue to use the upper left corner of the physical screen as the origin. If you omit the SCREEN keyword, all subsequent graphics statements use the upper left corner of the viewport as the origin, which is specified by (0, 0).

x1, *y1*, *x2*, *y2* are integer values that indicate the physical screen coordinates of opposite corners of the viewport being defined. *x1* and *x2* can range from 0 to the maximum horizontal resolution, and *y1* and *y2* can range from 0 to the maximum vertical resolution of the current screen mode.

attribute is an integer expression that specifies the background color. Using this parameter clears the viewport and sets it to the specified color. If you omit *attribute*, the viewport is not cleared, and any existing graphics or text within the viewport continues to be displayed.

border is an integer expression that when true (nonzero) draws a line in the specified color around the viewport. (If you use *border* but do not specify an attribute, you must include the first comma to hold the *attribute* position in the argument list.)

Using the VIEW statement without arguments cancels any previous VIEW statements and defines the entire screen as the current graphics viewport. However, VIEW does not clear the screen or change the display.

Usage

```
VIEW SCREEN (50, 20)-(150, 100)
```
Defines the specified physical coordinates as the new limits of the graphics viewport. Because SCREEN has been specified, subsequent graphics output uses absolute coordinates whose origin is located at the upper left corner of the physical screen.

Description

The VIEW statement lets you define the area of the screen in which graphics will appear. You can also use VIEW to remap the display coordinate system. Graphics locations are, by default, mapped in physical coordinates from an origin at the upper left corner of the screen—horizontally from left to right (*x*-axis) and vertically from top to bottom (*y*-axis). VIEW, when used with the SCREEN keyword, retains the physical coordinate system. Without the SCREEN keyword, VIEW changes the position of the origin to the upper left corner of the viewport.

VIEW does not display any graphics outside the viewport you specify, although any portion of a figure within the viewport is displayed. A figure that is not completely enclosed in a viewport is called a "clipped" figure.

You can use many VIEW statements in a program; however, graphics appear only in the currently active viewport, which is the area defined by the most recent VIEW statement. Because the coordinates specified in the VIEW statement are always interpreted as physical screen coordinates, you do not need to keep the new coordinates within the current viewport.

If you use VIEW to initialize a graphics viewport, the CLS statement clears only the contents of that viewport. However, if the program subsequently executes a VIEW PRINT statement, the defined text viewport becomes the active area, and a call to CLS clears only the text viewport. (See the CLS entry in Chapter 8, "Simple I/O," for details.)

Example

The following program graphs a profit-and-loss statement for an imaginary company. The program uses VIEW to create one viewport for the labels of the graph and another viewport for the contents of the graph.

```
SCREEN 9: LINE (0, 20)-(639, 349), 1, BF

VIEW (120, 180)-(510, 330), 0, 15  ' define viewport for labels of graph
WINDOW (0, -20000)-(12, 20000)
LOCATE 14, 33: PRINT "The Big Picture"
LOCATE 14, 18: PRINT "20000"
LOCATE 19, 16: PRINT "  0": LOCATE 23, 17: PRINT "-20000"
LINE (1, 0)-(12, 0), 15: LINE (1, -14000)-(1, 16000)

VIEW (153, 180)-(510, 330)         ' define viewport for the contents of graph
WINDOW (1, -20000)-(12, 20000)
PSET (0, 0)
RESTORE
FOR i% = 1 TO 12
    READ gainLoss!: LINE -(i%, gainLoss!), 15        ' get data for the graph
NEXT i%

PAINT (3, 2000), 14, 15: PAINT (10, -3000), 12, 15  ' draw the graph
PAINT (12, 800), 14, 15: VIEW: WINDOW
LOCATE 23, 30: PRINT "Profit"
LINE (300, 310)-(320, 320), 14, BF
LOCATE 23, 47: PRINT "Loss"
LINE (420, 310)-(440, 320), 12, BF
END

DATA 4013.28, 7269.88, 11152.75, 9327.08, 4148.20, 828.74
DATA -159.15, -788.61, -2693.80, -5164.02, -1176.53, 1297.63
```

WINDOW

See also

PMAP, VIEW

Purpose

The WINDOW statement defines a logical coordinate system for the current viewport. (The VIEW statement lets you define the screen boundaries of the viewport in which graphics will appear.) Use WINDOW to remap these physical coordinates into a logical coordinate system of your choice. You can also use the statement to reverse the normal, top-down orientation of the graphics display and use the Cartesian plotting system (with the origin at the bottom left corner of the viewport).

Syntax

WINDOW [[SCREEN] $(x1, y1)$-$(x2, y2)$]

$x1$, $y1$, $x2$, and $y2$ are single-precision values in the range $-3.37E+38$ through $3.37E+38$. They define the logical dimensions of the current viewport. The lesser of the two x-coordinates is the left boundary, and the greater x-coordinate is the right boundary. By default, the lesser y-coordinate specifies the bottom edge of the viewport and the greater y-coordinate specifies the top. If you use the SCREEN keyword, however, the lesser y-coordinate is the top of the viewport.

If you use WINDOW without any arguments, the graphics statement no longer uses logical coordinates but instead uses the default, physical coordinates of the viewport.

Usage

```
WINDOW (88.09, 1.5E+6)-(89.09, 2.5E+6)
```
Defines the logical coordinates for a viewport that displays a graph created from large numbers. Note that you can use both decimal and floating-point numbers as the logical coordinates.

Description

The WINDOW statement lets you translate real-world data into graphics coordinates without having to scale each value so that it fits into the boundaries of the physical screen. If your program calls WINDOW, the size and shape of the graphics drawn by your program appear approximately the same in screen mode 1 as in screen mode 9. (See the SCREEN (Statement) entry for a list of available screen modes.) The only differences between modes when WINDOW is used are that the colors differ and that lines and curves in screen modes with lower resolution are noticeably more jagged.

In the Cartesian coordinate system, the height of an object is measured from bottom to top, not from top to bottom as in the physical graphics coordinate system. WINDOW uses the Cartesian coordinate system by default, although you can override it by using the SCREEN option in the WINDOW statement.

After you define a logical coordinate system, subsequent graphics statements, such as LINE, CIRCLE, PAINT, PSET, PRESET, GET, and PUT use the values of this system as coordinates. QBasic translates these logical coordinates into physical screen locations when drawing an image. The DRAW statement is an exception because it accepts only physical screen coordinates.

If your program refers to points outside the logical dimensions of the viewport, QBasic plots them but does not display them on the screen. (This is called *clipping*.) Plotting the points ensures that any lines or curves that pass through the points are correctly drawn to their intersection with the screen boundaries.

If a graphics statement draws a figure so that the last point plotted is outside the viewport boundary, the position of the graphics cursor remains at that point even though it is outside the viewport. QBasic uses that point to plot subsequent graphics statements that use the STEP keyword to specify relative coordinates.

Example

You can use WINDOW to "zoom away" from a picture by drawing it within successively larger coordinate systems. The converse is also true: Defining smaller values for the logical dimensions of successive viewports magnifies the images in them. The following program uses this technique. It draws a figure six times, each time using smaller dimensions for the logical coordinates, which magnify the figure.

```
DECLARE SUB DrawPicture ()

SCREEN 9
LINE (0, 0)-(639, 349), 11, BF
x1 = 0: x2 = 1020: y1 = 0: y2 = 764
xPos% = 10: yPos% = 10: i% = 1

DO
    VIEW (xPos%, yPos%)-(xPos% + 200, yPos% + 155), 0, 15  ' define viewport
    WINDOW SCREEN (x1, y1)-(x2 / i%, y2 / i%)  ' define logical coordinates
    DrawPicture
    i% = i% + 1
    xPos% = xPos% + 210
    IF i% = 4 THEN xPos% = 10: yPos% = 175
LOOP UNTIL i% = 7
END

DATA 68, 4, 200, 76, 52, 12, 112, 44, 128, 52, 172, 76, 128, 52
DATA 68, 84, 112, 44, 84, 60, 128, 68, 100, 84, 68, 36, 96, 52
DATA 128, 68, 154, 84, 128, 68, 128, 116, 130, 54, 130, 68, 68
DATA 4, 52, 12, 172, 76, 142, 90, 142, 76, 142, 108, 142, 108
DATA 200, 76, 200, 76, 200, 92, 200, 92, 68, 164, 128, 116, 84
DATA 140, 52, 12, 52, 154, 52, 154, 68, 164, 68, 164, 68, 100
DATA 68, 36, 68, 84, 84, 45, 84, 76, 84, 109, 84, 140, 68, 100
DATA 96, 116, 84, 124, 112, 108, 68, 84, 128, 116, 85, 75, 113
DATA 91, 112, 77, 112, 108, 84, 119, 92, 115, 142, 86, 150, 82
DATA 180, 66, 186, 62, 186, 62, 236, 90, 236, 90, 68, 184, 68
DATA 184, 16, 154, 16, 154, 52, 133, 16, 154, 16, 160, 16, 160
DATA 68, 190, 68, 190, 68, 184, 68, 190, 236, 96, 236, 96, 236
DATA 90

SUB DrawPicture STATIC
    RESTORE
    FOR i% = 1 TO 40        ' read coordinates
        READ x1%, y1%, x2%, y2%: LINE (x1%, y1%)-(x2%, y2%), 1  ' draw outline
    NEXT i%
```

(continued)

continued

```
' paint figure
PAINT (56, 20), 1, 1: PAINT (136, 64), 1, 1
PAINT (120, 80), 1, 1: PAINT (152, 110), 14, 1
PAINT (76, 48), 14, 1: PAINT (124, 60), 14, 1
PAINT (68, 12), 2, 1: PAINT (80, 84), 2, 1
PAINT (92, 128), 2, 1: PAINT (36, 150), 12, 1
PAINT (150, 125), 12, 1: PAINT (80, 120), 14, 1
PAINT (36, 168), 1, 1: PAINT (150, 142), 14, 1
PAINT (88, 118), 12, 1: PAINT (144, 86), 12, 1
PAINT (100, 120), 2, 1: PAINT (165, 90), 2, 1
END SUB
```

CHAPTER 12

Sound

Introduction

Imagine that you've just written a flashy new QBasic program: It has colorful graphics, windows, and a friendly interface. But something seems to be missing. Is your program so quiet it's deafening? Music and sound effects can make games, educational programs, and other applications more interesting to the user. You can add a simple melody to the opening screen, a beep as a warning, or a pleasing tone for positive reinforcement. The statements and functions described in this chapter let your programs make sounds.

Table 12-1 lists QBasic's sound-related statements and functions.

Statement or function	Description
BEEP	Sounds a beep on the computer's speaker
ON PLAY GOSUB	Specifies the subroutine that adds notes to the music buffer when play event trapping is enabled; the notes are played in the background
PLAY (Function)	Returns the number of notes remaining in the music buffer
PLAY (Statement)	Plays the specified melody; executes commands for the octave, pitch, duration, tempo, and foreground or background
PLAY ON/OFF/STOP	Enables, disables, or suspends the play event trapping that occurs when the music buffer has fewer than the specified number of notes remaining
SOUND	Generates a tone of the specified frequency for the specified duration

Table 12-1.
QBasic sound-related statements and functions.

Using Music in Your Program

Before you decide what music to play in your program, first consider the purpose of the program: How will music help you entertain or communicate with the user? Aside from forming the core of programs whose explicit purpose is to teach or demonstrate music, music usually serves two purposes in programs.

The first—often used in games—is to provide atmosphere by playing music in the background while the program executes other statements. (A melody might also entertain the user while the program is not generating any visual output.)

The second purpose of music is to get the user's attention—to issue a cue, a warning, or a reward. In an educational program, for example, a triumphant "bugle call" might mean the student correctly answered a difficult question; or a melody might mean "Wrong—please try again." The program could also play a brief tune that lets the student know it's time to answer a question or enter some information; this would be helpful in programs for young children or for visually impaired persons.

In most cases you should use music sparingly. Most PCs have small speakers that can't generate very low or very high frequencies.

Translating a Musical Score into PLAY Statements

You probably won't be using QBasic to compose your own music—although the various statements for playing music aren't hard to use, they aren't as easily read as a musical score. More likely, you will transcribe music written in standard notation. Figure 12-1 shows the melody of the tune "Red River Valley" written on a musical staff. Below the staff are the commands you use with the PLAY statement to generate the notes.

The PLAY statement executes the tasks that are specified in a string of commands indicating the pitch (for example, A, C#, or E), duration, tempo, and other characteristics of the music. You don't have to use spaces to separate the commands in the string, but doing so makes the string easier to read. The following program uses one PLAY statement for each measure of music in "Red River Valley" to improve readability. When translating a note into PLAY commands, you must specify both the pitch and the duration of each note.

```
' Red River Valley
PLAY "O3" ' set octave 3, middle C
PLAY "L2 NO < L4 G > C"
PLAY "L2 E L4 E D"
PLAY "L2 C L4 D C"
PLAY "< L2 A > L1 C L4 < G > C"
PLAY "L2 E L4 E E"
PLAY "L2 G L4 F E"
PLAY "L1 D. < L4 G > C"
PLAY "L2 E L4 E D"
PLAY "L2 C L4 D E"
PLAY "L2 G L1 F < L4 A A"
PLAY "L2 G L4 > C D"
PLAY "L2 E L4 D D"
PLAY "L1 C. L2 NO"
```

Red River Valley

Figure 12-1.
"Red River Valley" in QBasic notation and in standard musical notation.

Specifying Pitch and Duration

Examine the listing of the program that plays "Red River Valley." The first statement (*PLAY "O3"*) sets the octave. (Note that the command begins with the letter O, not the number 0.) You can play music in any of seven octaves numbered from 0 through 6, with 0 corresponding to the lowest octave, 3 corresponding to the octave containing middle C, and 6 corresponding to the highest octave.

The commands in the string of the second PLAY statement specify the following actions:

L2 N0	Play a rest (note 0) for 2 beats (the length of a half note)
<	Shift subsequent notes down one octave
L4 G	Play the pitch G for 1 beat (the length of a quarter note)
>	Shift subsequent notes up one octave
C	Play the pitch C for 1 beat (the length of a quarter note)

Usually the most convenient approach is to specify the pitch of notes by using the standard letters—A through G; however, you can also use the N command to specify the absolute note number—N0 through N84. N30, for example, plays the 30th note in the seven-octave range. Table 12-2 lists the pitches and their corresponding numbers. N0 specifies a period of silence (a rest). You can also specify a rest by using the P command followed by a number that specifies the duration of the rest. For example, P4 specifies a quarter-note rest.

Although the "Red River Valley" example doesn't use sharps or flats to raise or lower pitches, QBasic lets you do so by following the note's letter name with a plus sign (+) or a number sign (#) for a sharp and a minus sign (–) for a flat. You cannot use the plus sign, number sign, or minus sign with a note specified by the N command and a number because every number corresponds to a different pitch. The command N38, for example, specifies the note C# in the third octave, as you can see in Table 12-2.

Octave	Pitch	Number	Octave	Pitch	Number
0	C	1	0	G#/A♭	9
0	C#/D♭	2	0	A	10
0	D	3	0	A#/B♭	11
0	D#/E♭	4	0	B	12
0	E	5	1	C	13
0	F	6	1	C#/D♭	14
0	F#/G♭	7	1	D	15
0	G	8	1	D#/E♭	16

Table 12-2.
Pitches and their corresponding number.

(continued)

Table 12-2. *continued*

Octave	Pitch	Number	Octave	Pitch	Number
1	E	17	4	D	51
1	F	18	4	D♯/E♭	52
1	F♯/G♭	19	4	E	53
1	G	20	4	F	54
1	G♯/A♭	21	4	F♯/G♭	55
1	A	22	4	G	56
1	A♯/B♭	23	4	G♯/A♭	57
1	B	24	4	A	58
2	C	25	4	A♯/B♭	59
2	C♯/D♭	26	4	B	60
2	D	27	5	C	61
2	D♯/E♭	28	5	C♯/D♭	62
2	E	29	5	D	63
2	F	30	5	D♯/E♭	64
2	F♯/G♭	31	5	E	65
2	G	32	5	F	66
2	G♯/A♭	33	5	F♯/G♭	67
2	A	34	5	G	68
2	A♯/B♭	35	5	G♯/A♭	69
2	B	36	5	A	70
3	C	37	5	A♯/B♭	71
3	C♯/D♭	38	5	B	72
3	D	39	6	C	73
3	D♯/E♭	40	6	C♯/D♭	74
3	E	41	6	D	75
3	F	42	6	D♯/E♭	76
3	F♯/G♭	43	6	E	77
3	G	44	6	F	78
3	G♯/A♭	45	6	F♯/G♭	79
3	A	46	6	G	80
3	A♯/B♭	47	6	G♯/A♭	81
3	B	48	6	A	82
4	C	49	6	A♯/B♭	83
4	C♯/D♭	50	6	B	84

You specify the length (duration) of a note with the L command followed by a number; for example, L2 N0 plays a half-note rest. The duration is specified as a fraction of a whole note: L1 specifies a whole note (4 beats), L2 a half note (2 beats), L4 a quarter note (1 beat), and so on to L64, a sixty-fourth note (⅛ of a beat). The L command sets the length of all subsequent notes until a new L command is given. Or you can specify a particular note's length (without affecting subsequent notes) by inserting only the length number after the note; for example, C8 plays the pitch C as an eighth note.

You can also make a note last half again as long as the specified length by following the note letter with a period. For example, L1 D. specifies a D whole note that is held for an additional half note, for a total duration of 1½ whole notes (6 beats). You can use this notation to transcribe any note in a musical score that has a dot after it.

Because notes in many songs range through several octaves, QBasic includes a convenient way to shift octaves: the greater-than sign (>) shifts the subsequent notes up one octave, and the less-than sign (<) shifts the subsequent notes down one octave. A shift remains in effect until a new shift is specified or until the O command specifies a particular octave. In "Red River Valley," the notes are in octaves 2 and 3.

Tempo and Other Modifiers

QBasic lets you control the speed, or tempo, of the music you compose. The T command in the PLAY statement specifies the tempo in terms of how many quarter notes will be played per minute, ranging from 32 through 255; the default is 120. Note that at a fast tempo (for example, T200) short notes such as sixty-fourth notes might not sound because the interval is shorter than the tick of the computer's clock, which QBasic uses for timing. (See Chapter 10, "Timing, Date, and Time.")

You can alter the length of notes by using the following commands:

ML (music legato)   Each note plays for full length

MN (music normal)   Each note plays for ⅞ length

MS (music staccato)   Each note plays for ¾ length

This lets you create effects that correspond to the spirit of the music.

Playing Commands from a String Variable

You can assign a series of PLAY commands to a string variable and then execute its contents by inserting it into a PLAY statement. For example, the following statements cause a scale to play:

```
scale$ = "CDEFGAB"
PLAY "X" + VARPTR$(scale$)
```

To use a string variable in a PLAY statement, you must first place an X in the PLAY command string, followed by a set of closing quotation marks, and then add a call to the VARPTR$ function. (This function returns the address of the string variable so that PLAY can find the commands in the string.)

Playing Music in the Background

The MB (music background) command for PLAY specifies that the music will play in the background while your program continues execution.

When music is to be played in the background, notes generated by the PLAY statements aren't played immediately—they are stored in an internal buffer. After the program executes a statement, it checks the music buffer to see whether there are any notes to be played. If there are, some notes might be played. The number of notes played is determined by the durations of the notes and whether any time has elapsed since the most recent note sounded.

The buffer can hold only 32 notes, so if you want to play more than a brief melody in the background, you must execute more PLAY statements to refill the buffer.

If you want to play background music continuously, you must set up a play event trap that refills the music buffer every time the number of notes in the buffer drops below a specified value. To do this, first create a subroutine containing the PLAY statements that will refill the buffer. (To be sure the music will be played in the background, include in your program a PLAY statement that contains the MB command.) Then specify that subroutine in an ON PLAY GOSUB statement. For example, the statement

```
ON PLAY(5) GOSUB MoreMusic
```

specifies that when fewer than five notes remain in the music buffer, the program will execute the subroutine *MoreMusic*. You might have to experiment with the number of notes you specify: If the number is too low, the buffer might empty before QBasic can check it; if the number is too high, the program might refill the buffer so frequently that program execution slows.

After you set up your music subroutine with an ON PLAY GOSUB statement, use the PLAY ON statement to turn on the play event-trapping mechanism. Then you must fill the buffer initially by calling the subroutine with a GOSUB statement. The program outline looks like the following listing:

```
ON PLAY(5) GOSUB MusicSub  ' set up music subroutine
PLAY ON                    ' turn on trapping
PLAY "MB"                  ' specify music in background
GOSUB MusicSub             ' begin the music
' other statements execute while music plays
' buffer is regularly refilled by MusicSub
END

MusicSub:
    ' PLAY statements
    RETURN
```

QBasic provides two other statements for use with PLAY. The PLAY OFF statement stops play event trapping. It prevents the program from executing the music subroutine so that the background music stops after all notes in the buffer have been played. The

PLAY STOP statement also prevents the music subroutine from being executed; however, the program remembers whether the number of notes in the music buffer goes below the specified threshold, and when the next PLAY ON statement is executed, the music subroutine executes and refills the buffer. Thus you can use PLAY STOP to temporarily disable the music subroutine (so that a critical part of the program won't be slowed down, for example) and then use PLAY ON to restore the background music.

If you would like to perform a task only when the music buffer has a certain number of notes in it, use the PLAY function to check the number of notes remaining in the buffer.

Other Sound-Producing Statements

The BEEP statement sounds a beep on the computer's built-in speaker, exactly as if you had executed the statement *PRINT CHR$(7)*.

The SOUND statement produces a sound of a specified frequency and duration and can be used for various sound effects. (The example program in the SOUND entry creates the sound of a police siren.) Follow the keyword SOUND with the frequency in cycles per second, or hertz, (a value in the range 37 through 32767), a comma, and the duration in clock ticks. (The computer's clock "ticks" 18.2 times per second.) Thus the statement

SOUND 440, 18.2

generates a 440-cycle tone (which is the pitch A) for 1 second. The SOUND statement is more versatile than PLAY because it is not limited to the recognized musical notes; on the other hand, the sounds produced by SOUND cannot be played in the background.

Related Reading

Enders, Bernd, and Bob Peterson. The Waite Group. *BASIC Primer for the IBM PC & XT.* New York, N.Y.: New American Library, 1984.

BEEP

See also
PLAY (Statement), SOUND

Purpose
The BEEP statement sounds a beep on the computer's speaker. A beep is often used to call attention to an error or to warn the user of the consequences of an action such as deleting a file.

Syntax
BEEP

Usage
BEEP

Sounds a beep on the speaker.

Description
The BEEP statement sounds a beep on the speaker for about half a second. You can achieve the same effect with the statement *PRINT CHR$(7)*.

You can't control the duration of a single beep, but you can make the beep seem longer by repeating the BEEP statement in a loop. You also can't control the pitch of the beep: To generate another sound or a musical note, you must use the SOUND statement or the PLAY statement.

Example
The following program uses a loop to request input of one of the following characters: A, B, C, or D (either lowercase or uppercase). If the user enters an invalid character, the program sounds a beep by calling BEEP and prompts the user to try again.

```
CLS
DO
    PRINT "Type A, B, C, or D."
    INPUT char$
    choice$ = UCASE$(char$)
    IF INSTR("ABCD", choice$) THEN
        PRINT "Very good!"
        EXIT DO
    ELSE
        BEEP
        PRINT "Please try again."
    END IF
LOOP
```

ON PLAY GOSUB

See also

PLAY (Function), PLAY (Statement), PLAY ON/OFF/STOP

Purpose

The ON PLAY GOSUB statement specifies the start of the subroutine that is executed whenever the number of notes left in the music buffer goes below a specified value. You can use this statement to specify the subroutine that fills the music buffer with notes to be played in the background while your program continues execution.

Syntax

ON PLAY(*notes*) GOSUB {*label* ¦ *line*}

notes is the number that specifies the fewest number of notes that can be in the music buffer before the program executes the subroutine. It must be an integer in the range 1 through 32.

label or *line* is the label or line number of the subroutine to be executed when fewer notes than specified by *notes* remain to be played in the buffer.

Usage

ON PLAY(3) GOSUB MoreMusic

Specifies that the subroutine *MoreMusic* will be executed when there are fewer than three notes left to be played in the music buffer.

Description

The ON PLAY GOSUB statement sets up play event trapping for filling the music buffer. It specifies the subroutine to which the program branches when the number of notes stored in the music buffer changes to one less than the specified value. Play event trapping keeps the music buffer full so that music can be played in the background until event trapping is disabled or paused. After you call the ON PLAY GOSUB statement, you must call PLAY ON to begin the event trapping.

Errors

If you specify a number of queued notes outside the range 1 through 32, QBasic displays an "Illegal function call" error message.

Example

See the example program in the PLAY ON/OFF/STOP entry for an illustration of the usage of the ON PLAY GOSUB statement.

PLAY (Function)

See also

ON PLAY GOSUB, PLAY (Statement), PLAY ON/OFF/STOP

Purpose

The PLAY function returns the number of notes that remain to be played in the music buffer. You can use this function to check the status of the buffer; if the buffer is almost empty, you can execute a PLAY statement to fill it.

Syntax

PLAY(*n*)

n is a dummy value that is used to distinguish the PLAY function from the PLAY statement. It can have any numeric value.

Usage

```
IF PLAY(1) < 10 THEN PLAY "C D E F G A B"
```

Puts the notes of a scale in the music buffer if fewer than 10 notes remain to be played.

Description

The PLAY function returns the number of notes remaining to be played in the music buffer. The music buffer holds notes only when music is being played in the background. By having your program check this value periodically, you can execute PLAY statements to refill the buffer and enable the background music to continue playing. The PLAY statement used with the MB command specifies that music is to be played in the background.

If music is being played in the foreground (the default for the PLAY statement when the MB command isn't specified), the PLAY function returns 0.

Comments

If your program is long or has considerable variation in its path of execution, the PLAY function might not be executed often enough to prevent the music buffer from being emptied (thus causing the music to stop playing). In these cases, use the ON PLAY GOSUB statement to make the program branch to a subroutine that refills the buffer when the buffer is nearly empty.

Example

The following program repeatedly plays a scale in the background. It calls the PLAY function each time through a loop and reports the number of notes in the music buffer. When the buffer contains fewer than three notes, the program refills it by calling the PLAY statement.

```
PLAY "MB"                    ' set background music mode
CLS

DO
    LOCATE 5, 1
    PRINT "Number of notes left to play: ";
    IF PLAY(1) < 3 THEN      ' refill music buffer if fewer than 3 notes remain
        PLAY "< C D E F G A B > C"
    END IF
    PRINT PLAY(1)
LOOP UNTIL INKEY$ <> ""       ' loop until user presses a key
END
```

PLAY (Statement)

See also

ON PLAY GOSUB, PLAY ON/OFF/STOP

Purpose

The PLAY statement plays specified musical notes. You can control the pitch and duration of each note and include pauses (rests). You can play the music in the foreground or in the background (while other statements of the program are being executed).

Syntax

PLAY *string*

string is a string literal, string variable, or string expression that contains a series of music commands. You can enter commands in uppercase or lowercase, and you can separate them with blank spaces or semicolons, although this merely makes the string more readable and is not a syntax requirement.

Usage

```
PLAY "C D E F G A B"
```
Plays a scale.

```
PLAY "X" + VARPTR$(cmd$)
```
Plays the commands in the string variable *cmd$*.

Description

The PLAY statement uses a "macro language" that enables your program to play melodies. The string in quotes (or in a string variable) following the PLAY keyword consists of a series of macro commands that specify the pitch and duration of notes, the overall tempo, and whether the music is to be played in the foreground or background.

Pitch

You can play notes in as many as seven octaves. Use the O command with a number in the range 0 through 6 to specify the octave of subsequent notes. (The fourth octave, or O3, contains middle C.) You can also use a greater-than sign (>) to specify the next-higher octave or a less-than sign (<) to specify the next-lower one. (Specifications above octave 6 or below octave 0 are ignored.)

You can use either of two methods to specify the pitch to be played: Use the N command followed by the note number (0 through 84), or merely specify the musical letter (A through G). (Remember, when you use note letters, QBasic plays that particular note within the last octave specified.) The command N0 indicates a rest (a period of silence). In the letter notation, a plus sign (+) or number sign (#) indicates a sharp, and a minus sign (−) indicates a flat. Sharps and flats affect only the current note.

You can also specify a pause by using the P command followed by the fraction of a whole note (in the range 1 through 64) that specifies the length of time to pause. See the "Duration" section for an explanation of the length.

Duration

Duration is the relative length of time for which a note sounds. Use the L command followed by the length of subsequent notes: 1 is a whole note, 2 a half note, 4 a quarter note, 8 an eighth note, 16 a sixteenth note, and 32 a thirty-second note. The shortest note value is 64 (a sixty-fourth note). After you specify a length with the L command, all subsequent notes use that length until you change it. If you want to change the length of only one note, specify a number after that note. For example, the command *PLAY "L4 C G A"* plays C, G, and A as quarter notes. If the next command were *PLAY "F8 B C"*, F would be an eighth note, and B and C would be played as quarter notes (the most recently specified length).

In accordance with musical notation, you can also follow a note with a dot to make its length 1½ times the last specified length. To do this, put a period after the note. For example, the command *PLAY "L8 G A."* plays G as an eighth note and then plays A as 1½ eighth notes (a "dotted eighth note").

The length of all notes being played can also be modified by the following commands:

ML (music legato)	Each note plays for full length
MN (music normal)	Each note plays for ⅞ length
MS (music staccato)	Each note plays for ¾ length

Any of these three commands remains in effect until you specify another one.

The length of a note is its relative duration—that is, how long the note plays in relation to a whole note. The actual amount of time (in seconds) that a note plays is determined by tempo, the rate at which the music is played. In PLAY, tempo is expressed in quarter notes per minute and is specified by T followed by a number in the range 32 through 255. The default is T120, which means 120 quarter notes can be played per minute.

Note that the interrupt rate of the system clock limits how short and fast individual notes can be. For example, if the tempo is set to 255, your program won't be able to play sixty-fourth notes (T255 L64) because the system cannot check the clock for the timing and produce the note in such a short interval.

Foreground and background music

PLAY includes two commands that specify the mode in which the program plays the specified notes. By default, music plays in the foreground (specified by MF). This means that a QBasic program executes PLAY statements and sounds the specified notes without executing any other statements until all the music has been played.

If you use the MB (music background) command, however, the notes specified in PLAY statements are put into a buffer and played in the background. Execution of the program continues while the music plays. After each statement in your program is executed, QBasic checks the buffer and might play some notes. (The number of notes played is determined by the durations of the notes and whether any notes are still being played; that is, QBasic tries to maintain the tempo you have set.) The buffer can hold a maximum of 32 notes; therefore, you must continually refill the buffer before it runs out of notes if you want the music to be played continuously. (See the tutorial and the ON PLAY GOSUB entry for details.)

Playing commands in a string variable

For convenience, you can assign a series of PLAY commands to a string variable and then use the variable in a PLAY statement. For example, the statement *cmd$ = "C D E"* assigns three PLAY commands to the variable *cmd$*. When you include this variable as a substring within a PLAY command string, QBasic executes the commands in the substring. To use the substring, type an X at the end of your PLAY command and add a call to the VARPTR$ function, as in the following statement:

```
PLAY "O3 A B- X" + VARPTR$(cmd$)
```

If you want to use an integer variable in the PLAY statement to specify the value following a command, you must follow the letter designating the command with an equal sign and a set of closing quotation marks. Then add the variable in a call to VARPTR$ to the command string. For example, if the variable *octave%* contains the number of the octave for a particular melody, you could set the octave with the following statement:

```
PLAY "O=" + VARPTR$(octave%)
```

Errors

If you specify an integer that is out of range for a particular PLAY command, QBasic displays an "Illegal function call" error message. QBasic displays the same message if you use a letter in the command string that isn't a command.

Example

The following program uses PLAY statements to play the song "Here Comes the Sun" by the Beatles (1969 Harrisongs, Ltd.).

```
PLAY "T255"   ' set tempo to 255 quarter notes per minute
PLAY "O3"
PLAY "< < L2 A > > > L4 C# < A B > L2 C#."
PLAY "L2 NO L4 C# < L2 B A F#"
PLAY "A B A F# L1 E."
PLAY "< < L2 A > > > L4 C# < A B > L2 C#."
PLAY "L2 NO L4 C# < L2 B A L2 F#."
PLAY "> L4 C# < L2 B A L1 B B L1 NO"

PLAY "< < L2 A > > > L4 C# < L2 B > L2 C# < L2 A."
PLAY "> L4 C# < A B > L2 C#."
PLAY "< < L2 A > > > L4 C# < L2 B > C# < L2 A."
PLAY "L4 NO A L2 B A"
PLAY "L2 NO > L2 C# < B A NO"
PLAY "L4 F# A B E A B D A B A G# F# E"
```

PLAY ON/OFF/STOP

See also
PLAY (Function), PLAY (Statement)

Purpose
The PLAY statements enable, disable, or suspend play event trapping. This statement lets you refill the music buffer continuously while music is being played in the background. Thus background music can continue while your program executes other statements.

Syntax
PLAY ON
PLAY OFF
PLAY STOP

Usage
```
ON PLAY(3) GOSUB Refill
PLAY ON
```
Refills the music buffer as specified in the ON PLAY GOSUB statement.

```
PLAY OFF
```
Stops the play event trapping that refills the music buffer.

Description
When you specify that music be played in the background (by including the MB command in a PLAY statement), the notes are stored in an internal buffer rather than played immediately. After a PLAY ON statement is executed, QBasic checks the buffer after

each subsequent statement is executed and plays as many notes as possible. When the number of notes remaining to be played falls below the number specified in the ON PLAY GOSUB statement, the subroutine specified in that statement is executed. (Usually this subroutine executes PLAY statements or calls subroutines that execute PLAY subroutines, thus refilling the buffer with notes.)

To completely disable background music, use the PLAY OFF statement. Executing PLAY OFF prevents the ON PLAY GOSUB subroutine from being executed. Thus the buffer soon runs out of notes, and the background music stops playing.

To temporarily suspend the background music (for example, while your program is executing instructions that might be affected by the repeated interruptions to refill the music buffer), use the PLAY STOP statement. The remaining notes in the buffer will be played, and then the background music will stop playing. To restart the background music, merely execute another PLAY ON statement. If the number of notes falls below the number specified in the ON PLAY GOSUB statement after PLAY STOP has been called, QBasic sets an internal flag indicating that the buffer needs refilling so that the program will execute the subroutine when PLAY ON is called.

Example

The following program uses a PLAY ON statement to turn on play event trapping and uses an ON PLAY GOSUB statement to send control to the *Replay* subroutine when the music buffer needs to be refilled. Note that the PLAY *"MB T255"* statement specifies that music be played in the background and sets a speedy tempo. The song played in this program is "Here Comes the Sun" by the Beatles.

The main FOR loop in the program draws progressively larger circles in changing colors to represent the sun. The outer DO loop executes the program until the user presses Esc.

The IF statements control the flag variable *music*. The first time a key (other than Esc) is pressed, *music* is set to 0 and a PLAY STOP statement is executed. This suspends event trapping and stops the music. The next time the user presses a key, *music* is set to 1, and a PLAY ON statement immediately refills the music buffer (because QBasic "remembers" the last event—the nearly empty buffer), and the music resumes. If you replace the PLAY STOP statement with PLAY OFF, the music does not resume.

The *Replay* subroutine contains the PLAY statements that fill the music buffer.

```
SCREEN 9        ' for EGA; use 1 for CGA, 12 for VGA
maxX% = 640     ' for EGA; use 320 for CGA
maxY% = 350     ' for EGA; use 200 for CGA, 480 for VGA

x = maxX% / 2
y = maxY% / 2               ' starting position for circle
maxColors% = 9
startRad = maxY% / 16      ' starting radius of circle
```

(continued)

continued

```
DIM colors(maxColors%)

FOR clr% = 1 TO 9          ' read the foreground color values
   READ colors(clr%)
NEXT clr%


' set up sound
ON PLAY(3) GOSUB Replay    ' refill buffer when three or fewer notes
GOSUB Replay               ' fill music buffer initially
PLAY ON                    ' turn on music event trapping
music = 1                  ' flag indicating whether music is played

DO                         ' main loop shows graphic
    FOR clr% = 1 TO maxColors%              ' FOR loop steps through values
        circleColor = colors(clr%)
        rad = startRad * clr%
        CIRCLE (x, y), rad, (circleColor)    ' draw circle
        PAINT (x, y), circleColor            ' fill in the circle
    NEXT clr%
    inky$ = INKEY$
    IF inky$ = CHR$(27) THEN EXIT DO        ' exit loop if user presses Esc
    FOR n = 1 TO 500: NEXT n
    PAINT (x, y), 0           ' erase circle
    IF inky$ <> "" THEN       ' toggle PLAY status
        IF music THEN
            PLAY STOP         ' pause event trapping
            music = 0
        ELSE
            PLAY ON           ' enable event trapping
            music = 1
        END IF
    END IF
LOOP UNTIL inky$ = CHR$(27)                 ' exit loop if user presses Esc
PLAY OFF
END


' subroutine to fill music buffer
Replay:
    PLAY "MB T255"
    PLAY "O3"
    PLAY "< < L2 A > > > L4 C# < A B > L2 C#."
    PLAY "L2 NO L4 C# < L2 B A F#"
    PLAY "A B A F# L1 E."
    PLAY "< < L2 A > > > L4 C# < A B > L2 C#."
    PLAY "L2 NO L4 C# < L2 B A L2 F#."
    PLAY "> L4 C# < L2 B A L1 B B L1 NO"

    PLAY "< < L2 A > > > L4 C# < L2 B > L2 C# < L2 A."
    PLAY "> L4 C# < A B > L2 C#."
```

(continued)

continued

```
      PLAY "< < L2 A > > > L4 C# < L2 B > C# < L2 A."
      PLAY "L4 NO A L2 B A"
      PLAY "L2 NO > L2 C# < B A NO"
      PLAY "L4 F# A B E A B D A B A G# F# E"
      RETURN

   ' foreground colors of the circles
   DATA 4, 12, 5, 13, 5, 12, 14, 12, 14
```

SOUND

See also

BEEP, PLAY (Statement)

Purpose

The SOUND statement generates a tone of a specified frequency and duration on the computer's speaker. You can use this statement to create sound effects other than the standard musical notes generated by the PLAY statement.

Syntax

SOUND *frequency, duration*

frequency is an integer expression in the range 37 through 32767; it represents the sound's frequency in cycles per second (hertz).

duration is an integer expression in the range 0 through 65535; it represents the length of the sound in clock ticks. (The computer's clock ticks 18.2 times per second.)

Usage

```
SOUND 440, 18.2
```

Sounds a 440-cycle tone (musical A) for 1 second (18.2 clock ticks).

```
SOUND 500, 0
```

Terminates the current sound. Any 0 duration turns off the sound currently being generated.

Description

The SOUND statement generates a sound of the specified number of cycles per second (hertz) for the specified number of clock ticks. The human ear can hear approximately 20 through 20,000 hertz, so be sure to limit the sounds to this range. A duration of 0 ticks in a SOUND statement turns off any SOUND statement currently running.

The computer's speaker isn't designed to reproduce sounds higher than a few thousand hertz. Unlike the PLAY statement, the SOUND statement can't run in the background. However, the current sound continues for its full duration while QBasic executes subsequent statements.

SOUND

Errors

If you use a string value with SOUND, QBasic displays a "Type mismatch" error message. Any numeric value that is out of range results in an "Illegal function call" error message.

Example

The following program plays a rising and falling glissando, which produces a "police siren" sound effect. To create the glissando, the program calls the SOUND statement in a FOR loop that modifies, by 4 hertz each iteration, the note played.

```
CLS
PRINT "PULL OVER!"
PRINT "<Press any key to stop>"
DO
    FOR i% = 440 TO 880 STEP 4
        SOUND i%, i% / 880
        IF INKEY$ <> "" THEN EXIT DO
    NEXT
    FOR i% = 880 TO 440 STEP -4
        SOUND i%, i% / 880
        IF INKEY$ <> "" THEN EXIT DO
    NEXT
LOOP UNTIL INKEY$ <> ""
```

CHAPTER 13

Light Pen and Joystick

Introduction

This chapter discusses two auxiliary input devices that can be connected to personal computers—the light pen and joystick. Like the mouse, trackball, and touch pad, the light pen and the joystick are pointing devices.

The basic concepts you use to program the light pen are virtually identical to those you use for the joystick; therefore, this tutorial introduces these devices separately but discusses programming for them together. Table 13-1 lists the QBasic light pen and joystick statements and functions in alphabetic order.

Statement or function	Description
ON PEN GOSUB	Specifies the subroutine to be executed when the light pen is activated and light-pen event trapping is enabled
ON STRIG GOSUB	Specifies the subroutine to be executed when a specified joystick button is pushed and joystick event trapping is enabled
PEN	Returns the x or y (column or row) position of the light pen
PEN ON/OFF/STOP	Enables, disables, or suspends event trapping for the light pen
STICK	Returns the x or y (column or row) position of the joystick
STRIG	Determines whether a specified joystick button has been (or is being) pressed
STRIG ON/OFF/STOP	Enables, disables, or suspends event trapping for a specified joystick button

Table 13-1.
Light pen and joystick statements and functions.

Light Pens

A light pen is a pen-shaped pointer that you use to interact directly with the monitor's screen. You activate the push-tip type by pressing the tip against an appropriate area of the screen (such as a menu selection). You activate the touch-ring type by holding it slightly above the appropriate area of the screen and pressing on the cliplike touch ring.

Light pens are used primarily in point-of-sale operations and computer-aided design, and occasionally in educational software. The advantage of using the light pen is that you merely point at what you want and activate the pen to make your choice. Unlike the mouse, the light pen doesn't require the computer to convert mechanical motion (on the desk) to cursor motion (on the screen). Although using the pen is perhaps more intuitive than using the mouse, when using the pen you must reach to the screen to issue a command. In addition, the push-tip type can scratch or smear the screen surface.

Joysticks

Joysticks are used more often than light pens; in fact, anyone who has played computer games has probably used a joystick. You can use either one or two joysticks with a PC. Although a few educational applications accept input from joysticks, joysticks are used mainly in games and simulations. In addition to their uses in flight simulators and arcade games, joysticks can also be used to move pieces in games of strategy. Joysticks vary in the number of buttons they provide and in their layout. You might have to experiment to determine how your joystick buttons correspond to the "upper" and "lower" buttons recognized by QBasic.

Setting Up Event Trapping

The programming concept you need to master to use the light pen or joystick in your programs is event trapping. A program performs event trapping by checking for input from the light pen or joystick and then executing the correct subroutine when that input occurs.

First you set up event trapping by specifying the names of the subroutines to which you want execution to branch when the light pen or joystick is activated. To set up event trapping for the light pen, use the ON PEN GOSUB statement. For the joystick, use the ON STRIG GOSUB statement. In addition to specifying the subroutine in the ON STRIG GOSUB statement, you include a number that specifies the joystick and the joystick button to which the event trapping will respond. Table 13-2 lists the numbers and the corresponding buttons.

Number	Button
0	Lower button on the first joystick
2	Lower button on the second joystick
4	Upper button on the first joystick
6	Upper button on the second joystick

Table 13-2.
Numbers used with ON STRIG GOSUB and the button to which each corresponds.

Next you enable the event trapping by calling PEN ON for light pens and STRIG ON for joysticks. You must specify the joystick button that will be trapped by including in the STRIG ON statement the appropriate number listed in Table 13-2. Note that even if you don't use light-pen event trapping, you must use the PEN ON statement before calling any statements (other than ON PEN GOSUB) that work with the light pen.

To summarize, the following program skeleton outlines a program that uses the light pen:

```
ON PEN GOSUB DoChoice    ' specify subroutine for light-pen event trapping
PEN ON                   ' enable light-pen event trapping
⋮
END     ' stop execution before it moves to the subroutines

DoChoice:
    ' statements executed when user activates light pen
    ⋮
    RETURN
```

The following program skeleton outlines a program that uses a single joystick:

```
ON STRIG(0) GOSUB DoChoice1    ' subroutine for lower button, joystick 1
ON STRIG(4) GOSUB DoChoice2    ' subroutine for upper button, joystick 1
STRIG(0) ON                    ' enable trapping for lower button
STRIG(4) ON                    ' enable trapping for upper button
⋮
END        ' stop execution before it moves to the subroutines

DoChoice1:
    ' statements executed when user presses lower button
    ⋮
    RETURN

DoChoice2:
    ' statements executed when user presses upper button
    ⋮
    RETURN
```

Because the button configuration can vary from joystick to joystick, a program that uses the joystick should direct the user or users to press each button of each joystick to define which is the upper button and which is the lower. If your program uses two joysticks and you want the program to respond to either joystick, simply trap the actions of both of them—use one subroutine for both lower buttons and another subroutine for both upper buttons.

If you want to disable light-pen or joystick event trapping during part of your program, you can turn off trapping by using the PEN OFF or STRIG OFF statement. Program execution will speed up because the program will no longer monitor the light pen or joystick. If you want to suspend event trapping but direct the program to remember whether the light pen or joystick was used during the time trapping was suspended, use PEN STOP or STRIG STOP. When the program executes the next PEN ON or STRIG ON statement, the program will branch to the correct subroutine if the light pen or joystick was activated.

Reading Position Values

Of course, your program must be able to determine the location at which the light pen or joystick is positioned when it triggers an event trap. When the program knows the location, it can perform the appropriate task, such as activating a menu choice or moving a game piece.

For the light pen, use the PEN function with a number that specifies the information PEN returns. (See the PEN entry for the list of numbers.) Note that the PEN function can return the coordinates of a location in either character format (character-cell location) or graphics format (pixel location). PEN can return either the position at which the light pen was activated or the position at which it was last aimed. (The two are not necessarily the same.) PEN can read the position of the light pen even when the light pen is not activated. Thus a drawing program can let the user activate the light pen at the starting point and then draw a line of points as the pen moves. This action is demonstrated in the following program segment:

```
SCREEN 1
PEN ON

DO
    IF PEN(0) = -1 THEN PSET (PEN(4), PEN(5))
LOOP UNTIL INKEY$ = CHR$(27)
```

For the joystick, use the STICK function with a number that specifies the *x*- or *y*-coordinate that STICK will return. (See the STICK entry for the list of numbers.) The joystick uses a coordinate system that is independent of the coordinate system used in the current screen mode. Different joysticks vary in the values they return. Some return coordinates in the range 1 through 80; others can use coordinates even higher than 200. The STICK function returns values only in the range 1 through 200. If you assume that the variables *maxX%* and *maxY%* contain the greatest *x*- and *y*-coordinates in the present graphics mode and that *maxXJoy%* and *maxYJoy%* contain the greatest joystick return values, you can calculate the scale factor for converting from joystick coordinates to screen coordinates by using the following statements:

```
xScale% = maxX% / maxXJoy%
yScale% = maxY% / maxYJoy%
```

Then, to convert a joystick coordinate to a screen coordinate, multiply the joystick coordinate by the scale factor. For example, to assign the position of joystick number 1 to the variables *xPos%* and *yPos%*, use the following statements:

```
xPos% = STICK(0)
yPos% = STICK(1)
```

Then, if you want to use the PUT statement to display an image at the position specified by the joystick, use the following statement:

```
PUT (xPos% * xScale%, yPos% * yScale%), graphArray%, PSET
```

Because of the variations in joystick design and configuration, your program should let the user calibrate the joystick by aiming it at specific points on the screen. During calibration, the program can use the values returned by STICK to perform the scaling.

The STRIG function returns information about the joystick buttons. You include a number in the call to STRIG to specify which button STRIG examines. This function is especially useful if the program contains a subroutine to which execution branches when any button is pressed. By using STRIG, the subroutine can determine which button was pressed.

Using the Mouse as a Light Pen

If you don't have a light pen attached to your computer but you do have a mouse with a driver installed, you can use the mouse somewhat like a light pen. Although you can't point the mouse at the screen, the PEN function will return the character row and column at which the mouse cursor is positioned if both buttons on the mouse are pressed. Using the mouse as a light pen is useful for testing statements such as *PRINT PEN(4), PEN(5)* which are in programs you expect will be used with a light pen.

Related Reading

Microsoft Press and the Hardware Division of Microsoft Corporation. *Microsoft Mouse Programmer's Reference*. Redmond, Wash.: Microsoft Press, 1989.

Prata, Stephen, with Harry Henderson. *The Waite Group's Microsoft QuickBASIC Primer Plus*. Redmond, Wash.: Microsoft Press, 1990.

Schneider, David L. *Handbook of BASIC*. 3d ed. Boston, Mass.: Brady, 1988.

ON PEN GOSUB

See also
PEN, PEN ON/OFF/STOP

Purpose
The ON PEN GOSUB statement specifies the subroutine to which execution branches when a light pen is activated. Use the ON PEN GOSUB statement when you want the program to respond to the light pen by performing light-pen event trapping that executes a certain task.

Syntax
ON PEN GOSUB {*line* ¦ *label*}

line or *label* specifies the line number or label that begins the subroutine to which execution branches.

Usage
ON PEN GOSUB HandlePen

Specifies that the *HandlePen* subroutine will be executed when the light pen is activated.

Description
You can use light-pen event trapping in your program to execute a specified subroutine when the program detects that a light pen has been activated. First call the ON PEN GOSUB statement to specify the subroutine to be executed. Then use a PEN ON statement to enable trapping (detection) of the light pen.

Errors
If the light pen is not connected or is not properly calibrated, QBasic displays an "Illegal function call" error message.

Warnings
QBasic will not respond to the light pen if a mouse driver is also installed in your system. You can use the mouse to emulate a light pen. See the tutorial for a discussion about how the light-pen statements and functions work with a mouse.

Example
The following program demonstrates light-pen event trapping. It specifies in an ON PEN GOSUB statement that the subroutine *Active* will be executed when the pen is activated. The subroutine merely sounds a beep, prints a message, and exits the program. If you have a two-button mouse, you can press both mouse buttons simultaneously to trigger the subroutine.

```
CLS
ON PEN GOSUB Active    ' specify subroutine for light-pen event trapping
PEN ON                 ' enable light-pen event trapping

DO
    LOCATE 1, 1
    PRINT "Activate the light pen."
LOOP UNTIL INKEY$ = CHR$(27)       ' exit loop when user presses Esc
END

Active:                ' light pen has been activated
    BEEP
    PRINT "The light pen has been activated."
    SYSTEM             ' quit program
    RETURN
```

ON STRIG GOSUB

See also

STRIG, STRIG ON/OFF/STOP

Purpose

The ON STRIG GOSUB statement specifies a subroutine to which execution branches when a particular joystick button is pressed. Use this statement when you want the program to respond to a joystick button press by performing joystick event trapping that executes a certain task.

Syntax

ON STRIG GOSUB(*button*) {*line* ¦ *label*}

button is either 0, 2, 4, or 6. 0 specifies the lower button on the first joystick, 2 specifies the lower button on the second joystick, 4 specifies the upper button on the first joystick, and 6 specifies the upper button on the second joystick.

line or *label* specifies the line number or label that begins the subroutine to which execution branches.

Usage

ON STRIG(4) GOSUB Fire

Specifies that the *Fire* subroutine will be executed when the upper button on the first joystick is pressed.

Description

You can use joystick event trapping in your program to execute a subroutine when the program detects that a certain joystick button has been pressed. (QBasic supports either one or two joysticks with one or two buttons on each.) The ON STRIG GOSUB statement specifies which of the four buttons to respond to and the subroutine that will be executed. The button numbers 0 and 4 refer to the lower and upper buttons on the first joystick; 2 and 6 refer to the lower and upper buttons on the second joystick. Some joysticks have one or two buttons on the base and a button on top of the stick. The latter is usually called an upper button. See your joystick documentation for details about button designations.

After calling ON STRIG GOSUB, you must use the STRIG ON statement to enable trapping (detection) of the specified joystick button.

Example

The following program traps both the lower and upper buttons of the first joystick. When a button is pressed, the program executes the subroutine specified by ON STRIG GOSUB. Each subroutine sounds a beep and displays a message. The subroutine for the upper button also exits the program by calling the SYSTEM statement.

```
CLS
ON STRIG(0) GOSUB Lower    ' specify subroutine for lower button, first joystick
ON STRIG(4) GOSUB Upper    ' specify subroutine for upper button, first joystick

STRIG(0) ON                ' enable trapping for lower button
STRIG(4) ON                ' enable trapping for upper button

PRINT "Press either joystick button."
PRINT "Pressing the upper button causes the program to end."

LOCATE 4, 1
PRINT "Press either joystick button."
DO
LOOP UNTIL INKEY$ = CHR$(27)
END

Lower:                     ' subroutine for lower button
    BEEP
    LOCATE 6, 1
    PRINT "You pressed the lower button."
    RETURN

Upper:                     ' subroutine for upper button
    BEEP
    LOCATE 6, 1
    PRINT "You pressed the upper button."
    SYSTEM
```

PEN

See also
ON PEN GOSUB, PEN ON/OFF/STOP

Purpose
The PEN function returns the current status of the light pen. Use this function to determine the location of the light pen on the screen.

Syntax
PEN(*number*)

number is an integer in the range 0 through 9.

Usage
```
lastX% = PEN(1)
lastY% = PEN(2)
```
Assigns the pixel coordinates of the location at which the light pen was last activated to the variables *lastX%* and *lastY%*.

Description
Use the PEN function to determine whether the light pen has been activated or is currently being activated; you can also use this function to find the graphics or text coordinates at which the pen was last activated or pointed. Before you can use the PEN statement, you must enable light-pen trapping by using a PEN ON statement.

Follow the keyword PEN with a number from 0 through 9 that is surrounded by parentheses. The number specifies the information that PEN will return. Table 13-3 describes the value that PEN returns for each number.

Number	Value returned
0	−1 if the light pen has been activated since the most recent call to PEN; 0 if not
1	x-coordinate of the pixel at which the light pen was most recently activated
2	y-coordinate of the pixel at which the light pen was most recently activated
3	−1 if the light pen is currently activated; 0 if not
4	x-coordinate of the pixel at which the light pen was most recently pointed
5	y-coordinate of the pixel at which the light pen was most recently pointed
6	character row in which the light pen was most recently activated
7	character column in which the light pen was most recently activated
8	character row in which the light pen was most recently pointed
9	character column in which the light pen was most recently pointed

Table 13-3.
Values returned by the PEN function.

The difference between the PEN(0) and PEN(3) functions is that PEN(0) returns a value of true (−1) if the pen has been activated since the most recent call to the PEN function, but the PEN(3) function returns a value of true only if the pen is active at the time PEN(3) is called.

The PEN function can be used in either graphics or text mode. In graphics mode, use the PEN(1) and PEN(2) functions to determine the approximate x- and y-coordinates of the pixel at which the light pen was last activated, and use PEN(4) and PEN(5) to determine the coordinates at which the light pen is currently aimed. The location coordinates are approximate because most light pens do not have as fine a resolution as the graphics screen. For example, the light pen might be able to gain access to only the x-coordinates 0, 8, 16, 24,...320 and the y-coordinates 0, 2, 4, 6,...200. A light pen aimed at the point (238, 149) might return the coordinates 240 and 150.

In text mode, use the PEN(6) and PEN(7) functions to determine the text row and column in which the light pen was most recently activated, and use PEN(8) and PEN(9) to determine the row and column at which the light pen was most recently pointed.

Warnings

QBasic does not respond to the light pen if a mouse driver is also installed in your system. You can use the mouse to emulate a light pen. See the tutorial for a discussion about how the light-pen statements and functions work with a mouse.

Example

The following program displays all the information provided by the PEN function. It also displays a small box and ends when the light pen is pressed against the box (or aimed at the box if the light pen is a touch-ring type).

```
PEN ON
CLS
LOCATE 10, 35
PRINT "Press the box to exit the program. "; CHR$(219)    ' box character
DO
    LOCATE 20, 1
    PRINT "Light pen has ";
    IF PEN(0) THEN                    ' check activation of light pen
        PRINT "been     activated";
    ELSE PRINT "not been activated";
    END IF

    LOCATE 20, 40
    PRINT "Switch currently ";
    IF PEN(3) THEN                    ' check whether light pen is active
        PRINT "    down";
    ELSE PRINT "not down";
    END IF
```

(continued)

continued

```
        LOCATE 21, 1
        PRINT "Last activated at X: "; PEN(1);
        LOCATE 21, 40
        PRINT "Last activated at Y: "; PEN(2);

        LOCATE 22, 1
        PRINT "Now at X: "; PEN(4);
        LOCATE 22, 40
        PRINT "Now at Y: "; PEN(5);

        LOCATE 23, 1
        PRINT "Activated at row: "; PEN(6);
        LOCATE 23, 40
        PRINT "Activated at col: "; PEN(7);

        LOCATE 24, 1
        PRINT "Now at row.: "; PEN(8);
        LOCATE 24, 40
        PRINT "Now at col: "; PEN(9);

        ' check whether light pen activated at the box
        IF (PEN(6) = 10) AND (PEN(7) = 70) THEN SYSTEM
    LOOP
```

PEN ON/OFF/STOP

See also

ON PEN GOSUB, PEN

Purpose

The three PEN statements enable, disable, or suspend the trapping of light-pen events. The PEN ON statement also enables the PEN function, which you can use to obtain information about the light pen's status.

Syntax

PEN ON
PEN OFF
PEN STOP

Usage

PEN ON
Enables both light-pen event trapping and the PEN function.

Description

Use the PEN ON statement to begin tracking the movements and status (activated or not activated) of the light pen. If the light pen is activated and an ON PEN GOSUB statement has been called, the program branches to the subroutine specified in the ON PEN GOSUB statement. (Use the PEN function to gain information about the light pen's position and status.)

The PEN OFF statement disables light-pen event trapping. The program will not branch to the subroutine when the light pen is activated. Also note that no information about the light pen is returned by the PEN function after the program calls PEN OFF. When you restore light-pen event trapping, the program does not remember events that occurred while trapping was off.

The PEN STOP statement suspends light-pen event trapping. The program continues to note light-pen activity but does not execute the subroutine specified in the ON PEN GOSUB statement. The next time a PEN ON statement is executed, the subroutine will be executed if the light pen was activated while event trapping was suspended.

The program executes an implicit PEN STOP whenever it enters the subroutine specified by ON PEN GOSUB. This ensures that another occurrence of the event does not cause the subroutine to be executed recursively. When the program encounters a RETURN statement and returns to the main program, it reinstates play event trapping by executing an implicit PEN ON statement.

Tips

Light-pen event trapping slows program execution slightly; you might want to turn off event trapping when you don't expect user input from the light pen.

QBasic will not respond to the light pen if a mouse driver is also installed in your system. You can use the mouse to emulate a light pen. See the tutorial for a discussion about how the light-pen statements and functions work with a mouse.

Example

The following example uses the PEN ON statement to enable light-pen event trapping. The program executes the *Active* subroutine when the light pen is first activated. The subroutine assigns 1 to the variable *trapped%*, which causes the program to execute the PEN STOP statement found in the main loop. Light-pen event trapping is enabled again when you exit the loop by pressing a key. The program, however, remembers whether you activated the pen after the PEN STOP, and it executes *Active* again if you did. Note that a call to PEN STOP is not effective if it is within the subroutine because the program always calls PEN ON when it exits the subroutine.

```
CLS
ON PEN GOSUB Active
PEN ON                    ' turn on event trapping for light pen
trapped% = 0              ' flag signaling whether event occurred

DO
    LOCATE 1, 1
    PRINT "Activate the light pen."
    IF trapped% = 1 THEN PEN STOP
LOOP UNTIL INKEY$ <> ""    ' exit if user presses any key

PEN ON      ' executes the Active subroutine if light pen has been activated
END

Active:     ' light pen has been activated
    BEEP
    PRINT "The Active subroutine will be executed one more time"
    PRINT "if you activate the light pen and then press any key."
    trapped% = 1
    RETURN
```

STICK

See also

ON STRIG GOSUB, STRIG, STRIG ON/OFF/STOP

Purpose

The STICK function returns the x- and y-coordinates pointed to by a joystick.

Syntax

STICK(*number*)

number is an integer in the range 0 through 3.

Usage

```
stick1X% = STICK(0)
```

Assigns the x-coordinate of the first joystick to the variable *stick1X%*.

Description

The STICK function returns information about the x- and y-coordinates pointed to by a joystick. The coordinate returned depends on the specified number. Table 13-4 on the following page lists each number and the corresponding value that STICK returns.

Number	Value returned
0	x-coordinate of the first joystick
1	y-coordinate of the first joystick
2	x-coordinate of the second joystick
3	y-coordinate of the second joystick

Table 13-4.
Values returned by the STICK function.

Different joysticks vary in the values they return. Some return coordinates in the range 1 through 80; others can use coordinates of 200 or more. The x- and y-coordinates returned by STICK are always in the range 1 through 200, regardless of the screen mode. If you want to draw (or redraw) a cursor to be moved by the joystick (as the sample program does, below), you must scale the joystick coordinates to the actual screen coordinates. For example, if you are using a 640-by-480-pixel graphics screen and a joystick whose coordinates range from 1 through 200, the x value returned by the STICK function must be multiplied by $640/200$, or 3.2, and the y value must be multiplied by $480/200$, or 2.4.

Use the STRIG function to determine whether a joystick button has been pressed.

Comments

The 1-through-200 coordinate range limits the resolution of joystick coordinates and therefore, the accuracy of the joystick. However, the result is still adequate for letting users make menu selections and for tracking motion in simple arcade-style games.

If no joystick is connected to your system, any call to the STICK function returns the value 0 and does not produce an error message.

Example

The following program draws a "gunsight" that you can move on the screen by using the joystick. When you press the lower joystick button, the program uses the STICK function to display the current joystick coordinates at the bottom right corner of the screen. When you press the upper button, the program ends. You might have to change the values of the scaling variables *xScale* and *yScale* if your joystick can return coordinates outside the range 1 through 80.

```
CLS
PRINT "Move gunsight with joystick number 1."
PRINT "Press lower button to see the coordinates."
PRINT "Press upper button to exit the program."
PRINT "< Press any key to begin. >"
DO
LOOP UNTIL INKEY$ <> ""

ON STRIG(0) GOSUB ShowCoords    ' show current coordinates
ON STRIG(4) GOSUB ExitProg      ' exit the program
```

(continued)

continued

```
STRIG(0) ON        ' trap lower button of first joystick
STRIG(4) ON        ' trap upper button of first joystick

' global variables
oldX = 0           ' x-coordinate of last gunsight drawn
oldY = 0           ' y-coordinate of last gunsight drawn
newX = 0           ' x-coordinate of new gunsight
newY = 0           ' y-coordinate of new gunsight

' the scale factors assume the joystick goes to 80 in each direction
xScale = 4         ' scaling factor for x in CGA
yScale = 2.5       ' scaling factor for y in CGA


SCREEN 1           ' CGA screen mode

DO                 ' loop until upper button pushed
    GOSUB Gunsight ' call subprogram to draw gunsight
LOOP

ShowCoords:        ' show coordinates when lower button is pushed
    LOCATE 24, 20
    PRINT "X = "; STICK(0);
    LOCATE 24, 30
    PRINT "Y = "; STICK(1);
    RETURN

Gunsight:          ' draw gunsight
    newX = STICK(0) * xScale
    newY = STICK(1) * yScale

    ' erase old gunsight
    LINE (oldX, oldY)-(oldX + 5, oldY), 0
    LINE (oldX, oldY)-(oldX - 5, oldY), 0
    LINE (oldX, oldY)-(oldX, oldY + 3), 0
    LINE (oldX, oldY)-(oldX, oldY - 3), 0

    ' draw new gunsight
    LINE (newX, newY)-(newX + 5, newY), 1
    LINE (newX, newY)-(newX - 5, newY), 1
    LINE (newX, newY)-(newX, newY + 3), 1
    LINE (newX, newY)-(newX, newY - 3), 1

    oldX = newX
    oldY = newY
    RETURN

ExitProg:
    SYSTEM
    RETURN
```

STRIG

See also

ON STRIG GOSUB, STRIG ON/OFF/STOP

Purpose

The STRIG function returns the status of a joystick button. You can use this information to process a user menu selection or to execute a "fire" command for a game.

Syntax

STRIG(*number*)

number is an integer in the range 0 through 7.

Usage

```
IF STRIG(0) GOSUB FireA
```

If the user presses the lower button of joystick 1, the program executes the subroutine *FireA*.

Description

Use the STRIG function with a number from 0 through 7 to determine whether a particular joystick button either has been pressed since the most recent call to STRIG with the same number or is currently being pressed. Table 13-5 lists each number and the corresponding value that STRIG returns. In each case, QBasic returns a value of −1 (true) if the button is being pressed and 0 (false) if the button is not being pressed. QBasic supports two joysticks with two buttons each.

Number	Value returned
0	−1 if the lower button on joystick 1 has been pressed since the most recent STRIG(0) call; 0 if not
1	−1 if the lower button on joystick 1 is currently being pressed; 0 if not
2	−1 if the lower button on joystick 2 has been pressed since the most recent STRIG(2) call; 0 if not
3	−1 if the lower button on joystick 2 is currently being pressed; 0 if not
4	−1 if the upper button on joystick 1 has been pressed since the most recent STRIG(4) call; 0 if not
5	−1 if the upper button on joystick 1 is currently being pressed; 0 if not
6	−1 if the upper button on joystick 2 has been pressed since the most recent STRIG(6) call; 0 if not
7	−1 if the upper button on joystick 2 is currently being pressed; 0 if not

Table 13-5.
Values returned by the STRIG function.

As an alternative to using an IF or other conditional statement to test the value of a STRIG call, you can use the ON STRIG GOSUB statement to set up joystick event trapping that executes a specific subroutine when the user presses a particular button.

If the joystick referred to in a STRIG function call isn't installed, the call returns the value 0 (false). QBasic does not display an error message.

Example

The following program tells you which button you have pressed on the first joystick and sounds the computer's built-in speaker.

```
DO
    IF STRIG(0) THEN PRINT "Lower button pressed "; CHR$(7)
    IF STRIG(4) THEN PRINT "Upper button pressed "; CHR$(7)
LOOP UNTIL INKEY$ <> ""    ' exit loop when user presses a key
```

STRIG ON/OFF/STOP

See also

ON STRIG GOSUB, STICK, STRIG

Purpose

The three STRIG statements enable, disable, or suspend the trapping of joystick button presses.

Syntax

STRIG(*button*) ON
STRIG(*button*) OFF
STRIG(*button*) STOP

button is either 0, 2, 4, or 6. 0 specifies the lower button on the first joystick, 2 specifies the lower button on the second joystick, 4 specifies the upper button on the first joystick, and 6 specifies the upper button on the second joystick.

Usage

```
STRIG(C) ON
```
Enables trapping for the lower button on the first joystick.

Description

Use the STRIG ON statement to begin tracking the status (pressed or not pressed) of the joystick button specified by the given number. See Table 13-6 on the following page for a list of the numbers and the buttons to which they correspond.

Number	Button
0	Lower button on the first joystick
2	Lower button on the second joystick
4	Upper button on the first joystick
6	Upper button on the second joystick

Table 13-6.
Joystick numbers and the button to which each corresponds.

If a button is pressed, the program executes the subroutine specified in the ON STRIG GOSUB statement for that button. (Use the STICK function to return information about the joystick position; use the STRIG function to check whether the joystick button is pressed.)

The STRIG OFF statement disables event trapping of the specified joystick button. To resume trapping a joystick button, you must execute a STRIG ON statement for that button. Any button presses that occurred while trapping was off will not be remembered by the program.

The STRIG STOP statement suspends joystick trapping. The program continues to note joystick activity but does not execute the subroutine specified by the corresponding ON STRIG GOSUB statement. The next time a STRIG ON statement for the button is executed, the subroutine will be executed if the button was pressed while event trapping was suspended.

The program executes an implicit STRIG STOP whenever it enters the subroutine specified by ON STRIG GOSUB. This ensures that another occurrence of the event does not cause the subroutine to be executed recursively. When the program encounters a RETURN statement and returns to the main program, the program reinstates joystick event trapping by executing an implicit STRIG ON statement.

Tips

Joystick event trapping slows program execution slightly; you might want to turn off event trapping when you don't expect user input from the joystick.

Example

The following program demonstrates joystick event trapping. The trapping is set so that if the lower or upper button is pushed, the program will execute the *Lower* or *Upper* subroutine. If you press the lower button, *Lower* uses a STRIG OFF statement to turn off trapping for the lower button, so this subroutine won't be executed for subsequent presses of the lower button. If you then press the upper button, *Upper* uses a STRIG(0) ON statement to re-enable trapping of the lower button, so the program will again respond to the lower button (and then turn it off again).

```
CLS

ON STRIG(0) GOSUB Lower    ' set up trapping for lower button, joystick 1
ON STRIG(4) GOSUB Upper    ' set up trapping for upper button, joystick 1

STRIG(0) ON                ' enable trapping for lower button
STRIG(4) ON                ' enable trapping for upper button

LOCATE 1, 1
PRINT "Either press a joystick button or press any key to quit."
PRINT STRING$(56, "_")

VIEW PRINT 3 TO 7          ' set text viewport to rows 3 through 7
DO
LOOP UNTIL INKEY$ <> ""    ' loop until user presses any key
END

Lower:                     ' subroutine for lower button
    BEEP
    PRINT "You pressed the lower button."
    PRINT "The lower button will not be trapped again"
    PRINT "until you press the upper button."
    PRINT STRING$(55, "_")
    STRIG(0) OFF           ' disable trapping for lower button
    RETURN

Upper:                     ' subroutine for upper button
    BEEP
    STRIG(0) ON            ' re-enable trapping for lower button
    PRINT "You pressed the upper button."
    PRINT STRING$(55, "_")
RETURN
```

SECTION III

DEVICES

CHAPTER 14

Keyboard

Introduction

The QBasic statements that manage keyboard input provide an essential link between the user and the program. Most IBM PCs and compatible computers have keyboards that include 10 or 12 function keys; the keyboard statements in QBasic let you offer shortcuts to users by assigning long key sequences to each of these keys. The keyboard event-trapping statements let you set up a routine that is called whenever the user presses a specific key. Many programs, for example, use an event trap to display a Help screen whenever the user presses the F1 function key.

This tutorial summarizes QBasic's keyboard-management statements and offers some suggestions for their use. Table 14-1 lists the keyboard-management statements.

Statement	Description
KEY	Sets up soft (shortcut) keys
KEY(n) ON/OFF/STOP	Enables, disables, or suspends keyboard event trapping set up by the ON KEY(n) GOSUB statement
ON KEY(n) GOSUB	Sets up keyboard event trapping

Table 14-1.
QBasic keyboard statements.

Soft Keys

If you have used GW-BASIC or BASICA, you are probably familiar with the list specifying function keys and corresponding abbreviated statements that is displayed on the bottom line of the screen. These keys are called soft keys, or shortcut keys, and they let you use the function keys to enter common statements with a single keypress. You can create soft keys for your programs by using the QBasic KEY statement.

By using the following statement, for example, you can make the F1 function key a soft key that is an abbreviation for the string "HELP":

```
KEY 1, "HELP"
```

Now, whenever the user presses the F1 function key while the program executes, any keyboard input function or statement (including INKEY$, INPUT, and LINE INPUT) accepts the word "HELP" as input.

Use the KEY LIST statement to display the current soft-key settings, which appear one per line on the screen. The KEY ON statement displays your soft-key settings on the bottom line of the screen, and the KEY OFF statement erases this display. The soft keys can be used even if they are not displayed.

Although they appear similar to the KEY(*n*) ON and KEY(*n*) OFF event-trapping statements, the KEY ON and KEY OFF statements apply only to the soft-key display.

Keyboard Event Trapping

QBasic provides a set of statements that enable and manage keyboard event trapping. You can trap a certain key so that the program executes a subroutine every time the user presses the key. For example, you might use the keyboard event trap to display context-sensitive help whenever the user presses the F1 function key. QBasic lets you trap function keys, direction keys, and user-defined key combinations.

You set up event trapping by first calling the ON KEY(*n*) GOSUB statement that specifies the name of the subroutine to which you want execution to branch when the user presses the specified key. Next you enable event trapping by calling the KEY(*n*) ON statement.

The following lines set up an event trap and enable it to execute the subroutine that begins at the label *ShowHelp* whenever the user presses the F1 key:

```
ON KEY(1) GOSUB ShowHelp
KEY(1) ON
```

Related Reading

Norton, Peter, and Richard Wilton. *The* New *Peter Norton Programmer's Guide to the IBM PC & PS/2*. Redmond, Wash.: Microsoft Press, 1988.

Prata, Stephen, with Harry Henderson. *The Waite Group's Microsoft QuickBASIC Primer Plus*. Redmond, Wash.: Microsoft Press, 1990.

KEY

See also

KEY(n) ON/OFF/STOP, ON KEY(n) GOSUB

Purpose

The KEY statement lets you initialize a soft key (that is, assign a string to a function key) and display the soft keys. You can use the KEY statement to give the user a method of generating a long sequence of keypresses by pressing one key.

Syntax

KEY *num, string*
KEY LIST
KEY ON
KEY OFF

num is the number of a function key; valid numbers are 1 through 10, 30 (for F11), and 31 (for F12).

string is a string expression of 1 through 15 characters; a null string disables the corresponding soft key.

Usage

```
KEY 1, "EXIT" + CHR$(13)
```
Sets the F1 function key as a soft key that generates the word EXIT and a carriage return.

```
KEY LIST
```
Displays the string assignments for all soft keys.

Description

The KEY statement manages soft keys, which are function keys that you press to produce strings. To create or change soft keys, follow the keyword KEY with a function key number and a string. The function key number specifies the soft key: Use 1 through 10 for function keys F1 through F10 and 30 and 31 for function keys F11 and F12 on 101-key keyboards. The string parameter to KEY must be a string expression of no more than 15 characters; KEY ignores any characters following the first 15. After you use the KEY statement to make an assignment, pressing that function key generates the corresponding string, exactly as if the user had typed it at the keyboard.

You can display all the current soft-key settings by using the KEY LIST statement. This 12-line list (one line for each function key) displays all 15 characters of each setting.

The KEY ON statement displays the first six characters of the first 10 soft-key settings on the bottom line of the screen. The soft-key settings for function keys 11 and 12 are not displayed. The KEY OFF statement disables the display at the bottom of the screen but does not prevent the soft keys from producing their corresponding strings.

Comments

The string parameter to KEY can include control characters such as CHR$(13), the Enter key. You can use a variant of the KEY statement to define a key combination for use with keyboard event trapping. See the KEY(*n*) ON/OFF/STOP entry for more details.

Errors

In a KEY statement that specifies a number and a string, if the number parameter is not 1 through 10 or either 30 or 31, QBasic displays an "Illegal function call" error message.

Example

The following program uses the KEY statement to provide users with shortcut keys. The program displays a menu of options that can be chosen by pressing a function key or typing a word.

```
' set up soft keys
KEY 1, "Add" + CHR$(13)         ' F1-add records
KEY 2, "Change" + CHR$(13)      ' F2-change record
KEY 3, "Quit" + CHR$(13)        ' F3-quit program

MainMenu:
    CLS
    PRINT : PRINT : PRINT
    PRINT "<Add>......Add records......[F1]"
    PRINT "<Change>...Change records...[F2]"
    PRINT "<Quit>.....Quit program.....[F3]"
    PRINT
    PRINT "Type a word and press Enter or press a function key: ";
    LINE INPUT selection$

    SELECT CASE UCASE$(selection$)
        CASE "ADD"
            PRINT : PRINT : PRINT
            PRINT "Add records."

        CASE "CHANGE"
            PRINT : PRINT : PRINT
            PRINT "Change records."

        CASE "QUIT"
            PRINT : PRINT : PRINT
            PRINT "Quit the program."

        CASE ELSE
            PRINT : PRINT : PRINT
            PRINT "Invalid selection--try again."
            BEEP
            SLEEP 1
            GOTO MainMenu
    END SELECT
```

KEY(n) ON/OFF/STOP

See also
KEY, ON KEY(*n*) GOSUB

Purpose
The KEY(*n*) statements enable, disable, or suspend event trapping for specific keys. Use keyboard event trapping to direct your program to execute a subroutine when the user presses a specified key.

Syntax
KEY(*n*) ON
KEY(*n*) OFF
KEY(*n*) STOP

n is a number that corresponds to a function key, a direction key, or a user-defined key; valid numbers are 0 through 25, 30, and 31. If *n* is 0, the trapping for all function keys, direction keys, and user-defined keys are affected.

Usage
```
ON KEY(1) GOSUB GetHelp
KEY(1) ON
```
Enables event trapping for the function key F1 so that execution will branch to *GetHelp* when the user presses F1.

Description
Use the KEY(*n*) ON statement to enable event trapping of a particular key. After executing a KEY(*n*) ON statement, the program checks after every statement to see whether the specified key was pressed. If it was, the program executes the routine specified in the ON KEY(*n*) GOSUB statement.

Table 14-3 lists the numbers that can be used in the KEY(*n*) statements.

Key numbers	Keyboard keys
0	All keys listed in this table
1 through 10	Function keys F1 through F10
11	Up direction key
12	Left direction key
13	Right direction key
14	Down direction key
15 through 25	User-defined keys
30 and 31	Function keys F11 and F12

Table 14-3.
Valid key numbers.

User-defined keys (key numbers 15 through 25) can be defined by using the following variant of the KEY statement:

KEY *num*, CHR$(*shift*) + CHR$(*scan*)

num indicates a user-defined key for keyboard event trapping and must be in the range 15 through 25.

shift is a combination of any of the hexadecimal values listed in Table 14-4. These values indicate the state of the various "shift" keys on the keyboard. You can use the sum of two or more of these values to indicate that several shift keys must be held down at the same time before the user-defined key can be trapped. For example, a *shift* parameter of *&H04* + *&H08* would indicate that both the Ctrl and Alt keys must be held down. QBasic does not make a distinction between left and right Shift keys; therefore, codes *&H01*, *&H02*, and *&H03* are handled identically.

scan is a scan code of one of the standard 83 keys of the keyboard. See Table 14-5 on the following pages for a complete list of IBM PC scan codes.

Value	Shift key
&H00	None
&H01 through &H03	Either or both Shift keys
&H04	Ctrl
&H08	Alt
&H20	Num Lock
&H40	Caps Lock
&H80	Extended keys on the 101-key keyboard

Table 14-4.
The hexadecimal values for shift states.

The KEY(*n*) ON statement enables event trapping for the key specified in the statement.

The KEY(*n*) OFF statement disables event trapping for the specified key. No event trapping of the key occurs until the program executes another KEY(*n*) ON statement. No events that occurred while trapping was off are remembered by the program.

The KEY(*n*) STOP statement suspends event trapping for the specified key. No event trapping occurs until the program executes another KEY(*n*) ON statement. However, if an event occurs while trapping is suspended, the program remembers the event and, the next time a KEY(*n*) ON statement is executed, the program branches to the appropriate subroutine.

The program executes an implicit KEY(*n*) STOP whenever it enters the subroutine specified by ON KEY(*n*) GOSUB. This ensures that another occurrence of the event does not cause the subroutine to execute recursively. When the program encounters a RETURN statement and returns to the main program, it reinstates keyboard event trapping by executing an implicit KEY(*n*) ON statement.

Key	Scan code	Key	Scan code
Esc	&H01	K	&H25
! or 1	&H02	L	&H26
@ or 2	&H03	: or ;	&H27
# or 3	&H04	" or '	&H28
$ or 4	&H05	~ or `	&H29
% or 5	&H06	Left Shift	&H2A
^ or 6	&H07	¦ or \	&H2B
& or 7	&H08	Z	&H2C
* or 8	&H09	X	&H2D
(or 9	&H0A	C	&H2E
) or 0	&H0B	V	&H2F
− or _	&H0C	B	&H30
+ or =	&H0D	N	&H31
Left	&H0E	M	&H32
Tab	&H0F	< or ,	&H33
Q	&H10	> or .	&H34
W	&H11	? or /	&H35
E	&H12	Right Shift	&H36
R	&H13	PrtSc or *	&H37
T	&H14	Alt	&H38
Y	&H15	Spacebar	&H39
U	&H16	Caps Lock	&H3A
I	&H17	F1	&H3B
O	&H18	F2	&H3C
P	&H19	F3	&H3D
{ or [	&H1A	F4	&H3E
} or]	&H1B	F5	&H3F
Enter	&H1C	F6	&H40
Ctrl	&H1D	F7	&H41
A	&H1E	F8	&H42
S	&H1F	F9	&H43
D	&H20	F10	&H44
F	&H21	Num Lock	&H45
G	&H22	Scroll Lock	&H46
H	&H23	Home or 7	&H47
J	&H24	Up or 8	&H48

Table 14-5.
Scan codes for the IBM PC keyboard.

(continued)

Table 14-5. *continued*

Key	Scan code	Key	Scan code
PgUp or 9	&H49	End or 1	&H4F
– (keypad)	&H4A	Down or 2	&H50
Left or 4	&H4B	PgDn or 3	&H51
5	&H4C	Ins or 0	&H52
Right or 6	&H4D	Del or .	&H53
+ (keypad)	&H4E		

Errors

If the value of the specified key number is not in the range 0 through 25 or either 30 or 31, QBasic displays an "Illegal function call" error message.

Tips

Using event-trapping statements makes your programs run more slowly. Avoid using event-trapping statements that are not essential.

Example

See the sample program in the ON KEY(*n*) GOSUB entry.

ON KEY(*n*) GOSUB

See also

KEY, KEY(*n*) ON/OFF/STOP

Purpose

The ON KEY(*n*) GOSUB statement specifies a subroutine that is executed whenever the user presses a certain key. You can use the ON KEY(*n*) GOSUB statement to set up keyboard event trapping so that the program prints a help message when the user presses the F1 key.

Syntax

ON KEY(*n*) GOSUB {*line* ┊ *label*}

n is a number that corresponds to a function key, a direction key, or a user-defined key; valid numbers are 1 through 25, 30, and 31.

line or *label* indicates the first program line of the event-trapping subroutine.

Usage

```
ON KEY(1) GOSUB ShowHelp
```

Specifies that the *ShowHelp* subroutine will be executed when the user presses the F1 function key.

Description

Use the ON KEY(*n*) GOSUB statement to set up an event trap that executes a subroutine when a specified key is pressed. Only function keys, direction keys, and user-defined keys can be specified in the statement. When the specified key is pressed, the program executes the subroutine.

When the subroutine begins, the program executes an implicit KEY(*n*) STOP so that another event trap doesn't cause the subroutine to execute recursively. However, if another timer event occurs while the subroutine is executing, the program remembers it. When the subroutine finishes, the program executes a KEY(*n*) ON statement (unless the subroutine explicitly executed a KEY(*n*) OFF statement) and immediately executes the suspended event.

The specified subroutine can end with a RETURN statement that branches to a specified line in the program. However, this version of the RETURN statement can cause serious problems because the event-trapping subroutine might have interrupted a critical operation. Also, you cannot use the RETURN statement with a specified line number or label to branch to a subprogram, function, or DEF FN function. (See the GOSUB...RETURN entry in Chapter 4, "Procedures," for details.)

QBasic performs keyboard event trapping in the following order:

1. The line printer echo-toggle key (Ctrl-PrtSc); redefining this key as a user-defined key has no effect.
2. Function keys and direction keys; redefining these keys does not affect QBasic key trapping because they are predefined.
3. User-defined keys.

The ON KEY(*n*) GOSUB statement can trap any key combination, including Ctrl-Break and Ctrl-Alt-Delete. You could, therefore, use it to prevent a user from breaking out of your program or even to perform a "warm" reboot of the computer. After you trap a key, you cannot use an INPUT or INKEY$ statement to retrieve the value of the key that caused the event.

Errors

If the value of the specified key number is not in the range 1 through 25 or either 30 or 31, QBasic displays an "Illegal function call" error message.

Tips

Using event-trapping statements makes your programs run more slowly. Avoid using event-trapping statements that aren't essential.

Example

The following program uses keyboard event trapping to display helpful information when the user presses the F1 key. The program also traps the PrtSc (print screen) key as well as the PrtSc key pressed with a Shift key, the Num Lock key, or both. When any of these key combinations is pressed, the program executes the *NoPrintScreen* subroutine.

```
CLS
LOCATE , , 1

ON KEY(1) GOSUB ShowHelp               ' F1 function key
KEY(1) ON

KEY 15, CHR$(&H80) + CHR$(&H37)        ' PrtSc key
ON KEY(15) GOSUB NoPrintScreen
KEY(15) ON

KEY 16, CHR$(&H83) + CHR$(&H37)        ' Shift-PrtSc key combination
ON KEY(16) GOSUB NoPrintScreen
KEY(16) ON

KEY 17, CHR$(&HA0) + CHR$(&H37)        ' PrtSc with Num Lock on
ON KEY(17) GOSUB NoPrintScreen
KEY(17) ON

KEY 18, CHR$(&HA3) + CHR$(&H37)        ' Shift-PrtSc with Num Lock on
ON KEY(18) GOSUB NoPrintScreen
KEY(18) ON

PRINT "Enter a new patient's name: "
name$ = ""
DO
    keybd$ = INKEY$
    IF keybd$ = CHR$(8) THEN           ' check for Backspace key
        LOCATE CSRLIN, POS(0) - 1
        PRINT " ";
        LOCATE CSRLIN, POS(0) - 1
        name$ = LEFT$(name$, LEN(name$) - 1)
    ELSE
        PRINT keybd$;
        name$ = name$ + keybd$
    END IF
LOOP UNTIL keybd$ = CHR$(13)           ' exit loop when user presses Enter
PRINT "You entered the name: "; name$
END

ShowHelp:
    LOCATE 5, 1
    PRINT "Enter the name of a new patient in the following form:"
    PRINT
    PRINT "     last name, first name"
    LOCATE 2, 1
    RETURN

NoPrintScreen:
    LOCATE 5, 1
    PRINT "Sorry, but you can't print this screen!"
    BEEP
    LOCATE 2, 1
    RETURN
```

CHAPTER 15

Printer

Introduction

QBasic provides a group of statements that offer a convenient way to print and to manage printed output. You can, of course, open the printer as a file and use a PRINT statement, as in the following example:

```
OPEN "LPT1:" AS #1
PRINT #1, "The quick brown fox"
```

But using the LPRINT statement is more intuitive and convenient, as shown in the statement

```
LPRINT "The quick brown fox"
```

(Note that opening a printer file and then using the LPRINT and LPRINT USING statements produces unpredictable output.)

Table 15-1 lists printer-related statements and functions in alphabetic order.

Statement or function	Description
LPOS	Returns the current position of the output column within the printer buffer.
LPRINT	Prints output on the printer attached to the LPT1: parallel port.
LPRINT USING	Prints a formatted string or other value on the printer. A special string specifies the format.
WIDTH LPRINT	Sets the column width of the printer output.

Table 15-1.
QBasic printer statements and functions.

Printing Text

The operation of the LPRINT and LPRINT USING statements, which direct output to the printer, is the same as that of PRINT and PRINT USING, which direct output to the screen. Therefore, you can find further discussion and related examples in the PRINT and PRINT USING entries in Chapter 8, "Simple I/O." The tutorial in this chapter addresses matters involving only the printer.

Using LPRINT with no parameters directs the printer to skip a line. When you use LPRINT with a numeric or string variable or with a constant string, such as "The quick brown fox," the printer prints the value and then prints a carriage return and a linefeed

(CR/LF), which moves the print head to the beginning of a new line. If you don't want the print head to move to a new line after printing, use a semicolon at the end of the LPRINT statement. For example, the statement

```
LPRINT "No new line yet.";
```

suppresses the CR/LF so that subsequent output is printed on the same line. QBasic doesn't insert spaces between items; if you want blank spaces, you must include them. For example, the statement

```
LPRINT firstName$; " "; lastName$
```

inserts a space between the first and last names. You can space items at regular intervals by using a comma after each item in the LPRINT statement. Each new item is printed at the beginning of the next 14-space print zone. Thus the statement

```
LPRINT "Widely", "Spaced", "Text"
```

results in the output

```
Widely          Spaced          Text
```

A comma at the end of an LPRINT statement moves the print head to the next print zone and suppresses the CR/LF.

The LPRINT USING statement specifies a format string and the item or items to be printed. For example, the following statement prints *****$29.99:

```
LPRINT USING "**$#####.##", 29.99
```

(Format strings are described in the PRINT USING entry in Chapter 8, "Simple I/O.")

Printer Control

The LPRINT statement is also useful for sending to the printer special control sequences that make it possible for a QBasic program to gain access to your printer's special features.

QBasic assumes the printer is a line printer. On almost all printers (including page printers such as laser printers), the statement *LPRINT CHR$(12)* prints a formfeed character, thus advancing the print head to the top of the next page. On most printers, the default length of one page is 66 lines.

Note that the LPRINT statement appends a carriage return (ASCII character 13) and a linefeed (ASCII character 10) to a line of output. If you use LPRINT with a printer that is set up to insert its own linefeeds, the output will contain extra blank lines. You can correct this by using the DOS printer device in binary mode—for example,

```
OPEN "LPT1:" FOR BINARY AS #1
```

Then, to send the output to the printer, use the PUT statement as shown in the following program segment:

```
words$ = "The quick brown fox"
PUT #1, words$
```

The PUT statement does not append a carriage return or a linefeed to the output.

The QBasic WIDTH LPRINT statement sets a width for the printer. When output reaches the specified width, the printer prints a CR/LF.

If you need more exact control over the position of the print head, use the LPOS function to determine the location of the print head in the current line. Your program can then decide whether it needs to begin a new line. You can also use LPOS to format output on the page by calling LPOS and then moving the print head a specific number of spaces, which depends on the value the function returns.

Related Reading

Schneider, David L. *Handbook of BASIC*. 3d ed. New York, N.Y.: Brady, 1988.

LPOS

See also

POS

Purpose

The LPOS function returns the position of the current output column for the printer at the specified port. Your program can use this information to determine when to start a new line of output, "wrap" words, and so on.

Syntax

LPOS(*port*)

port must be the number 1, 2, or 3, which refers to port LPT1: (or PRN:), LPT2:, or LPT3:.

Usage

```
LPRINT name$
col = LPOS(1)
```

Sends the string in *name$* to the printer and then stores the current output column of LPT1: in the variable *col*.

Description

In most cases, characters sent to the printer are not immediately printed. Rather, they are stored in the printer's buffer until an entire line or a linefeed is received from the computer. (LPRINT and PRINT send a carriage return and a linefeed to the printer unless the statement ends in a comma or a semicolon.) Immediately after a linefeed, a call to LPOS returns a 1 to indicate that the printer is beginning a new line of output.

The LPOS function does not actually return the print head position; instead, it returns the number of characters that have been output on the current line.

Warnings

The LPOS function counts a tab character as only one character; however, the printer normally prints a tab character as several spaces. Thus the value returned by LPOS does not correspond to the actual print head position after a tab is printed.

Turning the printer off resets the print head position to the left margin and clears any characters in the print buffer. When you turn the printer on again, QBasic is unaware that the buffer has been cleared, and the value of LPOS is the same as it was before the printer was turned off.

Example

The following program prompts you to specify the column numbers of the left and right margins and to type words at the keyboard. The program prints the entered line of text, one word at a time, using the specified margins. Before a word is printed, the program checks its length against the difference between the right margin position and the value of LPOS; if the word requires space beyond the margin, the program instead prints it at the beginning of a new line.

The *NextWord* subprogram parses each line of input into words, one word at a time, and returns the word (*word$*) and the remaining portion of the string. Notice that this subprogram is defined with the keyword STATIC because it must maintain the values of its variables between calls.

```
DECLARE SUB NextWord (aString$, sep$, word$)

sep$ = " "                    ' use a space to separate words
INPUT "Left margin column "; leftMargin
INPUT "Right margin column "; rightMargin
PRINT "Type text a line at a time."
PRINT "Press <Enter> by itself to exit the program."
GOSUB NewLine                 ' start printing on a new line
DO
    LINE INPUT line$
    IF LEN(line$) = 0 THEN
        LPRINT              ' LPRINT to flush buffer
        LPRINT CHR$(12)
        SYSTEM
    END IF
    GOSUB Justify
LOOP
END

Justify:
    DO
        CALL NextWord(line$, sep$, word$)       ' get next word
        IF (LEN(word$) > (rightMargin - LPOS(1))) THEN
            GOSUB NewLine   ' move to next line if word hits right margin
        END IF
        LPRINT word$; " ";
    LOOP UNTIL LEN(word$) = 0
    RETURN

NewLine:
    LPRINT                      ' move to next line
    FOR space% = 1 TO leftMargin
        LPRINT " ";     ' print spaces to the left margin
    NEXT space%
    RETURN

SUB NextWord (aString$, sep$, word$) STATIC
    word$ = ""
    strlen% = LEN(aString$)
    IF aString$ = "" THEN EXIT SUB

    FOR char1% = 1 TO strlen%
        IF INSTR(sep$, MID$(aString$, char1%, 1)) = 0 THEN EXIT FOR
    NEXT char1%
```

(continued)

continued

```
    FOR char2% = char1% TO strlen%
        IF INSTR(sep$, MID$(aString$, char2%, 1)) THEN EXIT FOR
    NEXT char2%

    FOR char3% = char2% TO strlen%
        IF INSTR(sep$, MID$(aString$, char3%, 1)) = 0 THEN EXIT FOR
    NEXT char3%

    IF char1% > strlen% THEN
        aString$ = ""
        EXIT SUB
    END IF

    IF char2% > strlen% THEN
        word$ = MID$(aString$, char1%)
        aString$ = ""
        EXIT SUB
    END IF

    word$ = MID$(aString$, char1%, char2% - char1%)

    IF char3% > strlen% THEN
        aString$ = ""
    ELSE
        aString$ = MID$(aString$, char3%)
    END IF
END SUB
```

LPRINT

See also

LPRINT USING, PRINT, PRINT USING

Purpose

The LPRINT statement prints the contents of numeric or string variables or literals on the printer. QBasic assumes the printer is connected to the first parallel port (LPT1: or PRN:). You can also use LPRINT to send control codes to the printer.

Syntax

LPRINT [*data*[{; ¦ ,}*data*...]] [; ¦ ,]

data can be any numeric or string constant, expression, or variable. If you specify more than one item, separate them with commas or semicolons.

If you use a semicolon between two items, the second item will be printed immediately after the first one. If you use a comma between items, the second item will be printed in the next print zone. (Each print zone is 14 characters long.) A semicolon or comma at the end of an LPRINT statement keeps the print head from moving to the next line after printing.

Usage

```
LPRINT "Hello";
```
Prints the word "Hello" but does not move the print head to a new line.

```
LPRINT subtotal + tax
```
Prints the sum of the variables *subtotal* and *tax*.

```
LPRINT CHR$(12)
```
Sends a formfeed character to the printer.

Description

The LPRINT statement works in exactly the same way as the PRINT statement does except that its output is sent to the parallel printer instead of the screen. LPRINT can also use the CHR$ function to send any character (including nonprinting characters) to the printer. This lets your program send control commands to the printer in order to gain access to the printer's special features.

Each kind of printer has a different set of control commands. See your printer manual for details.

Errors

If the printer is not connected or is not online, QBasic displays a "Device timeout" error message.

Tips

QBasic has no statement equal to LPRINT for printing directly to a serial printer. However, if you use the DOS command

```
MODE LPT1=COM1
```

to redirect parallel printer output to a serial printer connected to port COM1:, the output of LPRINT and LPRINT USING is sent to the serial printer. Or you can open the device COM1:, assign it a file number, and then print to it by using the PRINT $NO statement.

Example

The following program uses LPRINT to set up an HP LaserJet printer to print a disk file in landscape (sideways) orientation and with a compressed typeface. This format might be useful for printing program listings on which you will be making extensive notes.

```
DECLARE SUB DoHeader ()
CONST linesPerPage% = 20          ' lines per page, including header
CONST TRUE = 1
CONST FALSE = NOT TRUE
firstTime% = TRUE                 ' flag used to avoid formfeed before first page
```

(continued)

continued

```
' set up printer
LPRINT CHR$(27); "&l1O";        ' set landscape orientation
LPRINT CHR$(27); "(sOT";        ' set line printer typeface
LPRINT CHR$(27); "&k2S";        ' set compressed size
LPRINT CHR$(27); "&l3d";        ' set double spacing
LPRINT CHR$(27); "&l2E";        ' set 2-line top margin

INPUT "Name of file to print: "; file$  ' specify a file to be printed
ON ERROR GOTO BadFile

OPEN file$ FOR INPUT AS #1      ' open specified file

DoHeader                        ' print header for first page
firstTime% = FALSE             ' turn off flag so formfeeds are printed

DO                              ' print a page
    LINE INPUT #1, line$        ' get next line from file
    LPRINT line$                ' print the line
    currentLine% = currentLine% + 1      ' count the lines printed
    IF currentLine% = linesPerPage% THEN DoHeader
LOOP WHILE NOT EOF(1)

CLOSE #1                        ' close input file
LPRINT CHR$(27); "E";           ' reset printer for next job
END

BadFile:                        ' error-handling routine
    errnum% = ERR
    SELECT CASE errnum%
    CASE 29
        PRINT "Write fault."
    CASE 30
        PRINT "Read fault."
    CASE 52
        PRINT "Bad filename."
    CASE 53
        PRINT "File not found."
    CASE 68
        PRINT "Device not available. Be sure printer is ";
        PRINT "connected and turned on."
    END SELECT
    SYSTEM                      ' exit to operating system on error
END

SUB DoHeader STATIC
    SHARED firstTime%, currentLine%
    IF firstTime% = FALSE THEN
        LPRINT CHR$(12)                 ' formfeed
    ELSE
        pageNum% = 1
    END IF
```

(continued)

continued

```
      LPRINT UCASE$(file$); SPC(10);      ' print filename
      LPRINT DATE$; SPC(10);              ' print current date
      LPRINT TIME$; SPC(5);               ' print current time
      LPRINT SPC(5);
      LPRINT "Page "; pageNum%            ' print page number
      pageNum% = pageNum% + 1             ' increment page number
      currentLine% = 1                    ' set current line
  END SUB
```

LPRINT USING

See also
LPRINT, PRINT USING

Purpose
The LPRINT USING statement prints formatted numbers or strings on the printer and specifies the length and format of each item printed.

Syntax
LPRINT USING *template*; *var* [; *var*…][, ¦ ;]

template is a string constant or a string variable that can contain literal text and one or more special formatting characters that determine how the variables are to be printed.

var is a numeric or string expression that will be printed in the format specified by *template*.

A comma at the end of a statement causes the print head to remain on the current line and to move to the next print zone. A semicolon causes the print head to remain on the space immediately after the last character printed.

Usage
```
LPRINT USING "##.#"; 24.99
```
Prints *25.0*. Each number sign holds a place for a numeric digit. Because *template* specifies only three digits, LPRINT USING rounds off the number.

```
LPRINT USING "&"; "QBasic"
```
Prints *QBasic*.

Description
The LPRINT USING statement requires a special formatting string that is either in a string variable or enclosed in quotation marks. The formatting string provides great versatility in formatting numbers and strings. You can use it to print numbers rounded to a specified number of decimal places, preceded by dollar signs or other special characters, or printed in scientific notation. You can also use it to print strings in various

formats, such as truncated or justified. (See the PRINT USING entry in Chapter 8, "Simple I/O," for a complete discussion of formats.)

As with PRINT, ending the expression to be printed with a semicolon suppresses the carriage return and linefeed, and ending it with a comma causes the next LPRINT statement to begin printing in the next 14-character print zone.

Errors

If the printer is not connected or is not on line, QBasic displays a "Device timeout" error message.

Example

The following program lets the user enter numbers and formatting strings to see the effect. You can use this program to practice using the print formats. To use the program with string rather than numeric values, simply change the variable *num#* to a string variable (for example, *aString$*).

```
CLS
DO
    INPUT "Number to be printed (0 to quit) "; num#
    IF num# = 0 THEN EXIT DO
    INPUT "Format to use "; format$
    IF format$ = "" THEN
        LPRINT "You must enter a formatting string."
    ELSE
        LPRINT USING format$; num#
    END IF
LOOP
```

WIDTH LPRINT

See also

LPOS, POS, WIDTH (File I/O), WIDTH (Screen)

Purpose

The WIDTH LPRINT statement specifies the width of a printed line. QBasic begins a new line whenever the print head reaches the end of a line.

Syntax

WIDTH LPRINT *col*

col is an integer in the range 1 through 255 that specifies the maximum number of columns in each printed line.

Usage

WIDTH LPRINT 40

Prints all output in no more than 40 columns per line.

Description

The WIDTH LPRINT statement specifies the column at which the printer will issue a carriage return and linefeed (CR/LF). Any additional CR/LF sent by an LPRINT statement sends the print head to the next line. After you call WIDTH LPRINT, a line cannot exceed the specified width.

If the width you set is greater than the width of the paper in the printer, the printer truncates the characters specified in the LPRINT or LPRINT USING statement that fall between the edge of the paper and the specified width before printing a CR/LF. Specifying a width of 255 columns suppresses the CR/LF. Even if the output of an LPRINT or LPRINT USING statement extends past 255 columns, the print head does not move to the next line. It moves to the next line only when the program calls another LPRINT or LPRINT USING statement.

Example

The following program prompts the user to set a column width for the printer and to type lines of text that the program sends to the printer.

```
INPUT "Enter the line width of the printer: "; column%
WIDTH LPRINT column%
PRINT "Type one line at a time. Press Enter to quit."

DO
    LINE INPUT line$     ' get a line
    IF LEN(line$) = 0 THEN EXIT DO
    LPRINT line$;        ' don't force a linefeed
LOOP
LPRINT CHR$(12)          ' print a formfeed character
```

CHAPTER 16

Communications Port

Introduction

Personal computer communications involve the transfer of data between a personal computer and another computer system. The data might be program (binary) files, spreadsheet and database records, text documents, electronic mail, messages from bulletin boards, graphics images, or any other information that can be encoded in a digital format. The other computer might be a personal computer or a giant mainframe thousands of miles away. It might be running DOS, OS/2, UNIX, or some other operating system. The data might be transmitted through a cable directly connected to the other computer, or it might be sent through the phone lines by way of a modem.

As a QBasic programmer, you don't need to know many details about the transmitting and receiving systems themselves; all you need to know is that PC communications lets you transfer data to and from a serial communications port, which is a physical connection to the PC and its associated memory buffer. As far as QBasic is concerned, you communicate with the serial port, not with another computer or another operating system.

This chapter shows you how to use the QBasic statements that open the serial port connection, establish a temporary memory buffer to hold data, signal when data has been received, and close the connection when it is no longer needed. Table 16-1 lists QBasic's communications statements.

Statement	Description
COM ON/OFF/STOP	Enables, disables, or suspends communications event trapping.
ON COM GOSUB	Specifies the subroutine to which control branches when a specified communications port receives data.
OPEN COM	Opens a serial port connection and assigns a buffer and file number to it. The statement also lets you specify characteristics of communication, such as baud rate, parity, number of data bits, number of stop bits, and modem control.

Table 16-1.
QBasic communications statements.

Ports and Buffers

A port in a PC consists of three elements: a physical (electronic) connection, a particular location in memory for status information about the connection, and a memory buffer for the temporary storage of incoming or outgoing data. QBasic can transmit or receive data by way of the PC's standard serial ports. QBasic supports only the COM1: and COM2: serial ports.

QBasic assigns a memory area, called a buffer, to each port. This temporary storage area is necessary because usually a program must do other work while it transfers characters to and from a communications port. If the program had to stop whatever it was doing every time a character arrived at the port, execution would slow to a crawl—and at higher transmission speeds, characters would be lost before they could be used in the program. To make the data more manageable, the input buffer accumulates characters until it is full (or nearly full); the program then transfers the contents of the buffer to the screen, a file, or a string array, depending on the application. Similarly, outgoing characters are accumulated in the output buffer and then are sent when the buffer is full.

Establishing the Connection

When you send information from QBasic, the first step is to call the OPEN COM statement to specify both the serial port you want to use and the status of the connection. For example, the statement

```
OPEN "COM1:1200,N,8,1" FOR RANDOM AS #1
```

specifies that the port COM1: will be used and that the speed of character transmission will be 1200 baud (approximately 1200 bits per second). The transmission speed and other characteristics of the connection must be the same for both sender and receiver. That is, if you want your QBasic program to connect to a system that allows 300-baud, 1200-baud, or 2400-baud connections, you can pick one of these speeds but not, for example, 9600 baud.

The example statement uses the arguments N, 8, and 1 to indicate no parity bit, 8 data bits per character, and 1 stop bit. Parity checking is a method of detecting transmission errors by ensuring that the number of bits in a character with a value of 1 (or 0, depending on the type of parity checking) is even (or odd); you perform parity checking by setting a parity bit. The value of the parity bit indicates whether the number of bits should be even or odd. If the character arrives at the destination without the appropriate even or odd number of bits, the receiver requests that the character be sent again. The data bits are bits that actually contain the data being transmitted (such as ASCII characters). Note that 7 bits are enough to transmit any of the 128 ASCII characters but that 8 bits are needed for numeric data or for the characters in the IBM extended character set. Stop bits indicate the end of one set of data bits. You will most often use only 1 stop bit; use 2 bits only for the slowest transmission speeds (110 baud or less). Use the 1.5-bit setting only when you specify 5 data bits.

Use the FOR clause in the OPEN COM statement to specify how the program will use the data sent to and received from the port. FOR RANDOM, the default in QBasic, means the data will be treated like records in a random-access file. You can specify the record length by using a LEN clause. Random-access mode is convenient for sending fixed-length blocks of data—for example, when implementing error-correcting protocols such as XMODEM, which protect against transmission errors. You can also specify FOR INPUT in the OPEN COM statement so that the program receives only sequential input, and FOR OUTPUT so that it sends only sequential output.

The AS clause is the final part of the example OPEN COM statement. AS #1 specifies that the COM1: port can be accessed as file #1. Note that QBasic treats the communications port as a file. Thus you can open it and then either receive input from or send output to its buffer. QBasic uses separate transmit (TB) and receive (RB) buffers; the default size of each buffer in QBasic is 512 bytes.

Additional Communications Settings and Modem Control

The OPEN COM statement also lets you change other communications settings: the way data is treated (as ASCII characters or binary values), the size of the receive and transmit buffers, the printing of linefeeds on a serial printer, and the interval between when the modem control signal is monitored and when a time-out occurs. A time-out is the termination of communication that occurs when the time allowed for establishing the connection or performing an operation has been exceeded. Without time-outs, the program would simply hang if it encountered a problem with the connection. If you don't specify time-outs, QBasic uses default time-outs of 1 second. These options are discussed in detail in the OPEN COM entry. If you have trouble with time-outs caused by poor connections or by differences between the sending and receiving hardware, try increasing the time-out values.

Retrieving and Sending Characters

To retrieve characters from the input buffer, first use the EOF function to determine whether there are any characters to process. (Because QBasic treats the communications device as a file, the "end-of-file" status means there are no more characters to retrieve.) Next, use the INPUT$ (File I/O) function with the LOC function to retrieve all the characters in the buffer. Do not use the INPUT or LINE INPUT statements because they might not retrieve all the characters: INPUT stops at a comma, new line, and sometimes at a space or pair of double quotation marks; LINE INPUT stops at a new line. Do not use the GET statement because it waits for the buffer to fill, and the buffer might overflow before the characters can be transferred.

The following loop shows the recommended technique for retrieving characters. The loop waits until there are characters at the COM1: port (assuming the port has been opened properly) and displays them on the screen:

```
DO
    IF NOT EOF(1) THEN                    ' port was opened as file #1
        PRINT INPUT$(LOC(1), #1)
    END IF
LOOP
```

To send characters to the serial port (and thus to the connected system), you can use any appropriate PRINT or PUT statement. If you assign each line of input to a string called *line$*, the statement

```
PRINT #1, line$
```

will store the characters in *line$* in the transmit buffer. QBasic sends the contents of the buffer to the port.

Because a communications session uses files for serial input and output, use a CLOSE statement at the end of your program to close the files.

Managing Communications with Event Trapping

In many cases, you do not want your program to begin waiting for data from the communications buffer until communication occurs. QBasic includes a set of statements that branch control to a designated subroutine when data is received. Executing a subroutine when an event occurs is called event trapping.

The ON COM GOSUB statement specifies the subroutine to which execution branches when characters are available for processing in the communications buffer. Your program must also execute a COM ON statement to activate communications event trapping. The COM STOP statement suspends communications event trapping; characters continue to arrive at the buffer, but control does not branch to the subroutine. You might use this statement to turn off communications event trapping while your program performs a time-critical function, but be sure that you enable trapping again before the buffer overflows. When a buffer overflows, data is lost, and the program might halt. When you use another COM ON statement to resume event trapping, QBasic remembers any events that occurred while communications event trapping was off and executes the subroutine. This lets your program catch up with communications activity. The COM OFF statement simply turns off communications event trapping and does not remember any communications events.

In each communications event-trapping statement, the keyword COM is followed by the number of the communications port (either 1 or 2) in parentheses. (This number refers to either the COM1: or COM2: port. Do not confuse it with the file number you assign in the OPEN COM statement.)

A program that includes communications event trapping uses the following schematic form (this example uses the COM1: port):

```
OPEN "COM1:1200,N,8,1" FOR RANDOM AS #1     ' open the connection
ON COM(1) GOSUB DoCom           ' specify subroutine
COM(1) ON                       ' begin event trapping

DO                              ' program's main processing loop
    :
    COM(1) STOP                 ' begin time-critical activity
    :
    COM(1) ON                   ' restore event trapping
LOOP
CLOSE
END

DoCom:                          ' event-handler subroutine
    :
    RETURN
```

Further Explorations

You don't need two modems (or even one modem) to perform serial communications. If you have two DOS computers, you can connect their serial ports with a null modem cable (available at most electronics or computer stores) and run QBasic programs simultaneously on the two machines; this approach lets you test output from one and input to the other. You can test your connection by using the sample programs provided in the "Example" section of the ON COM GOSUB entry.

Sophisticated communications programs can be difficult to develop because they have to deal with matters of timing, file-transmission protocols, terminal emulation, and so on. See the books in the following bibliography to further your understanding of this subject.

Related Reading

Barkakati, Nabajyoti. "Programming the Serial Port with C," in *MS-DOS Papers*, by The Waite Group. Indianapolis, Ind.: Howard W. Sams & Co., 1988.

The Waite Group. *MS-DOS Developer's Guide*. 2d ed. Indianapolis, Ind.: Howard W. Sams & Co., 1989.

Willen, David C., and Jeffrey I. Krantz. *8088 Assembler Language Programming: The IBM PC*. 2d ed. Indianapolis, Ind.: Howard W. Sams & Co., 1984.

COM ON/OFF/STOP

See also

ON COM GOSUB, OPEN COM

Purpose

The COM statements enable, disable, or suspend communications event trapping. Use communications event trapping if you want the program to execute a subroutine whenever the specified communications port receives characters.

Syntax

COM(*port*) ON
COM(*port*) OFF
COM(*port*) STOP

port must be either 1 or 2. It specifies the communications port (either COM1: or COM2:) that will be used.

Usage

COM(1) ON

Enables communications event trapping at the COM1: port.

Description

QBasic lets you trap the arrival of characters at the communications (serial) port. Use the COM ON statement to enable trapping so that when a character arrives, control transfers to the subroutine designed to handle the communications input. (The subroutine is specified by an ON COM GOSUB statement.)

Note that you must open the serial port you want with an OPEN COM statement before a communications event will be available for trapping.

If your program is performing some other time-critical activity (such as working with another device), you might need to use the COM OFF statement to turn off event trapping at a specified port. Incoming characters will continue to be placed in the receive buffer, but if the buffer overflows, data will be lost and a fatal error might halt the program.

Use the COM STOP statement to suspend the trapping of events from the specified communications port. Until you execute a subsequent COM ON statement, incoming data continues to arrive at the input buffer for the specified port; however, the subroutine specified in an ON COM GOSUB statement is not executed. QBasic sets a flag recording that an event occurred so that the trap is triggered after the next COM ON statement is executed.

The program executes an implicit COM STOP whenever it enters the subroutine specified by ON COM GOSUB. This action ensures that another occurrence of the event does not cause the subroutine to be executed recursively. When the program encounters a RETURN statement and returns to the main program, it reinstates communications event trapping by executing an implicit COM ON statement.

Warnings

When you write communications programs and subprograms, use the ON ERROR GOTO statement to trap any errors that occur. Always test your communications programs under a variety of conditions (different speeds, different degrees of line noise, and so on) to ensure dependable performance.

Be sure your buffer is large enough to hold all characters that might arrive while trapping is suspended or off. Note that you might have to increase the buffer size at higher communications speeds (2400 baud and higher). You can set the communications buffer size by using the TB and RB parameters in the OPEN COM statement.

Example

The following program uses the COM ON statement to enable communications event trapping and the COM STOP statement to suspend communications event trapping until a key is pressed. The program begins by executing the subroutine *Event* every time characters arrive at the COM1: port. If you press a key, however, trapping is suspended, and the program will stop displaying the message "Trapped an event at the COM1: port." When you press another key, trapping resumes. Press Esc to exit the loop.

```
COM(1) ON                        ' enable trapping for port COM1:

ON COM(1) GOSUB Event            ' specify subroutine for event trapping
OPEN "COM1:1200,N,8,1" FOR INPUT AS 2     ' open port

toggle = -2                      ' start with toggle off
DO
    PRINT "Waiting for something to happen..."
    inky$ = INKEY$
    IF inky$ <> "" AND inky$ <> CHR$(27) THEN
        toggle = NOT toggle      ' reverse toggle setting
    END IF
    IF toggle THEN
        PRINT "Suspending event trapping."
        COM(1) STOP
    END IF
    IF NOT toggle THEN
        COM(1) ON
        PRINT "Event trapping resumed."
    END IF
LOOP UNTIL inky$ = CHR$(27)   ' exit loop if user presses Esc
CLOSE
END

Event:
    PRINT "Trapped an event at the COM1: port. "
    RETURN
```

ON COM GOSUB

See also

COM ON/OFF/STOP, OPEN COM

Purpose

The ON COM GOSUB statement specifies the subroutine to which execution branches whenever data is received at the specified communications port. This feature lets your program perform other tasks without having to check constantly for communications activity.

Syntax

ON COM(*port*) GOSUB {*line* | *label*}

port must be either 1 or 2. It specifies the communications port (either COM1: or COM2:) that will be used.

line or *label* specifies the line that begins the subroutine to which execution branches.

Usage

```
ON COM(1) GOSUB DoComm
```

Specifies that the *DoComm* subroutine will be executed when data arrives at the COM1: port.

Description

The ON COM GOSUB statement specifies the event-handling subroutine for a serial communications port. Event handling is the ability of the program to respond automatically to signals from the hardware—in this case, the signals indicate that data was received at a serial communications port.

To set up communications event handling, you must perform the following steps:

- Open a communications port by using the OPEN COM statement.
- Specify the open port and the subroutine that will handle communications events by using an ON COM GOSUB statement.
- Activate event handling, or event trapping, with a COM ON statement that specifies the open port.
- Define the subroutine that will process the communications.

The programs in the "Example" section demonstrate how these steps can be used with the COM1: serial port. Note that the QBasic communications statements support only two serial ports—1 refers to COM1: and 2 refers to the COM2: serial port.

Example

This section contains two programs. The first one opens the COM1: port for output and sends the string "This is a test..." to that port until you press a key. The second program opens the COM1: port to receive input, specifies that the subroutine

HandleComm be executed whenever data arrives at the port, and activates communications event trapping. The subroutine uses the INPUT$ function to retrieve any waiting characters. (The LOC function returns the number of characters in the buffer.) If you have two computers, you can connect a null modem cable (which is available at most electronics or computer stores) to their serial ports and run the first program on one and the second on the other. If you have two computers connected by modem, you can have one dial the other to establish the connection. After you have opened the communications port as file #1, for example, the statement

```
PRINT #1, "ATDT1234567"
```

instructs a Hayes-compatible modem at that port to dial the number 123-4567.

In the OPEN COM statements used in these programs, the parameters *CD0*, *CS0*, *DS0*, *OP0*, and *RS* prevent time-outs and waiting for the Request to Send lines. If you don't use these parameters (or you don't specify larger time-out values), one of the programs would probably issue a time-out while waiting for the other to send or receive characters.

```
' open the port
OPEN "COM1:1200,N,8,1,CD0,CS0,DS0,OP0,RS" FOR OUTPUT AS #1

DO
    PRINT #1, "This is a test..."
LOOP WHILE INKEY$ = ""
CLOSE       ' close the port
END
```

```
' open the port
OPEN "COM1:1200,N,8,1,CD0,CS0,DS0,OP0,RS" FOR INPUT AS #1

ON COM(1) GOSUB HandleComm          ' specify event-handling subroutine
COM(1) ON                           ' activate trapping

CLS
DO
    LOCATE 1, 1
    PRINT "Waiting for data at the COM1: port. "
    PRINT "Press any key to quit."
    IF INKEY$ <> "" THEN SYSTEM
LOOP
CLOSE       ' close the port
END

HandleComm:
    DO WHILE NOT EOF(1)
        PRINT INPUT$(LOC(1), #1);    ' display the data
    LOOP
    RETURN
```

OPEN COM

See also

COM ON/OFF/STOP, ON COM GOSUB

Purpose

The OPEN COM statement establishes a serial communications connection to a QBasic program. You can set many characteristics of the connection, including baud rate (transmission speed), parity, number of data and stop bits, buffer sizes, and time-out values for modem lines.

Syntax

OPEN "COM*port:params1 params2*" [FOR *mode*] AS [#]*file* [LEN=*length*]

port must be either 1 or 2. This number specifies the communications port (either COM1: or COM2:) that will be opened.

params1 is a list of the four parameters described in Table 16-2. You must use a comma as a placeholder for any parameter you do not use.

params2 is a list of the parameters described in Table 16-3. You can specify these parameters in any order, provided you separate them by using commas.

mode is the keyword RANDOM, INPUT, or OUTPUT.

file is the number of the file from which you access the communications port.

length is an integer that specifies the record size used with the port. You can use *length* if the value of *mode* is RANDOM.

Usage

```
OPEN "COM2:2400,E,7,1,BIN,CD0,CS0,DS0,OP0" FOR RANDOM AS #2
```
Opens a serial port connection and supplies data-communication specifications. COM2: is opened so that it has a transmission speed of 2400 baud, performs even parity checking, and uses 7 data bits and 1 stop bit. The port does not expand tabs or force carriage returns. The port does not use any time-outs, so it will wait for transmission and reception. The port is opened as a random file that can be accessed by #2.

Description

You must use the OPEN COM statement before your program can access a serial communications port. The syntax of the statement requires you to follow the keyword OPEN with the port number to be used (either COM1: or COM2:), and the parameters you want, which are separated by commas. You can specify any parameters listed in Tables 16-2 and 16-3.

Table 16-2 lists the first four parameters of the parameter list. They must appear in the order shown; if you skip a parameter, you must insert a comma as a placeholder.

Use the parameters listed in Table 16-3 after setting those in Table 16-2; you can enter these parameters in any order.

Parameter	Meaning	Comments
Speed	Baud rate (bits per second).	Use the value 75, 110, 150, 300, 600, 1200, 2400, 4800, or 9600. Most dial-up connections are 1200 or 2400 baud. The modem you use must support the speed you specify.
Parity	Type of parity checking used for error detection.	Use the N (none), E (even), O (odd), S (space), M (mark), or PE (enable error checking). If you do not know which to use, try N first.
Data bits	Number of bits in each group that represent actual data.	Use the value 5, 6, 7, or 8. Use 8 only if parity checking is not performed; use 7 if it is.
Stop bits	Number of bits used to mark the end of each word.	Use 1, 1.5, or 2. The appropriate choice is usually 1. Use 2 for slow transmission rates, and use 1.5 only if the number of data bits is 5.

Table 16-2.
The first four parameters for the OPEN COM statement.

Parameter	Meaning	Comments
ASC	Specifies characters as ASCII, expands tabs, forces a carriage return at the end of each line, and considers Ctrl-Z the EOF marker.	The standard setting for sending and receiving ASCII text files.
BIN	Performs none of the actions specified by ASC.	This is the default setting. Use either ASC or BIN but not both.
CD*ms*	Specifies the milliseconds to wait for the time-out on the Data Carrier Detect (DCD) line.	*ms* must be a number in the range 0 through 65535; A value of 0 disables the time-out. The default is 0.
CS*ms*	Specifies the milliseconds to wait for the time-out on the Clear to Send (CTS) line.	*ms* must be a number in the range 0 through 65535. The default is 1000 (1 second).
DS*ms*	Specifies the milliseconds to wait for the time-out on the Data Set Ready (DSR) line.	*ms* must be a number in the range 0 through 65535. The default is 1000 (1 second).
LF	Adds a linefeed character to each carriage return.	This setting is used for printing with serial printers.
OP*ms*	Specifies the milliseconds to wait for OPEN COM statement to be successful.	*ms* must be a number in the range 0 through 65535. The default is 10000 (10 seconds).
RB*bytes*	Allocates a number of bytes to the receive data buffer.	*bytes* must be a number in the range 0 through 32767. The default is 512.

Table 16-3. *(continued)*
The remaining parameters for the OPEN COM statement.

Table 16-3. *continued*

Parameter	Meaning	Comments
RS	Suppresses detection of the Request to Send (RTS) signal.	
TB*bytes*	Allocates a number of bytes to the transmit data buffer.	*bytes* must be a number in the range 0 through 32767. The default is 512.

Following the parameter list, use the keyword FOR and one of the following keywords:

RANDOM	For random input and output
INPUT	For sequential input
OUTPUT	For sequential output

RANDOM is the most commonly used option, and QBasic uses it as the default if you don't specify another mode. If you use RANDOM, you can follow it with the keyword LEN and the record size (in bytes) that will be used. The default record size is 128 bytes.

Comments

Timing problems can be difficult to handle. Start by using the most relaxed conditions your application can tolerate. Specify the time-out parameters as 0 so there will be no time-outs, set generous buffers, and start with a low speed (such as 1200 baud rather than 2400 or higher). The most commonly used setting specifies no parity, 8 data bits, and 1 stop bit. When you feel more comfortable using communications, begin varying the OPEN COM statement to meet the needs of your program.

Errors

A "Bad file name" error message displayed during the compilation of an OPEN COM statement usually indicates a syntax error of some sort. In addition, many other errors can occur during communications. DOS errors referring to "read fault" or "write fault" on device COM1: or COM2: usually indicate that the port was not opened. A "Device time-out" runtime error message indicates that a required signal took too long to arrive at the port. A "Fatal error" message might indicate a buffer overflow (usually the receive buffer); you might have to increase the buffer size to avoid this problem.

Warnings

Note that the ASC (ASCII text) parameter in the OPEN COM statement does not support XON/XOFF handshaking. The Ctrl-S and Ctrl-Q characters are treated as ordinary characters rather than as signals to start or stop data transmission.

Example

The following program prompts the user to enter the port number, baud rate, data bits, and stop bits values and then executes an OPEN COM statement with those values.

```
CONST TRUE = 1, FALSE = NOT TRUE
CLS

DO
valid% = TRUE
PRINT "Which port do you want to use"
INPUT "1) COM1:   2) COM2:   3) Quit program "; choice%
SELECT CASE choice%
    CASE 1
        port$ = "COM1:"
    CASE 2
        port$ = "COM2:"
    CASE 3
        SYSTEM
    CASE ELSE
        PRINT "Choose 1, 2, or 3."
        valid% = FALSE
END SELECT
LOOP UNTIL valid% = TRUE

PRINT
DO
valid% = TRUE
PRINT "What transmission speed"
INPUT "1) 300 baud   2) 1200 baud   3) 2400 baud   4) 9600 baud "; choice%
SELECT CASE choice%
    CASE 1
        speed$ = "300"
    CASE 2
        speed$ = "1200"
    CASE 3
        speed$ = "2400"
    CASE 4
        speed$ = "9600"
    CASE ELSE
        PRINT "Choose 1, 2, 3, or 4."
        valid% = FALSE
END SELECT
LOOP UNTIL valid% = TRUE

PRINT
DO
valid% = TRUE
PRINT "What parity should be used"
INPUT "1) Even   2) Odd   3) None "; choice%
SELECT CASE choice%
    CASE 1
        parity$ = "E"
    CASE 2
        parity$ = "O"
```

(continued)

continued

```
        CASE 3
            parity$ = "N"
        CASE ELSE
            PRINT "Choose 1, 2, or 3."
            valid% = FALSE
    END SELECT
    LOOP UNTIL valid% = TRUE


    PRINT
    DO
    valid% = TRUE
    PRINT "How many data bits per byte"
    INPUT "1) 5    2) 6    3) 7    4) 8 "; choice%
    SELECT CASE choice%
        CASE 1
            dataBits$ = "5"
        CASE 2
            dataBits$ = "6"
        CASE 3
            dataBits$ = "7"
        CASE 4
            dataBits$ = "8"
            IF parity$ <> "N" THEN
                PRINT "Must use 'no parity' with 8 data bits."
                PRINT "Setting parity to none (N)."
                parity$ = "N"
            END IF
        CASE ELSE
            PRINT "Choose 5, 6, 7, or 8."
            valid% = FALSE
    END SELECT
    LOOP UNTIL valid% = TRUE


    PRINT
    DO
    valid% = TRUE
    PRINT "How many stop bits"
    INPUT "1) 1    2) 1.5    3) 2 "; choice%
    SELECT CASE choice%
        CASE 1
            stopBits$ = "1"
        CASE 2
            stopBits$ = "1.5"
        CASE 3
            stopBits$ = "2"
        CASE ELSE
            PRINT "Choose 1, 2, or 3."
            valid% = FALSE
    END SELECT
    LOOP UNTIL valid% = TRUE
```

(continued)

continued

```
portSpec$ = port$ + speed$ + "," + parity$ + "," + dataBits$ + "," + stopBits$
PRINT "Your communications settings are: "; portSpec$

' open the communications port
OPEN portSpec$ FOR RANDOM AS #2
```

CHAPTER 17

Files

Introduction

The QBasic statements that manage file input and output provide an essential link between your program and the outside world. Most applications programs are useful because data that the user enters can be saved; after it is initially entered, the data is always available on file. By storing a form letter, a payroll register, or an inventory list, you can instantly gain access to information that took days or weeks to produce.

A file, stored in any manner, is merely a collection of bytes. The way those bytes are interpreted gives them meaning, as a patient history file, a record of sales transactions, or the like. Usually, programmers group information by using the following structures:

- *Fields*. A field is an individual piece of information, analogous to a simple variable. A field might contain a name, a birthdate, an inventory number, and so on. (The field length is the length of the field; it is usually measured in bytes.)

- *Records*. A record is a collection of fields that constitute a set of related information, analogous to a record variable defined by TYPE...END TYPE. A record might include a name, an address, and employment information. (The record length is the length of a single record; it is usually measured in bytes.)

- *Files*. A file is a set of records, analogous to an array of record variables. A file might comprise records for all of the employees of a company. (The "file length" is the combined length of all the records in the file; it is usually measured in bytes.)

Sequential Files

A sequential file is a continuous stream of characters that has no fields or records. A sequential file is line oriented rather than record oriented. This means that the exact location of information in a sequential file is unpredictable—to find line number 100, for example, you must first look through lines numbered 1 through 99. Sequential files are a lot like cassette tapes: To find a song in the middle of the tape, you must fast-forward through all the previous songs.

Sequential files can contain only ASCII or IBM extended characters. Each number in a sequential file is represented by 1 byte per digit.

Random-Access Files

A random-access file fully supports record structures. In fact, a random-access file contains a sequence of records, and a program can read only records from it or write only records to it. All records in a random-access file are the same length, so QBasic can calculate the exact location of any record in the file. Gaining access to a record is as easy as accessing the last song on a compact disk; because you know where every record (song) begins and ends, you can merely skip to the appropriate location.

Binary Files

A binary file is a variation of both random-access and sequential files. A binary file *can* support fields and records, but it can also do without them. If you want to ignore the field and record structures that are normally present in a random-access file, you can open the file as a binary file instead. QBasic treats a binary file as a sequence of bytes (not characters, as in a sequential file), so you can use a binary file to hold any type of information.

QBasic provides statements and functions to efficiently manage the different file types and their structures. This tutorial summarizes QBasic's file I/O abilities and offers some suggestions for their use. Table 17-1 lists QBasic's file I/O statements and functions in alphabetic order.

Statement or function	Description
CLOSE	Closes an open file or device
CVD	Converts an 8-byte string (created by MKD$) to a double-precision value
CVDMBF	Converts an 8-byte string containing a double-precision value (created by MKDMBF$) from Microsoft Binary format to IEEE format
CVI	Converts a 2-byte string (created by MKI$) to an integer value
CVL	Converts a 4-byte string (created by MKL$) to a long-integer value
CVS	Converts a 4-byte string (created by MKS$) to a single-precision value
CVSMBF	Converts a 4-byte string containing a single-precision value (created by MKSMBF$) from Microsoft Binary format to IEEE format
EOF	Returns −1 (true) when the file pointer is at the end of a file
FIELD	Defines a buffer for a random-access file
FILEATTR	Returns information about a file
FILES	Displays the filename of each file in the current or specified directory
FREEFILE	Returns the next available file number
GET (File I/O)	Reads data from a random-access or binary file
INPUT #	Reads data from a sequential file
INPUT$ (File I/O)	Reads the specified number of bytes from the keyboard or from a file
LINE INPUT #	Reads data from a sequential file

Table 17-1. *(continued)*
QBasic file I/O statements and functions.

Table 17-1. *continued*

Statement or function	Description
LOC	Returns the current location in a file
LOCK	Prevents other programs from accessing a file
LOF	Returns the length of a file in bytes
LSET	Puts data in a random-access file buffer
LTRIM$	Removes blank spaces from the left end of a string
MKD$	Converts a double-precision value to an 8-byte string for output to a random-access file
MKDMBF$	Converts a double-precision value stored in IEEE format to an 8-byte string containing the value in Microsoft Binary format for output to a random-access file
MKI$	Converts an integer value to a 2-byte string for output to a random-access file
MKL$	Converts a long-integer value to a 4-byte string for output to a random-access file
MKS$	Converts a single-precision value to a 4-byte string for output to a random-access file
MKSMBF$	Converts a single-precision value stored in IEEE format to a 4-byte string containing the value in Microsoft Binary format for output to a random-access file
NAME	Renames a file or directory
OPEN	Opens a file
PRINT #	Writes data to a sequential file
PRINT # USING	Writes formatted data to a sequential file
PUT (File I/O)	Writes data to a random-access or binary file
RESET	Closes all files
RSET	Puts data in a random-access file buffer
RTRIM$	Removes blank spaces from the right end of a string
SEEK (Function)	Returns the current location in a file
SEEK (Statement)	Moves to a specified location in a file
UNLOCK	Unlocks a file so other programs can access it
WIDTH (File I/O)	Sets the maximum width of a sequential file
WRITE #	Writes data to a sequential file

Opening a File or Device

QBasic references files by means of a file number. The OPEN statement associates a file with a file number so you can later access the file by specifying that number. If you are not certain which number to use, call the FREEFILE function, which returns the next free file number. The OPEN statement also performs several other functions—it creates a file if the specified file does not exist, sets access modes, manages the file buffer, and manages file access in a multiuser environment.

The access mode specified in an OPEN statement determines the way your program can use the file. Use one of the following keywords to specify the access mode: INPUT, OUTPUT, APPEND, RANDOM, or BINARY.

The keywords INPUT, OUTPUT, and APPEND open a file as a sequential file containing a sequence of characters. Your program can retrieve data from a sequential file only by opening it with INPUT and can write data to a sequential file only by opening it with OUTPUT or APPEND. The OUTPUT keyword specifies that a new sequential file will be created; the APPEND keyword specifies that an existing file will be opened and that data will be added to the end of it.

Using the RANDOM keyword in an OPEN statement opens a file in random-access mode. If you do not specify an access mode, OPEN uses random access by default. Using the BINARY keyword opens a file in binary mode.

A buffer is an area of memory in which a program places data that will be written to the file and data that is read from the file. Because reading information from a disk is a mechanical (and therefore slow) process, QBasic uses the buffer to hold data while the program continues execution. To further speed up program execution, each time a program accesses a disk file by using a read operation, it fills the buffer with data. When the program executes another read operation, the program does not need to access the disk; instead it gets the data from the buffer.

Programs that run on a network can either share files or restrict access to files. The lock clause in the OPEN statement lets you specify the kind of access other programs can have to an open file. Table 17-2 lists QBasic's lock specifications.

Lock clause	Description
(Default)	No other process can open the file.
SHARED	Any process can open the file in any mode.
LOCK READ	No other process can open the file with an ACCESS READ clause; no other process can already have ACCESS READ privileges.
LOCK WRITE	No other process can open the file with an ACCESS WRITE clause; no other process can already have ACCESS WRITE privileges.
LOCK READ WRITE	No other process can open the file with an ACCESS READ WRITE clause; no other process can already have ACCESS READ WRITE privileges.

Table 17-2.
Network-access lock definitions.

In a networking environment, you can specify the kind of access you want by including an ACCESS clause in the OPEN statement. You can choose from ACCESS READ, ACCESS WRITE, and ACCESS READ WRITE for input only, output only, and both input and output access. If another program uses an OPEN statement with a lock clause to open a file, and if your program tries to open the same file by using an OPEN statement with an ACCESS clause specifying the same access as the one specified in the lock clause, your program cannot open the file.

Closing a File or Device

The OPEN statement lets you access a file; the CLOSE statement ends communication with a file and clears all data from the associated buffer space. If the data in the buffer is output from the program, CLOSE writes the data to the file. The CLOSE statement either closes specific files or closes all files at once. The RESET statement, however, always closes all files and clears the file buffers.

Managing Random-Access Files

A random-access file contains a sequence of records that are broken into fields. QBasic's TYPE...END TYPE statement lets you create a user-defined type that specifies a number of fields and then declare record variables of that type. (See the TYPE...END TYPE entry in Chapter 1, "Variables and Types," for details.) Random-access files can contain records defined in this manner.

Early versions of Basic do not support the TYPE...END TYPE statement. With these versions of Basic you must use the FIELD statement to specify the fields of the records in a random-access file. The fields of these records must be strings. Because the FIELD statement allocates space for each field in the buffer that is associated with the file, you must use the LSET and RSET statements to assign values to the fields.

The "L" in LSET stands for left-justify, and the "R" in RSET stands for right-justify. LSET places a value at the left end of a string field and adds spaces to fill the right side of the field. RSET places a value at the right end and adds spaces to the left side of the field.

Because the FIELD statement can define only string fields, Basic provides several functions that convert numbers to strings; corresponding functions convert the strings back into numbers. QBasic supports these functions to maintain compatibility with other versions of Basic. Table 17-3 summarizes the string-conversion functions and number-conversion functions.

Numeric type	From number to string	From string to number
Integer	MKI$	CVI
Long integer	MKL$	CVL
Single precision	MKS$	CVS
MBF* single precision	MKSMBF$	CVSMBF
Double precision	MKD$	CVD
MBF* double precision	MKDMBF$	CVDMBF

*MBF stands for Microsoft Binary format, the numeric format used in GW-BASIC, BASICA, and QuickBASIC versions 3.0 and earlier; subsequent versions of QuickBasic and QBasic use IEEE numeric format.

Table 17-3.
QBasic string-conversion and number-conversion functions.

The conversion functions MKSMBF$ and MKDMBF$ convert numbers in IEEE format to strings containing numbers in Microsoft Binary format. The functions CVSMBF and CVDMBF convert strings containing numbers in Microsoft Binary format to numbers in IEEE format. These functions let you access files created by earlier versions of BASIC that support only the Microsoft Binary format.

For example, if your program includes a field named *pastDueAmount$* that was defined in a FIELD statement, you might use the following statements to write a numeric value to the disk file:

```
LSET pastDueAmount$ = MKD$(169.85)
PUT #1
```

The MKD$ function converts the number 169.85 into a string, and LSET places the string in the *pastDueAmount$* field, which can then be written to the file. The PUT statement writes the current record to the disk file.

To read the value of this field from the file, you can use the following statements:

```
GET #1
pastDueAmt# = CVD(pastDueAmount$)
```

The GET statement retrieves a record from the disk. *pastDueAmt#* is a double-precision variable, and the CVD function converts *pastDueAmount$* from a string back into a double-precision value.

Reading Data from Random-Access or Binary Files

You use the GET statement to read records from random-access and binary files. You specify in the GET statement both the record number (the byte number in a binary file) and the variable to be read. For example, to read the first record of a random-access file whose file number is 3 and assign it to the record variable *info*, you use the statement

```
GET #3, 1, info
```

Reading data from a binary file is just as simple. The following statement begins reading at byte number 129 in a binary file whose file number is 2 and assigns the value it reads to a variable named *invoices*:

```
GET #2, 129, invoices
```

When you define a record by using a FIELD statement and then you read that record from a random-access file, you cannot specify a record variable in the GET statement that will be assigned the values. When no record variable is specified, GET retrieves a record and places it in the file buffer. You must then use an INPUT #, LINE INPUT #, or PRINT # statement after the GET statement to read the values from the file buffer. Using record variables is much more convenient than working with the FIELD statement. If your version of Basic supports the TYPE...END TYPE statement, be sure to use it when you work with random-access files.

You can also use the INPUT$ function to read values from a random-access or binary file. The INPUT$ function reads the specified number of characters in a file. The maximum number of characters is the length of a record in a random-access file or 32,767 bytes in a binary file.

Writing Data to Random-Access or Binary Files

You use the PUT statement to write records to random-access and binary files. You specify in the PUT statement both the record number (the byte number in a binary file) and the variable to be written. For example, to write the values contained in the record variable *info* to record 31 of the random-access file whose file number is 1, you use the statement

```
PUT #1, 31, info
```

Writing to a binary file is also a simple operation. The following statement writes the contents of the variable *inventory* to a binary file whose file number is 12, beginning at byte number 1537:

```
PUT #12, 1537, inventory
```

When you write a record defined by a FIELD statement, you do not specify a variable in the PUT statement. If no variable is specified, the PUT statement writes to the file any values placed in the file buffer by LSET or RSET statements.

Reading Data from Sequential Files

You can use one of two statements or a function to read sequential files—INPUT #, LINE INPUT #, and INPUT$. Generally, you use the INPUT # statement to read numbers from a sequential file and the LINE INPUT # statement to read an entire line of text. The INPUT$ function reads the specified number of characters from a sequential file.

The INPUT # statement reads data from a sequential file until it reaches a delimiter—a space, comma, carriage return, or linefeed. (See the INPUT # entry for an explanation of the usage of delimiters in this statement.) The following statement, for example, uses the INPUT # statement to read a string variable and an integer variable from the file whose file number is 3:

```
INPUT #3, studentName$, grade%
```

The LINE INPUT # statement is more flexible because it recognizes only one delimiter—the carriage return and linefeed pair. Therefore, LINE INPUT # can read an entire line into a variable and include any delimiters in that line. A single LINE INPUT # statement, however, cannot read multiple lines. Also, LINE INPUT # can assign the data from the file only to a string variable, not to a numeric one. (See the LINE INPUT # entry for a description of the usage of delimiters in this statement.) The following statement illustrates how you might use the LINE INPUT # statement. It reads a line from the file whose file number is 5 and assigns it to the variable *code$*:

```
LINE INPUT #5, code$
```

The INPUT$ function reads a specified number of characters from a sequential file. You cannot specify more than 32,767 characters. You also must not specify more characters than are in the file. The INPUT$ function, unlike INPUT # and LINE INPUT #, recognizes no delimiters; you can read *any* character by using INPUT$. The following statement demonstrates the use of the INPUT$ function. It reads one character from the file whose file number is 3 and assigns the character to the variable *character$*:

```
character$ = INPUT$(1, #3)
```

Writing Data to Sequential Files

The PRINT # statement is the most commonly used statement for writing sequential output. It works much like the PRINT statement, which displays output on the screen. (See Figures 17-7 and 17-8 in the PRINT # entry for examples of the output of this statement.) For example, the following statement writes the number 123.15 to the file whose file number is 1:

```
PRINT #1, 123.15
```

The WRITE # statement is similar to the PRINT # statement, but it places a comma between expressions in the file and includes sets of quotation marks around string variables. The punctuation enables the INPUT # statement to read the file more easily. (See the INPUT # entry.) For example, the statement

```
WRITE #1, "DOE, JOHN", 012170, 150.25
```

writes to the file corresponding to file number 1 the following output (including all punctuation):

```
"DOE, JOHN",12170,150.25
```

Removing Blank Spaces from Strings

If a string includes spaces on either end (as happens when you use the LSET or RSET statement for random-access files), you can use the LTRIM$ or RTRIM$ function to remove them. For example, if you use one variable for a person's first name and another for his or her last name, and if you are creating forms in which the first and last names appear together, remove the extra spaces from the right end of the string that contains the person's first name. To do so, you might use the following statement:

```
PRINT #checks, "Pay to the order of "; RTRIM$(firstName$); " "; lastName$
```

If you want to remove the spaces from both ends of a string, you can use both the LTRIM$ and RTRIM$ functions, as shown in the following statement:

```
patient$ = LTRIM$(RTRIM$(patient$))
```

Moving Within a File

For every open file, QBasic maintains a pointer that indicates a location in the file. Any input or output that the program performs begins at this location unless you specify another location in the input or output statement. You can move the file pointer to any location in the file by calling the SEEK statement. If you use SEEK for a random-access file, you specify the number of the record to which you want to move the pointer. On the other hand, if you use SEEK for a sequential or binary file, you specify the number of the byte to which you want the pointer to move. For example, to position the pointer at record 256 of a random-access file whose file number is 17, you would use the following statement:

```
SEEK #17, 256
```

Determining File Characteristics

Although QBasic shields you from having to know the low-level details about files, it does let you access some of that information. The FILEATTR function, for example, returns the mode (INPUT, OUTPUT, APPEND, RANDOM, or BINARY) in which a file was opened; it can also be used to return the DOS file handle for that file. DOS uses the DOS file handle number to access the file, just as QBasic uses the file number; you probably need to know the file handle number only if you are using routines written in assembly language in your QBasic programs.

The EOF function tests to see whether the file pointer is positioned at the end of a file. You can use this function in a loop that reads the entire contents of a file, as shown in the following example.

```
DEFINT A-Z

fileNum = FREEFILE
OPEN "REPORT.RPT" FOR INPUT AS #fileNum

DO UNTIL EOF(fileNum)
    LINE INPUT #fileNum, text$
    LPRINT text$
LOOP

CLOSE
```

The LOF function returns the size of a file, in bytes. You can use LOF to calculate the number of records in a specified random-access file by using the following formula:

$$numRecords = \text{LOF}(file) \setminus recordLength \qquad \text{' note integer division}$$

QBasic also provides the LOC and SEEK functions. The LOC function returns the number of the record that was most recently written or read, for a random-access file; the current byte number divided by 128, for a sequential file; or the byte position of the last byte read or written, for a binary file. The SEEK function, however, returns the position of the *next* record that will be written or read, for a random-access file, or the byte position of the next byte to be written or read, for a sequential or binary file.

Managing Files on Disk

QBasic includes several statements that help you manage files. Chapter 18, "DOS and Program Management," discusses additional statements that manage files and directories.

The QBasic FILES statement displays a listing of the current or specified directory. It is similar to the DOS DIR /W command, which displays filenames in several columns across the screen. You can use the FILES statement to let the user see which data files are available.

The NAME statement changes the name of an existing file, much as the DOS command RENAME does. The NAME statement is more powerful than RENAME, however, because you can also use it to move files between directories on a disk. For example, the following statement moves a file to the REPORTS directory and changes its name to REPORT01.RPT.

```
NAME "C:\ACCT\REPORT.RPT" AS "C:\REPORTS\REPORT01.RPT"
```

Locking and Unlocking Files

When programs are used on a local area network, conflicts can arise if several programs try to access the same file. DOS versions 3.1 and later support file locking and record locking. If you lock a file or record, only your program can access the file or record. If another program wants access to a locked file or record, it must wait until your program unlocks the file or record.

QBasic provides the LOCK and UNLOCK statements to manage locking. The LOCK statement can lock an entire file or merely a portion of it. The UNLOCK statement complements the LOCK statement and must be used to release the lock.

Note that Microsoft guarantees support for QBasic only on the Microsoft LAN Manager, IBM PC Network, MS-Network systems, and compatible systems. Although limited success has been reported using some other networks, such as Novell and 3Com, problems can occur. If much of your programming is for networks other than those supported by Microsoft, you might consider using a third-party file manager that supports them.

Setting the Maximum
Width for Sequential Files

If you are creating sequential files to be printed on a printer that uses narrow paper, you must limit the width of each line in the file so that it will fit within the paper's margins. You can do this by using the WIDTH (File I/O) statement. When used with a file number, WIDTH limits lines to a specified width. Long lines are wrapped to the next line of the file when they exceed the specified width. This saves you the work of calculating maximum widths yourself.

Related Reading

Dettmann, Terry. *DOS Programmer's Reference.* Indianapolis, Ind.: Que, 1988.

Duncan, Ray, et al. *The MS-DOS Encyclopedia.* Redmond, Wash.: Microsoft Press, 1988.

Norton, Peter, and Richard Wilton. *The* New *Peter Norton Programmer's Guide to the IBM PC & PS/2.* Redmond, Wash.: Microsoft Press, 1988.

Prata, Stephen, with Harry Henderson. *The Waite Group's Microsoft QuickBASIC Primer Plus.* Redmond, Wash.: Microsoft Press, 1990.

The Waite Group. *MS-DOS Developer's Guide,* 2d ed. Indianapolis, Ind.: Howard Sams & Co., 1989.

The Waite Group. *Using PC DOS.* Indianapolis, Ind.: Howard Sams & Co., 1989.

CLOSE

See also

OPEN

Purpose

The CLOSE statement closes an open file or device. Use CLOSE after you conclude all input and output operations with a file or device.

Syntax

CLOSE [[#] *filenum*[, [#] *filenum*]...]

filenum is the file number associated with an open file.

Usage

```
CLOSE
```

Closes all open files and devices.

```
CLOSE 5, #15
```

Closes the files or devices that were opened as file numbers 5 and 15. Note that the number sign is optional.

Description

The CLOSE statement lets you close a file you previously opened with an OPEN statement. The OPEN statement allocates buffer space for the records in a file. The CLOSE statement writes any data remaining in the buffer space to the appropriate file or device and then releases the memory space reserved for the buffer. Using a CLOSE statement with no parameters closes all open files and devices.

After you close a file, you cannot reference it with another I/O statement until you specify the file in another OPEN statement. When you close a file, you can use the file number associated with that file when you reopen it or open any other file. That is, any closed file can be reopened under any unused file number.

When a program executes its last statement or executes a CLEAR, END, RESET, RUN, or SYSTEM statement, QBasic closes all open files and devices. Still, good programming practice dictates that you issue a CLOSE statement at the end of your program.

Comments

Closing a file that has not been opened will not cause an error.

Warnings

All fields defined by a FIELD statement are set to null strings after you close a file. If you want to save the contents of the fields, you must assign them to variables.

Example

The following program opens a sequential file and the printer device, writes the date and time to both, and then closes them.

```
OPEN "REPORT.TXT" FOR OUTPUT AS #5      ' open a sequential file for output
OPEN "LPT1:" FOR OUTPUT AS #6           ' open the printer device

PRINT #5, "Today's date is "; DATE$     ' write the date to the file
PRINT #5, "and the time is "; TIME$     ' write the time to the file

PRINT #6, "Today's date is "; DATE$     ' write the date to the printer
PRINT #6, "and the time is "; TIME$     ' write the time to the printer
PRINT #6, CHR$(12)                      ' write a formfeed to the printer

CLOSE #5, #6                            ' close the file and the device
```

CVD

See also

CVDMBF, DOUBLE, FIELD, MKD$, MKDMBF$

Purpose

The CVD function converts an 8-byte string returned by the MKD$ function to its double-precision numeric value. You use the CVD function after reading the string representation of a double-precision number in a random-access file that contains records defined by the FIELD statement.

Syntax

CVD(*string*)

string is an 8-byte string variable created by the MKD$ function.

Usage

```
past# = CVD(pastDue$)
```

Assigns the double-precision value contained in the string variable *pastDue$* to the variable *past#*.

Description

The CVD function converts an 8-byte string to its double-precision numeric value. The string that CVD converts must be contained in a string variable that was created by the MKD$ function.

Comments

If you specify the command-line switch /MBF, QBasic assumes that the string parameter to the CVD function is a number in Microsoft Binary format. (See the CVDMBF entry for details.) Otherwise, QBasic assumes that the string parameter in the CVD function contains a double-precision number in IEEE format.

Example

The following program converts values into strings, writes the strings to the random-access file SOL.DAT, and then converts each string stored in the file to a numeric value. The file contains information about the solar system, including the planet name, its diameter, its perihelion and aphelion, its highest and lowest temperatures, and the year in which it was discovered. (The perihelion of an orbit is the closest distance from the planet to the sun. The aphelion is the farthest distance from the planet to the sun.)

The program first lets you choose the number of the record that you want the program to read from the file. The program uses the functions CVL, CVD, CVDMBF, CVS, CVSMBF, and CVI to display the values of the record's fields. The program then uses the functions MKL$, MKD$, MKDMBF$, MKS$, MKSMBF$, and MKI$ to prepare new field values to write to the file.

```
OPEN "SOL.DAT" FOR RANDOM AS #1 LEN = 45
FIELD #1, 15 AS name$, 4 AS diameter$, 8 AS perihelion$, 8 AS aphelion$
FIELD #1, 35 AS dummy$, 4 AS highTemp$, 4 AS lowTemp$, 2 AS yearDiscovered$


CLS
INPUT "Information about which planet"; planetNum%
GET #1, planetNum%

PRINT "The diameter of planet "; RTRIM$(name$); " is";
PRINT CVL(diameter$); "kilometers"
PRINT "The perihelion of planet "; RTRIM$(name$); " is";
PRINT CVD(perihelion$); "kilometers"
PRINT "The aphelion of planet "; RTRIM$(name$); " is";
PRINT CVDMBF(aphelion$); "kilometers"
PRINT "The highest temperature of planet "; RTRIM$(name$); " is";
PRINT CVS(highTemp$); "degrees"
PRINT "The lowest temperature of planet "; RTRIM$(name$); " is";
PRINT CVSMBF(lowTemp$); "degrees"
PRINT "The planet was discovered in"; CVI(yearDiscovered$)
PRINT


INPUT "Do you want to change the record [Y/N] ", response$
IF UCASE$(response$) = "Y" THEN
    INPUT "Name: ", newName$
    INPUT "Diameter: ", newDiameter&
    INPUT "Perihelion: ", newPerihelion#
    INPUT "Aphelion: ", newAphelion#
    INPUT "Highest temperature: ", newHighTemp!
    INPUT "Lowest temperature: ", newLowTemp!
    INPUT "Year of discovery: ", newYear%
```

(continued)

continued

```
      LSET name$ = newName$
      LSET diameter$ = MKL$(newDiameter&)
      LSET perihelion$ = MKD$(newPerihelion#)
      LSET aphelion$ = MKDMBF$(newAphelion#)
      LSET highTemp$ = MKS$(newHighTemp!)
      LSET lowTemp$ = MKSMBF$(newLowTemp!)
      LSET yearDiscovered$ = MKI$(newYear%)
      PUT #1, planetNum%
   END IF

   CLOSE #1
```

CVDMBF

See also

CVD, DOUBLE, FIELD, MKD$, MKDMBF$

Purpose

The CVDMBF function converts an 8-byte string containing a value in Microsoft Binary format to its double-precision numeric value in IEEE format. You use the CVDMBF function after reading the string representation of a double-precision number in a random-access file that contains strings in Microsoft Binary format; the file must contain records defined by the FIELD statement.

Syntax

CVDMBF(*string*)

string is an 8-byte string variable created by the MKDMBF$ function or by the MKD$ function in a version of Basic that supports only the Microsoft Binary format.

Usage

```
past# = CVDMBF(pastDue$)
```

Assigns the double-precision value contained in the string variable *pastDue$* to the variable *past#*.

Description

The CVDMBF function converts an 8-byte string to its double-precision numeric value in IEEE format. The string that CVDMBF converts must be contained in a string variable that was created either by the MKD$ function in a version of Basic that supports only the Microsoft Binary format or by the MKDMBF$ function.

Comments

QBasic assumes that the string parameter in the CVDMBF function is a number in Microsoft Binary format.

Example

See the "Example" section in the CVD entry.

CVI

See also

FIELD, INTEGER, MKI$

Purpose

The CVI function converts a 2-byte string returned by the MKI$ function to its integer numeric value. You use the CVI function after reading the string representation of an integer in a random-access file that contains records defined by the FIELD statement.

Syntax

CVI(*string*)

string is a 2-byte string variable created by the MKI$ function.

Usage

```
acct% = CVI(acctNum$)
```

Assigns the integer value contained in the string variable *acctNum$* to the variable *acct%*.

Description

The CVI function converts a 2-byte string to its integer value. The string that CVI converts must be contained in a string variable or expression that was created by the MKI$ function.

Example

See the "Example" section in the CVD entry.

CVL

See also

FIELD, LONG, MKL$

Purpose

The CVL function converts a 4-byte string returned by the MKL$ function to its long-integer numeric value. You use the CVL function after reading the string representation of a long-integer number in a random-access file that contains records defined by the FIELD statement.

Syntax

CVL(*string*)

string is a 4-byte string variable created by the MKL$ function.

Usage

```
serial& = CVL(serialNum$)
```

Assigns the long-integer value contained in the string variable *serialNum$* to the variable *serial&*.

Description

The CVL function converts a 4-byte string to its long-integer value. The string that CVL converts must be a string variable that was created by the MKL$ function.

Example

See the "Example" section in the CVD entry.

CVS

See also

CVSMBF, FIELD, MKS$, MKSMBF$

Purpose

The CVS function converts a 4-byte string returned by the MKS$ function to its single-precision numeric value. You use the CVS function after reading the string representation of a single-precision number in a random-access file that contains records defined by the FIELD statement.

Syntax

CVS(*string*)

string is a 4-byte string variable created by the MKS$ function.

Usage

```
past! = CVS(pastDue$)
```

Assigns the single-precision value contained in the string variable *pastDue$* to the variable *past!*.

Description

The CVS function converts a 4-byte string to its single-precision numeric value. The string that CVS converts must be contained in a string variable that was created by the MKS$ function.

Comments

If you specify the command-line option /MBF, QBasic assumes that the string parameter to the CVS function is a number in Microsoft Binary format. (See the CVSMBF entry for details.) Otherwise, QBasic assumes that the string parameter in the CVS function contains a single-precision number in IEEE format.

Example

See the "Example" section in the CVD entry.

CVSMBF

See also

CVS, FIELD, MKS$, MKSMBF$, SINGLE

Purpose

The CVSMBF function converts a 4-byte string containing a value in Microsoft Binary format to its single-precision numeric value in IEEE format. You use the CVSMBF function after reading the string representation of a single-precision number in a random-access file that contains strings in Microsoft Binary format; the file must contain records defined by the FIELD statement.

Syntax

CVSMBF(*string*)

string is a 4-byte string variable created by the MKSMBF$ function or by the MKS$ function in a version of Basic that supports only the Microsoft Binary format.

Usage

```
past! = CVSMBF(pastDue$)
```

Assigns the single-precision value contained in the string variable *pastDue$* to the variable *past!*.

Description

The CVSMBF function converts a 4-byte string to its single-precision numeric value in IEEE format. The string that CVSMBF converts must be contained in a string variable that was created either by the MKS$ function in a version of Basic that supports only the Microsoft Binary format or by the MKSMBF$ function.

Comments

QBasic assumes that the string parameter in the CVSMBF function is a number in Microsoft Binary format.

Example

See the "Example" section in the CVD entry.

EOF

See also

LOC, LOF, SEEK

Purpose

The EOF function returns −1 (true) if the file pointer is positioned at the end of a file; it returns 0 (false) if the file contains information past the location of the file pointer. You use EOF to decide whether to continue processing a file.

Syntax

EOF(*filenum*)

filenum is the file number associated with an open file.

Usage

```
IF EOF(1) THEN GOTO EndOfJob
```

Branches execution to the line labeled *EndOfJob* if the file pointer is at the end of the file associated with file number 1.

Description

When processing the contents of a file, you need to know when to stop processing because the program has reached the end of the file. For sequential files, EOF returns −1 (true) when the most recent input statement reaches the end of the file. For random-access and binary files, the EOF function returns −1 (true) only if the most recent GET statement couldn't read an entire record. If GET cannot read an entire record, you specified in the GET statement a record number that was beyond the end of the file.

The QBasic devices SCRN:, KYBD:, CONS:, and LPT*n*: have no logical end of file.

EOF performs differently if the specified file number is the file associated with a communications device (COM1: or COM2:) and if the COM*n*: device was opened in ASCII or binary mode. When you use COM1: or COM2: in ASCII communications mode, the EOF function returns −1 (true) only after it reads a Ctrl-Z character (ASCII code 26). EOF then continues to return −1 until the file is closed. In binary communications mode, the EOF function returns −1 when the input queue is empty; otherwise, it returns 0 (false). (See the LOC entry for details about communication input queues.)

Errors

Unlike most QBasic file I/O statements, EOF does not accept a number sign (#) with the file number. If you precede the number with #, QBasic displays an "Expected: expression" error message.

If you use EOF with a file number that has not been specified by an OPEN statement, QBasic displays a "Bad file name or number" error message.

Example

The following program uses EOF to merge the lines of two sequential files into a third file. The resulting file contains (in order) the first line from file #1, the first line from file #2, the second line from file #1, and so on.

```
OPEN "FIRST" FOR INPUT AS #1      ' open the first source file
OPEN "SECOND" FOR INPUT AS #2     ' open the second source file
OPEN "THIRD" FOR OUTPUT AS #3     ' open the destination file

DO
    IF NOT EOF(1) THEN            ' check whether at the end of the file
        LINE INPUT #1, first$     ' get a line of text
        PRINT #3, first$          ' write the line to the destination file
    END IF

    IF NOT EOF(2) THEN            ' check whether at the end of the file
        LINE INPUT #2, second$    ' get a line of text
        PRINT #3, second$         ' write the line to the destination file
    END IF
LOOP UNTIL EOF(1) AND EOF(2)      ' repeat until both files have been read

CLOSE 1, 2, 3
```

FIELD

See also

CLOSE, GET (File I/O), LSET, OPEN, PUT, RSET

Purpose

The FIELD statement defines the structure of records to be used in a random-access file. If possible, however, use the TYPE…END TYPE structure to define the structure of records in a random-access file.

Syntax

FIELD [#] *filenum*, *width* AS *var*[, *width AS var* …]

filenum is the file number assigned to a file in an OPEN statement. It can be preceded by a number sign (#).

width is the size, in bytes, of *var*.

var is a field that will contain a string to be written to or read from the file.

Usage

```
OPEN "CUSTOMER.DAT" FOR RANDOM AS #1 LEN = 200
FIELD #1, 32 AS custName$, 32 AS custAddress$, 32 AS custCityStZip$
```

Opens a file named CUSTOMER.DAT and defines a record that contains three fields, each of which contains a 32-character string.

Description

Each record in a random-access file can consist of many different fields. A field is a location in a record that can be accessed by a field name. The records defined by the FIELD statement are analogous to the structures defined by the TYPE...END TYPE statement.

You can specify a single file number in multiple FIELD statements. This approach lets different variables share the same data in a record at the same time. Because a FIELD statement defines the record structure for a file, using more than one FIELD statement lets you define a record whose FIELD statement would be too long for a single line. Consider the following example:

```
FIELD #1, 10 AS firstName$, 20 AS lastName$
FIELD #1, 30 AS dummy$, 6 AS birthDate$ ' 30=sum of previous line's widths
FIELD #1, 36 AS dummy$, 32 AS address$  ' 36=sum of prevoius line's widths
```

When these statements specify *dummy$* as a field, they assign to the variable the number of bytes used in the previous FIELD statements. These FIELD statements perform the same task as the following single statement:

```
FIELD #1, 10 AS firstName$, 20 AS lastName$, 6 AS birthDate$, 32 AS address$
```

When you define fields in a FIELD statement, QBasic positions them within the file buffer's memory space. Because fields are not regular QBasic variables, you must use them with caution. QBasic frees a file's buffer space when you close the file, so fields defined in FIELD statements become undefined after the file is closed. Also, fields defined in FIELD statements cannot be used in the INPUT, LINE INPUT, or variable-assignment (*field = value*) statements because these statements relocate the field's pointer into normal string space so that the field becomes a regular variable. You can, however, safely reference variables defined in FIELD statements in an arithmetic or logical expression.

Comments

The FIELD statement can define only fields that are variable-length strings; to use numeric variables, you must perform extra steps to convert the numbers to their string equivalents and then back to numbers again. The functions MKD$, MKDMBF$, MKI$, MKL$, MKS$, and MKSMBF$ convert numbers to strings, and the functions CVD, CVDMBF, CVI, CVL, CVS, and CVSMBF convert these strings back to numbers. Using the TYPE...END TYPE statement to define a record eliminates the need to perform this complicated procedure.

Errors

The sum of sizes of the fields defined in a FIELD statement must not exceed the record length specified in the LEN clause when you opened the file. If it does, QBasic displays a "Field overflow" error message.

Example

The following program uses two random-access files that include records defined by FIELD statements. It copies data from an old file into a new file that uses a different record structure.

```
OPEN "PATIENTS.OLD" FOR RANDOM AS #1 LEN = 128
FIELD #1, 25 AS oldPatientName$, 25 AS oldInsuredsName$

OPEN "PATIENTS.NEW" FOR RANDOM AS #2 LEN = 256
FIELD #2, 32 AS newPatientName$, 32 AS newInsuredsName$

IF LOF(1) > 0 THEN
    FOR recNum% = 1 TO LOF(1) \ 128              ' note integer division
        GET #1, recNum%
        LSET newPatientName$ = oldPatientName$    ' assign information from
        LSET newInsuredsName$ = oldInsuredsName$  ' the old file to the new one
        PUT #2, recNum%
    NEXT

    PRINT "Conversion complete."
ELSE
    PRINT "You have no records in PATIENTS.OLD to convert."
END IF

CLOSE
```

FILEATTR

See also

OPEN

Purpose

The FILEATTR function returns either the file mode or the DOS file handle of an open file. You can use FILEATTR, for example, to determine whether a file is read only so that if it is, your program doesn't attempt to write to it.

Syntax

FILEATTR(*filenum*, *attribute*)

filenum is the file number assigned to a file in an OPEN statement.

attribute can be 1 or 2. If it is 1, FILEATTR returns information about the mode in which the file was opened; if it is 2, FILEATTR returns the file's DOS file handle.

Usage

```
OPEN "INFO.TXT" FOR INPUT AS #1
PRINT "The file mode of INFO.TXT is"; FILEATTR(1, 1)
```

Displays the number 1, which indicates that the file was opened in input mode.

Description

The file number you use to open a file in QBasic is not directly related to the DOS file-accessing number—the file handle. However, some assembly-language subroutines require you to supply the file handle, and FILEATTR lets you obtain this information. FILEATTR can also provide information for programs that need the mode of the file to determine what type of I/O they can perform.

To obtain the mode in which the file was opened, use the number 1 as the second parameter to FILEATTR. For example,

```
fileMode% = FILEATTR(4, 1)
```

returns the value that indicates the mode for the file opened as file number 4. The value that FILEATTR returns will be one of those listed in Table 17-4. For example, if *fileMode%* was assigned the value 32 in the above statement, the file was originally opened as a binary file.

Returned value	File mode
1	Input
2	Output
4	Random
8	Append
32	Binary

Table 17-4.
Values returned by FILEATTR.

To obtain the DOS file handle, use the number 2 as the second parameter to FILEATTR. For example,

```
fileHandle% = FILEATTR(4, 2)
```

returns the DOS file handle for the file opened as file number 4.

Errors

Unlike most QBasic file I/O statements, FILEATTR does not accept a number sign (#) with the file number. If you precede the number with a number sign, QBasic displays an "Expected: expression" error message.

If you use FILEATTR with a file number that has not been specified by an OPEN statement, QBasic displays a "Bad file name or number" error message.

Example

The following program uses the FILEATTR function to determine a file's DOS file handle and file mode.

```
CLS
OPEN "GARFIELD.DAT" FOR APPEND AS #7

fileMode% = FILEATTR(7, 1)
fileHandle% = FILEATTR(7, 2)

PRINT "GARFIELD.DAT has DOS file handle"; fileHandle%; "and was opened as a ";

SELECT CASE fileMode%
    CASE 1
        PRINT "sequential file for input.";
    CASE 2
        PRINT "sequential file for output.";
    CASE 4
        PRINT "random-access file for input or output.";
    CASE 8
        PRINT "sequential file for appending.";
    CASE 32
        PRINT "binary file for input or output.";
END SELECT

CLOSE
```

FILES

See also

CHDIR

Purpose

The FILES statement displays names of files that match a given file specification. You use FILES to display all or some of the files in the current directory or in a specified directory.

Syntax

FILES [*filespec*]

filespec is a string expression that specifies the files you want to display. *filespec* can contain a drive name, pathname, and filename; the filename can include the ? and * wildcard characters.

Usage

FILES

Displays the filenames of all files in the current directory (on the current drive).

FILES "C:\BIN*.*"

Displays the filenames of all files in the directory BIN on drive C.

Description

The FILES statement is similar to the DOS command DIR /W. It displays in a columnar format the names of either all files in the current directory or the specified files. For example, if you place all the example programs in this chapter in the CHAP17 directory on drive C, the statement FILES "C:\CHAP17*.*" displays the following:

```
C:\CHAP17
         .   <DIR>          ..  <DIR> CLOSE    .BAS      CVD      .BAS
EOF     .BAS      FIELD    .BAS      FILEATTR.BAS      FILES    .BAS
FREELINE.BAS      GET      .BAS      INPUT#   .BAS      INPUT$   .BAS
LINEINPT.BAS      LOC      .BAS      LOCK     .BAS      LOF      .BAS
LTRIM$  .BAS      NAME     .BAS      OPEN     .BAS      PRINT#   .BAS
PRT#USNG.BAS      PUT      .BAS      RESET    .BAS      RSET     .BAS
RTRIM$  .BAS      SEEK(FN).BAS      SEEK(ST).BAS      UNLOCK   .BAS
WIDTH   .BAS      WRITE#   .BAS
 19511296 Bytes free
```

The file-specification parameter is an optional string expression that specifies the files you want to display. It can contain a drive name, pathname, and filename; the filename can contain the ? and * wildcard characters. In DOS, filenames can have no more than eight characters for a name, a period, and three characters for an extension. The wildcard character ? matches any character in the same position in the filename, and the wildcard character * matches one or more characters beginning in the same position in the filename.

If you omit the drive name from the file specification, the FILES statement uses the current drive. If you omit the pathname, FILES uses the current directory. If you omit the file specification altogether, FILES displays all files in the current directory on the current drive.

Unlike the DOS DIR /W command, the FILES statement displays a one-line header that contains the current directory even if you specify another pathname in the FILES statement. After FILES lists all filenames that match the specification, it displays a line containing the number of free bytes that remain on the specified drive.

Comments

You can use wildcards only in the filename of the file specification. QBasic doesn't recognize wildcards in the drive name or pathname.

If a listing contains more than a single screen of filenames, the FILES statement scrolls the first names off the top of the screen.

Errors

If the file specification matches no files, QBasic displays a "File not found" error message. If you specify the letter of an external drive that does not contain a disk, QBasic displays a "Disk not ready" error message. If you specify a disk drive that does not exist, QBasic displays a "Device unavailable" error message.

Example

The following program uses the FILES statement to display a listing of the directory and drive the user specifies. It also performs error trapping so that if a user enters a file specification incorrectly the program does not end.

```
ON ERROR GOTO CheckError

DO
    PRINT "Enter a drive name, pathname, and file specification"
    PRINT "(file specification may include wildcards)"
    PRINT
    LINE INPUT fileSpec$

    IF fileSpec$ = "" THEN EXIT DO

    PRINT
    FILES fileSpec$
    PRINT
LOOP UNTIL fileSpec$ = ""
END

' perform error handling of user input
CheckError:
    numError% = ERR
    SELECT CASE numError%
        CASE 53
            PRINT "The file does not exist."
            RESUME NEXT
        CASE 64
            PRINT "The filename is in the wrong format."
            RESUME NEXT
        CASE 68
            PRINT "The device is unavailable."
            RESUME NEXT
        CASE 71
            PRINT "The drive does not have a disk in it."
            RESUME NEXT
        CASE ELSE
            ON ERROR GOTO 0       ' disable error handling for any other errors
    END SELECT
```

FREEFILE

See also

OPEN

Purpose

The FREEFILE function returns the lowest file number that is not associated with an open file. You use FREEFILE when you need to open a file and you don't know which file numbers are available.

Syntax

FREEFILE

Usage

```
filenum% = FREEFILE
OPEN "CONFIG.DAT" FOR RANDOM AS #filenum%
```

Opens a file and assigns the next available file number to it.

Description

You must access a QBasic file by using a file number in the range 1 through 255; however, you cannot specify a file number that has already been assigned a file in an OPEN statement. FREEFILE solves this problem by returning the lowest available file number (in the range 1 through 255). Simply assign the value FREEFILE returns to a numeric variable, and use that variable in subsequent OPEN, CLOSE, and other I/O statements.

Warnings

QBasic allows no more than 15 files to be open at once. If you try to open a 16th file, QBasic displays a "Too many files" error message.

Example

The following program uses the FREEFILE function to assign file numbers to five data files.

```
OPEN "BUFF1.DAT" FOR OUTPUT AS #1

FOR i% = 1 TO 5
    fileNum% = FREEFILE
    fileName$ = "BUFF" + MID$(STR$(fileNum%), 2) + ".DAT"
    OPEN fileName$ FOR OUTPUT AS #fileNum%
    PRINT fileName$
NEXT i%
CLOSE
```

GET (File I/O)

See also

FIELD, INPUT #, LINE INPUT #, OPEN, PUT (File I/O), TYPE...END TYPE

Purpose

The GET statement reads information from a random-access or binary file into the fields defined by a FIELD statement or into a record variable defined by a TYPE...END TYPE statement.

Syntax

GET [#] *filenum*[, [*position*][, *variable*]]

filenum is the file number assigned to a file in an OPEN statement.

position is the number of the record (in random-access files) or byte (in binary files) at which the program begins reading data. The number is in the range 1 through 2147483647.

variable is the variable that receives the data from the file.

Usage

```
GET #1, 1
```

Retrieves the first record in a random-access file that contains records defined by a FIELD statement.

```
GET #1, , info
```

Retrieves the next record (if one exists) in a random-access file and assigns it to the record variable *info*.

Description

With random-access and binary files, you must use GET to read from the file.

When you use GET with a random-access file, you can specify the number of the record to be read. Each record consists of as many bytes as the record length that was specified in the LEN clause of the OPEN statement for that file. The first record number in a file is record number 1. If you do not specify a record number, GET reads the record that follows the record used in the most recent GET or PUT operation or that was specified in the most recent SEEK statement.

When you use GET with a binary file, you can specify the number of the byte at which reading begins. The first byte in a file is byte number 1. If you do not specify a byte number, GET reads the byte that follows those used in the most recent GET or PUT operation or that was specified in the most recent SEEK statement.

When you use GET with a random-access file containing records defined by a TYPE...END TYPE statement, you can specify any variable whose size in bytes is no larger than the record length specified when the file was opened. The GET statement reads the data into this variable. For example, if the variable is a long integer, the GET statement reads 4 bytes from the file into the variable. You will most often specify a record variable whose structure matches the structure of the file's records.

You cannot use a variable in a GET statement if the records in the file were defined by a FIELD statement. QBasic displays a "FIELD statement active" error message if you specify a variable. If you do not specify a variable, GET assumes that the records contained in the file were defined by a FIELD statement. After calling GET, you can access the values that were read by using the field names in an output statement or by reading the values into other variables with an INPUT # or LINE INPUT # statement.

When you use GET with a binary file, you can specify a variable of any type and length. As long as there are enough bytes in the file, GET reads as many bytes as necessary to fill the variable.

When you specify a variable-length string variable in a GET statement, GET reads only the number of characters already in the variable. For example, if you use a string variable that has five characters, GET reads five characters into the variable, overwriting the original characters.

The largest possible string or record-variable size is 32,767 bytes. Therefore, 32,767 bytes is also the largest possible size for each record in a file and for the variable that QBasic accepts for the GET statement from a random-access or binary file.

Tips

If you specify a record or byte number beyond the end of the file, QBasic does not return an error message as it would with other file I/O statements, such as INPUT # and LINE INPUT #. If you specify a record or byte that is beyond the end of a random-access or binary file, GET either fills the specified variable with blank spaces or sets it to 0. You must use EOF or LOF to explicitly test whether the program has reached the end of the file.

Warning

Although GET and the PUT statement allow fixed-length access from a file opened as a communications device, a communications failure causes GET to wait indefinitely for characters. Instead, use the INPUT # statement or the INPUT$ function to read data from a communications device.

Example

The following program creates a record variable that stores the color choices used in a program. This example uses PUT to store and GET to retrieve the variable from a configuration file.

```
CLS
TYPE ConfigType
    normal AS INTEGER                 ' color of box internal area
    highlight AS INTEGER              ' color of letter highlight
    inverseHighlight AS INTEGER       ' color of the inverse of letter highlight
    inverse AS INTEGER                ' color of highlight bar
    help AS INTEGER                   ' color of help line
    cursorNormal AS INTEGER           ' cursor size when overstriking
    cursorInsert AS INTEGER           ' cursor size when inserting
END TYPE
DIM config AS ConfigType              ' define the record variable config

OPEN "CONFIG.DAT" FOR BINARY AS #1    ' open the file
    IF LOF(1) = 0 THEN                ' set default colors if file is empty
        config.normal = 7
        config.highlight = 15
        config.inverseHighlight = 126
        config.inverse = 112
        config.help = 1
        config.cursorNormal = 7
        config.cursorInsert = 15
        PUT #1, 1, config             ' write the defaults to the file
    ELSE
        GET #1, 1, config             ' read current configuration information
    END IF
CLOSE #1

' display current configuration information
PRINT "Normal color = "; config.normal
PRINT "Highlight color = "; config.highlight
PRINT "Inverse highlight color = "; config.inverseHighlight
PRINT "Inverse color = "; config.inverse
PRINT "Help color = "; config.help
PRINT "Overstrike cursor size = "; config.cursorNormal
PRINT "Insert cursor size = "; config.cursorInsert

END
```

INPUT

See also

INKEY$, INPUT, INPUT$ (File I/O), LINE INPUT, LINE INPUT #

Purpose

The INPUT # statement reads data values from a sequential file or device into variables. You can use INPUT # to read either formatted data from an ASCII file or ASCII data from a device.

Syntax

INPUT #*filenum, var*[, *var*...]

filenum is the file number with which the file was opened for sequential input.

var is the numeric or string variable that receives the data from the file.

Usage

```
INPUT #1, title$
```
Reads a value into the string variable *title$* from the sequential file associated with file number 1.

```
INPUT #10, x%, y%, z%
```
Reads values into the integer variables *x%*, *y%*, and *z%* from the sequential file associated with file number 10.

Description

The INPUT # statement is useful for reading numeric variables from sequential files. INPUT # ignores leading spaces, carriage returns, and linefeeds when it reads data into the specified variables. INPUT # stops reading a number if it encounters a space, carriage return, linefeed, comma, or the end of the file. INPUT # stops reading a string when it encounters quotation marks, a carriage return, a linefeed, a comma, or the end of the file.

You can specify a variable that is a simple variable, an array element, or a record-variable element. You can specify several variables in one statement by separating them with a comma.

The INPUT # statement reads data in ASCII format as if you had entered the data from the keyboard in response to an INPUT statement.

Figure 17-1 illustrates the contents of a sequential file.

Figure 17-1.
A sequential file.

After QBasic executes the following INPUT # statements, in which file number 1 specifies the file shown in Figure 17-1, *x%* and *y%* contain the values 12 and 8. The variable *a$* contains the string "This", and *b$* contains "that".

```
INPUT #1, x%, y%
INPUT #1, a$
INPUT #1, b$
```

Figure 17-2 shows the position of the file pointer after each of the above statements is executed.

`INPUT #1, x%, y%`

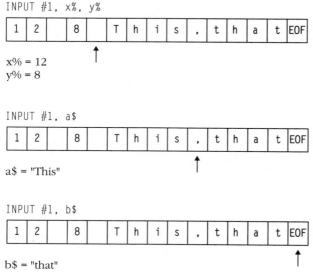

x% = 12
y% = 8

`INPUT #1, a$`

a$ = "This"

`INPUT #1, b$`

b$ = "that"

Figure 17-2.
Using INPUT # to read a sequential file.

Comments

If INPUT # reads a floating-point number (containing a decimal) from a sequential file into an integer or long-integer variable, INPUT # rounds off the floating-point number to fit the integer.

Using INPUT # to read an alphabetic character into a numeric variable does not cause an error. However, QBasic sets that numeric variable to 0.

Warnings

Because INPUT # uses commas to separate data items in a file, a string cannot contain embedded commas unless the entire string is enclosed in sets of quotation marks. For example, *Goodbye, all.* is read as two strings: *Goodbye* and *all*. However, INPUT # reads *"Goodbye, all."* as one string.

Example

The following program writes to a file a line of text and the values of 2 raised to the exponents 1 through 25. It then uses the INPUT # statement to read the contents of the file.

```
CLS
OPEN "2EXP.DAT" FOR OUTPUT AS #1

WRITE #1, "2EXP.DAT contains the value of 2 raised to the powers 1 through 25."
FOR i% = 1 TO 25
    result& = 1
    FOR j% = 1 TO i%
        result& = result& * 2
    NEXT j%
    WRITE #1, result&
NEXT i%
CLOSE #1

OPEN "2EXP.DAT" FOR INPUT AS #1

INPUT #1, description$
PRINT description$

PRINT "Press any key to continue."
DO: LOOP UNTIL INKEY$ <> ""

FOR i% = 1 TO 25
    INPUT #1, value&
    PRINT value&
NEXT i%
CLOSE #1
```

INPUT$ (File I/O)

See also

INPUT, LINE INPUT

Purpose

The INPUT$ function reads a specified number of bytes from the keyboard, a file, or a device. You can use INPUT$ to strictly control the amount of input.

Syntax

INPUT$(*num* [, [#] *filenum*])

num is the number of characters to be read. (The largest string that INPUT$ can read is 32,767 bytes.)

filenum is the file number you can associate with the file or device from which characters will be read.

Usage

```
PRINT "Press any key to continue: "; INPUT$(1);
```
Prompts the user to press a key and then uses INPUT$ to read the keystroke.

Description

The INPUT$ statement is useful when a program needs to retrieve a specified number of characters rather than process strings (as INPUT # and LINE INPUT # do). Note, however, that INPUT$ isn't a reasonable choice if you do not know the number of characters you need to read.

If you specify a file number, INPUT$ retrieves characters from the associated file or device. If you omit a file number, INPUT$ reads characters from the keyboard. If the file was opened as a random-access file, the number of characters that INPUT$ reads can be no more than the number of characters in each record that is specified in the OPEN statement for that file (in the LEN clause). If the file was opened as a binary or sequential file, INPUT$ can read no more than 32,767 characters.

INPUT$ does not display any characters it reads from the keyboard, file, or device. Your program can, of course, use the PRINT statement to echo the characters. The program in the "Example" section, however, demonstrates the advantages of not echoing characters. Note that INPUT$ reads all characters except the Ctrl-Break combination, which interrupts the program.

Errors

If you specify the file number of an unopened file, QBasic displays a "Bad file name or number" error message. Note that the number of characters must be available from the specified file. If the file doesn't contain enough characters, QBasic displays an "Input past end of file" error message. If the number of characters specified for a random-access file is greater than the record length, QBasic displays a "Field overflow" error message. If the number of characters specified for a sequential or binary file is greater than 32,767, QBasic displays an "Overflow" error message.

Tips

The INPUT$ function is the preferred method for communication device I/O because it lets you specify the number of characters to retrieve. When used with the LOC function, INPUT$ can always keep up with incoming communications.

Warnings

If you omit a file number, the number of characters specified must be entered at the keyboard—Enter does not indicate the end of input, as it does with the INPUT and LINE INPUT statements.

Example

The following program uses INPUT$ to retrieve an eight-character password from a file and then to accept an eight-character password from the keyboard. If the two passwords do not match, the program displays the message "Access denied."

```
OPEN "PASSWORD.DAT" FOR INPUT AS #1

password$ = INPUT$(8, #1)      ' read a password from the file

PRINT "Enter password:";
userPassword$ = INPUT$(8)      ' read a password from the keyboard

IF password$ = userPassword$ THEN
    PRINT "Access granted."
ELSE
    PRINT "Access denied."
    STOP
END IF
CLOSE
```

LINE INPUT

See also
INPUT, INPUT #, INPUT$ (File I/O), LINE INPUT

Purpose
The LINE INPUT # statement reads data from a sequential file or device into a string variable. Unlike the INPUT # statement, which reads strings separated by delimiters, LINE INPUT # reads the contents of a sequential file line by line. For example, you can use LINE INPUT # to read instructions from an ASCII file.

Syntax
LINE INPUT #*filenum*, *var*

filenum is the file number with which the file was opened for sequential input.

var is the string variable that receives the data read from the file.

Usage
```
LINE INPUT # 1, title$
```
Reads a line of the file associated with file number 1 and assigns it to the string variable *title$*.

Description
Usually, you use the LINE INPUT # statement to read a line of text from a sequential file or a device. LINE INPUT # reads all the characters on a line. LINE INPUT # cannot read more than 32,767 characters because that is the maximum number of characters that can be assigned to a string variable. The INPUT # statement ignores leading spaces and stops reading if it encounters a comma or a carriage-return/linefeed pair. However, LINE INPUT # doesn't ignore leading spaces and reads all characters—including commas—to the carriage return/linefeed pair, which indicates the end of the line.

The LINE INPUT # statement is often used for reading a text file from a word processor or database. If you can read the characters in a file when you use the DOS TYPE command, you can use the LINE INPUT # statement to read the file.

Figure 17-3 illustrates the contents of a sequential file. The initials CR and LF in the figure represent the carriage return and linefeed characters.

Figure 17-3.
A sequential file.

After executing the following statements, in which file number 1 specifies the file shown in Figure 17-3, the variable *x$* contains the string "12 8" and the variable *a$* contains the string "This,that".

```
LINE INPUT #1, x$
LINE INPUT #1, a$
```

Figure 17-4 shows the position of the file pointer after each of the above statements is executed.

```
LINE INPUT #1, x$
```
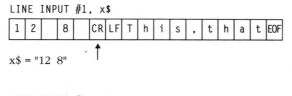

x$ = "12 8"

```
LINE INPUT #1, a$
```
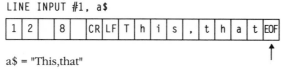

a$ = "This,that"

Figure 17-4.
Using LINE INPUT # to read a sequential file.

Comments
The only way you can delimit text in a file that will be read by LINE INPUT # is to place data on separate lines. LINE INPUT # reads commas in the middle of strings as characters, not delimiters.

Tips
Because string variables can contain any characters, including numeric digits, reading a number from a file doesn't cause an error; LINE INPUT # simply reads the numeric digits into the string variable. You can use VAL to convert the digits into numeric variables. (See the VAL entry in Chapter 5, "Strings," for details.)

Example

The following program shows some of the differences between using INPUT # and LINE INPUT # with text. Note that LINE INPUT # returns the file line by line, exactly as the file appears when displayed with the TYPE command in DOS.

```
OPEN "TEXT.DAT" FOR INPUT AS #1

PRINT "INPUT # sample:"
PRINT
number = 0
DO
    number = number + 1
    INPUT #1, text$
    PRINT number; text$
LOOP UNTIL EOF(1)

PRINT
PRINT "LINE INPUT # sample:"
PRINT

number = 0
SEEK #1, 1          ' move to beginning of the file
DO
    number = number + 1
    LINE INPUT #1, text$
    PRINT number; text$
LOOP UNTIL EOF(1)

CLOSE
```

LOC

See also

GET (File I/O), OPEN, PUT (File I/O)

Purpose

For every open file, QBasic maintains a pointer that shows where the next read or write operation will take place. The LOC function returns the current position of this pointer in an open file. You can use LOC to determine whether you are at the proper location in the file before executing a PUT or GET statement.

Syntax

LOC(*filenum*)

filenum is the file number with which the file was opened.

Usage

```
PRINT "Current position in file 1 is"; LOC(1)
```
Displays the location in the file that will be accessed by the next file I/O statement.

Description

The GET and PUT statements for file I/O let you input from or output to the current file position. You can use the LOC function to check the current position so that you don't retrieve the wrong record or write over another record.

The values that LOC returns depend on the mode in which the file was opened and whether the file is a communications device. If the file was opened for random access, LOC returns the number of the record last read from or written to the file.

If the file was opened for sequential input or output access, LOC returns the current byte position divided by 128 and rounded to an integer. Because a QBasic buffer is 128 bytes long, this operation returns the current position in the buffer.

If the file was opened for binary access, LOC returns the number of the byte most recently read from or written to the file. For example, if your program reads from a binary file a string variable 100 bytes long named *title$*, LOC returns 100. The next byte position is 101.

If the file is a communications device (COM1: or COM2:) opened in binary mode, LOC returns the number of characters remaining in that device's input buffer. If the file is a communications device opened in any other mode, LOC returns the number of characters remaining in that device's input buffer up to but not including the Ctrl-Z end-of-file character. (This information is important because if you try to input characters beyond the end-of-file marker, QBasic displays an "Input past end of file" error message.)

Comments

Before you read from or write to a file, the LOC function returns 0 because no I/O has taken place. The maximum value that LOC can return is 2147483647.

Warnings

The LOC function returns 0 when used with the QBasic SCRN:, KYBD:, CONS:, or LPT*n*: device. The LOC function returns meaningful values only when used with a file or a COM*n*: device.

Example

The following program uses the LOC function to determine the number of bytes used in each output operation to a binary file.

```
CLS

OPEN "EX-LOC.DAT" FOR BINARY AS #1

FOR size% = 1 TO 23
    currentPosition& = LOC(1) + 1           ' find current position in the file

    stringVariable$ = STRING$(size%, "*")   ' assign asterisks to the variable
    PUT #1, , stringVariable$               ' write the variable to the file

    newPosition& = LOC(1)                    ' find the next position in the file
    PRINT "Adding asterisks to the file from position ";
    PRINT USING "### to position ###."; currentPosition&; newPosition&
NEXT

CLOSE
```

LOCK

See also

OPEN, UNLOCK

Purpose

The LOCK statement prevents other processes on a network from accessing all or part of a shared file. A shared file is one that different processes or users on a multitasking, multiuser, or networking system can gain access to. You can use the LOCK statement to prevent access to a record after your program alters that record.

Syntax

LOCK [#]*filenum*[, {*record* ¦ [*start*] TO *end*}]

filenum is the file number of an open file.

record is the number of the record or byte to be locked.

start and *end* are integers that specify a range of records or bytes to be locked.

Usage

LOCK #1

Locks the entire file opened as file number 1. No other process can access this file until the program unlocks the file with the UNLOCK statement.

```
OPEN "VENDORS.DAT" FOR RANDOM AS #4
LOCK #4, 10
```

Locks record 10 of the random-access file opened as file number 4.

Description

In a networked environment in which several users or processes share the same files, you must prevent different processes from updating the same record simultaneously. If you don't, only one process's update takes effect; changes made by other processes are overwritten. The LOCK statement prevents this by allowing one process to have exclusive rights to a file or a record in a file and denying other processes access to that record or file while the process is using it. A LOCK statement must always be followed by a matching UNLOCK statement. (See the UNLOCK entry for details.)

In a binary file, you specify the bytes to be locked. The first byte in the file is byte number 1. In a file opened for random access, you specify the records. The first record in the file is record number 1.

If you include only one record or byte number, only that record or byte is locked for exclusive use by your program. If you include the TO keyword, the records or bytes in the range specified by the numbers surrounding TO are locked for exclusive use by your program. If you omit a number for the beginning of the range, LOCK uses record or byte 1 as the default starting position. If you don't specify any records or bytes, the LOCK statement locks the entire file for exclusive use by your program.

You can lock individual records or bytes only in random-access and binary files. With sequential files, you can lock only the entire file.

LOCK functions at runtime only with the SHARE.EXE program activated. SHARE.EXE is a program supplied with DOS that supports file sharing and locking for Microsoft networks.

Errors

Locked portions of files can be accessed only by the program that performed the LOCK statement. If another QBasic program tries to read from or write to the locked portion of that file, QBasic displays a "Permission denied" error message.

Warnings

Note that Microsoft supports QBasic only on Microsoft LAN Manager, IBM-PC Network, MS-Network, and compatible systems. Although limited success has been reported using other networks, such as Novell and 3Com, problems can occur.

If you lock a file and then either lose power or reboot your computer before you execute the matching UNLOCK statement, data in the locked file might be lost. To minimize the danger of losing data, use LOCK to lock records only as long as necessary.

Example

The following example uses the LOC and LOCK statements to protect portions of a binary file while the program updates them.

```
CLS

OPEN "EX-LOCK.DAT" FOR BINARY AS #1

FOR size% = 1 TO 23
    currentPosition& = LOC(1) + 1              ' find current position in file
    newPosition& = currentPosition& + size%    ' find next position in file

    LOCK #1, currentPosition& TO newPosition&    ' lock a portion of the file
    stringVariable$ = STRING$(size%, "*")
    PUT #1, , stringVariable$                    ' output the variable
    UNLOCK #1, currentPosition& TO newPosition&  ' unlock the portion

    PRINT "Adding asterisks to the file from position ";
    PRINT USING "##### to position #####."; currentPosition&; newPosition&
NEXT

CLOSE
```

LOF

See also
LOC, OPEN

Purpose
The LOF function returns the number of bytes in an open file. You use the LOF function when you need to know the length of a file before you begin processing it.

Syntax
LOF(*filenum*)

filenum is the file number with which the file was opened.

Usage
```
PRINT "The file is"; LOF(1); "bytes long."
```
Displays a message that gives the length of the file opened as file number 1.

Description
Use LOF to determine the current size of an open file. LOF returns the size, in bytes, of a file that has been opened in any mode. The maximum value that LOF can return is 2147483647.

If the open file is a communication device (COM1: or COM2:), LOF returns the number of characters available in that device's output buffer. You cannot use LOF with a number associated with the QBasic SCRN:, KYBD:, CONS:, LPT1:, or LPT2: device.

Example

The following program uses the LOF function to monitor the size of a file.

```
CLS

OPEN "EX-LOF.DAT" FOR OUTPUT AS #1

FOR size% = 1 TO 23
    PRINT "Current file size is"; LOF(1); "bytes."

    stringVariable$ = STRING$(size%, "*")  ' assign asterisks to the variable
    PRINT #1, stringVariable$              ' write the variable to the file
NEXT

CLOSE #1
```

LSET

See also

FIELD, MKD$, MKDMBF$, MKI$, MKL$, MKS$, MKSMBF$, PUT (File I/O), RSET

Purpose

The LSET statement puts the value of an expression or a variable into a specified field of a random-access file's buffer. LSET also left-justifies this expression or variable. LSET can also be used to left-justify any string variable or to assign one record variable to another.

Syntax

LSET *var* = *expr*

var and *expr* must both be strings if LSET is being used for left-justification or for placing a value into a field. They must both be record variables if LSET is being used to assign one record variable to another.

Usage

LSET address$ = "123 PARK ST."

Left-justifies the string constant "123 PARK ST." and places it into the *address$* field if *address$* is the name of a field defined by a FIELD statement. If *address$* is a string variable, LSET only left-justifies it within the current length of *address$*.

LSET amtDue$ = MKD$(total#)

Places the string representation of the contents of *total#* into *amtDue$*, which can be either the name of a field defined by a FIELD statement or a string variable.

Description

The FIELD statement allocates a special storage buffer when it defines the record for a random-access file. Because of this special allocation, you cannot use the equal sign (=) or the LET statement to assign values to the fields defined by the FIELD statement. Instead, you must use the LSET or RSET statement to make the assignment. Note that you can also use LSET with string variables and record variables.

Using LSET with fields

When you specify a field name as the first parameter in an LSET statement, the LSET statement copies the value of the second parameter (which must be a string) into the location in a random-access buffer allocated for the specified field.

If the length of the field is greater than the length of the string value, LSET left-justifies the value in the buffer. That is, LSET adds spaces to the right end of the string until the string is the same length as the field.

If the length of the field is less than the length of the string value, LSET copies only enough characters to fill the field and ignores the remaining characters.

Figure 17-5 shows how the LSET statement places a string in a field.

```
FIELD 1, 20 AS patientName$
LSET patientName$ = "Robert Anderson II"
```

| R | o | b | e | r | t | | A | n | d | e | r | s | o | n | | I | I | | |

```
LSET patientName$ = "Robert Lloyd Anderson II"
```

| R | o | b | e | r | t | | L | l | o | y | d | | A | n | d | e | r | s | o |

Figure 17-5.
The LSET statement with fields.

Using LSET with string variables

When the first parameter to LSET is a string variable (not a field name), LSET performs a different task. Because the length of the variable is not set by a FIELD statement, LSET uses the current length of the string variable to calculate the justification it will perform.

If the current length of the string variable is greater than the length of the value specified in the second parameter, LSET left-justifies the value. That is, LSET adds spaces to the right end of the string value until the string is the same length as the string variable.

If the current length of the string variable is less than the length of the value specified in the second parameter, LSET copies only enough characters to fill the string variable and ignores the remaining characters.

You can determine the current length of a string variable by using the LEN function. (See the LEN entry in Chapter 5, "Strings," for details.)

Figure 17-6 shows how the LSET statement works with string variables.

```
patientName$ = SPACE$(20)
LSET patientName$ = "Robert Anderson II"
```

```
LSET patientName$ = "Robert Lloyd Anderson II"
```

Figure 17-6.
The LSET statement with string variables.

Using LSET with record variables

The usual means of assignment (the equal sign or LET) can't copy record variables defined by different TYPE…END TYPE statements. To copy different record variables, you must use the LSET statement. However, the LSET statement merely copies from one record variable to another—it doesn't left-justify the data. (See the TYPE…END TYPE entry in Chapter 1, "Variables and Types," for details.)

When you use LSET in this way, the two parameters to LSET must both be record variables. The LSET statement copies as many bytes as it can from the record variable specified in the second parameter into the record variable specified in the first parameter. For example, if the length of the second record variable is 40 bytes and the length of the first is 30 bytes, LSET copies only 30 bytes from the second to the first. Because the LSET statement copies individual bytes to a record variable, the values of the elements of the record variable are not accurately copied unless the elements of the record variable to which bytes are being copied have the same type and location within that record variable as they have in the second record variable.

The following program segment demonstrates the use of LSET with record variables:

```
TYPE Type1
    x AS INTEGER
    y AS LONG
    z AS DOUBLE
END TYPE

TYPE Type2
    x AS INTEGER
    y AS LONG
END TYPE

DIM a1 AS Type1, a2 AS Type2

a1.x = 100
a1.y = 10000
a1.z = 100.1
```

```
a2.x = 200
a2.y = 200000

LSET a1 = a2
```

After the LSET statement is executed, *a1.x* equals 200, *a1.y* equals 200000, and *a1.z* equals 100.1. Because the record variable *a2* has fewer bytes than the record variable *a1*, the value of *a1.z* does not change.

Comments

Remember that you must convert numeric values to strings before you place them in a field defined by a FIELD statement. (See the MKD$, MKDMBF$, MKI$, MKL$, MKS$, and MKSMBF$ entries for details.)

Example

See the CVD entry for a program that uses the LSET statement to place strings into fields that will be stored in a random-access file.

LTRIM$

See also

RTRIM$

Purpose

The LTRIM$ function returns a copy of a string expression without leading spaces (spaces on the left). You use the LTRIM$ function to format data in which leading spaces would either cause misaligned output or be misinterpreted as literal characters.

Syntax

LTRIM$(*string*)

string is any string expression.

Usage

```
PRINT #1, LTRIM$(description$)
```

Writes the variable *description$* without leading spaces to the file associated with file number 1.

Description

QBasic provides the LTRIM$ function to let you delete extra spaces that might have been inserted by the user or the program. The LTRIM$ function accepts any string expression and returns the same string without leading spaces.

Example

The following program uses the LTRIM$ and RTRIM$ functions to delete the leading and trailing spaces from lines in a text file.

```
CLS
PRINT "This program deletes leading and trailing spaces from each line of "
PRINT "a file and writes the resulting lines to another file."
PRINT

LINE INPUT "Enter name of input file:  "; filename$
LINE INPUT "Enter name of output file: "; output$

OPEN filename$ FOR INPUT AS #1
OPEN output$ FOR OUTPUT AS #2

DO UNTIL EOF(1)
    LINE INPUT #1, inputLine$
    PRINT #2, LTRIM$(RTRIM$(inputLine$))
LOOP

CLOSE
```

MKD$

See also

CVD, CVDMBF, DOUBLE, FIELD, MKDMBF$

Purpose

The MKD$ function converts a double-precision number to an 8-byte string. The MKD$ function complements the CVD function. You use the MKD$ function to convert a double-precision number to a string that will be assigned to a field defined by the FIELD statement.

Syntax

MKD$(*number*)

number is any numeric expression in the range $-1.7976931D+308$ through $1.7976931D+308$.

Usage

```
LSET amountDue$ = MKD$(265.98)
```

Places the string representing the double-precision value 265.98 into the field *amountDue$*.

Description

The MKD$ function converts a double-precision value to an 8-byte string. Note that the specified number can be any numeric expression; MKD$ converts the number to double precision. The MKD$ function returns a value that you must either assign to a variable or use in an expression. Usually, you use MKD$ in an LSET statement.

Comments

If you specify the command-line switch /MBF, QBasic assumes that the value that MKD$ converts is a number in Microsoft Binary format. (See the MKDMBF$ entry for details.) Otherwise, the MKD$ function converts a number in IEEE format.

Example

See the "Example" section in the CVD entry.

MKDMBF$

See also

CVD, CVDMBF, DOUBLE, FIELD, MKD$

Purpose

The MKDMBF$ function converts a double-precision number in IEEE format to an 8-byte string containing the number in Microsoft Binary format. The MKDMBF$ function complements the CVDMBF function. You use the MKDMBF$ function to convert a double-precision number to a string that will be assigned to a field defined by a FIELD statement.

Syntax

MKDMBF$(*number*)

number is any numeric expression in the range −1.7976931D+308 through 1.7976931D+308.

Usage

```
LSET amountDue$ = MKDMBF$(265.98)
```

Places the string representing the double-precision value 265.98 into the field *amountDue$*.

Description

The MKDMBF$ function converts a double-precision value in IEEE format to an 8-byte string in Microsoft Binary format. Note that the specified number can be any numeric expression; MKDMBF$ converts the number to double precision. The MKDMBF$ function returns a value that you must either assign to a variable or use in an expression. Usually, you use MKDMBF$ in an LSET statement.

Example

See the "Example" section in the CVD entry.

MKI$

See also

CVI, FIELD, INTEGER

Purpose

The MKI$ function converts an integer number to a 2-byte string. The MKI$ function complements the CVI function. Use the MKI$ function to convert an integer number to a string that will be assigned to a field defined by the FIELD statement.

Syntax

MKI$(*number*)

number is any numeric expression in the range −32768 through 32767.

Usage

```
LSET age$ = MKI$(19)
```

Places the string representing the integer value 19 into the field *age$*.

Description

The MKI$ function converts an integer value to a 2-byte string. Note that the specified number can be any numeric expression in the range for integers (−32768 to 32767). MKI$ converts the number to an integer. The MKI$ function returns a value that you must either assign to a variable or use in an expression. Usually, you use MKI$ in an LSET$ statement.

Example

See the "Example" section in the CVD entry.

MKL$

See also

CVL, FIELD, LONG

Purpose

The MKL$ function converts a long-integer number to a 4-byte string. The MKL$ function complements the CVL function. You use the MKL$ function to convert a long integer to a string that will be assigned to a field defined by the FIELD statement.

Syntax

MKL$(*number*)

number is any numeric expression in the range −2147483648 through 2147483647.

Usage

```
LSET population$ = MKL$(225102963)
```

Places the string representing the long-integer value 225102963 into the variable *population$*.

Description

The MKL$ function converts a long-integer value to a 4-byte string. Note that the specified number can be any numeric expression in the range for long integers (−2147483648 through 2147483647). MKL$ converts the number to a long integer. The MKL$ function returns a value that you must either assign to a variable or use in an expression. Usually, you use MKL$ in an LSET statement.

Example

See the "Example" section in the CVD entry.

MKS$

See also

CVS, CVSMBF, FIELD, MKSMBF$, SINGLE

Purpose

The MKS$ function converts a single-precision number to a 4-byte string. The MKS$ function complements the CVS function. You use the MKS$ function to convert a single-precision number to a string that will be assigned to a field defined by a FIELD statement.

Syntax

MKS$(*number*)

number is any numeric expression in the range −3.402823E+38 through 3.402823E+38.

Usage

```
LSET wholesale$ = MKS$(ourCost!)
```

Places the string representing the value of *ourCost!* into the field *wholesale$*.

Description

The MKS$ function converts a single-precision value to a 4-byte string. Note that the specified number can be any numeric expression; MKS$ converts the number to single precision. The MKS$ function returns a value that you must either assign to a variable or use in an expression. Usually, you use MKS$ in an LSET statement.

Comments

If you specify the command line option /MBF, QBasic assumes that the value MKS$ converts is a number in Microsoft Binary format. (See the MKSMBF$ entry for details.) Otherwise, the MKS$ function converts a number in IEEE format.

Example

See the "Example" section in the CVD entry.

MKSMBF$

See also

CVS, CVSMBF, FIELD, MKS$, SINGLE

Purpose

The MKSMBF$ function converts a single-precision number in IEEE format to a 4-byte string containing the number in Microsoft Binary format. The MKSMBF$ function complements the CVSMBF function. You use the MKSMBF$ function to convert a single-precision number to a string that will be assigned to a field defined by a FIELD statement.

Syntax

MKSMBF$(*number*)

number is any numeric variable or numeric expression in the range −3.402823E+38 through 3.402823E+38.

Usage

```
LSET amountDue$ = MKSMBF$(265.98)
```
Places the string representing the single-precision value 265.98 into the field *amountDue$*.

Description

The MKSMBF$ function converts a single-precision value in IEEE format to a 4-byte string in Microsoft Binary format. Note that the specified number can be any numeric expression; MKSMBF$ converts the number to single precision. The MKSMBF$ function returns a value that you must assign to a variable or use in an expression. Usually, you will use MKSMBF$ in an LSET statement.

Example

See the "Example" section in the CVD entry.

NAME

See also

CHDIR

Purpose

The NAME statement changes the name or the location of a file. You use the NAME statement to let your program efficiently manage files.

Syntax

NAME *oldfilespec* AS *newfilespec*

oldfilespec is the existing filename. It can also include a pathname.

newfilespec is the new filename for the file. It can also include a pathname.

Usage

```
NAME "CUSTOMER.DAT" AS "OLD-CUST.DAT"
```
Renames the file CUSTOMER.DAT as OLD-CUST.DAT.

```
NAME "\CONFIG.SYS" AS "\BIN\OLDCONFIG.SYS"
```
Moves the file CONFIG.SYS from the root directory to the directory \BIN and changes the name of the file to OLDCONFIG.SYS.

Description

Like the DOS RENAME command, the QBasic NAME statement changes the name of a file on a disk. The NAME statement can also move a file from one directory to another directory on the same drive. However, NAME cannot rename directories.

The two parameters to NAME must be string constants or expressions that contain a filename, which can be preceded by a pathname. If the pathname of the new name is different than that of the old name, NAME moves the file to the specified directory and, if the filename is different, renames the file.

Errors

The NAME statement doesn't physically transfer a file's data; it merely changes DOS's directory information about the file. If the two parameters do not both use the same drive, QBasic displays a "Rename across disks" error message.

If the file to be renamed doesn't exist, QBasic displays a "File not found" error message; if the new filename already exists, QBasic dislays a "File already exists" error message.

You must close an open file before you use the NAME statement to rename or move it. If the file to be renamed is currently open, QBasic displays a "File already open" error message.

Example

The following program uses the NAME statement to make a backup copy of an existing file before overwriting it with new data.

```
CLS
ON ERROR GOTO ErrorHandler                 ' branches to ErrorHandler for errors

NAME "REPORT.RPT" AS "REPORT.BAK"          ' if file exists, rename it

OPEN "REPORT.RPT" FOR OUTPUT AS #1         ' open file for output

PRINT #1, "REPORT.RPT"
PRINT "Information has been written to the file REPORT.RPT"
CLOSE
END

ErrorHandler:
    SELECT CASE ERR
        CASE 53
            PRINT "REPORT.RPT not found. No backup has been made."
            RESUME NEXT
        CASE 58
            KILL "REPORT.BAK"
            PRINT "Old backup file has been replaced by new one."
            RESUME
        CASE ELSE
            ON ERROR GOTO 0
    END SELECT
```

OPEN

See also

CLOSE, FREEFILE, IOCTL, OPEN COM

Purpose

The OPEN statement opens a file or device so that the program can perform input and output operations with the file or device. The OPEN statement prepares a file that will be either read from or written to. You must use OPEN before using a QBasic file I/O statement such as GET, PUT, PRINT #, or INPUT #, for example.

Syntax

New syntax:

OPEN *file* [FOR *accessmode*] [ACCESS *access*] [*lock*] AS [#] *filenum* [LEN = *reclen*]

Traditional syntax:

OPEN *mode*, [#] *filenum*, *file*[, *reclen*]

file is the name of the file that will be opened.

accessmode is a keyword that specifies the way the program will use the file. It can be one of the following keywords: INPUT, OUTPUT, APPEND, RANDOM, and BINARY.

access is a keyword that specifies the kind of access that the program will have to the file being opened. It can be one of the following keywords: READ, WRITE, or READ WRITE.

lock is a clause that specifies the kind of access other programs can have to an open file. It can be one of the following clauses: SHARED, LOCK READ, LOCK WRITE, or LOCK READ WRITE.

filenum is the number (in the range 1 through 255) that is associated with the file. It is used to access the file.

reclen is the length of each record in a sequential or random-access file. It must be in the range 1 through 32767.

mode is a single letter that specifies the way the program will use the file. It can be one of the following letters: I, O, A, R, or B.

Usage

```
OPEN "A:STUFF.DAT" FOR INPUT AS #1
```
Opens the sequential file STUFF.DAT on drive A: as file number 1 and specifies that data will be read.

```
OPEN "D:\PATIENTS.DAT" FOR RANDOM ACCESS READ WRITE LOCK WRITE AS #3 LEN = 1024
```
Opens the random-access file PATIENTS.DAT on the D: drive. The current process can read from or write to the file, but other processes are prevented from opening the file for writing. This file was opened as file number 3, and each record in the file is 1024 bytes long.

Description

Before you can read to or write from a file, you must first open the file. The OPEN statement can communicate with DOS and a local area network to set access mode and file locking, thus allowing several QBasic programs to access the same files.

The file to be opened must be specified by a string constant or expression that contains a DOS or QBasic device or filename. Note that you can precede a filename with a drive name or directory name or both, according to DOS file conventions. See Table 17-5 for a list of valid QBasic device names.

The LEN clause in the OPEN statement, which is optional, lets you specify either the length, in bytes, of records in the file or the size, in bytes, of QBasic's buffer for that file. For random-access files, the LEN clause specifies the number of bytes in each record of the file; if omitted, the length by default is 128 bytes. QBasic ignores the LEN clause for binary files. For sequential files, the LEN clause specifies the size (in bytes) of the buffer QBasic uses when reading from or writing to the file; 512 bytes is the default size. Specifying a larger buffer speeds up I/O operations. However, QBasic allocates a little more than the specified number of bytes from the available memory, so you must determine whether increases in speed are worth the additional memory that the buffer requires. If the file is a character device, QBasic ignores the length because the buffer of a character device is always 1 byte and cannot be changed.

Device	Description
CONS:	Console; screen output and keyboard input
KYBD:	Keyboard; keyboard input only
SCRN:	Screen; screen output only
COM*n*:	Communications port *n*; input and output
LPT*n*:	Parallel printer port *n*; input and output

Table 17-5.
QBasic devices.

The FOR clause

In the new OPEN syntax, you specify the access mode by using a FOR clause with one of the following keywords: INPUT, OUTPUT, APPEND, RANDOM, or BINARY.

In the traditional OPEN syntax, you specify the access mode by specifying the first letter of one of the new syntax keywords (I, O, A, R, or B). If you use the traditional syntax, you must specify an access mode.

Table 17-6 lists the definitions of the access modes. If you omit the FOR mode clause when using the new syntax, QBasic opens the file for random access.

New syntax	Traditional syntax	Description
INPUT	I	Sequential input
OUTPUT	O	Sequential output
APPEND	A	Sequential output to the end of the file
RANDOM	R	Random-access I/O (default mode) to any record position
BINARY	B	Binary I/O to any byte position

Table 17-6.
Access modes specified by the FOR clause.

When you open a file using the keyword BINARY in the FOR clause, variables can be read from and written to any byte position in the file regardless of the file's internal structure. (See the GET and PUT entries for details about binary mode I/O.)

If a file consists of ASCII text entered on separate lines or separated by spaces or commas, use the INPUT keyword in the FOR clause to open the sequential file for accessing the contents. In input mode, the data in a file can be unstructured and of different types (numeric and text) because the I/O routines INPUT # and LINE INPUT # read the file and make the necessary conversions (from ASCII characters to numeric variables, for example). (See the INPUT # and LINE INPUT # entries for details about input mode I/O.)

Specify the keyword OUTPUT in the FOR clause to create a sequential file. The data written to a file opened for output can be unstructured and of different types. (See the PRINT # and WRITE # entries for details about output mode I/O.)

Specify APPEND to open a sequential file to which you need to add information. When you do so, any data you write to the file appears at the end of the file; the original data remains untouched. Otherwise, append mode is the same as output.

Specify RANDOM in the FOR clause to open a random-access file that stores records of data that have the same structure. These records can be defined by either a FIELD statement or a TYPE...END TYPE statement. You can gain access to any record in a random-access file directly; you don't have to start a search at the beginning of the file to find the record. (See the GET and PUT entries for details about random mode I/O.)

The ACCESS clause

The ACCESS clause can include one of the following keywords: READ, WRITE, or READ WRITE. These specify that the file is to be opened for reading only, for writing only, or for both reading and writing. ACCESS READ WRITE is valid only for files opened with the keywords RANDOM, BINARY, or APPEND in the FOR clause.

If the process that opens a file denies read access, any attempt by another process to open that file with ACCESS READ or ACCESS READ WRITE results in the runtime error message "Permission denied." If the process that opens a file denies write access, any attempt by another process to open that file with ACCESS WRITE or ACCESS READ WRITE results in the runtime error message "Permission denied."

If you don't specify an ACCESS clause with a random-access or binary file, QBasic makes three attempts to open the file—one with an implicit ACCESS READ WRITE clause, the next with an implicit ACCESS WRITE, and the final attempt with an implicit ACCESS READ. If a file-sharing conflict arises with another process, the next attempt is made. If all three attempts fail, QBasic displays a "Permission denied" error message.

The lock clause

The lock clause of OPEN notifies the operating system which access privileges any other process can use for the file. For example, if the lock clause is LOCK READ, no other process can access the file with read privileges. Table 17-7 lists the keywords you can specify in the lock clause.

Lock clause	Description
(Default)	No other process can open the file.
SHARED	Any process can open the file in any mode.
LOCK READ	No other process can open the file with an ACCESS READ clause; no other process can already have ACCESS READ privileges.
LOCK WRITE	No other process can open the file with an ACCESS WRITE clause; no other process can already have ACCESS WRITE privileges.
LOCK READ WRITE	No other process can open the file with an ACCESS READ WRITE clause; no other process can already have ACCESS READ WRITE privileges.

Table 17-7.
Network-access lock definitions.

Errors

If you use the OPEN statement with the INPUT keyword (or I) and the file does not exist, QBasic displays a "File not found" error message. In any other mode (specified by OUTPUT, APPEND, RANDOM, or BINARY), if you use the OPEN statement and the file does not exist, QBasic merely creates the file with a length of 0 bytes; no error message is displayed.

Tips

Because each open file buffer uses available memory space, always close a file when you no longer need it.

Warnings

If you use a user-defined function or a DEF FN function as a parameter to any QBasic I/O statement, that function must not use an I/O statement itself; such use can cause unpredictable results.

When you open a file with the APPEND keyword, the ACCESS clause, if used, must be READ WRITE, not merely WRITE; the OPEN statement must have read privileges to be able to find the end of the file.

Example

The following example, which uses three OPEN statements, converts a text file to hexadecimal and octal formats.

```
OPEN "INPUT.DAT" FOR INPUT AS #1
OPEN "HEX.DAT" FOR OUTPUT AS #2
OPEN "OCTAL.DAT" FOR OUTPUT AS #3

DO UNTIL EOF(1)
    LINE INPUT #1, text$         ' get a line
    PRINT text$

    PRINT #2, text$,
    FOR x = 1 TO LEN(text$)
        PRINT #2, HEX$(ASC(MID$(text$, x, 1))); " ";    ' print the hex value
    NEXT
    PRINT #2,

    PRINT #3, text$,
    FOR x = 1 TO LEN(text$)
        PRINT #3, OCT$(ASC(MID$(text$, x, 1))); " ";    ' print the octal value
    NEXT
    PRINT #3,
LOOP

CLOSE                            ' close all open files
```

PRINT

See also
INPUT #, PRINT, PRINT # USING, PRINT USING, WRITE #

Purpose
The PRINT # statement writes unformatted data to a sequential file. You can use the PRINT # statement to add text and numbers to a sequential file.

Syntax
PRINT #*filenum*[, *expr* [{;¦,}*expr*...]][;¦,]

filenum is the file number of the open sequential file to which you are writing data.

expr is a numeric or string expression that contains the value to be written to the file; you can specify several expressions, separating them with semicolons or commas.

If you use a semicolon between two expressions, the second expression will be written immediately after the first one. If you use a comma between two expressions, the second expression will be written in the next print zone. (Each print zone is 14 characters in length.) A semicolon or comma at the end of the statement keeps the file pointer on the same line of the file so the output of the next PRINT # statement begins on the same line.

Usage
```
PRINT #5, "Today's date is "; DATE$
```
Writes a string constant and the value returned by the DATE$ function to the file opened as file number 5.

Description
Sequential file output is useful for creating files that users can view or edit, such as report or mail-merge files. In QBasic, you can use the PRINT # statement to write characters to a sequential output file. Note that the file to which you will write data must have been previously opened by using the OUTPUT or APPEND keyword in the OPEN statement.

The value written to the file can be specified by either a constant (quoted text or a constant defined by CONST) or an expression of any simple type, such as an array element, a record element, a simple variable, or a mathematical or string expression that uses QBasic functions. If you do not specify any values in a PRINT # statement, PRINT # writes a blank line to the file.

The PRINT # statement writes data to the file exactly as PRINT writes data to the screen. If you need to read a file later, you must insert delimiters (such as a carriage-return/linefeed pair, spaces, or commas) between data items.

Writing numeric values

If a parameter to PRINT # is any type of numeric variable or expression, PRINT # writes the value of that variable or expression to the file. When PRINT # writes numbers to a file, it inserts a space after each number. PRINT # also precedes positive numeric values with a space and negative numeric values with a minus sign.

If the parameter is an integer or long-integer variable or expression, PRINT # writes the value of that variable or expression to the file, using as many digits as necessary to represent the number. Except as specified in the previous paragraph, no extra leading spaces or zeros precede the value when it is written to the file. Figure 17-7 illustrates this procedure.

Figure 17-7.
Using PRINT # to write integers to a file.

If a parameter to PRINT # is a single-precision or double-precision variable or expression, PRINT # writes the value of that variable or expression to the file, using as many digits as necessary to represent the number. If QBasic can represent the value of a single-precision number in seven or fewer digits (plus the decimal point) without loss of accuracy, PRINT # writes the value to the file in fixed-point format; otherwise, PRINT # writes the single-precision value in scientific notation. If QBasic can represent the value of a double-precision number in 16 or fewer digits (plus the decimal point) without loss of accuracy, PRINT # writes the value to the file in fixed-point format; otherwise, PRINT # writes the double-precision value in scientific notation. Figure 17-8 illustrates this procedure.

```
PRINT #1, 123.15!
```
| | 1 | 2 | 3 | . | 1 | 5 | |

```
PRINT #1, 100#
```
| | 1 | 0 | 0 | |

```
PRINT #1, -985.45!
```
| - | 9 | 8 | 5 | . | 4 | 5 | |

Figure 17-8.
Using PRINT # to write single-precision and double-precision numbers to a file.

(continued)

Figure 17-8. *continued*

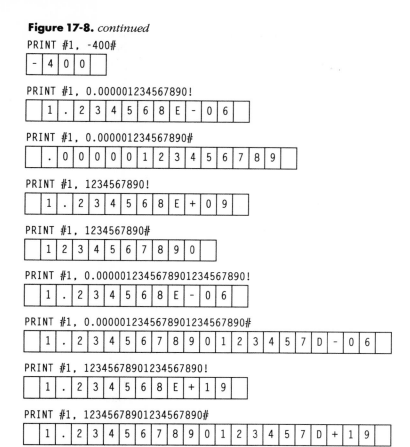

PRINT #1, -400#

| - | 4 | 0 | 0 | |

PRINT #1, 0.000001234567890!

| 1 | . | 2 | 3 | 4 | 5 | 6 | 8 | E | - | 0 | 6 | |

PRINT #1, 0.000001234567890#

| . | 0 | 0 | 0 | 0 | 0 | 1 | 2 | 3 | 4 | 5 | 6 | 7 | 8 | 9 | |

PRINT #1, 1234567890!

| 1 | . | 2 | 3 | 4 | 5 | 6 | 8 | E | + | 0 | 9 | |

PRINT #1, 1234567890#

| 1 | 2 | 3 | 4 | 5 | 6 | 7 | 8 | 9 | 0 | | |

PRINT #1, 0.00000123456789012345678901

| 1 | . | 2 | 3 | 4 | 5 | 6 | 8 | E | - | 0 | 6 | |

PRINT #1, 0.00000123456789012345678901#

| 1 | . | 2 | 3 | 4 | 5 | 6 | 7 | 8 | 9 | 0 | 1 | 2 | 3 | 4 | 5 | 7 | D | - | 0 | 6 | |

PRINT #1, 12345678901234567890!

| 1 | . | 2 | 3 | 4 | 5 | 6 | 8 | E | + | 1 | 9 | |

PRINT #1, 12345678901234567890#

| 1 | . | 2 | 3 | 4 | 5 | 6 | 7 | 8 | 9 | 0 | 1 | 2 | 3 | 4 | 5 | 7 | D | + | 1 | 9 | |

Comments

If you use commas to separate parameters, PRINT # inserts spaces in the file to position the next tab stop. Because this can waste disk space, however, it is better to use semicolons between numeric values and quoted commas between string variables, as in the following example:

```
PRINT #1, stringVar$; ","; numericVar%; dollarVar#
```

Errors

If you use an array or a record variable as a parameter, QBasic displays a "Type mismatch" error message.

Tips

To speed up sequential file output, you can increase the size of the buffer by using the LEN clause in the OPEN statement of a file. However, remember that an increased buffer size reduces the available memory for the program.

Example

The following program uses the PRINT # statement to write the contents of the 80-by-25-character text screen to a sequential file.

```
OPEN "SCREEN.DAT" FOR APPEND AS #1

FOR y% = 1 TO 25
    FOR x% = 1 TO 80
        PRINT #1, CHR$(SCREEN(y%, x%));
    NEXT x%

NEXT y%

PRINT #1, STRING$(80, 196)
PRINT #1, "This screen was written on "; DATE$; " at "; TIME$; "."
PRINT #1, STRING$(80, 196)

CLOSE
```

PRINT # USING

See also

INPUT #, PRINT, PRINT #, PRINT USING, WRITE #

Purpose

The PRINT # USING statement writes formatted data to an open sequential file, just as PRINT USING writes formatted data to the display. (See Chapter 8, "Simple I/O.") You can use PRINT # USING to write numbers and text to a file that will, for example, be used to fill in specific portions of a form.

Syntax

PRINT #*filenum*, USING *templateString*; *expr*[; *expr*...][; ! ,]

filenum is the file number of an open file to which data will be written.

templateString is either a string constant or a string variable. It can contain literal text, which is printed unchanged, and one or more special formatting characters (described in the PRINT USING entry in Chapter 8, "Simple I/O") that determine how the variables or expressions following the template string are to be printed.

expr is a numeric or string expression that contains the value to be written to the file; you can specify several expressions by separating them with semicolons. A comma at the end of the statement causes the file pointer to remain on the current line of the file and to move to the next print zone. (Each print zone is 14 characters in length.) A semicolon at the end of the statement causes the file pointer to remain on the current line, positioned immediately after the most recent character written.

Usage

```
PRINT #1, USING "######"; numVar%
```
Writes six digits of the contents of the variable *numVar%* to file number 1.

```
PRINT #1, USING "Pay to the order of !. !. &"; firstName$, middleName$, lastName$
```
Writes two single-character strings and a variable-length string to file number 1.

Description

The PRINT # USING statement writes data to a file exactly as PRINT USING writes data to the screen. If you must later read the file as a sequential file opened with the keyword INPUT, you must insert delimiters between data items. (For a complete list of formatting characters, see the PRINT USING entry in Chapter 8, "Simple I/O.")

Errors

If you use an array or a record variable as a parameter, QBasic displays a "Type mismatch" error message.

Tips

To speed up sequential file output, you can increase the size of the buffer by using the LEN clause in the OPEN statement of a file. However, remember that an increased buffer size reduces the available memory for the program.

Example

The following program uses the PRINT # USING statement to write data to a file that might later be printed onto checks.

```
CLS
DEFINT A-Z                ' define variables as integer by default

file = FREEFILE                       ' get next available file number
OPEN "CHECKS" FOR APPEND AS #file     ' open the file for additional output

DO
    PRINT
    PRINT "When you're finished, press Enter."
    PRINT

    LINE INPUT "Enter payee's first name:  "; first$
    IF first$ = "" THEN EXIT DO        ' quit if user presses Enter
    LINE INPUT "Enter payee's middle name: "; middle$
    LINE INPUT "Enter payee's last name:   "; last$
    INPUT "Enter amount to be paid:   ", amount!

    PRINT #file, "The Acme Novelty Company", , , DATE$   ' commas specify tabs
    PRINT #file, : PRINT #file, : PRINT #file,           ' skip three lines

    PRINT #file, "Pay to the order of: "
    PRINT #file, USING "!. !. \            \ "; first$; middle$; last$;
    PRINT #file, USING "             **$#,###,###.##"; amount!
```

(continued)

continued

```
      dollars& = FIX(amount!)              ' calculate the number of whole dollars
      cents = (amount! - dollars&) * 100   ' calculate the number of cents

      PRINT #file, USING "#,###,### and ##/100 dollars"; dollars&; cents
      PRINT #file, : PRINT #file, : PRINT #file,
      PRINT #file, , , "Jill Acme, President"
      PRINT #file, : PRINT #file, : PRINT #file,
   LOOP

   CLOSE #file
```

PUT (File I/O)

See also

FIELD, GET (File I/O), INPUT #, LINE INPUT #, OPEN, TYPE...END TYPE

Purpose

The PUT statement writes information to a random-access or binary file from fields defined by a FIELD statement or from record variables defined by a TYPE...END TYPE statement.

Syntax

PUT [#] *filenum*[, [*position*][, *variable*]]

filenum is the file number assigned to a file in an OPEN statement.

position is the number of the record (in random-access files) or byte (in binary files) at which writing data begins (in the range 1 through 2147483647).

variable is the variable that contains the data to be written to the file.

Usage

```
PUT #1, 1
```
Writes the contents of the fields associated with a random-access file to the first record in the file opened as file number 1.

```
PUT 1, , info
```
Writes the record variable *info* to the next record in a random-access file.

Description

You can use the PUT statement to write simple variables or entire records to a random-access or binary file.

When you use the PUT statement with a random-access file, you can specify the number of the record at which writing begins. Each record consists of the number of bytes specified in the LEN clause of the OPEN statement. The first record number in a file is record number 1. If you do not specify a record number, PUT writes the record after the one used in the most recent GET or PUT operation or after the record specified in the most recent SEEK statement.

When you use PUT with random-access files, you can specify any variable whose size in bytes is no larger than the record length specified when you opened the file. Specify a variable that matches the structure of the file's records.

If you use the PUT statement with a binary file, you can specify the number of the byte at which writing begins. The first byte in a file is byte number 1. If you do not specify a byte number, PUT writes the byte after the one used in the most recent GET or PUT operation or after the byte specified in the most recent SEEK statement.

The variable that you specify for a binary file parameter can be of any type and length. The PUT statement writes the number of bytes contained in the variable.

If you use the PUT statement when the record for the file has been defined by a FIELD statement, you cannot specify a variable. QBasic displays a "FIELD statement active" error message if you do specify a variable. To write values to the file, you must first assign the values to the fields of the record by using the LSET or RSET statement. Then use PUT without a variable to write the values to the file.

Warnings

Because the maximum size of a record in a file is 32,767 bytes, the maximum size of the variable in a PUT statement to a random-access or binary file is also 32,767 bytes.

If the specified variable is a variable-length string, PUT precedes the data in the string with a 2-byte header that specifies the length of the string. Therefore, each variable-length string extends the length of a record by 2 bytes. This might cause a problem if you must share data files with a program written in another version of Basic. To prevent this, used fixed-length strings in your GET and PUT statements.

Example

The following program uses the GET and PUT statements to update a file that contains the user's color choices for the screen.

```
TYPE ConfigType
    normal AS INTEGER             ' color of box internal area
    highlight AS INTEGER          ' color of letter highlight
    inverseHighlight AS INTEGER   ' color of the inverse of letter highlight
    inverse AS INTEGER            ' color of highlight bar
    help AS INTEGER               ' color of help line
    cursorNormal AS INTEGER       ' cursor size when overstriking
    cursorInsert AS INTEGER       ' cursor size when inserting
END TYPE

DIM config AS ConfigType          ' define the record variable config

OPEN "CONFIG.DAT" FOR BINARY AS #1  ' open the file
```

(continued)

continued

```
GET #1, 1, config                       ' read current configuration information

CLS
PRINT "Enter new colors."
PRINT

PRINT "Normal color = "; config.normal;
INPUT "  Change to: ", config.normal

PRINT "Highlight color = "; config.highlight;
INPUT "  Change to: ", config.highlight

PRINT "Inverse highlight color = "; config.inverseHighlight;
INPUT "  Change to: ", config.inverseHighlight

PRINT "Inverse color = "; config.inverse;
INPUT "  Change to: ", config.inverse

PRINT "Help color = "; config.help;
INPUT "  Change to: ", config.help

PRINT "Overstrike cursor size = "; config.cursorNormal;
INPUT "  Change to: ", config.cursorNormal

PRINT "Insert cursor size = "; config.cursorInsert;
INPUT "  Change to: ", config.cursorInsert

PUT #1, 1, config                       ' write the information to the file
CLOSE

END
```

RESET

See also

CLOSE, END, SYSTEM

Purpose

The RESET statement closes all open files and writes the data in the corresponding buffers to the appropriate file or device. You can use RESET at the end of your program to be sure all files are closed before the program ends.

Syntax

RESET

Usage

```
PRINT "All tasks have been completed."
RESET
```

Displays a shutdown message, clears all data from the current file buffers, and then closes all open files.

Description

The RESET statement closes all open files and clears any data still in the file buffers that were allocated by the OPEN statement. The RESET statement works the same as the CLOSE statement without any parameters.

Comments

The RESET statement (and the CLOSE, END, and SYSTEM statements) clears pending I/O by writing the contents of the current file buffers to the appropriate file or device; however, RESET doesn't execute a PUT statement to update a file containing fields (defined by FIELD) to a random-access file. Therefore, if you have changed any fields, you must execute a PUT statement to add the changes to the file before executing the RESET statement.

Example

The following program uses the RESET statement to close all files when the user quits the program.

```
OPEN "FIRST" FOR INPUT AS #1
OPEN "SECOND" FOR INPUT AS #2
OPEN "THIRD" FOR OUTPUT AS #3
OPEN "GARFIELD.DAT" FOR APPEND AS #7

INPUT "Do you want to quit the program?"; yesNo$

DO
    IF UCASE$(LEFT$(yesNo$, 1)) = "Y" THEN
        RESET
        END
    END IF
LOOP
```

RSET

See also

FIELD, LSET, MKD$, MKDMBF$, MKI$, MKL$, MKS$, MKSMBF$, PUT (File I/O)

Purpose

The RSET statement puts the value of an expression or a variable into a specified field of a random-access file's buffer. RSET also right-justifies this expression or variable. RSET can also be used to right-justify any string variable.

Syntax

RSET *var* = *expr*

var and *expr* must both be strings.

Usage

```
RSET address$ = "123 PARK ST."
```

Right-justifies the string constant "123 PARK ST." and places it into the *address$* field if *address$* is the name of a field defined by a FIELD statement. If *address$* is a string variable, RSET only right-justifies it within the current length of *address$*.

```
RSET amtDue$ = MKD$(total#)
```

Places the string representation of the contents of *total#* variable into *amtDue$*, which can be either the name of a field defined by a FIELD statement or a string variable.

Description

The FIELD statement allocates a special storage buffer when it defines the record for a random-access file. Because of this special allocation, you cannot use the equal sign (=) or the LET statement to assign values to the fields defined by the FIELD statement. Instead, you must use the LSET or RSET statement to make the assignment. Note that you can also use RSET with string variables.

Using RSET with fields

When you specify a field name as the first parameter in an RSET statement, the RSET statement copies the value of the second parameter (which must be a string) into the location in a random-access buffer allocated for the specified field.

If the length of the field is greater than the length of the string value, RSET right-justifies the value in the buffer. That is, RSET adds spaces to the beginning of the string until it is the same length as the field.

If the length of the field is less than the length of the string value, RSET copies only enough characters to fill the field and ignores the remaining characters.

Figure 17-9 shows how the RSET statement places a string in a field.

```
FIELD 1, 20 AS patientName$
RSET patientName$ = "Robert Anderson II"
```

		R	o	b	e	r	t		A	n	d	e	r	s	o	n		I	I

```
RSET patientName$ = "Robert Lloyd Anderson II"
```

R	o	b	e	r	t		L	l	o	y	d		A	n	d	e	r	s	o

Figure 17-9.
The RSET statement with fields.

Using RSET with string variables

When the first parameter to RSET is a string variable (not a field name), RSET performs a different task. Because the length of the variable is not set by a FIELD statement, RSET uses the current length of the string variable to calculate the justification it will perform.

If the current length of the string variable is greater than the length of the value specified in the second parameter, RSET right-justifies the value. That is, RSET adds spaces to the beginning of the string value until it is the same length as the string variable.

If the current length of the string variable is less than the length of the value specified in the second parameter, RSET copies only enough characters to fill the string variable and ignores the remaining characters.

You can determine the current length of a string variable by using the LEN function. (See the LEN entry in Chapter 5, "Strings," for details.)

Figure 17-10 shows how the RESET statement works with string variables.

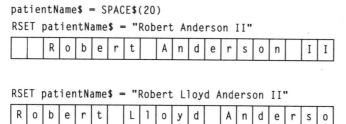

```
patientName$ = SPACE$(20)
RSET patientName$ = "Robert Anderson II"
```

```
RSET patientName$ = "Robert Lloyd Anderson II"
```

Figure 17-10.
The RSET statement with string variables.

Comments

Remember that you must convert numeric values to strings before you place them into a field defined by a FIELD statement. (See the MKD$, MKDMBF$, MKI$, MKL$, MKS$, and MKSMBF$ entries for details.)

Example

The following program uses RSET to right-justify user input. It writes job titles and people's names to a file, positioning the job title on the left side and the corresponding name on the right. The program then displays the contents of the file.

```
OPEN "CREDITS.TXT" FOR OUTPUT AS #1

DO
    job$ = SPACE$(40)
    person$ = SPACE$(40)

    LINE INPUT "Job title:    "; jobTitle$
    IF jobTitle$ = "" THEN EXIT DO
```

(continued)

continued

```
    LINE INPUT "Person's name: "; personName$
    PRINT

    LSET job$ = jobTitle$
    RSET person$ = personName$
    PRINT #1, job$; person$          ' write the information to the file
LOOP UNTIL jobTitle$ = ""

CLOSE #1

OPEN "credits.txt" FOR INPUT AS #1

DO UNTIL EOF(1)
    LINE INPUT #1, credit$           ' display the contents of the file
    PRINT credit$
LOOP
CLOSE #1
```

RTRIM$

See also
LTRIM$

Purpose
The RTRIM$ function returns a copy of a string expression without trailing spaces (spaces on the right). You use the RTRIM$ function to format data in which trailing spaces would either cause misaligned output or be misinterpreted as literal characters.

Syntax
RTRIM$(*string*)

string is any string expression.

Usage
```
PRINT #1, RTRIM$(description$)
```
Writes the variable *description$* without trailing spaces to the file associated with file number 1.

Description
QBasic provides the RTRIM$ function to let you delete extra spaces that might have been inserted by the user or the program. The RTRIM$ function accepts any string expression and returns the same string without trailing spaces.

Example
The following program uses the RTRIM$ function to delete the trailing spaces from user input.

```
CLS

LINE INPUT "Enter your first name:  "; first$
LINE INPUT "Enter your middle name: "; middle$
LINE INPUT "Enter your last name:   "; last$

PRINT
PRINT "Pay to the order of: "; RTRIM$(first$); " ";
PRINT LEFT$(middle$, 1); ". "; RTRIM$(last$)
```

SEEK (Function)

See also

GET (File I/O), OPEN, PUT (File I/O), SEEK (Statement)

Purpose

The SEEK function returns the number of the current record or byte position in a file. You can use SEEK, for example, to determine how close the current record is to the end of the file.

Syntax

SEEK(*filenum*)

filenum is the file number of an open file.

Usage

```
PRINT "The current file position is"; SEEK(1)
```

Displays the current file position for the file opened as file number 1.

Description

The value that the SEEK function returns for random-access files is the number of the next record that will be read from or written to when you use the PUT and GET file I/O statements. Note that the first record in a file is record number 1.

If the file is a sequential or binary file, the SEEK function returns the byte number at which the next I/O operation (such as a PUT or a GET statement) will take place. Note that the first byte in a file is byte number 1.

Comments

The largest value the SEEK function can return is 2147483647 because that is the largest file that QBasic and DOS support.

Warnings

The SEEK function returns 0 when used with the QBasic SCRN:, KYBD:, CONS:, COM*n*:, and LPT*n*: devices. The SEEK function returns meaningful values only when it is used with files.

Example

The following program uses the SEEK function to determine which record is current in a random-access file.

```
TYPE Planets                        ' type definition for planet information
    nam AS STRING * 20              ' name
    diameter AS LONG                ' diameter
    perihelion AS DOUBLE            ' orbital point closest to sun
    aphelion AS DOUBLE              ' orbital point farthest from sun
    highTemp AS SINGLE              ' highest surface temperature
    lowTemp AS SINGLE               ' lowest surface temperature
    yearDiscovered AS INTEGER       ' year discovered
END TYPE

DIM planet AS Planets               ' define a variable of type Planets

CLS
OPEN "SOL.DAT" FOR RANDOM AS #1 LEN = 50     ' open the data file

FOR planetNum% = 1 TO 9
    PRINT : PRINT : PRINT

    SEEK #1, planetNum%                      ' move to the correct record
    GET #1, , planet                         ' read the record
    PRINT "Planet number"; SEEK(1) - 1       ' display the record number

    PRINT : PRINT "Information about planet "; planet.nam
    PRINT STRING$(79, 45): PRINT

    ' get information from the user if the record is empty
    IF planet.nam = STRING$(20, 0) THEN
        INPUT "Name"; planet.nam
        INPUT "Diameter (km)"; planet.diameter
        INPUT "Perihelion (km)"; planet.perihelion
        INPUT "Aphelion (km)"; planet.aphelion
        INPUT "Highest temperature"; planet.highTemp
        INPUT "Lowest temperature"; planet.lowTemp
        INPUT "Discovered in"; planet.yearDiscovered
        PUT #1, planetNum%, planet           ' write the information to the file
        PRINT : PRINT "Information saved": PRINT : PRINT
    ELSE                                     ' display the information
        PRINT "Diameter is"; planet.diameter; "kilometers."
        PRINT "Perihelion is"; planet.perihelion; "kilometers."
        PRINT "Aphelion is"; planet.aphelion; "kilometers."
        PRINT "Highest temperature is"; planet.highTemp; "degrees."
        PRINT "Lowest temperature is"; planet.lowTemp; "degrees."
        PRINT "Discovered in"; planet.yearDiscovered; "."
    END IF
NEXT

CLOSE
```

SEEK (Statement)

See also

GET (File I/O), OPEN, PUT (File I/O), SEEK (Function)

Purpose

The SEEK statement sets the current position in an open file. The current position is the location at which the next I/O operation (such as a GET or a PUT operation) will take place.

Syntax

SEEK [#] *filenum, position*

filenum is the file number of an open file.

position is the number of the record or byte that you want to move to within the file. It must be in the range 1 through 2147483647.

Usage

```
OPEN "FILE.DAT" FOR RANDOM AS #1
SEEK 1, 128
```

Sets the current position for the file opened as number 1 to record number 128.

Description

QBasic's GET and PUT file I/O statements let you omit which record or byte in the file to read from or write to; if you do not specify a record or byte number, the statement reads from or writes to the current position in the file. The current position is updated to the next location in the file after a read or write operation. You can use the current position to gain access to files sequentially, should you need to. However, the SEEK statement lets you change the current file position to any other record or byte. After you execute the SEEK statement, the next I/O operation is performed at the new location provided that it doesn't include a specific record or byte number.

The specified position for a random-access file is the record number that will become the current position. The first record in a file is record number 1. The specified position for a sequential or binary file is the byte number that will become the current position. The first byte in a file is byte number 1.

Comments

QBasic ignores the SEEK statement if the *filenum* parameter is the file number of the SCRN:, KYBD:, CONS:, COM*n*:, or LPT*n*: QBasic device.

Errors

If you specify a position that is less than or equal to 0, QBasic displays a "Bad record number" error message.

Example

The following program uses the SEEK statement to change the current position to a specific record in a random-access file.

```
TYPE Planets                        ' type definition for planet information
    nam AS STRING * 20              ' name
    diameter AS LONG                ' diameter
    perihelion AS DOUBLE            ' orbital point closest to sun
    aphelion AS DOUBLE              ' orbital point farthest from sun
    highTemp AS SINGLE              ' highest surface temperature
    lowTemp AS SINGLE               ' lowest surface temperature
    yearDiscovered AS INTEGER       ' year discovered
END TYPE

DIM planet AS Planets               ' define a variable of type Planets

CLS
OPEN "SOL.DAT" FOR RANDOM AS #1 LEN = 50      'open the data file

DO
    PRINT : PRINT : PRINT
    INPUT "Information about which planet"; planetNum%    ' get a record number

    ' exit if user presses Enter or planetNum% out of range
    IF planetNum% < 1 OR planetNum% > 9 THEN EXIT DO

    SEEK #1, planetNum%                     ' move to the correct record
    GET #1, , planet                        ' read the record

    PRINT : PRINT "Information about planet "; planet.nam
    PRINT STRING$(79, 45): PRINT

    ' get information from the user if the record is empty
    IF planet.nam = STRING$(20, 0) THEN
        INPUT "Name"; planet.nam
        INPUT "Diameter (km)"; planet.diameter
        INPUT "Perihelion (km)"; planet.perihelion
        INPUT "Aphelion (km)"; planet.aphelion
        INPUT "Highest temperature"; planet.highTemp
        INPUT "Lowest temperature"; planet.lowTemp
        INPUT "Discovered in"; planet.yearDiscovered
        PUT #1, planetNum%, planet          ' write the information to the file
        PRINT : PRINT "Information saved": PRINT : PRINT
    ELSE                                    ' display the information
        PRINT "Diameter is"; planet.diameter; "kilometers."
        PRINT "Perihelion is"; planet.perihelion; "kilometers."
        PRINT "Aphelion is"; planet.aphelion; "kilometers."
        PRINT "Highest temperature is"; planet.highTemp; "degrees."
        PRINT "Lowest temperature is"; planet.lowTemp; "degrees."
        PRINT "Discovered in"; planet.yearDiscovered; "."
    END IF
LOOP
CLOSE
```

UNLOCK

See also

LOCK, OPEN

Purpose

The UNLOCK statement lets other network programs access a shared file or sections of that file. You use UNLOCK to let other programs share a file or a portion of a file that was previously locked during a critical I/O operation.

Syntax

UNLOCK [#] *filenum*[, {*record* ┊ [*start*] TO *end*}]

filenum is the file number of an open file.

record is the number of the record or byte to be unlocked.

start and *end* are integers that specify a range of records or bytes to be unlocked.

Usage

```
UNLOCK #1
```
Unlocks the entire file opened as file number 1.

```
OPEN "VENDORS.DAT" FOR RANDOM AS #4
⋮
UNLOCK #4, 10
```
Unlocks record 10 of the random-access file opened as file number 4.

Description

You use UNLOCK with programs that will be used in a network environment in which several users or processes share the same files. After you use the LOCK statement to prevent conflicts that can occur when different programs try to access the same data simultaneously, you must use the UNLOCK statement to release the locks on the file.

In a random-access file, you specify the numbers of the records to be locked. The first record in a file is always record number 1. In a binary file, you specify the bytes to be locked. The first byte in the file is always byte number 1. You can unlock individual records or bytes only in binary or random-access files; with sequential files you can unlock only the entire file.

Comments

You must use the LOCK and UNLOCK statements in *exactly* matching pairs. That is, you cannot combine the UNLOCK statements of more than one LOCK statement to form an "equivalent" UNLOCK statement; you must instead use UNLOCK statements that correspond exactly to the original LOCK statements. For example, the two statements

```
LOCK #3, 1 TO 10
LOCK #3, 11 TO 20
```

require the two UNLOCK statements

```
UNLOCK #3, 1 TO 10
UNLOCK #3, 11 TO 20
```

You cannot simply combine the two UNLOCK statements into the single statement

```
UNLOCK #3, 1 TO 20
```

Note that QBasic lets you issue the above single UNLOCK statement without returning an error; however, the statement has no effect, and the 20 bytes or records remain locked.

Errors

If you specify the UNLOCK statement before you use the LOCK statement, QBasic displays a "Permission denied" error message.

Warnings

Note that Microsoft supports QBasic only on Microsoft LAN Manager, IBM PC Network, MS-Network, and compatible systems. Although limited success has been reported using other networks, such as Novell and 3Com, problems can occur.

If you lock a file and then either lose power or reboot your computer before you execute the matching UNLOCK statement, data in the locked file might be lost. To minimize the danger of losing data, use LOCK to lock records only as long as necessary.

Example

The following program uses the LOCK statement to guarantee that no other program can access the file CONFIG.DAT while the program is running. Before the program ends, it releases its lock on the file by issuing the matching UNLOCK statement.

```
TYPE ConfigType
    normal AS INTEGER              ' color of box internal area
    highlight AS INTEGER           ' color of letter highlight
    inverseHighlight AS INTEGER    ' color of the inverse of letter highlight
    inverse AS INTEGER             ' color of highlight bar
    help AS INTEGER                ' color of help line
    cursorNormal AS INTEGER        ' cursor size when overstriking
    cursorInsert AS INTEGER        ' cursor size when inserting
END TYPE

DIM config AS ConfigType           ' define the record variable config

CLS
PRINT "Enter new colors."
PRINT

OPEN "CONFIG.DAT" FOR BINARY ACCESS READ WRITE LOCK WRITE AS #1  ' open file

LOCK #1                            ' lock the entire file
GET #1, 1, config                  ' read the current configuration information
```

(continued)

continued

```
PRINT "Normal color = "; config.normal;
INPUT "  Change to: ", config.normal

PRINT "Highlight color = "; config.highlight;
INPUT "  Change to: ", config.highlight

PRINT "Inverse highlight color = "; config.inverseHighlight;
INPUT "  Change to: ", config.inverseHighlight

PRINT "Inverse color = "; config.inverse;
INPUT "  Change to: ", config.inverse

PRINT "Help color = "; config.help;
INPUT "  Change to: ", config.help

PRINT "Overstrike cursor size = "; config.cursorNormal;
INPUT "  Change to: ", config.cursorNormal

PRINT "Insert cursor size = "; config.cursorInsert;
INPUT "  Change to: ", config.cursorInsert

PUT #1, 1, config              ' write the information to the file
UNLOCK #1                      ' unlock the entire file

CLOSE #1

END
```

WIDTH (File I/O)

See also

LPOS, LPRINT, POS, PRINT, TAB

Purpose

The WIDTH statement sets a maximum line width for sequential files. You can use the WIDTH statement, for example, to limit the line lengths in a file containing a report.

Syntax

WIDTH {#*filenum* ¦ *device*}, *width*

filenum is the file number of an open sequential file.

device is a string expression that specifies the name of a QBasic device.

width is the desired width (in characters) of a line for either *filenum* or *device*.

Usage

```
WIDTH #1, 40
```
Sets the width of the specified file to 40 characters.

```
WIDTH "CONS:", 32
```
Sets the width of the QBasic device CONS: to 32 characters.

Description

Usually, you write data to sequential files without formatting. However, you can use the WIDTH statement to prevent text from being written beyond a specified right margin. The WIDTH statement accomplishes this by wrapping any long line to the next line. Figure 17-11 illustrates the effects of a WIDTH statement.

```
WIDTH, #1, 25
sample$ = "ABCDEFGHIJKLMNOPQRSTUVWXYZABCDEFGHIJKLMNOPQRSTUVWXYZABCDEFGH"
PRINT #1, sample$
```

A	B	C	D	E	F	G	H	I	J	K	L	M	N	O	P	Q	R	S	T	U	V	W	X	Y

Z	A	B	C	D	E	F	G	H	I	J	K	L	M	N	O	P	Q	R	S	T	U	V	W	X

Y	Z	A	B	C	D	E	F	G	H															

Figure 17-11.
The use of the WIDTH statement.

Using the WIDTH statement with a filename lets you set the line width for an opened file or for a QBasic device opened as a file. This is, in fact, the only way to change the line width of a file. Note that the file or device opened as a file must be open before you issue the WIDTH statement.

Using the WIDTH statement with a device name lets you set the line width for a QBasic device. You cannot use the WIDTH statement to affect a DOS device. Note that WIDTH does not effect output to the device until the next time you open it.

Errors

If the specified device is not a QBasic device (CONS:, SCRN:, LPT*n*:, or COM*n*), QBasic displays an "Illegal function call" error message.

Example

The following program creates a report whose lines do not exceed 80 characters.

```
OPEN "SALES.RPT" FOR OUTPUT AS #1          ' open report file
WIDTH #1, 80                               ' set line width to 80

PRINT #1, "Sales report as of "; DATE$     ' print heading

FOR region% = 1 TO 30
    PRINT #1, USING "Region ##: "; region%;  ' print line heading
```

(continued)

continued

```
    salesAmt% = RND * 50              ' calculate fictitious sales
    FOR i% = 1 TO salesAmt%
        PRINT #1, "* ";               ' write the graph to the file
    NEXT
    PRINT #1,                         ' move to next report line
NEXT                                  ' move to next region

CLOSE
```

WRITE

See also

INPUT #, PRINT #

Purpose

The WRITE # statement writes delimited, unformatted data to a sequential file. You can use the WRITE # statement to quickly write data to a file so that it can be easily read by the INPUT # statement.

Syntax

WRITE # *filenum*[, *expr* [, *expr*...]]

filenum is the file number of a currently open file.

expr is a numeric or string expression that contains the value to be written to the file. Separate multiple entries with commas.

Usage

```
WRITE #2, patientName$, patientBirthday%, pastDueAmount#
```

Writes the values of three variables to the file opened as file number 2; the value of *patientName$* is enclosed in quotation marks in the file, and all the values are separated by commas.

Description

The QBasic file input statement INPUT # requires that data be formatted and delimited. If you use the PRINT # statement to write data to a file, you must explicitly include spaces, quotation marks, or commas for delimiters. This can be difficult to enter and to read, as you can see in the following example:

```
PRINT #2, CHR$(34); patientName$; CHR$(34); ","; birthday%; ","; pastDueAmount#
```

You can perform the same operation with the following simpler and more readable WRITE # statement:

```
WRITE #2, patientName$, birthday%, pastDueAmount#
```

WRITE #

The specified file number is the number associated with the file to which the data will be written. Note that the file must have been opened as a sequential file by using the keyword OUTPUT or APPEND in the OPEN statement.

The value written to the file can be specified by a constant (quoted text, a numeric value, or a constant defined by CONST) or by an expression of any simple type, such as an array element, a record element, a simple variable, or a mathematical or string expression that uses QBasic functions. If you don't use parameters in a WRITE # statement, the statement writes a blank line to the file.

When the WRITE # statement writes data to a file, it uses the least amount of space, while still allowing the INPUT # statement to later read what was written. As shown in Figure 17-12, WRITE # encloses string variables in quotation marks. Unlike the PRINT # statement, however, WRITE # writes numeric variables to the file without leading or trailing space. It writes negative numeric variables to the file with a preceding minus sign. Unlike the PRINT # statement, WRITE # inserts commas between all variables in the file. Figure 17-12 illustrates the actions of the WRITE # statement.

```
patientName$ = "Doe, John"
birthday! = 12170
pastDueAmount# = 150.25
```

| " | D | o | e | , | | J | o | h | n | " | , | 1 | 2 | 1 | 7 | 0 | , | 1 | 5 | 0 | . | 2 | 5 |

Figure 17-12.
Using WRITE # to write to a file.

After writing the last specified value to the file, the WRITE # statement inserts a newline character in the file. Therefore, the next WRITE # or PRINT # statement writes data to the next line in the file. Unlike the PRINT # statement, the WRITE # statement always writes a newline character.

Comments
The WRITE # statement does not have a corresponding WRITE # USING statement to provide formatted output. If you must format data, use the PRINT # USING statement.

Because the WRITE # statement encloses strings in quotation marks, the INPUT # statement cannot correctly read strings that have been written to the file by using WRITE # and that already have quotation marks in them. If you need to read strings that include quotation marks, use the LINE INPUT # statement instead.

Example
The following program uses the WRITE # statement to write the contents of the current screen to a file; the program encloses each line in quotation marks so that you can later use the INPUT # statement to read the file one line at a time.

```
OPEN "SCREEN.DAT" FOR APPEND AS #1

FOR y = 1 TO 25
    screenLine$ = ""

    FOR x = 1 TO 80
        screenLine$ = screenLine$ + CHR$(SCREEN(y, x))
    NEXT

    WRITE #1, screenLine$
NEXT

WRITE #1, STRING$(80, 196)
WRITE #1, "This screen was written on ", DATE$, " at ", TIME$
WRITE #1, STRING$(80, 196)

CLOSE
```

SECTION IV

DEVELOPMENT

CHAPTER 18

DOS and Program Management

Introduction

QBasic includes many commands and functions that help you control the interaction between your program and the DOS environment. For example, the program management routines discussed in this chapter let you perform the following operations:

- Use any of several methods to exit a QBasic program
- Pass control to a second QBasic program
- Examine QBasic's copy of the DOS environment and change or add to the variables in it
- Create, change to, or remove a disk directory
- Delete files from a disk
- Run the DOS command processor, execute any DOS commands or other programs, and then resume execution of a QBasic program
- Send control instructions to or receive them from a device driver

Table 18-1 lists the QBasic program-management statements and functions in alphabetic order.

Statement or function	Description
CHDIR	Makes the specified directory the current (default) directory.
CLEAR	Reinitializes (clears) all program variables; can also set the size of the QBasic stack, which maintains data during subroutine and procedure calls.
: (Colon)	Separates multiple statements on the same program line.
END	Ends a program and closes all open files.
ENVIRON	Adds, removes, or changes an environment variable.
ENVIRON$	Returns the value of QBasic's copy of a DOS environment variable.
IOCTL	Sends a control string to a device driver.
IOCTL$	Receives a status string from a device driver.
KILL	Deletes a disk file.

Table 18-1. *(continued)*
QBasic program-management statements and functions.

Table 18-1. *continued*

Statement or function	Description
MKDIR	Creates the specified directory on a disk.
REM	Begins a comment (remark) line. A single quotation mark also begins a comment line or begins a comment at the end of an executable statement.
RMDIR	Removes a directory from a disk. The directory must not contain any files.
RUN	Restarts the current program (optionally, from a specified line number) or runs another program; however, the second program cannot access data from the first.
SHELL	Runs a copy of COMMAND.COM, the DOS command processor, with which you can run any DOS command or program (memory permitting).
STOP	Ends execution of the QBasic program but does not close open files.
SYSTEM	Ends execution of the QBasic program and closes all open files.

The Statement Separator and Comments

You can place several QBasic statements on the same program line; merely separate the statements with a colon (:). Generally, putting several executable statements on the same line makes your code harder to read. Sometimes, however, putting multiple statements on one line makes your code easier to read, such as when you use multiple PRINT statements to force blank lines in a display:

```
PRINT : PRINT : REM skip two lines
```

This line includes two PRINT statements and a REM (remark, or comment) statement that explains the purpose of the line. Using a single quote mark symbol (') is a shorthand method for specifying a comment, as in the following statement:

```
PRINT : PRINT ' skip two lines
```

Note that you don't need to use a colon in front of a quoted comment on a line that contains executable statements. A comment introduced by a single quotation mark or by REM can occupy a complete line by itself, but if a comment follows executable code on the same line, the comment must be preceded either by single quotation mark or by a colon and the REM keyword.

Exiting a QBasic Program

QBasic implicitly calls the END statement after the last statement in a program. END closes all files and terminates the program. You can insert END statements in any part of your program to exit the program, as shown in the following program segment:

```
DO
    DisplayMenu
    INPUT ans$
    IF UCASE$(ans$) = "X" THEN END
    IF UCASE$(ans$) = "A" THEN AddFile
LOOP
```

This loop executes END only if the user enters *x* or *X*. Note that the keyword END is also used with the statements DEF FN, FUNCTION, IF, SELECT CASE, SUB, and TYPE...END TYPE to indicate the end of these structures or definitions.

The END statement is similar to the STOP and SYSTEM statements. END and SYSTEM close all open files. STOP leaves files open when you run the program.

Running Programs and Using DOS Commands in a Program

You can use both the CHAIN and RUN commands to run a second program from a QBasic program. CHAIN lets the second program access any variables declared in a COMMON statement; RUN does not. RUN, on the other hand, can either start a second program or restart the current program from the beginning or at a specified line number. CHAIN and RUN can run only Basic source files. (See the CHAIN and RUN entries for details about these statements.)

If you want your program to use a DOS command or run a batch file, you can specify the command or the batch file's name in a call to the SHELL statement. The SHELL statement exits the program, runs the DOS command processor COMMAND.COM, performs the specified task, and then returns to the program. If you don't specify a command or batch file in a call to SHELL, it exits the program and runs the command processor until the user enters the EXIT command.

Reinitializing Variables and Setting Stack Size

The CLEAR statement sets all numeric variables and numeric array elements to 0, sets all string variables and string array elements to the null string (""), and closes all files. If you execute a CLEAR statement before you use RUN, you can restart a program with a clean slate.

CLEAR also clears the stack and can also set its size. The stack is the area in memory that QBasic uses to store the contents of variables used in subroutine and function calls. For example, the statement

```
CLEAR , , 8000
```

reinitializes all variables and sets the stack to 8000 bytes. You might need to increase the size of the stack if your program has many deeply nested subroutines or procedures or if you use recursive procedures (subprograms or functions that call themselves). You cannot use CLEAR within a procedure or subroutine. The stack maintains the location to which the procedure or subroutine must return, so after CLEAR erases the stack, the procedure or subroutine can't return control to the statement that called it.

Reading and Setting Environment Variables

QBasic programs can obtain and modify information about the DOS environment. The environment is an area of memory that DOS copies into the data area of a QBasic program when it runs. The copy consists of a series of variables associated with strings of information.

QBasic provides a statement and a function that interact with your program's copy of the environment. The ENVIRON statement replaces the information in a DOS environment variable. For example,

```
ENVIRON "PATH=C:\ACCT;C:\TEMP"
```

changes the value of the PATH variable to *C:\ACCT;C:\TEMP*.

The ENVIRON$ function in QBasic returns the value of an environment variable. The statement *ENVIRON$(1)* returns the first variable and its value, *ENVIRON$(2)* returns the second one, and so on. Thus, if PATH is the third variable in the environment, the statement

```
PRINT ENVIRON$(3)
```

displays *PATH=C:\ACCT;C:\TEMP*

Or you can use a variable name with the ENVIRON$ statement to retrieve the value of the specified variable. The following statement displays the same string the previous example did:

```
PRINT ENVIRON$("PATH")
```

Remember that your QBasic program receives only a copy of the original DOS environment; any changes specified in ENVIRON statements do not change the original DOS environment, which is restored when your program completes execution. However, if your program runs another program with the CHAIN or RUN command or the SHELL statement, the new program receives a copy of your program's environment, including any changes or additions you've made. (See the ENVIRON entry for suggestions about how to prevent "Out of memory" errors.)

Communicating with Device Drivers

The IOCTL ("I/O control") statement sends a string of instructions to a device driver, which is a special program that DOS installs in memory (usually by means of a DEVICE statement in the CONFIG.SYS file). The program interprets instructions for a specific device (such as the printer, communications port, or mouse) and translates them into the low-level instructions that the hardware uses. In turn, you can request that the device driver report the status of the device (for example, whether the printer is ready to accept more text). When you specify the file number associated with an open device, the IOCTL$ statement returns the corresponding status report if the device supports IOCTL instructions. Unfortunately, most devices (including the common devices LPT1, LPT2, COM1, COM2, and so on) are not designed to accept IOCTL instructions.

Managing Files and Directories

QBasic provides many statements that let users manage files; Chapter 17, "Files," discusses most of these. QBasic provides three statements that let users manage directories: MKDIR creates a directory, CHDIR changes the current directory, and RMDIR removes a directory. These statements are similar to their DOS counterparts; however, you can't abbreviate them as you can in DOS.

Related Reading

Lesser, Murray. *Advanced QuickBASIC 4.0: Language Extension with Modular Tools.* New York, N.Y.: Bantam Computer Books, 1988.

Prata, Stephen, with Harry Henderson. *The Waite Group's Microsoft QuickBASIC Primer Plus.* Redmond, Wash.: Microsoft Press, 1990.

CHDIR

See also
MKDIR, RMDIR, SHELL, SYSTEM

Purpose
The CHDIR statement changes the current directory. You can use CHDIR to change the default directory for file-related commands (such as OPEN or CHAIN) so that the program doesn't have to specify a full directory path.

Syntax
CHDIR *directory*

directory is a string expression of no more than 63 characters that specifies a new directory or directory path.

Usage
```
TEMPDIR$ = "C:\TEMP"
CHDIR tempdir$
```
Changes the current directory on drive C to the directory specified in the string variable *tempdir$*.

Description
DOS maintains a current directory for each drive in the system. The current directory is the default that DOS and QBasic use if you don't specify path information in a command. For example, if the current directory on drive C (the current drive) is TEMP, the FILES statement lists the contents of the directory C:\TEMP.

Note that DOS keeps track of both the current drive and the current directory on each drive. Changing the current directory on a drive does not change the current drive. For example, if the current drive is A, the statements

```
CHDIR "C:\TEMP"
FILES
```

change the current directory on drive C, but they list the current directory of drive A, not that of C:\TEMP. You cannot change to a new drive by using the CHDIR statement. To change the current drive from within a Basic program, you must use the SHELL statement, as in the statement *SHELL "C:"*.

Your programs should not assume a particular drive or directory; instead, they should set the current drive and directory explicitly.

Comments
The QBasic CHDIR statement is similar to the DOS CHDIR command; however, it is different in that QBasic does not recognize the abbreviation CD.

Errors

If you specify in the CHDIR statement a path that doesn't exist, QBasic displays a "Path not found" error message. If you specify an expression that is not a string, QBasic displays a "Type mismatch" error message. If you do not specify a parameter, QBasic displays an "Expected: expression" error message.

Example

The following program prompts the user for a directory path and then uses a CHDIR statement to make that the current directory. A FILES statement then displays the contents of the specified directory.

```
INPUT "Enter the directory to which you want to change: ", dir$
CHDIR dir$     ' change the current directory

' display the contents of the directory
PRINT "*** Listing of files in "; dir$; " ***": PRINT
FILES
```

CLEAR

See also

DECLARE, DIM, ERASE, FRE, REDIM

Purpose

The CLEAR statement reinitializes all program variables (setting numeric values to 0 and strings to the null string, ""), clears the stack, closes all files, and optionally changes the size of the stack. You might use CLEAR to increase the stack size if a program has procedures that are recursive or deeply nested, or that include many parameters and automatic variables.

Syntax

CLEAR [, , *stack*]

stack is the number of bytes (in the range 0 through 32767) to be allocated for the stack used by the program. Note that you must always precede *stack* with two commas.

Usage

```
CLEAR
```
Reinitializes all variables, clears the stack, and closes all open files.

```
CLEAR , , 1024
```
Reinitializes all variables, clears the stack, closes all open files, and sets the stack size to 1024 bytes.

Description

The main use of the CLEAR statement is to reinitialize all variables (including array elements) to 0 (for numeric values) or to the null string (for string values). In a program that traps an error normally considered fatal (perhaps involving the corruption of data), you can use the CLEAR statement to clear all (potentially incorrect) variable values; you can then restart the program from the beginning with a clean slate. (You might also do this in a game, to begin a new game upon request.) Note that CLEAR closes all open files.

Do not use CLEAR simply to reinitialize arrays and other variables later in the program because CLEAR reinitializes *all* variables, not only the ones you want to reuse. You can use the ERASE statement to reinitialize specific arrays without affecting other variables.

You can also use CLEAR to change the size of the stack used by your program. In this case, be sure to call the CLEAR statement at the beginning of your program, before you dimension arrays or initialize other variables, because CLEAR reinitializes all variables. QBasic adds the amount of stack space it requires and the amount of stack space you specify to compute the size of the entire stack. The default size of the stack is 2048 bytes. The stack size remains at the most recently specified value until you run a different program.

Errors

If you use CLEAR in a subroutine, QBasic displays a "Return without GOSUB" error message. If you use CLEAR in a procedure, QBasic displays an "Illegal function call" error message when you run the program.

Example

The following program shows how to use the CLEAR statement at the beginning of a program to set the size of the stack. The program uses the recursive function *Factorial#* to calculate the factorial of a number (the product of all of the values from 1 through the number). The program calls the FRE function with the parameter −2 so that the function returns the amount of space currently available on the stack. Note that the stack space decreases with each recursive call to the *Factorial#* function.

```
DECLARE FUNCTION Factorial# (num%)

INPUT "Change stack size (y/n) "; ans$
IF UCASE$(ans$) = "Y" THEN
    INPUT "Stack size: ", size
    CLEAR , , size
END IF

PRINT "Stack space available "; FRE(-2); " bytes."

INPUT "Factorial of what number "; number%
fact# = Factorial#(number%)
PRINT "Factorial of "; number%; " is "; fact#
```

(continued)

continued

```
FUNCTION Factorial# (num%)
    PRINT "Stack space left: "; FRE(-2)
    IF num% = O THEN
        Factorial# = 1
    ELSE Factorial# = (num% * Factorial#(num% - 1))
    END IF
END FUNCTION
```

: (Colon)

See also
DATA, REM

Purpose
The colon (:) separates Basic statements on one line of source code.

Syntax
statement : *statement* [: *statement* ...]

statement is any valid QBasic statement.

Usage
```
FOR customer% = 1 TO numCustomers%
    PRINT custInfo(customer%).custName: PRINT custInfo(customer%).street
    PRINT custInfo(customer%).city: PRINT custInfo(customer%).zip
NEXT customer%
```
Uses the colon to place multiple PRINT statements on one line.

Description
If you use more than one statement in the same line of code, you must separate the statements by using a colon. Using more than one statement on a single line often makes code harder to read. In particular, it obscures the operation of branching and looping statements. Because of this, use the colon cautiously. You can more clearly reveal the structure of a loop, its conditions, and the statements affected by using block statements and indention.

Comments
QBasic does not let you enter a line more than 256 characters long; however, it accepts longer lines loaded from disk files. If you complete a line created outside the QBasic editor with an underscore character (_), then QBasic combines that line and the one that follows into a single line, no matter how long it is. Note that you cannot use the underscore character to continue a REM or DATA statement.

The colon can also be used in a program to signify that the word preceding it is a line label.

Example

The following example illustrates the use of multiple statements on a program line. In this program, the second PRINT statement on some program lines makes the text double spaced; including the second PRINT statement on the same line makes the listing more compact without sacrificing readability.

```
TYPE Information
    custName AS STRING * 20
    street AS STRING * 15
    city AS STRING * 15
    zip AS INTEGER
END TYPE

numCustomers% = 15
DIM custInfo(numCustomers%) AS Information

PRINT "Customer Mailing List": PRINT   ' double-spaced
PRINT "====================": PRINT
PRINT TAB(8); DATE$: PRINT
PRINT "====================": PRINT

FOR customer% = 1 TO numCustomers%
    PRINT custInfo(customer%).custName: PRINT custInfo(customer%).street
    PRINT custInfo(customer%).city: PRINT custInfo(customer%).zip
NEXT customer%
```

END

See also

FUNCTION, GOSUB... RETURN, GOTO, IF, SELECT CASE, SUB, TYPE...END TYPE

Purpose

The END statement terminates a QBasic program. The END keyword can also end a type, function, or subprogram definition or a block statement.

Syntax

END

Usage

```
PRINT "This is a very short program."
END
```

Terminates program execution at the second line.

Description

The END statement closes all open files and ends execution of a QBasic program.

If your program includes subroutines, place an END statement between the main program and the first subroutine; this prevents the subroutine from being executed inadvertently. QBasic executes an implicit END statement at the end of every program. Because of this, you need not use an END statement as the last statement. The END statement can, however, enhance the readability of the program.

Example

The following program uses two END statements. The one inside the loop causes the program to exit immediately if the user responds to the prompt by typing the letter Y.

```
CONST MILETOKILO = 1.61
PRINT "This program converts from miles per hour to kilometers per hour."
DO
    INPUT "Do you want to stop? "; ans$
    IF UCASE$(ans$) = "Y" THEN END
    INPUT "How fast are you driving (in miles per hour) "; mph
    PRINT "That's "; mph * MILETOKILO; " kilometers per hour."
LOOP UNTIL mph = 0
PRINT "You're out of gas!"
END
```

ENVIRON

See also

ENVIRON$, SHELL

Purpose

The ENVIRON statement either changes the value of an environment variable or adds an entry to the program's copy of the DOS environment (a list of systemwide variables and their values that QBasic makes available to every running program). You can, for example, use ENVIRON to change information (such as a directory search path) for a program run from the current program by using RUN or for DOS commands executed by a SHELL statement.

Syntax

ENVIRON "*varname*[=] [text ¦;]"

varname is a string that identifies the environment variable. To assign a value to the variable, follow the name with an equal sign or a space; then specify *text*, which is the variable's value.

If you use a semicolon in place of text or if you don't specify any text, ENVIRON deletes the variable from the environment.

Usage

```
ENVIRON "PATH=C:\QB45;C:\QB45\TEST;C:\ACCT\TEST"
```

Changes the value of the PATH environment variable in the QBasic copy of the environment.

```
ENVIRON "SOURCE= "
```
Deletes the environment variable SOURCE from the QBasic copy of the environment.

Description

DOS maintains a memory area that contains several variables your programs might need to access. These variables include PATH, the list of directories that DOS searches for executable files; COMSPEC, the location and name of the command processor; and PROMPT, the string of characters that DOS uses for its prompt. Each of these variable names is associated with a string that contains its value. To display a list of the currently defined environment variables, type SET at the DOS prompt.

When a QBasic program runs, it receives a copy of the DOS environment, that is, a list of the variables and their values. The ENVIRON statement lets you change the values of the variables and add or delete variables. Remember that this is only a copy of the DOS environment: You will see when you exit QBasic that the original DOS environment is unchanged. However, changes your program makes are passed to any programs run from the program and are inherited by other programs you run in the QBasic environment.

Comments

By default, the environment is usually small (128 or 256 bytes), so using the ENVIRON statement frequently generates an "Out of memory" error message. You can expand the DOS environment by using the DOS SHELL command in your CONFIG.SYS file. For example, the command

```
SHELL=C:\DOS\COMMAND.COM /p /e:512
```

places the COMMAND.COM command processor in memory *(/p)* and sets a maximum environment size of 512 bytes *(/e:512)*.

This statement does not in itself prevent "Out of memory" error messages because a QBasic program receives only a copy of the actual environment, not the full space allocated in the MS-DOS command SHELL. You cannot increase the amount of memory used by the copy. Before running your QBasic program, however, you can use the DOS SET command to allocate a "dummy" variable, as the following example shows:

```
SET EXPAND=12345678901234567890901234567890
```

Your program can then create available space in its copy of the environment by deallocating this variable as follows:

```
ENVIRON "EXPAND=;"
```

The space is then available for new environment variables and values.

Errors

If the environment cannot be expanded to include a new variable (or a longer value for an existing variable), QBasic displays an "Out of Memory" error message. If the parameter you specify with ENVIRON isn't a string (if, for example, you forgot to enclose it in sets of quotation marks), QBasic displays a "Type mismatch" error message.

Example

The following program changes the PROMPT environment variable and displays the new prompt and the changed environment list.

```
CLS
PRINT "Current environment is: "
SHELL "SET"     ' display the current environment

PRINT "Changing the prompt: "
ENVIRON "PROMPT=Type 'exit' to return to QBasic ==>"
SHELL           ' run the command processor with the new prompt

PRINT "This is the modified environment: "
SHELL "SET"     ' display the modified environment
```

ENVIRON$

See also

ENVIRON, SHELL

Purpose

The ENVIRON$ function returns the value of the specified DOS environment variable.

Syntax

ENVIRON$({*var* ¦ *num*})

var is the name of an environment variable.

num is an integer that specifies the position in the list of environment variables of the variable you want.

Usage

```
PRINT ENVIRON$("PATH")
```

Displays the value of the environment variable PATH, which specifies the current search path.

```
env$ = ENVIRON$(3)
```

Assigns to the variable *env$* the environment variable (and its value) that is third in the environment variable list.

Description

The ENVIRON$ function returns the value of the specified environment variable. ENVIRON$ accepts either the name of an environment variable or a number representing a position in the environment variable list. The function is case sensitive, so *ENVIRON$("PATH")* returns the search path, and *ENVIRON$("path")* returns a null (empty) string unless your environment includes a variable called *path*.

If you specify a number that is greater than the number of variables in the environment, ENVIRON$ returns a null string.

Comments

Remember that the environment examined by ENVIRON$ is the copy of the DOS environment that the program receives; it differs from the original DOS environment if you introduced changes by using the ENVIRON statement.

Example

The following program first uses ENVIRON$ in a loop to list all the variables in the environment. Note that the test for the null string terminates the loop after the last variable is listed. The second part of the program accepts an environment variable name from the user and then displays the value of the variable if the variable exists.

```
CLS
var = 1
DO WHILE (ENVIRON$(var) <> "")
    PRINT var; ": "; ENVIRON$(var)
    var = var + 1
LOOP

DO
    PRINT : PRINT "Type 'q' to quit or "
    INPUT "the name of a variable to examine: "; varName$
    IF UCASE$(varName$) = "Q" THEN END
    PRINT varName$; " ";
    IF ENVIRON$(varName$) = "" THEN
        PRINT "is not defined"
        ELSE PRINT "is "; ENVIRON$(varName$)
    END IF
LOOP
```

IOCTL

See also

IOCTL$

Purpose

The IOCTL ("I/O Control") statement sends an instruction string to a device driver that supports such instructions. You might use IOCTL to initialize a modem or to send instructions to the mouse.

Syntax

IOCTL [#] *filenum, string*

filenum is the file number used in the OPEN statement that opened the device as a file.

string is a string that contains an instruction that is meaningful to the device driver; it must be enclosed in a set of quotation marks and cannot exceed 32,767 characters.

Usage

```
OPEN "SCANNER" FOR OUTPUT AS #4
IOCTL #4, "READPAGE"
```

Opens the device driver of a scanner so that it can receive output and then sends it a command.

Description

DOS supports any device driver that accepts IOCTL instructions. A device driver is a memory-resident program that translates the general instructions for a device (such as a printer, disk drive, or mouse) into the specific instructions that the hardware can use. Built-in drivers, such as LPT1 and COM1, do not support IOCTL instructions; however, you can replace the built-in drivers with enhanced drivers that do support IOCTL. If the driver in question supports IOCTL, its documentation should list the valid instructions. Note that most device drivers do not support IOCTL instructions.

You must first install the device driver (usually by using a DEVICE statement in the CONFIG.SYS file) and then open it with an OPEN statement in your program before you can use the IOCTL statement to send it instructions.

Errors

If the specified driver does not support IOCTL instructions, QBasic displays an "Illegal function call" error message.

Example

The following example demonstrates the use of IOCTL. It assumes that you have installed a driver named MYDRIVER.SYS, which can handle IOCTL instructions.

```
OPEN "C:\SYS\MYDRIVER.SYS" FOR OUTPUT AS #1     ' open device driver as a file
IOCTL #1, "BLOCK"       ' use block mode
IOCTL #1, "1024"        ' use a block length of 1024 bytes
IOCTL #1, "READ 4"      ' read four blocks
IOCTL #1, "SEND"        ' send the data
CLOSE                   ' close the driver
```

IOCTL$

See also

IOCTL, OPEN

Purpose

The IOCTL$ function returns status information from a device driver that supports IOCTL instructions. You can use IOCTL$, for example, to receive the status of a modem or mouse.

Syntax

IOCTL$([#] *filenum*)

filenum is the file number used in the OPEN statement that opened the device as a file.

Usage

```
OPEN "MODEM" FOR OUTPUT AS #1
PRINT IOCTL$(#1)
```

Opens the MODEM device driver and displays status information returned by the device driver.

Description

A device driver is a memory-resident program that translates general instructions for a device (such as a printer, disk drive, or mouse) into the specific instructions that the hardware can use. You can use the IOCTL$ function only with drivers that support IOCTL instructions.

An installed device driver that supports IOCTL can supply status information in the IOCTL$ function. The device driver usually supplies status information concerning an instruction sent with the IOCTL statement. (See the device-driver documentation for details about the status information that the device driver returns.) Note that most device drivers do not support IOCTL instructions.

You must first install a device driver (usually by using a DEVICE statement in the CONFIG.SYS file) and then open it with an OPEN statement in your program before you can use the IOCTL$ function.

Errors

If the specified device driver does not support IOCTL instructions, QBasic displays an "Illegal function call" error message.

Example

The following program assumes that you have installed a driver called MYDRIVER.SYS. It first opens the device as file number 1. If IOCTL$ returns a 0, the driver is not yet ready to receive input.

```
OPEN "C:\SYS\MYDRIVER.SYS" FOR OUTPUT AS #1    ' open the device driver

IF IOCTL$(#1) = 0 THEN    ' driver returns 0 if it is not enabled
    PRINT "Driver not enabled"
    END                   ' exit the program
ELSE
    ' use the driver
END IF

CLOSE #1
```

KILL

See also
FILES, RMDIR

Purpose
The KILL statement deletes a file and frees the space it occupied. You use KILL as you use the DOS DEL or ERASE command—to free space when a disk is full or to delete unnecessary files.

Syntax
KILL *filespec*

filespec is a string variable or constant that specifies the file or files to delete; *filespec* can include the wildcard characters, ? and *, to specify a group of files.

Usage
```
KILL "CONFIG.DAT"
```
Deletes the file CONFIG.DAT in the current directory.

```
KILL "*.DAT"
```
Deletes all files with the extension DAT in the current directory.

Description
The KILL statement deletes files; the required string variable or constant specifies the file or files to delete. Note that the filename portion can include the ? and * wildcard characters. The wildcard character ? matches any character in the same position in the filename. The wildcard character * matches zero or more characters in the filename.

If you omit a drive name from the file specification, KILL uses the current drive. If you omit a pathname, KILL uses the current directory of the current drive.

Comments
You can use wildcards only in the filename of the file specification. QBasic doesn't recognize wildcards in the directory, drive name, or pathname.

Errors
You can delete only closed files with the KILL statement. If you try to delete an open file, QBasic displays a "File already open" error message. KILL deletes only files; use the RMDIR statement to delete empty directories.

If the file specification does not match any file, QBasic displays a "File not found" error message. If you specify the letter of an external drive that does not contain a disk, QBasic displays a "Disk not read" error message. If the specified disk does not exist, QBasic displays a "Device unavailable" error message.

Warnings
Unlike the DOS DEL command, the QBasic KILL statement will not prompt you if you are about to delete the entire contents of a directory. A single KILL statement can erase

an entire directory! KILL can also delete the currently running program file, so be careful when using this statement in your programs.

Example

The following program uses FILES to display the directory the user specifies and then uses KILL to delete all the files in the directory.

```
DO
    PRINT "Enter the pathname of a directory whose files you want to delete."
    PRINT "Press Enter to quit."
    LINE INPUT fileSpec$

    IF fileSpec$ = "" THEN EXIT DO

    PRINT
    FILES fileSpec$ + "\*.*"              ' display the files in the directory
    PRINT

    LINE INPUT "Delete these files? (Y/N) "; yesNo$

    IF UCASE$(yesNo$) = "Y" THEN
        KILL fileSpec$ + "\*.*"           ' delete the files in the directory
        PRINT "All files in the directory "; fileSpec$; " have been deleted."
        PRINT
        PRINT
    END IF
LOOP UNTIL fileSpec$ = ""
```

MKDIR

See also

CHDIR, RMDIR

Purpose

The MKDIR statement creates the specified directory. You can use MKDIR to let the user make a new directory from within your program and store it anywhere on disk.

Syntax

MKDIR *directory*

directory is a string expression of no more than 127 characters that specifies the subdirectory to be created.

Usage

```
MKDIR "C:\ACCT\TEMP"
```
Creates TEMP, a subdirectory of the ACCT directory, on drive C.

Description

The MKDIR statement works like the DOS command MKDIR. It creates a new directory on the specified disk. Note that MKDIR creates the directory as a subdirectory of the current directory unless you specify a pathname.

Be sure to trap errors that occur with the MKDIR statement so that the user will know whether the directory could not be created because it already exists or because a file has the same name. (See the ON ERROR GOTO entry in Chapter 9, "Error Trapping.")

Note that you cannot shorten the QBasic statement MKDIR to MD as you can the DOS command MKDIR.

Errors

If you specify a directory that already exists or if a file has the same name as the directory, QBasic displays a "Path/File access error" error message. If you specify an expression that is not a string, QBasic displays a "Type mismatch" error message.

Example

The following program prompts the user for a directory name and then attempts to create the directory. It prints an error message if the directory already exists or there is already a file by that name.

```
ON ERROR GOTO Errorhandler     ' set up error trapping

INPUT "Directory to create: "; dir$
MKDIR dir$                      ' attempt to create the directory
END

Errorhandler:
    errNum = ERR
    IF errNum = 75 THEN
        PRINT "Unable to create directory "; dir$
        PRINT "Directory already exists or "
        PRINT "there's already a file with that name. "
    END IF
    RESUME NEXT
```

REM

See also

$DYNAMIC, $STATIC

Purpose

The REM statement lets you include a comment in a program. You can use a single quotation mark in place of the keyword REM. A comment is a nonexecutable statement that describes or explains the operation of a program. REM can also introduce a meta-command (a special instruction to the compiler), such as $DYNAMIC.

Syntax

{REM ¦ '} *comment*

comment is text that has any combination of characters. If you use the REM keyword, a comment that follows an executable statement on the same line must begin with a colon; spaces before and after the colon are optional.

Usage

```
REM Perform the operation each day of the week
FOR day% = 1 to 7
    CALL Total(sales(day%))          ' call the subprogram Total
NEXT day%
```

The first comment explains the purpose of the section of code; the second describes the action of a line of code.

Description

The REM statement introduces a remark, description, explanation, or metacommand in your program. QBasic ignores text—except a metacommand—that follows the keyword REM or single quotation mark until you begin a new line. To add a remark to an executable statement, follow the statement with a colon and then begin the REM statement:

```
CALL Tree : REM catalog the hard disk
```

Note that you can also use a single quotation mark instead of a colon and the REM keyword:

```
CALL Tree ' catalog the hard disk
```

In a program that uses line numbers, you can use a REM statement as the destination line for a GOTO or GOSUB statement. Execution continues at the first executable statement after the REM statement.

Warnings

To include a comment within a DATA statement, you must use REM rather than a single quotation mark: QBasic treats a single quotation mark as part of the data.

Do not confuse the single-quote comment character with a set of double quotation marks. A double quotation mark indicates a string character.

Example

The following program includes comments by using the REM statement and the single quotation mark.

```
REM this program displays the string "Hello" 50 times

FOR i% = 1 TO 50
    PRINT "Hello";       ' display the string
NEXT i%

END
```

RMDIR

See also

CHDIR, FILES, KILL, MKDIR

Purpose

The RMDIR statement removes a directory from a disk. The directory cannot contain any files.

Syntax

RMDIR *directory*

directory is a string expression of no more than 127 characters that specifies the subdirectory to be deleted.

Usage

RMDIR "C:\ACCT\TEMP"

Removes the TEMP subdirectory from the ACCT directory on drive C.

RMDIR dir$

Removes the directory specified by the value of the string variable *dir$*.

Description

The RMDIR statement deletes a directory that contains no files; it works in the same way as the DOS RMDIR command, except that you can't use the abbreviation RD in QBasic. If your program creates a directory to store temporary files that hold intermediate steps in processing, for example, you can use RMDIR to remove the directory when your program no longer needs the files. First you must delete the temporary files by using the KILL statement. Then you can remove the directory by using RMDIR.

Errors

If the directory you specify in the RMDIR statement does not exist, QBasic displays a "Path not found" error message. If the specified directory is not empty, QBasic displays a "Path/File access error" error message. This error also occurs if you specify the name of a file rather than a directory. If you don't specify a string in the RMDIR statement, QBasic displays a "Type mismatch" error message.

Example

The following program lets the user remove a directory. The program uses the ON ERROR GOTO statement to trap for the "Path/File access error" error message, which usually indicates that the directory isn't empty. The error handler asks the user whether he or she wants to remove the files. Note that the program does not distinguish between a nonempty directory and a file. If the user enters the name of a file, the KILL statement fails, and QBasic displays a "Path not found" error message, so it is not necessary to make a distinction between a nonempty directory and a file.

```
ON ERROR GOTO Errhandler  ' set up error trapping

INPUT "Name of directory to remove: "; dir$
RMDIR dir$                ' attempt to remove the directory
END

Errhandler:
    errNum = ERR
    PRINT "Error number: "; errNum
    SELECT CASE errNum
    CASE 75                   ' the directory probably contains files
        PRINT dir$; " isn't empty."
        PRINT "Do you still want to remove it?"
        PRINT "(All files in the directory will be deleted.)"
        INPUT ans$
        IF UCASE$(ans$) = "Y" THEN
            delDir$ = dir$ + "\*.*"    ' construct a path containing wildcards
            KILL delDir$               ' delete all files in the directory
            RESUME                     ' try removing directory again
        END IF

    CASE 76                   ' the directory was not found
        PRINT dir$; " was not found."
    CASE ELSE
        ON ERROR GOTO 0    ' disable error trapping
    END SELECT
    RESUME NEXT
```

RUN

See also

CHAIN, CLEAR, GOTO, SHELL

Purpose

You can use the RUN statement either to restart the current program from the beginning or from a specified line number or to run a second program. You can use RUN, for example, to restart a program after an error or to run a series of self-contained programs that don't need to share variables.

Syntax

RUN [*line* ┆ *file*]

line is the line number in the current program at which execution restarts.

file is a string expression of no more than 127 characters that contains the name of the program to be loaded into memory and run.

Usage

```
RUN 100
```
Restarts the current program at line 100.

```
RUN "ENDGAME"
```
Loads the ENDGAME program into memory and runs it.

Description

The RUN statement transfers control either to the current program (at the beginning or at a specified line number) or to another program. Note that control does not return to the program that executed the RUN statement. If you specify a line number, RUN acts like a GOTO statement except that it closes all open files and clears all variables. In effect, RUN reruns the current program from the specified line. If you use RUN without a parameter, the current program executes from the beginning. You cannot use a non-numeric line label as the target of a RUN statement.

You can also use RUN to execute another program, beginning at the first line of the program. If the other program isn't in the current directory, you must specify its location by including a pathname. The specified program must be a QBasic source file. QBasic assumes that the program has the extension BAS, so you don't need to specify the extension.

Programmers today rarely use the RUN statement to run a second program because the CHAIN statement is much more versatile. It lets you run a second program, maintain open files, and access any variables specified by a COMMON statement—these are great advantages when you use a group of related programs.

Comments

RUN does not let you preserve or share variable values from the original program. It also closes all open files, so be aware that the second program might need to re-open them.

Errors

If the program you specify in the RUN statement does not exist, QBasic displays a "File not found" error message. If the line number that you specify does not exist or is not in module-level code, QBasic displays a "Label not defined" error message.

Example

The following program is the "front end" of an application program; it uses RUN to run the program PLANNER.BAS after displaying instructions (if the user requests them).

```
CLS
PRINT "Welcome to Project Planner."
INPUT "Do you need instructions (Y/N)"; ans$

IF UCASE$(ans$) = "Y" THEN
     PRINT "Instructions for using PLANNER.BAS"
     PRINT "More instructions...": PRINT
     PRINT "Press any key to continue..."
     ans$ = INPUT$(1)    ' wait for keypress
END IF
RUN "PLANNER.BAS"        ' assumes file in same directory
END
```

```
' PLANNER.BAS
CLS
PRINT "*** PLANNER MAIN MENU ***"
PRINT "Rest of PLANNER program runs here."
```

SHELL

See also
CHAIN, ENVIRON, RUN

Purpose
The SHELL statement lets you run a DOS command (or any executable or batch file) from a QBasic program. In effect, the SHELL statement adds all the capabilities of DOS to QBasic. For example, although no QBasic command lets you format a disk, you can use the SHELL statement to call the DOS command FORMAT.

Syntax
SHELL [*command*]

command is a string expression containing a command that DOS can execute. Without parameters, SHELL runs the DOS command processor; the user must type *EXIT* on the command line to resume execution of the program.

Usage
```
SHELL "FORMAT B:"
```
Formats the disk in drive B from a QBasic program; the DOS command FORMAT issues its usual prompts.

```
cmd$ = "DIR " + file$ + " /p"
SHELL cmd$
```
Executes the DOS command line contained in the variable *cmd$*.

Description

The SHELL statement runs a copy of the DOS command processor, COMMAND.COM, which inherits the DOS environment used by the current QBasic program. SHELL is therefore equivalent to the DOS command COMMAND with the /C switch. Any commands in the specified string following the keyword SHELL are passed to DOS as though you had typed them at the DOS command line.

If the SHELL statement specifies a command that does not have an extension, DOS looks first for a command file with the extension COM, then for an executable file with the extension EXE, and finally for a batch file with the extension BAT. Unless you specify a pathname, DOS assumes the file is in the current directory. However, if the environment includes a PATH environment variable, DOS also searches the specified directories for the file.

Although the DOS command or program that you run with SHELL does not have direct access to the variables in your QBasic program, you can convey information to the command or program by setting variables in the environment (discussed in the ENVIRON entry) or by specifying options in the SHELL statement's command string.

Errors

Because SHELL passes control to DOS, most errors (such as "File not found") are reported by DOS, not QBasic. (See your DOS documentation for an explanation of DOS errors.) If you specify a parameter in SHELL that is not a string, QBasic displays a "Type mismatch" error message.

Warnings

Because a QBasic program remains in memory when it executes a SHELL statement, you cannot run a program by using SHELL if the program uses more than the available amount of memory. DOS displays an "Insufficient memory" error message if there is not enough memory for the program.

Example

The following program provides a menu of several DOS commands that the program performs on request. The user must enter *E* to exit the program. The inner loop (around the menu) displays the menu until the user enters a valid character.

Note how the command line to be used with each SHELL statement is constructed. Because the statements *SHELL "DIR file$"* and *SHELL "DIR ";file$* are invalid, you must build the command string by concatenating the DOS command with the string that is input by the user. Note that you sometimes need to add spaces: For example, you must add a space between the DOS command COPY and the source filename and between the source and target filenames.

```
DO                  ' outer loop--loop until user enters E
    DO              ' inner loop--loop until user enters a valid letter
        CLS
        PRINT "Access DOS from QBasic to: "
        PRINT "V)iew a file"
        PRINT "D)irectory"
        PRINT "P)rint a file"
        PRINT "C)opy a file"
        PRINT "E)xit the program"
        INPUT choice$
        choice$ = UCASE$(choice$)
    LOOP UNTIL INSTR("VDPCE", choice$) <> 0

    CLS
    SELECT CASE choice$
    CASE "V"
        INPUT "View what file "; file$
        cmd$ = "MORE <" + file$
        SHELL cmd$
    CASE "D"
        INPUT "See which directory "; dir$
        cmd$ = "DIR " + dir$ + " /p"
        SHELL cmd$
    CASE "P"
        INPUT "Print what file "; file$
        cmd$ = "PRINT " + file$
        SHELL cmd$
    CASE "C"
        INPUT "File to be copied: ", source$
        INPUT "Copy to what file: ", dest$
        cmd$ = "COPY " + source$ + " " + dest$
        SHELL cmd$
    CASE "E"
        END
    CASE ELSE
        PRINT "Invalid Command: "; choice$
    END SELECT

    PRINT : PRINT "Press any key to continue"
    ans$ = INPUT$(1)
LOOP
```

STOP

See also

END

Purpose

The STOP statement terminates a QBasic program.

Syntax

```
STOP
```

Usage

```
PRINT "Executing first line"
STOP
```

Terminates the program after executing the PRINT statement.

Description

The STOP command stops execution of a program, leaving files open and returning control to the QBasic environment. STOP is the same as END, except that STOP leaves open files open, and END closes them.

The STOP keyword is also used with various event-trapping statements to suspend trapping for the specified event. (For more information, see the following entries: KEY(n) ON/OFF/STOP, PEN ON/OFF/STOP, PLAY ON/OFF/STOP, STRIG ON/OFF/STOP, and TIMER ON/OFF/STOP.)

Example

The following program executes three assignment statements that use the RND function; when control reaches the STOP statement, the program terminates. Note that the fourth assignment statement isn't executed unless you choose the Continue command from the Run menu to complete the program.

```
first = INT(3 * RND) + 1
second = INT(3 * RND) + 2
third = INT(3 * RND) + 3
STOP
fourth = first + second + third
```

SYSTEM

See also

END, SHELL, STOP

Purpose

The SYSTEM statement closes all open files and terminates a QBasic program.

Syntax

```
SYSTEM
```

Usage

```
PRINT "This program is running in the QBasic environment."
SYSTEM
```

Returns control to the QBasic environment.

Description

The SYSTEM statement ends execution of a QBasic program and removes the program from memory. If you run the program by specifying the program and the /RUN option when you start QBasic, control returns to the operating system. However, if you run the program in the QBasic environment, control returns to the environment. (If you enter a SYSTEM statement in QBasic's Immediate window, QBasic terminates and returns you to the operating system.)

Example

The following program demonstrates that the SYSTEM statement returns control to the environment from which the program is run. If you run this program from within the QBasic environment, it returns control to that environment. If you run the file by specifying the /RUN option when you start QBasic, it returns control to DOS.

```
PRINT "Program now running."
PRINT "Program still running";
FOR i% = 1 TO 10
    PRINT ".";
    SLEEP 1
NEXT i%

SYSTEM
```

CHAPTER 19

Port and Memory

Introduction

This chapter discusses how QBasic programs can gain access to the information stored in your computer's memory. It also shows how to communicate directly with the hardware by using the memory outside the normal address space—the set of input/output channels known as ports. Table 19-1 lists QBasic's port and memory statements and functions in alphabetic order.

Statement or function	Description
BLOAD	Loads a block of memory stored in a file into memory at an absolute address
BSAVE	Saves a block of memory to a disk file
FRE	Returns the amount of available stack space, string space, or memory
INP	Returns the byte at the specified port
OUT	Sends a byte to the specified port
PEEK	Returns the byte at the specified address
POKE	Writes a byte to the specified address
WAIT	Waits for a specific signal to be read from the specified port

Table 19-1.
Port and memory statements and functions.

Memory

Several QBasic statements and functions let you reference data stored at a specified address in your computer's memory. The PEEK function, for example, returns the contents of the byte at the specified location; the CALL ABSOLUTE statement lets you execute a machine-language program that begins at the specified address in memory. Note that these statements require the address to be an integer in the range 0 through 65535, so you can access a block of memory that contains only up to 64 KB. Each block of memory is called a segment. The QBasic data segment, DGROUP, is a 32-KB segment that you can gain access to.

Your computer probably has considerably more than 64 KB of memory. IBM PCs and compatible computers can have up to 640 KB of random-access memory and 384 KB of memory dedicated to the video display, disk-drive controller, and ROM BIOS programs. Therefore, you can gain access to as much as 1 MB (1024 KB) of memory.

Addressing Memory

You can specify any address in memory by using two 16-bit numbers: the segment and the offset. The number of the segment specifies the block of memory to be accessed; the number of the offset specifies the location of the address within the block of memory. Because the segment and the offset are both 16-bit numbers, programmers often write addresses as two 4-digit hexadecimal values separated by a colon. For example, the address at segment 15, offset 145, is expressed as 000F:0091.

Each segment in memory begins at a paragraph boundary. (A paragraph is a block of 16 bytes.) Because of this, the 1 MB of address space in the PC can be divided into 65,535 possible segments. Any segment larger than 16 bytes, of course, will overlap the segments beginning at the next and subsequent paragraph boundaries.

QBasic Programs in Memory

QBasic uses a single 32-KB segment, DGROUP, to hold all the simple variables that a program uses. This 32-KB segment limit is the main factor that limits the size of your programs. Only complex variables, such as dynamic arrays, are given their own segments outside of DGROUP.

Gaining Access to Memory

QBasic provides statements that let you examine and change memory directly. The PEEK function returns the value of the byte at a specified address, and the POKE statement lets you load a value into the byte at a specified address. The address, in both cases, is an unsigned integer value in the range 0 through 65535 that corresponds to the offset of the byte, which is measured from the beginning of the current segment. Because a byte consists of 8 bits, POKE can load only values in the range 0 through 255 into memory, and PEEK can return only values in the same range.

Unless otherwise specified, PEEK and POKE access DGROUP, the QBasic data segment. Because DGROUP stores strings and simple variables, PEEK and POKE let you read or modify these objects directly as long as you know the location at which they are stored. Indeed, QBasic supports a function that returns this information: the VARPTR function returns the offset address of a numeric variable. (See the VARPTR entry in Chapter 20, "QBasic and Machine Language," for details.)

Of course, QBasic offers easier ways of reading and loading variables in DGROUP than by using PEEK or POKE. Although PEEK is sometimes used to load a machine-code routine into a string (discussed in the CALL ABSOLUTE entry in Chapter 20, "QBasic and Machine Language"), the benefits of PEEK and POKE are not apparent until you use them outside the DGROUP data segment.

To access memory outside of DGROUP, you must first use the DEF SEG statement to select a new segment. (See Chapter 20, "QBasic and Machine Language," for details.) DEF SEG can specify any segment (0 through 65535) in the address space; because PEEK and POKE can address any offset within a full 64-KB segment, you can read data from or write data to any location in memory. The new segment you select becomes the current segment for all statements and functions that use absolute memory addresses—BLOAD, BSAVE, CALL ABSOLUTE, PEEK, and POKE.

Loading and Saving Blocks of Memory

QBasic provides two statements that let you transfer data between memory and disk. If, for example, your program uses an array to store data, you can save the array to a disk file by using the BSAVE command. The next time you execute the program, you can reload the array into memory by using the BLOAD command.

Perhaps the most common use for BLOAD and BSAVE is to load and store screen images. To BSAVE, the video buffer is exactly the same as any other part of memory. You can use BSAVE to capture a graphics screen your program has created and store it in a disk file; you can later retrieve the screen by using BLOAD. The BLOAD and BSAVE entries include sample programs that let you load and save graphics displays in any screen mode.

The Far Heap

QBasic also stores data in an area of memory above DGROUP. This area, called the far heap, contains large variables such as dynamic numeric arrays and dynamic arrays of fixed-length strings. The far heap uses the memory remaining after all other segments have been allocated up to a maximum of 128 KB.

The FRE function lets you examine your program's use of memory. If you specify −1 as the function's parameter, FRE returns the number of bytes available in the heap, which is the area of memory used to hold all variables. (The heap is described in two parts. The near heap is the section of memory that contains strings and simple variables. As described earlier, the far heap stores numeric arrays and arrays of fixed-length strings.) If you specify a parameter of −2, FRE returns the number of available bytes in the program stack. If you use any other number or a string as the parameter, the function returns the available string space. If you specify a string, FRE compacts the free string space into a single block of memory before returning the amount of available string space.

Ports

In addition to memory that holds data and active programs (including DOS and the ROM BIOS), your computer has an additional section of memory, which you can gain access to from within QBasic. This is the 64-KB block of memory used by hardware ports, which is outside the normal PC address space but which nevertheless can be read from and written to by your programs.

When you communicate by using a port, you are reading from and writing to this block of memory. The INP function and the OUT statement are the same as PEEK and POKE, with one exception: Before they access a port address, they send a signal on the system bus to indicate the address is not in normal PC address space but is the number of a port.

A port is an input/output (I/O) channel through which a hardware device sends information to your program and receives instructions in return. Hardware devices include the processor's support chips, the keyboard, disk controller, video adapter, math coprocessor, and so on. Every hardware device in your system is associated with one or more ports. Even so, because there are 65,536 port addresses available, many are not used. Table 19-2 lists the port addresses of the most common hardware devices.

Port address	Device description
000H–01FH	Direct memory access (DMA) controller
020H–03FH	Programmable interrupt controller
040H–05FH	Programmable interval timer
060H–06FH	Keyboard controller
070H–07FH	Real-time clock (PC/XT and PS/2 Model 30) CMOS configuration RAM (PC/AT and other PS/2s)
0A0H	NMI mask register (PC, PC/XT, and PS/2 Model 30)
0C0H–0CFH	Complex-sound generator (PCJr and Tandy 1000)
0E0H–0EFH	Real-time clock (PC/AT and PS/2 series)
0F0H–0FFH	Math coprocessor
1F0H–1F8H	Hard-disk controller
200H–207H	Game controller (joystick)
278H–27FH	Third parallel printer
2F8H–2FFH	Second serial port
300H–31FH	Prototype card
320H–32FH	Hard-disk controller (PC/XT and PS/2 Model 30)
360H–363H, 368H–36BH	PC network controller
378H–37FH	Second parallel printer
3A0H–3A9H	Bisynchronous adapter (mainframe link)
3B0H–3BBH	Monochrome Display Adapter (MDA); also used by EGA and VGA in monochrome video modes
3BCH–3BFH	First parallel printer port
3C0H–3CFH	Enhanced graphics adapters (EGA and VGA)
3D0H–3DFH	Color graphics adapters (CGA and MCGA); also used by EGA and VGA in color video modes
3F0H–3F7H	Floppy-disk controller
3F8H–3FFH	First serial port

Table 19-2.
Major I/O port addresses on PC systems.

The OUT statement writes a byte of information to a port address; the INP function returns the current setting of a port. The WAIT statement waits for a specific signal to be read from a port. If you have installed a data-acquisition device in your computer, such as a bar code reader, the WAIT statement can pause execution until that device is ready to transmit data. The INP function and the OUT and WAIT statements are rarely used in everyday programming because the higher-level QBasic I/O statements and functions let you control system devices indirectly. Nevertheless, these statements let you program hardware at its lowest level whenever the need arises.

Related Reading

Davies, Russ. *Mapping the IBM PC and PCjr.* Greensboro, N.C.: Compute! Books, 1988.

Norton, Peter, and Richard Wilton. *The* New *Peter Norton Programmer's Guide to the IBM PC & PS/2.* 2d ed. Redmond, Wash.: Microsoft Press, 1988.

BLOAD

See also

BSAVE, DEF SEG, VARPTR, VARSEG

Purpose

The BLOAD statement loads a memory-image file created by the BSAVE statement into memory at a specified location. Because using BLOAD retrieves files faster than any other method does, you can use the statement to load screen images that cannot be created quickly by QBasic graphics statements.

Syntax

BLOAD *name*[, *offset*]

name is the name of the device or file that contains the memory image. *name* can include a directory pathname and a drive name and can be either a string literal enclosed in quotation marks or a string expression.

offset is the address, in the current segment, at which the file is loaded. *offset* is a numeric expression in the range 0 through 65535. If you omit this parameter, the file is loaded into the segment and the offset address from which it was saved.

Usage

```
DEF SEG = freeSeg%
BLOAD mcFile$, &H400
```

Selects the memory segment specified in the integer variable *freeSeg%* and then loads a memory-image file into offset 1024 (400H) in that segment.

Description

QBasic provides two commands that let you transfer memory-image files between disk and memory. A memory-image file is a file containing binary data—an exact, bit-for-bit copy of a block of memory that can contain anything held in memory, such as an array of data or a screen image. The BSAVE statement saves a memory-image file to disk, and BLOAD loads it back into memory. By default, BLOAD restores the copy into the area of memory from which it was saved; however, you can also load the copy into any other part of memory. Because BLOAD uses a single binary read to transfer the entire file from disk to memory, it is faster than other file-retrieval methods.

BLOAD file header

Files loaded by the BLOAD statement use a common header format that always begins with the hexadecimal number &HFD (253 decimal), which identifies a file as a memory-image file. The next 4 bytes contain the segment and the offset address of the block of memory from which the file was saved. If you use the BLOAD statement without specifying an offset, QBasic uses this address to restore the file to memory. However, if you specify an offset value, BLOAD loads the file, beginning at that offset, into the segment specified by the last DEF SEG statement. The last 2 bytes in the header contain the length of the file, in bytes. Figure 19-1 shows the memory-image file header format.

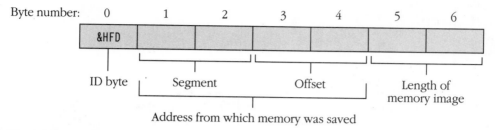

Figure 19-1.
The memory-image file header format.

The memory image itself begins immediately after the file header and is terminated by the Ctrl-Z character (ASCII 26), which is the standard DOS end-of-file marker. Because only 2 bytes are provided to hold the length of the file, the largest image that you can save in a single file is 64 KB, or one full segment.

Warnings

QBasic does not check to see whether the addresses specified in a BLOAD statement are free for your program to use; consequently, the image file you load might overwrite other programs or even the operating system itself.

When loading graphics images, be sure that the current screen mode is the same as the one in which the image was saved; otherwise, the display will not be correct.

Example

To load previously saved CGA graphics screens, simply use BLOAD with the name of the file you want to reload; the original BSAVE command stored the segment and the offset address of your screen buffer in the file header. Loading EGA and VGA screens is more difficult because each screen requires four BSAVE files—one for each bit plane that these video adapters use. The following subprogram uses BLOAD to load the four files that form an EGA or VGA color graphics display. (See the "Example" section in the BSAVE entry for the program that originally saved the image.)

The four bit planes used by EGA and VGA graphics adapters are mapped into the same segment of video memory. The four planes (blue, green, red, and intensity) control the appearance of the pixels on the graphics screen. (See the SCREEN (Statement) entry in Chapter 11, "Graphics," for a description of all screen modes.)

This program uses the port at address 3C4H, which is the EGA and VGA address register. The program first writes the value 2 to the port to enable the data register at port 3C5H to set the currently addressable bit plane. The program then selects one bit plane at a time by writing the values 1, 2, 4, and 8 to port 3C5H.

See the OUT entry for details about writing to hardware ports.

```
SUB VGALoad (title$) STATIC
    SHARED screenMode AS INTEGER

    IF LEN(title$) > 8 THEN title$ = LEFT$(title$, 8)
    IF screenMode% > 6 THEN
        IF screenMode% = 13 THEN
            BLOAD title$ + ".GRA"   ' load the only bit plane
        ELSE
            FOR i% = 0 TO 3
                OUT &H3C4, 2        ' enable port
                OUT &H3C5, 2 ^ i%   ' set the currently addressable bit plane
                BLOAD title$ + ".BP" + CHR$(49 + i%)   ' load the bit plane
                IF i% = 1 AND screenMode% = 10 THEN EXIT FOR
            NEXT i%
        END IF
    END IF
END SUB
```

BSAVE

See also
BLOAD, DEF SEG, SCREEN (Statement), VARPTR, VARSEG

Purpose
The BSAVE statement transfers a memory image to a disk file or a device. You can use BSAVE to save complex screen images created by graphics statements.

Syntax
BSAVE *name, offset, bytes*

name is a string expression that contains the name of the device or the file to which the memory image is to be saved; it can include a directory pathname and a drive name.

offset is the address, in the current segment, at which the block of memory to be saved begins; *bytes* is the length of the block of memory. *offset* and *bytes* are numeric expressions in the range 0 through 65535.

Usage
```
DEF SEG = &HB800
BSAVE "PICTURE.DAT", 0, 16384
```
Selects the video segment for computers that use a color adapter and writes a 16-KB screen image to the file PICTURE.DAT. Copying starts at offset 0 in the segment.

Description
Use BSAVE to transfer an exact copy of an area of memory to a memory-image file on disk. A memory-image file is a file containing binary data—an exact, bit-for-bit copy of a block of memory that can contain anything held in memory, such as an array of data

or a screen image. You must specify the name of the file to which you want to save the memory image, the file's starting address in memory, and the number of bytes to be transferred. If the file does not already exist, BSAVE creates it. Use the BLOAD statement to reload the file into memory.

You specify in a BSAVE statement only the offset of the address at which you want copying to begin. To copy from a segment other than the default data segment, DGROUP, you must first change segments by calling the DEF SEG statement. To save from the beginning of a segment, use an offset of 0.

The sum of the specified offset and number of bytes must not be greater than 65,535 (the number of bytes in a segment). If the total exceeds this number, QBasic will not report an error, but when BSAVE reaches the end of the segment it will wrap around and copy bytes from the beginning of the segment.

BSAVE is useful for saving screen displays, and it works equally well with text mode and high-resolution graphics. To use BSAVE for this purpose, you must know the segment address of video memory used by the display adapter you are using and the size (in bytes) of the screen image in the various screen modes. Table 19-3 lists this information.

Screen mode	Segment	Page size (in bytes)	Number of pages	Remarks
0	B000H	4096	1	MDA and HGC
	B800H	4096	4	80-column text
	B800H	2048	8	40-column text
1	B800H	16384	1	320 by 200, four colors
2	B800H	16384	1	640 by 200, two colors
3	B800H	32768	1	HGC only
11	B800H	65536	1	VGA and MCGA
13	B800H	65536	1	VGA and MCGA

Note: Computers with a CGA adapter and a monochrome monitor use the video buffer segment address B800H, not B000H.

Table 19-3.
Address and size of the display buffer in QBasic screen modes.

The screen modes that can be used only by EGA and VGA adapters support a different scheme of addressing video memory which uses bit planes. See the sample program in the "Example" section for a method of saving EGA and VGA screens.

Example

Saving screen images created in the screen modes used only by EGA and VGA adapters is complicated because BSAVE must create four files—one for each bit plane that these video adapters use. The following subprogram extracts each bit plane from the EGA or VGA video buffer and uses BSAVE to save it to a file.

The four bit planes used by EGA and VGA graphics adapters are mapped into the same segment of video memory. The four planes (blue, green, red, and intensity) control the appearance of the pixels on the graphics screen. (See the SCREEN (Statement) entry in Chapter 11, "Graphics," for a description of all screen modes.)

This program uses the port at address 3CEH, which is the EGA and VGA port. The program first writes the value 4 to the port to enable the data register at port 3CFH to set the currently addressable bit plane. The program then selects one bit plane at a time by writing the values 1 through 3 to port 3CFH. (See the OUT entry in this chapter for details about writing to hardware ports.)

```
' subprogram to save EGA and VGA screens from video memory
SUB VGASave (title AS STRING) STATIC
    SHARED screenMode AS INTEGER   ' current screen mode
    IF LEN(title$) > 8 THEN
        title$ = LEFT$(title$, 8)
    END IF
    SELECT CASE screenMode%          ' video buffer sizes
        CASE 7
            bytes& = 8000
        CASE 8
            bytes& = 16000
        CASE 9, 10
            bytes& = 28000
        CASE 11, 12
            bytes& = 38400
        CASE 13
            bytes& = 64000
        CASE ELSE
            bytes& = 0
    END SELECT

    IF bytes& THEN
        DEF SEG = &HA000             ' video buffer segment
        IF screenMode% = 13 THEN
            BSAVE title$ + ".GRA", 0, bytes&
        ELSE
            FOR i% = 0 TO 3
                OUT &H3CE, 4         ' enable port
                OUT &H3CF, i%        ' set the currently addressable bit plane
                BSAVE title$ + ".BP" + CHR$(49 + i%), 0, bytes&
                IF i% = 1 AND screenMode% = 10 THEN EXIT FOR
            NEXT i%
        END IF
        DEF SEG
    END IF
END SUB
```

FRE

See also

DIM, $DYNAMIC, ERASE, $STATIC

Purpose

The FRE function returns the amount of available stack space, string space, or memory. You can use FRE to determine whether your program has enough space to perform a task that requires a large amount of memory.

Syntax

FRE (*number* ¦ *string*)

If *number* is −1, the FRE function returns the amount of memory available in the heap; if it is −2, FRE returns the amount of available stack space; if you use any other numeric value, FRE returns the size of the next block of unused string space. If you specify *string*, FRE first compacts unused string space into the largest possible block and then returns the amount of available string space.

Usage

```
IF FRE(-2) < 256 THEN PRINT "Stack space is running out!"
```
Checks the available space in the stack and warns the user if the stack is smaller than 256 bytes.

Description

The FRE function returns the number of bytes available for use in one of three areas of memory that QBasic uses to store data for your program: the heap, the stack, and the string space. The heap, which is the memory that QBasic uses to hold all variables, is divided into two parts. The near heap is the section of memory that contains strings and simple variables. The far heap stores numeric arrays and arrays of fixed-length strings. The stack stores temporary variables and the return addresses of subroutines and functions. The string space is the part of the near heap that holds the values of variables containing strings.

The value that FRE returns depends on the parameter specified in the function call. If you specify −1, FRE returns the number of bytes available in the heap. The parameter −2 directs FRE to return the number of available bytes in the stack. If any other number or string is specified, FRE returns the amount of available string space.

If you specify a string as a parameter, FRE compacts the free string space into a single block of memory before returning the amount of available string space. Compaction clears the string space of all strings that are no longer in use and combines all fragmented portions of the string space.

Note that FRE used with the parameter −2 (for stack space) returns reliable results only when a running program executes it. Although you can execute *FRE(−2)* from the Immediate window, the results will not be accurate.

Example

The following program dimensions various kinds of arrays and then uses the FRE function to examine the changing amounts of available memory.

```
REM $DYNAMIC           ' make all arrays dynamic
DECLARE SUB MemAvail ()

CLS
MemAvail               ' show available memory
DIM array%(15000)      ' dynamic array of integers
PRINT "After defining a dynamic array of 15000 integers:"
MemAvail

DIM strArray$(1000)  ' dynamic variable-length string array
PRINT "After defining a dynamic array of 1000 variable-length strings:"
MemAvail

FOR i% = 1 TO 1000
    strArray$(i%) = "Test string"
NEXT i%
PRINT "After filling the array:"
MemAvail

DIM dynString(1000) AS STRING * 10     ' dynamic fixed-length string array
PRINT "After defining a dynamic array of 1000 fixed-length strings:"
MemAvail

FOR i% = 1 TO 1000
    dynString(i%) = "Test"
NEXT i%
PRINT "After filling the array:"
MemAvail

REM $STATIC
SUB MemAvail
    PRINT "Total heap space available: "; FRE(-1)
    PRINT "Total string space available: "; FRE(0)
    PRINT
END SUB
```

INP

See also

OUT, WAIT

Purpose

The INP function lets your program read a byte of data from a specified I/O port.

Syntax

INP(*port*)

port is the address of the specified port and is an integer in the range 0 through 65535 (or 0 through FFFF in hexadecimal).

Usage

```
IF INP(&H3D5) <> 255 THEN PRINT "Color adapter is installed"
```

Port 981 (3D5H) is the status register used by the CGA and by the EGA and VGA in color modes. If the value returned is 255, a monochrome display is installed.

Description

The central processor in the PC communicates with support chips and hardware devices by means of a series of ports. Ports are input/output (I/O) channels through which information passes between the CPU and the device it is controlling; QBasic associates one or more hardware ports with each device. QBasic provides statements and functions that handle most hardware-related tasks. However, if you want to program your display adapter at a low level or if your computer uses a digital scanner or other nonstandard device, INP and its companion statement, OUT (discussed in the OUT entry), let you control the device without having to use a machine-language routine.

The IBM PC and compatible computers allocate port addresses 0 through 3FFH to system hardware; however, not all of these addresses are actually used. Furthermore, because many ports are write only, INP does not always return meaningful data. Table 19-2, in the tutorial section, lists the port addresses associated with the major system devices. Before experimenting, however, consult your computer's technical reference manual for up-to-date information about ports.

INP reads data 1 byte at a time; therefore, each call to INP returns a value in the range 0 through 255. Many input ports require you to first write to another port associated with the device so that you can select which data item will be returned. For example, you can retrieve a pair of 8-bit random numbers by writing the value 0 to the system's timer control port at the address 43H and then reading the timer port (at address 40H) twice:

```
OUT &H43, 0
rand1% = INP(&H40): rand2% = INP(&H40)
```

The two values returned by INP in this example are the upper and lower bytes of a single 16-bit number; therefore, you need to read the port twice to retrieve the entire number.

Warnings

Because port addresses are hardware-specific, using INP and the OUT statement limits the portability of your programs to computers that have the same hardware configuration as yours. Moreover, because these statements directly manipulate the system hardware, writing incorrect data to a port can "lock up" the computer.

Example

PC/AT and PS/2-series computers store configuration data in RAM that is stored in CMOS circuits. This RAM can be read through hardware port 71H. The following program reads configuration information and reports the number and type of fixed disks installed in the system. Note that the program writes a byte to address 70H so that the byte that the INP function reads contains the required information.

```
CLS
OUT &H70, &H12              ' specify required information
diskType% = INP(&H71)       ' read fixed-disk data
PRINT diskType%
cDrive% = diskType% \ 16    ' drive C is specified in the first four bits
dDrive% = diskType% MOD 16  ' drive D is specified in the second four bits

IF cDrive% THEN
    PRINT "Fixed disk C is type"; cDrive%
ELSE
    PRINT "Fixed disk C is not installed"
END IF

IF dDrive% THEN
    PRINT "Fixed disk D is type"; dDrive%
ELSE
    PRINT "Fixed disk D is not installed"
END IF
END
```

OUT

See also

INP, WAIT

Purpose

The OUT statement sends a byte of data to a specified I/O port.

Syntax

OUT *port*, *byte*

port is the address of the specified port and is an integer in the range 0 through 65535 (or 0 through FFFF in hexadecimal).

byte is a value in the range 0 through 255.

Usage

```
OUT &H70, &H12
```

Writes the byte &H12 to the CMOS RAM port address. This prepares the port for obtaining a specific value with the INP function.

Description

A port is an input/output (I/O) channel through which a program can directly control a hardware device. Usually you don't need to access ports, because QBasic provides statements and functions that handle most hardware-related tasks. However, if you want to program your display adapter at a low level or if your computer uses a scanner or other nonstandard device, OUT and its companion function, INP, let you control the device without having to use a machine-language routine.

The IBM PC and compatible computers allocate port addresses 0 through 3FFH to system hardware; however, not all of these addresses are actually used. Furthermore, many ports are read only, so you cannot always use OUT. Table 19-2, in the tutorial, lists the port addresses associated with the major system devices. Before experimenting, however, consult your computer's technical reference manual for up-to-date information about the ports. Remember that OUT writes data 1 byte at a time; therefore, the value you send to the port must be in the range 0 through 255.

Warnings

Because port addresses are hardware specific, using the INP function and OUT limits the portability of your programs to computers that have the same hardware configuration as yours. Moreover, because these statements directly manipulate the system hardware, writing incorrect data to a port can "lock up" the computer.

Example

If the EGA and VGA adapters have enough memory, they can store more than one screenful of information at a time; QBasic lets you use the SCREEN statement to switch between these screen pages. The hardware itself, however, allows much finer control of the display; in fact, by programming the adapter's start address registers directly, you can specify the position of the visible part of the video buffer to the nearest pixel. The following subprogram draws a design on the screen and then lets the user press the direction keys to move the screen contents in any direction. The subprogram uses the OUT statement to scroll the screen.

```
DECLARE SUB PanDisplay (x%, y%)

CONST FALSE = 0, TRUE = NOT FALSE

SCREEN 9
LINE (0, 0)-(639, 349), 9, BF              ' draw the design
VIEW SCREEN (40, 25)-(600, 325), 0, 15
CIRCLE (319, 174), 150, 14: PAINT (319, 174), 14, 14

' initialize variables
x% = 0: y% = 0
esc$ = CHR$(27)
leftDirection$ = CHR$(0) + CHR$(75): rightDirection$ = CHR$(0) + CHR$(77)
upDirection$ = CHR$(0) + CHR$(72): downDirection$ = CHR$(0) + CHR$(80)
```

(continued)

continued

```
DO
    DO
        keyStroke$ = INKEY$
    LOOP WHILE keyStroke$ = ""
    pan% = TRUE
    SELECT CASE keyStroke$                  ' calculate new x- or y-coordinate
        CASE leftDirection$
            IF x% > 0 THEN x% = x% - 1
        CASE rightDirection$
            IF x% < 79 THEN x% = x% + 1
        CASE upDirection$
            IF y% > 0 THEN y% = y% - 1
        CASE downDirection$
            IF y% < 22 THEN y% = y% + 1
        CASE ELSE
            pan% = FALSE
    END SELECT
    IF pan% THEN PanDisplay x%, y% * 5     ' move the display
LOOP UNTIL keyStroke$ = esc$
END

' set display window coordinates
SUB PanDisplay (x%, y%) STATIC
    OUT &H3D4, 12: OUT &H3D5, y%            ' scroll screen vertically
    OUT &H3D4, 13: OUT &H3D5, x%            ' scroll screen horizontally
END SUB
```

PEEK

See also
DEF SEG, POKE, VARPTR

Purpose
The PEEK function returns the contents of the specified memory address in the current segment. You can, for example, use PEEK to find the current hardware configuration of the system.

Syntax
PEEK(*address*)

address is an integer expression in the range 0 through 65535 that specifies the offset of the byte you want to examine in the current segment of memory.

Usage
```
byte% = PEEK(&HF000)
```
Assigns the contents of address F000H to the integer variable *byte%*. Note that you can specify addresses in either hexadecimal or decimal notation.

Description

The PEEK function lets you directly examine data in memory. This data might be variables used by your program, characters on the screen, or information provided by the BIOS or DOS. You can use the DEF SEG statement to specify the memory segment you want PEEK to read from. If you do not define a new segment, QBasic uses DGROUP, the default data segment. (See the DEF SEG entry in Chapter 20, "QBasic and Machine Language," for details about changing the default segment.)

PEEK returns a value in the range 0 through 255, the contents of a single byte of memory. However, if you want to read a value other than a single character, you need to read the contents of two or more contiguous memory addresses. An integer, for example, is stored in 2 adjacent bytes, the least significant byte (LSB) preceding the most significant byte (MSB). The MSB is the number of times the integer value can be divided by 256, and the LSB is the remainder of this division. The number 1000, for example, would be stored in memory as shown in Figure 19-2.

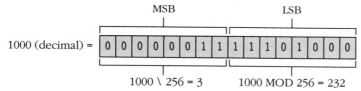

Figure 19-2.
How QBasic stores the number 1000.

Therefore, to obtain the value of the integer that begins at the address specified by the variable *loc%*, you need to use the following statement:

```
intValue% = PEEK(loc%) + (PEEK(loc% + 1) * 256)
```

Example

A program that will be used on different computers might need to determine what type of hardware a system has installed. It can easily find this information on an IBM PC compatible because the ROM BIOS in those computers maintains a 2-byte "equipment list" in low memory. The following program uses PEEK to read the equipment list and then displays its contents.

```
DECLARE FUNCTION SInt% (num&)
DECLARE FUNCTION BitTest% (number%, bit%)
DEF SEG = &H40          ' change default segment to low memory

lowByte = PEEK(&H10) ' get least significant byte of equipment list
hiByte = PEEK(&H11)   ' get most significant byte of equipment list
equipment% = SInt%(lowByte + (hiByte * 256))   ' form equipment list
```

(continued)

continued

```
DEF SEG                   ' change default segment to DGROUP
flag$ = STRING$(16, "0")
FOR i% = 15 TO 0 STEP -1
    IF BitTest%(equipment%, i%) THEN     ' extract each bit
        MID$(flag$, 16 - i%, 1) = "1"
    END IF
NEXT i%

' display equipment list
CLS : LOCATE 1, 1
PRINT "F E D C B A 9 8 7 6 5 4 3 2 1 0"
PRINT STRING$(32, CHR$(196))
FOR i% = 1 TO 16: PRINT MID$(flag$, i%, 1); " "; : NEXT
PRINT : PRINT STRING$(32, CHR$(196))

LOCATE 7, 1
PRINT "ROM BIOS equipment list at 0040:0010"
PRINT
PRINT "0:   Floppy drives installed?"
PRINT "1:   Math coprocessor installed?"
PRINT "2-3: Original PC motherboard RAM "
PRINT "4-5: Initial video mode "
PRINT "6-7: Number of floppy drives"
PRINT "9-B: Number of serial ports"
PRINT "C:   Game adapter installed?"
PRINT "E-F: Number of parallel printers"
END

FUNCTION BitTest% (number%, bit%)
    ' extract a bit from the number
    BitTest% = -SGN(number% AND 2 ^ bit%)
END FUNCTION

FUNCTION SInt% (num&) convert a long integer to a signed integer
    SInt% = -((num& > 32767) * (num& - 65536)) - ((num& < 32767) * num&)
END FUNCTION
```

POKE

See also

DEF SEG, PEEK, VARPTR

Purpose

The POKE statement writes a byte of data to a specified memory address in the current segment. You can use POKE, for example, to set the status of the Ctrl key.

Syntax

POKE *address, char*

address is an integer expression in the range 0 through 65535 that specifies the offset of the address to which you want POKE to write in the current memory segment.

char is the integer value in the range 0 through 255 to be written to the specified address.

Usage

```
POKE &HC000, ASC("A")
```

Writes the character A into offset C000H in the current segment. Note that you can specify addresses in either hexadecimal or decimal notation.

Description

The POKE statement inserts a single byte of data (a value in the range 0 through 255) into a specified address. The effect of this operation depends on the address you write to. Often, POKE simply stores a character in an unoccupied area of memory. Some addresses, however, are used by your computer for specific purposes; writing to these locations gives instructions to the hardware. For example, if you are using a color monitor, the contents of the screen are stored in memory in segment B800H; writing to the addresses in that area of memory displays characters on the screen. (The corresponding address for computers with monochrome monitors is segment B000H.)

You can use the DEF SEG statement to specify the memory segment you want POKE to write to. If you do not define a new segment, QBasic uses DGROUP, the default data segment. (See the DEF SEG entry in Chapter 20, "QBasic and Machine Languages," for details about changing the default segment.)

If you want to write any value other than a character, you need to write to two or more contiguous memory addresses. An integer, for example, is stored in two adjacent bytes, the least significant byte (LSB) preceding the most significant byte (MSB). The MSB is the number of times the integer value can be divided by 256, and the LSB is the remainder of this division. The number 1000, for example, would be stored in memory as shown in Figure 19-3.

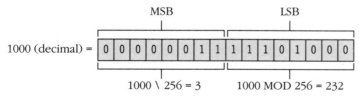

Figure 19-3.
How QBasic stores the number 1000.

Therefore, to store an integer in memory, you need to use POKE twice, as shown in the following statements:

```
POKE byte%, intValue% MOD 256
POKE byte% + 1, intValue% \ 256
```

Warnings

When using POKE, be careful not to overwrite any addresses used by DOS or other resident programs; doing this might cause your program to "crash" or your computer to "lock up."

Example

The following program uses POKE to turn on the Caps Lock key. The PC ROM BIOS records the status of the Shift keys and the Ctrl, Alt, Caps Lock, Num Lock, Scroll Lock, and Insert keys at location 0040:0017 (segment 40H, offset 17H) in memory. The program first switches to the BIOS data segment by using DEF SEG and then turns on the Caps Lock key by using POKE.

```
CLS
PRINT "This program turns on the Caps Lock key for you"

DEF SEG = &H40                  ' switch to BIOS data segment
POKE &H17, PEEK(&H17) OR 64     ' turn on Caps Lock
DEF SEG                         ' restore DGROUP

INPUT "Enter a line of text. It will be capitalized: ", text$
```

WAIT

See also

INP, OUT

Purpose

The WAIT statement reads data from a specified hardware port and suspends program execution until a specified bit pattern is read. You can use WAIT to pause execution until a device is ready for a particular event to take place.

Syntax

WAIT *port, andExpr*[, *xorExpr*]

port is the address of the port to be monitored; it can be an integer expression in the range 0 through 65535.

andExpr is an integer value that is used as an operand in a logical AND operation with the byte read from the port. You can also use the integer value *xorExpr* as an operand in a logical XOR (exclusive or) operation with the byte that is performed before the

AND operation. Program execution continues only when the result of these operations is a nonzero value.

Usage

```
WAIT &H60, 127
```
Polls the port at address 60H until the top bit of the byte read is set.

Description

The WAIT statement is most useful in real-time programs that let you communicate with other computers. For example, if you are writing a program that links your computer to another computer, you need to monitor the hardware port that connects the computers; otherwise, you might lose data.

WAIT suspends execution until the specified output port returns a byte of a specified bit pattern. Whenever you execute a WAIT statement, QBasic reads a byte from the specified port and performs an AND operation with the logical expression specified in the second parameter. For example, if you want program execution to pause until the sixth bit of the byte read is set, you specify the value 32 in the second parameter. This masks all bits but the sixth one. If WAIT reads the value 183 from a port, the AND operation masks the sixth bit, as follows:

```
WAIT port%, 32
```

```
      1  0  1  1  0  1  1  1  = 183
AND   0  0  1  0  0  0  0  0  = 32
      ─────────────────────
      0  0  1  0  0  0  0  0  = 32
```

Because the result of this operation is nonzero, WAIT completes and the program resumes execution.

To reverse the logic of the test—to wait until the sixth bit is *not* set—you can perform a preliminary XOR operation with the byte read by including a third parameter in the call to WAIT. You can use the XOR operation to toggle 1 or more bits, reversing their current settings. Again, suppose the byte read from a port is 183. If you then use 32 as the value for both the second and the third parameters of WAIT, the statement performs the following operations.

```
WAIT port%, 32, 32
```

```
      1  0  1  1  0  1  1  1  = 183          1  0  0  1  0  1  1  1  = 151
XOR   0  0  1  0  0  0  0  0  = 32     AND   0  0  1  0  0  0  0  0  = 32
      ─────────────────────                 ─────────────────────
      1  0  0  1  0  1  1  1  = 151          0  0  0  0  0  0  0  0  =  0
```

Note that the WAIT statement does not return a value. If you need to read the information that the port is transmitting, use the INP function. (See the INP entry.)

Warnings

If the specified bit pattern does not occur at the port being polled (for example, if a remote computer fails to reply to your message), WAIT remains in an endless loop. If this happens, you can regain control only by rebooting the computer.

Example

The following program uses the WAIT statement to pause program execution until the printer connected to the first parallel port is on line. Because the sixth bit of the byte at address 3BDH is 0 when the printer is ready, the call to WAIT uses the number 32 in the second and third parameters.

```
CLS
PRINT "Be sure that your printer is ready."
WAIT &H3BD, 32, 32          ' wait until first parallel printer is ready
PRINT "Now printing a message."
LPRINT "QBasic Programmer's Reference", DATE$, TIME$; CHR$(12)
```

CHAPTER 20

QBasic and Machine Language

Introduction

Although QBasic is powerful and rich in built-in features, it is not well suited to certain programming tasks. FORTRAN, for example, is better adapted to applications that must perform specialized scientific calculations and intensive number-crunching. C has a wealth of functions for manipulating and moving large blocks of memory, and assembly language produces the fastest and most efficient code for low-level applications and for controlling the PC hardware.

A QBasic program can call on the resources of other languages by including the machine language of routines written in those languages. Table 20-1 contains an alphabetic listing of QBasic's machine-language statements and functions.

Statement or function	Description
CALL ABSOLUTE	Executes a machine-language routine that begins at an absolute address in memory
DEF SEG	Defines the current segment in memory for statements and functions that use absolute addresses
VARPTR, VARPTR$	Return the offset address of a variable in the current data segment
VARSEG	Returns the segment address of a variable

Table 20-1.
Machine-language statements and functions.

Loading Machine-Language Routines into Variables

QBasic provides a method of incorporating non-Basic routines in QBasic programs. You can load a machine-language routine (which is a routine that has been translated into an executable format) into a QBasic variable and execute it by using the CALL ABSOLUTE statement.

You must convert the machine-language code into QBasic DATA statements before you can load the code into a variable. (See the following section, "Converting Machine Language into DATA Statements.") You will most often load the code into an integer array. You can call the CALL ABSOLUTE statement by using the following syntax:

CALL ABSOLUTE (*address*)

address is an integer that specifies the address in memory of the variable that contains the machine-language routine. QBasic provides the VARPTR function which returns the address of a numeric variable, an array, or a fixed-length string. The address returned by VARPTR is the offset of the specified variable in its memory segment.

Use the address returned by VARPTR for the array's first element; that is, use the following statement to retrieve the address:

```
address% = VARPTR(codeArray%(0))
```

However, because QBasic doesn't store dynamic arrays in DGROUP, you must change to the proper memory segment before you call the routine. The VARSEG function returns the segment address of a variable, and the DEF SEG statement lets you set that address as the current segment. To execute a machine-language routine that has been loaded into a dynamic array, use the following statements:

```
DEF SEG = VARSEG(codeArray%(0))
CALL ABSOLUTE(VARPTR(codeArray%(0)))
```

Each element of an integer array can hold 2 bytes of machine code, so when you dimension the array, you need to use only half the number of subscripts as the number of bytes in the routine. Use the POKE statement to load the code directly into the memory occupied by the array, as demonstrated in the following program segment:

```
DEF SEG = VARSEG(codeArray%(0))   ' change to the correct segment
offSet% = VARPTR(codeArray%(0))   ' find beginning of the array

FOR i% = 0 TO 30
    READ byte%
    POKE offSet% + i%, VAL("&H" + byte%)
NEXT i%

DATA   55, 8B, EC, 06, 1E, 57, 56, 2E, C7, 06
⋮
```

You must be careful when you load an array and call the routine. In particular, you must be sure that QBasic does not move the variable before you call the routine. You can prevent this from happening by using dynamic arrays to hold the routine; because QBasic places dynamic arrays in their own segments outside of DGROUP, they never move.

Converting Machine Language into DATA Statements

To use your machine-language routines with the CALL ABSOLUTE statement, you must convert them into DATA statements that can be used in your QBasic program. One way to convert a routine is to load it into a debugging program such as Debug or Microsoft CodeView and then copy the byte values from the display into DATA statements in your program. However, the following program provides a better way of making the conversion. It reads a file that contains machine language and translates each byte into QBasic DATA statements that you can then merge into your program. The program also calculates a checksum value that your loading routine can use to detect incorrectly typed data and then places the value by itself in the last DATA statement.

```
' BIN2DATA.BAS - translates binary files into DATA statements
binFile$ = "ROUTINE.COM"              ' change to machine-language filename
dataFile$ = "HEXDATA.INC"

OPEN binFile$ FOR BINARY AS #1 LEN = 1
OPEN dataFile$ FOR OUTPUT AS #2

DIM byte AS STRING * 1

dataLine$ = "DATA   "
count% = 0: checksum& = 0

DO UNTIL EOF(1)
    GET #1, , byte
    checksum& = checksum& + ASC(byte)
    dataLine$ = dataLine$ + RIGHT$("0" + HEX$(ASC(byte)), 2)
    count% = count% + 1
    IF count% < 15 THEN
        dataLine$ = dataLine$ + ", "
    ELSE
        PRINT #2, dataLine$
        dataLine$ = "DATA   "
        count% = 0
    END IF
LOOP

IF count% > 0 THEN
    dataLine$ = LEFT$(dataLine$, LEN(dataLine$) - 2)
    PRINT #2, dataLine$
END IF

dataLine$ = "DATA   " + STR$(checksum&)
PRINT #2, dataLine$
CLOSE
END
```

Related Reading

Craig, John Clark. *Microsoft QuickBASIC Programmer's Toolbox*. Redmond, Wash.: Microsoft Press, 1988.

Duncan, Ray. *Advanced MS-DOS Programming,* 2d ed. Redmond, Wash.: Microsoft Press, 1988.

Duncan, Ray. *IBM ROM BIOS: Programmer's Quick Reference*. Redmond, Wash.: Microsoft Press, 1988.

Norton, Peter, and Richard Wilton. *The* New *Peter Norton Programmer's Guide to the IBM PC & PS/2*. 2d ed. Redmond, Wash.: Microsoft Press, 1988.

The Waite Group. *MS-DOS Developer's Guide*. Indianapolis, Ind.: Howard W. Sams & Co., 1989.

The Waite Group. *MS-DOS Papers*. Indianapolis, Ind.: Howard W. Sams & Co., 1988.

CALL ABSOLUTE

See also

CALL, DEF SEG, VARPTR, VARSEG

Purpose

The CALL ABSOLUTE statement executes a machine-language routine that has been loaded into a variable at an absolute address in memory. This statement lets you use routines developed for earlier versions of Basic.

Syntax

CALL ABSOLUTE([*var*[, *var*...]] *address*)

var is one or more optional variables supplied as parameters to the machine-language routine.

address is a valid QBasic expression or variable name that evaluates to an integer value that is the offset of the called routine in the currently defined segment.

Usage

```
CALL ABSOLUTE(&HF000)
```

Transfers control to a machine-language routine in memory at offset 61440 (F000H) in the current segment.

Description

Most programmers who move to QBasic from an earlier version of Basic already have a collection of useful machine-language routines. These routines might enhance the display, speed up slow-moving sections of code, or perform an operation that is difficult to do in Basic. The CALL ABSOLUTE statement lets you port machine-language routines developed under Basic to QBasic programs.

Each dynamic array is stored in its own segment in the far heap. So if your program uses a machine-language routine stored in a dynamic array, you must use the VARSEG function to find the array's segment and then use the DEF SEG statement to change the current segment.

CALL ABSOLUTE provides a degree of compatibility with earlier versions of Basic, which often use the BLOAD statement to load machine-language files into an absolute address in memory.

Example

QBasic runtime errors commonly occur when a program tries to send output to a printer that has run out of paper or is not on line. The following program uses a machine-language routine that is stored in an array and used with CALL ABSOLUTE to test the printer status prior to output; the program then takes appropriate action if the printer is not available.

```
' $DYNAMIC                               ' make all arrays dynamic

DIM mCode(0 TO 11) AS INTEGER            ' dimension array for routine
printer% = 1                             ' 1 = LPT1:, 2 = LPT2: etc.
testSum& = 0                             ' set up for checksum test

DEF SEG = VARSEG(mCode(0))              ' set the array segment
offSet% = VARPTR(mCode(0))              ' get the array address
RESTORE Code

FOR i% = 0 TO 23                         ' read each machine-code byte
    READ byte%
    testSum& = testSum& + byte%
    POKE offSet% + i%, byte%            ' load the byte into the array
NEXT i%

READ checkSum&
IF testSum& <> checkSum& THEN            ' check for typing errors
    PRINT "CHECKSUM ERROR!!!"
    BEEP: PRINT "Can't continue"
    STOP
END IF

CALL ABSOLUTE (printer%, offSet%)        ' execute the routine
DEF SEG                                  ' restore default segment

IF printer% = 144 OR printer% = 208 THEN     ' indicates printer is ready
    PRINT "The printer is ready for output."
ELSE
    PRINT "The printer is not ready for output."
END IF
END

' machine-language routine data bytes and the checksum
Code:
    DATA &H55, &H8B, &HEC, &H8B, &H5E, &H06, &H8B, &H17
    DATA &H4A, &HB4, &H02, &HCD, &H17, &H8A, &HC4, &HB4
    DATA &H00, &H89, &H07, &H5D, &HCA, &H02, &H00, &H00
    DATA 2300
```

DEF SEG

See also

BLOAD, BSAVE, CALL ABSOLUTE, PEEK, POKE, VARPTR, VARPTR$, VARSEG

Purpose

The DEF SEG statement specifies the segment to be used by QBasic statements and functions that directly address memory. PC chip architecture divides memory into 64-KB areas; each is defined by the address at which it starts, which is called its segment number. You use DEF SEG to set the current segment address for subsequent PEEK functions and BLOAD, BSAVE, CALL ABSOLUTE, and POKE statements.

Syntax

DEF SEG [= *segment*]

segment is any constant, variable, or expression that evaluates to an integer in the range 0 through 65535. If you omit *segment*, QBasic uses the default data segment, DGROUP.

Note that because the largest signed decimal integer is 32767, hexadecimal numbers are often used to set the segment value.

Usage

```
DEF SEG = &HB800
```

Sets the current segment address to the video display buffer in systems using a Color Graphic Adapter (CGA).

```
DEF SEG
```

Resets the current segment to the QBasic default data segment, DGROUP.

Description

Several QBasic statements and functions let you reference data stored at an absolute address in your computer's memory. The PEEK function, for example, returns the contents of the byte at a specified location; the CALL ABSOLUTE statement executes a machine-language program stored at a specified address. These statements and functions require that the address be an integer in the range 0 through 65535, which is a value specifying a location in a 64-KB block of memory.

To gain access to a segment in the 1024 KB of addressable memory, you must first specify the starting address of a 64-KB block. The starting address is called the segment address. For example, you might need to gain access to the memory external to DGROUP to load (using the BLOAD statement) a graphics-image file directly into the video-display buffer. DEF SEG lets you specify the 64-KB segment in which this operation will take place. Until you issue another DEF SEG statement, QBasic interprets any address you specify in a PEEK function or a BLOAD, BSAVE, CALL ABSOLUTE, or POKE statement as an offset of this segment. Specifying a different segment does not disrupt your program unless you write over memory being used by the operating system, by QBasic, or by the program itself.

Errors

If you specify a segment address outside the range 0 through 65535, QBasic displays an "Illegal function call" error message and does not change the current segment.

Example

To help you better understand DEF SEG, let's examine how you might use the BIOS data area in low memory, beginning at segment 0040H. This area contains the keyboard buffer, information about the status of installed equipment, and information about the video display.

The following program uses the information in the BIOS data area to write text from QBasic directly to the bottom line of the computer screen without causing the screen to scroll. The program first checks the BIOS data area to see whether the program is running on a computer with a monochrome display or on a computer with a color display; this approach lets you determine which segment of memory to send output to. To perform this check, the program uses DEF SEG to set the current working segment to the BIOS data area, which starts at 40H.

The program also checks the screen dimensions, defined in the BIOS data segment, to determine whether the display is in 40-column or 80-column mode and whether the number of screen rows is 25, 43, or 50. This information lets you calculate the offset address (in video memory) of the bottom row of the screen.

Finally, the program sends text to the display; however, first it uses DEF SEG again to set the correct video segment. Note that each character output requires 2 bytes of video memory, one for the ASCII code of the character and the other for its display attribute, or color.

```
DEF SEG = &H40                    ' set segment to BIOS data area
IF PEEK(&H49) = 7 THEN            ' check video mode
    videoSegment% = &HB000       ' mode 7 indicates a monochrome display
ELSE
    videoSegment% = &HB800       ' any other mode indicates a color display
END IF

columns% = PEEK(&H4A) + (PEEK(&H4B) * 256)   ' get screen width
bytes% = PEEK(&H4C) + (PEEK(&H4D) * 256)     ' get screen size
rows% = bytes% \ (columns% * 2)              ' calculate number of rows
offSet% = (columns% * (rows% - 1)) * 2       ' get last row

DEF SEG = videoSegment%                       ' set segment to video memory
FOR i% = 0 TO columns% - 1
    POKE offSet% + (i% * 2), ASC("*")         ' write a character
    POKE offSet% + (i% * 2) + 1, 78           ' write an attribute
NEXT i%
DEF SEG                                        ' restore the DGROUP segment
SLEEP 3
END
```

VARPTR, VARPTR$

See also

DEF SEG, VARSEG

Purpose

The VARPTR function returns the offset address of a variable within its current memory segment. If you need to load a machine-language routine directly into memory, for example, you use VARPTR to find the address of the variable into which these statements can be loaded. The VARPTR$ function returns a string that contains the address of a variable. Use VARPTR$ in calls to DRAW or PLAY to execute substrings contained in variables.

Syntax

VARPTR(*var*)
VARPTR$(*var*)

var is any valid QBasic variable. If the specified variable does not exist, QBasic creates it before returning the address or the string containing the address.

Usage

```
offSet% = VARPTR(codeArray%(0))
```
Assigns the offset address of the first element in the integer array *codeArray%* to the variable *offset%*.

```
PLAY "X" + VARPTR$(cmd$)
```
Plays the music dictated by the commands contained in the string variable *cmd$*.

Description

Every reference to a location in memory consists of two parts—the segment, an integer value (in the range 0 through 65535) that specifies the 64-KB block of memory in which the object resides, and the offset, another integer value (in the range 0 through 65535) that specifies the location of the object within that 64-KB segment. The VARSEG function returns the segment part of a variable's address; the VARPTR function returns the offset part of the address. The VARPTR$ function returns the offset part as a string.

Because QBasic stores simple variables and strings in DGROUP, the default data segment, you need to use only VARPTR to address these variables. Numeric arrays and dynamic arrays of fixed-length strings, however, are stored in their own segments outside of DGROUP; therefore, you need to use both VARSEG and VARPTR to address these segments.

Note that when you use VARPTR (or VARSEG) to obtain the address of an array, you must specify an element number as well as the array name. Because array data is stored contiguously in memory, the address of an array's first element is actually the address of the entire array.

When you use VARPTR with a variable-length string, it does not return the address of the string itself; instead, it returns a pointer to a 4-byte string descriptor in DGROUP. The first 2 bytes of the descriptor hold the length of the string; the second 2 bytes hold the address of the string, which is offset from the beginning of DGROUP.

To simplify your programming tasks, always use both VARSEG and VARPTR when specifying the address of a numeric array.

Note that QBasic always stores arrays of variable-length strings in DGROUP.

Warnings

QBasic allocates storage in DGROUP dynamically. If you create a new variable, change the size of an existing variable, or use a variable inside a function or expression, QBasic might change the address of this or other variables. To avoid this problem, your program should always use the address returned by VARPTR immediately; if it doesn't, QBasic can move the variable, making the returned address incorrect.

Example

QBasic lacks a function that detects whether a particular file exists. If you try to open a nonexistent file, QBasic either creates it by using a length of 0 bytes or, if it is opened for input only, reports an error. You can trap for these error conditions, but the error-trapping code is often clumsy.

The DOS services include several functions that return information about specified files. The following program uses a machine-language routine that can be incorporated into other programs. The routine queries DOS for the size (in bytes) of a specified file. The routine accepts a filename containing wildcard characters (* and ?); if you supply such a filename, it returns the summation of the sizes of all matching files. If the routine returns 0, the file does not exist.

In order to be as compact as possible, the following program uses an assembly-language routine stored in an array variable.

The program leaves empty the first 29 elements of the array that contain the machine language; those elements form a temporary disk transfer address and filename buffer. The actual code of the routine begins at element 30, and the value returned by the routine is assigned to element 1.

```
' $DYNAMIC                    ' make all arrays dynamic

DIM mCode(1 TO 70) AS LONG    ' array for the machine-language routine
DIM byte AS STRING * 2        ' holds each data item

DEF SEG = VARSEG(mCode(1))    ' set the array segment
offSet% = VARPTR(mCode(30))   ' address of the 30th element

' load the machine-language data bytes into the array
RESTORE
FOR i% = 0 TO 161
    READ byte
    POKE offSet% + i%, VAL("&H" + byte)
NEXT i%

CLS
PRINT "THIS PROGRAM REPORTS THE SIZE OF FILES YOU SPECIFY"
PRINT "-------------------------------------------------"
PRINT
PRINT "The filename can include a directory path and can"
PRINT "use the wildcard characters ? and *."
```

(continued)

continued

```
PRINT "The program returns the size of the file, in bytes,"
PRINT "or, if it finds more than one match, the summation"
PRINT "of the sizes of all the files. If the size returned is 0,"
PRINT "the file does not exist (at least not in the specified"
PRINT "directory)."
PRINT
PRINT "Enter the pathname (up to 64 characters) of the file,"
PRINT "or press Enter to quit."

DO
    LOCATE 14, 1: PRINT SPACE$(240);
    LOCATE 14, 1: INPUT "Pathname"; pathName$
    IF LEN(pathName$) > 1 AND LEN(pathName$) < 65 THEN
        CALL ABSOLUTE(pathName$, VARPTR(mCode(30)))      ' call the routine
        LOCATE 16, 1: PRINT "Size = "; mCode(1)          ' display the size
        LOCATE 20, 1, 1: PRINT "Press any key to continue. ";
        r$ = INPUT$(1)
        LOCATE 20, 1: PRINT SPACE$(26);
    END IF
LOOP UNTIL pathName$ = ""
DEF SEG                          ' restore segment
END

' machine-language routine
    DATA  55, 8B, EC, 06, 1E, 57, 56, 2E, C7, 06, 00, 00, 00, 00, 2E
    DATA  C7, 06, 02, 00, 00, 00, 0E, 07, 8B, 5E, 06, 8B, 0F, 83, F9
    DATA  01, 72, 6F, 83, F9, 40, 77, 6A, 8B, 77, 02, BF, 33, 00, FC
    DATA  F3, A4, B0, 00, AA, 0E, 1F, B4, 2F, CD, 21, 2E, 89, 1E, 2F
    DATA  00, 2E, 8C, 06, 31, 00, BA, 04, 00, B4, 1A, CD, 21, BA, 33
    DATA  00, 33, C9, B4, 4E, CD, 21, 72, 2D, 2E, A1, 1E, 00, 2E, 8B
    DATA  16, 20, 00, 2E, A3, 00, 00, 2E, 89, 16, 02, 00, B4, 4F, CD
    DATA  21, 72, 15, 2E, A1, 1E, 00, 2E, 8B, 16, 20, 00, 2E, 01, 06
    DATA  00, 00, 2E, 11, 16, 02, 00, EB, E5, 2E, A1, 31, 00, 2E, 8B
    DATA  16, 2F, 00, 8E, D8, B4, 1A, CD, 21, 2E, 8B, 16, 02, 00, 2E
    DATA  A1, 00, 00, 5E, 5F, 1F, 07, 5D, CA, 02, 00, 00
```

VARSEG

See also

DEF SEG, VARPTR, VARPTR$

Purpose

The VARSEG function returns the segment part of a variable's address. You might use VARSEG, for example, to find the segment of a dynamic numeric array that you want to save on disk by using BSAVE.

Syntax

VARSEG(*var*)

var is any valid QBasic variable name. If the specified variable does not exist, QBasic creates it before returning the address.

Usage

```
segment% = VARSEG(codeArray%(0))
```

Assigns the segment of the first element in the integer array *codeArray%* to the variable *segment%*.

Description

VARSEG returns the segment occupied by any variable, thus enabling you to fully specify the variable's address. VARSEG returns an integer number that corresponds to the address of the segment containing the specified variable. If the specified variable is a simple numeric variable or a variable-length string, the returned value indicates the segment address of DGROUP. Because DGROUP is QBasic's default segment, you do not need to specify the segment part of the address when referring to data stored there. Usually all you need to specify is the offset from the beginning of the segment (which is returned by the VARPTR function).

If the variable is a dynamic numeric array or a dynamic array of fixed-length strings, VARSEG returns the segment address that QBasic allocated to that variable. Your programs must specify both the segment (by using VARSEG) and the offset (by using VARPTR) of such a variable when passing its address.

Example

See the "Example" section in the VARPTR entry for a program that uses both VARPTR and VARSEG.

CHAPTER 21

Debugging

A Sample Debugging Session

This tutorial documents an interactive debugging session with a sample program. Imagine that you created the file SORTFILE.BAS, listed below, which is intended to sort a fixed-length file in memory; however, SORTFILE.BAS contains several errors that prevent it from executing properly. You can use the QBasic environment to find these errors and correct them.

```
' SORTFILE.BAS - sorts a fixed-length file
DECLARE FUNCTION SortFile% (path$, recLen%, offSet%, fieldLen%, sortErr%)

CONST FALSE = 0, TRUE = NOT FALSE

TYPE Element
    sKey AS STRING * 10
    recNum AS INTEGER
END TYPE

PRINT : PRINT "SORTFILE - Random-access file sorter": PRINT

' acquire information needed to sort a file
LINE INPUT "Enter pathname of file to be sorted  ? "; path$
LINE INPUT "What is the record length of the file? "; temp$
recLen% = VAL(temp$)
LINE INPUT "Define sort field - starting position? "; temp$
offSet% = VAL(temp$)
LINE INPUT "                       - length of field  ? "; temp$
fieldLen% = VAL(temp$)

IF SortFile%(path$, recLen%, offSet%, fieldLen%, sortErr%) THEN
    PRINT "File successfully sorted"
ELSE
    PRINT "Unable to sort file": BEEP
END IF
END

' sort the file in memory
FUNCTION SortFile% (path$, recLen%, offSet%, fieldLen%, sortErr%) STATIC
    sortErr% = FALSE

    ' find file length
    OPEN path$ FOR RANDOM AS #1 LEN = recLen%
```

(continued)

continued

```
        fileLen& = LOF(1)
        CLOSE 1

        ' check whether sort is possible
        records& = fileLen& \ recLen%          ' (first definition of records&)
        IF (fieldLen% + offSet%) > recLen% THEN
            sortErr% = 1: EXIT FUNCTION
        END IF
        freeRam& = FRE(-1): wanted& = records& * 12
        IF fieldLen% > 10 OR wanted& > freeRam& THEN
            sortErr% = 2: EXIT FUNCTION
        END IF

        ' create a temporary file
        tempFile$ = UCASE$(path$)
        dotPosition% = INSTR(tempFile$, ".")
        IF dotPosition% > 0 THEN
            tempFile$ = LEFT$(tempFile$, dotPosition%) + "TMP"
        ELSE
            tempFile$ = tempFile$ + ".TMP"
        END IF
        cmd$ = "COPY " + path$ + " " + tempFile$ + " > nul"
        SHELL cmd$

        ' prepare for sort
        DIM array(1 TO records%) AS Element

        OPEN path$ FOR RANDOM AS #1 LEN = recLen%
        IF offSet% > 1 THEN                    ' define records for reading the file
            FIELD 1, offSet% - 1 AS dummy$, fieldLen% AS key1$
        ELSE
            FIELD 1, fieldLen% AS key1$
        END IF
        FIELD 1, recLen% AS finalRec$
        i% = 1

        ' fill the array with sort keys from the file
        DO
            GET 1, i%
            LSET array(i%).sKey = key1$        ' put each sort key in the array
            array(i%).recNum = i%              ' put each record number in the array
            i% = i% + 1
        LOOP UNTIL i% > records&

        ' perform the sort
        partition% = records% \ 2
        DO WHILE partition% > 0
            range% = records& - partition%
            DO
                swapped% = FALSE
                FOR i% = 1 TO range%           ' if necessary, swap array elements
                    IF array(i%).sKey > array(i% + partition%).sKey THEN
```

(continued)

continued

```
                    SWAP array(i%), array(i% + partition%)
                    swapped% = i%
              END IF
          NEXT i%
          range% = swapped%
      LOOP UNTIL NOT swapped%
      partition% = partition% \ 2
    LOOP

    ' use the sorted array to sort the file
    OPEN tempFile$ FOR RANDOM AS #2 LEN = recLen%     ' open temporary file
    FIELD 2, recLen% AS tempRec$              ' define records for the file
    FOR i% = 1 TO records&
        GET 2, array(i%).recNum               ' get one record from the file
        tempRecVar$ = tempRec$                ' assign record to temporary variable
        LSET finalRec$ = tempRecVar$          ' assign temporary variable to field
        PUT 1, i%                             ' write field to the file
    NEXT i%

    CLOSE : KILL tempFile$                    ' delete temporary file
    SortFile% = TRUE
END FUNCTION
```

The following listing shows file SAMPLE.DAT, which contains the unsorted data you will use to test the program.

```
89/03/01 1549 C00003 ICIPA    1000      2.50 B000001
89/03/01 1645 C00008 AAC       500      5.80 B000002  S000030
89/03/01 1646 C00013 CWC       250      5.00 B000003  S000044
89/03/01 1648 C00011 ALMO      500     10.00 S000004  B000006
89/03/01 1649 C00002 QCLGA     180      1.92 B000005  S000017
89/03/01 1651 C00005 ALMO      500     10.00 B000006  S000004
89/03/02 1648 C00011 ALMO     1000     10.00 S000004A B000009
89/03/02 1701 C00007 WPL       200      3.65 S000007  B000072
89/03/02 1703 C00012 CIG       700      5.80 S000008
89/03/02 1704 C00006 ALMO     1000     10.00 B000009  S000004A
89/03/02 1705 C00003 ASD       300     17.00 S000010
89/03/03 1706 C00009 ALMO      500     10.00 B000011  S000004
89/03/03 2042 C00002 POSO      100      6.00 S000014  B000073
89/03/04 2044 C00012 BUD       500      3.00 B000015
89/03/04 2045 C00013 ALMO      300     10.00 B000016  S000004C
89/03/04 2046 C00014 QCLGA     180      1.92 S000017  B000005
89/03/04 2047 C00007 BAB       300       .75 S000018
89/03/04 2049 C00001 ALMO      500     10.00 B000019  S000004D
89/03/05 2050 C00011 CCYOA    1000      2.24 B000020  A000023
89/03/05 2051 C00020 WOIPA    1000      6.65 S000021
89/03/05 2052 C00019 WIM      5000      0.10 B000022
89/03/06 2053 C00021 CCYOA    1000      2.24 S000023  B000020
89/03/07 2053 C00021 CCYOA    2000      2.24 S000023A B000026
89/03/07 1648 C00011 ALMO      500     10.00 S000004D B000019
```

(continued)

continued

```
89/03/08 1648 C00011 ALMO    2000    10.00 S000004E B000028
89/03/08 2125 C00018 WPL     2000     3.75 S000024
89/03/10 2126 C00025 ERA     8000      .05 S000025
89/03/11 2128 C00026 CCYOA   2000     2.24 B000026  S000023A
89/03/11 2129 C00014 AUP      100     5.18 B000027  S000041
89/03/11 2130 C00015 ALMO    2000    10.00 B000028  S000004E
89/03/12 2131 C00015 WLW      400     3.69 B000029
89/03/12 2132 C00018 AAC      500     5.80 S000030  B000002
```

Before you begin, make a working copy of this data file so that if the program corrupts the data in the working copy, you have a backup of the original file. Name the working copy SAMPLE.TST.

Now load the program SORTFILE.BAS into the QBasic environment. The best way to test the program is to try to run it. Press Shift-F5 (or choose Start from the Run menu) and see what happens.

You should now see a prompt in the Output window. The program seems to have compiled correctly; the QBasic editor would have caught any syntax errors before letting you get this far. The program is now asking for data. In response to the first prompt, "Enter pathname of file to be sorted," enter *SAMPLE.TST.* Then, in response to the next prompt, enter *64*, the length of each record in the file SAMPLE.TST. The program then prompts you for information about the sort field.

The program is designed to use any field of a file record as the sort key. Use the product code field in SAMPLE.TST, which starts at position 22 in the record and is five characters long. When you've finished responding to the prompts, your screen contains the following information:

```
Enter pathname of file to be sorted  ? SAMPLE.TST
What is the record length of the file? 64
Define sort field - starting position? 22
                  - length of field  ? 5
```

The program immediately produces an error. QBasic reports a "Subscript out of range" error in a dialog box and positions the cursor at the statement that caused the error. The dialog box informs you that when the program tried to dimension the array, a subscript was out of range.

Why do you get a "Subscript out of range" error message when the array is only now being dimensioned? To find the answer to this question, you must examine the array. It's a dynamic array because you're using a variable to dimension it. Look at the contents of that variable, *records%*. Press Enter or Esc to clear the error message dialog box from the screen.

The easiest way to examine the contents of a variable in QBasic is to use the Immediate window. After you clear the error dialog box, the cursor is on the line that caused the error. Move the cursor to the variable *records%* and select it. (The easiest way to select the variable is to move the cursor to the beginning of *records%*, hold down either Shift key, and press Ctrl-Right direction key.) Then copy what you've selected to the clipboard by pressing Ctrl-Ins (or by choosing the Copy command from the Edit menu).

The Immediate window lets you enter QBasic statements to be executed—without entering them as permanent parts of your program. This characteristic is especially useful in debugging because you can use the PRINT statement to display the current values in suspect variables such as *records%*. Press F6 to switch from the program's Edit window to the Immediate window. You can abbreviate the PRINT statement by using a question mark, so either type *PRINT* followed by a space or type a question mark. Then press Shift-Ins to copy the contents of the clipboard into the Immediate window. When you press Enter, QBasic displays the value of *records%* in the Output window. Because QBasic displays this value at the last position of the cursor in the Output window, sometimes it's hard to locate your output.

The Immediate window output shows the cause of the error. The variable *records%*, which you would expect to contain the number of records in the file, actually contains the value 0. Let's look at the section of code that sets the value of *records%*. Press any key to return to the Immediate window, and then press F6 to switch the cursor to the Edit window.

Look a few lines above the highlighted line in the Edit window, to the line that includes the comment (*first definition of records&*); there's the error. The variable that holds the number of records is actually called *records&* (a long-integer variable), not *records%* (a normal, or short, integer variable). Because you included an integer type-declaration character with the variable used to dimension the array, QBasic assumed you were referring to a new variable and created *records%*. That's why *records%* was set to 0.

To correct the problem, move the cursor back to the DIM statement (the highlighted line), and type *records&* instead of *records%*. As soon as you move the cursor off the line, QBasic displays a dialog box saying "You will have to restart your program after this edit. Proceed anyway?" This restart message tells you that the change you made affects the rest of the program, so you must restart the program if you want to maintain the change. Press Enter to accept the change, and then press Shift-F5 to start the program from the beginning. After you reenter the parameters, the program displays the following message:

```
File successfully sorted
```

If you exit QBasic (by choosing the Exit command from the File menu), you can use the DOS command TYPE to examine the file SAMPLE.TST. You'll notice that the file is exactly the same as it was before. The program didn't sort the file at all. Reload QBasic and the SORTFILE.BAS program.

The problem is not obvious because QBasic isn't reporting any errors. You now have to deal with a *logic error*, a design flaw in your sort subprogram. The best way to deal with this problem is to run the program step by step to see if you can find where it's going wrong. It would take too long to step through the entire program, so you should run the program at normal speed until it gets to the sort routine; then stop it.

QBasic can help by setting a *breakpoint*. Perhaps the best place to stop would be at the top of the FOR...NEXT loop in the *SortFile* subprogram. Move to the *SortFile* subprogram by pressing F2, choosing *SortFile* from the list box, and pressing Enter. Next move the cursor to the beginning of the first FOR...NEXT loop in the subprogram, and press F9 to set a breakpoint there. QBasic highlights the line to indicate that the program will pause when it reaches that line of code.

Now run the program. Press Shift-F5 to start the program, and type the parameters again. The program then displays the message "File successfully sorted."

What has happened? Execution never reached the breakpoint. Evidently the program is not running the sort routine at all. Put the breakpoint elsewhere—for example, immediately above the main sort loop. First press F9 again to clear the current breakpoint, and then move the cursor up a few lines, to the statement

```
DO WHILE partition% > 0
```

Press F9 to place a new breakpoint at that line. That is the beginning of the entire sort loop. The program must reach this statement.

Press Shift-F5 to start the program again. That breakpoint worked; the program stopped at the DO statement. Clear the breakpoint by pressing F9 again. Now begin stepping through the loop, one statement at a time, by pressing the F8 key.

What has happened? Instead of moving into the loop, execution jumped directly to the statement after the final LOOP instruction. This is an entry-condition loop, with the test at the top, so somehow the test must have failed.

The loop executes only while the variable *partition%* contains a value greater then 0. Move back to the DO statement, and check the actual value of *partition%* by using the Immediate window technique discussed earlier.

You can see that the value of *partition%* is 0. Now look at the previous line. The initial value of *partition%*, the partition size for the sort, is obtained by dividing the number of records by 2; however, you used the wrong type-declaration character for the variable *records%* again. It should be a long integer.

Wait. Before you try to sort the file again, check to see that you haven't made this same mistake elsewhere. Do a global search-and-replace operation.

You perform a global search-and-replace operation by using the Change command in the Search menu. Press Alt-S to gain access to the Search menu, and then press C to choose Change from this menu. QBasic displays a dialog box in which you can specify the appropriate change. Type *records%* in the "Find What:" field. Press the Tab key to move to the "Change To:" field. Type *records&* as the name that will replace *records%*, and then press Enter to begin the search. QBasic displays a dialog box when it finds *records%*. Press Enter to direct QBasic to change the variable to *records&*. Good—it found only one occurrence of the error.

Try sorting the file again by pressing Shift-F5 to restart the program. The program reports "File successfully sorted." The program took longer to run this time; but did it work? Exit QBasic, being sure to save your work, and use the DOS command TYPE to examine the file again. At first glance, the file appears sorted; however, on closer inspection, you can see that a few items are still out of place. The program partially sorted the file but didn't quite finish the job. Restore the file to its original order by copying the backup file SAMPLE.DAT into SAMPLE.TST as follows:

```
COPY SAMPLE.DAT SAMPLE.TST
```

Restart QBasic and reload SORTFILE.BAS. Now step through the sort again. Put the breakpoint back at the beginning of the DO statement so that when you restart the program, it will pause at that point. Press F9 to set the breakpoint. Now press Shift-F5 to start the program, and enter the data again. Good—execution stopped at the breakpoint. Press F9 to clear the breakpoint.

Now use the F8 key to step through the sort routine. Note that QBasic highlights the current statement as you move through the program. The current statement is

```
DO WHILE partition% > 0
```

When you press F8, the cursor moves into the outermost loop. This loop executes as long as the partition size is greater than 0. Now the current statement is

```
range% = records& - partition%
```

This statement sets the sort range for the current pass through the file data in memory.

When you press F8 again, the cursor moves to the beginning of another loop. This loop repeats until all the out-of-sequence data in the current partition has been exchanged. The next statement is

```
swapped% = FALSE
```

This statement prepares the variable *swapped%* for the next pass through the current partition.

Press F8 to move to the statement

```
FOR i% = 1 TO range%          ' if necessary, swap array elements
```

This statement is the beginning of the innermost loop, which performs all the sorting.

Press F8 again. Now execution pauses at the following statement, which is the test that determines whether a pair of records needs to be swapped:

```
IF array(i%).sKey > array(i% + partition%).sKey THEN
```

You might find it useful if you could see what is in each record when it's tested. Unfortunately, during debugging, QBasic provides only the Immediate window for displaying the values of variables. But luckily, QBasic retains the contents of the Immediate window, even when you switch to the Edit window. When you switch back to the Immediate window by pressing F6, you can execute statements you already typed. You can simply move your cursor to the line in the Immediate window that you want to execute and press Enter.

Move to the Immediate window, and use a PRINT statement to output the contents of the variables *array(i%).sKey* and *array(i% + partition%).sKey*. Notice that the ASCII value of the variable (ICIPA) is greater than that of the second variable (BAB); therefore, according to the logic of the program, the values of the two variables should have been exchanged using the SWAP statement. To see whether the program actually swaps them, press F8 several times to execute and move through the IF statement.

Switch back to the Immediate window and reexecute the PRINT statements on the variables *array(i%).sKey* and *array(i% + partition%).sKey*. Did the values change? The logic seems to be working correctly. Nothing appears to be wrong so far. Skip to the end of the FOR...NEXT loop, and see whether execution continues to the next pass. You don't want to single-step through the entire loop, so speed things up a little by moving the cursor to the statement after the *NEXT i%* at the end of the loop and then pressing F9 to set a breakpoint and F5 to continue.

Now step through the program again. The current statement is

```
range% = swapped%
```

This statement tells the program to sort through the partition of records that were exchanged last time. The program continues shuffling them until all are in order. (A pass is made without any swaps.)

Press F8 to move to the next statement:

```
LOOP UNTIL NOT swapped%
```

The next step should take you back to the top of the inner DO...LOOP. When you press F8 again, the cursor moves to the statement

```
partition% = partition% / 2
```

Something is wrong here: Execution dropped through the loop. This shouldn't have happened until *swapped%* equaled 0.

Use the Immediate window to display the value of the variable *swapped%*. You see the value 16—definitely a nonzero value. Why then did execution fall through the DO...LOOP statement? The program should have continued to loop until the variable *swapped%* became logically false, or 0.

Is the test correct? See what *NOT swapped%* evaluates to; you can do this with the Immediate window. The problem is that QBasic evaluates the expression as −17, which means *NOT swapped%* is true (nonzero). That's why execution fell through the loop.

The DO...LOOP statement is currently repeating until *NOT swapped%* is true:

```
LOOP UNTIL NOT swapped%
```

This is quite different from repeating until *swapped%* is false, which is what you want. How can you code it correctly? Reverse the logic, like this:

```
LOOP WHILE swapped%
```

Type the changed line and press Shift-F5 to restart the program. Once again, the program reports "File successfully sorted." Check the file to see for yourself. Exit QBasic and then use the DOS command TYPE to display the file. The program worked! The file is properly sorted in alphabetic order (using the product code field). You finally got all the bugs out of the program. Thank goodness for the QBasic environment interpreter; this process would have taken quite a long time if you'd had to debug the program without it.

This tutorial session illustrated many of the tools that the QBasic programming environment provides to help you manage and debug your programs. The rest of this chapter discusses these facilities individually and in greater detail. It also includes several features the tutorial did not discuss.

Clear All Breakpoints

See also
Toggle Breakpoint

Purpose
The Clear All Breakpoints command cancels all set breakpoints and lets the program run without interruptions. You use Clear All Breakpoints after you have found and corrected all the bugs in your program.

Selection
Keyboard
Press Alt-D to open the Debug menu. The Clear All Breakpoints command is the fifth command on the menu; use the direction keys to choose the Clear All Breakpoints command, and then press Enter. Or you can enter the shortcut sequence Alt-D-C.

Mouse
Use the mouse to move the cursor to the Debug menu on the menu bar, and click the left button. When the Debug menu opens, move the cursor to the Clear All Breakpoints command and then click the left button.

Description
Breakpoints are markers that the QBasic environment inserts into your code to cause the program to stop executing at a specific statement. The Clear All Breakpoints command instantly removes all the breakpoints that you set during a debugging session.

Procedure Step

See also
Step

Purpose
The Procedure Step command executes the next statement in your QBasic program, tracing over procedure calls. You use Procedure Step when you want to examine the flow of a program in fine detail.

Selection
Keyboard
Press Alt-D to open the Debug menu. The Procedure Step command is the second command on the menu; use the direction keys to choose the Procedure Step command, and then press Enter. Or you can enter the shortcut sequence Alt-D-P. You can also press the F10 function key.

Mouse

Use the mouse to move the cursor to the Debug menu on the menu bar, and click the left button. When the Debug menu opens, move the cursor to the Procedure Step command and then click the left button.

Description

You can use the Procedure Step command to start executing your program instruction by instruction. You normally set a breakpoint at a point in your program where you suspect a bug is located and then use Procedure Step to execute a few instructions to see whether the bug is actually there.

When you use the Procedure Step command, QBasic executes the statement, briefly switching to the Output window if the statement displays output and then returning to the Edit window. You can make changes to your program or use other QBasic menu commands as you step through the program.

The Procedure Step command will "skip" execution over a subprogram or function. For example, with this line of code

```
CALL PrintScreen
```

QBasic will execute the *PrintScreen* subprogram and continue with the statement following the CALL. Normally, if you've already debugged your subprograms and functions, you would use the Procedure Step command. However, if you want to "follow" execution into a subprogram or function, use the Step debugging command, which executes the subprogram or function one statement at a time.

Set Next Statement

Purpose

The Set Next Statement command lets you resume program execution (after temporarily interrupting it) at a statement other than the next in sequence. You can use this command to change the normal flow of execution or to examine the effect of alternative branchings in an IF or SELECT CASE statement.

Selection

Keyboard

Press Alt-D to open the Debug menu. Set Next Statement is the last command on the menu; use the direction keys to choose the Set Next Statement command, and then press Enter. Or you can enter the shortcut sequence Alt-D-S.

Mouse

Use the mouse to move the cursor to the Debug menu on the menu bar, and click the left button. When the Debug menu opens, move the cursor to the Set Next Statement command and then click the left button.

Description

The Set Next Statement command lets you select the first statement that will be executed when you restart the program after it was interrupted by a breakpoint or the Ctrl-Break key combination. QBasic does not execute any code between the last statement executed and the new statement you specify. Therefore, you must set any variables that the new section of code requires.

To specify a new statement, use the direction keys (or the mouse) to move the cursor to the appropriate program line, and then choose the Set Next Statement command from the Debug menu. The highlight that marks the current statement moves to the statement you have selected, and when you restart the program, execution will begin there. To resume execution, press F5; you can also use the F8 key to step through subsequent statements.

Step

See also

Procedure Step

Purpose

The Step command executes the next statement in your QBasic program. You use Step when you want to examine the flow of a program in fine detail.

Selection

Keyboard

Press Alt-D to open the Debug menu. Because the Step command is the first command on the menu, it is already chosen. Simply press Enter. Or you can enter the shortcut sequence Alt-D-S. You can also press the F8 key.

Mouse

Use the mouse to move the cursor to the Debug menu on the menu bar, and click the left button. When the Debug menu opens, move the cursor to the Step command and then click the left button.

Description

You can use the Step command to start executing your program instruction by instruction. You normally set a breakpoint at a point in your program where you suspect a bug is located and then use Step to execute a few instructions to see whether the bug is actually there.

When you use the Step command, QBasic executes the statement, briefly switching to the Output window if the statement displays output and then returning to the Edit window. You can make changes to your program or use other QBasic menu commands as you step through the program.

The Step command will "follow" execution into a subprogram or function. For example, with this line of code

```
CALL PrintScreen
```

QBasic will bring the *PrintScreen* subprogram into the Edit window, and the next statement to be executed is the first statement in that subprogram. If you want to "skip over" your subprograms and functions, trusting that they are bug-free, use the Procedure Step debugging command, which traces over the subprogram and function calls.

Toggle Breakpoint

See also
Clear All Breakpoints

Purpose
A breakpoint is a location in your program at which you want execution to stop. You can set breakpoints either to suspend the program execution before it enters a critical section of code; or you can set them to stop the program after it has executed a procedure you want to test, which lets you examine the contents of variables.

Selection

Keyboard
Press Alt-D to open the Debug menu. Toggle Breakpoint is the fourth command on the menu; use the direction keys to choose the Toggle Breakpoint command, and then press Enter. Or you can enter the shortcut sequence Alt-D-B. You can also press the F9 function key.

Mouse
Use the mouse to move the cursor to the Debug menu on the menu bar, and click the left button. When the Debug menu opens, move the cursor to the Toggle Breakpoint command and then click the left button.

Description
The Toggle Breakpoint command toggles a breakpoint: Choose it once to place a breakpoint at the line the cursor is on; choose it again to remove the breakpoint at the line the cursor is on. QBasic highlights any line that contains a breakpoint.

When a program running in the QBasic environment encounters a breakpoint, it stops immediately; it does not execute the statement in which the breakpoint is set. After the program stops, you can examine active variables or test the value of expressions by issuing a PRINT statement in the Immediate window to display them.

After you have tested the variables or expressions, you can resume program execution by pressing the F5 key. You can also use the F8 key to step through subsequent statements, one statement at a time. If the program is still stopped and you press F9 a second time to clear the breakpoint at the cursor, the program will not resume until you press F5. If your program contains more than one breakpoint, you can clear them all at once by choosing the Clear All Breakpoints command from the Debug menu. (See the Clear All Breakpoints entry.)

Trace On

See also
TROFF, TRON

Purpose
The Trace On command enables or disables program tracing in the QBasic environment. When tracing is enabled, QBasic selects each statement as it executes, displaying the statement in the environment's Edit window.

Selection

Keyboard
Press Alt-D to open the Debug menu. The Trace On command is the third command on the menu; use the direction keys to choose the Trace On command, and then press Enter. Or you can enter the shortcut sequence Alt-D-T.

Mouse
Use the mouse to move the cursor to the Debug menu on the menu bar, and click the left button. When the Debug menu opens, move the cursor to the Trace On command and click the left button.

Description
The Trace On command in the Debug menu toggles tracing: Choose it once to enable tracing; choose it again to disable tracing. When tracing is enabled, the Trace On command is preceded by a bullet symbol in the Debug menu.

Trace On turns on the "animated tracing" capabilities of QBasic, which cause QBasic to step through a program as it is executed. This gives you time to watch the details of program execution and lets you stop the program (by using Ctrl-Break) if it doesn't execute as you intended. Any breakpoints that were in effect before you chose Trace On will continue to stop execution at particular points in the program. As each statement executes, QBasic highlights the line in which it appears in the Edit window; this lets you check whether the program is executing in the proper sequence. Any output that the program generates is directed to the Output window as usual; however, as soon as the output operation finishes, the display switches back to the Edit window.

Tips
The program itself can also enable and disable tracing—merely insert the statements TRON (trace on) and TROFF (trace off) at appropriate places in the program code. You can use these statements to restrict tracing to the section of the program in which you suspect bugs exist.

You can also enter TRON and TROFF directly in the Immediate window. However, doing this has exactly the same effect as does enabling or disabling tracing from the Debug menu.

TROFF, TRON

See also

Trace On

Purpose

The TRON statement activates the QBasic Trace On command, which is used for debugging programs. When tracing is enabled, QBasic highlights each statement as it executes. The TROFF statement disables line tracing.

Syntax

TRON
TROFF

Usage

```
TRON          ' enables tracing
FOR i% = 1 to range%
    IF array(i%) > array(i% + gap%) THEN
        SWAP array(i%), array(i% + gap%)
        swapped% = i%
    END IF
NEXT i%
TROFF          ' disables tracing
```

Enables tracing, executes a FOR loop, and then disables tracing.

Description

The TROFF and TRON statements help you monitor program execution in the QBasic environment. They duplicate the effect of the Trace On command, which is found in the Debug menu.

TRON has the same effect as does choosing Trace On from the Debug menu. TRON turns on the animated tracing capabilities of QBasic, which cause QBasic to step through a program when it is executed. As each statement executes, QBasic highlights it in the Edit window; this lets you check whether the statements are executing in the proper sequence. If breakpoints are specified, they stop execution at particular points in the program. You can also press Ctrl-Break to stop the program.

TROFF turns off animated tracing; however, the program continues to execute. When used together, TROFF and TRON help you isolate a section of program in which you suspect bugs exist.

Note that you can also enter TROFF and TRON in the Immediate window to toggle program tracing directly.

The following program illustrates the use of the TRON and TROFF statements. This program toggles the QBasic tracing feature on and off when the user presses any key. It is usually easier to do control tracing yourself by using the Trace On command from the Debug menu.

```
CLS
counter& = 0
DO
    counter& = counter& + 1
    LOCATE 10, 10: PRINT counter&
    r$ = INKEY$: IF r$ = CHR$(27) THEN EXIT DO
    IF r$ <> "" THEN
        IF trace% THEN
            trace% = 0: TROFF            ' turn tracing off
            LOCATE 11, 1: PRINT SPACE$(80);
            LOCATE 10, 10
        ELSE
            trace% = -1: TRON            ' turn tracing on
        END IF
    END IF
LOOP WHILE 1
END
```

SECTION V

APPENDIXES

APPENDICES

APPENDIX A

Error Messages and Error Codes

QBasic Error Messages

Errors can occur during any of three stages of program development:

- When you start QBasic from the command line
- While you edit or compile a program
- While a program runs

When an error occurs, QBasic displays a dialog box that describes the error and enables you to gain access to complete online Help that explains the error. This appendix provides a handy alphabetic and numeric listing and an explanation of each error.

Invocation Errors

These errors occur when you run QBasic (QBASIC.EXE) from the DOS command line. The most common errors result from using incorrect option switches.

Syntax and Compile-time Errors

QBasic has a "smart" editor that incorporates all syntax rules and that parses your program code as you enter it. When you attempt to move the cursor off the current program line, the editor checks the syntax and notifies you of any error, such as missing function parameters, invalid variables, or unclosed parentheses. The error dialog box that appears displays a brief error message and lets you gain access to Help, which explains the error in more detail.

Runtime Errors

Some errors don't occur until a program is actually executed—for example, when an array index goes out of bounds, or when the program attempts to divide by 0 or runs out of stack space. If QBasic detects an error while a program is running, it displays an error dialog box.

Not all errors have error numbers, but most runtime errors do. Therefore, your ON ERROR GOTO statements can easily trap these errors to provide a safe and graceful way of handling them. The QBasic ERR statement returns the error number, or code, of the preceding error. You specify an error code in the ERROR statement to simulate the error corresponding to the code. Table A-1 on the following page lists the error codes and their descriptions.

The following section lists all invocation, compile-time, and runtime errors in alphabetic order. Because these types of error messages share a common format, this list is easy to use as a reference. Each error message is printed in boldface and is followed by the error type (invocation, compile-time, or runtime). An explanation of the error follows, sometimes with suggestions for correcting it. (Remember that QBasic notifies you of many compile-time errors before you actually compile the code.) Finally, if the error message has an error number, or code, it is shown in parentheses.

Code	Description	Code	Description
2	Syntax error	53	File not found
3	RETURN without GOSUB	54	Bad file mode
4	Out of DATA	55	File already open
5	Illegal function call	56	FIELD statement active
6	Overflow	57	Device I/O error
7	Out of memory	58	File already exists
9	Subscript out of range	59	Bad record length
10	Duplicate definition	61	Disk full
11	Division by zero	62	Input past end of file
13	Type mismatch	63	Bad record number
14	Out of string space	64	Bad file name
16	String formula too complex	67	Too many files
19	No RESUME	68	Device unavailable
20	RESUME without error	69	Communications-buffer overflow
24	Device timeout	70	Permission denied
25	Device fault	71	Disk not ready
27	Out of paper	72	Disk-media error
39	CASE ELSE expected	73	Advanced feature unavailable
40	Variable required	74	Rename across disks
50	FIELD overflow	75	Path/File access error
51	Internal error	76	Path not found
52	Bad file name or number		

Table A-1.
QBasic error codes.

Invocation, Compile-Time, and Runtime Errors

Advanced feature unavailable. Compile-time or runtime. You tried to use a feature that isn't available in this version of QBasic or the version of DOS on your system. Check online Help. (73)

Argument-count mismatch. Compile-time. You specified the wrong number of arguments to a subprogram or function. Compare the subprogram or function call with the header line or declaration of the subprogram or function.

Array already dimensioned. Compile-time or runtime. You used more than one DIM statement with a static array. This error also occurs if you use an OPTION BASE statement after dimensioning any array. Check the type of the array (static or dynamic) and the position of your OPTION BASE statement (if any).

Array not defined. Compile-time. You referred to an array with more than 10 elements without having first defined (dimensioned) it. (It is good practice to define all arrays, even those with fewer than 10 elements, but QBasic doesn't force you to do so.) If the array isn't defined anywhere, add an appropriate DIM statement. If the array is in another module, use the appropriate statement (such as COMMON, SHARED, and so on).

Array too big. Compile-time. You tried to dimension a static array that exceeds either 64 KB or the amount of space available in the default data segment (DGROUP). Reduce the size of the array, reduce other DGROUP data requirements (such as for strings), or declare the array to be dynamic so that it will be stored in the far heap.

AS clause required. Compile-time. You originally declared a variable by using an AS clause (for example, AS STRING) and then specified that variable in a DIM, REDIM, SHARED, or COMMON statement without including the AS clause.

AS clause required on first declaration. Compile-time. You referred to a variable name with an AS clause but did not include an AS clause in the original declaration. Add the appropriate AS clause to the declaration.

AS missing. Compile-time. The statement you used requires the AS keyword (for example, *OPEN "Filename" FOR OUTPUT AS #1*).

Asterisk missing. Compile-time. You tried to declare a fixed-length string but omitted the asterisk before the number of characters. Such a declaration should read STRING * *chars*.

Bad file mode. Runtime. You tried to do one of the following:

- Use a PUT or GET statement with a sequential file. (54)
- Execute an OPEN statement with a file mode other than I, O, or R. (54)
- Use a FIELD statement with a file not opened as a random-access file. (54)
- Output to a file that was opened as a sequential-access file for input. (54)
- Read from a file that was opened as a sequential-access file for output or for appending. (54)
- Load a binary program that has been corrupted. (54)

Bad file name. Runtime. The filename you specified violated one of the rules for DOS files (illegal characters, name too long, and so on). This message might also occur if you introduce a syntax error in an OPEN statement, such as by omitting quotation marks around the filename. (64)

Bad file name or number. Runtime. Either you tried to refer to a filename or file number that was not specified properly in an OPEN statement or you used a number that is out of range. (52)

Bad record length. Runtime. You specified a record in a GET or PUT statement whose length does not match the record length originally specified in the OPEN statement. (59)

Bad record number. Runtime. You used a record number less than or equal to 0 in a GET or PUT statement. (This message occurs if, for example, you forgot to initialize a variable.) (63)

BASE missing. Compile-time. You used the word OPTION without following it with the keyword BASE.

Binary source file. Compile-time. You tried to compile a binary (compressed-format, object, or compiled-code) file rather than an ASCII source file. If you want to compile a BASICA source file, you must first save it by using the ,A option.

Block IF without END IF. Compile-time. You began writing a block-style IF statement but didn't end it with END IF. (Any IF statement that has no statement on the line following the keyword THEN is considered a block IF statement.)

BYVAL allowed only with numeric arguments. Compile-time. You can specify only numeric variables with the BYVAL clause in a call to an external routine.

Cannot continue. Runtime. Stops program execution during debugging because you made a major change while editing. Choose either Start or Restart from the Run menu to run the program from the beginning.

Cannot start with 'FN'. Compile-time. You can't begin the name of a variable, subprogram, or function defined by FUNCTION with the letters FN. You can use these letters only for functions defined with the DEF FN statement.

CASE without SELECT. Compile-time. The keyword CASE at the start of a SELECT CASE statement must be preceded by the keyword SELECT.

Comma missing. Compile-time. The syntax of the statement in question requires a comma. (See the entry for the statement or use QBasic's online Help system to remind yourself of the syntax.)

COMMON and DECLARE must precede executable statements. Compile-time. You must place a COMMON or DECLARE statement before any executable statements.

Statements that define variables or compiler conditions or introduce comments (COM-MON, DEF*type*, DIM, OPTION BASE, REM, TYPE...END TYPE) are not executable statements. (DIM for static arrays is not executable; however, DIM for dynamic arrays is executable.) Metacommands (for example, $DYNAMIC) are also not executable.

Communications-buffer overflow. Runtime. The communications receive buffer overflowed. Try increasing the buffer size by increasing the value specified in the RB parameter in the OPEN COM statement, checking the buffer more frequently (by using the LOC function) to detect potential overflow, or reading the buffer more often by using the INPUT$ function. (69)

CONST/DIM SHARED follows SUB/FUNCTION. Compile-time. You placed a CONST or DIM SHARED declaration after a subprogram or function definition. Be sure to place these declarations at the beginning of the file. This message is a warning of potential trouble although your program might execute correctly.

Control structure in IF...THEN...ELSE incomplete. Compile-time. You used an unmatched END IF, END SELECT, LOOP, NEXT, or WEND statement within a single-line IF statement. Do not branch into a control structure without entering the control structure at its beginning.

Data-memory overflow. Compile-time. You used too much memory for static array elements, strings, or other variables. Make your arrays dynamic if that is possible. You can also conserve memory by omitting debugging switches. If all else fails, divide your program into parts that can be chained together.

DECLARE required. Compile-time. You performed an implicit subroutine or function call (by naming the subroutine or function directly in a statement rather than by using the CALL statement) and did not declare the subroutine or function before calling it.

DEF FN not allowed in control statements. Compile-time. You cannot define a function with a DEF FN statement inside a control structure (such as IF or SELECT CASE).

DEF without END DEF. Compile-time. You started defining a DEF FN function but did not end the definition with END DEF.

DEF*type* character specification illegal. Compile-time. You used an invalid type name with a DEF*type* declaration. The valid types are INT, SNG, DBL, LNG, and STR. You might have tried to define a DEF FN function without putting a space before the function name.

Device fault. Runtime. A device has signaled a hardware error; for example, a printer might have run out of paper. If this error arises during transmission to a communications port, it indicates that signals specified in the OPEN COM statement were not received within the allotted time. (25)

Device I/O error. Runtime. A device has signaled an I/O error, and the operating system could not recover from the error (could not continue writing, reading, and so on). (57)

Device timeout. Runtime. The program did not receive data or a signal from an I/O device within the allotted time. This usually occurs in communications using the serial ports. (24)

Device unavailable. Runtime. You attempted to gain access to a device that is not on line, is not properly configured, or does not exist. (68)

Disk full. Runtime. You tried to send data to the disk as part of a PRINT, WRITE, or CLOSE operation, and there wasn't enough room on the disk for the data. (61)

Disk-media error. Runtime. The disk controller found a problem with the disk surface when attempting to read or write to the disk. You might be able to "lock out" the bad sector by using the DOS FORMAT command after you back up all the data you can recover. (72)

Disk not ready. Runtime. Either the disk drive has no disk in it or you left the disk-drive door open. (71)

Division by zero. Compile-time or runtime. The program encountered a divisor of 0. You might have forgotten to initialize a variable or have misspelled a variable name. (11)

Document too large. Editor. You tried to edit a program or other document that was too large for the QBasic editor. Split the document into smaller pieces, and edit them separately.

DO without LOOP. Compile-time. Each DO statement must end with the LOOP keyword.

Duplicate definition. Compile-time or runtime. You are using an identifier that has already been defined. You can't use constants, variables, subprograms, or functions that have the same name. This message might also occur because you attempted to redimension a dynamic array by using a second DIM statement; use ERASE and DIM (or just REDIM) to redimension the dynamic array. (10)

Duplicate label. Compile-time. You used the same label (or line number) for more than one program line.

Dynamic array element illegal. Compile-time. You tried to use VARPTR$ with an element of a dynamic array. Because the address of such an element might change during program execution, you cannot reliably use its address.

Element not defined. Compile-time. You referred to a field in a user-defined type, but you did not define that field in the TYPE...END TYPE statement.

ELSEIF without IF. Compile-time. You used an ELSEIF clause without beginning the structure with an IF clause, or you deleted the IF clause.

ELSE without IF. Compile-time. You used an ELSE clause without beginning the structure with an IF clause, or you deleted the IF clause.

END DEF without DEF. Compile-time. You tried to end a function definition with END DEF without beginning it with a DEF FN clause, or you deleted the DEF FN clause.

END IF without block IF. Compile-time. You tried to end a block (multi-line) IF statement without beginning it with an IF clause, or you deleted the IF clause.

END SELECT without SELECT. Compile-time. You tried to end a SELECT CASE statement without beginning it with a SELECT CASE clause, or you deleted the SELECT CASE clause.

END SUB/FUNCTION without SUB/FUNCTION. Compile-time. You tried to end a subprogram or function definition without beginning it with the SUB or FUNCTION keyword, or you deleted the SUB or FUNCTION keyword.

END SUB or END FUNCTION must be last line in window. Compile-time. You tried to add code following a subprogram or function definition. Return to the main program (using the View menu in the editor).

END TYPE without TYPE. Compile-time. You tried to end a TYPE...END TYPE statement without beginning it with a TYPE clause, or you deleted the TYPE clause.

Equal sign missing. Compile-time. The syntax of the statement that prompted this message requires an equal sign (for example, in an assignment statement).

Error during QBasic initialization. Invocation. Usually this means there isn't enough memory in your system to load QBasic. Try removing unnecessary memory-resident programs. This error might also occur if your machine is not completely IBM compatible.

Error in loading file (*filename*)—Cannot find file. Invocation. You tried to redirect input from a file to QBasic from the command line, but the file wasn't in the specified location.

Error in loading file (*filename*)—Disk I/O error. Invocation. You tried to load a file into QBasic, but there was a problem with the disk drive (for example, the drive door was open).

Error in loading file (*filename*)—DOS memory-area error. Invocation. You tried to load a file into QBasic, but QBasic found that part of the memory needed by DOS was overwritten (possibly by an incorrect assembly-language routine or by a POKE statement).

Error in loading file (*filename*)—Out of memory. Runtime. An operation required more memory than was available (for example, for allocating a file buffer). Try to reduce the memory used by DOS buffers, memory-resident programs, or device drivers; or try to make large arrays dynamic rather than static. Reducing the amount of text in the QBasic editor also frees some memory.

EXIT DO not within DO...LOOP. Compile-time. You used an EXIT DO statement outside a DO...LOOP statement.

EXIT not within FOR...NEXT. Compile-time. You used an EXIT FOR statement outside a FOR...NEXT statement.

Expected: *item*. Compile-time. The syntax of the statement in question requires the *item* specified (for example, a closing parenthesis or a comma). If you are unsure of the correct syntax, look up the statement in the online Help system or in this book.

Expression too complex. Compile-time. You created an expression that has too many elements or whose elements are too deeply nested. The expression might require too many temporary strings for holding string literals. Try to simplify the expression, such as by assigning strings to variables and by using the variables rather than the literal strings in the expression.

Far heap corrupt. Compile-time. This message might be caused by a memory-resident program that conflicts with QBasic or by a POKE statement or a non-Basic routine that inadvertently modifies one of QBasic's internal memory locations.

FIELD overflow. Runtime. You tried to use the FIELD statement to specify more bytes than the record length of a random-access file. (50)

FIELD statement active. Runtime. You tried to specify a record variable in a GET or PUT statement, but the file being used had space allocated with a FIELD statement. GET and PUT cannot be used with a record variable that was specified in a FIELD statement. (56)

File already exists. Runtime. You tried to specify a file in a NAME statement, but the name specified is the same as that of an existing file or directory on the current disk. (58)

File already open. Runtime. You tried to open a file for sequential output, but the file was already open; or you tried to use KILL to delete an open file. (You must close the file before using KILL.) (55)

File not found. Runtime. In a program run from the QBasic environment, you referred to a nonexistent file in a FILES, KILL, NAME, OPEN, or RUN statement. (53)

File previously loaded. Compile-time. You tried to load a file that is already in memory.

Fixed-length string illegal. Compile-time. You tried to pass a fixed-length string to a subroutine or function. Use a variable-length string instead.

FOR index variable already in use. Compile-time. You tried to use the same index variable in more than one FOR loop in a set of nested FOR loops.

FOR index variable illegal. Compile-time. You used a variable other than a simple numeric variable as the index variable in a FOR loop.

Formal parameters not unique. Compile-time. You cannot use the same name more than once in a parameter list.

Formal parameter specifications illegal. Compile-time. You made an error in a subprogram or function parameter list. You might have specified the wrong number or type of parameters.

FOR without NEXT. Compile-time. You started a FOR loop and did not end it with a NEXT clause.

Function already defined. Compile-time. You tried to define a function that is already defined elsewhere.

Function name illegal. Compile-time. You tried to use a reserved keyword as the name of a user-defined function.

Function not defined. Compile-time. You tried to use a user-defined function before you defined or declared it.

GOSUB missing. Compile-time. You started an ON *event* GOSUB statement, but did not follow it with the keyword GOSUB (for example, ON COM GOSUB).

GOTO missing. Compile-time. You started an ON ERROR statement but did not follow it with the keyword GOTO.

GOTO or GOSUB expected. Compile-time. The syntax in question requires a GOTO or GOSUB statement.

Help not found. Editor. QBasic was unable to provide help because program errors prevented it from constructing a variable table for your program. Press F5 to display the line that caused the error.

Identifier cannot end with %, &, !, #, or $. Compile-time. You tried to use one of these type specifiers at the end of a user-defined type name, a subprogram name, or a name used in a COMMON statement.

Identifier cannot include period. Compile-time. Names of user-defined types and names of record elements cannot contain periods. A period, when used with record variables, can separate only the record name and the element name (for example, *address.street*). You also cannot use a period if the part of the name before the period matches the name of an existing variable defined with the clause *AS user-defined-type*. In general, avoid using periods to separate parts of variable names; instead, use mixed-case descriptive names (for example, *streetAddress*).

Identifier expected. Compile-time. You used an incorrect identifier (such as a number or a reserved keyword) where QBasic expected a valid identifier.

Identifier too long. Compile-time. You tried to use an identifier more than 40 characters long.

Illegal function call. Runtime. Usually this means that you passed an out-of-range parameter to a math or string function. (For example, you specified a negative number with the SQR function.) Other examples include array subscripts that are too large or are negative (unless the array was properly specified with a TO clause), negative record numbers, or invalid or nonexistent devices in I/O statements. (5)

Illegal in direct mode. Compile-time. You tried to use a statement in the Immediate window that can be used only in a program.

Illegal in procedure or DEF FN. Compile-time. The statement in question cannot be used inside a FUNCTION, SUB, or DEF FN statement.

Illegal number. Compile-time. QBasic expected a number, but you included non-numeric characters (such as most letters or punctuation).

Illegal outside of SUB, FUNCTION, or DEF FN. Compile-time. You can use the statement in question only in a FUNCTION, SUB, or DEF FN statement, not in module-level code.

Illegal outside of SUB/FUNCTION. Compile-time. You can use the statement in question only in a SUB or FUNCTION statement, not in module-level code.

Illegal outside of TYPE block. Compile-time. You can only use an AS clause in the form *name* AS *type* inside a TYPE...END TYPE statement.

Illegal type character in numeric constant. Compile-time. You used an inappropriate type-declaration character (%, &, !, #, or $)—for example, 1.34%.

INPUT missing. Compile-time. The syntax of the statement in question requires the keyword INPUT.

Input past end of file. Runtime. You tried to read past the end of a file. Before reading, check the return value of the EOF function to see whether you have reached the end of the file. (62)

Integer between 1 and 32767 required. Compile-time. The statement in question requires a positive-integer argument.

Invalid character. Compile-time. Your source file contains an invalid character. You might have inadvertently inserted a control character, or you might be using a file from a word processor or editor that uses formatting codes. A source file can contain only ASCII characters.

Invalid constant. Compile-time. The expression you tried to assign to a constant is invalid. Numeric expressions can contain numeric constants or literals and any arithmetic operators except exponentiation (^). A string expression assigned to a constant must always be a single string literal.

Label not defined. Compile-time. You specified a line label in a GOTO or GOSUB statement, but the label doesn't exist in your program.

Label not defined: *label.* Compile-time. A GOTO statement referred to a nonexistent line label.

Left parenthesis missing. Compile-time. Either the syntax for the statement in question needs a left parenthesis or a REDIM statement tried to reallocate space for a variable that is not an array.

Line number or label missing. Compile-time. You used a statement (such as GOTO or GOSUB) that requires a line number or label, but you did not specify one.

Line too long. Compile-time. Your source code contains a line more than 255 characters long.

LOOP without DO. Compile-time. You used the keyword LOOP, but you did not start the structure with the DO keyword.

Math overflow. Compile-time. You tried to perform a calculation whose result was larger than can be represented in QBasic's number format.

$Metacommand error. Compile-time. You incorrectly specified a metacommand; you might have spelled it wrong.

Minus sign missing. Compile-time. The syntax of the statement in question requires a minus sign.

Module level code too large. Compile-time. Your module-level code (main program) exceeds QBasic's internal limit. Convert some of the code into subprograms or functions.

Must be first statement on the line. Compile-time. You tried to use another keyword in front of an IF, ELSE, ELSEIF, or END IF clause in a block IF statement. Only a line number or label can precede one of these clauses on the line.

Name of subprogram illegal. Compile-time. You either used a reserved keyword as the name of a subprogram or tried to use the same name for two different subprograms.

Nested function definition. Compile-time. You tried to insert a FUNCTION statement inside another FUNCTION statement or inside an IF statement.

NEXT missing for *variable*. Compile-time. You didn't use the NEXT keyword in a FOR loop. *variable* is the index variable of the loop in question.

NEXT without FOR. Compile-time. You used a NEXT keyword, but you didn't precede it with a FOR clause.

No RESUME. Runtime. The program ended while executing an error-handling routine. Insert a RESUME statement to return control from the error handler. (19)

Numeric array illegal. Compile-time. You cannot use the VARPTR$ function to retrieve the address of a numeric array. (You can use only simple numeric variables and string arrays.)

Only simple variables allowed. Compile-time. You tried to use READ or INPUT with a user-defined type or an array of a user-defined type. (Elements of other arrays are acceptable. You can also read individual fields of a user-defined type one at a time.)

Operation requires disk. Compile-time. You specified a read or write operation that requires a disk device rather than a keyboard, printer, or communications device.

Out of DATA. Runtime. You tried to execute a READ statement, but the DATA statements didn't contain any more items to be read. (You can use RESTORE to reread data items.) (4)

Out of data space. Compile-time or runtime. You ran out of space in QBasic's default data segment (DGROUP), which contains variable-length strings and simple variables. Try to reduce buffers or the stack, use data types (such as integers) that don't require more space than necessary, or consider using alternative algorithms.

Out of memory. Invocation, compile-time, or runtime. An operation required more memory than was available (for example, the allocating of a file buffer). Try to reduce the memory used by DOS buffers, memory-resident programs, or device drivers. Reducing the amount of text loaded into the QBasic editor will also free some memory. (7)

Out of paper. Runtime. The printer is either out of paper or not turned on. (27)

Out of stack space. Runtime. Either the program contains too many active subprograms or functions or a recursive function has called itself too many times. You cannot trap this error.

Out of string space. Runtime. You ran out of space for static strings in the default data segment (DGROUP). Try using dynamic arrays of fixed-length strings. (14)

Overflow. Runtime. A program calculation exceeded the allowable range for integer or floating-point numbers. (6)

Overflow in numeric constant. Compile-time. You used a numeric constant that is too large for the type of number represented (for example, an integer greater than 32767).

Parameter type mismatch. Compile-time. You tried to call a subprogram or function with a parameter whose data type doesn't match the one defined in the parameter list.

Path/File access error. Compile-time or runtime. During an OPEN, MKDIR, CHDIR, or RMDIR operation, DOS was unable to gain access to the specified file using the path you specified. Check the pathname and (if you are trying to write to or delete a file) the file attributes. (75)

Path not found. Runtime. You tried to execute an OPEN, MKDIR, CHDIR, or RMDIR statement with a path that DOS could not find. (76)

Permission denied. Runtime. You tried to write to a write-protected disk, or you tried to gain access to a locked file on a network. (70)

Procedure too large. Compile-time. A procedure is larger than QBasic allows. Split the procedure into several smaller procedures.

Program-memory overflow. Compile-time. The compiled code for your program exceeded 64 KB. Use the CHAIN statement to connect parts of your program.

Record/string assignment required. Compile-time. You used an LSET statement without specifying an assignment to a string or a record variable.

Redo from start. Runtime. The response to an INPUT statement provided the wrong number or type of data items. Retype the response, using the correct form.

Rename across disks. Runtime. You used a different drive designator when you tried to rename a file; QBasic does not allow this. Copy the file to the new disk drive, and then use KILL to delete the original file. (74)

RESUME without error. Runtime. You placed a RESUME statement outside an error-trapping routine. (20)

RETURN without GOSUB. Runtime. QBasic executed a RETURN statement without having encountered a previous, unmatched GOSUB statement. (3)

Right parenthesis missing. Compile-time. The syntax of the statement in question requires a right, or closing, parenthesis.

SELECT without END SELECT. Compile-time. You began a SELECT CASE statement but omitted (or misspelled) the END SELECT clause.

Semicolon missing. Compile-time. The syntax of the statement in question requires a semicolon.

Separator illegal. Compile-time. You used a character other than a semicolon or a comma as a delimiter in a PRINT USING or WRITE statement.

Simple or array variable expected. Compile-time. QBasic requires a variable argument in the statement in question. You can use either a simple variable or an array.

Skipped forward to END TYPE statement. Compile-time. An error in a TYPE... END TYPE statement caused QBasic to ignore the remaining statements in the type definition. Although compilation will continue, the program will probably not work correctly.

Statement cannot precede SUB/FUNCTION definition. Compile-time. Only a REM statement or DEF*type* statement can precede a subroutine or function definition.

Statement illegal in TYPE block. Compile-time. You can use only a REM statement or an *element* AS *typename* clause within a TYPE...END TYPE statement.

String assignment required. Compile-time. You used an RSET statement without specifying an assignment to a string.

String expression required. Compile-time. The syntax of the statement in question requires a string expression. You might have used a numeric variable or a numeric literal. Usually when QBasic requires a string expression, you can use any combination of string variables, string constants, or string literals.

String formula too complex. Runtime. You used a string expression that was too long, or you specified more than 15 variables in an INPUT statement. Either assign part of the expression to a string variable and then use the variable in another expression or use two INPUT statements. (16)

String space corrupt. Runtime. This error can be caused by one of the following problems:

- An incorrect POKE or DEF SEG statement changed a string pointer or descriptor.
- Two chained programs contain mismatched COMMON declarations.

String variable required. Compile-time. The syntax of the statement in question requires a string variable, not a string literal or a numeric value.

SUB/FUNCTION without END SUB/FUNCTION. Compile-time. You started a subprogram or function but didn't end the definition with an END FUNCTION or END SUB statement.

SUB or FUNCTION missing. Compile-time. You specified a subprogram or function in a DECLARE statement, but the program contains no definition for the subprogram or function.

Subprogram error. Compile-time. This error is most likely to occur when you try to define a subprogram or function that is already defined in your program. Either try to insert a subprogram or function definition within another such definition or omit the END SUB or END FUNCTION statement.

Subprogram not defined. Compile-time. You called a subprogram that you haven't defined. You might need to load the program module or library that contains the definition.

Subprograms not allowed in control statements. Compile-time. You can't define a subprogram or function within an IF or SELECT CASE statement. (You can, of course, call a subprogram or function within a control statement.)

Subscript out of range. Runtime. The program tried to reference an array element beyond the defined subscript boundaries of the array. Also, you might have attempted to gain access to an element of an undimensioned dynamic array (for example, if the array was erased), or you might have used an array that exceeded 64 KB in size. (9)

Subscript syntax illegal. Compile-time. A syntax error occurred in an array subscript specification (for example, you tried to use a string value for a subscript).

Syntax error. Compile-time or runtime. At compile time, this message usually indicates a typographical error or incorrect punctuation in a statement. QBasic reports these errors as soon as you move the cursor from the current line. At runtime, a syntax error usually indicates an improperly formatted item in a DATA statement. (2)

Syntax error in numeric constant. Compile-time. A numeric constant or literal contains invalid punctuation or other invalid characters.

THEN missing. Compile-time. You started writing an IF statement, but you forgot to include the THEN clause.

TO missing. Compile-time. Usually this means you tried to specify a range of array subscripts but omitted the TO keyword.

Too many arguments in function call. Compile-time. You tried to use more than 60 arguments when calling a function—an unlikely situation.

Too many dimensions. Compile-time. You tried to specify more than 60 dimensions in an array definition.

Too many files. Runtime. This error means that your program tried to create a new file (with SAVE or OPEN) in a directory that already has 255 files in it. (67)

Too many labels. Compile-time. At compile time, this message means you used more than 255 line labels in an ON...GOSUB or ON...GOTO statement.

Too many TYPE definitions. Compile-time. You cannot define more than 240 user-defined data types.

Too many variables for INPUT. Compile-time. You cannot specify more than 60 variables in an INPUT statement.

Too many variables for LINE INPUT. Compile-time. You cannot specify more than one variable in a LINE INPUT statement.

Typed variable not allowed in expression. Compile-time. You cannot use a record variable in the statement in question. You might have tried to pass a variable of a user-defined type to a subprogram or function.

Type mismatch. Compile-time or runtime. You used the wrong type of variable for an operation. (For example, you can't use the LEFT$ function with a numeric argument or the ABS function with a string argument.) (13)

TYPE missing. Compile-time. You used the END TYPE clause but didn't include a preceding, unmatched TYPE clause. You might have inadvertently deleted that line.

Type more than 65535 bytes. Compile-time. A user-defined type cannot contain more than 64 KB of data.

Type not defined. Compile-time. You referred to another user-defined type within a TYPE...END TYPE statement, but the type you referred to is not defined in your program. You might need to load the module or library that contains the definition.

TYPE statement improperly nested. Compile-time. You cannot include a definition of a user-defined type within a subprogram or function.

TYPE without END TYPE. Compile-time. You started writing a user-defined type definition but did not end it with an END TYPE clause.

Unexpected end of file in TYPE declaration. Compile-time. You embedded an end-of-file character in a user-defined type definition. If you use an editor that can search for control characters, search for and delete any Ctrl-Z characters.

Unprintable error. Runtime. No error message corresponds to the error code that was generated. You might have used the ERROR statement without including a defined error code.

Variable-length string required. Compile-time. You tried to use a fixed-length string in a FIELD statement; QBasic does not allow this.

Variable name not unique. Compile-time. You tried to define a variable as a user-defined type after the variable was used as a record variable.

Variable required. Compile-time or runtime. During compile time, you used an IN-PUT, LET, READ, or SHARED statement without specifying the name of a variable. At runtime, you used a GET or PUT statement that didn't specify a variable when used with a file opened in binary mode. (40)

WEND without WHILE. Compile-time. You used a WEND statement without a preceding, unmatched WHILE keyword. You might have inadvertently deleted that line.

WHILE without WEND. Compile-time. You started writing a WHILE statement but didn't end it with a WEND statement.

Wrong number of dimensions. Compile-time. You referred to an array element using a number of dimensions different from the number you specified in the array definition.

APPENDIX B

Control Codes

Ctrl-key combinations represent the first 32 ASCII codes, which originally controlled peripherals. Now the IBM PC also uses them to display special characters.

ASCII codes Dec	Hex	Control abbreviation and function		IBM character	DOS display
0	0	NUL	(Null)		∧@[1]
1	1	SOH	(Start of heading)	☺	∧A
2	2	STX	(Start of text)	☻	∧B
3	3	ETX	(End of text)	♥	∧C (Break)[2]
4	4	EOT	(End of transmission)	♦	∧D
5	5	ENQ	(Enquiry)	♣	∧E
6	6	ACK	(Acknowledge)	♠	
7	7	BEL	(Bell)	•	∧G
8	8	BS	(Backspace)	◘	Backspace
9	9	HT	(Horizontal tab)	○	Tab
10	A	LF	(Linefeed)	◙	Linefeed
11	B	VT	(Vertical tab)	♂	∧K
12	C	FF	(Formfeed)	♀	∧L
13	D	CR	(Carriage return)	♪	Enter
14	E	SO	(Shift out)	♫	∧N
15	F	SI	(Shift in)	☼	∧O
16	10	DLE	(Data link escape)	►	Printer toggle[3]
17	11	DC1	(Device control 1)	◄	∧Q (or resume)
18	12	DC2	(Device control 2)	↕	∧R
19	13	DC3	(Device control 3)	‼	Pause (or ∧S)
20	14	DC4	(Device control 4)	¶	∧T
21	15	NAK	(Negative acknowledge)	§	∧U
22	16	SYN	(Synchronous idle)	▬	∧V
23	17	ETB	(End transmission block)	↨	∧W
24	18	CAN	(Cancel)	↑	∧X
25	19	EM	(End of medium)	↓	∧Y
26	1A	SUB	(Substitute)	→	∧Z[4]
27	1B	ESC	(Escape)	←	\ (or ∧[)[5]

(continued)

599

continued

| ASCII codes | | Control abbreviation | | IBM | DOS |
Dec	Hex	and function		character	display
28	1C	FS	(File separator)	∟	^\
29	1D	GS	(Group separator)	↔	^]
30	1E	RS	(Record separator)	▲	^^
31	1F	US	(Unit separator)	▼	^_

[1] Only by pressing F7; Ctrl-@ produces ^C (Break).

[2] Same as Break (Ctrl-Pause; on pre-101-key keyboards, Ctrl-Scroll Lock).

[3] Same as Ctrl-Print Screen (turns on and off echoing of screen characters to printer).

[4] Also by pressing F6; used as ASCII end-of-file marker.

[5] At the DOS command line, pressing the Esc key displays a backslash followed by a new, blank command line. However, the escape character is often displayed as ^[.

APPENDIX C

ASCII Characters

ASCII	Dec	Hex	Control		ASCII	Dec	Hex
	0	0	NUL (Null)		`<space>`	32	20
☺	1	1	SOH (Start of heading)		!	33	21
●	2	2	STX (Start of text)		"	34	22
♥	3	3	ETX (End of text)		#	35	23
♦	4	4	EOT (End of transmission)		$	36	24
♣	5	5	ENQ (Enquiry)		%	37	25
♠	6	6	ACK (Acknowledge)		&	38	26
•	7	7	BEL (Bell)		'	39	27
◘	8	8	BS (Backspace)		(	40	28
○	9	9	HT (Horizontal tab)		)	41	29
◙	10	A	LF (Linefeed)		*	42	2A
♂	11	B	VT (Vertical tab)		+	43	2B
♀	12	C	FF (Formfeed)		,	44	2C
♪	13	D	CR (Carriage return)		–	45	2D
♫	14	E	SO (Shift out)		.	46	2E
☼	15	F	SI (Shift in)		/	47	2F
►	16	10	DLE (Data link escape)		0	48	30
◄	17	11	DC1 (Device control 1)		1	49	31
↕	18	12	DC2 (Device control 2)		2	50	32
‼	19	13	DC3 (Device control 3)		3	51	33
¶	20	14	DC4 (Device control 4)		4	52	34
§	21	15	NAK (Negative acknowledge)		5	53	35
▬	22	16	SYN (Synchronous idle)		6	54	36
↨	23	17	ETB (End transmission block)		7	55	37
↑	24	18	CAN (Cancel)		8	56	38
↓	25	19	EM (End of medium)		9	57	39
→	26	1A	SUB (Substitute)		:	58	3A
←	27	1B	ESC (Escape)		;	59	3B
∟	28	1C	FS (File separator)		<	60	3C
↔	29	1D	GS (Group separator)		=	61	3D
▲	30	1E	RS (Record separator)		>	62	3E
▼	31	1F	US (Unit separator)		?	63	3F

(continued)

continued

ASCII	Dec	Hex	ASCII	Dec	Hex	ASCII	Dec	Hex
@	64	40	`	96	60	Ç	128	80
A	65	41	a	97	61	ü	129	81
B	66	42	b	98	62	é	130	82
C	67	43	c	99	63	â	131	83
D	68	44	d	100	64	ä	132	84
E	69	45	e	101	65	à	133	85
F	70	46	f	102	66	å	134	86
G	71	47	g	103	67	ç	135	87
H	72	48	h	104	68	ê	136	88
I	73	49	i	105	69	ë	137	89
J	74	4A	j	106	6A	è	138	8A
K	75	4B	k	107	6B	ï	139	8B
L	76	4C	l	108	6C	î	140	8C
M	77	4D	m	109	6D	ì	141	8D
N	78	4E	n	110	6E	Ä	142	8E
O	79	4F	o	111	6F	Å	143	8F
P	80	50	p	112	70	É	144	90
Q	81	51	q	113	71	æ	145	91
R	82	52	r	114	72	Æ	146	92
S	83	53	s	115	73	ô	147	93
T	84	54	t	116	74	ö	148	94
U	85	55	u	117	75	ò	149	95
V	86	56	v	118	76	û	150	96
W	87	57	w	119	77	ù	151	97
X	88	58	x	120	78	ÿ	152	98
Y	89	59	y	121	79	ö	153	99
Z	90	5A	z	122	7A	Ü	154	9A
[	91	5B	{	123	7B	¢	155	9B
\	92	5C	¦	124	7C	£	156	9C
]	93	5D	}	125	7D	¥	157	9D
^	94	5E	~	126	7E	Pt	158	9E
_	95	5F	△	127	7F	ƒ	159	9F

(continued)

ASCII	Dec	Hex	ASCII	Dec	Hex	ASCII	Dec	Hex
á	160	A0	└	192	C0	α	224	E0
í	161	A1	┴	193	C1	β	225	E1
ó	162	A2	┬	194	C2	Γ	226	E2
ú	163	A3	├	195	C3	π	227	E3
ñ	164	A4	─	196	C4	Σ	228	E4
Ñ	165	A5	┼	197	C5	σ	229	E5
ª	166	A6	╞	198	C6	µ	230	E6
º	167	A7	╟	199	C7	τ	231	E7
¿	168	A8	╚	200	C8	Φ	232	E8
⌐	169	A9	╔	201	C9	Θ	233	E9
¬	170	AA	╩	202	CA	Ω	234	EA
½	171	AB	╦	203	CB	δ	235	EB
¼	172	AC	╠	204	CC	∞	236	EC
¡	173	AD	═	205	CD	φ	237	ED
«	174	AE	╬	206	CE	ε	238	EE
»	175	AF	╧	207	CF	∩	239	EF
░	176	B0	╨	208	D0	≡	240	F0
▒	177	B1	╤	209	D1	±	241	F1
▓	178	B2	╥	210	D2	≥	242	F2
│	179	B3	╙	211	D3	≤	243	F3
┤	180	B4	╘	212	D4	⌠	244	F4
╡	181	B5	╒	213	D5	⌡	245	F5
╢	182	B6	╓	214	D6	÷	246	F6
╖	183	B7	╫	215	D7	≈	247	F7
╕	184	B8	╪	216	D8	°	248	F8
╣	185	B9	┘	217	D9	•	249	F9
║	186	BA	┌	218	DA	·	250	FA
╗	187	BB	█	219	DB	√	251	FB
╝	188	BC	▄	220	DC	η	252	FC
╜	189	BD	▌	221	DD	²	253	FD
╛	190	BE	▐	222	DE	■	254	FE
┐	191	BF	▀	223	DF		255	FF

INDEX

Note: Italicized page numbers refer to figures or tables.

Special Characters

! (single-precision floating-point data type) 6, 16, 26, 99

" (string) 121

(double-precision floating-point data type) 6, 16, 19, 99

(music generation) 342, 351

$ (string data type) 6, 16, 27, 99

$ (variable-length string) 121

% (integer data type) 6, 16, 21, 99

& (long-integer data type) 6, 16, 24, 99

' (comment) 502, 520

* (fixed-length string) 123

* (wildcard character) 443

+ (concatenation operator) *55*, 61, 64–65, 126

+ (graphics cursor movement) 295

+ (music generation) 342, 351

, (with INPUT statement) 217, 218

- (graphics cursor movement) 295

- (music generation) 342, 351

: (colon) *501*, 502, 509–10

; (with INPUT statement) 217, 218

< (less-than operator) 56–57

< (music generation) 342, 351

<= (less-than-or-equal-to operator) 56–58

<> (not-equal-to operator) 56–57

= (equal-to operator) 56–58

= (string expression) 121

> (greater-than operator) 56–58

> (music generation) 342, 351

>= (greater-than-or-equal-to operator) 56–57

? (wildcard character) 443

\ (integer division operator) 60

A

ABS function *179*, 184–85

adapters. *See* display adapters

ampersand (&) 6, 16, 24, 99

AND operator *55*, 58–59, 62–64

angle brackets (<>) 56–57

animation 283, 311, 324–26

APPEND keyword 422, 472–73

arcs 287–88

arctangent 180, 185–86

arrays 151–58

   DATA statement *152*, 156, 159–60

   declaring 152–55, 160–64

   dimensions of 153–55

   DIM statement *152*, 152–55, 157, 160–64

   dynamic 95, 158, 166

   $DYNAMIC metacommand *152*, 158, 164–65

   elements in 153–56

   ERASE statement *152*, 158, 165–66, 508

   in functions 157

   gaining access to elements in 154–55, 156

   LBOUND function *152*, 166–68

   OPTION BASE statement *152*, 154, 168–69

   READ statement *152*, 155–56, 169–71

   REDIM statement *152*, 158, 171–73

   RESTORE statement *152*, 173–74

   $STATIC metacommand *152*, 158, 175–76

   static vs. dynamic 95, 157–58

   storing data in 155–56

   string 122, 131–32

   in subprograms 157

   subscripts in 153–56

* Integer division operator is " \ "

＊ Integer division operator is " \ "

SPACE$ function *120,* 126, 142–43
SPC function *208,* 209, 235–36
SQR function *179,* 181, 204
square root 181, 204
stack 503, 507–9, 531, 539
$STATIC metacommand *152,* 158,
    175–76
STATIC statement *85,* 87, 88, 105, 111–13,
    158
static variables. *See* STATIC statement
static vs. dynamic arrays 95, 157–58
Step command 574–75
STICK function *359,* 362–63, 371–73
STOP statement *502,* 503, 526–27
STR$ function *120,* 127, 144–45
STRIG function *359,* 363, 374–75
STRIG ON/OFF/STOP statements *359,*
    360–61, 375–77
STRING$ function *120,* 128, 145–47
string arrays 122, 131–32
string constants 121–22
string expressions 121
STRING keyword *4,* 27–28
strings 119–28
    ASC function *120,* 129–30
    changing parts of 127, 139–41
    CHR$ function *120,* 130–32
    comparing 124
    concatenating 61, 64–65, 126
    converting numbers from 128, 148–50
    converting numbers to 128, 144–45
    defining 121–24
    extracting parts of 124–25, 135–36,
        138–39, 141–42
    filler 126–27, 142–45
    finding characters in 126, 132–34
    fixed-length 123–24
    INSTR function *120,* 126, 132–34
    LCASE$ function *120,* 127, 134–35
    LEFT$ function *120,* 124, 135–36
    LEN function *120,* 124, 136–38

strings, *continued*
    MID$ function *120,* 125, 138–39
    MID$ statement *120,* 127, 139–41
    RIGHT$ function *120,* 125, 141–42
    SPACE$ function *120,* 126, 142–43
    storing 122–24
    STR$ function *120,* 127, 144–45
    STRING$ function *120,* 128, 145–47
    UCASE$ function *120,* 127, 147–48
    VAL function *120,* 128, 148–50
    variable-length 122–23
string variables 5, 7, 119–20, 121
    and LSET statement 461–62
    and PLAY statement 344, 352
    and RSET statement 485
subprograms 86–87, 113–17
    arrays in 157
    calling 87, 90–92, 114
    declaring 87, 98–100, 114
    exiting 86
    recursive 114–15
subroutines 87–88, 106–8
SUB statement *85,* 86–87, 113–17
SWAP statement *4,* 8, 28–29
syntax errors 245, 581
SYSTEM statement *502,* 503, 527–28

T

TAB function *208,* 209, 236–37
TAN function *179,* 180, 205
tangent 180, 205
terminating programs 502–3, 510–11,
    526–28
text output 209, 228–37, 242–43
text viewport 211, 238–40
tiling colors 305–8
TIME$ function *261,* 262, 269–71
TIME$ statement *261,* 262, 269–71
TIMER function *261,* 262, 271–72
TIMER ON/OFF/STOP statements *261,*
    263, 272–73

Robert Arnson has been programming for eight years in BASIC, Pascal, C, and FORTRAN. He has developed several large business applications for professional insurance and statement billing, using QuickBASIC versions 2.0 through 4.5 and BASIC compilers 6.0 and 7.0.

Christy Gemmell has been writing software professionally for nine years. His programs are used by stockbrokers, accountants, and direct-mail companies. He is a founding member of Qbug, the British QuickBASIC Users Group, and the author of the Assembly Language Toolbox for QuickBASIC, a shareware utilities package. He works for Arden Microsystems in Leicester, England. He has written several articles on computer topics and programs for British user-group magazines such as *80 Micro*.

Harry Henderson is a freelance technical writer and editor. He writes documentation for a major software manufacturer and has coauthored many Waite Group books, including *Microsoft QuickC Programming* and *The Waite Group's Microsoft QuickBASIC Primer Plus*, published by Microsoft Press; and *Understanding MS-DOS*, 2d ed., *The Waite Group's Using PC-DOS*, and *UNIX Communications*, published by Howard W. Sams & Co.

Arnson, **Gemmell**, and **Henderson**, along with Mitchell Waite, are the authors of *The Waite Group's Microsoft QuickBASIC Bible*, published by Microsoft Press.

The manuscript for this book was prepared and submitted to Microsoft Press in electronic form. Text files were processed and formatted using Microsoft Word.

Word processors: Judith Bloch and Debbie Kem
Principal proofreader: Jean Zimmer
Principal typographer: Ruth Pettis
Interior text designer: Darcie S. Furlan
Principal illustrator: Rebecca Geisler-Johnson
Cover designer: Thomas A. Draper
Cover photographer: Lisa Irwin
Cover color separator: Rainier Color Corporation

Text composition by Microsoft Press in Garamond with display type in Futura Bold, using the Magna composition system and the Linotronic 300 laser imagesetter.

Printed on recycled paper stock.

OTHER TITLES FROM MICROSOFT PRESS

The Classic Bestseller on DOS

RUNNING MS-DOS, 5th ed.

Van Wolverton

"This book is simply the definitive handbook of PC-DOS and MS-DOS...written for both novices and experienced users." **BYTE magazine**

Now updated to include DOS 5, RUNNING MS-DOS 5th ed. is the ideal book for all levels—from novices to advanced DOS users. For novices, this is a solid introduction to basic DOS concepts and applications. For seasoned users this book provides all you need to achieve DOS mastery—precise, real-world examples, thoughtful discussions, and understandable descriptions. Throughout, the author addresses the exciting improvements in DOS 5 while providing in-depth coverage of every major version of DOS. You'll discover how to control your entire computer system—manage a hard disk, use the built-in text editor, increase your productivity with batch files, and even tailor the system to your needs and preferences. The example-rich command reference—completely revised and updated—is an invaluable resource for every DOS user.

592 pages, softcover   7³/₈ x 9¹/₄ $24.95   Order Code RUMS5

Handy Microsoft® Quick Reference Guides

MS-DOS, 5th ed.
Microsoft® Quick Reference

Van Wolverton

The perfect companion to RUNNING MS-DOS. This handy alphabetic reference—with examples—covers the commands and editing keys for DOS versions 2.0 through 5. You'll learn how to use the DOSKEY macro-creating utility, edit text with the new menu-based Editor, and more.

144 pages, softcover   4³/₄ x 8 $7.95   Order Code QRMS5

MS-DOS® BATCH FILES, 2nd ed.
Microsoft® Quick Reference

Kris Jamsa

Batch files offer an easy and instantly rewarding way to significantly increase your productivity. Now updated to DOS 5, this handy guide is perfect for for all levels of users. If you're a novice computer user, you'll learn the fundamentals of batch files. For seasoned users, you'll discover exciting new uses for batch files: how to use them to control printer output, to set screen colors, to redefine functions, and to back up your hard disk. Create menu-driven batch files, use DEBUG to enhance your batch files, and create batch files that prompt the user to respond to questions and then process the responses.

176 pages, softcover   4³/₄ x 8 $7.95   Order Code QRMSB2

MS-DOS® QBASIC
Microsoft® Quick Reference

Kris Jamsa

Now you can have instant answers to your MS-DOS QBasic questions! This is the perfect computer-side reference for any beginning to advanced MS-DOS QBasic programmer. This handy guide is both a concise overview of the new MS-DOS QBasic programming environment and a ready alphabetic reference to each statement and function.

135 pages, softcover   4³/₄ x 8 $7.95   Order Code QRMSQB

MS-DOS® QBasic is a fine stepping-stone to the more powerful Microsoft QuickBASIC™ programming environment. Add to your programming library with these authorized editions from Microsoft Press.

THE WAITE GROUP'S
MICROSOFT QUICKBASIC™ PRIMER PLUS
Stephen Prata with Harry Henderson

This is the ideal introduction—and more—for anyone eager to explore the Microsoft QuickBASIC environment. Covering Microsoft QuickBASIC version 4.5, this book provides step-by-step instructions, clear and helpful explanations, superb programming examples, and expert advice. You'll also find detailed information on topics not fully covered in standard introductions—graphics, debugging, sound, error trapping, interaction with DOS, and mixed-language programming. In addition, each chapter includes a series of review questions and answers so that you can chart your progress.

624 pages, softcover   7³/₈ x 9¹/₄ $24.95   Order Code QBPRPL

THE WAITE GROUP'S
MICROSOFT QUICKBASIC™ BIBLE
Mitchell Waite, Robert Arnson, Christy Gemmell, and Harry Henderson

Covering Microsoft QuickBASIC through version 4.5, this is the definitive reference, the cornerstone—indeed, the "bible"—on Microsoft QuickBASIC. It makes a perfect companion to *The Waite Group's Microsoft QuickBASIC Primer Plus*. This book features up-to-date, detailed information on every QuickBASIC keyword, function, and feature, compatibility information for 8 other versions of BASIC, in addition to hundreds of instruction and useful programming examples and tutorials. Recommended for novice programmers, programmers moving to the Microsoft QuickBASIC modern programming system from another version of BASIC, and seasoned professionals in search of the ultimate QuickBASIC reference.

960 pages, softcover   7³/₈ x 9¹/₄ $27.95   Order Code QBBI

THE MICROSOFT QUICKBASIC™ PROGRAMMER'S TOOLBOX
An Essential Library of More Than 250 Functions, Routines, and Utilities for Supercharging QuickBASIC Programs
John Clark Craig

Multiply the power and speed of your QuickBASIC programs with this unrivaled collection of more than 250 helpful subprograms, functions, and utilities designed for both novice and intermediate programmers. The routines are practical and easy to reference. They creatively exploit QuickBASIC's capabilities to tackle both common and unusual programming tasks: ANSI.SYS screen control, printer control, mouse interface routines, pop-up windows, fonts, graphics, editor routines, and more. THE MICROSOFT QUICKBASIC PROGRAMMER'S TOOLBOX comes complete with a detailed section that explains and demonstrates interlanguage calling techniques. A valuable resource, this book will enhance your skills and reinforce sold programming techniques.

512 pages, softcover   7³/₈ x 9¹/₄ $22.95   Order Code QBPRTO

*Microsoft Press books are available wherever quality computer books are sold.
Or call **1-800-MSPRESS** for ordering information or placing credit card orders.*
*Please refer to **BBK** when placing your order.*

---

*In Canada, contact Macmillan of Canada, Attn: Microsoft Press Dept., 164 Commander Blvd., Agincourt, Ontario, Canada M1S 3C7.
In the U.K., contact Microsoft Press, 27 Wrights Lane, London W8 5TZ.

KEYWORDS, STATEMENTS, AND FUNCTIONS BY CATEGORY